DATA MINING FOR INTELLIGENCE, FRAUD, & CRIMINAL DETECTION

Advanced Analytics & Information Sharing Technologies

CHRISTOPHER WESTPHAL

CRC Press
Taylor & Francis Group
Boca Raton London New York

CRC Press is an imprint of the
Taylor & Francis Group, an **informa** business

CRC Press
Taylor & Francis Group
6000 Broken Sound Parkway NW, Suite 300
Boca Raton, FL 33487-2742

No claim to original U.S. Government works
Printed in the United States of America on acid-free paper
10 9 8 7 6 5 4 3 2 1

International Standard Book Number-13: 978-1-4200-6723-1 (Hardcover)

Library of Congress Cataloging-in-Publication Data

Westphal, Christopher R. (Christopher Ralph), 1965-
Data mining for intelligence, fraud & criminal detection : advanced analytics & information sharing technologies / Christopher Westphal.
p. cm.
Includes bibliographical references and index.
ISBN 978-1-4200-6723-1 (alk. paper)
1. Law enforcement--United States. 2. Data mining--United States. I. Title.

HV7921.W47 2008
363.25'6--dc22 2008021209

Visit the Taylor & Francis Web site at
http://www.taylorandfrancis.com

and the CRC Press Web site at
http://www.crcpress.com

Dedication

This book is dedicated to the analysts around the world who work diligently to secure the borders, critical infrastructure, and integrity of their homelands. It is for all those people who support law enforcement, the intelligence community, and corporate security. It is for the police officers, special agents, and criminal investigators who ensure our safety every day. It is for all the heroes who have given their lives to uphold our laws, protect our rights, and guarantee our freedoms.

All royalty proceeds from this book are being donated to the National Law Enforcement Officers Memorial Fund (NLEOMF) in honor of those individuals who have made the ultimate sacrifice to the service, protection, and security of others. More than 18,200 names, representing law enforcement officers who died in the line of duty, are engraved on the National Law Enforcement Memorial located in Washington, D.C. To learn more about NLEOMF and to further contribute to the fund, please visit their site at www.nleomf.com.

National Law Enforcement Officers
MEMORIAL FUND

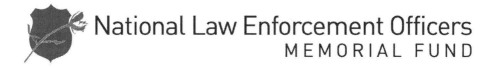

Contents

Foreword

A lot has occurred in the world during the 10 years since I wrote my last book, *Data Mining Solutions,*[1] with Teresa Blaxton: Google is formally incorporated and Viagra is approved for prescription sale (1998); the euro currency is introduced into Europe and Y2K software concerns loom (1999); America Online buys Time Warner for $162 billion and Bon Jovi is still topping the music charts (2000); 9/11 shakes the world and *Shrek* is released into movie theaters (2001); the United States invades Afghanistan and Kelly Clarkson wins on the first season of *American Idol* (2002); the United States declares war with Iraq and Arnold Schwarzenegger gets elected the governor of California (2003); a massive tsunami in Southeast Asia kills more than 200,000 people and the Boston Red Sox win the World Series after 86 years (2004); Hurricane Katrina devastates New Orleans and gas prices in the United States inflate to more than $3 a gallon (2005); Saddam Hussein is hanged for his crimes against humanity and Microsoft formally releases the Vista operating system (2006); the iPhone is brought to market and Evel Knievel finally meets his maker (2007). In 2008 and beyond, we now have global warming concerns, the emergence of China as an economic powerhouse, and ever-expanding terrorist threats and incidents.

So, when Taylor & Francis Group approached me about doing another book, I had to ask myself, what has *really* changed in this field and is it worth writing about? There are already a number of data-mining books in the marketplace that briefly touch on a few of the topics that I would want to cover in a new book. However, most of the coverage is "simple" at best

[1] Christopher Westphal and Teresa Blaxton, *Data Mining Solutions: Methods and Tools for Solving Real-World Problems* (New York: John Wiley & Sons, 1998).

and there is little discussion of the real-world detail required to understand and implement the concepts presented. Additionally, many of these books are geared toward a more generalized audience and I wanted to focus on homeland security professionals and consultants, law enforcement officials, the intelligence community, corporate security personnel, intelligence analysts, special agents, special investigative units, private investigators, financial-crimes units, and broadly to corporate information technology (IT) professionals.

To write another book I would have to draw on my experience from a "real world" perspective—as someone who has been in the trenches implementing and structuring the analytical and information-sharing systems in use across a number of government programs and commercial industries. There would have to be little hype or dramatization with respect to how the systems are described and, if anything, I would have to err on the side of being too honest about the positive and negative aspects of what is really being done behind the closed doors of our intelligence and law enforcement agencies.

I thought about all the systems I have been involved with implementing, the different technology companies I have worked with over the years, and the numerous types of requirements defined by the user communities, and determined that there was enough advancement in the market to create a publication. Thus, I agreed to write this book, and after a number of iterations with the publisher, we decided to title it *Data Mining for Intelligence, Fraud, & Criminal Detection: Advanced Analytics & Information Sharing Technologies.*

Even though there have been many changes in the world, a lot has stayed the same, specifically in the context of information sharing and data analytics. The post-9/11 era has brought about many promises of sharing information, performing better analysis, and generally making the world a safer place for everyone. Every organization, bureau, agency, and corporation has fundamental analytical needs that traditionally require a significant amount of data integration and resources to best understand the data. Whether trying to identify money laundering, insider trading, insurance fraud, terrorist behavior, or other forms of criminal activity, the analytical processes and system architectures are very similar to each other. In fact, the types of patterns exposed in one domain can frequently be used in another, and it is often not necessary to reinvest and re-create these capabilities across different industries when a common approach can be used. This book will address these topics in depth and review the commonalities, framework, and infrastructures necessary to implement and deploy complex analytical systems.

In 2004, the Government Accountability Office (GAO) provided a report[2] detailing approximately 200 government-based, data-mining projects. In 2005, they issued a follow-up report[3] discussing privacy protections. These and other reports[4] show that there are many controls in place to ensure the systems are documented, audited, and accountable for the types of analytics they are delivering. What they do not state is the overall effectiveness of these systems—successes or pitfalls. This book will review several such systems and explain both how they function and how they produce results, and will provide an overall review of their capabilities and relative limitations (data, representation, and structure).

In addition to analytical approaches (technologies and methodologies), this book will also cover the topic of information sharing. Law enforcement agencies are always looking for better ways to conduct their investigations. On TV, shows like *CSI* (Crime Scene Investigation) and *NCIS* (Naval Criminal Investigative Service) depict elite teams of special investigators quickly resolving cases by accessing different high-tech resources to analyze the evidence. With a few clicks of a button, they search through their data archives to find the smoking gun—case solved. Traditionally, law enforcement agencies have not been as proficient with advanced technologies and although intriguing, these TV shows do not reflect what occurs in the mainstream community. This book will shed light on the current state of affairs within law enforcement, as well as within the intelligence and commercial communities.

A significant gap exists between local- and state-level investigative efforts of counterdrug, financial crimes, terrorism, and fraud. While sharing a common and collective goal of combating crime, there is currently little, if any, analytical collaboration and minimal data sharing among state and local law enforcement agencies because each organization operates independently. Although politics, jurisdictional boundaries, and other factors all play into how much one agency is willing to support the sharing of its resources, many agencies embrace the ability to make effective use of their data resources. This book will address a number of information-sharing issues and why no large-scale capabilities are currently deployed throughout the government. It will also review several commercial efforts that have had limited success.

[2] "Data Mining: Federal Efforts Cover a Wide Range of Uses," U.S. Government Accountability Office, GAO-04-548, May 2004, http://www.gao.gov/new.items/d04548.pdf.

[3] "Data Mining: Agencies Have Taken Key Steps to Protect Privacy in Selected Efforts, but Significant Compliance Issues Remain," U.S. Government Accountability Office, GAO-05-866, August 2005, http://www.gao.gov/new.items/d05866.pdf.

[4] "Data Mining Report," Office of the Director of National Intelligence, February 15, 2008.

In the rapid pace of our changing world, it is difficult to keep up-to-date with industry trends in complex fields, such as data mining, text processing, crime mapping, link analysis, and other forms of advanced analytics. Many investigators are not adequately trained in the IT field—although this is changing as more advanced training is being provided to investigators coming up through the ranks. To better foster cooperation and data sharing among different agencies, and to alleviate the current noncollaborative investigative situation, fusion centers and programs have been proposed, are under development, or are actively operating to address these issues. This book will dedicate a fair amount of time to discussing how current fusion centers are really being designed and will review their Achilles' heel in terms of being able to meet their stated objectives.

Currently, there is very little in published literature that truly defines real-world systems, how they are deployed, and the positive and negative aspects of their operations. Other books only briefly touch the surface of what is possible, or potentially can be done, leaving the reader wondering what the true status and capabilities are in today's high-end analytical systems. Most importantly, this book provides a significant number of examples based on real-world data, systems, and operations. Specifically, the analytical approaches presented throughout this book are heavily based on graph theory (e.g., connect the dots) because it holds the most promise for understanding large quantities of discrete-valued information.

The book is organized into three parts: Part 1 provides an overview of the main topics involved with understanding the types of data that can be used in current analytical and information-sharing systems. This section covers the fundamental approaches to analyzing data and clearly delineates how to connect the dots among different data elements. Part 2 is exclusively focused on providing real-world examples of how data is used, manipulated, integrated, and interpreted. All scenarios presented in this section are derived from operational systems. Finally, Part 3 provides an overview of many information-sharing systems, organizations, and task forces as well as data interchange formats. It also discusses more ideal information-sharing and analytical architectures for use across a broad spectrum of applications.

I feel it is important to stress that the content, opinions, explanations, discussions, and materials presented in this manuscript do not necessarily reflect the official views of, or make endorsements for, any government or private organization or product. The interpretations of the data, patterns, and results presented herein are entirely based on my personal observations and opinions and alternative interpretations are certainly encouraged. Reasonable efforts have been made to present the material in the most objective fashion possible; however, it is still derived from a subjective understanding and viewpoint. The accuracy of this content is made according to the best materials publicly and readily available at the time of research. There may be omissions or errors in the descriptions of some systems, laws, or processes, but they do not materially affect the concepts being conveyed to the readership. Additionally, this field is rapidly changing and new or updated statistics, numbers, or laws and regulations may be introduced after the period of research and writing of this book has been concluded; therefore all information should be revalidated if it will be used for more in-depth discussion or related research.

Acknowledgments

There are a number of people I would like to personally thank for helping to support the content, writings, background, research, review, and comments on this book. The book is a culmination of my experiences and exposure to different environments, situations, cultures, and scenarios. Many people have provided me with invaluable support throughout my career and helped define the approaches, methodologies, and techniques presented in this book. I am certainly indebted to all who have contributed to this material. Specifically, I would like to thank the following:

Mark Listewnik, my editor from Taylor & Francis, who was the catalyst in identifying the need for this book and pulling together the resources necessary to turn it into a reality. I appreciate the encouragement, support, and guidance he provided throughout this endeavor. Additionally, I would like to acknowledge my project editor, Ari Silver, for his coordination and our interactions throughout this process. Also, thanks to Susan Lagerstrom-Fife and Sharon Palleschi from Springer for their quick responses and permission to use important content from a previous publication.

Cameron "Kip" Holmes, chief of the Financial Remedies Section of the Arizona Attorney General's Office (AZAG), for his years of dedicated service combating financial crimes, and his innovative approaches to prosecuting money laundering activities. I would also like to thank Kip for supplying the breadth of materials documenting a number of the anti–money laundering operations on the Southwest Border. Detective John Shallue of the Phoenix Police Department for his service to law enforcement and for the case reference materials generously provided. Also, thanks to Hal

White from the AZAG for his insightful research, behind-the-scenes work, and for his dedication to law enforcement.

David R. Dugas, United States Attorney's Office for the Middle District of Louisiana, for his insight into several cases and prosecutions related to Hurricane Katrina. Michael Delafosse, director of the Office of Unemployment Insurance Administration, Louisiana Department of Labor, for his inputs on how the automated safeguards implemented in their systems help flag anomalies in their claims data.

Vicente S. Aquino, executive director, Anti–Money Laundering Council (AMLC) Secretariat (Philippines), for his diligence in combating financial crimes and for his input regarding the operations at AMLC. Agus "Gooseman" Surachman from Pelaporan dan Analisis Transaksi: Keuangan (PPATK) (Indonesia) for his energy and enthusiasm in wanting to expand his knowledge of the world and for contributing to this manuscript. Alejandro Rocchetti, Pablo Aliaga, and Danielle Iriarte of Systech S.A. (Argentina) for their support with Financial Intelligence Units (FIUs) throughout Latin America including Conselho de Controle de Atividades Financeiras (COAF) (Brazil), Secretaría de Prevención de Lavado de Dinero o Bienes (SEPRELAD) (Paraguay), and Unidad de Investigaćion Financiera (UIF) (El Salvador). Pavel Cherkashin from Security Problems Institute (SPI2) for his comments, inputs, and background on the Russian Financial Monitoring Service (FMS). Police Col. Seehanat Prayoonrat, the deputy secretary-general at the Anti–Money Laundering Office (AMLO) in Thailand, for his dedication and pursuit of prosecuting criminal enterprises and for positioning his country in a leadership role.

Andrew Shankman, Financial Crimes Enforcement Network (FinCEN), for his stimulating conversations, his realistic viewpoints on all matters large and small, and his voice of reason. Christina Klinger, FinCEN, for her steadfastness, realism, and unwavering support to do what is right. Thank you for the many years of support and for all the discussions and conversations we have had throughout those years. Shawn Polonet, acting Assistant Special Agent in Charge (ASAC), Immigrations and Custom Enforcement, New York, and Gary Murray, former director, New York High Intensity Financial Crime Area (HIFCA) for their devoted support to law enforcement and for their inputs and feedback on the El Dorado Task Force. Also, thanks to Mark A. Marshall, chief of police, Smithfield, Virginia, for his edits/comments as well as his involvement in creating information-sharing systems and for his perseverance in ensuring cooperation among law enforcement agencies.

Special thanks to Debbie Tyler from Visual Analytics Inc. (VAI) for her technical editing, insightful inputs, direct comments, and overall support during this process. David O'Connor (VAI) for his brilliance, his stellar programming abilities, and his ingenuity in creating VisuaLinks®—by far the best visualization and link discovery tool available in the open marketplace. Bennett McPhatter (VAI) for his determination and resolve to implement DIG® (Digital Information Gateway), perhaps one of the most successful real-world and operationally proven information-sharing tools in existence. Also, in memory of Carl Antonelli, a member of my staff at VAI, for his positive attitude, creative personality, vast intellect, and off-sense of humor; he is missed by many people.

The following also deserve my thanks for their continued support over the years: Dick Baer, Tom Carr, Leo Urbaniak, Kevin Hohn, Ken Middleton, Phil Canter, Robert Dintino, Brad King, Johan du Plooy, Peter Fryer, K. J. Min, Andrea Garavaglia, Paolo Consonni, Karl Eiselsberg, John Carbaugh, Jesus Cruz, Al Brandenstein, Mustafa Cem Arpaci, Frank Doe, Paul Bernier, Len Starling, as well as the entire staff at VAI.

To my son, Fletcher, who made sure that I had enough breaks and playtime to keep things properly balanced in the house. Finally, my biggest "thank you" is to my beautiful wife, Libby, for the support she provided throughout this whole undertaking. I appreciate her inputs and comments, her guidance, and most of all, her patience and endurance to ensure I had the time to dedicate to completing this book. I love you.

—Chris Westphal

The Author

Christopher Westphal is cofounder and CEO of Visual Analytics, Inc. (VAI—http://www.visualanalytics.com). Since its inception in 1998, he has guided the growth of the company from a fledgling start-up into a world-class provider of visualization software, information-sharing systems, and advanced analytical training. His clients include federal, state, and local law enforcement, all major intelligence agencies, the Department of Defense, civilian agencies, international Financial Intelligence Units (FIUs), and large corporations. VAI is a recognized leader in the intelligence and law enforcement industries and has garnered industry recognition and accolades, including Deloitte's Technology Fast 50 (Maryland), Maryland's International Leadership Award, and Maryland Muscle Award, and was named a finalist for the Ernst & Young Entrepreneur of the Year Award.

Prior to starting VAI, Mr. Westphal held key roles at the BDM Corporation, the Institute for Defense Analyses (IDA), Syscon (Logicon), and several other high-tech companies. During his collective tenures, he designed analytical systems and provided management expertise to critical government programs addressing organized crime, narcotics trafficking, money laundering, terrorism, tax evasion, insider trading, border crossings, smuggling, and criminal enterprises. He has supported a number of government offices and programs including the Office of National Drug Control Policy (ONDCP), Financial Crimes Enforcement Network (FinCEN), Internal Revenue Service (IRS) Criminal Investigations Division (CID), Drug Enforcement Administration (DEA), U.S. Army, Department of Justice (DOJ), Defense Intelligence Agency (DIA),

Federal Bureau of Investigation (FBI), and Bureau of Alcohol, Tobacco and Firearms (ATF), and has consulted with government agencies in more than thirty countries on six continents.

Mr. Westphal has defined and created a number of unique and innovative approaches for performing visual data mining on large volumes of disparate data acquired from multiple sources. He is a recognized authority in the detection and exposure of complex patterns. Some of his investigative background stems from his early operational experience implementing anti–money laundering and fraud detection systems. He has also applied his expertise to help fight white-collar crimes and various forms of corruption, which has resulted in criminal convictions.

Mr. Westphal has worked personally with the banking and financial ministries throughout Europe, Asia, the Middle East, and South America in relation to fraud, anti–money laundering, embezzlement, asset forfeiture investigations, and various regulatory matters. He has worked to coordinate foreign regional practice areas across industry segments to aid enforcement and compliance. Fortune 1,000 companies, government agencies, high-tech companies, and consulting firms have sought advice from Westphal relating to compliance, risk management, data governance issues, and systems modernization.

He has authored numerous publications and several books including *Data Mining Solutions: Methods and Tools for Solving Real-World Problems* (Westphal/Blaxton, John & Wiley Sons, 1998) and *Readings in Knowledge Acquisition: Current Practices and Trends* (McGraw/Westphal, Ellis Horwood Limited, 1990), and a chapter in *Net-Centric Approaches to Intelligence and National Security* (Ladner/Petry, Springer, 2005). He has served as a referee, editor, and reviewer for large international journals and conferences on topics, such as data mining, expert systems, decision support, and data visualization.

Addressing data visualization, data mining, and the associated challenges and benefits of analyzing complex data sets, Mr. Westphal speaks frequently on these matters before government, banking, legal, compliance, and academic audiences. He has lectured internationally to thousands of business and information technology professionals. He is routinely asked to speak and participate on technology panels and sought out for his expert opinion on advanced analytical systems and data-mining methodologies.

Mr. Westphal was born and raised in New York. He received his B.S. in computer science from the School of Engineering at Tulane University. He can be reached at westphal@visualanalytics.com or chris_westphal@yahoo.com.

PART 1

INTERPRETING PATTERNS AND ANALYTICAL METHODOLOGIES

The goal of this section is to provide some fundamental insight into real-world scenarios, issues, and problems commonly encountered with operational analytical environments. There are all sorts of definitions for the intelligence production process, intelligence cycles, and intelligence analysis, along with a breadth of tools and technologies. There are programs to access, sort, and filter data; systems to perform advanced analysis and correlation; and packages that present, report on, and help disseminate the information. Several integrated environments, using a cadre of technologies to support the intelligence production cycle, have also been developed for both government and commercial purposes. These environments increase productivity by enabling faster processing and contextual analyses, which are paying off by providing timely, accurate, and more detailed results.

When we discuss the intelligence production cycle, we are talking about the *process* used to generate results for dissemination, which is ultimately used to make actionable decisions (e.g., seize accounts, arrest people, or even launch missiles). These results are derived from multiple iterations of accessing, analyzing, and presenting information within these environments. Typically, intelligence production begins with identifying source data and creating a repository in which information can be structured, stored, and reviewed. Unfortunately, in many systems, the actual analysis and reporting stages represent only a small fraction of the overall effort and tend to occur at the end of a fairly comprehensive process.

Perhaps one of the most overlooked, and certainly one of the most important dimensions associated with performing analysis, is the quality of the data being processed. This is critical for highly discrete data values, such as names (people, organizations), addresses, identification numbers, and incident details associated with fraud and criminal detection data sets. In fact, many published reports estimate that the amount of time applied to normalizing, formatting, and cleansing data in preparation for analysis takes between 50 and 90 percent of the time applied to the overall process. An overwhelming number of agencies and organizations have created databases without giving the proper forethought to how the information is eventually used. This directly impacts how the information is collected and stored, and, ultimately, analyzed. Without the proper collection interfaces to enforce the recording of, say, a telephone number, there can be many different formats presented. For example, 1-123-555-1212, 123-555-1212, (123) 555-1212, and 1235551212 represent several variations of the same number. The less consistent the collection method, the more post-processing is required to ensure reliable and accurate analytics.

Once the inconsistencies, incompleteness, and quality issues are addressed, the data can be analyzed to expose patterns and trends. Interpreting the data requires a thorough understanding of the underlying content, including its core representations, how it was collected, how it is stored, and how it is accessed. Additionally, it requires an analytical perspective in terms of what questions can be answered from the data. Often, knowing what questions to ask is half the battle in exposing new patterns and trends. Important to note is the fact that each pattern can be broken down into its fundamental network structures, temporal sequences, and/or geospatial relationships and interpreted in context (e.g., financial crimes, point-of-sale fraud, embezzlement, etc.). Ultimately, there is little difference between the types of patterns associated with different activities (e.g., money laundering versus insurance fraud) because there are many similarities in their data structures and the primary differences are often based on the interpretation of the results in the context of their respective domains.

This section will review a number of data quality issues, including value errors, missing data, bad structures, and uniqueness of specific data types. It also introduces approaches to standardizing representations and discusses entity resolution and anonymity techniques. The section then goes on to present different types of patterns and their interpretations (importance, reliability, and consistency), and then wraps up by presenting scenarios based on real-world data sources and environments. The discussions are based heavily on entity analytics and the use of network diagrams to convey results and interpret data. Once a person has a good analytical foundation, it can easily be migrated between different industries and domains, and, more importantly, used to expose new patterns and trends.

Chapter 1

Overview[1]

[1] Much of this section was derived from a previous book chapter, reprinted with permission: Christopher Westphal, "Analyzing Intelligence Data: Next Generation Technologies for Connecting the Dots," in *Net-Centric Approaches to Intelligence and National Security,* ed. Roy Ladner and Fred Petry, 83–101 (New York: Springer, 2005).

Introduction

The information technology (IT) boom of the 1990s left many organizations and companies awash in data. With the popularity of the Internet, data sets were collected on virtually every topic, for every purpose, for every mouse click, for every reason imaginable. Often, multiple databases or huge data warehouses were built to store these immense quantities of data. Although billions of dollars are spent every year to collect and store information, data owners, paradoxically, often spend only pennies on analysis. What has been missing from the IT landscape is a way in which all of the data can be effectively analyzed—a way to *connect the dots*. Without a means to use and understand the data that has been collected, the owners of the data will never realize the potential benefits of these resources. This has already been evidenced by the events of 9/11 and the government's limited effort to share, combine, analyze, and report on the pre- and postindicators.

Since the disastrous events of September 11, 2001, governments and businesses around the world are operating in a state of heightened security and awareness of the possibility of additional terrorist attacks. While these unfortunate events changed our lives forever, they have also alerted us to the dangers of fanatical individuals and groups who are willing to go to any lengths and face any and all consequences for what they believe. This situation has caused government agencies and corporations to focus more seriously on issues of security, information sharing, and collaborative analyses. These themes have been repeatedly emphasized by many top officials in the world's leading democratic governments and private industries because terrorism and similar threats[2] are an international concern.

In light of these and other events, it has become increasingly clear that the intelligence community is not a collaborative set of organizations. In fact, the reality is that there has been little sharing of intelligence information between agencies. Had there been a more collaborative atmosphere between intelligence agencies and better analytical systems in place, some people would argue that September 11th might have been avoided. This reality has caused the government to seek new tools and techniques that allow faster, better, and more effective ways of understanding and analyzing data contained within home agencies as well as data gathered and owned by other agencies.

Corporations are also operating on a heightened sense of awareness of external and internal threats to their business. Critical areas of analysis, like fraud detection in the banking, insurance, and healthcare industries, must utilize better and more powerful systems to detect the anomalies

[2] Including, for example, money laundering, narcotics trafficking, and serious fraud.

and patterns contained in their data sources—that is, they must work smarter. Other areas of analysis, such as understanding consumer spending patterns, are becoming increasingly important as firms attempt to maximize revenues through targeted marketing and cross-selling while minimizing click fraud and other detriments to their operations.

As companies become increasingly aware of their vulnerabilities, they look for new ways to identify, quantify, and protect themselves from the huge losses that fraud and security breaches can cause. Others want to stay abreast or ahead of their competition in the marketplace by managing their data more efficiently to identify improvements to their business processes and activities. All of these scenarios and situations are based on the ability to effectively access, integrate, and analyze data to expose new patterns.

Sharing Data

Sharing data is not a new concept nor is it technically difficult. In fact, the capabilities have been in place for quite some time. It is somewhat ironic that freeware, such as Napster, Gnutella, Morpheus, BearShare, and KaZaA, is readily downloadable from the Internet and allows millions of people across the globe to share files, documents, pictures, videos, and music with the click of a button, whereas the intelligence community and law enforcement agencies have little capability or impetus to share information. Many of the obstacles have to do with the limitations on the application of the technologies required to facilitate the analyses, and some can be attributed to politics, stovepipe systems, isolated processes, or compartmented procedures (and related security) that dominate how these organizations operate.

The analytical landscape has changed over the past decade. Traditional approaches were focused on processing standardized reports and fixed types of output where the interfaces were static and the queries largely predetermined and unsophisticated. However, the amount of data currently being generated by today's systems far exceeds our capacity to analyze it. Many organizations and agencies have been collecting data for long periods of time and have built up vast databases, information stores, and data warehouses.

The goal is to determine how to "connect the dots" in these data repositories to discover the important patterns and relationships. It is such a simple concept—connect the dots. In fact, many children play this game early in their development process as part of learning their ABCs and/or numbers. Each correct connection between a set of points reveals more

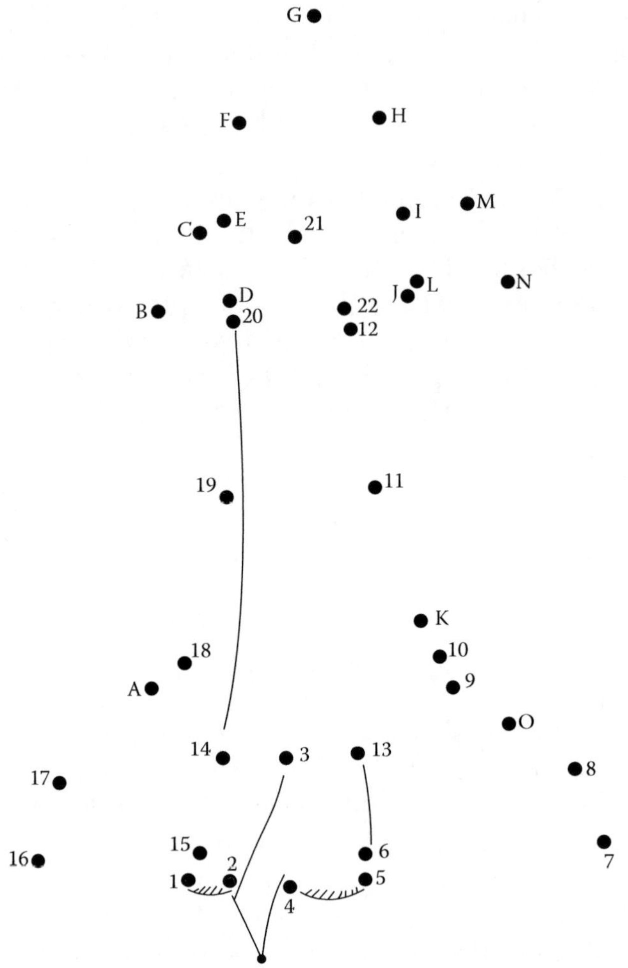

Figure 1.1 Connect the dots.

of a hidden pattern. As long as the correct sequence of numbers or letters is followed, the final diagram is eventually completed—exposing the "big picture." How hard can it be? See if you can figure out what is shown[3] in Figure 1.1—start connecting the numbers followed by the letters.

As we have all heard from post-9/11 analyses, there were plenty of indicators based on known processes or suspicious activities. For example, we learned that if someone enters the country on a student visa, then attends flight training for commercial aircraft, and has indirect linkages to known terrorists, they are most likely a prime target for a follow-up investigation. Connect the dots—the picture is clear, right?

[3] http://lsda.jsc.nasa.gov/docs/kids/shuttledot2.gif.

Unfortunately, connecting the dots would indicate that we already know the pattern and that it would be a simple matter of generating a query to report on all known instances of the pattern. Suppose Figure 1.1 did not have any numbers or letters. Would the pattern still be recognizable? Hindsight plays an important role in exposing certain previously unknown patterns. Thus, we must constantly ask ourselves:

What does a terrorist look like?
What does a money launderer look like?
What does a criminal look like?
What does a fraudster look like?

Simply identifying the data to answer these questions can help determine what "dots" need to be connected. Regrettably, for many organizations, it is not known what sources of data are even available, how to combine those sources that are ultimately identified, or, fundamentally, what patterns are of importance. Often, the data is not readily accessible, is controlled by a different group, or does not contain the proper information. So the question becomes: What is the sequence or order in which the dots are connected and what happens when there are missing dots?

The templates (or rules) ultimately created to derive the answers (e.g., connect the dots) will be based on known scenarios and can certainly be automated wherever possible. However, the real threat lies in the "unknown." Changes in the existing patterns or different approaches to circumventing the systems will ultimately compromise the templates that are in place. Instead of airline training, the subjects apply for commercial driving licenses or explosive permits, purchase large storage containers, or simply rent a truck. Will the existing templates flag these events? Will the data be available? Will the analyst know what to look for?

It is critical that the analytical methodologies used in these types of environments are flexible and adaptive to help find different variations in the patterns of interest. Keep in mind that there are no *right* answers and there are *no* wrong answers. Any templates defined to help expose probable targets of interest should ultimately be reviewed by a human analyst to determine if the template was properly applied, and most important, to determine if there are any exceptions to the rule. The results must always be verified and should never be determined 100 percent by computer algorithms.

A good example of this occurred when developing a data-centric application for the Department of the Treasury where a number of different data sources (over a dozen) were being integrated to target a particular area in the southeastern region of the United States for exposing noncompliant tax filers. Two of the primary data sources processed exposed a "subject" as a well-qualified target, a high-value asset (i.e., a residence worth over $1,000,000) with a low reported means of income (i.e., less than $10,000).

In this case, the house was located in a very affluent suburb of Atlanta and had a market value of more than $1.5 million (circa 1995). The subject had a reported income of only $4,000. However, the system performed according to expectations. Once the target was identified, special agents performed a more thorough review of the data to confirm the circumstances of the pattern and quickly discovered additional "dimensions" to it that were, as of yet, not factored into the discovery process. As it turns out, the pattern was triggered by one of the children (junior) where the income amount was the total interest reported from a savings account. The father (senior), with the exact same name, had properly and correctly reported an income required to afford and support the residence.

In this case, the rules were perfectly valid and exposed circumstances that would normally result in an active investigation; however, there are always exceptions to the rule(s), as this scenario showed.[4] One might think one has defined a very good pattern (e.g., conditions), but until it can be tested and confirmed using real-world data and circumstances, it is just a concept that may never trigger, might trigger too often, or could, indeed, be perfect. The due diligence naturally performed by the special agents avoided a situation that could have gotten unpleasant, at best, and provided valuable feedback in terms of how the pattern can be modified to better reflect the reality of their operating environment.

Connect the Dots

State and local law enforcement agencies are always looking for a better "mousetrap" to use in conducting their investigations. Often, a lone investigator tirelessly searches through the clues, putting all of the pieces together to solve the crime. Each clue is critical in and of itself, but more important is knowing how each applies to the overall case. Although data-centric technologies have been deployed in a variety of law enforcement agencies (LEAs) to help them better comprehend and understand their case data, integrate datasets, and pursue leads, historically, LEAs have not fully embraced[5] the use of advanced information and analytical technologies to help them understand and manage large quantities of data.

[4] There are also, many times, exceptions to the exceptions.

[5] Often citing budgetary limitations or the high cost of implementing analytical systems.

Law enforcement is a unique challenge in the analytical world because each organization operates independently while trying to achieve a common and collective goal of combating crime. Although many issues surround each agency's willingness to support the sharing of their resources, many desire additional capabilities to make more effective use of their resources. Collaborative data sharing among different agencies is an idea whose time has come and represents a win–win situation for all involved. There are a growing number of programs, funding sources, and mandated requirements that have targeted the incorporation of information-sharing technologies into their underlying architectures.

The following example and related diagrams show how an investigator might pursue a case where multiple sources of data are accessed across a variety of different agencies. Usually, there is a known starting point from a past crime, arrest, or some type of situation. This type of investigation typically represents a "reactive" situation.

Reactive analyses are based on the preselection of an entity, such as a person (as in this case), organization, account, location, shell casing, DNA sample, or criminal event. The entity of interest is already known and becomes the center, or focus, of the analysis. Ultimately, the goal of a reactive analysis is to expand on the known network to find additional clues and leads where the investigator would look at all aspects of the subject to determine other people who are related to him or her through family, business dealings, criminal records, or any other source, to show unusual connections or associations that might expose important connections to other criminal activities. Indirect relationships, through addresses, phone numbers, or vehicles, may also be pursued by the investigator.

Following the path of connections, additional entities can be identified based on their connection(s) to the original entity. To maintain the context of the analysis, any new entities then become the source for the next level of inquiry. One of the most fitting technologies used by LEAs and intelligence communities throughout the world is link analysis to visually depict the entities and their connections. This technology helps the investigator see the big picture and understand how the entities are related, and helps to expose hidden relationships. As such, the majority of the examples presented in this book are based on the representation, presentation, and interpretation of network diagrams to exposed patterns and trends.

The first source utilized in this example is based on criminal arrest data, usually provided by the local police department. Police departments have access to a number of different sources, including computer-aided dispatch (CAD) systems, incident reports, record management systems

Figure 1.2 The Suspect.

(RMSs), prison records, and booking/arrest data, to name just a few. Some of these systems are home-grown to meet the specific needs of the organization while others are adapted from commercial software packages. Often, there is no consistency among the sources, the values represented, or their internal structures.

The investigation starts off where a subject[6] with the name "Brad Q. Billings" has been causing some problems around town and is currently under suspicion for a number of narcotics-related incidents including burglary, assault, and the intent to distribute methamphetamines. The entity shown in Figure 1.2 is depicted with a specific date of birth used to help distinguish him from other people with similar names. Any other supporting information, such as physical data (e.g., height, weight, hair color, etc.), scars/tattoos, known aliases, are represented as descriptive "attributes" of the entity and can be viewed[7] through other reporting and detailing mechanisms.

Keep in mind that many organizations and agencies that collect information often do not fully understand how the data will be used or analyzed. The real challenge is in improving the accuracy of the data through better collection and representation methods. In this case, the only uniquely identifying information is the combination of the name and date of birth. For local or regional analytics, this may not cause too much concern; yet, nationally, there may be multiple people with the same name and birth date. While all facets should be considered when reviewing suspect information, investigators also don't want to exclude a potential candidate because of missing information.

Continuing with the example, Figure 1.3 shows the first level of connections, revealing that the subject has relationships with a variety of

[6] As with all examples throughout this book, all names, addresses, and numbers have been made up and do not reflect any ongoing investigations nor intentionally reflect any real-world entities. This example represents a fictitious investigation and does not reflect or detail many of the interim steps required for accessing the data.

[7] Different commercial tools in the marketplace support different methods for performing a drill-down on any displayed entities or objects.

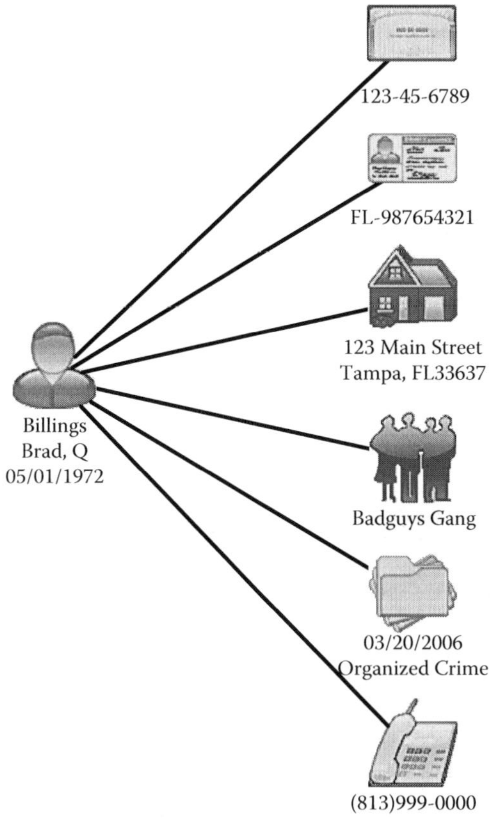

Figure 1.3 First level of connections.

different objects, including a criminal organization called the "Badguys Gang." There is also a criminal file (represented by the folder icon) that contains all of the details, dates, times, locations, and descriptions associated with the case. Additionally, the subject's driver's license, Social Security number (SSN), phone number, and last known address are depicted in this diagram.

Additional searches to try and identify any associates, gang members, or family members living at the same address come up negative from the criminal database. Thus, there is no other information in this particular source that will further extend the network. However, because this agency has access to other sources of data, the investigator cross-references all of the information with another online source. In this example, the phones, ID numbers, and addresses are checked against a federal database containing Suspicious Activity Reports (SARs) filed by banks, financial institutions, casinos, and money service businesses (MSBs—see sidebar) throughout the United States.

Money Service Business

On January 1, 2002, as part of the changes enacted by the U.S. Patriot Act, requirements went into effect for MSBs to submit SARs. According to the U.S. Department of the Treasury, an MSB is defined as a money transmitter or issuer, or seller or redeemer of money orders or traveler's checks, which also includes the U.S. Postal Service. MSBs are required to report suspicious activity within 30 days by filing the SAR-MSB Form when a transaction (or series of transactions) exceeds, $2,000 and is believed to be derived from illegal activity, serves no business or apparent lawful purpose, or is attempting to evade any requirements of the Bank Secrecy Act (BSA).

The basic business process of MSBs is to transfer money within a network of authorized agents. There is always a sender and a receiver of the money, and reviewing the flow of money between the actual participants (i.e., the subjects) in the network is the basis for performing money-laundering investigations. However, it is also a duty of the MSB to monitor the individual agents to ensure they remain compliant with their reporting requirements and are not trying to circumvent any controls within the system. At the end of 2007, there were a little over 38,000 registered MSBs[8] within the United States.

[8] Estimates suggest that fewer than 20 percent of MSBs are registered with FinCEN; from 2007 National Money Laundering Strategy.

Figure 1.4 shows that a match was made in the SAR database on the driver's license number. As it turns out, our suspect was involved in three separate suspicious financial transactions where the driver's license number was listed along with a different Social Security number that was off by one digit, a different phone number, and an address that appears to match the first address (Street = St.). Interestingly, our suspect also listed a different date of birth during these transactions, resulting in a new icon depicting the differences.

The thicker linkages indicate that the same driver's license, Social Security number, address, and telephone were all used for each of the three suspicious transactions. Thus, the investigator has a high degree of confidence that he or she is still targeting the same suspect from the criminal investigation. Of further interest is that all of the transactions occurred on the same account.[9] This entity becomes the focus

[9] Technically, SAR-MSB forms to not utilize account information.

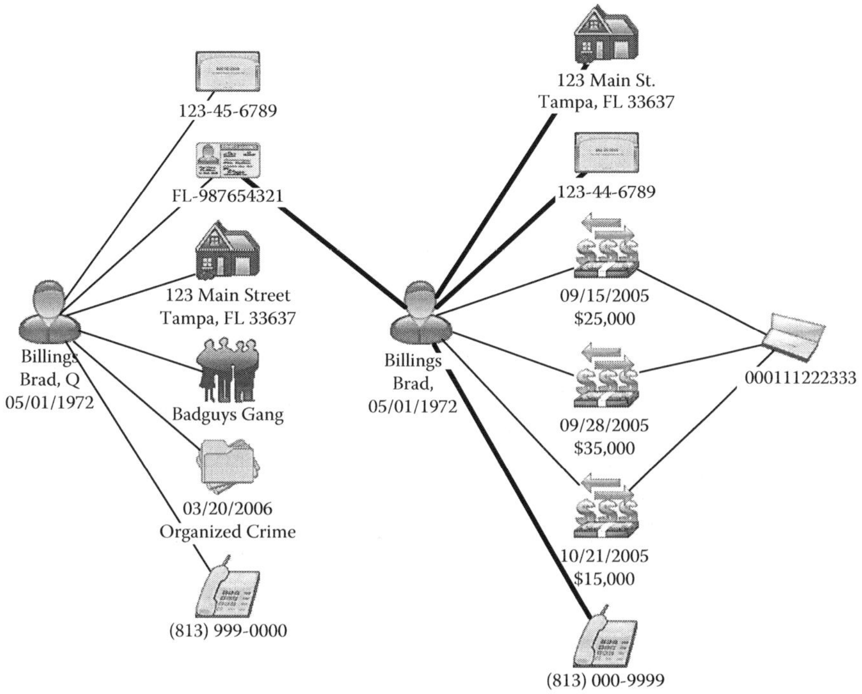

Figure 1.4 Money transfers related to subject.

of the next inquiry: To check for any wire transfers made against that account.

Figure 1.5 shows that there were six transactions (wires) on this account. Each wire was a deposit for an amount less than $10,000. A quick review of the transfer dates showed that they occurred within a few weeks of one another. Most likely, a counterpart (e.g., another gang member) in a different city wired the proceeds of criminal activity, such as narcotics trafficking, prostitution, or extortion, to the account maintained by our suspect.

The bank became suspicious of these wire transfers and filed SARs on the suspect when he came to withdraw the money from this account. From this information, the investigator concludes that the money is most likely being used to fund the operations of the criminal organization (the Badguys Gang). With all of the detail being shown, this diagram is getting fairly complex. Some cleanup is performed by merging together similar entities and collapsing the transactions into a composite representation. The results are presented in Figure 1.6.

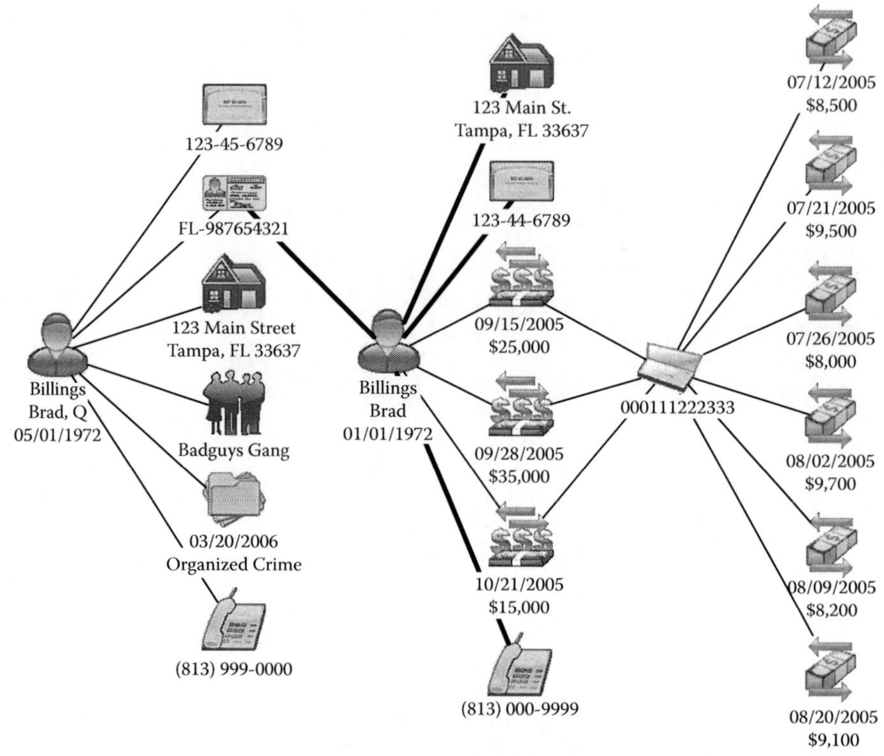

Figure 1.5 Suspect's account receives wire transfers.

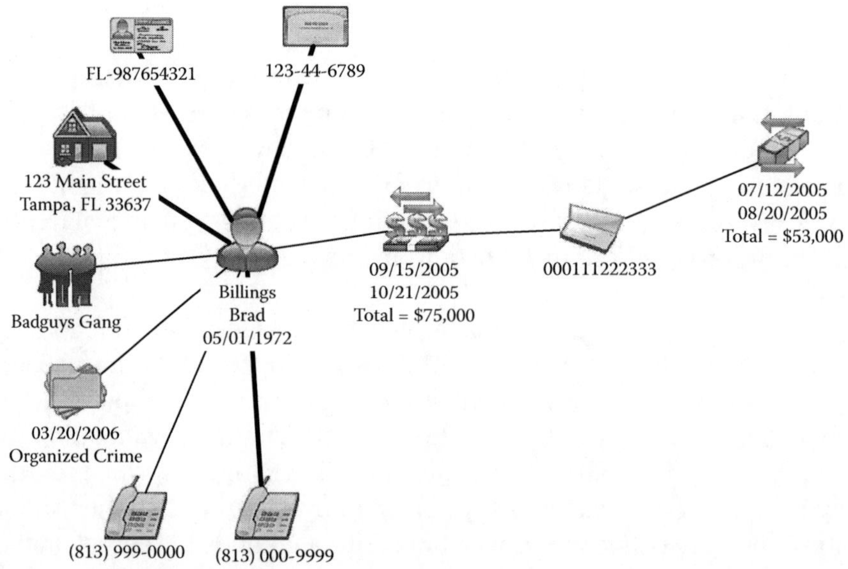

Figure 1.6 Cleaned-up interim network diagram.

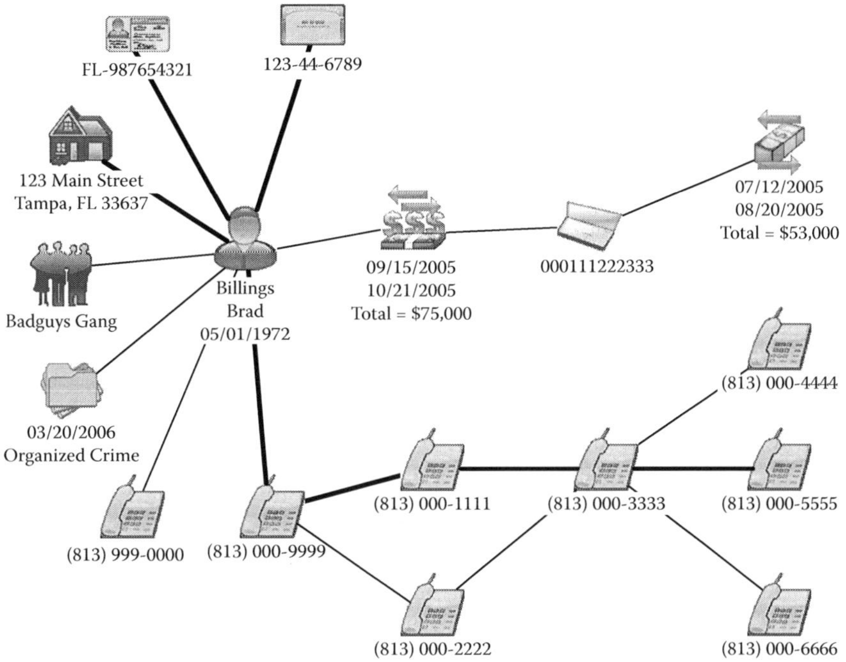

Figure 1.7 Telephone toll calls.

With no additional suspects at this time, the investigator opts to search some other sources that relate to the criminal case associated with the suspect. At this point in the investigation, the focus turns to the telephone numbers[10] associated with the subject.

Figure 1.7 shows that there are several different phone numbers that are indirectly connected to our suspect's phone. In this case, the thicker linkages indicate more frequent communication (i.e., more phone calls) between the two numbers. Often in the narcotics trade, trust relationships are built up between the different players, promoting frequent communications regarding product and payment. Although phone numbers are commonly discarded to help avoid being tracked, our current suspect has used his number exclusively to call a "lieutenant" in the gang to coordinate their activities.

---

[10] Often during investigations, pen registers and trap/trace devices are used to record the numbers dialed to/from a phone. Additionally, the phone companies maintain very accurate call records that can be obtained through court orders. Ultimately an investigator can obtain Title III phone intercepts to listen to the actual calls once there is enough justification and a court order signed by a judge to warrant this type of approach. An interesting note about Title IIIs is that there are privileged conversations that are excluded from monitoring, such as those between the attorney and client, husband and wife, priest and penitent, and doctor and patient, unless the privilege has been waived or there are discussions regarding criminal activities.

The network of phone calls expands for three levels. Each new phone number will have to be individually verified to determine the subscriber and their role in the gang (if any) or other related entity. Using this type of representation, the investigator gets an understanding of how a phone interacts with other phones. What it does not tell the investigator is the pattern of interaction among the phones. Generally, there will be some type of temporal component (i.e., time and date) associated with the event (e.g., the phone call) that can be used to establish a pattern.

When detecting temporal behaviors, one must reflect on the type of data that is available for supporting such patterns. Typically, we think of "transactional" data as events, such as financial deposits and withdrawals, border crossings, credit card purchases, travel events, terrorist actions, narcotics dealing, and, of course, telephone tolls. The common thread between all transactions is that they support a time/date characteristic. A single transaction is usually not significant. However, when all transactions for a specific type of data (e.g., a phone number, a credit card, an account) are viewed collectively, we can infer behavior based on how the transactions occurred. Viewing transactions in the context of other transactions can lead to some very interesting results.

The patterns exposed through a temporal analysis will show when the phone calls tend to occur. Examples would include absolute temporal references (e.g., every Tuesday between 2:00 and 3:00 p.m.) and sequential temporal references (e.g., phone X calls phone Y only after a call from phone Z). In this example, the investigator is interested only in exposing additional subjects and, therefore, is concerned only with how the phones connect with one another.

The focus of this investigation, targeting additional suspects, can be achieved by checking local Department of Motor Vehicles (DMV) records. Because the phone data contains the addresses of the subscribers, the investigator can cross-reference the addresses to vehicles (identified by vehicle identification numbers or VINs). Figure 1.8 shows how the data might be presented for one of the phone entities.

This investigation reveals an additional subject. The ultimate goal of the investigator is to connect the dots to expose as many potential targets as possible, and then select the most "well-qualified target" for additional review and follow up. This process can continue for as long as there are data sources available to query. Each time a new entity appears within the display, any of the prior sources can, and should, be requeried to determine if the entity has other connections. Figure 1.9 illustrates the concept of cross-referencing among different sources.

As shown in the diagram, the investigation starts in Source A with a specific target, A1, who is shown connected (1) to another suspect, A2.

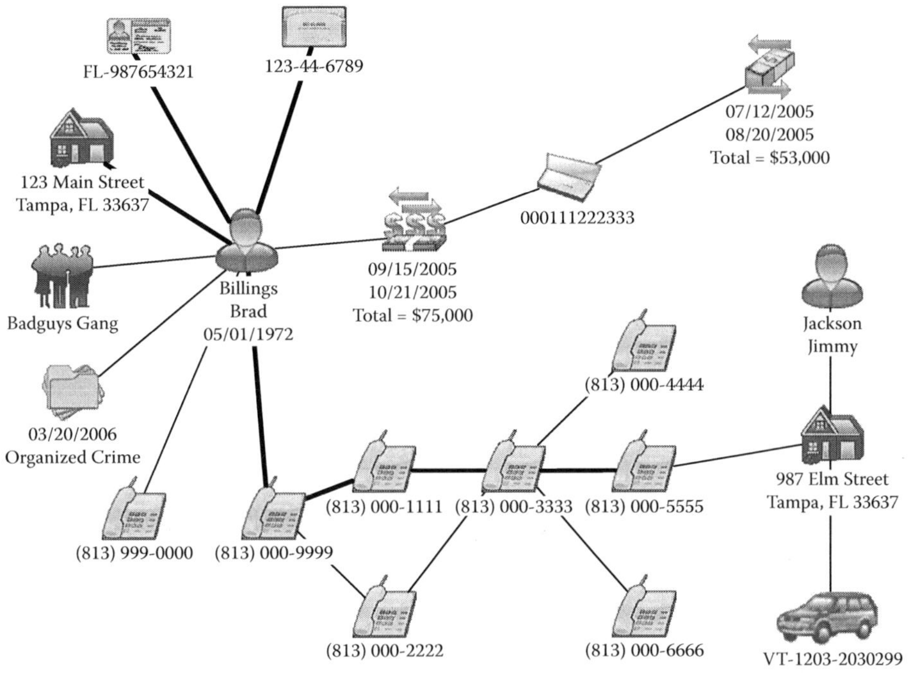

Figure 1.8 Vehicle registration data referenced.

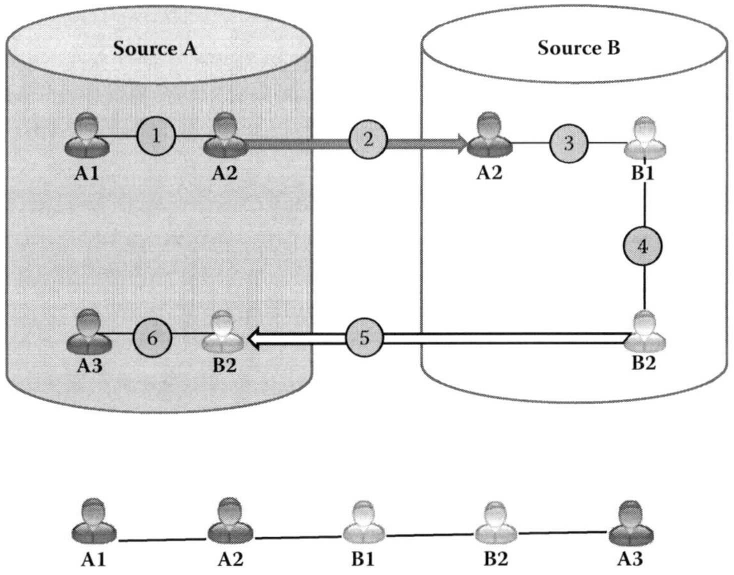

Figure 1.9 Cross-referencing data entities across different data sources.

A search of both A1 and A2 within Source B, as referenced by (2), shows a match for A2. Expanding the network (3) shows that A2 and B1 are connected and B1 is further connected (4) to B2. Both B1 and B2 can then be searched back in Source A, as presented by (5), where B2 is matched. Further expansion (6) shows that B2 and A3 are connected. Therefore, indirectly A1, A2, and A3 in Source A are all related, but only with information supplied by Source B. These types of cross-references have proven to be invaluable and help to expose larger and more complex criminal patterns.

State and local agencies can provide a wide range of data—from real property and utility records to driver's licenses and criminal arrests. The volumes of data maintained by state and local governments provide more detail (resolution) on individuals to help round out data collected at the federal level. Furthermore, commercial information providers (e.g., subscription services) are also invaluable resources in providing timely access across a large number of different sources, although many have been slow in offering a real-time batch query capability (e.g., a type of proactive search). Other private sources of data, including rental car companies, commercial airlines, and banks, can also be used to gain a better understanding of certain subjects.

Analytical Versus Referential Data

As seen in the previous example, five sources of data were effectively combined to expose important patterns of interest and help connect the dots. The sources used in this example represented "analytical data" such that, individually, they could all be analyzed independently of one another because each has its own patterns and trends. However, there are sources of data used to supplement the analysis that are defined as "referential," meaning they contain no analytical value, only supplemental information with respect to the analytical sources.

A referential source is used almost exclusively to determine if specific characteristics exist for certain entities and usually does not support the ability to expose interesting relationships or networks of value. Time permitting, referential sources are often included as additional datasets that are typically accessed in a passive fashion when the investigator previews the data. For example, if any of the people in the prior example were wanted on outstanding warrants, they could be flagged with a special icon indicating a prior murder, narcotics conviction, or money-laundering indictment. The importance of this fact would be shown graphically because the checks were made automatically in the background by the system.

For example, one federal agency maintains a database of all investigations conducted on various financial crimes and money-laundering operations. The primary reference for pulling case files from this system is a document control number, which is associated with each financial transaction housed in their primary analytical databases. Every case in this database of approximately 100,000 entries consists of one or more unique document control numbers that can be matched against the main data source comprising more than 200,000,000 records. The control number defines the original source, the date of the filing, and a unique sequence number. As an analyst reviews the 200,000,000 records, and finds a match in the case database, the case reference is added to the transaction as a special attribute and its image is overridden with a special icon (as shown in Figure 1.10), giving the analyst a quick visual clue that his or her current analytical data contains information that has been worked in a prior case. This helps maximize the analyst's time because he or she doesn't need to pursue leads that have already been worked in another investigation.

In another example, the reference source is the Social Security Death Master (SSDM) Index, which is acquired from the U.S. government—interestingly, from the Department of Commerce. This source contains more than 80,000,000 records of people who are deceased and have received a death benefit from the government.[11] The record format is fairly

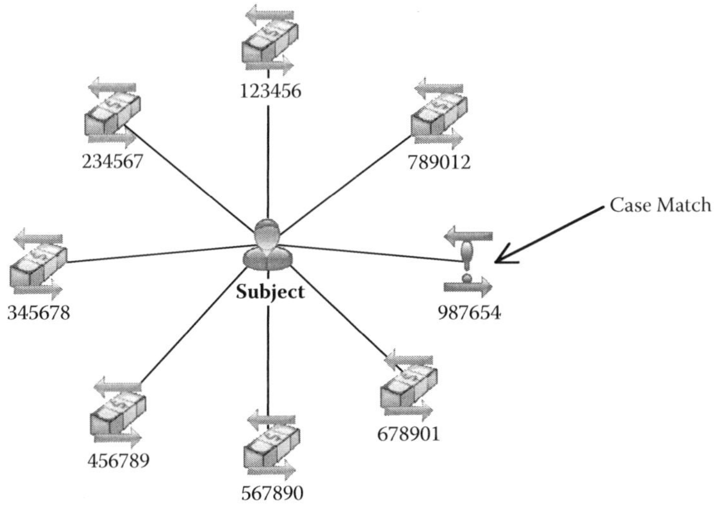

Figure 1.10 Case information reference.

[11] A one-time Lump Sum Death Benefit payment of $255 is payable to the surviving spouse if he or she was living with the beneficiary at the time of death.

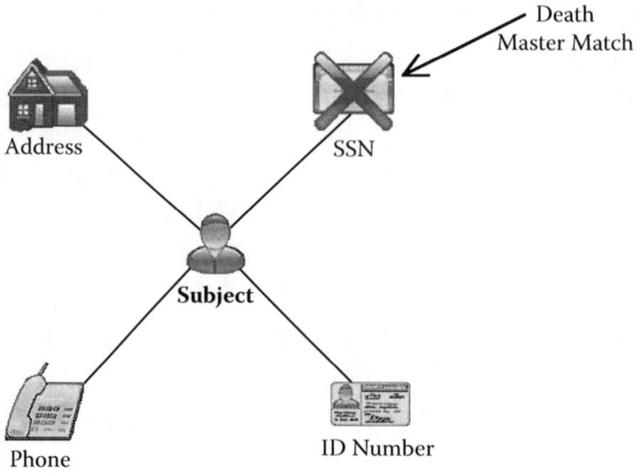

Figure 1.11 Death master reference.

basic and contains the SSN, last/first/middle name, date of birth, date of death, and region of death. For any database utilizing an SSN, the SSDM can be checked for anyone conducting, say, financial transactions with the SSN of a deceased person. If a match is found, the icon for the SSN (as shown in Figure 1.11) can be changed to reflect this fact and the analyst can investigate further.

In this next example, a particular State Attorney General's office annually subpoenas all of the public pay phones within the state to obtain phone numbers, operating organizations, and physical locations. This database contains more than 45,000 entries[12] and is used as a reference source to determine if people have listed pay phones as either their home or work phone number when, say, conducting financial transactions, providing criminal arrest data, or applying for welfare/food stamps. When a match is encountered in the pay phone reference database, the icon is changed (as shown in Figure 1.12) to reflect this fact and the investigator then has a well-qualified target to pursue.

Another important referential data check is categorized under "watch lists." There are several different watch lists for various industries, countries, and agencies for a wide number of reasons. A watch list simply flags an entity that has a characteristic considered important. Watch lists can be applied to virtually anything, including account numbers, such as stolen credit cards, stock symbols considered to be hot picks, countries/regions with a high incidence of malaria, or products that have been flagged for recall. One of the more widely recognized watch lists has traditionally

---

[12] Once common on every street corner, the number of public pay phones is declining and ultimately becoming obsolete due to the wide utilization of cell phones.

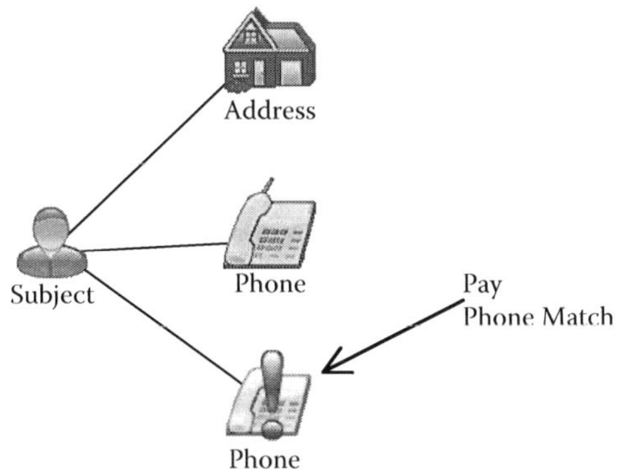

Figure 1.12 Public pay phone reference.

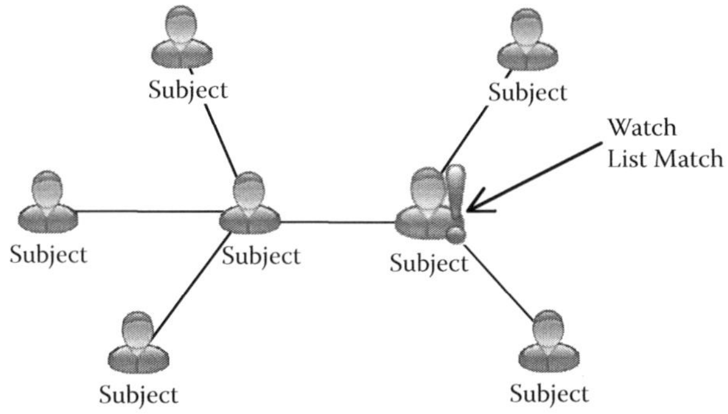

Figure 1.13 Watch list reference.

been the FBI's 10 Most Wanted Fugitives list, originally established in 1950. However, post-9/11, the most active watch lists focus on terrorists and people with ties to terrorism. Figure 1.13 shows a diagram where a person's icon has been changed because a name match was found in a watch list reference source.

The following list represents some of the published watch lists, available in the public domain, that include terrorists, criminals, and sanctioned entities such as people and organizations. This list should not be considered in any way complete, and it should be noted that these sources are constantly changing, meaning that the references may become invalid over time or be decommissioned, and/or new lists may be added. There are also commercial companies that offer subscription services for identifying Politically Exposed/Influenced Persons (PEP/PIPs), who are classified as senior members and officials from foreign government organizations and political parties along with their immediate family members and close associates.

Treasury's Office of Foreign Assets Control (OFAC)
Specially Designated Nationals (SDN)
http://www.treas.gov/offices/enforcement/ofac/sdn/index.html

Department of State
Terrorist Exclusion List:
http://www.state.gov/s/ct/rls/fs/2004/32678.htm
Debarred Parties
http://www.pmddtc.state.gov/debar059.htm

United Nations
The Consolidated List of The Security Council's Al-Qaida/Taliban Sanctions Committee:
http://www.un.org/sc/committeees/1267/consolist.shtml

Australian Department of Foreign Affairs and Trade (DFAT)
The Consolidated List:
http://www.dfat.gov/au/icat/regulation8_consolidated.xls

Bank of England (HM Treasury)
Consolidated List
http://documents.treasury.gov.uk/financialsanctions/sanctionsconlist.txt

Bureau of Industry and Security, U.S. Department of Commerce
Denied Persons List
http://www.bis.doc.gov/dpl/dpl.txt
Unverified List
http://www.bis.doc.gov/enforcement/unverified_parties.html

EAR License Requirements
http://www.access.gpo.gov/bis/ear/txt/744spir.txt

Office of the Superintendent of Financial Institutions (OSFI) Canada
Consolidated List
http://www.osfi-bsif.gc.ca/app/DocRepository/1/eng/issues/terrorism/entstld_e.txt

European Commission
Consolidated List
http://ec.europa.eu/external_relations/cfsp/sanctions/list/version4/global/e_ctlview.html

Federal Bureau of Investigations

Top Ten Most Wanted Fugitives

http://www.fbi.gov/wanted/topten/fugitives/fugitives.htm

War on Terrorism

http://www.fbi.gov/terrorinfo/terrorismsi.htm

Crime Alerts

http://www.fbi.gov/wanted/alert/alert.htm

Hong Kong Monetary Authority List

United Nations Sanctions Ordinance

http://www.info.gov/hk/hkma/eng/guide/circu_date/attach/20050506e1a.doc

Interpol

Most Wanted

http://www.interpol.int/Public/Wanted/Search/Recent.asp

World Bank

Ineligible Firms

http://www.worldbank.org/debarr

U.S. Marshals Service

Top 15 Most Wanted

http://www.usmarshals.gov/investigations/most_wanted/index.html

Major Fugitive Cases

http://www.usmarshals.gov/investigations/major_cases/index.html

U.S. Drug Enforcement Administration

Major International Fugitives

http://www.usdoj.gov/dea/fugitives/internl/internllist.htm

Most Wanted Fugitives

http://www.usdoj.gov/dea/fugitives/fuglist.htm

Immigration and Customs Enforcement

Most Wanted

http://www.ice.gov/pi/investigations/wanted/fugitives.htm

U.S. Postal Inspection Service

Most Wanted

http://www.usps.com/postalinspectors/wanted/wantmenu.htm

U.S. Secret Service
Most Wanted
http://www.ustreas.gov/usss/mostwanted.shtml

Bureau of Alcohol, Tobacco, Firearms, and Explosives
Most Wanted
http://www.atf.treas.gov/wanted/index.htm

Air Force Office of Special Investigations
Wanted Fugitives
http://www.osi.andrews.af.mil/library/fugitives/index.asp

Naval Criminal Investigation Service
Wanted Fugitives
http://www.ncis.navy.mil/wanted.asp

Royal Canadian Mounted Police (RCMP)
Wanted Persons
http://www.rcmp-grc.gc.ca/wanted/index_e.htm

As the list demonstrates, there are numerous watch lists that can be incorporated into any system for virtually any type of analysis. Unfortunately, referential sources based solely on people's names are fraught with potential problems including inaccurate and incomplete data that can result in a number of false-positive matches. For example, using the OFAC SDN (referenced in the watch list table), the following record appears for a man named Cesar Lopez:

> LOPEZ, Cesar (a.k.a. ARROYAVE RUIZ, Elkin Alberto), Carrera 9 No. 71D-10, Cali, Colombia; DOB 3 Sep 1968; POB Caucasia, Antioquia, Colombia; Cedula No. 4652820 (Colombia) (individual) [SDNTK]

Based on the information provided, this Colombian national is approximately 40 years of age and can be uniquely defined by his Cedula number (a national identification similar to a Social Security number). However, this name is fairly common and can be found throughout the United States, Central America, and South America. In fact, a quick check of the white pages[13] at the beginning of 2008 shows that there are several states where multiple people have the name Cesar Lopez, as shown in the following table:

[13] http://www.whitepages.com.

Count	State
25	New Jersey
36	Illinois
41	New York
56	Florida
156	Texas
268	California

This makes it difficult to rely purely on a matched name, although sometimes it is the only data provided and, therefore, represents the lowest common denominator from which to perform referential matching. Additionally, the name may not be a 100 percent match and often a degree of closeness must be factored into these processes. These topics will be covered more in-depth in Chapter 2, as related to uniqueness and entity resolution techniques.

Considering all of these facets collectively can add a lot of value to the information. Figure 1.14 presents a diagram that is somewhat generic, shows some basic connections as well as a few indirect associations, and overall represents a vanilla network without too much fanfare.

Adding just the referential checks previously discussed, Figure 1.15 depicts a much more interesting and actionable network: Our main subject has been involved in a prior case, the primary phone is a pay phone located at the corner convenience store, one of the subjects is using a dead person's SSN number, and a subject matching a name on the terrorist watch list is involved in a majority of the defined events. Needless to say, this additional information spices up the analysis considerably and adds tremendous value to the overall analytics. What might have been discounted as an uninteresting network using just the analytical data became a high-priority investigation after the referential data was added.

Information Sharing

In the post-9/11 era, many organizations have expressed the need to share data in order to "connect the dots" to see the bigger picture. A number of systems, networks, and approaches have been deployed to help provide this capability to the community. Until now, the progress has been somewhat limited and in the years that have passed, many agencies are still not actively sharing information.

A variety of different approaches have been proposed to address this problem, including one highly publicized project by the U.S. government that aimed to "copy" information from virtually every law and government

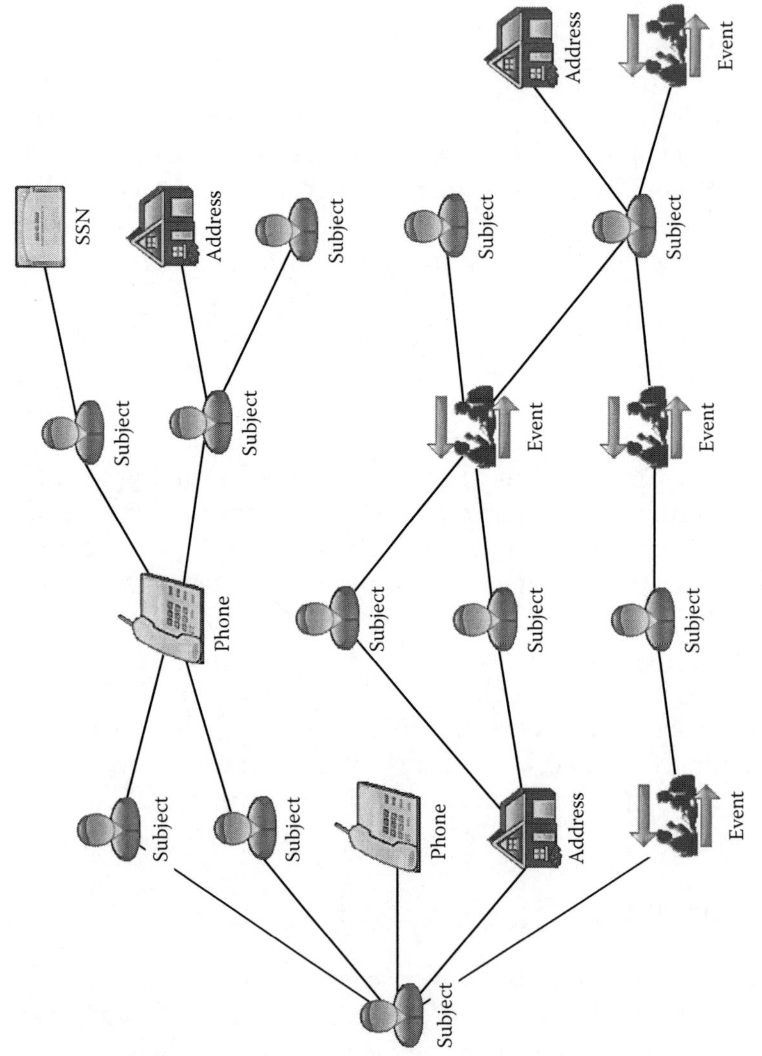

Figure 1.14 Network showing only analytical data.

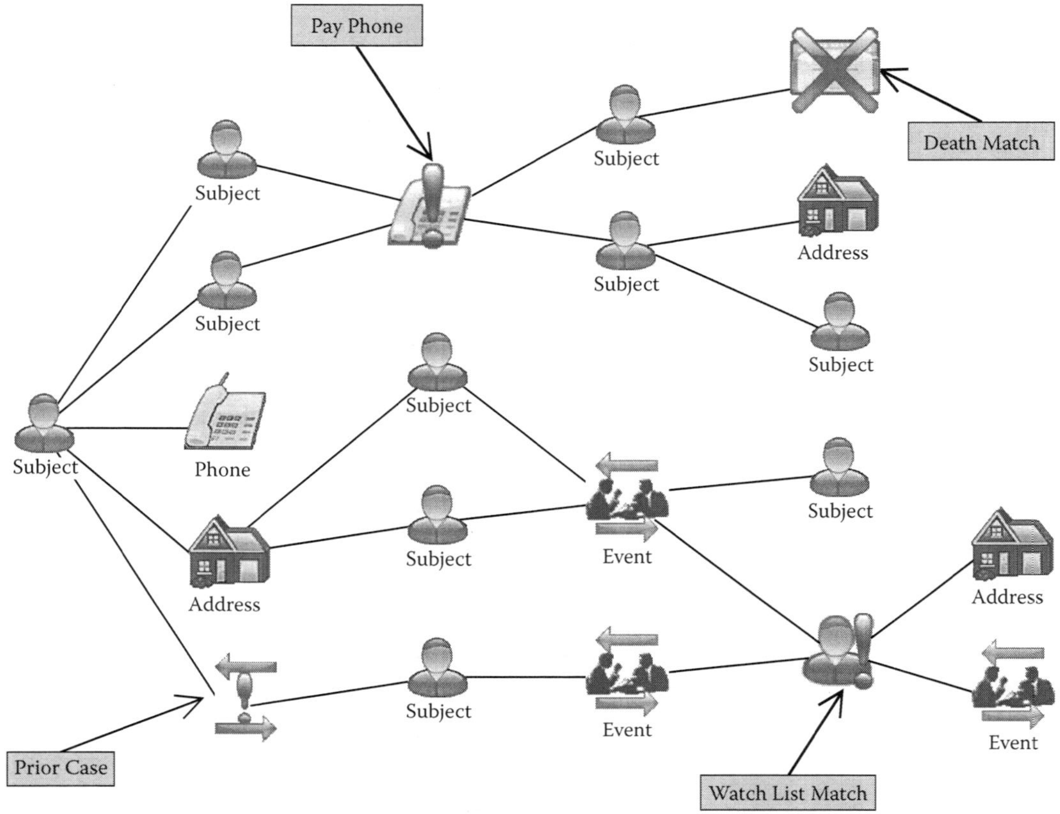

Figure 1.15 Network overlaid with referential data.

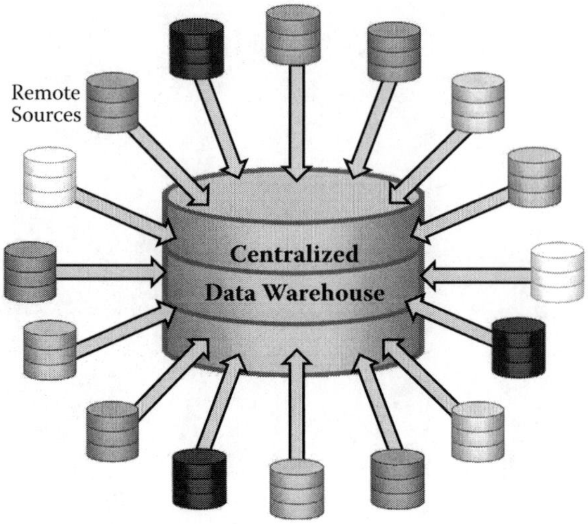

Figure 1.16 Large, centralized data warehouse.

agency into a behemoth, nationwide data warehouse where it would be analyzed by experts and properly disseminated through appropriate channels. The concept is fairly straightforward—to bring it all together in one place where it could be collectively analyzed. This approach presents many technical challenges that must be overcome, including data aggregation, scalability, security, sheer physical storage of the masses of information, and issues associated with control and accountability—not to mention the timeliness with which the data is updated and that it tends to flow in only one direction. Overall, it represents an overcomplicated, outdated, and expensive proposition that does not scale very well. Figure 1.16 provides an abstraction of this type of approach.

Analysts operating throughout many government organizations that are chartered with analyzing data routinely print out all of the reports and filings in hard-copy format and then laboriously read through each one to determine if additional investigation and analysis should be considered. There are more modern methods to quickly address and better deal with this task. Not utilizing automated methods is a fundamental flaw in this process that not only reduces the volume of data that can be analyzed, but involves more resources than is necessary, hinders information sharing, and—most importantly—severely limits the scope of the investigations that can be pursued.

Large budgets and discretionary funds are used to create customized, home-grown systems that are neither scalable nor adaptive and most likely will not meet the current or future needs of their creators. Sadly, most customized systems are reinventing the wheel each time and they quickly become legacy systems before the project period of performance ends. Large system integrators have their talents, but are not necessarily the best choice for achieving the "right" system due to the fundamental conflict of interest (COI) of being paid for delivering services and personnel, rather than reliable, robust, and operational systems that take minimal tuning and resources to operate.

There are no standard collection methods, no predefined database schemas, no analytical products, and no reporting capabilities that are configured, documented, and accepted globally in the community.[14] Additionally, there are no consolidated watch lists, no common patterns, and no accepted reporting formats shared across different agencies or countries for that matter. There has been little investment made by the community in the creation of a framework that can be deployed throughout the nation, much less the world, to better address this complex and comprehensive undertaking.

What happens when hundreds or thousands of data sources can be accessed and queried simultaneously? A different approach and methodology are required to provide members within a community the means to easily share their information without the headache or overhead associated with a massive data warehouse. A distributed architecture, similar to the peer-to-peer systems mentioned previously, can be used to allow organizations to selectively and securely share data with others. Figure 1.17 presents a simplified view of this concept.

In a distributed model, information (databases, documents, etc.) can stay in its current location, eliminating the need to copy to new locations for the sake of "integration." This approach has generally been termed a "virtual data warehouse" and provides a commonsense approach to data

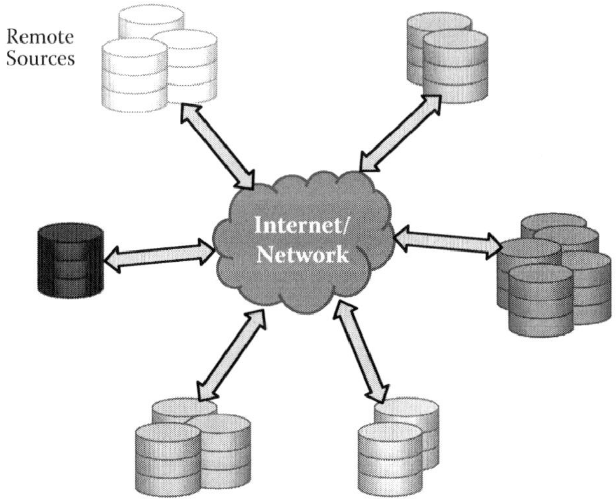

Figure 1.17 Distributed framework.

[14] Several recent frameworks are presented in chapters 8 and 9, including GJXDM, NIEM, R-DEx, and N-DEx.

sharing that can be implemented on a very large scale, connecting hundreds or thousands of data sources. This distributed system approach has many advantages over its conventional counterpart, including security, real-time access, and robustness.

- **Security:** Consider access control with regard to data sharing. In part, this means keeping data safe from unauthorized access, and regulating that access to appropriate segments of information depending on the user. For instance, organization "X" may have 10 databases and 2 million documents it wants to make available to its own local users and several external organizations with their own groups of users. Further, some of these databases are sensitive within organization "X" such that only a small group of users can see them. A granular security model is needed that enforces the permissions for each data source. Additionally, the security model itself must also support a distributed approach where organization "X" can delegate some authority for sharing its data to administrators in remote organizations whom they trust to apply appropriate permissions to their users.
- **Real-Time Access:** The nature of a distributed system lends itself to real-time information access. Consider a data warehouse approach where information from many sources must be copied into a centralized warehouse. Depending on the methods used, each of these sources may be copied at various intervals ranging from hours to days to weeks. In contrast, the distributed model doesn't need to copy data because it connects to the "live" data providing real-time, peer-to-peer data sharing. If any of these services worked off of a static, clumsy, centralized data repository, the service would not be dynamic or very useful to many users.
- **Robustness:** Consider a system where data from 50 sites around the nation is copied to a single location, then searched and analyzed remotely by users from those same 50 sites. What happens if that single location becomes unavailable? Potentially, hundreds or thousands of users will be offline because that single location is a single point of failure. Now, consider that same data in the same 50 locations where instead of copying data, each of the 50 locations offered a data-sharing hub that enabled secure sharing to both local users and each of 49 affiliate locations. This model is much more robust because there is no single point of failure for the entire system. Moreover, the entire system of 50 locations is real-time and each location retains full control over the dissemination of their data.

Additionally, using a traditional data warehouse approach requires that the format of the data be changed into a single composite representation. This makes users subject to the decisions made by a remote party, which may not reflect their particular needs. In a distributed approach, each format remains intact while utilizing access and transformation features to add value to the end results.

In a distributed environment, each server can broker a search or other request on behalf of an authenticated user to another server in an affiliate organization. Information sent between servers can be encrypted and sent via standard Internet protocols[15] in order to help traverse firewalls that exist between different locations. This means that users in one location will be able to search for and analyze data that physically resides in multiple locations. This type of integrated technology is unprecedented and considered mandatory in the next-generation analytical systems.

Although agencies have shared data using other types of remote data access including terminal emulations, Web portals, or specialized applications/protocols, the use of a real-time, distributed approach for creating a virtual data warehouse is a somewhat novel approach for government and law enforcement organizations. The owners of the data control who is allowed to access it and how much they are allowed to see for any given request. Requests are made from a network of distributed servers that are responsible for the authentication, security, and load balancing of the system. This approach allows for *n*-way sharing of data where any number of agencies can share data thereby allowing for data producers, consumers, or both.

The following topics should be considered when sharing data:

Avoid the creation of a centralized warehouse: Consolidating data can be expensive and time consuming. Using a virtual warehouse through a distributed data-sharing model provides a more flexible, adaptable, and scalable system.

Utilize existing data formats and layouts: Systems should be capable of mapping to the existing database schemas and formats. Very little, if any, preprocessing of the data should be required to prepare data for sharing.

Automate accounting: Systems should have a strong accounting model such that all data requests are logged into a separate data repository that can be reviewed and reported on for security, case support, or deconfliction. Accounting must be enabled at each source/site by the owner of the data.

Manage the volume and detail returned: Reasonable limitations should be placed on the amount and type of information returned

[15] For example, HTTP, SOAP, and XML.

by each query to avoid overburdening resources and limit abuse. Pointer indexes should be used when sensitive data can't be generically shared.

Control access: System access should always be controlled by the owner of the data. Those sites that post a source of data should remain in total control over who gains access, the type of access, and the volume of data returned.

As agencies start to reap the benefits of sharing data, they can also expect the quality of the results, analyses, and reports to improve dramatically. The costs associated with many types of operations can be reduced because the manpower required to access and collect the information can be minimized. Additionally, duplication of efforts, such as hosting the same sources, performing the same analytics, and generating the same reports, can be curtailed thereby freeing up more resources to perform other work. The ROI (return on investment) for information sharing is immediate, significant, and measurable.

Conclusion

The analytical community is changing every day. New methods, approaches, and technologies are being applied to help improve how data is accessed, combined, analyzed, and reported. This is a never-ending and constantly changing paradigm where new techniques and methods must be developed to keep pace with the threats that emerge every day. Terrorism has changed how governments and businesses operate, and our adversaries are constantly changing how they will plan and execute the next attack. Information sharing is key to facilitating better analytics. Over the next decade, there will be massive efforts to clean up, standardize, and share data. Already in the works is the creation of fusion systems, analytical centers, information standards, and collaborative task forces—all designed to connect the dots.

The next several chapters present a wide range of concepts with a heavy focus on analytical methodologies. Some of the topics discussed may seem trivial; however, when applied to real-world operational systems, they have a significant impact on the quality of the analyses performed, which directly impacts the type of patterns exposed. There is a lot of food for thought in the cases, examples, and materials presented. Next time you are boarding a plane, investing in the stock market, or purchasing items online, remember that the event or transaction is only as safe and secure as the analysts (and systems) identifying patterns can make it.

Chapter 2

The Quality of Data

Introduction

Computer processors are faster than ever, storage is fairly cheap, network bandwidth is continually expanding, and information technologies are capable of integrating massive amounts of data. With all of these high-end systems and capabilities, there is still a limitation on performing effective analytics and much of this has to do with the quality of the data collected throughout the years. The real challenge lies in improving the accuracy of the data through better collection and representation methods. Only when this problem is appropriately addressed can one realistically expect to see improvement in the detection and analytics of fraud, terrorism, money laundering, and other critical areas.

One high-profile situation emphasizes this point. It was reported[1] that Senator Edward Kennedy (Massachusetts) was stopped while boarding airline flights on five different occasions because his name matched an entry on a government no-fly list. Additionally, Congressman John Lewis (Georgia) claims he was required to submit to additional security checks because his name also matched one on a watch list. In both cases, the data processed by these systems represented only a limited portion of what was necessary to properly perform an appropriate match. Ultimately the situations were resolved, but only after direct intervention from top-ranking officials at the Department of Homeland Security (DHS).

In another case,[2] Sister McPhee, a 62-year-old nun and education advocate for the Catholic Church was repeatedly stopped over a nine-month period (starting in 2003) because her last name matched that of an Afghani man using McPhee as an alias, with supposedly no first name for this man. There are even reports of infants and toddlers being stopped from boarding planes because their names positively matched one on a watch list. A little common sense, or better oversight, would resolve these types of situations. According to reports,[3] the "Transportation Security Administration, which administers the lists, instructs airlines not to deny boarding to children under 12 years of age—or select them for extra security checks—even if their names match those on a list."

Obviously, the quality of data in terms of consistency, correctness, and precision impacts the accuracy and reliability of analytical and monitoring systems. In the financial industry, simple mistakes, such as spelling errors, phonetic interpretations, or abbreviations, account for a large

---

[1] Rachel Swarns, "Senator? Terrorist? A Watch List Stops Kennedy at Airport," *The New York Times*, August 20, 2004, http://www.nytimes.com/2004/08/20/national/20flight.html.

[2] Ryan Singel, "Nun Terrorized by Terror Watch," *Wired*, September 26, 2005, http://www.wired.com/politics/security/news/2005/09/68973.

[3] Leslie Miller, "No-Fly List Grounds Some Unusual Young Suspects: Similarly-Named Babies Were Barred. *Associated Press*, August 16, 2005, http://www.boston.com/news/nation/articles/2005/08/16/no_fly_list_grounds_some_unusual_young_suspects/.

amount of the inconsistent data recorded. In one financial database analyzed, a large West Coast city was entered with 13 different spellings, a venerable bank had 18 unique name variations, and the number of permutations for certain industry occupations (e.g., chef, cook, waiter, worker at a restaurant, etc.) were almost unmanageable. Also, under certain circumstances, people will not be entirely truthful with their information while others will outright lie or intentionally misrepresent themselves to a financial institution. The quality of this data directly impacts the types of analyses that are conducted and ultimately the value of results.

The old adage "garbage in, garbage out" continues to ring true. Therefore, whenever possible practitioners should evaluate and change the collection process to minimize errors or inconsistencies, thus better facilitating the analytics that will be performed. The quality of the data will forever play a critical role within the analytical and investigative communities.

Value Errors

Errors and inconsistencies in the data are most often seen as the result of typos, misspellings, or abbreviations in the data. Generally, without strong validation controls (e.g., lookup tables, entry masks, etc.), and especially when data can be entered in a free-form format, there will be problems with the quality of the data. Additionally, in adversarial collections (e.g., money laundering, terrorism, fraud) there is often intentionally misrepresented data.

Value errors represent one of the largest problems typically encountered in collecting data. Small value variations can have a significant impact on how the final results are interpreted. The list following Figure 2.1 shows an example of more than 80 variations in the spelling of the city value in data returned from a query targeting Lower Manhattan in New York City using the following ZIP codes: 10004, 10005, 10006, 10007, 10038, and 10280 (as outlined in the bottom portion in Figure 2.1).

MANHA HAN	MANHANHATTAN
MANHANTAN	MANHANTHAN
MANHANTTAN	MANHATAN
MANHATTAN	MANHATTAN K
MANHATTAN N Y	MANHATTAN NY
MANHATTEN	MANHATTON
MEW YORK	N Y
NEW Y ORK	NEW Y ORK
NEW YO RK	NEW YOEK
NEW YOIK	NEW YOK

NEW YOKR	NEW YOORK
NEW YOR	NEW YOR K
NEW YOR,	NEW YORJ
NEW YORK	NEW YORK 10017-1011
NEW YORK 10031	NEW YORK 725
NEW YORK 806	NEW YORK 806
NEW YORK 987	NEW YORK BK
NEW YORK CITY	NEW YORK N
NEW YORK NEW YORK	NEW YORK NY
NEW YORK NY	NEW YORK NY 10001
NEW YORK NY 10002	NEW YORK NY 10009
NEW YORK NY 10016	NEW YORK NY 10018
NEW YORK NY 10019	NEW YORK NY 10022
NEW YORK NY 10023	NEW YORK NY 10028
NEW YORK NY 10029	NEW YORK NY 10036
NEW YORK NY 10036-3619	NEW YORK QUEENS
NY ROOSEVELT ISLAND	NEW YORK STATE
NEW YORK Y	NEW YORK,
NEW YORK,	NEW YORK, NEW YORK
NEW YORK, NY	NEW YORK, NY 10017
NEW YORKCITY	NEW YORKD
NEW YORKE	NEW YORKJ
NEW YORKK	NEW YORKQ
NEW YORKS	NEW YORKY
NEW YORK|	NEW YORL
NEW YORY	NEW YOTK
NEW YOUR	NEW YOURK
NEW YOYK	NEW YRK
NEW YROK	NEWYORK
NY	NY NY
NY PLAZA	NYC
YN	Y

Clearly, this amount of variation is unacceptable for any system—commercial or government—especially when trying to target criminal activities, generate accurate sales reports, track inventory, or allocate investigatory resources. One approach to minimizing these variations is to simply use a reverse lookup—where the city and state for the respective address are derived from the ZIP code. For the five ZIP codes used in this example, a search on the United States Postal Service's Web site[4]

[4] http://zip4.usps.com/zip4/citytown_zip.jsp.

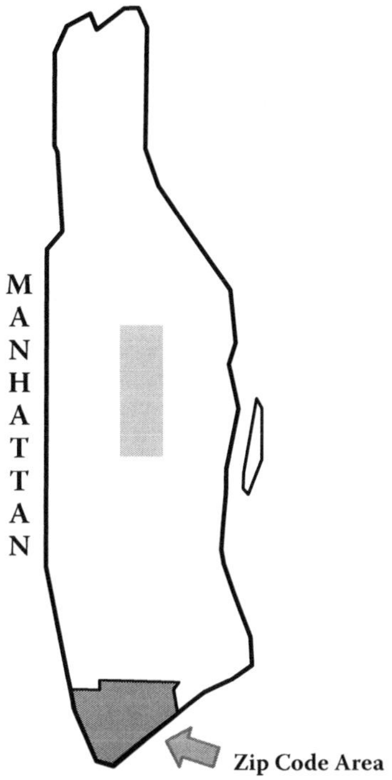

Figure 2.1 Zip codes used for Lower Manhattan query.

shows them as New York, NY, and clearly specifies that Manhattan and NYC are unacceptable and should not be used. Although simple ETL (extract, transform, load) procedures can help fix these types of values after the fact, these are additional steps, incurring more costs, and are subject to certain limitations, especially if the ZIP code entered is not valid (e.g., 10000, 01234, 54321, 11111, etc.).

Other value errors include situations where the information entered is simply wrong. Many people have a hard time with geography and are typically not familiar with places outside of their immediate vicinity, which tends to be amplified when dealing with data entry clerks, point-of-sale stations, or systems without any input controls or cross-validation procedures. This next example is derived from a database that involves international money transactions. The country of interest is Saudi Arabia; the correct country abbreviation is SA. Unfortunately, a considerable number of bank employees (e.g., tellers) are not aware of this fact. Figure 2.2 represents a sample of the city/country values contained in the database using the SA country code.

While not all of the entries are wrong, there are a number of cases where the SA code was erroneously applied, including Salt Lake City (where the country was most likely USA and the *U* was dropped because of the

Salt Lake City	SA
Madina	SA
Riyadh	SA
Dharan	SA
Jeddah	SA
Riyadh	SA
Jeddah	SA
johannesburg	SA
Jeddah	SA
Johannesburg	SA
San Salvador	SA
North Adelaide	SA
Bogota	SA
Madina, Saudi Arabia	SA
Medellin, Columbia S.Amer.	SA
Johannesburg	SA
Jeddah	SA

Figure 2.2 City/country code value pairings for country = SA.

two-character limit), Dharan[5] (which is in Nepal and is most likely a typo in the city name), Johannesburg (located in South Africa where the country code is ZA), San Salvador (which is in El Salvador, Central America, not South America where the country code is SV), North Adelaide (the most populous city of the Australian state of South Australia with a country code of AU), and both Bogota and Medellin (which are South American cities located in Colombia, which has a country code of CO).

To be fair, some country codes are simply not obvious (e.g., El Salvador = SV) and systems without proper lookup methods are prone to these quality issues. Therefore, it is vital that systems without the required entry controls are updated to reduce these types of errors from entering the underlying databases. The table below is provided to see if you can match the country to the correct code abbreviation. Draw a line between the pairings you think are correct.

[5] This also represents an alternative transliteration of Dhahran, which is actually located in Saudi Arabia.

SWITZERLAND	IS
CHINA	DE
ICELAND	IE
GERMANY	SG
SINGAPORE	CH
UNITED ARAB EMIRATES	CN
IRELAND	AE

The answers are not always apparent and, therefore, supplemental procedures and methods need to be implemented to help minimize these types of errors. If country code information was important to the organization or agency maintaining this data source, it would be imperative to validate and double-check all entries before any type of detailed analytics was performed, otherwise the results would be erroneous and not reflect the true state of their affairs. The answers to the country and its correct code can be found in the footnote.[6]

Missing Data and Bad Structures

In a perfect world, all information would be collected consistently and we would always have valid data. Often the processes, controls, and mechanisms in place do not enforce certain collections. Inevitably, there will be values missing from the data, such as middle names, dates of birth, country codes, and ZIP codes. The analytical process must accommodate for these types of situations.

Sometimes data can be loaded into the wrong database fields entirely, resulting in a truly inconsistent database. For example, the name of a person should be loaded into three different fields (first, last, and middle), but is often entered into a single field, usually the last-name field, especially when representing DBA (doing business as) values. Other examples include more than one value entered per field or improper use of remarks or notes fields. In one case, data submitted (from a bank to the federal government) using a particular commercially available anti–money laundering software package exposed an issue where the transaction date/time values were being transmitted in the violation amount column, resulting in billion-dollar filings. As expected, these transactions were immediately flagged and, after some preliminary review, the analysts were able to identify the root of the problem and notify the bank. In another example, the

[6] Switzerland = CH, China = CN, Iceland = IS, Germany = DE, Singapore = SG, United Arab Emirates = AE, and Ireland = IE.

decimal points for the cents were not being inserted properly, multiplying each value by 100 (e.g., 15,000.00 entered as 1,500,000). These types of issues have big impacts on the quality of the analytics being conducted on the data and need to be addressed promptly.

Another problem quickly noted was that an overwhelming number of people did not provide a date of birth (DOB) in their transaction data. Those who did tended to list 12/30/1900, 11/11/1911, or 01/01/1960 (including 1970 and 1980). The data reflected a considerable number of people born after the year 2000, which is impossible since persons[7] conducting these transactions must be over the age of 18. The data also included transpositions in years such as 9154 (1954), 7971 (1971), 4969 (1969), and 2086 (1986). These types of entries result in questionable reliability and usefulness—of the data, the collection instruments, and the overall processes used to ensure accurate data.

In this next example, when reviewing the sales data from a Ford, Lincoln, and Mercury car dealership located in the Washington, D.C., metropolitan region, it was surprising to see all the variations of the "make" of vehicle entered for their primary line of vehicles. The following are the variations of Mercury and Lincoln as entered into their sales system:

MERCURY	LINCOLN
MERUCRY	LONCOLN
MERRCURY	LINCOLM
MERCURT	LINCOL N
MERCURH	LINCOL
MERCRUY	LINCLON
MECURY	LINCLN
MERC	LICOLN

Other data quality issues include inaccuracies in the finance company address. As shown in Figure 2.3, there are at least 20 different variations of the address in the database. There are many variations, including missing periods (.) between the post office abbreviation (e.g., P.O. versus PO), incorrect state codes (e.g., MA, VA), different ZIP codes, and even considerable variations in the box number.

Generally, addresses tend to be one of the most inconsistent types of data because there are multiple parts (e.g., street, city, state, ZIP) that can be misrepresented. As shown in Figure 2.3, items, such as street names

[7] The comparisons for age used 2008 as the year for establishing whether an individual was over 18 years of age. Many of the DOBs encountered for this pattern were related to businesses or organizations and most likely represented the year of incorporation—which is not allowed for the DOB field in this particular system.

Figure 2.3 Automotive finance company address variations.

and abbreviations (St./Street, Blvd./Boulevard, Ln./Lane, etc.), can easily change the proper representation of an address. Below are some additional variations found in the city and state values contained in the sales data.

WASHTINGTON	DC	VIENNA	VCA
WASHNGTON	DC	VIENNA	VA
WASHINGTON D	DC	VIENNA	V
WASHINGTON	VA[8]	VIENNA	CA
WASHINGTON	DV	VIENNA	BA
WASHINGTON	DC	VIENJNA	VA
WASHINGTON	D.C.	VIENAA	VA
WASHINGOTN	DC	MECLEAN	V
FALLSCVHURCH	VA	MCLENA	VA
FALLS CHURCHA	VA	MCLEAN VA	22102
FALLS CHURCH	VA	MCLEAN	VBA
FALLS CHURCH	VA	MCLEAN	VA
FALLS CHURCH	CA	MCLEAN	RD
FALLS CHURCH	AV	MCLEAN	MD
FALLS CHUCH	VA	MCLEAN	BVA
FALLS CHRUCH	VA	MCLEAN	BA
FALL CHURCH	VA	MCLAEN	VA

[8] This is actually a proper city/state pairing, which is located about 70 miles from Washington, D.C.; http://town.washington.va.us/

There can be lots of problems with data, and detailing all of the specific conditions and inconsistencies is outside the scope of this book. However, these types of issues fundamentally impact how data is represented, and ultimately the quality of the analysis that is performed. Depending on the end results, poor data quality can wind up wasting significant resources, time, money, and ultimately people's lives (for LEA applications). Thus, when working with data, it is important to know the overall quality and where the pitfalls may lie. This can influence how the data is modeled and interpreted in the final analytics. For example, consider each of the objects presented in Figure 2.4. Determine if they represent unique entities or if there can be duplicated values in the data. Mark the box with a true (T) or false (F) based on your assumptions.

Unique Addresses

Starting from the top, addresses, as previously discussed, are perhaps some of the most inconsistent values encountered in most data sources;

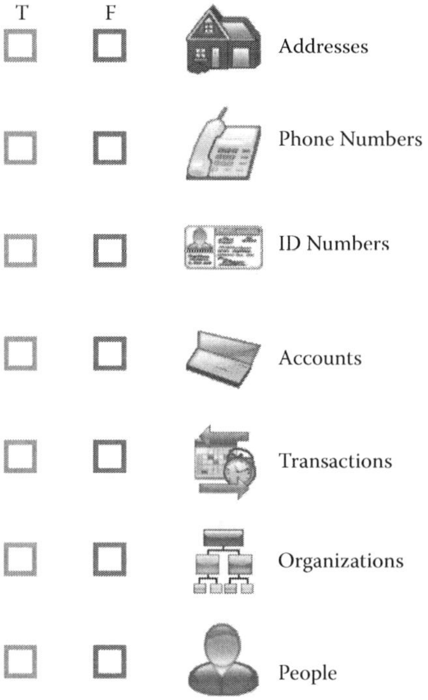

Figure 2.4 What entities are unique?

however, they are by definition considered unique. Whether or not 123 Main St. or 123 Main Street is entered consistently into a database, they ultimately refer to the same physical address regardless of their spelling and assuming the same city,[9] state, and country information is referenced. With basic ETL functions and some geo-coding processes, the address can be standardized and validated, resulting in only one address in the world with the specific combination of street, city, state, ZIP/postal code, and country.

The only real issue to factor in is the time frame for which the information has been reported because the relationships (e.g., ownership, renter, leaser, etc.) may change over time. Furthermore, additional checks regarding the real-world classification of the address (e.g., vacant lot, bus terminal, office building, residential, etc.) or even if the address actually exists would prove vital for many types of analyses to help expose questionable activities, patterns, and misrepresentations. However, the fact remains that an address is always considered unique regardless of whether it is real or was fabricated—interpreting its value

[9] The top five cities in the United States show that 29 states have a city named Washington, 28 have a Salem, 27 have a Springfield, 27 have a Marion, and 27 have a Madison.

is a different matter. Consider the following addresses[10] and determine if they would be legitimate or appropriate if encountered during an analysis where they were listed as the home address for, say, a criminal investigation:

(1) 1060 West Addison Street, Chicago, Illinois 60613
(2) 1301 E. 12th Street, Wilmington, DE 19801
(3) 801 Mount Vernon Place, NW, Washington, D.C. 20001

Distinct Phone Numbers

Phone numbers are also considered unique entities because there can be only one phone with the assigned number.[11] For example, dialing 202-456-1414 will connect you to the main switchboard for the West Wing of the White House. Of course, this remains true only if the country code is considered part of the number because, within a country, the core phone number will always be unique, but across different countries, there could be some confusion if the country code is not included.

For example, the phone number 1-800-323-3331 represents the main line to the Sheraton Hotel (Millennium Hotel) at the Buffalo Airport located in upstate New York. The same number, 1800-3233331, is assigned to the quality service manager for the Ministry of National Development (MND) located in Singapore. If this number showed up in a database being analyzed, depending on the context or origin of the data, there might be some confusion as to where this number is actually resolved to represent. Ideally, if the number is being referenced in a database used by U.S. agencies, it would most likely represent the Sheraton, and if it indeed was for the MND, then it would be preceded with a "65" for the country access code for Singapore.

Just as with addresses, care must be taken to factor in the time frames for any telephone-related data, such as subscriber information and operating regions, especially with the number of disposable phone numbers being consumed today. Also, the collection instruments used to obtain phone numbers can affect the nature of the data being

---

10 (1) Wrigley Field Ball Park, the address was also used by Elwood Blues (Dan Akroyd) in the movie *The Blues Brothers* (1980) as his home address on his Illinois driver's license; (2) physical address for the Howard R. Young Correctional Institution (aka Gander Hill Prison); (3) Washington, D.C., Convention Center.

11 Some telcos allow multiple devices to be associated with the same phone number (e.g., account); however, only one will be active at any time. From "Two Phones—One Number Comes to Bahrain," *cellular-news,* April 1, 2002, http://www.cellular-news.com/story/6302.php.

represented, particularly if dialed number recorders[12] (DNRs) are used to capture the detail of a call. Depending on what information is presented in the dialed number, the nature of the equipment used, and the country laws, there can be varying degrees of information captured in the call record, so some care must be taken when analyzing this data in its context. The format can vary considerably and some numbers are entirely complete, others are missing the country code (when dialed in-country), and sometimes area codes are missing. These matters can certainly complicate the analyses; however, a complete phone number is always considered unique.

Furthermore, validity of the phone number should always be considered. There are a number of online sources and services that can be used to check phone numbers, perform reverse lookups of the subscribers, or find out more about the number. Depending on the nature of the database, there will be varying degrees of accuracy in terms of how truthful individuals will be in disclosing their contact information (e.g., listed on a mortgage application versus collected for a retail store point-of-sale system). Depending on the analytics being performed (e.g., money laundering, terrorism, fraud), this additional information can prove critical to detecting anomalies and intentional misrepresentations of people trying to avoid detection.

For example, consider the following phone numbers[13] and their representation. They all appear as legitimately structured numbers; however, where they are located (and the usage) might raise some concerns during, say, a fraud investigation:

(1) 240-314-8900
(2) 703-522-3333
(3) 202-844-1111

Individual ID Numbers

ID numbers are also considered unique entities when the actual number and its type (e.g., driver's license, passport, etc.) are represented collectively. There are a few exceptions that have an impact on their interpretation. For example, in the United States, the SSN is a nine-digit number issued by the Social Security Administration that is used to collect

[12] Also referred to as pen-registers (regulated under 18 U.S.C., CHAPTER 206—PEN REGISTERS AND TRAP AND TRACE DEVICES).

[13] (1) Nonemergency number for the Rockville City Police Department, Maryland; (2) Red Top Cab Service in Arlington, Virginia; (3) Automated time recording for Washington, D.C., area.

retirement and disability benefits, but is also widely used as a form of identification. However, the IRS also issues TINs/EINs (Taxpayer/Employer Identification numbers) to corporations, which are also nine digits. In many databases, it is very hard to distinguish between SSNs and TINs/EINs and, therefore, duplication and confusion can result if these are not properly separated. Furthermore, almost two dozen states have nine-digit driver's license numbers, which if not properly defined as such also risk the potential of being confused[14] with SSNs.

Anomalous Accounts

Accounts are also considered unique when paired with their financial institution. Every bank defines their own account number using some type of internal code or format. With more than 7,500 banks in the United States, there are certainly going to be several that share the same encoding and representation. Therefore, to uniquely distinguish one account from another, the institution should be referenced along with the account number.

Other similar types of representations include serial numbers for products. Every manufacturer sets their own serial number for the products they make and there is no guarantee that one company won't use the same numbers assigned by a different company. However, if the serial number and the product are referenced together, then uniqueness is guaranteed in the final representation. This also holds true for order numbers for different manufacturers, invoice numbers for different companies, and reference numbers for service organizations.

One-of-a-Kind Transactions

Transactions, by definition, are always unique because there can only ever be a single instance of an event. Of course, there may be many events that are identical in their descriptions, attributes, and values, but they are still considered unique. For example, a lightning strike is a unique event; the same object can be struck multiple times, but each instance is considered a separate event. The same holds true for phone calls, terrorist activities, financial transactions, border crossings, e-mail transmissions, meetings, and virtually any other type of event.

[14] States like New York, Georgia, and Louisiana are all numeric, whereas Virginia, Arizona, and Idaho are a mixture of alphanumeric characters.

The representation of an event is also all-encompassing such that all details and descriptions are specific for the event. For example, the date, time, and duration of a phone call between Phone A and Phone B would be described with potentially five attributes: (1) date of call, (2) time of day the call was made, (3) duration or length of call, (4) calling number (originator), and (5) number called (destination). These phones could have 50 different calls between them; however, each is considered a separate and unique transaction, even if a majority of the details are exactly the same.

Defining the uniqueness of transactions is fairly straightforward. Many people consider only the attributes describing the transaction as the unique identifier (e.g., combining the date, time, etc.); however, a serially incrementing number will suffice, just as long as it does not repeat or get reused for another transaction. Most credible databases will automatically assign a unique ID to a transaction in their load/creation process and some systems have specific methods for creating and assigning unique ID (one method is described later in this book). Unique IDs can be assigned to existing data with a simple database auto-indexing method where every row gets a unique line count. Any derivative entities that stem from the transaction (e.g., the two phone numbers) can be directly related because of the transaction and all of its respective attributes.

Original Organizations

What about the names of organizations? Are they unique? The short answer is no. Laws vary by country, and in the United States you can incorporate a business with a specific name in one state and a different business in a different state can have the exact same name. Yellow Cab, Acme Liquor, Sparkies Electric, and A1 Plumbing are a few examples. However, no two corporations within the same state can have the same name and so in most cases it would be important to represent the company with its associated state reference to guarantee a unique entity. Furthermore, a company can reuse a name within a state if the previous company is no longer in business (e.g., not active), making time frames a factor in determining if an entry is a duplicate. Of course, companies that have a trademarked name[15] are considered unique as there will only be a single company with a trademarked name.

[15] John Stossel and Alan B. Goldberg, "Starbucks vs. Sambucks Coffee: Beverage Giant Wants Shop Owner to Change Her Name," *20/20 ABC News*, December 9, 2005, http://abcnews.go.com/2020/GiveMeABreak/story?Id=1390867.

Additionally, there is great potential for variation in the way and manner an organization's name is captured due to abbreviations, typos, and other factors. The following list represents some of the ways that the name of a credit union[16] was depicted in a financial database, and these values come directly from the credit union itself based on required filings made according to government regulations.

AAB-XYZ FEDERAL CREDIT UNION	ABC XYZ
ABC XYZ FCU	ABC XYZ FEDERAL CREDIT UNION
ABC-CREDIT UNION	ABCFCU
ABCXYZ	ABC-XYZ
ABC-XYZ FCU	ABC-XYZ FEDERA CREDIT UNION
ABC-XYZ FEDERAL CREDIT	ABC-XYZ FEDERAL CREDIT UNION
ABC-XYZ FEDERAL CU	ABC-XYZ-FCU
ABC-XYZ-FEDERAL CREDIT UNION	ABD-XYZ FCU

Just as in the previous example, the context of the analysis plays a significant role in terms of the importance of how the company names are interpreted. Assuming the following company names are unique, and assuming they are being reviewed by an intelligence agency for counterterrorism operations, what makes them different, makes them stand out, or binds[17] them together in some fashion?

Caribbean Happy Lines
Modern Electronic Company
Sacks Factory

Perspicuous People

Finally, we discuss whether or not people are considered unique. There is no doubt that each individual, living, breathing person on the face of this planet is considered unique. However, distinctly representing them within data sources can prove to be quite challenging, with many of the problems stemming from incomplete information, poor collection standards, and intentional misrepresentation. In a perfect world, all data would be complete and properly entered. Unfortunately, that day is far off. In the real

[16] The identifying part of the credit union name was changed, but the inconsistencies are structurally and syntactically accurate.

[17] They are all listed on the OFAC/SDN (Office of Foreign Assets Control/Specially Designated Nationals) found at https://www.treas.gov/offices/enforcement/ofac/sdn/sdnlist.txt.

world, one has to take what one can get and many times cater to the lowest common denominator.

Consider the following data entries representing a person:

1.	John Smith			
2.	John Q. Smith			
3.	John Q. Smith	11/30/1950		
4.	John Q. Smith	11/30/1950	Brooklyn, NY	
5.	John Q. Smith	11/30/1950	Brooklyn, NY	123-45-6789

Which one of these entries would be most useful for uniquely identifying someone from a database? The first entry is simply a name—a very common name.[18] If that was all the information an investigator had to solve a murder case, it would be a long row to hoe—especially with the number of false-positives that would be encountered during the search. If the name were something like Maximilienne MacDhubhshith, then the odds are greatly improved because there would be less chance of multiple real-world people sharing that uncommon name. The second name entry on the list improves the odds somewhat because the middle initial allows the investigator to immediately dismiss certain candidates from consideration. Although not ideal, it is a lot better than the first option.

The third entry includes the DOB. With this information, the number of candidates is greatly reduced because the chances of multiple people having the same name and same DOB are diminished. The fourth entry introduces a regional delineation to the identity of the person by providing a specific city and state. This further narrows down the gene pool from which to identify the person and the more specific the geographic area,[19] the more reliable the results.

With all of these conditions met, there is still no guarantee that a name, DOB, and location combination is unique to a single individual.

[18] In the United States, common names include Smith, Johnson, Williams, and Jones. In Korea, with a population approaching 50 million people, common names include Kim, Lee, Park, and Choi. In fact, the government estimates that approximately 20 percent of the population (almost 10 million people) share the surname of Kim, making it nearly impossible to target/analyze data utilizing the name of a subject. Thus, an alternative primary reference, such as their Resident Registration Number loosely translated as "Jumin deungrok beonho," is often used to uniquely identify people in Korea. The Resident Registration number, which is similar to the U.S. Social Security number, is a 13-digit number based on a combination of birth date, gender, and registration-related data (region/order).

[19] In 2006, Brooklyn (Kings County) had over 2.5 million residents, which still represents a large collection where false-positives may be encountered. Further refinement down to a neighborhood, such as Flatbush, Coney Island, or Manhattan Beach, would provide a more ideal situation for uniquely identifying the person of interest.

The investigator needs to consider and question his or her results if things seem still uncertain. This leads us to the fifth entry where the SSN is included. With this last piece of data provided, there is high reliability that the person is properly identified. While the SSN itself is considered unique and could be used as a substitute for the person, the more dimensions that are presented provide some fault tolerance should information get skewed due to character transpositions, use of nicknames, abbreviations, or other data variations.

Entity Resolution

The previous discussions regarding the reliability of different types of real-world entities (e.g., people, places, things) are important because there can be so many variations contained in a database, or increasingly, across multiple sources of data. Identifying the same, or potentially the same, entities within data sources becomes vital for intelligence, law enforcement, and criminal analytics (e.g., fraud). The term entity resolution is also referred to as *data de-duplication* in some circles and although this concept is not new,[20]

there are a number of different approaches being pursued within the research and commercial communities with increasingly elaborate systems being defined each year.

Unfortunately, many databases are fraught with errors and inconsistencies, further compounding the problem and making entity resolution imperative for any critical systems (e.g., counterterrorism). A balance must also be achieved with respect to what is definitively determined to be the same entity, what is likely or potentially the same entity, and what is simply a false positive. Those systems that do this best will deliver a more effective baseline for analytics and ultimately better results. There are no hard-and-fast rules defined for performing entity resolution. Much of the process is based on the particulars or details of the data being collected, the quality of the data, and the scope of the data (e.g., global, national, regional, local).

In most applications, the goal is to identify a target of interest. In intelligence, law enforcement, and special investigative units (e.g., fraud), the primary target is usually a person. Of course, other industries using entity resolution can be focused on identifying similar retail products

[20] The concept of data scrubbing or data cleaning has been utilized within bulk mailing lists for quite some time. Generally, the content or data is standardized; the data columns properly aligned; and then the results are merged–purged to produce a final list. Unfortunately, purging is not a viable component in today's analytical systems.

for price comparisons,[21] copyrighted materials, publications via author referrals,[22] and corporate operations (e.g., ownership, doing-business-as, subsidiaries, etc.). Focusing on people and their related attributes and descriptions, the following presents a generic overview of some techniques used for performing entity resolution.

As previously discussed, people are highly characterized by their names. When reviewing a name, there is a certain amount of information that can be reasonably calculated (or estimated), including, for example, their gender, ethnicity, and surname. These types of calculations can help determine similar entities, but are somewhat superficial with respect to how much value they add to the process. Given a name such as John, most people would recognize this as a predominantly male name; however, names like Chris or Tracy, which can be used by both men and women, would result in little value added to the computation. From a U.S. perspective, the gender attribute is certainly helpful for interpreting unfamiliar names from places like Scandinavia,[23] Africa, or Asia, especially if the names look similar. Although gender categorization on many names can be easy, its utility in the overall entity resolution process is just one facet of many that can add some value depending on the circumstances.

The ethnicity or cultural aspects of a name can also be determined using certain techniques. There are many baby-naming sites[24] on the Internet chock full of these names, their origins, and even the gender. These types of lookup tables can easily be incorporated into analytical tools to add value to the target entity. Other approaches are focused on classifying the ethnicity of a last name (surname), where, for example, Hertz would generally be classified as a German, Gomez as Hispanic, and L'Enfant as French. Of course, the use of this information for entity resolution can be debated, but it must be factored into the nature of the system operations and how the data is being processed.

Perhaps one of the most useful techniques used in identifying duplicate entities is the use of name aliases. Aliases are vital in helping to standardize the interpretation of a name because people will often use a nickname or abbreviation to represent themselves in different situations. For example, some aliases of Jonathan include John, Jon, Johnny, and Juan. Aliases also help to account for various spelling differences, such as

---

[21] Omar Benjelloun, Hector Garcia-Molina, Hideki Kawai, Tait Eliott Larson, David Menestrina, Qi Su, Sutthipong Thavisomboon, and Jennifer Widom, "Generic Entity Resolution in the SERF Project," *IEEE Data Engineering Bulletin* 29, no. 2 (June 2006).

[22] Indrajit Bhattacharya and Lise Getoor, "Query-Time Entity Resolution," *Journal of Artificial Intelligence Research* 30 (2007): 621–57.

[23] For example, Finnish female names include Pirkko, Sisko, and Tove; male names include Mika, Kimi, and Samsa.

[24] http://www.babycenter.com/baby-name-finder.

Kris, Chris, Cris or Stacy, Stacey, Stacie, Staci, Stacy, and so forth. Many times, utilizing an alias is the first step in identifying duplicate entities.

As previously demonstrated using the Manhattan spelling example, the data in many government systems is acquired from sources that might not be the most reliable or consistent, thereby leading to a large number of alternative representations. According to some sources,[25] there are over 300 different spellings of Mohammed, based on background, origin, and other regional influences. Depending on who encodes the information into the data source, there can obviously be a number of variations present. Recently in Britain it was reported[26] that Mohammed is the number two ranked name given to newborn boys when all spelling variations are taken into account. The following represents some of these alternative spellings:

Mohammed	Muhammad
Mohammad	Muhammed
Mohamed	Mohamad
Mahammed	Mohammod
Mahamed	Muhammod
Muhamad	Mohmmed
Mohamud	Mohammud

Incorporating an aliasing method within the entity resolution process is important to help address the variations that can occur within databases. However, names alone are not the best indicator of uniqueness and virtually every system utilizes other factors, including DOB, identification numbers, phones, and addresses. Consider Table 2.1, which shows the details of a particular name of interest. In the First Name, Last Name,

Table 2.1 Sample Record Structure – Ref #1

#	*FIRST*	*LAST*	*MID*	*DOB*	*OCCP*
1	Becky	Reis	D	11/16/1976	Sales
2	Becky	De Vries			Employee
3	Becka	Vreis		06/16/1976	Waitress
4	Becky	Ress	D	11/16/1976	Housekeeper
5	Becky	Vries	D	11/16/1976	
6	Becky	Vries		11/16/1967	
7	Rebecca	Vreese	D	11/16/1976	
8	Rebecca	DeVries		11/16/1976	Employee
9	Becky	Vreis	D	11/16/1976	Sales
10	Rebecca	De Vries		11/16/1976	Employee

[25] Described in the LAS (Language Analysis Systems) marketing literature (since acquired by IBM).
[26] http://www.timesonline.co.uk/tol/news/uk/article1890354.ece.

Middle Name, Date of Birth (DOB), and Occupation (OCCP) columns, is there enough information present to warrant considering all of these people to be the same? If so, which columns or combination of columns are deemed most valuable in this case?

Sometimes judgment calls play a role in resolving entities and it really comes down to factoring in how precise or general the matching conditions are defined. Some arguments could be made that records 1 and 4 form an entity; 2, 8, and 10 another entity; and 5, 7, and 9 a third entity. Think about what this means for analytics on terrorism, money laundering, criminal events, or corporate fraud versus mailing lists, customer surveys, or publication references. How tolerant are the false-positives or the overgeneralized matches and what is the potential cost if not all entities are considered?

In this example, the most important columns are Last Name followed by DOB. If these were the only two fields initially present, the decisions made about which entities to resolve would be consistent. The First Name and Middle Name columns are somewhat useful because they help validate the combination of Last Name and DOB by providing better resolution or detail to the entities. Finally, the Occupation column is nice to have, but it does not add much value to the overall interpretation of the entities, partially because the values are so generic (a waitress and a housekeeper are types of an employee as is someone in sales). With these overarching descriptions, it is hard to place much value on their meaning.

Now, consider Table 2.2, where the Occupation column is replaced by a Phone column. A quick glance at these values proves to be extremely disappointing as there is no new commonality as a result of these phone numbers. Furthermore, none of the phone numbers are close enough to each other where a simple digit transposition could be held accountable

Table 2.2 Sample Record Structure – Ref #2

#	*FIRST*	*LAST*	*MID*	*DOB*	*PHONE*
1	Becky	Reis	D	11/16/1976	201-111-1111
2	Becky	De Vries			201-222-2222
3	Becka	Vreis		06/16/1976	
4	Becky	Ress	D	11/16/1976	201-333-3333
5	Becky	Vries	D	11/16/1976	201-444-4444
6	Becky	Vries		11/16/1967	201-555-5555
7	Rebecca	Vreese	D	11/16/1976	201-666-6666
8	Rebecca	DeVries		11/16/1976	
9	Becky	Vreis	D	11/16/1976	212-999-9999
10	Rebecca	De Vries		11/16/1976	

Table 2.3 Sample Record Structure – Ref #3

#	FIRST	LAST	MID	DOB	PHONE	ADDRESS
1	Becky	Reis	D	11/16/1976	201-111-1111	815 Liberty Street, Trenton, NJ 08611
2	Becky	De Vries			201-222-2222	63 Butler St, Trenton, NJ 08611
3	Becka	Vreis		06/16/1976		61 Conrad St, Trenton, NJ 08611
4	Becky	Ress	D	11/16/1976	201-333-3333	324 S Clinton Ave, Trenton, NJ 08609
5	Becky	Vries	D	11/16/1976	201-444-4444	815 Liberty St, Trenton, NJ 08611
6	Becky	Vries		11/16/1967	201-555-5555	815 Liberty Street, Trenton, NJ 08611
7	Rebecca	Vreese	D	11/16/1976	201-666-6666	815 Liberty Street, Trenton, NJ 08612
8	Rebecca	DeVries		11/16/1976		815 Liberty Street, Trenton, NJ 08611
9	Becky	Vreis	D	11/16/1976	212-999-9999	815 Liberty St., Trenton, NJ 08610
10	Rebecca	De Vries		11/16/1976		815 Liberty Street, Trenton, NJ 08611

for any of the different values. Although unusual that there is no commonality, these circumstances do happen in the real world.

Continuing to expand the various fields associated with these entities, Table 2.3 presents the Address associated with each entity. Things are starting to get a little bit complicated with respect to seeing the relationships and connections among the entities. Additionally, very small or subtle differences are almost impossible to pick up in the data through manual observations. This is somewhat of a double-edged sword because to a human the values look the same, but to a computer they are completely different.

To emphasize this point, the information provided in Table 2.3 has been converted into a link diagram, presented in Figure 2.5, to show exactly how a computer sees these values. Taken at face value, without

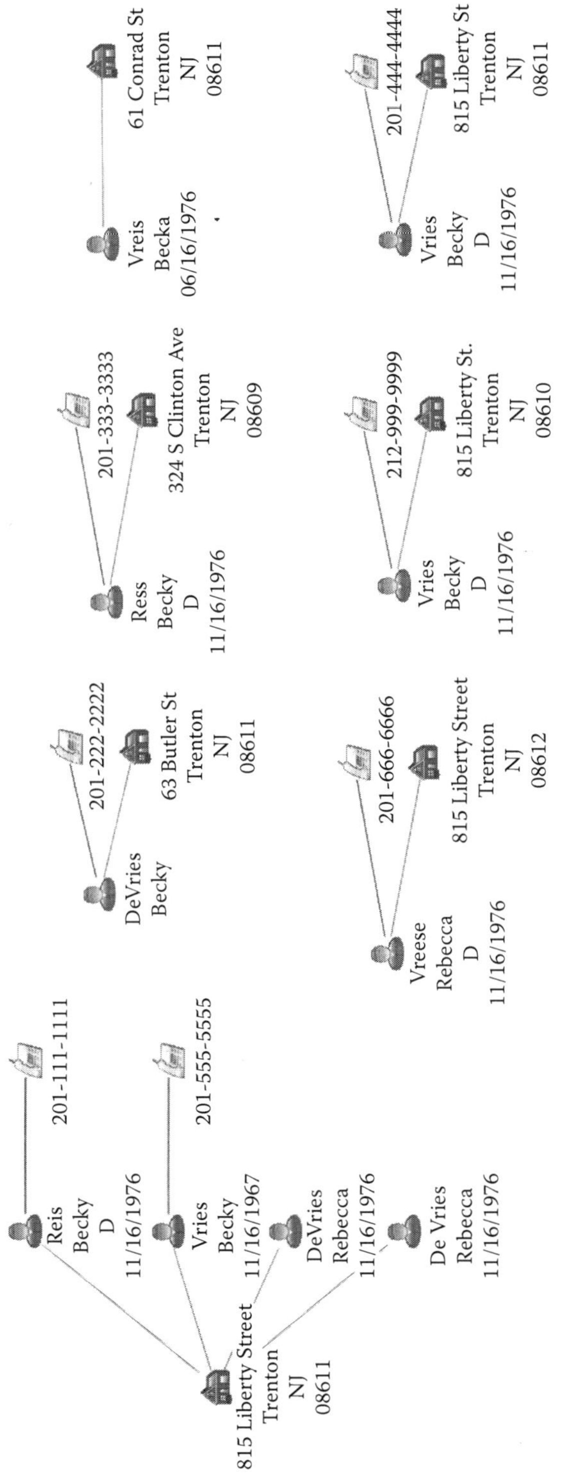

Figure 2.5 Link diagram for entity resolution using raw values.

any type of standardization or cleanup performed, the diagram shows seven distinct clusters.

Closer inspection of both the table and the diagram reveals that the addresses located at Liberty Street are virtually identical except that there are abbreviations used for the word 'Street' (St.) and there are different ZIP codes being used for two of the addresses. One can feel fairly confident that the addresses depicted by the four unique address objects are truly the same location. At this point, they can be considered identical and merged together as is shown in Figure 2.6.

This is a somewhat secondary entity resolution by-product on an address type in the fulfillment of identifying subject entities. Automating the cleanup of the addresses would normally take place within an entity resolution system, but the point here is to show the diversity of seemingly unique or similar entities using the raw data values.

Another point to make is that plotting the four different addresses onto a map (not included here) would show that they are in fairly close proximity to one another. Simple distance functions can be applied to the latitude and longitude coordinates of the addresses using some basic geo-coding techniques. It would then be clear that these addresses are less than a mile from each other, providing additional confidence that the person is most like the same entity. From here, an additional column representing the driver's license (LICENSE) is included into the data set for consideration and shown in Table 2.4.

With this additional information a new diagram is presented, in Figure 2.7, showing a total of three network clusters. Close inspection of the driver's license numbers reveals that they all appear to be a variation of one another. The relationships formed (e.g., indirect connections) among the subjects are strengthened by the new information. In the cluster in the lower left of the diagram, the driver's license number is off by a single digit; and in combination with the rest of the detail for the subject, it can be safely assumed that this is the same entity as described in the larger network. The cluster in the lower right still remains independent and somewhat isolated from the rest of the data because there is not enough overlap to warrant merging this entity with the others. The lack of a middle initial, a different date of birth (although the same year), and a different address all factor into keeping this entity separated.

After merging together the subject entities, the final network diagram is presented in Figure 2.8. What initially appeared as potentially ten unique records was narrowed down to two primary subjects through an entity resolution process. The remaining two driver's licenses are different enough to keep separated even though they are connected to the same person entity. There was, unfortunately, no consolidation from the phone numbers in

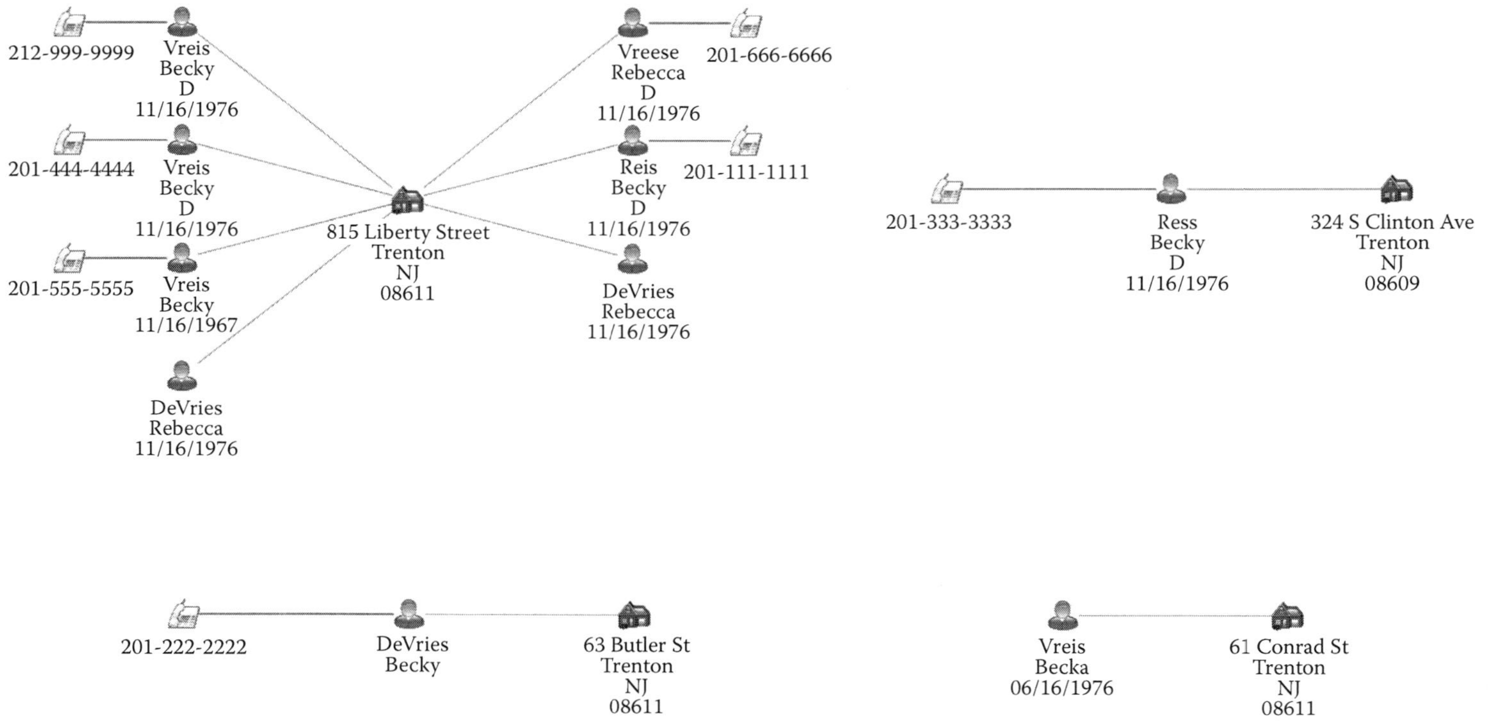

Figure 2.6 Link diagram for entity resolution after merging addresses.

Table 2.4 Sample Record Structure – Ref #4

#	*FIRST*	*LAST*	*MID*	*DOB*	*PHONE*	*ADDRESS*	*LICENSE*
1	Becky	Reis	D	11/16/1976	201-111-1111	815 Liberty Street, Trenton, NJ 08611	D12345678
2	Becky	De Vries			201-222-2222	63 Butler St, Trenton, NJ 08611	D12345678
3	Becka	Vreis		06/16/1976		61 Conrad St, Trenton, NJ 08611	
4	Becky	Ress	D	11/16/1976	201-333-3333	324 S Clinton Ave, Trenton, NJ 08609	D1234569
5	Becky	Vries	D	11/16/1976	201-444-4444	815 Liberty St, Trenton, NJ 08611	
6	Becky	Vries		11/16/1967	201-555-5555	815 Liberty Street, Trenton, NJ 08611	
7	Rebecca	Vreese	D	11/16/1976	201-666-6666	815 Liberty Street, Trenton, NJ 08612	D87654321
8	Rebecca	DeVries		11/16/1976		815 Liberty Street, Trenton, NJ 08611	
9	Becky	Vreis	D	11/16/1976	212-999-9999	815 Liberty St., Trenton, NJ 08610	D12345678
10	Rebecca	De Vries		11/16/1976		815 Liberty Street, Trenton, NJ 08611	D12345678

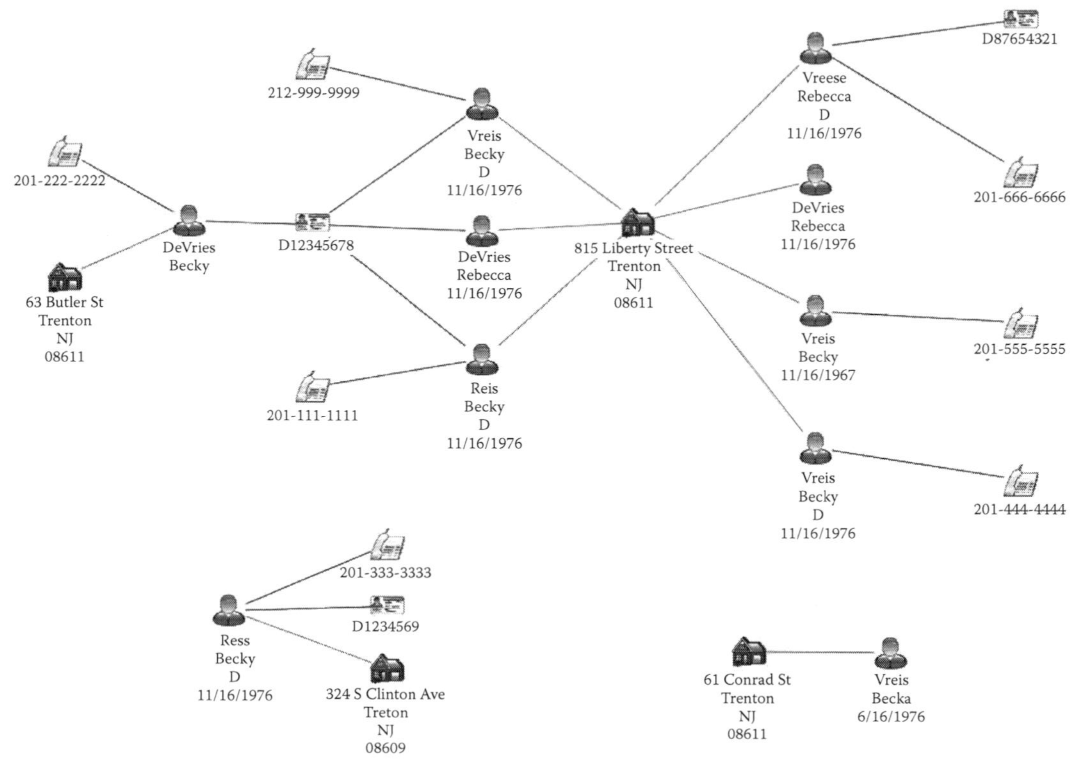

Figure 2.7 Link diagram for entity resolution presenting driver's licenses.

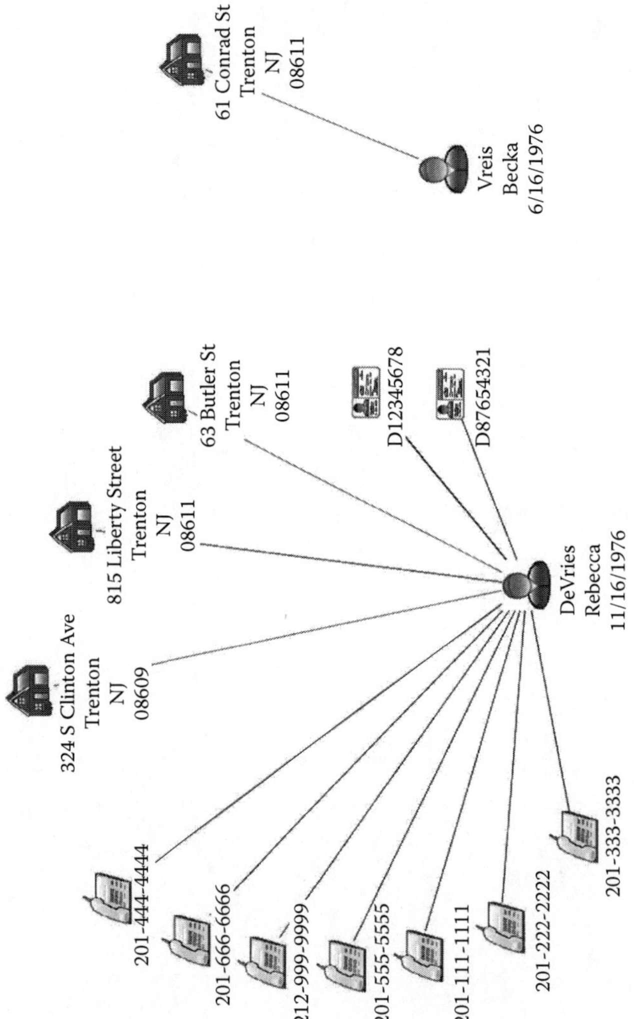

Figure 2.8 Link diagram for final entity resolution.

this example,[27] however, the addresses and driver's licenses were key to establishing more confidence regarding the true identities of the people.

Of course, any system resolving, combining, and merging entities would need to keep track of their original representations, sources, and related information to guarantee the integrity of the data. This is also critical because there are cases where entities are deemed the same; however, when new information is presented, there is an inconsistency in the logic and the entities must be unbundled. Often, this negative information does not support the facts and must be backed out of the process. For example, as shown in Figure 2.9, there are three person entities presented along with their descriptive data. Assume each entity is created from a separate database, respectively called A, B, and C. The goal is to determine if there are one, two, or three distinct entities.

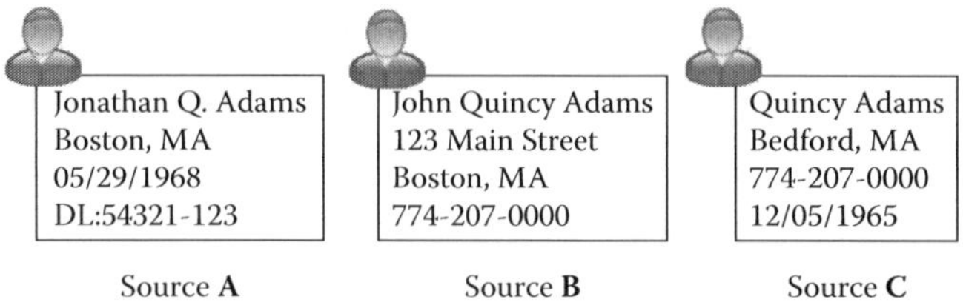

Figure 2.9 The resolution of three person entities.

Given that Sources A and B are processed first, it can reasonably be assumed that Jonathan Q. Adams and John Quincy Adams are the same entity based on the similarity of their names and locations. With the information provided, it would be a sensible decision to make a logical match. Now Source C is factored into the equation and its descriptive information is compared against the other data elements. In Source C, there is a name similarity found with Source B as well as a common phone number, which tends to provide a higher degree of credibility to the match. Although Bedford, MA, and Boston, MA, is not an exact location match, they are only about 20 miles apart and the area code (774) and exchange (207) of the phone number are from the Bedford, MA, area. Given this information, there proves to be a good match between Sources B and C.

Now, consideration is given to the entity from Source A to see if it is a potential match for the entity from Source C. In this case there is some overlap based on the name; however, the date of birth for these two entities is more than two years apart and, therefore, does not constitute a reliable match. At this point, the entity resolution process shows that

[27] Most data samples have common phone numbers, as is exemplified in other examples in this book.

A = B, B = C, and A ≠ C, which means that some housekeeping needs to be performed to produce a final output because the results must be transitive. The relationship between A and B must be uncoupled[28] because B more closely matches with C, and the conflict on the date of birth between A and C means that A is left as a single entity when all three sources are combined.

Anonymous Resolution

There is a lot of value in being able to identify and match similar entities within or across data sources, especially in the law enforcement and intelligence communities. Even though the concept of information sharing has been discussed quite heavily in the post-9/11 era, there has been limited progress with respect to organizations effectively sharing data in an automated fashion, and given the billions of records being acquired by government agencies every year, it becomes more important with every record that is processed. Fortunately, there are some methods that provide a way to share data without exposing the identities or details of data targets being queried.

This is a somewhat sensitive area for many government agencies. If an investigator needs to run a background check, or search for the name of a terrorist or a subject of interest, the mere act of running the query in a source or environment controlled by a third party could easily expose their intentions. Often, more secure government agencies won't even allow Internet access to their analytical resources and the ones that do typically shun the process of searching open-source resources for additional detail or information because the queries could potentially be linked back to the agency.

One highly critical incident[29] occurred in 2004 when the European Commission agreed to provide the United States with access to the personal information collected on airline passengers for the sake of terrorist screening. The Passenger Name Records (PNRs) provided included 34 fields of information, such as the names, passports, dates of birth, and flight details. The data was shared with an understanding that the U.S. authorities would provide appropriate protections and access controls for the data.

---

28 Uncoupling a match should be trivial because a system should maintain all details for each entity including its attributes and source references.

29 Chris Williams, "EU Court Stomps Passenger Data Sharing," *The Register,* May 30, 2006, http://www.theregister.co.uk/2006/05/30/pnr_eu_judgment/.

The agreement was struck down in 2006[30] by the European Court of Justice because they deemed that it was illegal and that it violated the privacy and civil rights of European citizens. Even the Information Commissioner's Office (ICO),[31] the United Kingdom's independent authority to promote access to official information and protect personal information, stated, "It is important that there are proper data protection safeguards surrounding the transfer of airline passenger details to foreign government authorities..."

Utilizing an approach that incorporates an anonymous resolution[32] would simplify these types of matters as well as domestic concerns raised by civil libertarians regarding unintentional disclosure or misuse of the data. The concept is fairly simple: To encrypt the names in a way so they are not presented in an interpretable format, are not reversible, and can be used only by basic matching routines. Essentially any detail, including names, dates of birth, addresses, credit cards, and other collected data,[33] can be encoded into a unique "hash" that will match only identical values. In theory, no two input conditions should generate the same hash encoding.

There are countless hashing algorithms published in the marketplace, and research communities publish new findings frequently. Each approach has its own strengths and weaknesses, and a specific review of various approaches' capabilities, vulnerabilities, and virtues is outside the scope of this discussion. However, the most prevalent hash techniques in use at the time of this writing include Message Digest algorithm 5 (MD5) and the Secure Hash Algorithm (SHA) series. Of course, an appropriate hash should be matched to the problem space being perused for development.

The output values produced by different hash techniques are typically 128, 160, 256, and 512 bits long, where a bit is a standard on/off value. Generally, the higher the bit value, the more secure the algorithm. In Table 2.5, several different hash algorithms[34] are applied to an input value for "John Smith" and the resulting hash values are clearly indecipherable and bear no resemblance to the input values.

In Table 2.6, the input value is changed to "Jon Smith" and the resulting hash values are distinctly different from those presented in the previous table. Thus, any variation in the input value will result in a completely

[30] Nicola Clark, "European Court Bars Passing Passenger Data to U.S," *The New York Times,* May 30, 2006, http://www.nytimes.com/iht/2006/05/30/world/30cnd-air.html.

[31] http://www.ico.gov.uk/.

[32] For additional material, see Damiaan Zwietering, "Entity Analytics Solutions," IBM Corporation.

[33] This technique is also used in forensic accounting (e.g. electronic discovery) practices to identify duplicate files and e-mail messages. It is also used for validating downloaded files to see if the checksums are equivalent to ensure the files have not been altered.

[34] Results produced by http://passcracking.com/.

Table 2.5 Hash Value Maps for John Smith

Hash Type	*Hash Value for John Smith*
md5_128bit	6117323d2cabbc17d44c2b44587f682c
md5_64bit	6117323d2cabbc17
md5(md5_lcase)	d986b8c066286e4093b45ee1994db104
md5(md5_Ucase)	44e4b2bcd9576f2691ede4bfcf6c5a21
sha1_160bit	e61a3587b3f7a142b8c7b9263c82f8119398ecb7
MySQL_64bit	43ef225a165961bc
MySQL_160bit	*cc420ae08bfa1d0ba7392a520976f7dc4253e291

Table 2.6 Hash Value Maps for Jon Smith

Hash Type	*Hash Value for Jon Smith*
md5_128bit	f9bde240549bfb86ebdeeb3dd1f49345
md5_64bit	f9bde240549bfb86
md5(md5_lcase)	ef65102db1b101f13000792a6a928d77
md5(md5_Ucase)	702f9de97ae2d05f085bbb2365f37fd3
sha1_160bit	d3a4fc04e25bed2f840be6aec3e8d22911ff9003
MySQL_64bit	583d8ce253fc9e75
MySQL_160bit	*1d570594d82db5e64e3b0ce0d6a4a6d7240175c8

different hash value and ultimately in a different set of entity matches or nonmatches being encountered.

In fact, even the case (i.e., upper or lower case) of the data affects the hash algorithm. For example, the MD5-128 bit for encoding "John" is 61409aa1fd47d4a5332de23cbf59a36f and the encoding for "JOHN" is e2577c04131c5b0c7e7580f978322b31. So, in the context of anonymous resolution, the structure and content of the entities must be well defined because slight variations on the input values can result in a false-negative match occurring, which potentially could prove catastrophic.

When processing data for anonymous entity resolution, all parties involved must be in agreement on the approach to representing and encoding their data. Therefore, the same alias lists must be used along with any format changes (e.g., dropping parentheses, commas, dashes, etc.), and the order of the descriptive attributes (e.g., data columns) must be known. Generally, encrypting the entire record structure may not be necessary as long as any identifying information, such as names, ID numbers, credit cards, or other sensitive details, is not disclosed.

For example, given the records from Airline A (passenger-screening data) shown in Table 2.7 and from Agency B (a watch list maintained by a counterterrorist agency) shown in Table 2.8, and assuming the same encoding techniques are used, matches can be made based on criteria set forth for weighing different attributes according to the task.

In this example, the Full Name of the passenger matches the identity of a known terrorist and the agency can pull the Raw Value to determine who was actually matched. Normally, such a condition would set off alarms and red flags; however, given the rest of the information transmitted it appears, overall, to be an unsubstantiated match. An important consideration to factor into this example is that if the Birth Date were also encrypted, it would be a binary value (match/does not match) to any automated system or human analyst because they would never know if the date was off by a single day or by one hundred years. Because it does not compromise the identity of the person, it makes sense to leave it in a standard format, allowing additional business logic to be included in the entity resolution systems and helping to result in confidence in these kinds of disparate values.

Citizenship is another field that does not compromise the identity of a passenger and, therefore, can be transmitted without any type of encoding. As can be expected, there are certain countries that tend to be safe harbors for terrorist activities, and therefore knowing explicitly where the passenger is from will factor into the overall analytics. Encoding the passport number can be debated because the number itself does not truly expose the identity of an individual—at least not without proper

Table 2.7 Passenger-Screening Data for Airline A

COLUMN	*RAW-VALUE*	*PROCESSED-DATA*	*ENCODED-VALUE*
FULL NAME	John Smith	JON SMITH	231f79d8ff3504de
BIRTH DATE	04/15/70	1970/04/15	1970/04/15
CITIZENSHIP	United States	USA	USA
PASSPORT#	023456789	1234567890	e807f1fcf82d132f

Table 2.8 Passenger-Screening Data for Agency B

COLUMN	*RAW-VALUE*	*PROCESSED-DATA*	*ENCODED-VALUE*
FULL NAME	Smith, Jonathon	JON SMITH	231f79d8ff3504de
BIRTH DATE	07/21/1982	1982/07/21	1982/07/21
CITIZENSHIP	Pakistani	PAKISTAN	PAKISTAN
PASSPORT#	555-22222-1	555222221	c003df6a954c9af4

government access. However, in this example, the information is deemed sensitive and is therefore, encoded.

Conclusion

The *quality* of data has a tremendous impact on the *quality* of the analytics that can be performed. Value errors, missing data, and bad structures directly, and usually in a negative fashion, affect the outcomes and results of a system. Seemingly simple searches can be fraught with challenges due to misspelled words, transposed characters, or improperly formatted content. The level of trust placed in using the results from such systems is marginal at best.

Fortunately, there are ways to help deal with these situations by transforming, cleaning up, and restructuring the data to better accommodate the analyses. Additionally, the use of entity resolution techniques within the law enforcement and intelligence communities will begin to transition from the larger, well-funded projects to become a more commonplace offering across all systems. These advancements also lay the foundation for expanding the use of anonymous resolution capabilities to enable sharing among systems with different security requirements as well as with external agencies, including foreign allies. However, a lot of the disparity encountered in the data can be addressed during its collection.

The data collection instruments (e.g., processes, interfaces, structure, and storage) act as the primary gateway for allowing bad data to be captured and recorded and should be reevaluated regularly. When data quality issues are encountered within the underlying data sources, those interfaces and processes responsible for the problems should be prioritized and addressed quickly. Unfortunately, this is easier said than done in many organizations. Thus, the long-term impact for not correcting these problems is that the quality of the analyses will potentially be compromised.

Chapter 3

What Are Patterns?

Introduction

We have all heard stories about advanced computing and analytical systems being capable of exposing hidden patterns contained in data—whether it is for uncovering credit card frauds, identifying money launderers, or tracking terrorists. The process is usually very mysterious and avant-garde, where the specific parameters, values, and conditions of the patterns are closely guarded secrets for the agencies and organizations that have placed them into operation.

But what are the "patterns" that these industries keep referring to? Patterns can be any combination of values that contain meaning within the context or domain for which they are being reviewed. There are many different ways to expose patterns, including clusters, sequences, or relationships. Remember that there are no right answers and there are no wrong answers. Patterns are based on individual interpretation of the data, the environment, the circumstances, and the quality of the data collected. One must also take into account that not all patterns hold true 100 percent of the time, that there are always exceptions to the patterns, that there are always exceptions to the exceptions, and that the patterns are always evolving.

Patterns, such as fraud, exist in data because the controls established by the organization, business, or entity have allowed the situation to exist in the first place—albeit unintentionally. In many cases fraud, malpractice, and malfeasance succeed because people do not know how to interpret their datasets or recognize the telltale symptoms.[1] Most theft and fraud is usually achieved through a series of frequent claims or transactions with relatively modest amounts of money being stolen on any one occasion, rather than in a single, large, obvious heist.

Over an extended time period, an organization may pay out millions of dollars in small chunks. This sort of fraud is subtle and not directly detectable through usual methods of oversight. Of course, upon detecting a pattern, the goal is to determine what processes need to change to remove or minimize future occurrences of the fraud. Practically speaking, detecting patterns is useless unless the corporation or agency affected is in a position to change their processes (collection, enforcement, or audit)—otherwise, it is a waste of money, time, and resources to even initiate.

Patterns can often be exposed simply by generating special reports to see what values or counts tend to fall out of normal bounds. In one

[1] Christopher Westphal and Teresa Blaxton, *Data Mining Solutions: Methods and Tools for Solving Real-World Problems* (New York: John Wiley & Sons, 1998), 18.

Medicare fraud case, a doctor was targeted for investigation due to the large number of claims he filed. To deliver the number of services billed, he would have had to work 36 hours a day, every day—an unlikely situation that was easy to spot. Some approaches are focused on improved data collection protocols where more consistent and reliable methods result in better patterns. One example is to standardize addresses so there is little variation in how the street, city, state, and ZIP code are represented. Yet others will update business logic to deal with situations, minimizing their exposure to loss/fraud. Limiting the use of the same credit card multiple times (typically twice) at the same gas station during a 24-hour time period is one such approach.

Data analysis requires practitioners to think creatively. As much as we would like to believe in the unexplained, there are no silver bullets or magic wands that exist to expose patterns. What is required is a fundamental understanding of the domain, basic logic, and the ability to ask the right questions to expose the patterns of interest. Unfortunately, many times the clients themselves don't even know what questions to ask, where to start, or how to proceed. A few of the questions asked by clients on some high-end engagements include:

Client: We think we have fraud occurring in our company. Can you find it?
Reality: We have expense reports and charge card statements and want to expose patterns of questionable reimbursements (e.g., multiple submissions, inflated costs, etc.).
Client: We can't account for $5 million this quarter. Where did it go?
Reality: We want to expose patterns of questionable payments in our accounts payable system (e.g., duplicate payments, unallowed costs, etc.).
Client: How can we improve our bottom line?
Reality: We want to create common profiles of our customers across different divisions to support cross-selling initiatives (e.g., minimize fraud, increase consumption, etc.).

The majority of examples, descriptions, and discussions presented throughout this book are based on entity relationship diagrams (e.g., networks), commonly interpreted using link analysis techniques and technologies. Keep in mind that networks are generally meant to be analyzed in the context of their parts as well as collectively as a whole. There are going to be different types of patterns exposed based on the values, relationships, and pathways defined within the network, and not all objects within a network necessarily add to the value of the information.

When describing networks, their structures can take many different formats, meanings, and interpretations. To quickly define the concepts of a network, objects, also referred to as entities or nodes, represent the fundamental building blocks of a network. By definition, objects are generally considered mutually exclusive of one another such that there are no direct influences, biases, or dependencies among their underlying representations. For example, an object can represent, say, a person, and as in nature, every person is considered a unique and separate being; so Mary is different from John. Many times, analysis can be performed using just objects where various clustering techniques are used to expose patterns based on their underlying attributable representations (e.g., hair color, last name, gender, ethnicity, etc.).

The introduction of relationships (also called linkages, associations, or connections) ties together a pair of objects. If we have two people objects, such as Mary and John, they may be related as brother/sister, husband/wife, boss/employee, or some other type of value. Relationships are finite in that they only exist between pairs of objects. If 10 people were all part of the same family, each person would have their own unique relationships to other members of the family. If multiple relationships are required between any pair of objects, each is considered a separate instance and unrelated. For example, if John calls Mary on the phone several times, each call (e.g., the relationships) is considered distinct because a phone call, by definition, is a unique event. Unlike objects, relationships can't exist by themselves; they must be defined in the context of objects.

Generally a single relationship does not define a network, nor do multiple relationships between a single pair of objects—although one could argue the latter when trying to detect any type of sequence patterns that exists within the data. Nevertheless, for this discussion networks are considered to exist only when there are multiple pairs or tuples of relationships present among the objects. Simply stated, there must be at minimum of three objects to define a basic network. Therefore, at least one of the objects will be connected to two or more other objects and, based on this premise, we can then start to look for commonalities among the objects that might indicate a pattern of interest.

Consider the representation shown in Figure 3.1, where there are three objects connected by two distinct relationships. This is one of the most basic, generic, and prevalent types of structures that can be defined within a network. The question is: *Does this represent an important pattern?*

The answer is: *It depends on the context for which the pattern is being interpreted.* For example, if the objects are all telephone numbers, then

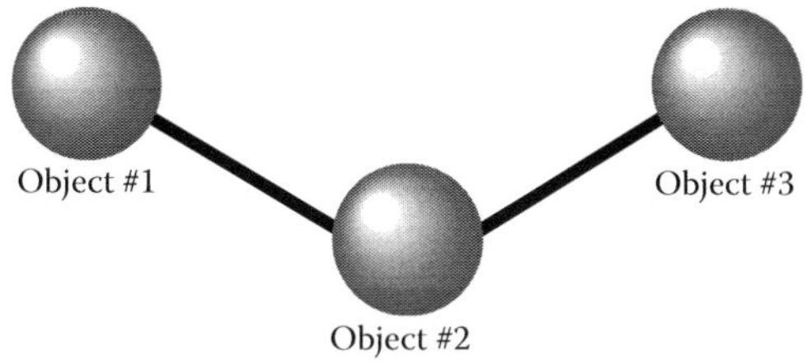

Figure 3.1 A basic network diagram.

the phone in the middle will represent the most active, assuming only a single link (e.g., call) between each of the phones and assuming that it also indirectly connects the two other phones. In a different example, if the objects represent people, then the person at the center of the network could be interpreted as having the more influence and/or control over the other two people.

If we take this concept and interpret it in a different context, where two objects of a certain type are connected to a single object of a different type, then additional patterns can be exposed within the network. For example, if a person is connected to two addresses, then we need to ask ourselves, is this an important pattern? If we are a retail organization, it might indicate that our customer has recently moved and the different addresses represent the old and new addresses, which means we might want to send coupons for new curtains or towels in the expectation that they are setting up a new household. If we are an insurance company and we see this pattern, it may be indicative of fraud because the same claim is filed for each address, indicating a duplicate or fraudulent claim. There is no right answer and there is no wrong answer—it all depends on the context of the data and analysis and the overall expectations of the client. Figure 3.2 shows some additional combinations and interpretations of this simple network pattern.

Many times the initial interpretation or understanding of a pattern is at face value. Until all the permutations, combinations, and different interpretations are explored, a final recommendation or action should not be initiated. There are always exceptions to the pattern and there are exceptions to the exceptions. This chapter presents an overview of different types of network patterns that have several different interpretations. Sometimes it is important to know the nature of the data source as well as the circumstances of the collection, or simply to look at the pattern from a different perspective. Much of this is common sense, but until one is actively engaged in these types of analytics, it can take some time before it comes natural—just like learning tennis, skiing, or golf.

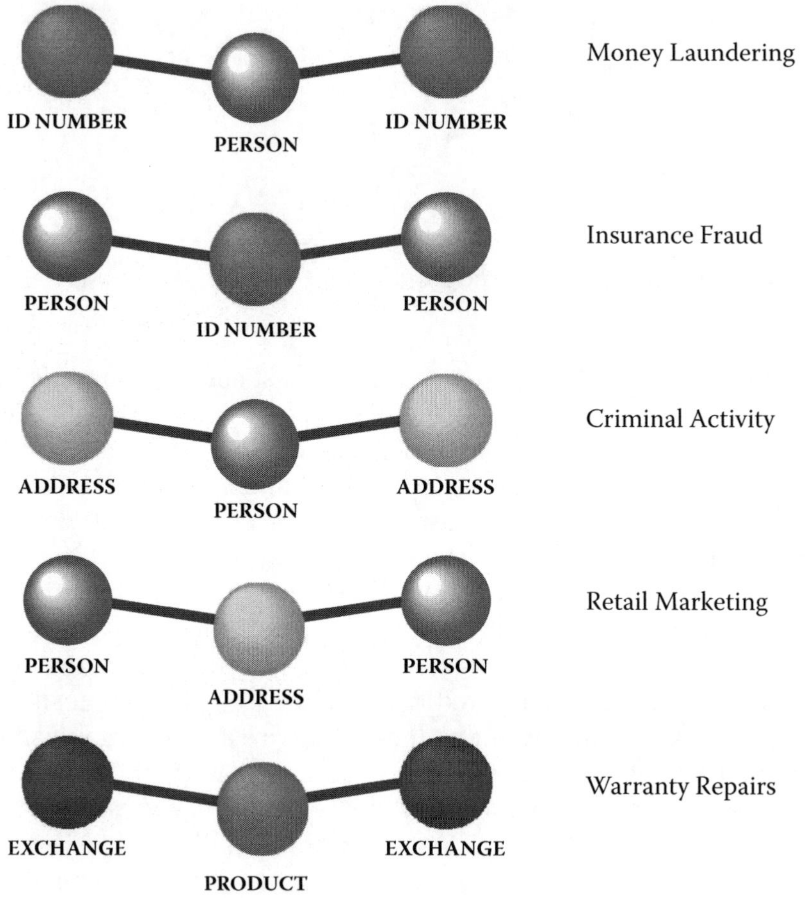

Figure 3.2 Different instantiations of a basic network pattern.

Which Pattern Is More Important?

In the following example, suppose an agent from the special investigations unit (SIU) of a large, national insurance carrier is reviewing recent claim submissions. Upon reviewing the data, two different network structures appear as shown in Figure 3.3. These networks represent a subset of the data derived from claims[2] submitted for property damage that occurred during a recent natural disaster and consist of different combinations of *Subjects* (e.g., the claimants) and their related *SSNs* (Social Security numbers). The question faced by the investigator is: *Which pattern/network is more important?*

[2] The same concept is applied to financial institutions reviewing their transactions for potential money-laundering activities, revenue service agencies exposing complex tax schemes, or even state welfare agencies processing benefit claims.

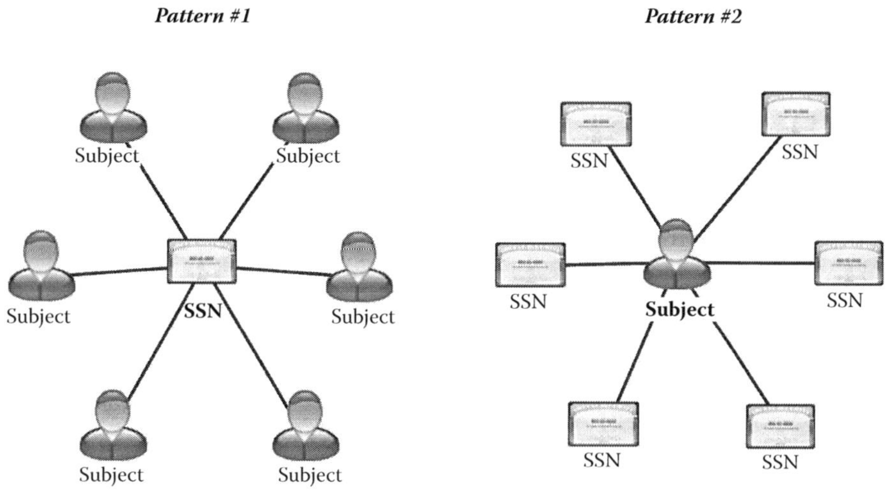

Figure 3.3 Qualifying important patterns.

The network on the left shows a single *SSN* connected to six policy holders (i.e., the *Subjects*). At face value, most investigators would consider this a very questionable and suspicious situation. However, before any action can be taken, the investigator must check all the facts and verify the validity of the data. First, this network may not be considered suspicious if the *SSN* represents an invalid or common number such as 999-99-9999, 000-00-0000, 123-45-6789, UNKNOWN, or NOT PROVIDED. Often, this can be attributed to faulty data collection, improper collection interfaces, flawed data entry systems, or poorly trained staff. This type of situation is quite common in most real-world data sources, especially those without strong controls or a centralized system to check for these conditions. If "dirty" data is present in the display, the entire network would be disregarded because there is no reliable connection among the *Subjects*. Basically this equates to a "short circuit," and the implied link expressed through the use of a common *SSN,* in this case, is considered invalid.

Let's assume the *SSN* presented in Figure 3.3 is actually a valid number and it passes all the relevant checks (see sidebar for validating SSNs). A different interpretation would arise if each of the *Subjects* had a similar name. In this case, the investigators may discount the severity of the pattern if the names represented, say, John Smith, Johnny Smith, J. Smith, Jon Smithe, Smith Jonathan, or J J Smith. Obviously, these names most likely reflect the same *Subject* because they are all similar and tied to the same *SSN,* which then raises the question: Is this person trying to avoid detection by intentionally varying his name? It would be highly unusual for each claim to have a different name spelling and it would certainly be suspicious if the network was formed from claim data provided from the same insurance carrier, assuming they utilized their customer relationship management (CRM) system to control their claim content.

What is not explicitly conveyed in the diagram is that each linkage between a *Subject* and an *SSN* is generated based on the occurrence of a separate and unique claim. A thicker link between the *SSN* and any *Subject* would indicate usage of that name on more than one claim. Thus, there are at least six claims involved in creating this network, using six different names, and this fact[3] alone would most likely form the basis for starting an investigation.

One final interpretation of the diagram shown in Figure 3.3 is when the *SSN* is indeed a valid number and each of the *Subjects* represents a distinct and unique name (e.g., John Smith, Betty Jones, Joe Johnson, Mary Doe, Dan Walters, and Tom Willis). When initially presented with this "generic" diagram, most people expect that this is the only interpretation of the pattern without really giving much regard to the variations or alternative ways in which the data can be represented (e.g., flawed). However, until the details are checked there should be no assumption that the network is either valid or invalid, and jumping to conclusions can often lead to undesirable outcomes. Remember that there are always exceptions to the pattern, and exceptions to the exceptions. Now, let's take what we learned and see if it can be applied to the network shown on the right in Figure 3.3.

A completely different interpretation can be made using a variation on this particular pattern. In this case, the center of the network represents a *Subject* that is related to six *SSNs*. This pattern is of most interest to the investigator when the *Subject* has a unique name and the *SSN* values are also distinct (and valid). An exception to this pattern occurs when the *SSNs* appear as variations of the same number—possibly off by a few digits, have transposed digits, or appear as misinterpreted digits.[4] Often, this type of pattern represents an intentional misrepresentation of the *SSNs* by the *Subject* and would be of particular interest to the investigator.

Another exception comes when a common name such as John Smith is used as the *Subject* because the *SSNs* are most likely valid and the network is formed based on too general a representation of the *Subject's* name. Thus, the pattern does not reveal any type of explicit fraud or

[3] For analytical purposes, clean data is always desirable; however, sometimes a pattern exists because of the variations presented due to intentional misrepresentation.

[4] Often numbers can be mistakenly transposed based on how they are written—specifically 1 and 7, 4 and 9, 3 and 8, and sometimes 2 and 5.

wrongdoing; rather, it actually represents six different and unique people named John Smith. But without any other type of *Subject* discriminator such as a date of birth, city, or physical description, they are all generically represented as the same *Subject.* Luckily, there are techniques and solutions for dealing with these types of situations through the use of better data representation and disambiguation functions; these are discussed later in the book.

In reality, the data will most likely show a combination of patterns where different numbers of *Subjects* and *SSNs* are interrelated, forming a more intricate and complex network structure. The patterns grow more involved when the phone numbers, addresses, and other pertinent claim data are represented within the network. These patterns are not unique to the insurance fraud world. They also appear in money-laundering networks, terrorist cells, and organized crime rings. Ultimately, the investigator will have to know how to interpret these structures and act accordingly.

The problem becomes even more complex when analysis requires the integration of multiple sources of data obtained from different insurance carriers. The insurance industry[5] has long recognized that providing a reliable and effective means of integrating multiple sources of data is important to exposing larger fraud rings. The ability to combine data from different companies and different sources is essential for fraud detection. As these trends continue, it becomes increasingly critical to integrate public record data, other insurance carrier data, and nontraditional sources including law enforcement (narcotics, theft/burglary, and arrests), telephone subscribers, death indexes, and other references.

Accessing billions of records from across potentially thousands of databases provides a very challenging environment from which to conduct analysis. Making sense of all this data can be overwhelming—especially with the amount of variation in content and representation, to name but one of the major challenges. The good news is that the technologies already exist to access, query, integrate, combine, and present data in these types of environments. The twin challenges will be maintaining a focus on the analytical methodologies used to determine which patterns are most important and leveraging the extensive work done in other areas, such as financial crimes, counterterrorism, and law enforcement that can be applied to insurance fraud (and vice versa).

[5] Places like the National Insurance Crime Bureau (NICB) in the United States and the Financial Supervisory Service (FSS) in Korea are chartered with combining claim data from multiple insurance carriers to help identify fraud across the industry.

SSN Validation

Many data sources contain Social Security numbers (SSNs) as a form of identity or descriptive information about an individual and SSNs are, by definition, unique to the person they are issued to by the Social Security Administration (SSA). However, there are instances where SSNs are not properly entered or are made up by people to avoid being tracked or monitored. Luckily, the process used to create SSNs helps isolate certain types of abuses from occurring. Somewhat similar to a credit card with checksum digits (e.g., the Luhn algorithm[6]), an SSN has a specific structure and encoding[7,8,9], dictating how it is created and thereby providing a basic foundation for understanding and validating how it gets issued. An SSN consists of nine digits where the first three digits are called the Area Number and indicate the state or region where the SSN was issued. In Table 3.1, several examples (does not present all mappings) show how SSNs are related to their issuance locale.

The next two digits (the middle two numbers) are called the Group Number and reflect a specific ordering[10] used to help validate whether the SSN was ever issued. The Group Number is assigned using a sequence of odd numbers for 01–09 and even numbers for 10–98. Group codes of "00" are not assigned and considered invalid. Initially the numbers are assigned as shown in Table 3.2.

The Group Numbers are validated using a "high" number that is posted on the SSA Web site[11] and updated monthly. This high-number list indicates the most recent group assignments for each state/region code and can technically be used to determine when an SSN was issued. 05 (odd 01–09) precedes the number 50 (even 10–98), which precedes the number 06 (even 02–08), which precedes the number 15 (odd 11–99). So, a high number of

Table 3.1 Area Number and State Issued for SSNs

Area Number	*State Issued*
050-134	New York
261-267	Florida
526-527	Arizona
545-573	California
530	Nevada
574	Alaska
580	Virgin Islands

[6] http://en.wikipedia.org/wiki/Luhn_formula.
[7] http://www.cpsr.org/prevsite/cpsr/privacy/ssn/ssn.structure.html.
[8] http://en.wikipedia.org/wiki/Social_security_number.
[9] http://www.socialsecurity.gov/history/ssn/geocard.html.
[10] http://www.socialsecurity.gov/employer/ssnweb.htm.
[11] http://www.ssa.gov/employer/highgroup.txt.

Table 3.2 Group Numbers and Orderings for SSNs

Group Number	*Ordering*
odd numbers:	01 to 09
even numbers:	10 to 98
even numbers:	02 to 08
odd numbers:	11 to 99

92 would invalidate SSN XXX-04-XXXX, a high number of 07 invalidates SSN XXX-15-XXXX, and a high number of 20 validates SSN XXX-03-XXXX.

Finally, the last four digits are consecutively assigned (0001–9999), defined as a Serial Number, and do not have any sort of check digit or lookup values. Bear in mind, this algorithm is used only to determine if an SSN has ever been issued—it can't tell if the person is alive or dead or the name of the person to whom the number was originally issued.

To give a real-world example, consider the SSN 480-07-7456, which belonged to Ronald Reagan, the 40th president of the United States. He was born on February 6, 1911, and died on June 5, 2004, at 93 years of age. To interpret this SSN, we examine the first three digits (i.e., the Area Number) using a Social Security Number Allocation table[12] and see that 480 is part of the range 478–485 assigned to the state of Iowa. A review of the Wikipedia entry[13] on Ronald Reagan shows that he worked at various radio stations in Iowa during the 1930s and talks about his enlistment in the U.S. Army Reserves, which is most likely when he applied for his SSN. As a matter of record, the SSA first started issuing numbers in 1936, so obviously the number was assigned sometime after this date.

The next two digits 07 (i.e., the Group Number) are cross-referenced using the high list. The most recent entry shows that number is currently set at 37. Using the formula described above, 37 falls into the final category of odd numbers (11–99), which means that Reagan's Group Number assignment of 07 (part of the first category 01–09) makes it a valid entry. Also, 07 is a number that was assigned early on in the SSA issuance process, indicating it would most likely be an older number. Actually, this type of comparison is important in validating SSNs in situations where, say, a 21-year-old person is trying to use an SSN issued to someone that is 50 years old.

The final Serial Number, 7456, merely distinguishes the assigned numbers from others in the Area/Group. The number of SSNs issued each year changes based on demand, and historically[14] there are some years with fairly large fluctuations including 1937 (with more than 37 million issued in the first year of the SSA), 1973, and 1987.

---

12 http://www.ssa.gov/employer/stateweb.htm.

13 http://en.wikipedia.org/wiki/Ronald_Reagan.

14 http://www.socialsecurity.gov/history/ssn/ssnvolume.html.

SSN validation checks are a simple and effective way to find obvious issues, errors, and anomalies in data and form a good foundation for detecting various precursors to aberrant behaviors and fraud-related activities. Unfortunately, sometimes due to careless data entry or other factors, inconsistencies are introduced through transposed digits, so care must be taken when validating the data to ensure the accuracy of the data.

In continuing with the interpretation of patterns and the use of additional sources of data, we switch our discussions from fighting insurance fraud to combating money laundering.[15] These two industries share a considerable amount of the same challenges with respect to understanding their respective patterns.

Do These Patterns Make Sense?

Many times pattern interpretation needs to be done within certain types of domain context. It is important to know the origins of the data, the value transformations involved, and what can logically be presented. Given the two networks shown in Figure 3.4, determine which one is of most interest to the analysts performing the investigation.

The first pattern shows a standard financial transaction where all the related information is shown connected to the *Subject*. For a complete

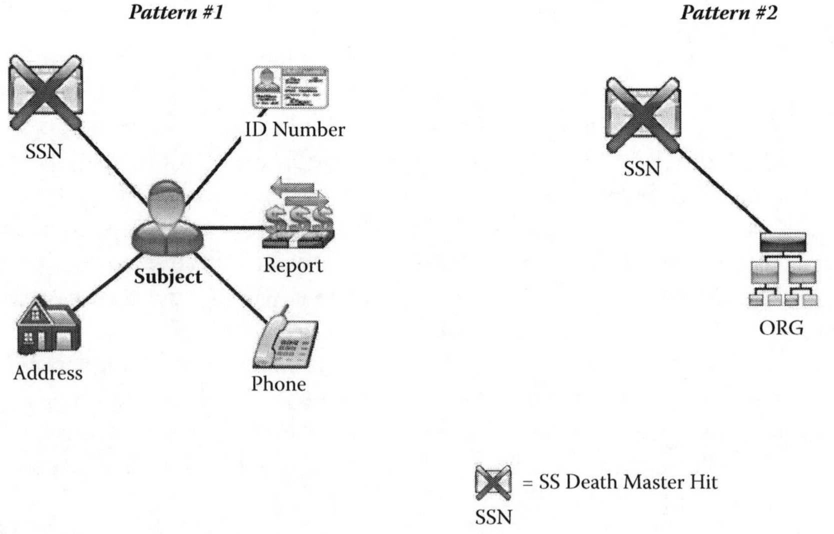

Figure 3.4 Interpreting the patterns.

[15] The previous pattern discussed is also routinely seen in financial data, especially Bank Secrecy Act (BSA) data, and most patterns presented in this section are interchangeable between domains.

transaction, generally there will be information on the home *Address,* a work or a home *Phone* (or both), some type of *ID Number* used to conduct the transactions (e.g., a driver's license, passport, alien registration, or other form), and most important, an *SSN.* However in this case, a special icon is assigned to the *SSN* because it was found to be an exact match of an entry in the Social Security Death Master (SSDM) Index[16] (see sidebar on SSDM). This type of matching is routinely done in organizations such as FinCEN (Financial Crimes Enforcement Network) and the IRS-CID (Criminal Investigations Division) when performing money laundering-related analytics.

Death Master Index

The Social Security Administration Death Master Index (DMI), also referred to as the Social Security Death Master (SSDM) Index, is a database offered for sale by the Department of Commerce, Technology Administration through their National Technical Information Service (NTIS), a division responsible for the collection and dissemination of various scientific and technical information sources created by the government for release to the public as well as special research services to other federal agencies. The DMI is a database with over 80,000,000 records (circa 2008) that simply contain the name, SSN, dates of birth and death, and some basic address data on any person who has died with an assigned SSN. The following sample shows the basic layout of a record in the death master file:

Code A/C/D (add/change/delete)
Social Security Number
Last Name
Name Suffix (e.g., Jr., III)
First Name
Middle Name
Code V/P (verify or proof—for confirming death)
Date of Death
Date of Birth
State/Country of Residence
ZIP Code of Last Residence
ZIP Code of Payment Benefit

Once a person is reported deceased, their SSN should no longer be used for any type of income reporting, finance application, or other type of official benefit. Although not authorized, use of the SSNs of the deceased for these types of purposes occurs on a fairly routine basis. Many of the financial intelligence units operating in the United States utilize the DMI/SSDM to

16 http://www.ntis.gov/products/ssa-dmf.aspx.

cross-check cash transaction reports and other types of financial dealings to ensure people are not listing the SSNs of dead people. Often, unintentional errors occur due to character transpositions. Additionally, intentional misrepresentations occur when people make up their own SSNs to avoid government reporting and filing requirements.

At first glance, this looks to be a promising pattern where someone was involved in a financial transaction using the *SSN* of a dead person. However, before we can definitively state that this is the case, there are a few additional items that must be checked. First, for this to be of any interest to an investigator, the date of the financial transaction must occur after the date of death. People do die, the databases are updated routinely, and eventually everyone in the database will reflect a match on the death master index, but the value of these records will long be past their term of usefulness and most likely purged from the system. As a side note, most of the investigations to identify new patterns and targets of interests tend to be on more current data sources, say, within the last two years. Investigators typically check only the older data sources (e.g., five or more years) once they have an initial suspect and are reviewing background and backup materials for their case—but rarely would older data be used to initiate a new case.

So, if the date of death is *after* the date of the transaction, the pattern is discounted and the investigator moves on to the next target. If the dates are not in the right sequence, then the next item to check is whether the name from the SSDM matches the name of the *Subject* in the transaction. Often when the SSN is improperly coded during the collection process, a single misrepresented digit can cause a false match. Therefore, it is important that the investigator checks the names for consistency to see if it is the same person. If the names don't match, then there is a good chance it was a collection issue—and most likely the SSN listed is not truly the one assigned to the *Subject*. This becomes a judgment call for the investigator, because in this example there is only one transaction on which to base the decision. If there were several transactions, each consistently listing the same SSN (the diagram would show a thicker link between the *Subject* and the *SSN*), then we would know it was an intentional misrepresentation and appropriate actions could be taken against the subject. If a match on the names is encountered, then our suspect is indeed dead and it reflects an interesting situation, most likely some type of identify theft. Regardless, it becomes an actionable pattern.

The other pattern displayed represents an *Organization* connected to an *SSN* that has a death master match. The question is: Does this pattern make sense? The short answer is "no," because in the United States, corporate entities have a Taxpayer Identification number[17] (TIN), also referred to as an Employer Identification number[18] (EIN), that is structured as a nine-digit number, which, as mentioned previously, is the same number of digits as an SSN. On many financial data collection forms[19] used by the government, it is often confusing and ambiguous whether a person or an organization is being represented. Thus, an EIN and an SSN are equivalent values within many financial datasets because there is no clear way to tell them apart. Unfortunately, the IRS did not require some type of encoding for corporate identifications (e.g., where they always start with a certain sequence) and, therefore, a company and an individual can technically have the same number, yet not be related in any way. As you can imagine, this complicates the analytics that are performed on such data sources because there is no sure way to know what value is truly being represented.

Therefore, the diagram where the *Organization* is connected to an *SSN* with a death master hit represents a situation that can't logically exist and so is considered invalid, and the investigator continues on to the next target of interest. There are circumstances where a *Subject* is connected to an *SSN* (with a death master match) that is also connected to an *Organization* because the *Subject* was DBA (doing business as) the *Organization*.

Is This a Reliable Pattern?

Look closely at the information presented in Figure 3.5 and determine if the contents present a reliable pattern. The first pattern to consider is the indirect relationship between the two *Subjects* through the *Phone* and the second pattern is through the *Address*.

Without having to look at any of the details presented in this diagram, if the names of the two *Subjects* are similar, then the pattern is considered reliable. But for this exercise, assume the names are completely different from one another, focusing instead on other clues from which to make an evaluation. The three transactions on the left side of the diagram all occurred in 2005 and the four on the right occurred in 2008, representing a three-year difference in the filings for these *Subjects*. From the information presented, can the pattern be deemed reliable?

Factoring real-world circumstances and realistic interpretations of the data, there are a number of dimensions that need to be considered. Often

---

[17] http://www.irs.gov/businesses/small/international/article/0,,id=96696,00.html.

[18] http://www.irs.gov/businesses/small/article/0,,id=98350,00.html.

[19] This reference is based on observations associated with the Bank Secrecy Act Data (BSA).

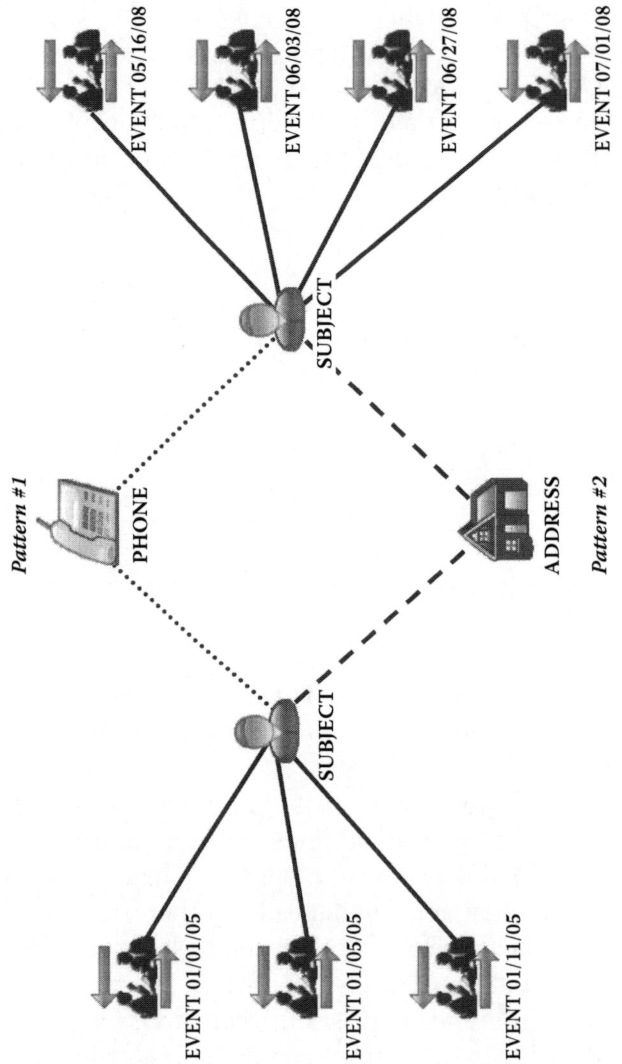

Figure 3.5 Pattern reliability.

phone numbers are recycled[20] and reused[21] within the telecommunications industry—normally in about 90 days once a number (e.g., an account) has been deactivated, but for some carriers it is as short as 30 days. Additionally, the investigator would want to know if this is a home or a work phone number because common numbers for large organizations would promptly discount the value of the pattern.[22] Given the situation presented, more than likely the two *Subjects* are not related because of the time gaps.

Now, interpret the diagram using only the *Address* as the basis for the connection. Is this a reliable pattern? All the same conditions hold true for the *Address* as for the *Phone* because people tend to move and apartments can be rerented to other people, so the same rationale for discounting the *Address* pattern is made as it was for the *Phone* pattern. Additionally, the investigator would want to double-check the *Address* to make sure it is not a generic location, such as a large apartment complex, a major office building, or some other public address. If it is, then the pattern would almost be guaranteed to be dismissed as too common.

Having gone through the individual pieces of this pattern and defining why they would not be very reliable, consider the pattern when both the *Address* and *Phone* are connected between the *Subjects*. Would this then be a reliable pattern? In almost all circumstances, yes, it would be—if the data represented valid values (e.g., not unknown (UNK)) and they did not represent the address and main phone number of a large business. It is important to review all aspects of a pattern and not merely interpret the results as valid or valuable. Analysis is a process that takes time, reasoning, and a lot of insight into the data being reviewed. Small variations in the data can yield vastly different outcomes, and good analysts understand these subtle differences.

Here is another real-world pattern that puts a slightly different spin on this type of pattern. The network shown in Figure 3.6 comes from two different *SARs* (suspicious activity reports) filed by completely independent financial institutions. The first *SAR* (shown at the top of the diagram) was filed in 2000 with a violation type of check kiting,[23] which is a way to cover funds between multiple accounts by using the float as the balance

---

[20] David Lazarus, Service providers recycling cell phone numbers is a dirty little secret. *San Francisco Chronicle*, February 3, 2006, http://www.sfgate.com/cgi-bin/article.cgi?file=/chronicle/archive/2006/02/03/BUGA7GTHKM91.DTL.

[21] Cosmin Turcu, Calling Paris, Wrong Number, *Softpedia*, July 9, 2007, http://news.softpedia.com/news/Calling-Paris-Wrong-Number-59331.shtml.

[22] The main phone number associated with a large corporation, such as AOL (703) 265-1000, would not constitute a direct or even implied relationship among its employees as it might in a smaller business (e.g., under 200 people).

[23] http://en.wikipedia.org/wiki/Check_kiting.

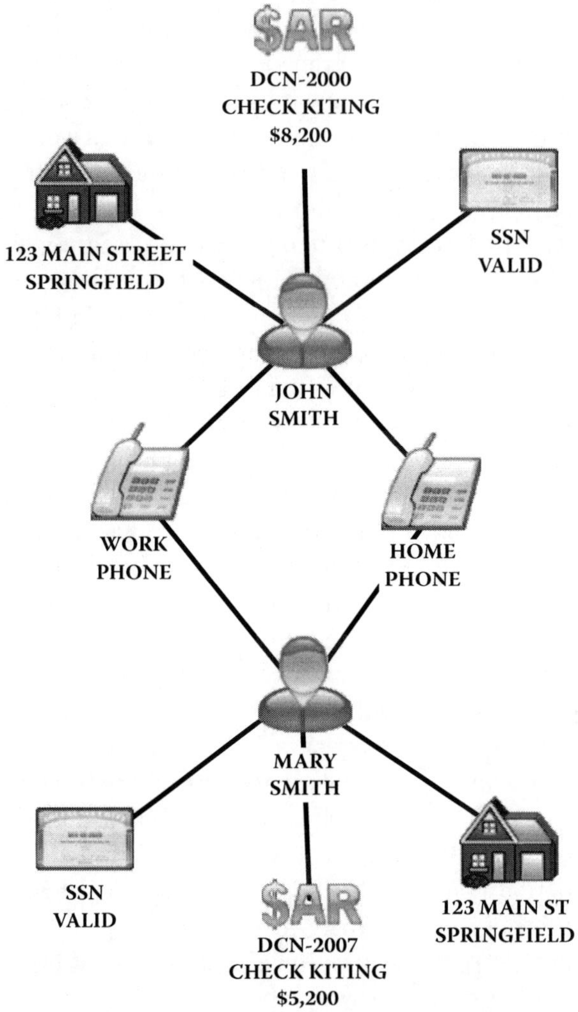

Figure 3.6 Repeated behavior—check kiting.

for uncollected checks.[24] This *Subject* owns/operates a gas station. All of the other information related to this *Subject* checks out properly against public sources and online references—so the investigator knows the *Address, Phone,* and *SSN* are all valid.

The *SAR* at the bottom of the diagram was filed in 2007 by a different bank—almost seven years to the day after the first *SAR*—and it was also for check kiting. The major difference is that it was filed on the spouse

[24] Laura Bruce, Anatomy of check-kiting fraud. *Bankrate.com*, December 3, 2002, http://www.bankrate.com/brm/news/chk/20021203b.asp.

(wife) of the person referenced in the first *SAR*, thereby providing the investigator with some consistency based on their last names. The network commonality in this diagram is founded on the work and home *Phone* numbers and if you look closely at the *Address* detail, the two are identical except for the abbreviation of "Street" to "St." There are mechanisms that can be applied to correct these types of inconsistencies in the data to help make the diagrams and networks more reliable for interpretation.

The net–net value of this diagram shows that even though a fairly long period of time has lapsed between the *SAR* events, the emerging big picture tells us the operators of this gas station are involved with illegal (rather, undesirable) banking practices and the financial community needs to impose very strict oversight and limitations on their business accounts. Certainly, with prior knowledge of such activities, any new financial institutions where this business might apply for credit or banking services would apply more diligence and oversight on the business to ensure there was no unethical or illegal behaviors or activities.

Is This an Actionable Pattern?

Continuing to build on interpreting the structures, commonalities, frequencies, and values encountered in the data, this next pattern provides a more complex network with several additional dimensions to review. Specifically, this pattern reveals more details about the objects themselves via their assigned labels. While the data presented has been sanitized and does not in any way reflect the original source data, the structural integrity is kept the same. The first objective when reviewing the diagram presented in Figure 3.7 is to determine if the data represents an important pattern.

Immediately, the investigator sees that there is a common or shared *SSN* between the two *Subjects*. In financial data, an SSN can be shared by a husband and wife in certain transactions. A quick check shows that they are different people based on their names and dates of birth, so the investigator considers these people unrelated. At this point the other details of this network come into play, mainly that there are no other objects in common—no addresses, no ID numbers, and no phones. The premise is that a common phone number or a shared driver's license, in conjunction with the SSN, would guarantee a strong connection between the two *Subjects*. Yet there is no additional overlap observed in this network.

Addresses are perhaps the most widely varying data encountered in any system. There are many abbreviations, spellings, and formats used to encode an address. It is not unusual to see three, four, or five variations of the same address—often differentiated only by extra periods, commas,

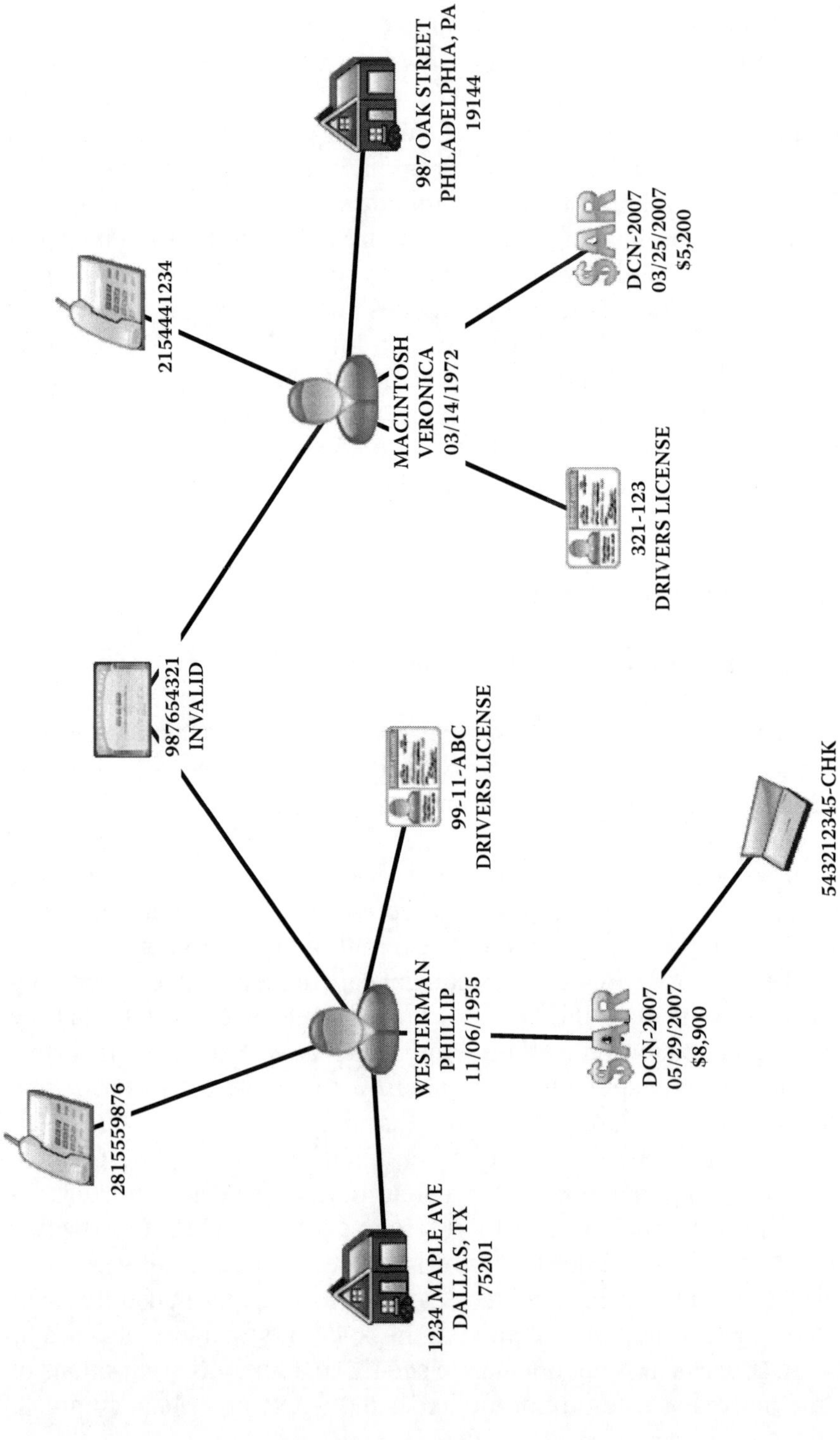

Figure 3.7 Pattern misinterpretation.

or directional encoding (e.g., NW, N., or North). The investigator quickly realizes that the two *Addresses* shown in the diagram are not even close to one another. If they were in the same city or state, there would be more of a chance the *Subjects* were related. In this case these two *Addresses* are more than 1,300 miles apart, which dramatically diminishes the likelihood that they are related.

As shown in the diagram, each *Subject* has only a single *SAR* transaction. This tells the investigators that the *Subjects* are not actively engaged in multiple transactions and, therefore, the common *SSN* is most likely a data entry problem, which can be further justified because the "INVALID" label shown under the *SSN* indicates it failed a Social Security validation check. In short, the entire network can be discounted. This network would warrant further investigation if the *Subjects* each had more than one transaction because it would be highly unlikely that the same transposition for the *SSNs* would occur for every transaction. If that were the case, the investigators would aggressively pursue these targets.

Which Pattern Is More Valuable?

In many agencies and organizations there are often multiple patterns of interest that can be pursued at any given time, and the investigators must prioritize their time and resources to follow up on those that will provide the greatest return on the investment. Sometimes the more valuable pattern is based on the total amount of money lost to a fraud or scheme, and at other times the more valuable pattern is based on how quickly an indictment or charges can be brought against the perpetrators. Ideally, all patterns should be pursued, but budgets are limited so it becomes a judgment call for the investigators.

The first network in Figure 3.8 shows a complex structure based on the total number of objects and how they are related. For this example, assume the *Subjects'* names are completely different from each other and their addresses are located in different cities. Similar to patterns shown in the previous examples, there is a common *SSN* shared by all three *Subjects*. The main difference is that there are multiple *Transactions* (e.g., SARs) defined for two of the *Subjects,* which changes the interpretation of this pattern.

The upper-left *Subject* was involved in two *Transactions* with a single *SSN*. In this case, both transactions used the same *SSN* and the two *Addresses* are also the same with just a slight variation (Ave/Avenue). The upper-right *Subject* has five *Transactions* all using the same *SSN*. Additionally, there is an *ID Number* that is shared with the *Subject* at the bottom, along with the same *SSN*.

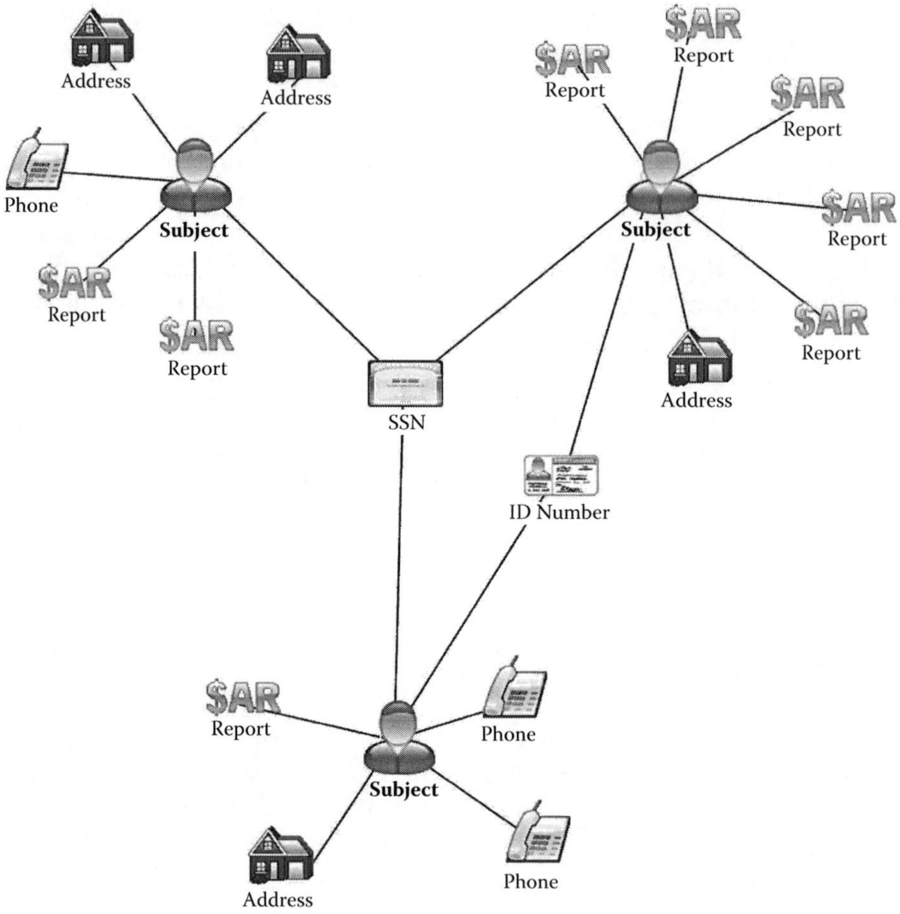

Figure 3.8 Interpreting the value of network #1.

Although the *Subject* at the bottom of the network has only a single *Transaction,* he is strongly tied into the network because he shares both an *SSN* and an *ID Number* with the other *Subject.* If there had been only one connection, it might be attributed to a data quality problem. The additional connection indicates that this is not a coincidence or the result of a data error. This network clearly shows the intentional use of the same *SSN* by different *Subjects*. Furthermore, the *Addresses* listed for these *Subjects* are in different cities, strongly indicating that they are operating as an organized group. If we tally up the actual dollar amount of the *Transactions* involved in this network (assuming each is valued at \$10,000), they are worth about \$80,000. Considering the locations of the *Subjects,* pursuing this lead will require the cooperation of multiple jurisdictions to prosecute.

The second network shown in Figure 3.9 presents a more centralized arrangement of connections because all the activity is tied to a single

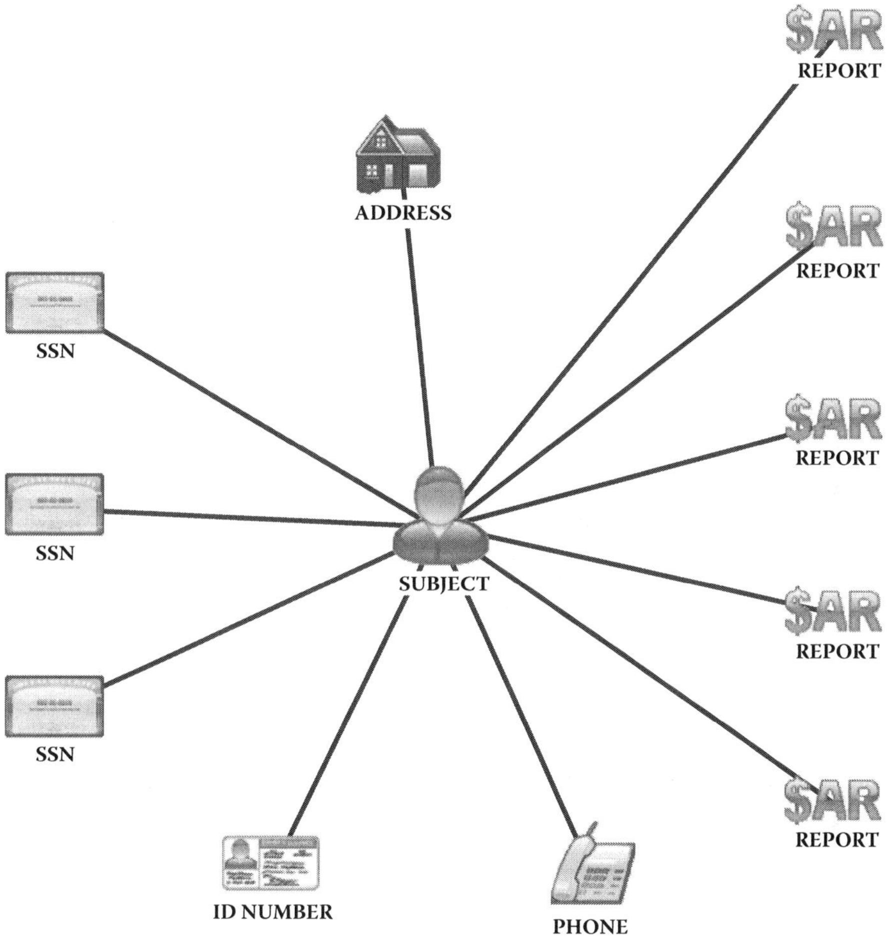

Figure 3.9 Interpreting the value of network #2.

Subject. The most noteworthy feature of this network is that there are multiple (three) *SSNs* used by this one *Subject*. As we have learned, the variations in the *SSNs* could be innocent data entry errors or they could be intentional misrepresentations. The most unusual factor in the diagram is that there is only one *Address, Phone,* and *ID Number*. The investigator finds this inconsistent with the number of *SSNs* shown, reviews the *SSNs* to find that the variations are not simple transpositions, and, therefore, determines the *Subject* is trying to avoid detection by altering his *SSN*.

When using object representations for network diagramming, the uniqueness of, say, a *Subject* is limited to the combinations of first, last, and middle names. Therefore, common names (e.g., Mary Smith, Jose Gonzalez, Tran Nguyen, and Mohammed Fayyad) may produce a composite representation of more than one *Subject*. In these cases, it is common to see multiple *SSNs*; however, there will also be multiple *Addresses,* or *Phones,* and/or *ID Numbers*.

Even though the value of this network is only $50,000 (based on the five *Transactions* worth $10,000 each), it is more attractive for prosecution purposes because it involves only a single *Subject* that is operating out of a specific *Address* and the level of resources required to pursue this case can be minimized.

What Does this Pattern Show?

In this next example, we change the domain to a vehicle sales database, and discover that there are some larger commonalities among the objects than are to be expected. Think about the last time you went to a car dealership and purchased a new or used vehicle. There may have been some haggling on the price and desired options, but more than likely there was a lot of standard paperwork to fill out including the vehicle registration, warranty information, and finance applications. Depending on the efficiency and automation of the dealership, this can simply be a matter of signing a number of forms. However, the data collected not only completes the sale, but also serves as a marketing tool for scheduling maintenance, providing service reminders, issuing recall/safety notices, and cross-selling different dealership products.

In Figure 3.10, a network was discovered interconnecting a large number of *Customers* (see, not all examples are based on trying to find a "bad person") that share a common *Phone*[25] number. This pattern was discussed previously in the context of money-laundering activities, but the interpretation for this domain is somewhat different. Also, for readability, a number of the *Customers* were removed so the network detail would be more explicit.

There are several important dimensions to point out in this network to help interpret its meaning. First, each of the *Customers* appears to be connected to at least two phone numbers and common sense dictates that the *Phones* are either a work or a home phone number. The number at the center of the network is most likely a work phone number because it is shared by all the subjects and the other phones are more of a one-to-one connection to specific customers with the exception of the phone number at the top of the network, indicating that these people are perhaps related or possibly roommates.

[25] The phone numbers represented in this diagram were "randomly" generated to cleanse the original data and protect the identity of the original customer. The relationships of the phone numbers are structurally accurate, and as such, their connections to the customers have been left intact.

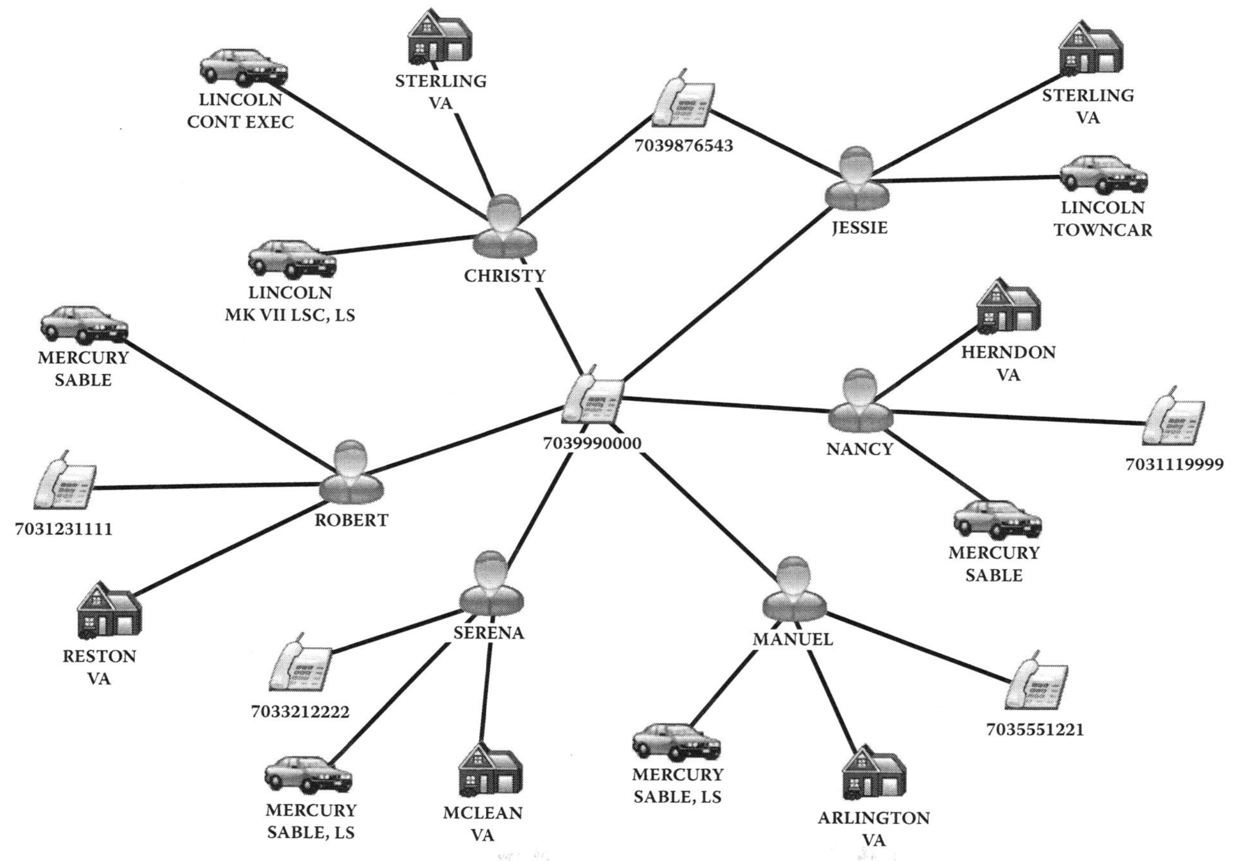

Figure 3.10 Phone-centric network of customers.

Clarification of the role of the phone can be determined from how the linkages were encoded when modeled from the original data schema. Remember, *a phone is a phone is a phone* (see sidebar) regardless of whether it is a home, work, cell, fax, or other type of commission. The "role" of the phone is defined in how it is used and how it relates to the other entities being represented. Thus, a home phone can double as a fax and can also be used for work purposes; therefore, the phone number does not change, only the role or its usage for the different activities. The same holds true for cell phones and voice over Internet protocol (VoIP) configurations.

Generic Data Types

In the play *Romeo and Juliet,* written by William Shakespeare (circa 1594), Juliet states "What's in a name? That which we call a rose by any other name would smell as sweet." Essentially, how we refer to objects is somewhat irrelevant because they will exhibit their basic and underlying characteristics regardless of what we call them. Perhaps even more apropos is the phrase: "A rose is a rose is a rose," which comes from Gertrude Stein's poem "Sacred Emily" (circa 1913). When representing data, one must think about defining the "type" of an object in terms of how it will be used during the analytics. Fundamentally, the role of an object, as defined within a system, should not be its type but rather its "real-world" interpretation. If there is a potential that more than one of the same object types defined within an analytical model could represent the same entity, then they all should be cast as the same type.

For example, when defining the calling parties associated with a phone call, it is generally more appropriate to represent both sides as a phone rather than a caller (calling phone = 123) or a callee (called phone = 456). Consider the case when a caller for one phone call (123 → 456) is then the callee in a subsequent phone call (456 → 123). From an analytical perspective, when searching for a specific phone number, the end user does not typically want to create multiple queries to find all callers = 123 in addition to all callees = 123. Ideally, the number(s) would be represented as phones and their roles within a phone call transaction recorded as caller (phone = 123) and callee (phone = 456), respectively.

The same concepts hold true for a number of scenarios, including, for example, husband (Bob) and wife (Mary). Both represent people in the real world, and their roles, with respect to one another, are husband and wife. The husband can also be a son, brother, father, employee, volunteer, or even a perpetrator or victim in a criminal event. The intent here is not to create a different representation (e.g., instance) of the same entity, but rather to be smart about how to fulfill the analytical requirements. Thus, Bob = Person and Mary = Person and the role they have in the relationship is as husband/wife. Figure 3.11 shows some additional roles/types that should be considered generic when modeling data, including, for example, vehicles (rented, owned, or leased cars) and addresses (home, work, remote, HQ, staging, or demonstration).

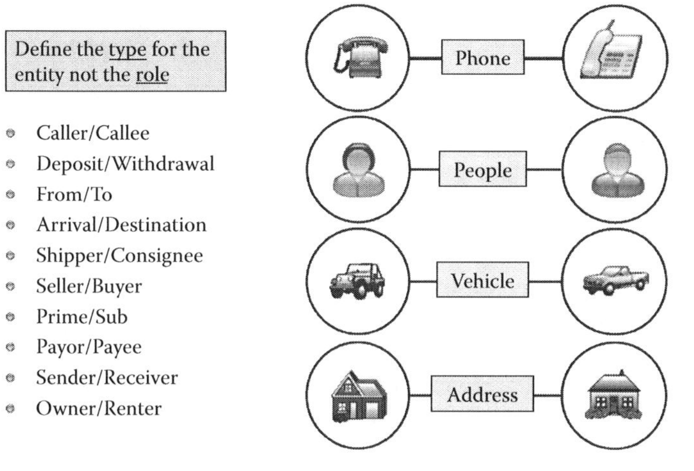

Figure 3.11 Defining consistent data types.

Second, the *Addresses* associated with each of the *Customers* are located within a fairly well-defined region in the Washington, D.C. metropolitan area. These *Addresses* are also within about 30 miles of the location of the car dealership. Third, the types of cars sold to this community are consistent (e.g., Lincoln and Mercury brands) for this category of customers.

Instead of discounting this pattern for being too general due to the common work number, the dealership owner can utilize this situation for offering a better product/service. Most dealerships provide loaner cars, which are an expensive overhead cost and take up valuable time for paperwork processing on behalf of the customer. Additionally, many dealerships in the Washington metropolitan region offer scheduled shuttle service to the closest Metro station. The business associated with this phone number is, unfortunately, not located near a Metro facility, but is located about 15 minutes away from the dealership. Thus, due to the large volume of customers employed at this location, the dealership not only can offer a door-to-door shuttle directly to their place of employment and but also can send out special discounts for servicing their vehicles to take advantage of this shuttle offer. So what would be a "short circuit" in one domain proves to be a valuable pattern in a different domain.

In continuing with the dealership scenario, there is another commonality pattern that is based on the *Customer* and his/her *Address*. When reviewing the network structures for this dealership, it was discovered that certain "home" addresses appeared frequently in the database. Immediately, this raised a red flag because the home address of the customer should be somewhat unique and should not be linked to hundreds of different customers. Figure 3.12 shows a high-level view of the top three networks.

The objects at the center of each network represent a single *Address* and the objects spanning the circumference of the circle are the *Customers*. A quick review showed the addresses in question were the post office boxes associated with two of the primary finance companies used by the dealership. The *Addresses* represented in Network #2 and Network #3 in Figure 3.12 actually reference the same location, except one used PO Box (without periods) and the other used P.O. Box (with periods). Somehow the addresses of the customers (142 + 340 = 482) were entered as that of the finance company. This shows a fundamental flaw in the collection process either through a faulty computer program (unlikely) or because of a poorly trained sales department. Luckily, this situation was detected and could be easily fixed. Unfortunately, there were thousands of records that had to be manually reentered to ensure the accuracy of the database. Furthermore, before this pattern was found the dealership mailed out sales and maintenance flyers that often were not delivered to the intended party and cost the dealership in production and delivery costs in addition to the lost sales. Thus, finding this pattern was an immediate return on investment (ROI) for the dealership.

Other patterns that were found in this dealership's data included several of the same invoice number being used to represent different car sales (based on vehicle identification numbers [VINs]; also see sidebar), exposing a flaw in their sales tracking system/process. As shown in Figure 3.13, there are seven sales transactions with the same invoice number (16350)

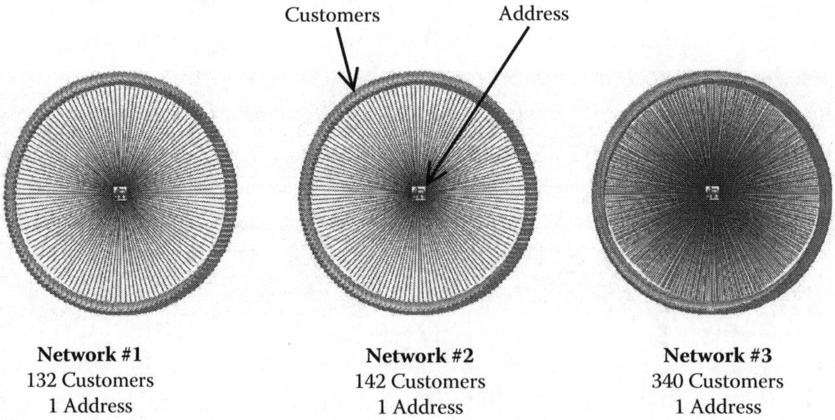

Figure 3.12 Top three address-centric networks.

Figure 3.13 Duplicate sales invoice numbers.

and dates that occur over a two-day period. The same salesperson (not shown) appeared on at least three of these invoices and each was for a unique VIN. There were dozens of instances of this type of pattern in the database.

Another example from this dataset showed numerous patterns where a VIN was utilized by multiple *Customers.* As is shown in Figure 3.14, a single *Vehicle,* defined by the VIN, was involved in three different sale *Transactions,* which all occurred on the same day and involved three completely independent *Customers* (shown along with their *Addresses* and *Phone* numbers). Logically this situation does not make sense because the people are not related in any way, removing the possibility that perhaps someone co-signed for another or they all jointly purchased the vehicle together. Certainly the car was not sold to three separate people on the same day. One observation for all instances of this pattern is that the salesperson (name not shown) responsible for the transactions is the same. Therefore, it must be concluded that there is a flaw in their sales-processing database and perhaps test drives were mistakenly entered as bona fide sales.

Certainly, exposing this type of pattern helped the dealership improve their processes and procedures, which in turn reduced costs due to improper forecasts and erroneous reporting of inventory. The ability to view the data from different aspects helped expose patterns that affect the day-to-day operations of the dealership and ultimately provided a means to improve business processes.

VIN Validation

Since 1981, all vehicle identification numbers (VINs) have been standardized to 17 characters that encode specific details about the vehicle. Knowing this information can help verify the legitimacy of the vehicle, especially for insurance-related applications or law enforcement checkpoints at border crossings. Each character represents a unique aspect about the vehicle, as shown in Table 3.3.

Another way to look at this layout in a more refined grouping is shown in Table 3.4.

Table 3.3 VIN Structure (Vertical)

Character Location	*Reference*
1	Country
2	Manufacturer
3	Make
4–6	Engine
7	Body/Transmission
8	Trim Level/Restraint
9	Check Digit
10	Model Year
11	Assembly Plant
12–17	Serial Number

Table 3.4 VIN Structure (Horizontal)

1	2	3	4	5	6	7	8	9	10	11	12	13	14	15	16	17
WMI			Model					*	Y	P	Serial Number					

WMI = World Manufacturing Identification
* = Check Digit
Y = Year Manufactured
P = Plant Code

The Check Digit (position #9) is based on a mathematical calculation. Generally, each character in the VIN is assigned a number, which in turn is multiplied by a position-weight factor as defined in a standardized lookup table. The products are then added together and the total divided by 11. The remainder becomes the check digit (the value 10 = X). Without the proper knowledge of each VIN value or how the check digit is calculated, it is difficult to just make up a fake VIN.

Although a full discussion of VIN decomposition is outside the scope of this book, there are a number of programs[26] and Web sites[27] that are useful for looking up the actual values for each of these fields, and some

[26] http://www.autobaza.pl/ab/en/web/productaa0100.
[27] http://en.wikipedia.org/wiki/Vehicle_identification_number.

further define the raw calculations involved in computing the Check Digit. So, for instance, a VIN such as ZHWBU26S95LA01701 represents a 2005 LAMBORGHINI MURCIELAGO with a ROADSTER body style having a 6.2L V12 DOHC 48V engine that was manufactured in ITALY.

Who Is the Most Important Person?

There has recently been a lot of emphasis placed on social networking analysis (SNA) in a number of intelligence areas, including communications, such as lawful intercept, politically exposed persons, and corporate governances. SNA approaches seek ways to better classify critical objects within a network, and the concepts of centrality, closeness, and betweenness have been used extensively to help organizations better understand their underlying interpersonal operating behaviors.

Centrality is designed to expose those entities that are most interrelated and potentially exhibit a high degree of control within a network. The centrality of an object defines how many connections it has with other objects, where more connections indicate more centrality. Very centralized networks tend to be dominated by a few entities and, therefore, are subject to failure should these "central" nodes be terminated or removed. Less central networks tend to be more resilient. Depending on the application, knowing this fact can prove very useful when disrupting the operations of a network.

Closeness calculates how "close" objects are with respect to the overall coverage or distance within the network. Objects that are "closest" have the fewest direct and/or indirect relationships to all other objects within the network. They can reach another object in the shortest number of steps, hops, or linkages. Detecting the closest object in a network can provide an ideal vantage for monitoring the operations of a network or spreading information throughout the network.

Betweenness represents a way to identify objects that support the largest number of pathways within a network. There can be any number of pathways (e.g., multiple routes) between objects in a network and the most "between" object ties together the largest number of possible routes. The object with the largest number of connections does not necessarily represent the object with the best betweenness factor. These types of objects can exhibit a great deal of influence within a network.

There are many additional aspects to SNA theory[28] regarding the types of calculations, statistics, and dimensions that can be calculated from a network. However, when trying to best understand the structure

[28] An in-depth discussion of SNA theory is outside the scope of this book.

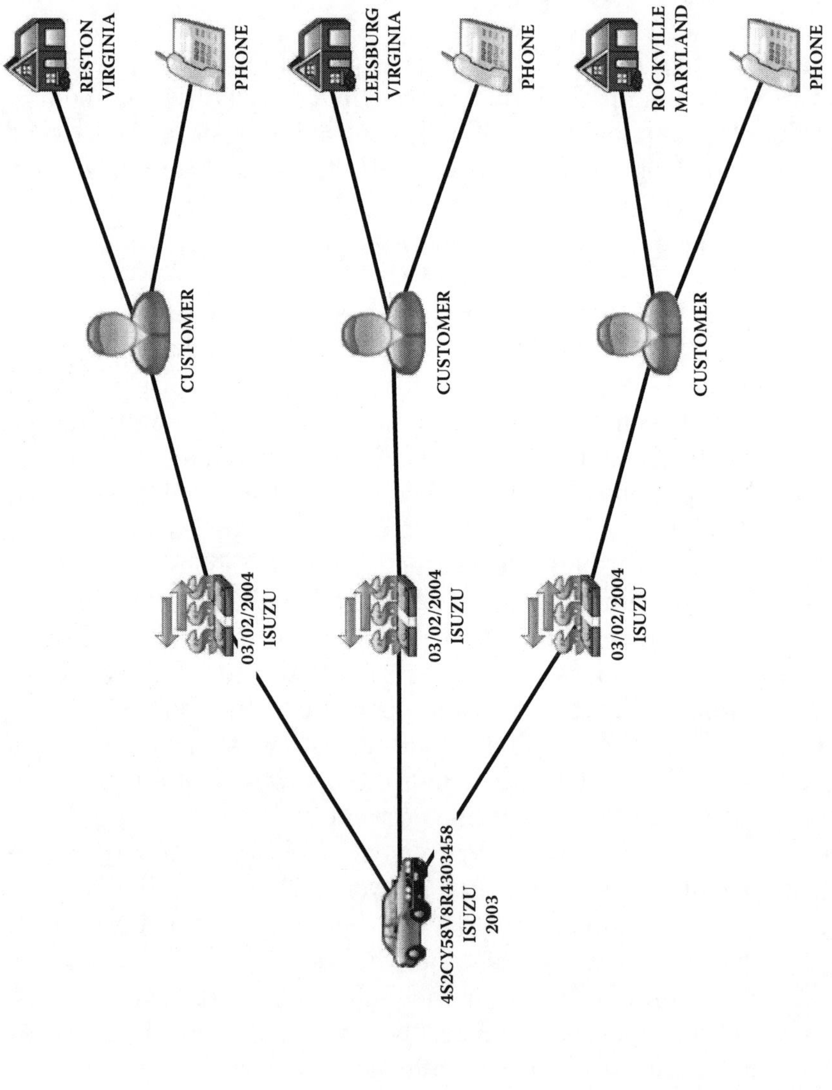

Figure 3.14 Multiple sales transactions for the same vehicle.

of a network utilizing real-world data sources, the SNA process certainly provides great utility for helping to expose important network factors, but good old common sense is also a big part of properly interpreting the network. Therefore, given the network presented in Figure 3.15, consider which person represents the most important person in the network.

There are actually a number of good candidates to nominate from this network. Remember that there are no right answers or wrong answers; it depends on the context and the interpretation of the data. Many people immediately think Boris is the most important person in the network because he clearly is responsible for bridging two subnetworks (acting as an articulation point or a gatekeeper) and, if removed, the entire network would no longer be connected. Depending on Boris's role in the organization, he might be the top-level commander or could be just an intermediate grunt conveying orders among parts of the group.

Alternatively, Nokolai or Igor could be considered the most important people in the network because they connect (e.g., influence) the most number of other people. Removing either of these people from the network would have a strong negative effect on the overall viability of the network (i.e., it would completely fall apart). People such as Nokolai and Igor can react quickly to personnel changes and new information, or pass on orders because they are, respectively, the closest to all the other people in the network.

Finally, an unlikely member of the group, Petrik, could be considered the most important even though he is on the perimeter of the network. Although not explicitly shown, the roles of these members (e.g., leader or follower) need to be taken into account when the network is being analyzed. The directionality of the connections also needs to be factored into these analytics. These have a big influence on how "important" the objects are considered. One minor difference with Petrik is the thicker link shown between him and Nokolai. This could indicate that Petrik is passing on orders (as the boss) to direct Nokolai (a lieutenant) to carry out certain actions.

Based on SNA calculations[29] performed on this network, Nokolai is the most "between," followed by Igor then Boris, and the same holds true for the degree of "connected." Nokolai and either Boris or Igor are respectively the most "close" in terms of network connections. Thus, the interpretations of the network are subjective to the domain and the context in which the analysis is being performed.

[29] These values were derived using the SNA procedures offered in the VisuaLinks software product.

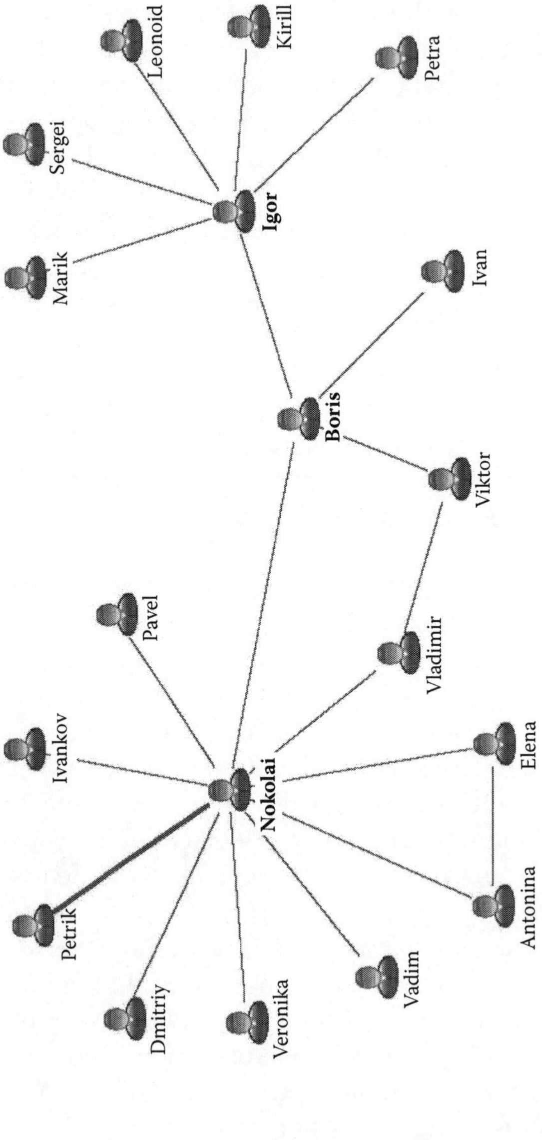

Figure 3.15 Interpreting social network patterns.

Conclusion

A number of different networks were presented throughout this section and each had a specific interpretation based on the domain and/or circumstances under which it was being evaluated. Generally, the structure of the networks was fairly simple, yet conveyed a large amount of detail, some explicitly and some implied. Subtle clues in the network representations, such as labels, values, proximities, frequencies, and commonalities, were used to summarize and convey the most logical explanation for their existence. As was reiterated many times, there are no right or wrong answers, only interpretations and subjective opinions.

In addition to exposing patterns and trends using network diagrams, the presentations often help expose issues and problems in the quality of the underlying data collection systems and acquisition interfaces. Inevitably, core business processes will need to be updated, upgraded, and adjusted to respond to these circumstances. New interfaces and value checks will be implemented to minimize collection mistakes, reduce data entry errors, and improve the overall quality of the data. Furthermore, the patterns themselves need to be vetted, and all relevant, repeatable, and actionable patterns need to be addressed and new procedures put in place to deal with the findings. Thus, patterns related to fraud would require existing business processes to be adjusted to minimize their occurrences and reduce losses resulting from these schemes (e.g., add new data checks to validate the SSN), where as patterns exposing new market segments or identifying customers likely to purchase new products would be maximized. It is all a matter of perspective.

PART 2

AMPLES
S

wonderful people, perhaps
gagement is learning about
all operations of a program,
ering the unknown. To see
ad stimulating, while at the
ng and make one somewhat
e bad guy" scenarios where
interest and uncovering the
vident, where, for example:

ation or industry can cost
ased premiums or taxes,

cumvent bank reporting
s of crime, thereby under-
rketplace.
across a border without
y, well-being, and futures

nforcement agencies and
n people's property and

uld kill large numbers of
e intelligence community.

There is also a personal challenge associated with performing these types of analyses, especially when it comes to detecting criminals trying to outsmart "the system" by taking advantage of the loopholes, flaws, or vulnerabilities inherent in any process. A small percentage of dishonest people adversely affect the millions of people who lead decent and honest lifestyles. For some, they have been lucky, avoided detection, and gotten away with their scams, frauds, and embezzlements for personal gain. Everyone has a rationale and justification for their actions and many feel they are entitled to the money or benefits they steal.

At the end of each day, someone's life changes—for better or worse—depending on the outcomes of the analyses performed by reviewing the data sources. Ultimately, the goal is to improve detection capabilities by providing better, faster, and more effective analytics against the data and enabling the investigators to be more timely and efficient with their limited resources. Small improvements in detection can result in significant levels of returns.

This section overviews a number of different industries and the solutions that have been implemented to help deal with some of these problem areas. Specifically, there are descriptions of fraud patterns, narcotics trafficking and interdiction, border crossings, and money-laundering operations. Each scenario provides some fundamental background regarding the nature of the operations, the issues (e.g., frauds, smuggling, laundering), and the approaches contrived to deal with the problems at hand.

Although the analytical approaches presented in this section may appear somewhat disjointed and unrelated, they all follow the same logic, processes, and protocols as were discussed in Part 1. Try to generalize the problem space when reading through this section and you will quickly learn that there are a lot of similarities among the different industries presented. In fact, many of the same patterns exist within all of these domains. The trick is in recognizing the commonality and generalizing the results so that they can be applied globally. Therefore, even though the underlying technology is based on graph theory and network visualization, the true value is in knowing the proper analytical methodologies to employ when working on a new data source.

Chapter 4

Border Protection

Introduction

In our global economy, with affordable air transportation along with convenient routes and schedules across the world, many more people are traveling internationally these days. Some people travel for pleasure or vacation while others travel solely for business reasons. According to the data posted on the Transportation Department's Bureau of Transportation Statistics,[1] there were more than 650 million domestic passengers and over 150 million international passengers flying in and out of U.S. airports in 2005. There are also hundreds of millions of border-crossing events between the United States and Canada[2,3] and Mexico.[4] Many people entering the United States are not citizens and, therefore, are required to file an Arrival/Departure Record (I-94 Form) to document their admission into the country, as is also required by other nations (where it is often called a Landing Card).

I-94 Arrival/Departure Records

The I-94 form,[5] shown in Figure 4.1 (front and back), has two parts—one for the arrival, which is collected at the immigration desk upon entering the country, and one for the departure, which must remain with the passport until the person leaves the country, at which point it must be surrendered back to an authorized official. Not returning the second part of the I-94 form can cause problems with being readmitted to the country.

The information collected on an I-94 form is fairly standard and includes the most common types of data including names, dates, and addresses; it is actually recorded manually on paper by the individual entering the country—usually during the last part of the flight—before landing.[6] Thus, there are a number of vulnerable points in the collection process. The data can be misinterpreted by the passenger due to language conflicts, intentionally made inaccurate, or transposed by the data entry operators when converted into the Treasury Enforcement Communication System (TECS), a mainframe computer database operated by the Department of Homeland Security's (DHS) U.S. Customs

[1] http://www.bts.gov/.

[2] http://canada.usembassy.gov/content/can_usa/didyouknow.pdf.

[3] http://www.bts.gov/programs/ international/border_crossing_entry_data/us_canada/.

[4] http://www.bts.gov/programs/international/border_crossing_entry_data/us_mexico/.

[5] http://www.cbp.gov/xp/cgov/travel/id_visa/i-94_instructions/arrival_departure_record.xml.

[6] Some countries now require this information to be entered online when purchasing tickets.

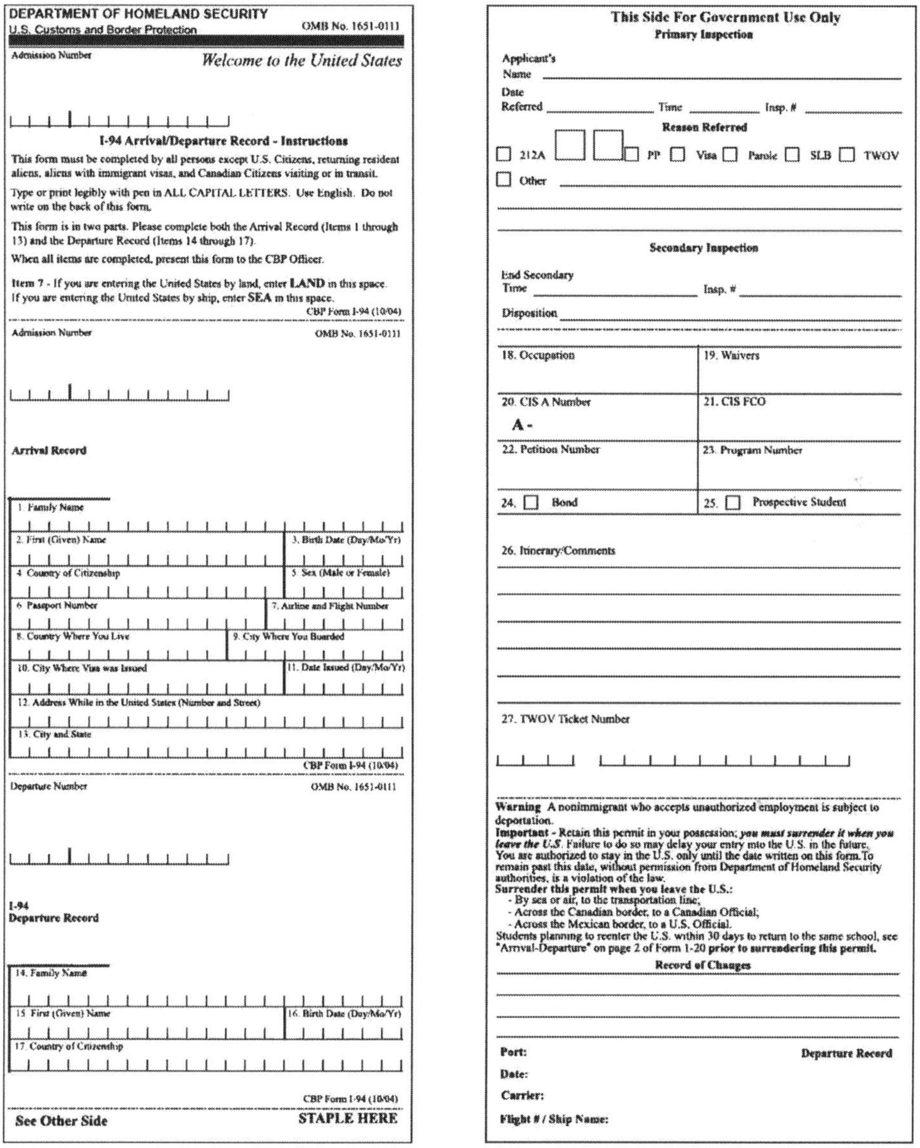

DEPARTMENT OF HOMELAND SECURITY
U.S. Customs and Border Protection OMB No. 1651-0111

Admission Number

Welcome to the United States

I-94 Arrival/Departure Record - Instructions

This form must be completed by all persons except U.S. Citizens, returning resident aliens, aliens with immigrant visas, and Canadian Citizens visiting or in transit.

Type or print legibly with pen in ALL CAPITAL LETTERS. Use English. Do not write on the back of this form.

This form is in two parts. Please complete both the Arrival Record (Items 1 through 13) and the Departure Record (Items 14 through 17).

When all items are completed, present this form to the CBP Officer.

Item 7 - If you are entering the United States by land, enter LAND in this space. If you are entering the United States by ship, enter SEA in this space.

CBP Form I-94 (10/04)

Admission Number OMB No. 1651-0111

Arrival Record

1. Family Name
2. First (Given) Name
3. Birth Date (Day/Mo/Yr)
4. Country of Citizenship
5. Sex (Male or Female)
6. Passport Number
7. Airline and Flight Number
8. Country Where You Live
9. City Where You Boarded
10. City Where Visa was Issued
11. Date Issued (Day/Mo/Yr)
12. Address While in the United States (Number and Street)
13. City and State

CBP Form I-94 (10/04)

Departure Number OMB No. 1651-0111

I-94
Departure Record

14. Family Name
15. First (Given) Name
16. Birth Date (Day/Mo/Yr)
17. Country of Citizenship

CBP Form I-94 (10/04)

See Other Side STAPLE HERE

This Side For Government Use Only
Primary Inspection

Applicant's Name
Date Referred Time Insp. #

Reason Referred

212A PP Visa Parole SLB TWOV
Other

Secondary Inspection

End Secondary Time Insp. #
Disposition

18. Occupation
19. Waivers
20. CIS A Number A -
21. CIS FCO
22. Petition Number
23. Program Number
24. Bond
25. Prospective Student
26. Itinerary/Comments
27. TWOV Ticket Number

Warning A nonimmigrant who accepts unauthorized employment is subject to deportation.
Important - Retain this permit in your possession; *you must surrender it when you leave the U.S.* Failure to do so may delay your entry into the U.S. in the future.
You are authorized to stay in the U.S. only until the date written on this form. To remain past this date, without permission from Department of Homeland Security authorities, is a violation of the law.
Surrender this permit when you leave the U.S.:
- By sea or air, to the transportation line;
- Across the Canadian border, to a Canadian Official;
- Across the Mexican border, to a U.S. Official.
Students planning to reenter the U.S. within 30 days to return to the same school, see "Arrival-Departure" on page 2 of Form I-20 prior to surrendering this permit.

Record of Changes

Port: Departure Record
Date:
Carrier:
Flight # / Ship Name:

Figure 4.1 I-94 arrival/departure form.

and Border Protection (CBP) containing mostly border-oriented and immigration-focused repositories. The data fields captured off the I-94 forms specifically include the following:

- Family Name
- First Name
- Date of Birth

- Country of Citizenship
- Sex (Male or Female)
- Passport Number
- Airline and Flight Number
- Country Where You Live
- City Where You Boarded
- City Where Visa was Issued
- Date Issued (Day/Mo/Yr)
- Address in the United States (Number and Street)
- City and State

Other fields are also captured in TECS for I-94 data, including the date/time, port of entry, inspector references, and other administrative data. All of this is collectively stored and made available in a relational format from which to perform analysis. In 2005, more than 175 million nonimmigrant admissions[7] (e.g., foreign nationals) entered the United States and over 32 million of them were required to file an I-94 form (an increase of 4 percent from 2004).

In an analysis of some I-94 data (containing about 85 million border-crossing events), an analytical model was created that reflected the general nature of the data on the form (as is shown in Figure 4.2) as a subject-centric model. The key values (e.g., what uniquely identifies a target object) for the *Subject* rely on a combination of their first, last, and middle names and their dates of birth (DOBs)—keeping in mind that there could potentially be *Subjects* who share the same information. Every record, by definition, reflects a different I-94 filing (e.g., *Event*) and one would expect to see an individual with multiple filings associated with different airline carriers and flight numbers.

There are quite a number of pattern types that can be exposed from I-94 data. One of the most prevalent patterns is *the usage of multiple passports by a single individual.* Using some basic data decomposition, grouping, and counting, it was quickly discovered that there were thousands of instances of this pattern present in the database. Not surprisingly, the top 10 results were due to "bad" data where improper names were entered. Luckily, these were easy to spot and remove from consideration before any additional investigative resources were committed to the review and follow-up of their actions.

[7] Elizabeth M. Grieco. Temporary Admissions of Nonimmigrants to the United States: 2005 Annual Flow Report, Department of Homeland Security, July 2006. Report available at: http://www.dhs.gov/xlibrary/assets/statistics/publications/2005_NI_rpt,pdf.

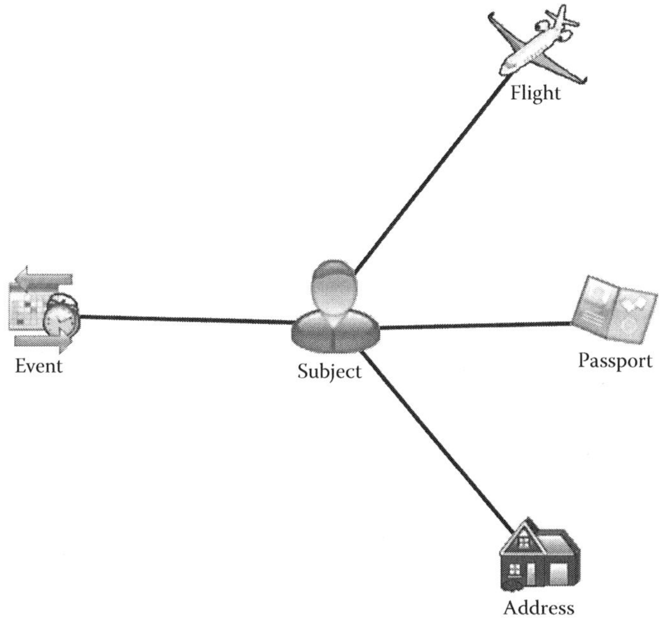

Figure 4.2 I-94 analytical model representation.

The 11th highest-ranking value turned out to be an individual with 54 different passport numbers used in more than 240 flights made from/to a foreign country[8] over the course of a single year. This volume of travel is somewhat high, even for a person in his line of business as an international courier. However, the number of misrepresentations made in recording his passport number, whether accidental or intentional, occurred so frequently that it could not be overlooked. Most of the variations, almost identical to those we see with miscoding Social Security numbers (SSNs), came from the data entry process where the numbers 2 and 5, 4 and 9, and 1 and 7 can be easily mistaken or transposed, especially with someone who has bad penmanship—particularly since the forms are usually filled out on the plane, generally during final descent. The good news in this selected case was that the poor quality of the data actually worked in favor of the investigators for exposing the subject's actions.[9]

Initially, it was suspected there may be more than one person with the same name and DOB—considering the number of different passport

[8] This individual was a Mexican national and he routinely flew in/out of Mexico City and in/out of Los Angeles.

[9] Sometimes patterns are exposed through the intentional misrepresentation of the data and for these types of environments, the analytics should also be conducted before any type of data cleanup is performed.

numbers. Viewing the results as a network diagram was not very helpful in this scenario because it generated a "death star" type of display (e.g., a single entity in the middle surrounded by a larger number of indistinguishable objects) due to the 240 directly connected travel events (i.e., the flights). However, presenting them in a timeline representation, as shown in Figure 4.3, helped clarify the nature and pattern (e.g., behavior) of his actions.

For this analysis, each of the horizontal lines in the display[10] was selected to depict a different passport number used by the subject. The variations are clearly shown, and one unexpected observation was that in July/August of that year the subject actually changed his passport number. It is unclear why someone would be issued a new passport number; however, the digits associated with the new number were completely different from the original. Again, it was thought that more than one person was represented using the same name and DOB, but because the change in numbers was so evident it was easy to reach this conclusion. Also, for a week during the changeover, it appeared that a third number was emerging, but there were not enough I-94 events to clearly make that determination.

At this point, the subject was becoming a well-qualified target for investigation, and additional information from the I-94 database was pulled to show his address, per the analytical model in Figure 4.2. Although there were some inconsistencies due to street abbreviations in the representations of the addresses, they all pointed back to a single location in a warehouse district in Orange County, California, just south of Los Angeles. This provided further evidence that it was the same individual using all of these different passport numbers.

A reverse lookup was conducted on the address listed and it turned out to be registered to a courier business, which is presumably why the individual was thought to be a courier. The address was then checked against the I-94 data to see if anyone else used the same address in their filings. As luck would have it, there were four other individuals listed (shown in Figure 4.4), also Mexican nationals. Naturally, a check of their specific crossings revealed a very similar pattern to that of our original target, albeit not as abusive—the number of passport variations used by each of these new targets was 38, 26, 24, and 18.

The nature of this situation clearly shows that the controls over U.S. immigration are fallible because individuals are able to list different

[10] Due to obvious security concerns, this diagram is a re-creation of what was presented at the government site involved in performing this analysis (the original indeed had 54 horizontal lines one for each passport number).

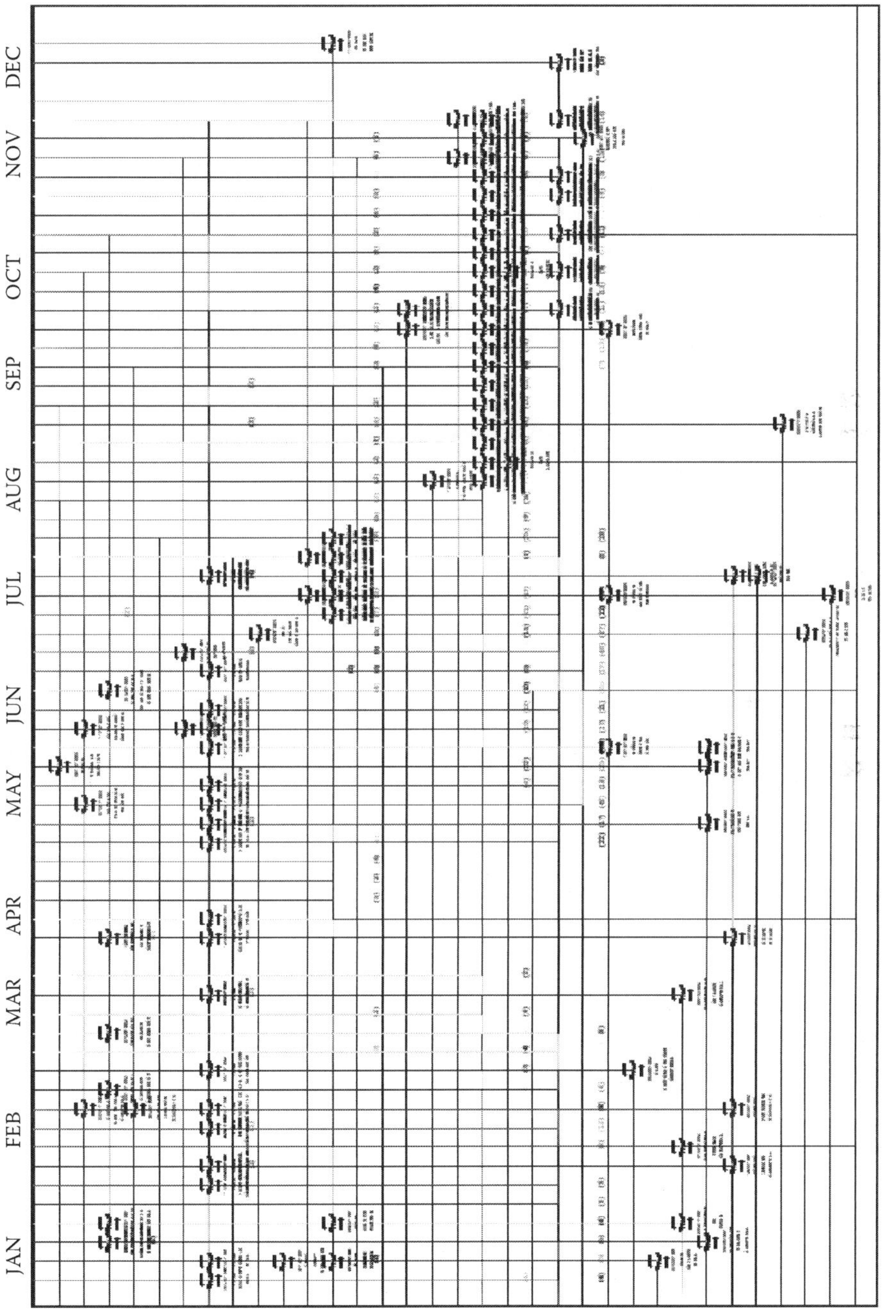

Figure 4.3 Timeline display of I-94 travel event.

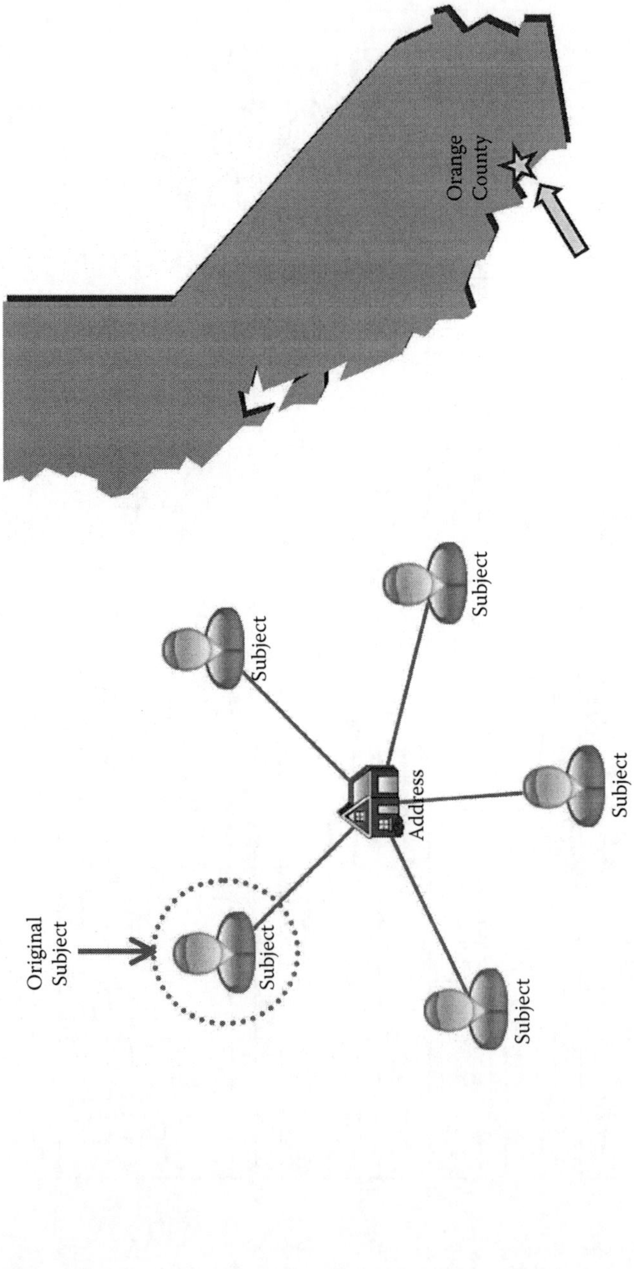

Figure 4.4 Additional linkages to suspect address.

passport numbers without being cross-checked, verified, or validated in any way. Some of this can be resolved with automated collection processes and/or more manual diligence, but either way these particular targets were able to circumvent the existing procedures and most likely were couriers of the proceeds of drugs or other illegal operations.

The I-94 data has other types of valuable patterns. The reverse of the pattern described above also exists, where *the same passport number is used by multiple people*. This is an equally important pattern because it helps expose unexpected behaviors. Other patterns include flight co-occurrence, which looks for unusual levels of commonality among passengers (as approximated by Figure 4.5), especially on different flight routes or carriers (as shown in Figure 4.6). Although it would not be unusual to see the same names appear on commuter flights (e.g., from New York to Chicago every Monday morning), it would be of interest for international flights dealing with foreign nationals. This pattern exposes many typical business relationships (e.g., representatives from the same company flying to the same client location) as well as mules/spotters (for drug or money movement), and perhaps even covert terrorist planning operations looking for a soft spot in the airline operations. The conditions of the pattern vary based on:

- The number of shared flights
- Use of noncommuter flights
- Sharing different flight origins
- Common flight destinations
- External connections (same addresses, credit cards, and phones)
- Flight dependencies/sequences (e.g., flight *x* followed by flight *y*)

Land Border Targeting

In continuing the discussion of border crossings and detecting unusual behaviors, this example overviews another system that was researched[11] for the U.S. Customs Service (now Customs and Border Protection) to help spot narcotics-smuggling activities through land border ports of entry (POEs). The system was used to access, integrate, and analyze multiple sources of data to identify high-value targets (e.g., vehicles) that were smuggling narcotics into the United States.

[11] System was utilized as a prototype under pre-9/11 conditions and is *not* currently part of any strategic plan involving Customs and Border Protection or any Homeland Security Program. Funding for the project was originally provided by the Deputy Assistant Secretary of Defense for Drug Enforcement Policy (ASD/DEP&S), the Counter-Drug Integration Division (CDID–D64) of the Defense Information Systems Agency (DISA).

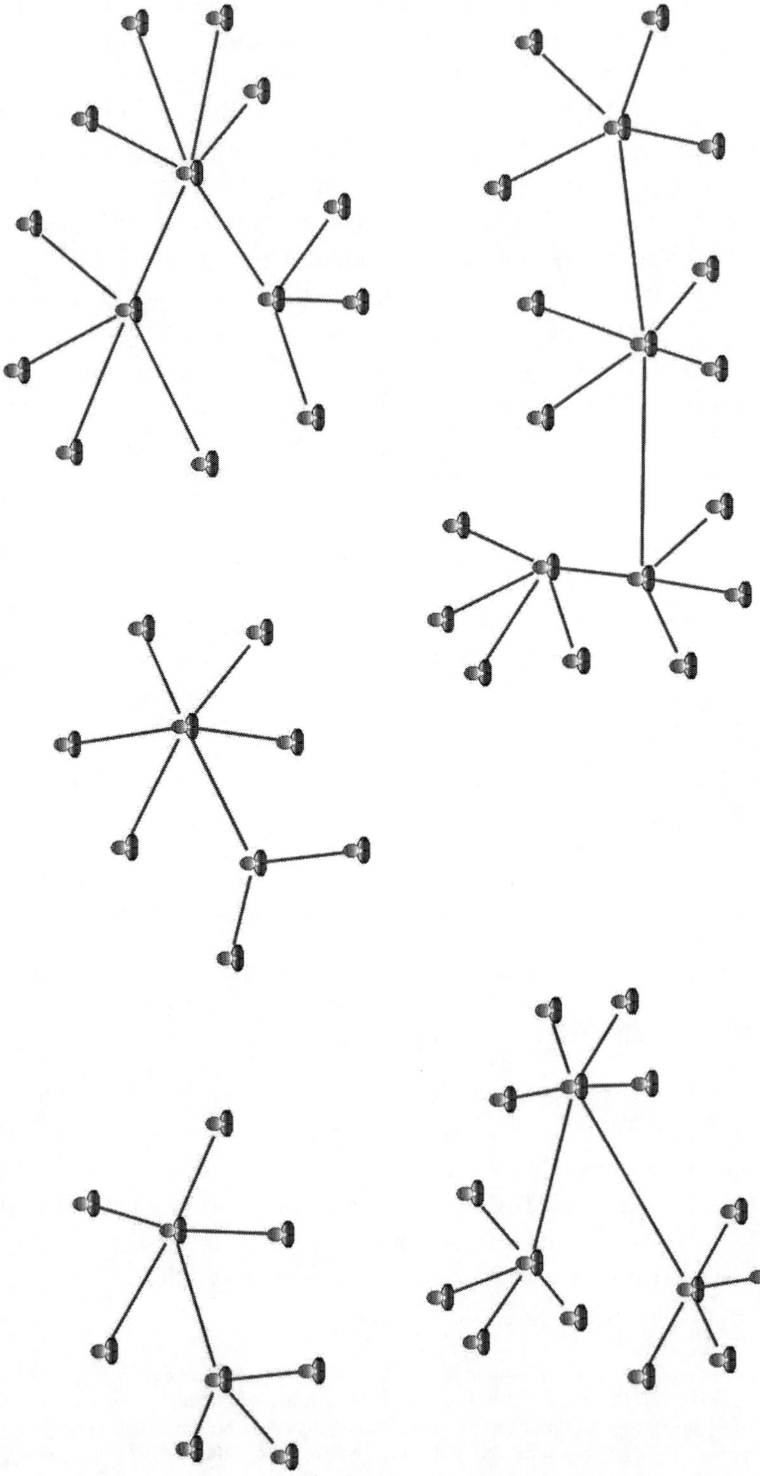

Figure 4.5 Commonality of passengers based on I-94 forms.

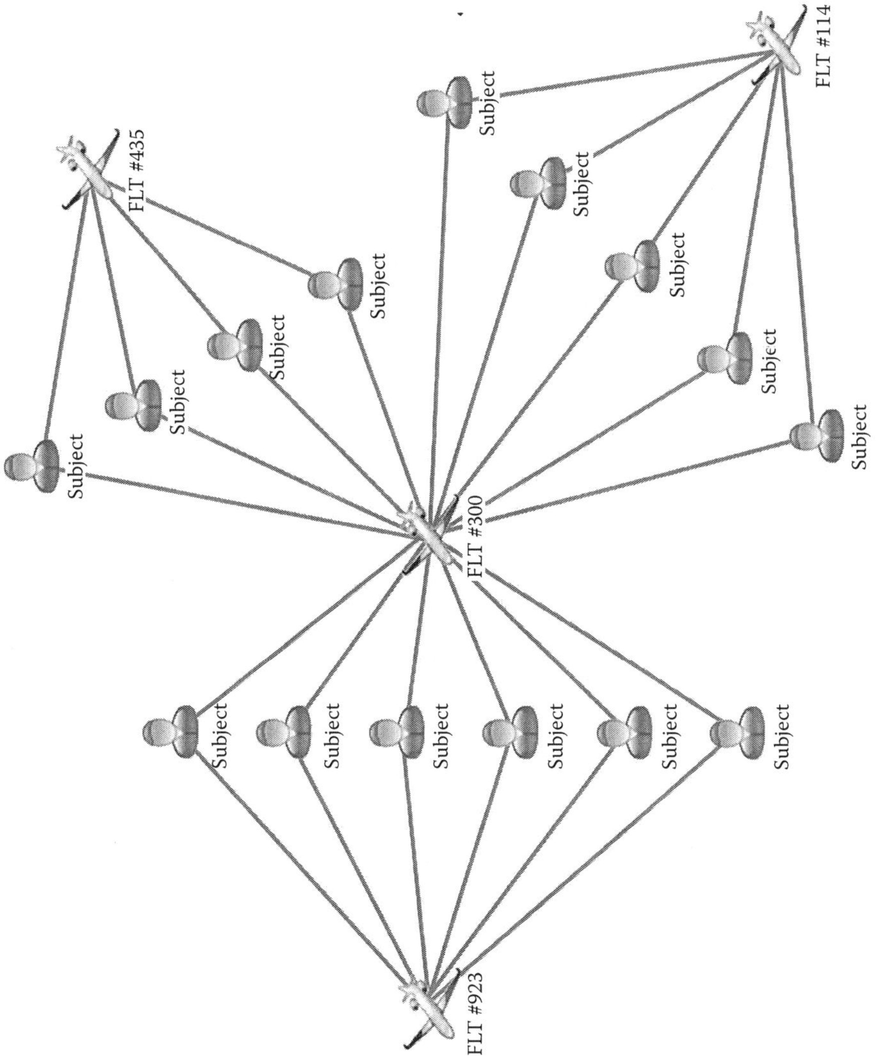

Figure 4.6 Commonality of flights using I-94 data.

The sheer number of vehicles, both passenger and cargo, that cross U.S. land borders each and every day presents a very difficult challenge when trying to identify those vehicles that are transporting narcotics.[12] It is physically impossible to adequately search every vehicle and still maintain a reasonable traffic throughput along U.S. borders. Thus, this system was focused on applying new approaches and advanced systems to better target narcotics traffickers.

The border between the United States and Mexico spans 1,951 miles and the border with Canada is 5,522 miles. There are approximately 1,000 Border Patrol agents assigned to the northern border (Canada) and about 9,500 on the southern border (Mexico).[13] In total, there are 325 ports of entry (POEs) located throughout the United States[14] including airports, seaports, and vehicle-crossing areas, of which 116 are designated as land borders.[15] Each day, approximately 333,000 privately-owned vehicles cross into the United States at the land borders, which accounts for almost 75 percent of all the people coming into the United States.[16] In 2005, there were more than 319 million people who entered the United States through a land border POE.

The system was initially deployed at the San Ysidro port of entry where more than 14 million cars pass through its borders annually. San Ysidro is located between San Diego and Tijuana and is the largest land border crossing in the world, consisting of 24 northbound lanes and six southbound lanes that operate 24/7. According to the Bureau of Transportation Statistics,[17] at any given time there are about 250 customs agents/inspectors and more than 200 immigration inspectors working at San Ysidro (see sidebar for a comparison between agents and inspectors).

In Figure 4.7, the San Ysidro POE (referred to as port code L255) is marked with a (1). This is where all of the inspector booths are located as well as the detention facilities and the administrative and management offices associated with its operations. It basically looks like a large interstate toll booth plaza. The area marked with a (2) represents the preprimary (northbound into the United States) lanes where cars are initially screened by inspectors and agents looking for narcotics and hidden contraband, usually with the help of canine units that patrol the area.

---

12 The challenges and patterns are virtually identical to those encountered in analyzing the I-94 data.

13 http://hsc-democrats.house.gov/SiteDocuments/20060912174839-94357.pdf.

14 http://www.cbp.gov/xp/cgov/toolbox/contacts/ports/ (provides a list of ports, points-of-contact, and port codes).

15 http://www.gao.gov/htext/d031084r.html.

16 Securing America's Borders at Ports of Entry: Office of Field Investigations, Strategic Plan FY 2007–2001. U.S. Customs and Border Protection. September 2006. Washington, D.C.: http://www.cbp.gov/xp/cgov/border_security/port_activities/securing_ports/.

17 http://www.bts.gov/publications/north_american_trade_and_travel_trends/boxes/box3.html.

Agents Versus Inspectors

Based on the job descriptions[18] provided by the U.S. Department of Labor, Bureau of Labor Statistics, the distinction between Immigration and Customs inspectors is detailed below:

"*Immigration inspectors* interview and examine people seeking entrance to the United States and its territories. They inspect passports to determine whether people are legally eligible to enter the United States. Immigration inspectors also prepare reports, maintain records, and process applications and petitions for immigration or temporary residence in the United States."

"*Customs inspectors* enforce laws governing imports and exports by inspecting cargo, baggage, and articles worn or carried by people, vessels, vehicles, trains, and aircraft entering or leaving the United States. These inspectors examine, count, weigh, gauge, measure, and sample commercial and noncommercial cargoes entering and leaving the United States. Customs inspectors seize prohibited or smuggled articles; intercept contraband; and apprehend, search, detain, and arrest violators of U.S. laws. Customs agents investigate violations, such as narcotics smuggling, money laundering, child pornography, and customs fraud, and they enforce the Arms Export Control Act. During domestic and foreign investigations, they develop and use informants; conduct physical and electronic surveillance; and examine records from importers and exporters, banks, couriers, and manufacturers. They conduct interviews, serve on joint task forces with other agencies, and get and execute search warrants."

It is important to make this distinction in roles because the system described was designated to support Customs in detecting vehicles loaded with narcotics due to their law enforcement responsibilities and powers. The focus was not necessarily on immigration issues, but rather on the smuggling of people, illegal substances, and contraband, such as narcotics, agriculture (plants and animals), and cash or other financial instruments.

[18] http://www.bis.gov/oco/ocosl60.htm (*Occupational Outlook Handbook*).

The southbound lanes, marked with a (3), are the entry point back into Mexico and, though the United States has a right to search outbound traffic for drug money, stolen vehicles, weapons, and wanted persons, it seldom occurs due to limited resources. The covered parking areas, marked with (4) and (5), represent the secondary inspection areas where vehicles are sent for a more thorough evaluation and examination. People are required to exit their cars while the inspectors perform manual searches and apply various detection technologies, such as fiber optic scopes to inspect for loaded gas tanks, vapor tracing devices to sample

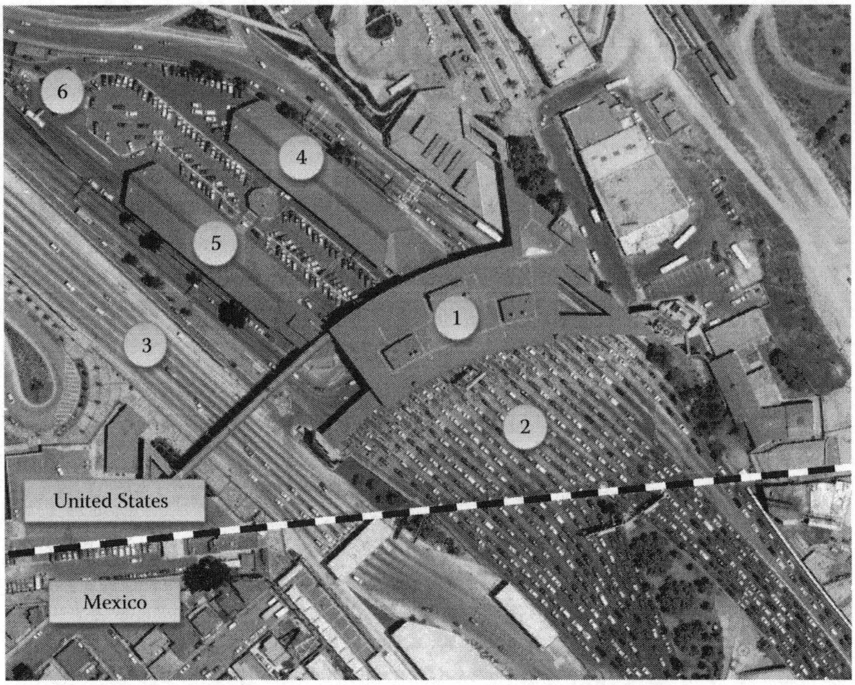

Figure 4.7 Aerial view[19] of the San Ysidro port of entry.

the air for drugs, laser range finders for detecting false walls, surface density measurement devices to help identify hidden compartments, or as is done on a regular basis, use of a canine unit for a more extensive screening. Once the vehicle has cleared all of its inspections, it must exit through a controlled-access area (6) with well-defined traffic control barriers, and the drivers must present the proper clearance from the inspectors to show that they have been authorized for release. From here the vehicle then gets on Interstate 5 and heads north toward San Diego.

For those vehicles that make it through the scrutiny of San Ysidro inspectors, there are additional checkpoints permanently located about 65 miles north of the border as shown in Figure 4.8. The first is in San Clemente[20] on the south side near Camp Pendleton on Interstate 5, which represents one of the busiest checkpoints in the United States with more than 144,000 vehicles transiting through its control daily.[21]

[19] Image courtesy of the United States Geological Survey: http://www.usgs.gov/.

[20] http://www.cbp.gov/xp/cgov/border_security/border_patrol/border_patrol_sectors/sandiego_sector_ca/stations/sandiego_sanclemente.xml.

[21] GAO Report, Border Patrol: Available Data on Interior Checkpoints Suggest Differences in Sector Performance, Appendix II: San Diego Sector Profile, pp. 55–61, July 2005. http://www.gao.gov/new.items/d05435.pdf.

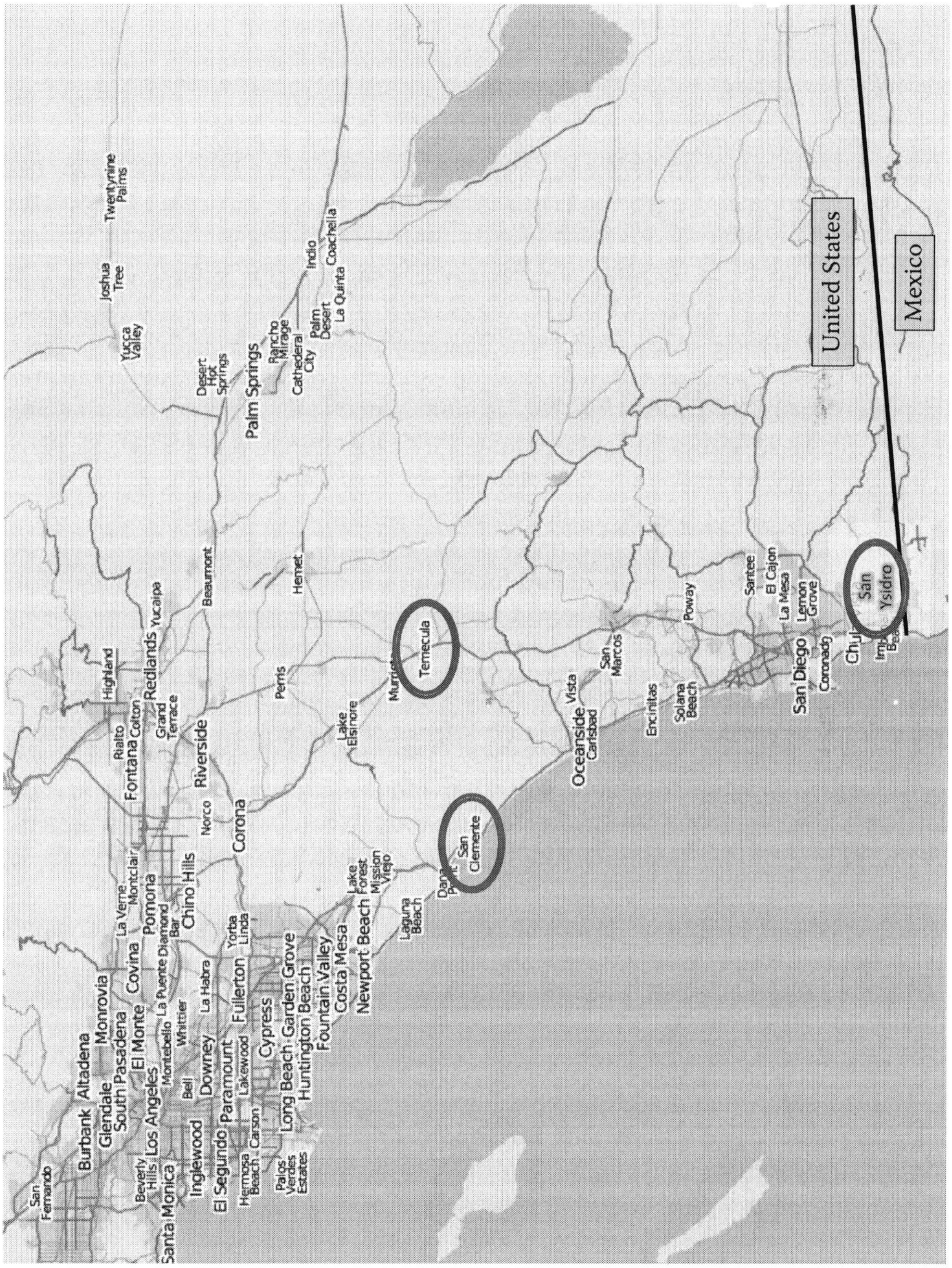

Figure 4.8 Southern California checkpoints.

A second checkpoint, about 25 miles due east of San Clemente, is located in Temecula, California, and covers traffic operating on Route 15. This region also has additional, permanent checkpoints and a number of tactical checkpoints that are mobile units operated on an as-needed basis to cover secondary roads, side roads, and other thoroughfares. Thus, there is a fairly tight network of checkpoints constantly reviewing vehicles and the related behavior of their occupants.

The system was heavily based on the use of the TECS database that contains all of the crossing data and any reported seizure data for the border POEs. The system also integrated the Department of Motor Vehicle (DMV) data for the state of California. Most of the crossing data in TECS was acquired through license plate readers (LPRs) that recorded and captured individual crossings for each vehicle. At the time of the prototype, there were over 280 LPRs operating[22] on both the southern and northern borders of the United States, including all 24 northbound lanes at San Ysidro; today there are more than 400 LPRs operating at 65 POEs.[23] The LPR function is almost identical to that used in red-light violation cameras, speeding cameras, and other security-related applications.[24] Most recently,[25] CBP agreed to provide the National Insurance Crime Bureau (NICB)[26] the raw LPR data as a tool in its efforts to prevent and investigate vehicle theft and insurance fraud.

The basic premise of the system is that vehicles that cross through a POE will exhibit a variety of characteristics that can be exploited through both automated and manual analytical methods. While looking for narcotics, there are three primary categories of methodologies that are used by the inspectors and agents to determine whether a vehicle is of interest with respect to performing a more in-depth search—also called a secondary inspection. These include physical indicators, behavioral indicators, and crossing history. Unless a particular feature or behavior is extremely explicit, inspectors will most likely use a combination of traits on which to base their decision.

The first method is based on the physical indicators of the vehicles themselves. There are some obvious signs that a car may be transporting narcotics, ranging from unusual odors or smells and bulging compartments (or wobbling tires) to fresh paint or new screws and bolts (indicating work was performed on the vehicle to potentially hide/seal narcotics into hidden compartments). There are wide ranges of physical indicators,

[22] http://www.cbp.gov/xp/CustomsToday/200 1/December/custoday_lpr.xml.
[23] http://www.dhs.gov/xlibrary/assets/mgmt/e300-cbp-lpr2008.pdf.
[24] http://www.licenseplaterecognition.com/.
[25] http://www.oea.das.state.or.us/OSP/CJIS/docs/NLETS_PLATE_READERS_LOC.pdf.
[26] http://www.nicb.org.

such as dashboard Bibles,[27] personal effects,[28] and specific makes and models,[29] that can be used for these purposes and the inspectors tend to rely on a personalized and select set of them to help make their decisions. There is no centralized database containing this type of information to analyze because it is rooted entirely on physical observations made at the time the vehicle crosses the border and on the experiences of the individual investigators.

The second method is based on the behaviors and actions of the drivers and passengers in the vehicles at the time of crossing. People that won't make eye contact, tend to be overly friendly, or appear nervous are most often going to catch the interest of the inspector. It is the degree of interaction exhibited by the drivers and passengers that is used as the basis for determining whether or not there is enough suspicion to select them for a more thorough inspection. Again, there is no qualified database to reference for this information and the inspectors will form their own ideas and opinions based on their specific experiences and exposure to a wide range of crossing events.

The third method is based on the crossing history of the vehicle itself. There are several types of existing checks in place within TECS, including the display of the crossing history (usually limited to the last 72 hours), a process that identifies any crossing co-occurrence for the selected vehicle, and other on-demand inquiries. However, the crossing behavior of a vehicle can be quite extensive and there have been observations that some cars cross more than 400 times in any given year. Trying to understand this volume of crossing data can quickly become a monumental task, for which there is little time while the vehicle is passing through the lane. Thus, the system was focused on providing more intuitive mechanisms and interfaces by which to interpret the crossing data, thereby allowing the inspector to make more accurate and reliable decisions.

Generally, Customs likes to keep a rolling 20 to 30 minute backup at the port to provide time to review the vehicles and behaviors of their passengers. It also provides an opportunity to run the canine units around the vehicles to help detect narcotic loads. Sometimes vehicles that have loaded their gas tanks with packaged narcotics will run out of fuel waiting

[27] A Bible on the dashboard is interpreted by the inspector that the driver is sending a message that he or she is an honest and God-fearing person and would not try to do anything illegal; except that exposing the Bible to the harsh sun, and the related wear and tear of its being placed on the dashboard, would potentially be considered disrespectful in many religions.

[28] Use of a single key on a key chain (e.g., no home or office keys, only the car key) might indicate limited use of the vehicle and/or no personal effects in the car, such as maps/papers, CDs/tapes, or loose change to show regular use of the vehicle.

[29] Loaded vehicles tend to be older models or lower-value vehicles due to the risk of seizure.

in these artificial backups. Even during nonpeak times (e.g., 2:00 a.m.), a number of lane closures ensures there is still a reasonable waiting period for review and inspection of the vehicles.

The goal of the system was to provide a well-integrated picture of all of the known data for a vehicle when it arrives at or departs from a POE. Thus, it presented the inspectors with a set of diagrams from which to make a decision about whether or not to submit the vehicle to a more detailed search (i.e., a secondary inspection). Because the crossing behavior associated with a vehicle has quite a large number of dimensions (e.g., ports, lanes, times, dates, etc.), a series of diagrams was created to summarize the important points. Based on the configurations of all the diagrams, the inspectors could draw conclusions about the "suspiciousness" of the vehicle they were reviewing.[30]

At the time, the databases used in the system contained more than 200 million records that were derived from the TECS and the DMV. The system was configured to support both proactive (any value) and reactive (license plate) centric analyses. The system was designed not to explicitly make decisions by itself, but rather, it presented its data to the inspectors/agents in a way that was easy to interpret so that decisions could be made in a confident and timely fashion. This allowed the inspectors to form their own opinions with respect to the data being presented so that they could rely on those diagrams (e.g., patterns) they felt more comfortable interpreting instead of treating all the patterns equally.

Mapping the underlying data into their appropriate analytical models was critical and required a bit of foresight with respect to the types of conditions, anomalies, and inconsistencies that could be encountered. The analytical models supported by this system included entities for *License Plates, Addresses, People,* and *Border Crossings* (transactions) that are connected (i.e., linked together) based on what was contained in the underlying data when using the *License Plate* as the primary entity. Figure 4.9 shows an example of the analytical model used in this system.

Keep in mind that the LPRs are not 100 percent accurate and misreads can be made when the vehicle passes through the screening area due to bent license plates, dirt or mud on the plates, or spare tires (SUVs) and trailers partially blocking the plates from the readers. Additionally, the LPRs (at the time) were not able to record the issuing authority of the plate (e.g., the

---

[30] All information presented was based on known connections and crossing histories and, therefore, decisions were made interpreting these behaviors rather than any type of static profiling where the gender, age, ethnicity, or other physical characteristics of the driver or passengers was presented.

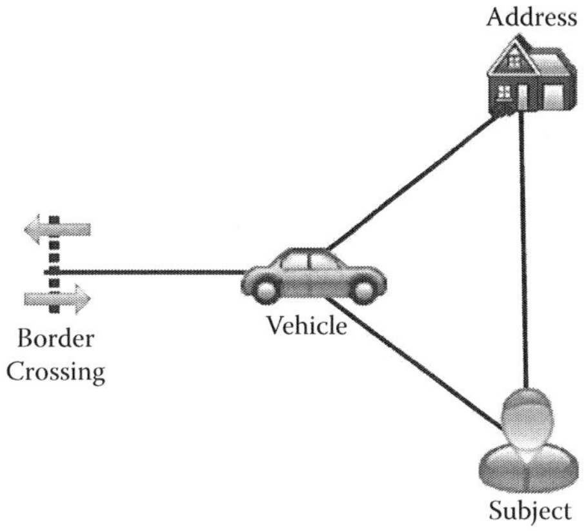

Figure 4.9 Land border crossing analytical model.

state in the United States or the province in Mexico/Canada); therefore, the same plate number could legitimately exist for different vehicles.

The data schema acquired for the DMV provided only those fields that were pertinent to the analyses being performed. These fields and their mappings to the analytic objects are shown in Figure 4.10 and are fairly intuitive. The *Vehicle* is keyed off of the license plate field, as opposed to the VIN, because it represents the only value by which to integrate with the other sources, and all of the self-described fields of this table/database are also applied as attributes to the *Vehicle* object. The *Subject* is keyed off the owner name field, which represents a composite value of first, middle, and last names of the registered owner of the vehicle. The *Address* object is keyed off the street, city, state, ZIP, and country, which are also applied as attributes of the object.

Within the DMV schema, *Subjects (Owners)* own *Vehicles* that are registered to *Addresses.* As can be anticipated, there are numerous cases where multiple *Vehicles* are registered to a single *Address* or where an *Owner* has multiple *Vehicles,* or even where an *Owner* has multiple *Addresses.* We must also consider that *Owner*s can be individuals or businesses and that not all *Vehicles* captured in the system will have a relationship to an *Owner* or *Address* because they are registered in a state other than California or in another country (e.g., Mexico or Canada). There should be no conditions where either an *Owner* or *Address* exist without a corresponding *Vehicle.*

The schema[31] derived from the TECS for the *Border Crossing* object shown in Figure 4.11 is used to create all the details for the event. The

[31] The schema presented in the diagram is modified from its original structure to hide sensitive fields and values relating to TECS's operations.

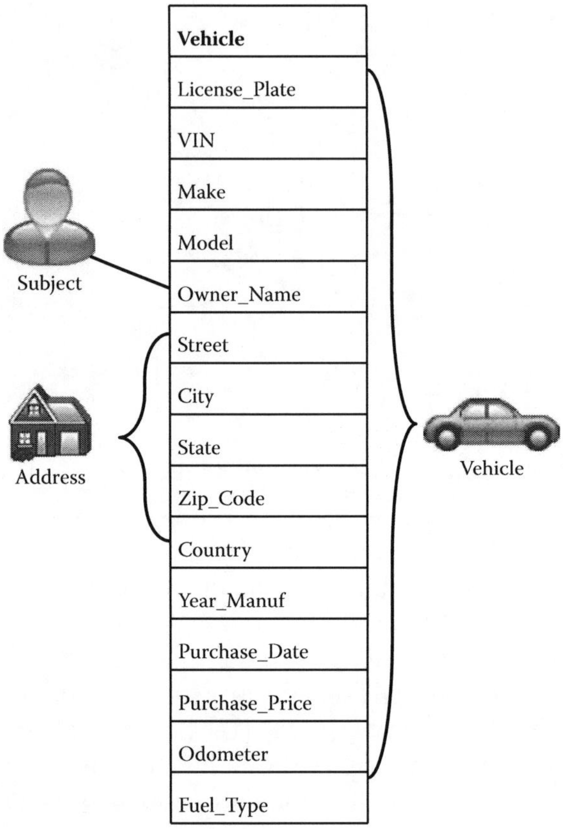

Figure 4.10 DMV database schema.

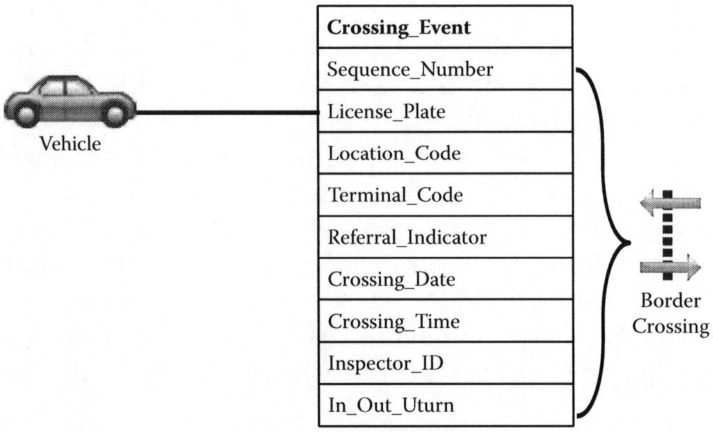

Figure 4.11 Schema for TECS crossing event.

object is keyed using the Sequence Number because it guarantees a unique value for each event. Additionally, all of the fields are applied to the *Border Crossing* object as attributes:

LOCATION_CODE = The unique POE identifier where the vehicle is crossing.
TERMINAL_CODE = Refers to the lane at the POE used in the crossing.
REFERRAL_INDICATOR = Tells if the vehicle was referred to a secondary inspection.
CROSSING_DATE = Date the vehicle crossed through the POE.
CROSSING_TIME = Time of day the vehicle crossed through the POE.
INSPECTOR_ID = Unique code for the inspector assigned to the lane.
IN_OUT_UTURN = Shows the direction[32] of travel of the vehicle.

This schema is also used to create an instance of the *Vehicle* object using the license plate as the key. This is an important part of the analytical model because the crossings are directly associated with a vehicle and are entirely defined in the TECS data that form the foundation for all the analytics performed by the system. Thus, every crossing theoretically has a corresponding license plate and any matches found in the DMV data using the same license plate add more value to the overall result set (as a referential source).

Finally, the Seizure Event schema[33] from the TECS is shown in Figure 4.12. Interpreting this schema presents a challenge with respect to its final utilization in the analytical model because it can be defined as a new object type, used as an attribute of the *Vehicle* object, or both. There is no hard and fast rule for which representation approach is considered

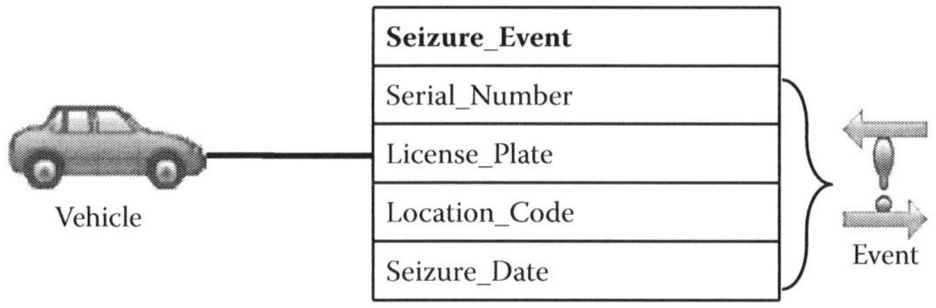

Figure 4.12 Seizure schema.

[32] Not all southbound lanes are outfitted with LPRs and the UTURN refers to a special area where cars can return to Mexico without officially going through the POE.
[33] This also represents a modified schema to hide sensitive field values.

better in this particular case, and, therefore, both methods were used. Finally, a *Vehicle* object is also created from this table to connect with the *Seizure* object.

As the number of entities increases, so does the complexity of the visual displays created from this data. Thus, it becomes important to present the targeted data in a timely fashion using display techniques that allow for quick interpretation of what is being presented. Because a reactive analytical approach was selected as the main use of the system, the amount of data presented is limited only to the vehicle crossing through a POE where the displays present all of the data related directly to the *Vehicle,* including *Addresses, Owners,* and *Crossings* (as well as *Seizures*).

Within the system, every aspect of the diagram conveys a piece of information. Not only are the entities themselves presented as objects, but their display characteristics, such as sizes, colors, positions, and labels, are all configured to show more detail regarding specific values associated with the entities. For example, Figure 4.13 shows five vehicles registered to the same address and one of the vehicles was marked as *seized.* Because this is an important fact to communicate to the inspector, a different shape and color are used to make this entity more prevalent in the display. Thus, if a vehicle passing through a lane were associated with an address or owner of a previously seized vehicle, it would make sense to more closely scrutinize that vehicle because there is recorded proof of previous wrongdoings that can be indirectly associated with the vehicle.

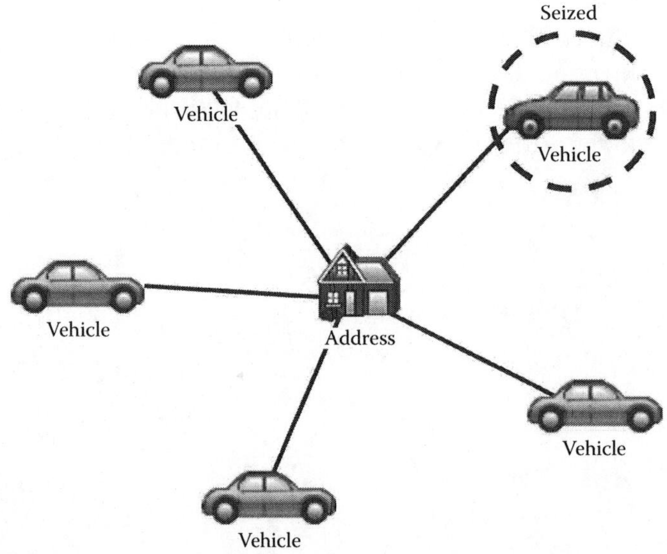

Figure 4.13 Conveying seizure detail using visual indicators.

The system was also designed to show the actual crossing events for a specified vehicle. Every time a vehicle crosses the border, a record is created for its license plate and includes the time, date, lane, port, and many other descriptive features detailing the conditions of the particular crossing. Because most vehicles regularly cross the border, a history of crossing events can be reviewed to better understand their crossing behaviors. Figure 4.14 shows an example of a *Vehicle* with 15 *Crossing* events. The system takes advantage of this crossing data to expose patterns to the investigator.

The main interactions with the system were through a license plate entry interface and a results-based visualization system. All interactions with the system were focused on a license plate, which means that the information presented was directly related to the license plate of the vehicle of interest. By utilizing this approach, the visual displays were structured to maximize the information presented.

Due to the large number of crossings at the POEs, realistically it would take too much time to review every last piece of information to determine if a vehicle should be referred to a secondary inspection. Thus, the system was designed to graphically present large quantities of data in very concise and well-formatted diagrams to shorten the review process. The goal was to provide an inspector with the ability to quickly interpret the diagrams and make a decision about whether or not there was enough cause to perform a more in-depth search, trunk inspection, or other type of examination.

The concept was to look for anomalies, inconsistencies, or other factors that don't seem to be associated with regular and acceptable border-crossing behavior. Keep in mind that there are numerous documented examples of people with "legitimate" crossing patterns who are involved in the movement and smuggling of narcotics or immigrants, and examples of these patterns are shown throughout this section. The inspectors were expected to derive their own set of characteristics and beliefs from the diagrams produced by the system so that they could be more effective in their targeting activities.

To use the system,[34] a license plate was introduced to seed the extraction process so all activity was based on its respective *Crossing* events and the *Vehicle* involved became the primary entity, enabling other TECS and

[34] It is important to note that all interactions with the system were recorded into a database. Thus, any entities that were reviewed could have comments/notes placed on them for future reference and recall purposes. Additionally, by tracking this data, the CBP received important feedback regarding its operations and could make adjustments where necessary to improve the targeting capabilities of the system. This feedback was also tied into the display parameters shown every time a *Vehicle* was presented.

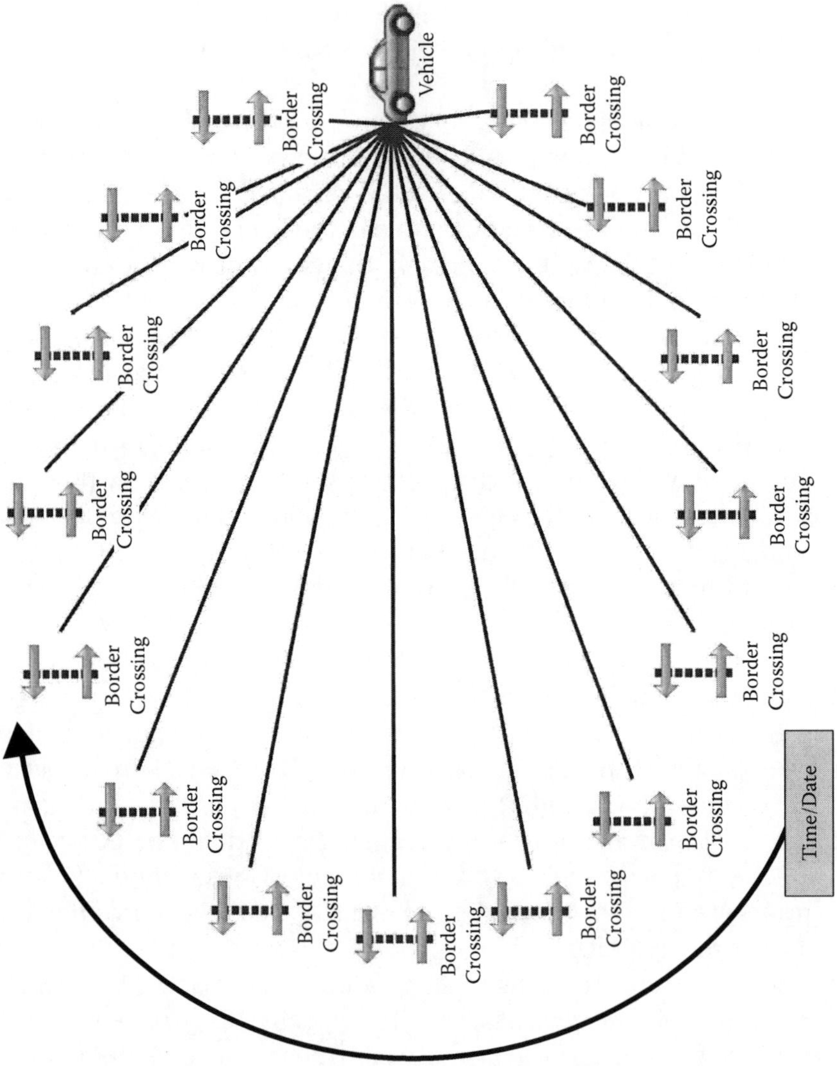

Figure 4.14 Vehicle with 15 border crossings.

DMV records to be extracted based on a matched license plate. Any data derived from the system was always started with the specification of a *Vehicle* (i.e., a license plate) as it was observed for a *Crossing* event.

It is the combinations of these sources and their respective values that determine the type of crossing pattern exhibited by the vehicle being reviewed. Within the visualization there are indicators, including size and color of the entities, that are used to convey other types of information. As described in Table 4.1, colors–states were used for presenting additional detail regarding the *Crossing* entities. Additionally, the label for all *Crossing* entities shows the lane, date, time, day of week, POE, country, and registered state (if known) of the license plate when it crossed the border.

The other entities within the visualizations also had unique presentation characteristics to convey their contents: *Vehicles* displayed the make, model, and year in the label; *Addresses* had the street, city, and state as part of their label. All three entities (*Vehicles, Addresses,* and *Owners*) also contained special counts to indicate the number of other entities to which they were connected. This value helped determine the degree of connectivity among the data elements. There were additional colors defined for the *Address* entities as defined in Table 4.2.

Depending on how the information was presented the display, different types of information (e.g., behavior) could be determined. Several examples are provided for each configuration to show both "normal" and "unusual" patterns for each, with a short discussion about their interpretation and meaning. The inspectors formulated their own conclusions based on how the data was presented within the different displays. Keep in mind that the type of data shown in each display format may overlap somewhat, especially with respect to time- and date-based data.

Table 4.1 Color Codes for Special Crossing Indicators

Color	*Meaning*
Gold	Special Crossing Date (e.g., holidays)
Brown	DMV Expiration Date < Crossing Date
Blue	Outbound Crossing
Yellow	Hit Flag Set (e.g., has a lookout set in TECS)
Purple	Special Operations Flag (i.e., intelligence group)
Pink	Referral Flag (e.g., vehicle was referred to secondary)
Red	Seized Vehicle

Table 4.2 Color Codes for Special Crossing Indicators

Color	*Meaning*
Yellow	Has a Post Office Box Representation
Blue	Address not within California
Green	Name Contains Auto, Motor, Dealer, or Rental

Cluster by Hour of the Day (HOD)

The hour of the crossing has proven to be important with respect to establishing a known pattern of crossings for a vehicle. All crossing events have an associated time that is usually represented as HH:MM. Since it is difficult for a vehicle to cross at exactly the same time (e.g., traffic backups, running late, etc.), it was decided to round the time frames into the hour in which the crossing has occurred. Thus, there will be at most 24 groups, and often a lesser number, represented in this display. It is important to realize that people who tend to cross regularly will keep to fairly standard behaviors (morning, lunchtime, etc.). What is being looked for here are vehicles that tend to cross at extreme times or tend to be erratic in their crossing times. Figure 4.15 shows an example of different crossing times based on the hour of the day for a select vehicle.

A slight variation in layout shows a diagram utilizing a combination of dates and times to represent the crossing behavior associated with a vehicle. In this diagram, 24 hours are placed on the *x*-axis and 52 weeks of the year on the *y*-axis. This placement represents an "absolute" temporal representation of the data because any gaps in time are clearly displayed, and provides insight into how regular the crossing behaviors are or how much they change over time.

This display explicitly shows commuter trends, shift changes, and other combinations of crossing patterns. The grid on the left in Figure 4.16 provides an example of crossing patterns using this display type and shows a very consistent behavior, where the crossing times overwhelmingly occur between 8:00 and 9:00 a.m. for the better part of a year, indicative of a daily commuter. There are also some weeks where they are running early/late (shown by rows with four filled boxes indicating 7:00, 8:00, 9:00, and 10:00 a.m.), some weeks they don't cross (depicted by empty rows), and one early-morning/late-night crossing at the beginning of the year. The darker line down the middle represents the noon transition.

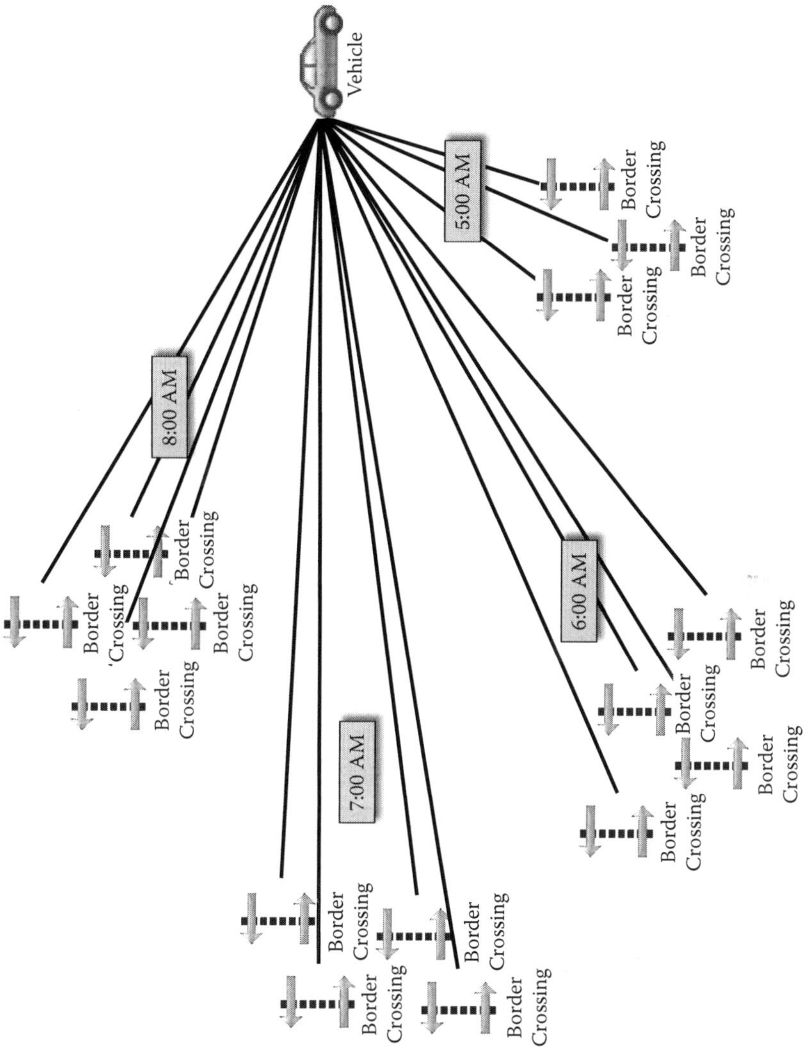

Figure 4.15 Crossing clusters based on hour of the day.

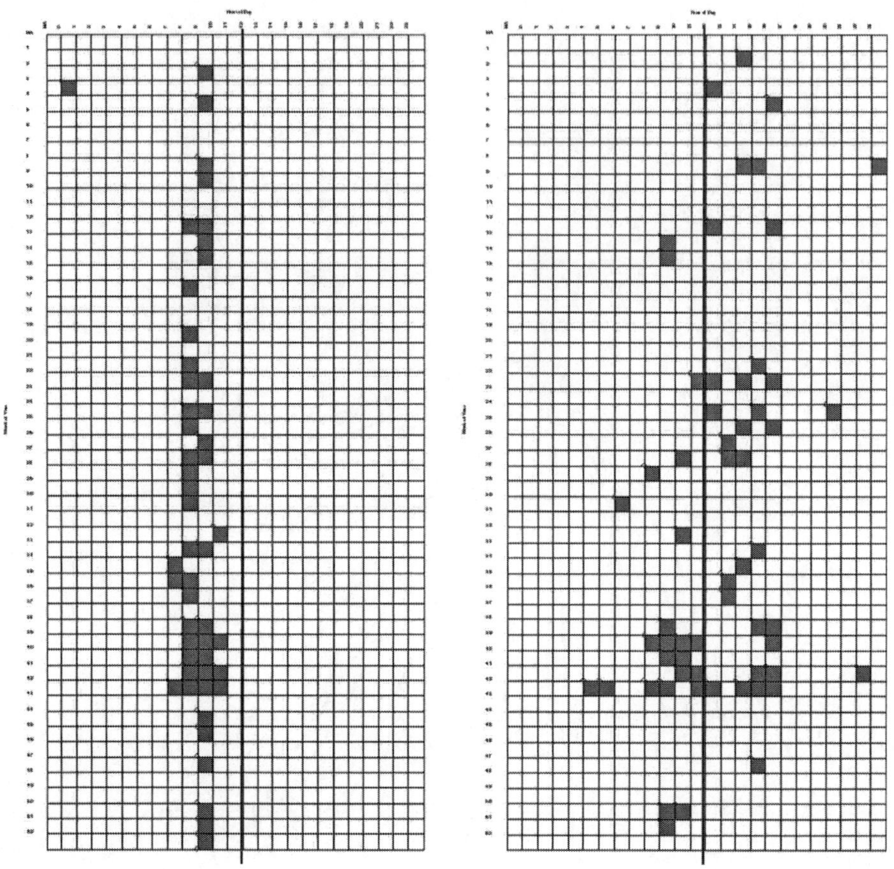

Figure 4.16 Date grid showing crossing behavior by hour/week.

The grid on the right in Figure 4.16 shows the crossing behavior of a different vehicle. This grid shows large gaps in the dates of the crossings with no regularity in terms of the times. This represents very inconsistent and nonpredictable behavior. Based on the detail presented, there are a few minor observations to be made, including an increase in crossings during June and July and then again in August and September. The three filled grid boxes on the far right appear to occur in a regular interval indicating some type of schedule or established crossing that occurs later at night[35] after 10:00 p.m.

[35] Traditionally, ladies nights at bars in Tijuana were held on Wednesday nights, which would result in certain crossings occurring later than normal.

Cluster by Day of the Week (DOW)

The day of week associated with a crossing can reveal some basic fundamental crossing patterns with respect to a vehicle. Within the database, the dates are converted to reveal the day of the week as one of seven values (Sunday through Saturday). It has been noticed that people who are regular commuters tend to have very heavy Monday through Friday crossing patterns. Others appear to prefer weekend crossings with some Monday or Friday times. The DOW is used to see if there is regularity with respect to which days a vehicle crosses. When the DOW does not appear to be regular, more consideration should be given to its overall rating. Figure 4.17 represents an example of DOW crossing patterns for a vehicle.

Again, a variation to this display shows how a temporal grid can be used to present crossings arranged by the seven days of the week (x-axis) by the 52 weeks in a year (y-axis). Using the 7×52 layout clearly shows what crossing days are of importance to the vehicle and if there are any significant gaps in their crossing times (e.g., days or weeks). Figure 4.18 shows two very different crossing patterns. The diagram on the left is very consistent and represents a typical commuter pattern where all the crossings occur Monday through Friday with some gaps for time taken off for illness, holiday, or other purposes. The diagram on the right shows a much more inconsistent crossing pattern because there are large gaps between crossing dates, no continuity, and generally no correlation to any type of known crossing pattern.

Cluster by Date

The date a vehicle crosses can expose a number of activities, especially when combined with other perspectives and specifically when multiple crossings occur within a single day. This is not unusual because many people cross to go to work, to come home for lunch, to drop the kids off at day care, and so forth. However, when you see this crossing behavior associated with multiple ports, co-occurring with other vehicles, or not following any type of regular pattern, then it becomes a pattern of interest. The date of a crossing is also partially reflected in the DOW and other date placement routines built into this application. Figure 4.19 represents the crossing patterns of a vehicle, grouped by the date of the actual crossings, and shows both a relative placement (circle on left) and an absolute placement (grid on right) for this temporal data. Groups with more than one crossing entity are easily identifiable (also highlighted

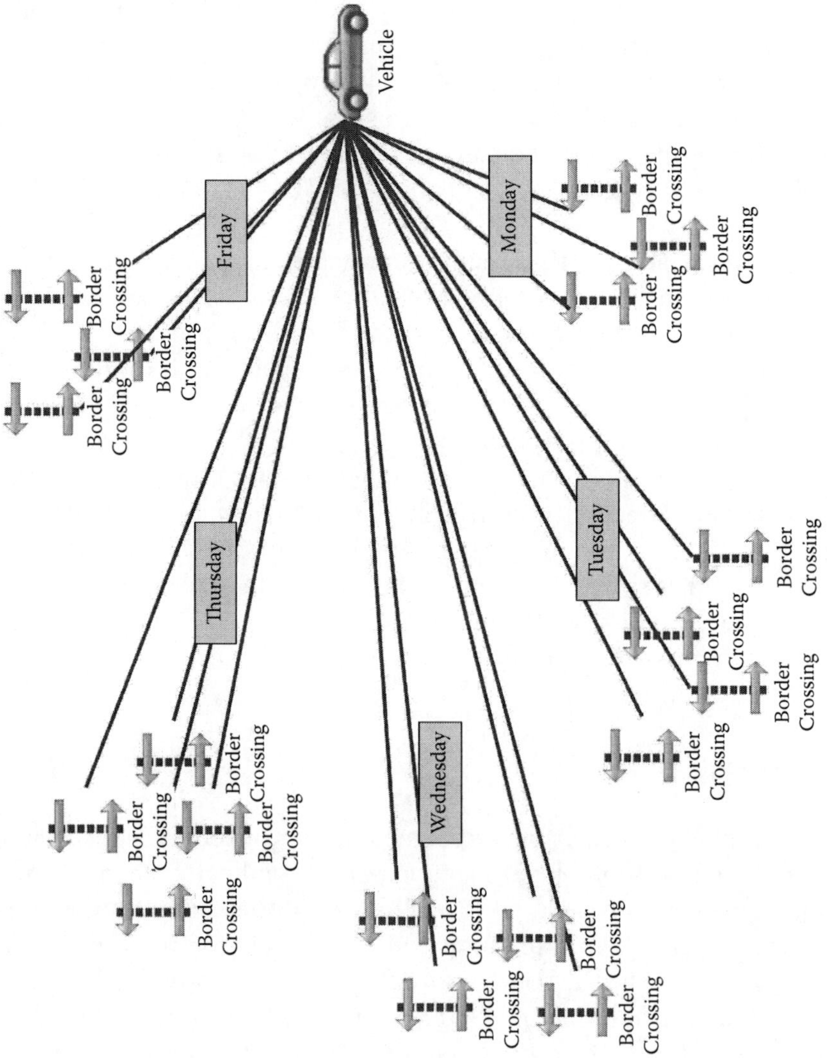

Figure 4.17 Crossing clusters based on day of the week.

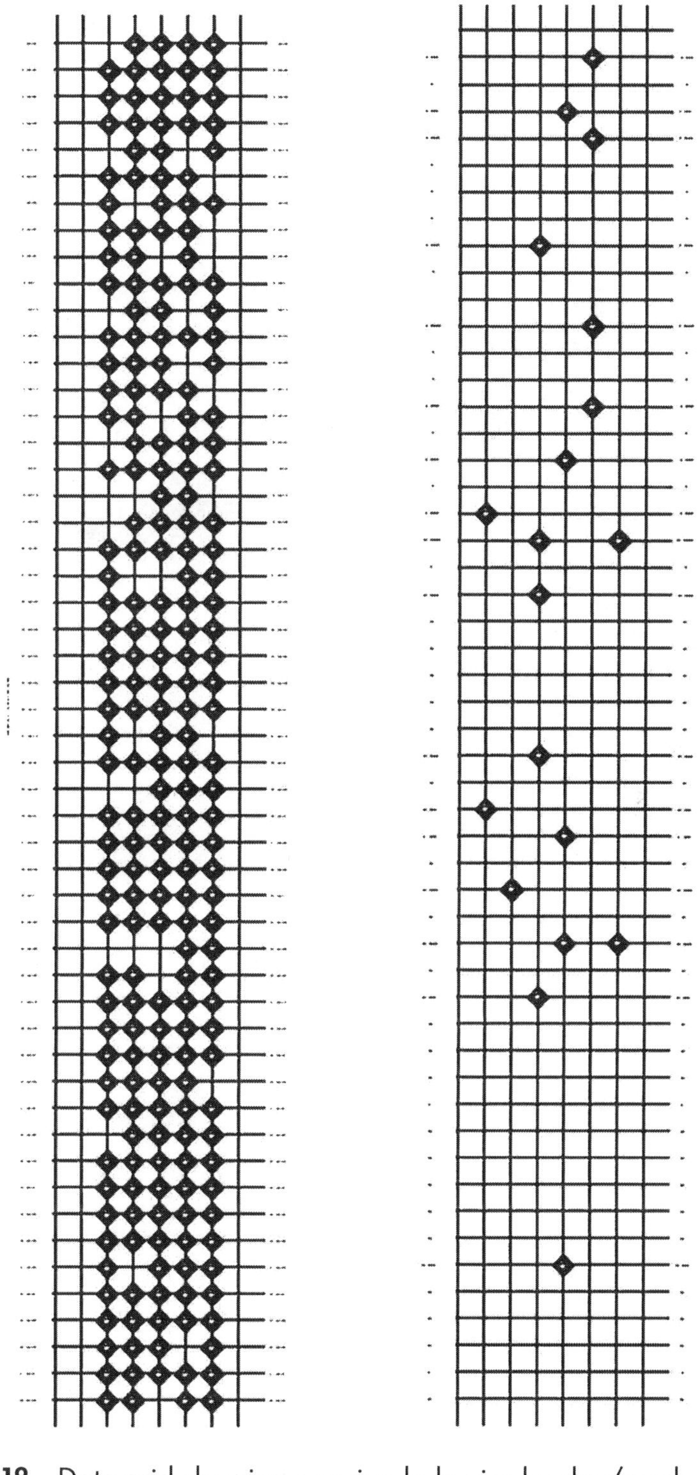

Figure 4.18 Date grid showing crossing behavior by day/week.

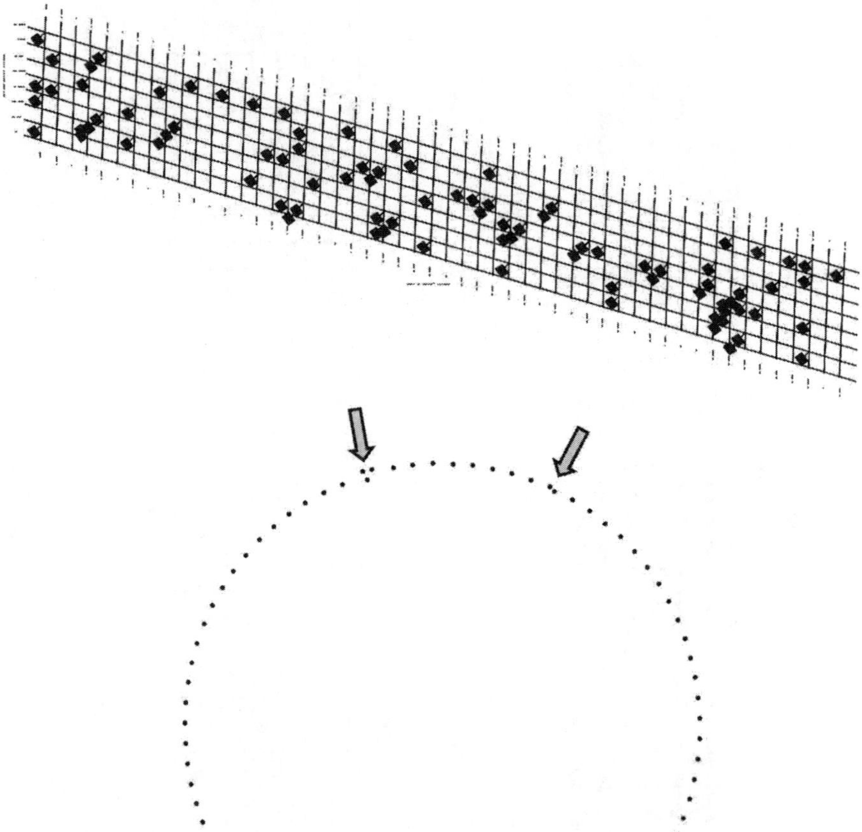

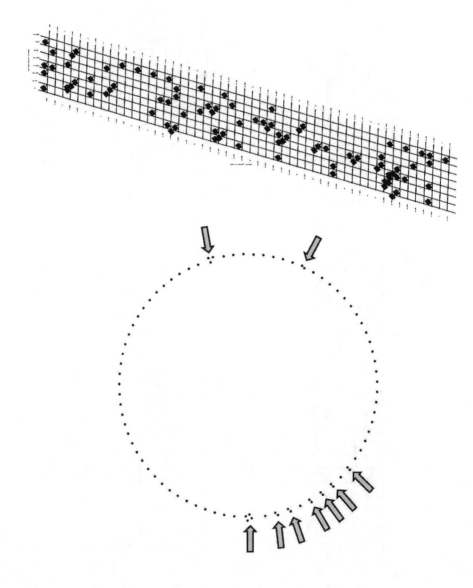

Figure 4.19 Crossing clusters based on the date.

with arrows) and indicate there have been multiple crossings on that specific day. The majority of the multicrossings appear as doubles (e.g., two crossings a day); however, there is one day with three crossings and even a day with four crossings. Also of note, a number of the double crossings occur sequentially (crossings are arranged in the circle according to the date, starting at the 12:00 position and increasing in a clockwise order) in a very short time span, which obviously indicates increased activity and should potentially raise concern about the reasoning behind this changed behavior.

Cluster by Port of Entry (POE)

There has been a lot of attention paid to those vehicles that have crossed through multiple ports, especially when it occurs in a relatively short time/date frame. The usefulness of this dimension depends heavily on the POE[36] where the crossings occurred.[37] Certain POEs are co-located together,[38] such that the actual terminal site codes are different, even though they may be entry points (e.g., bridges[39]) only a few miles apart. In these cases, it is less important than when the POEs are a reasonable distance apart. Keep in mind that the link colors within the displays of the operational systems reflect the terminal site codes. Figure 4.20 shows a vehicle with a number of different POE crossings. The link colors (represented by different gray scales) as well as the link style (dotted, dashed, etc.) are representative of the POE.

Clusters by Lane

The lane associated with passing through a POE represents a dimension that is highly subjective in terms of what may be considered questionable behavior because it will depend on the POE. It has been noticed that certain people will select specific lanes when they cross (e.g., Lane 7 or 11) for reasons of good luck or other cultural superstitions. Some people tend to regularly pick the inner or outer lanes. Certain biases may appear

[36] http://apps.cbp.gov/bwt/(shows POE operating hours and wait times).

[37] http://en.wikipedia.org/wiki/United_States–Mexico_border.

[38] San Ysidro and Otay Mesa are approximately 5 miles apart and Tecate is located about another 40 miles away.

[39] http://en.wikipedia.org/wiki/Laredo,_Texas (see International Bridges reference), Gateway to the Americas International Bridge, Juárez-Lincoln International Bridge, World Trade International Bridge (commercial traffic only), Colombia-Solidarity International Bridge, and Texas-Mexican Railway International Bridge.

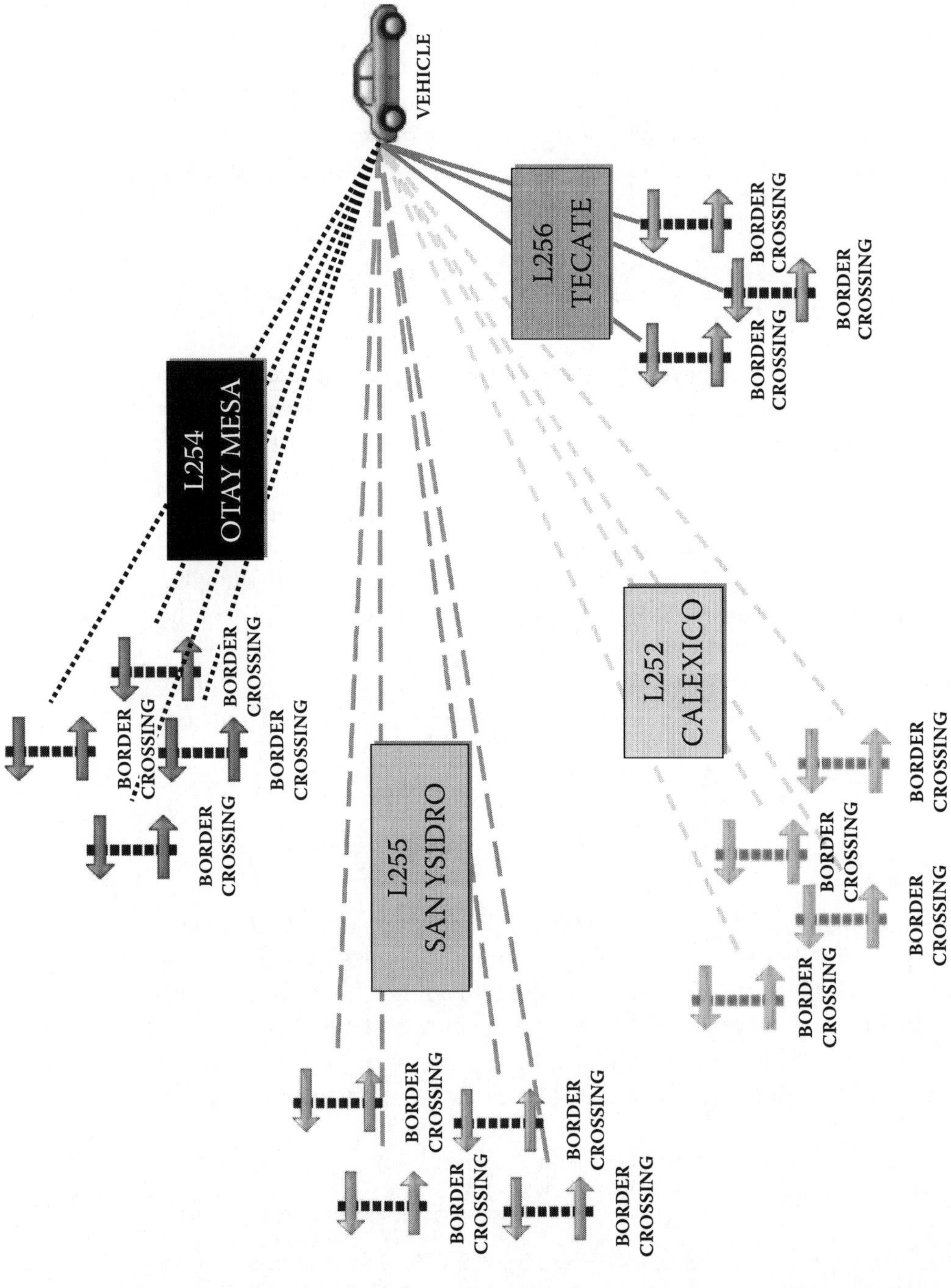

Figure 4.20 Crossing clusters based on the POE.

when people are using the commuter lane. This is not suspicious, but it does reveal another aspect of their crossing behavior for consideration in the overall analysis.

Cluster by Inspector

The ID of the inspector operating the lane is another factor that can be incorporated into the analysis. This represents a special display that was only used by the port management authority. The use of the inspector ID within this system was to help expose any biases that vehicles may have with respect to utilizing a particular inspector. There has been very little evidence of this within the data that has been viewed, except when dealing with the commuter lanes because they are manned by only a select set of specially trained inspectors who remain logged into the system. The primary concern here is to identify some type of collusion between the inspector and a target vehicle where a blind eye may be turned to allow a narcotics-loaded vehicle to cross into the country. Port regulations also ensure that the inspectors change their lane assignments approximately every 20 minutes to help minimize the chance of this situation occurring (remember, there are intentional traffic backups to help mitigate this situation).

Cluster by City/State

The "city" dimension is useful only when there is registered owner information for a license plate. The system returned a wide range of data, including all of the vehicles registered to a specific address. To ensure the vehicles were indeed located at the same address, this dimension was supported because a street number and name (especially PO Boxes) can appear in more than one city within a state. By clustering on the city code contained in the database, it can be determined if there are multiple addresses being represented.

Sometimes it can be difficult to tell if a single vehicle actually exhibits a detected crossing behavior, especially if multiple ports are involved. This can occur when the same license plate is registered to different vehicles (in different states or countries). For example, personalized plates are specific to the state where they are issued. Additionally, sometimes the LPRs will misinterpret characters in the layout of a license plate and cause this type of problem to occur. Therefore, grouping by state will show if a misclassification or a duplicate tag number exists within the database.

Cluster by VIN

It has been noticed that many vehicles within the database have been replated at one time or another. What this means is that the VIN remains the same but the plates themselves change, which is not uncommon if a vehicle is bought or sold. However, it was observed that this behavior was prevalent at those addresses where there were multiple plates registered to different individuals. Inspecting for this situation can quickly show if there are occurrences of replating for an individual or an address. Replating vehicles is somewhat of an anomaly, especially if there are border-crossing events associated with the vehicle and the times/dates of the crossings are close to each other.

Putting It Together

Once a review of the displays has been performed on a plate, the decision about what to do with the vehicle must be communicated back to the system. There are two choices available to control the data actions associated with a plate: low risk and high risk. Those crossing behaviors that do not appear to warrant any further investigation can be set to "low-risk" and the vehicle will not be targeted. Low-risk vehicles do not exhibit any type of unusual crossing behaviors and their general crossing trends tend to be fairly consistent. It is expected that the majority of the vehicles reviewed will be tagged with a low-risk rating. This rating can change at any time and should not be considered a permanent value.

A vehicle that received a "high risk" rating will be more closely reviewed by the lane inspector, the secondary inspection, or a member of a roving team situated in the preprimary areas of the POE. A high-risk rating would indicate that the crossing patterns of the vehicle were somewhat inconsistent with respect to several of the displays presented. Remember that the accounting and auditing mechanisms built into the system record the evaluation of the vehicles for future reference and recall. Any vehicles referred to as high risk in the system must be called in or entered as a lookout in TECS.[40]

Examples that would prompt a high-risk classification may include a common registered address with a previously seized vehicle, multiple vehicle replatings, addresses with multiple replates, or addresses with excessive registrations. Another high-risk situation is when the registered address for the vehicle is greater than 200 miles away from the POE and

[40] No automated feeds into TECS existed at the time this system was implemented.

there are multiple daily crossings for the vehicle. Yet another example would include large date gaps in between crossings with multiple port visits. It is ultimately up to the inspector to decide how to classify the vehicle based on its TECS crossing behavior or related DMV data.

The system was designed to provide a method to visually present the crossing behavior associated with any vehicle. The interfaces developed were optimized for speed, interactivity, and volume. Inspectors were expected to formulate their own interpretations of the displays in order to determine if the crossing behavior and/or DMV data associated with a vehicle is considered suspect.

Conclusion

The systems described in this chapter are conceptually very similar to one another because they both depict highly transactional data sources. The methodologies used for understanding and exposing the patterns contained within these sources are derived from both structural (e.g., how different objects are associated) as well as temporal (e.g., the date and times when the events occur) configurations. In reality, there is no one single pattern that is used to confirm suspicious behavior, but rather a combination of different dimensions that are interpreted within the context of the environment. The analytical approaches overviewed for these domains are also seen throughout a number of other examples provided in this section. Ultimately, those analysts and investigators who can generalize their approach for examining data will be more adept at expanding their capabilities into other areas. This point is critical when factoring in the sharing and integration of multiple sources of data as well as the collaboration with other agencies.

Chapter 5

Money Laundering and Financial Crimes

Introduction

Much attention and funding has been given to anti–money laundering (AML) efforts in the post-9/11 era. New rules, laws, and regulations are geared toward collecting more information in an effort to thwart terrorist activities and other related and undesirable operations. The amount of money laundered globally is thought to easily exceed $1 trillion[1] annually. To help combat this volume of financial crimes, a majority of international governments have created financial intelligence units (FIUs) to defend the integrity of worldwide financial markets.

Money laundering occurs when financial transactions are conducted involving assets representing the proceeds of some type of unlawful activity. Depending on the jurisdiction, it can include activities such as illegal drug trafficking, organized crime operations, credit card scams, tax evasion, illegal gambling, mispriced trade/invoicing, insider trading and securities fraud, and terrorist financing. If left unchecked, money laundering can undermine the integrity of any financial institution and may affect the social, economic, and political structure of a country through corruption and crime. Money laundering is also an international problem that crosses multiple jurisdictions, which often do not have reciprocal laws or the resources to deal with this immense problem.

Oversight of the world's financial marketplaces and the movement of money throughout its related institutions has traditionally been dominated by the Group of Seven (G7),[2] which comprises the heads of state of Canada, France, Germany, Italy, Japan, the United Kingdom, and the United States, which ultimately established the Financial Action Task Force (FATF[3]) on Money Laundering in 1989. The FATF[4] has evolved a list of 40 recommendations and 9 special recommendations on terrorist financing that form an essential baseline and guidance from which to create an effective AML program. Those countries not in compliance with FATF recommendations are considered Non-Cooperative Countries and Territories (NCCTs) and can have economic and trade sanctions placed against them. Sanctions against an NCCT may include blocked accounts and other assets as well as the prohibition of trade and financial transactions with the country. Thus, there are strong incentives for all countries to enact the necessary laws, regulations, and systems to combat money laundering.

[1] Activities can encompass a wide range of illegal activity including narcotics trafficking, insider trading, organized crime, embezzlement, hiding gambling wins, tax evasion, mispriced trade activity, illegal real estate transfers, securities fraud, wire fraud, and terrorist financing, to name just a few.

[2] Russia formally joined in 1997, making it the G8.

[3] Also known in French as the Groupe d'Action Financiére (GAFI).

[4] http://www.fatf-gafi.org.

Within the United States, a number of laws[5] have been enacted to fight financial crimes and money-laundering operations. In response to reports of people carrying bags full of money for deposit into banks, in 1970 the United States passed a number of rules and regulations called the Financial Recordkeeping and Reporting of Currency and Foreign Transactions Act (31 U.S.C. 1051 et seq.). This is often referred to as the Bank Secrecy Act (BSA) because it pertains to the movement and flow of cash and other negotiable instruments throughout the financial system. It was primarily designed to create a paper trail to help track the flow of the money, which often had questionable origins.

When the BSA[6] was enacted, it put a mandatory requirement on banks and financial institutions, such as credit unions, savings and loans, and thrift institutions to file a Currency Transaction Report (CTR)[7] for any amounts that were deposited, withdrawn, transferred, or exchanged that exceeded $10,000 in cash or coin (31 CFR 103.22). The activity has to be conducted by or on behalf of the same individual and the daily aggregate amount must exceed $10,000. Thus, if an individual went to three separate branches of a bank on the same day and deposited, say, $5,000 at each branch, the bank would be required to submit a CTR on the individual for the cumulative $15,000 deposited because it exceeds the $10,000 reporting level. The information collected on a CTR is fairly straightforward[8]; and a sample form is shown in Figure 5.1.

Keep in mind that being involved with cash transactions over $10,000 is not illegal, unless the money represents proceeds from unlawful activities, and this type of data collection is done on a fairly routine basis. CTRs currently represent the largest type of BSA filing based on the volume of transactions, with approximately 15 million CTR forms filed with the Financial Crimes Enforcement Network (FinCEN) each year from all the regulated financial institutions located in the United States.

Similar laws have been enacted in over 100 countries[9] and although each has their own interpretation, terms, and conditions, the concept of a CTR is universal. For example, there are about 4.5 million CTRs filed yearly with the KoFIU (Korean Financial Intelligence Unit); the Financial Transactions and Reports Analysis Centre of Canada (FINTRAC) receives almost 5.5 million Large Cash Transaction Reports annually; the Federal

[5] Some statutes define money laundering to include the movement or transaction of criminal proceeds and other related conduct.

[6] http://www.sec.gov/about/offices/ocie/aml2007/31cfr103.22.pdf.

[7] http://www.fincen.gov/forms/files/fin104_ctr.pdf (FinCEN Form 104).

[8] Ironically, the CTR forms do not collect the work and home phone numbers of the individuals involved in the transaction. Although the forms go through periodic revisions and are reviewed by government advisers, this type of critical data is not currently collected for CTRs.

[9] http://www.egmontgroup.org/.

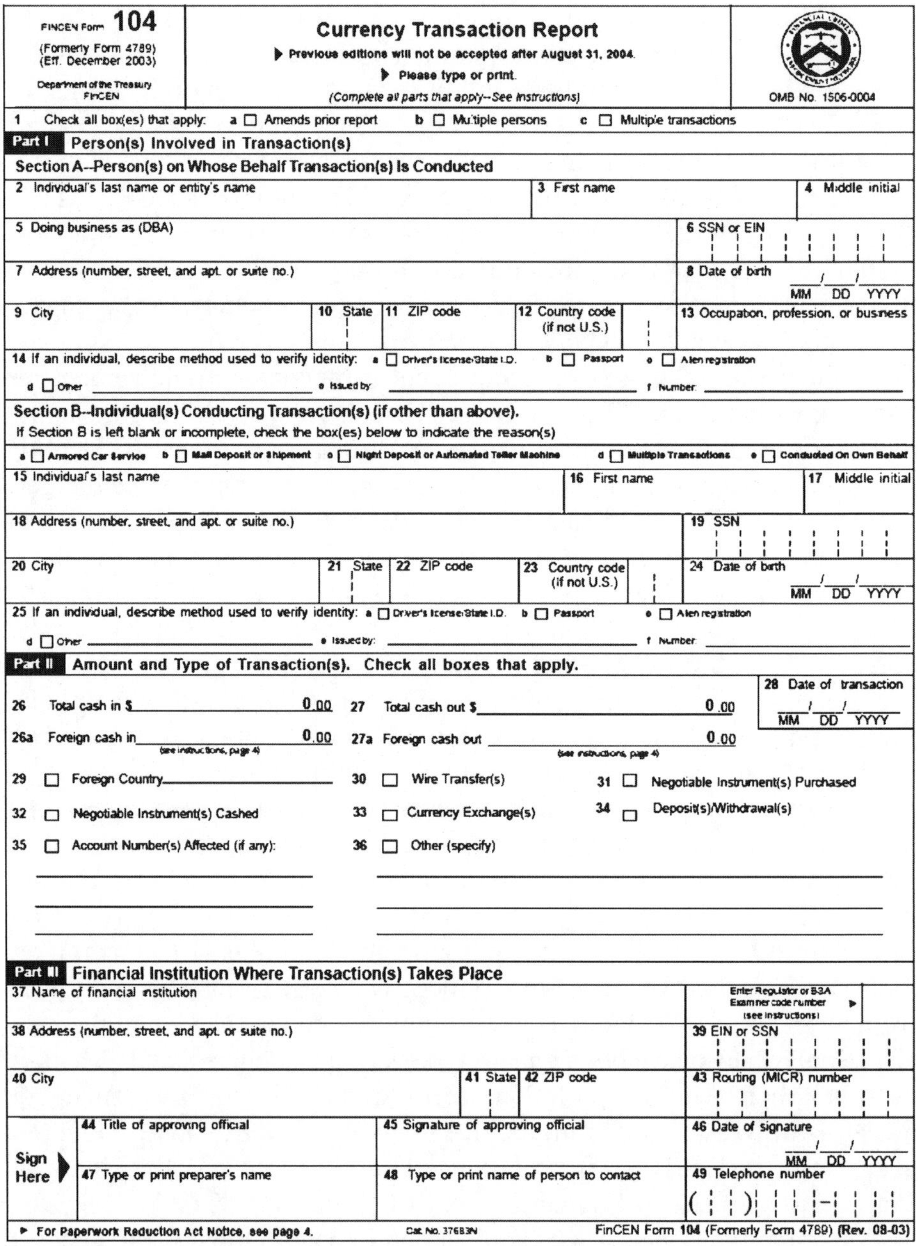

FINCEN Form 104
(Formerly Form 4789)
(Eff. December 2003)
Department of the Treasury
FinCEN

Currency Transaction Report
▶ Previous editions will not be accepted after August 31, 2004.
▶ Please type or print.
(Complete all parts that apply--See Instructions)

OMB No. 1506-0004

1 Check all box(es) that apply: a ☐ Amends prior report b ☐ Multiple persons c ☐ Multiple transactions

Part I Person(s) Involved in Transaction(s)

Section A--Person(s) on Whose Behalf Transaction(s) Is Conducted

2 Individual's last name or entity's name | 3 First name | 4 Middle initial
5 Doing business as (DBA) | 6 SSN or EIN
7 Address (number, street, and apt. or suite no.) | 8 Date of birth MM/DD/YYYY
9 City | 10 State | 11 ZIP code | 12 Country code (if not U.S.) | 13 Occupation, profession, or business
14 If an individual, describe method used to verify identity: a ☐ Driver's license/State I.D. b ☐ Passport c ☐ Alien registration
d ☐ Other ______ e Issued by: ______ f Number: ______

Section B--Individual(s) Conducting Transaction(s) (if other than above).
If Section B is left blank or incomplete, check the box(es) below to indicate the reason(s)
a ☐ Armored Car Service b ☐ Mail Deposit or Shipment c ☐ Night Deposit or Automated Teller Machine d ☐ Multiple Transactions e ☐ Conducted On Own Behalf

15 Individual's last name | 16 First name | 17 Middle initial
18 Address (number, street, and apt. or suite no.) | 19 SSN
20 City | 21 State | 22 ZIP code | 23 Country code (if not U.S.) | 24 Date of birth MM/DD/YYYY
25 If an individual, describe method used to verify identity: a ☐ Driver's license/State I.D. b ☐ Passport c ☐ Alien registration
d ☐ Other ______ e Issued by: ______ f Number: ______

Part II Amount and Type of Transaction(s). Check all boxes that apply.

26 Total cash in $ ______ 0.00 | 27 Total cash out $ ______ 0.00 | 28 Date of transaction MM/DD/YYYY
26a Foreign cash in ______ 0.00 (see instructions, page 4) | 27a Foreign cash out ______ 0.00 (see instructions, page 4)

29 ☐ Foreign Country ______ 30 ☐ Wire Transfer(s) 31 ☐ Negotiable Instrument(s) Purchased
32 ☐ Negotiable Instrument(s) Cashed 33 ☐ Currency Exchange(s) 34 ☐ Deposit(s)/Withdrawal(s)
35 ☐ Account Number(s) Affected (if any): 36 ☐ Other (specify)

Part III Financial Institution Where Transaction(s) Takes Place

37 Name of financial institution | Enter Regulator or BSA Examiner code number (see instructions) ▶
38 Address (number, street, and apt. or suite no.) | 39 EIN or SSN
40 City | 41 State | 42 ZIP code | 43 Routing (MICR) number

Sign Here ▶
44 Title of approving official | 45 Signature of approving official | 46 Date of signature MM/DD/YYYY
47 Type or print preparer's name | 48 Type or print name of person to contact | 49 Telephone number ( )

▶ For Paperwork Reduction Act Notice, see page 4. Cat. No. 37683N FinCEN Form 104 (Formerly Form 4789) (Rev. 08-03)

Figure 5.1 Currency transaction report (CTR) form 104.

Financial Monitoring Service in Russia reports about 10 million transactions (cash/noncash) per year; the Australian Transaction Reports and Analysis Centre (AUSTRAC) reports 2.6 million Significant Cash Transaction Reports; the Pelaporan dan Analisis Transaksi Keuangan

(PPATK), also known as the Indonesian Financial Transaction Reports and Analysis Centre, receives 1 million CTRs annually; the Anti–Money Laundering Office (AMLO) in Thailand also logs about 1 million transactions; the Conselho de Controle de Atividades Financeiras (COAF) in Brazil receives only 170,000 CTRs per year because they have their thresholds set at R$100,000 Brazilian Reais[10]; and in the Philippines, there are approximately 26 million CTRs filed yearly with the Anti–Money Laundering Council (AMLC), which not only includes cash transactions, but any type of transaction over $10,000 (equivalent in pesos) including, for example, payroll charges, real estate transfers, and car purchases.

In the United States, customers who routinely exceed the CTR thresholds can be listed on a Designation of Exempt Person (DEP) form[11] (FinCEN 110). Legitimate organizations dealing with high volumes of cash, such as restaurants, bars, convenience stores, and gas stations, that have a proven track record with their respective financial institution can have a DEP form filed on them to avoid the routine filing of a CTR every time the $10,000 limit is exceeded. DEP forms are reviewed and potentially renewed biennially (every other year). Of course, the DEP filing becomes of particular interest when the individual or business appears in other types of financial transactions within the BSA datasets.

CTRs are instrumental in combating all types of financial crimes and, although very powerful, their utility is somewhat limited due to certain conditions and restrictions placed on their reporting requirements. As with any system, the criminal element finds ways to circumvent the laws and new ways to launder their proceeds. Specifically, the drug dealers and organized crime members would enlist runners, mules, or smurfs to visit different banks to make deposits or purchase monetary instruments just under the $10,000 limit to avoid the filing requirements.

Breaking the deposits into identical, smaller, and repeated transactions (e.g., smurfing or structuring) was essentially a simple means to get around the CTR reporting requirements. To help fill in the gaps and plug the holes within the financial-reporting community, the Money Laundering Control Act[12] (MLCA) of the Anti-Drug Abuse Act of 1986 was passed, which criminalized the act of money laundering, prohibited the structuring of transactions to avoid CTR filing requirements, and imposed civil and criminal penalties/forfeitures on BSA violations.

---

[10] At the time of this writing, R$100,000 = U.S.$55,900 (1 USD = 1.788 BRL).

[11] http://www.fincen.gov/forms/files/fin110_dep.pdf.

[12] http://www.occ.treas.gov/BSA/documents/regulations/ML_Control_1986.pdf.

To deter any type of circumvention, avoidance, or interference of the CTR reporting requirement, Congress enacted an antistructuring provision.[13] Title 31 (Money and Finance), Subtitle IV (Money), Subchapter II (Records and Reports on Monetary Instruments and Transactions), Section 5324 (Structuring transactions to evade reporting requirement prohibited) it states:

> *Any person who for the purpose of evading the CTR reporting requirements, (1) cause or attempt to cause a domestic financial institution to fail to file a report; (2) cause or attempt to cause a domestic financial institution to file a report that contains a material omission or misstatement of fact; or (3) structure or assist in structuring, or attempt to structure or assist in structuring, any transaction with one or more domestic financial institutions.*

Thus, it is a violation of federal law to walk into a bank to deposit an amount over $10,000, realize the bank is going to file a CTR on the transaction, and adjust the amount deposited to a value less than $10,000 to avoid the CTR filing. Alternatively, breaking up a large transaction into smaller amounts and depositing them over several days is still structuring deposits to avoid the filing requirements and, is still therefore, a violation of these laws. Additionally, providing invalid information, such as a false identification number, an incorrect name, a different date of birth, or any other type of other erroneous description, is a willful violation of this statute. Any of these violations can result in fines or even prison time.

The MLCA is primarily composed of two sections found under U.S. Code Title 18 (Crimes and Criminal Procedure), Part I (Crimes), Chapter 95 (Racketeering) called § 1956, Laundering of monetary instruments and § 1957, Engaging in monetary transactions in property derived from specified unlawful activity. The primary effect of this law makes it illegal to conduct or attempt to conduct a financial transaction with proceeds known to be from specified unlawful activity, or to transport or attempt to transport monetary instruments or funds in or out of the United States with:

- Intent to promote, conduct, or the carrying on of specified unlawful activity.
- Intent to evade taxes.
- Knowing that the monetary instrument or funds involved in the transaction or transportation are designed in whole or in part to conceal or disguise the nature, the location, the source, the

[13] http://www.irs.gov/irm/part4/ch26s05.html.

ownership, or the control of the proceeds of specified unlawful activity, or to avoid a transaction reporting requirement under state or federal law.

To ensure these new statues would have the necessary impact, they carry penalties including a fine of not more than $500,000 or twice the value of the property involved in the transaction (whichever is greater), or imprisonment not to exceed 20 years, or both. These types of penalties coupled with new forms of regulations, asset seizures, and reporting requirements help form the foundation for a comprehensive AML blueprint.

The government has kept pace with refining and expanding the scope of its AML arsenal of laws, statutes, and regulations. Over the years, additional legislation was implemented to provide more control over the types of information being reported and collected, oversight of different market segments being regulated, and even the scope and nature of the crimes governed under these laws. The following represent milestone acts implemented since the original BSA rules were enacted:

- 1986 The Money Laundering Control Act (of 1986)
- 1988 The Anti-Drug Abuse Act (of 1988)
- 1988 Money Laundering Prosecution Improvement Act
- 1990 Bank Fraud Prosecution and Taxpayer Recovery Act of 1990 (Crime Control Act)
- 1991 Federal Deposit Insurance Corporation Improvement Act; Section 206
- 1992 Annunzio–Wylie Money Laundering Suppression Act
- 1994 Money Laundering Suppression Act
- 1998 Money Laundering and Financial Crimes Strategy Act
- 2001 USA PATRIOT Act (Title III, International Money Laundering Abatement and Anti-Terrorist Financing Act of 2001)

It is outside the scope of these discussions to review the details of these acts; however, each has left its own mark and contributed positively to establishing the current BSA regulations governing the U.S. financial marketplace. There are reporting and record-keeping requirements for a breadth of industries ranging from banks and credit unions to casinos and security dealers. There are literally hundreds of thousands of businesses currently subject to BSA filing requirements and this list is continually expanding as new means, methods, and technologies are employed to launder money in the commercial marketplace.

Currently, under the BSA, the U.S. government requires submission of a number of different forms depending on the industry and the nature of the transaction. There are general reporting forms for foreign account information, forms for transactions over $10,000, and forms that are submitted when questionable or suspicious behavior is encountered during the conduct of a transaction. Each one has been designed to help monitor and minimize the abuses that can occur within regulated financial systems. Although the details of each form are beyond the scope of this discussion, Table 5.1 lists those forms currently required by the U.S. government.

Virtually any industry dealing with cash, or a means by which to transfer value, will be reviewed by federal regulators to determine if there should be controls established to help thwart potential money-laundering abuses. In fact, there are rules in place for insurance companies[14] to submit suspicious activity reports (pending: SAR-IC FinCEN 108) because specific products, such as life insurance policies, annuity contracts, and other products with cash value or investment features, are at risk for exploitation by criminal elements. Simply put, policies can be paid for using dirty money, and once cashed out, they become legitimized funds in the form of an insurance check.

Table 5.1 BSA Forms Required by Government Regulations

ABBR:	*FORM REF:*	*FULL FORM NAME*
CTR-DI	FinCEN 104	Currency Transaction Report by Depository Institutions
CTR-C	FinCEN 103	Currency Transaction Report by Casinos and Card Clubs
SAR-DI	TD F 90-22.47	Suspicious Activity Report by Depository Institutions
SAR-SF	FinCEN 101	Suspicious Activity Report by Securities and Futures Industries
SAR-C	FinCEN 102	Suspicious Activity Report by Casinos and Card Clubs
SAR-MSB	FinCEN 109	Suspicious Activity Report by Money Services Business
CMIR	FinCEN 105	Report of International Transportation of Currency or Monetary Instruments
8300	IRS-8300	Cash over 10K Rcv'd in Trade/Business
FBAR	TD F 90-22.1	Foreign Bank Account Report
DEP	FinCEN 110	Designation of Exempt Person

[14] http://www.fincen.gov/news_room/nr/pdf/20051031.pdf.

Other industries subject to AML compliance include dealers in precious metals, stones, or jewels,[15] and certain antique dealers, but not industrial machinery or equipment businesses, pawnbrokers, or toll refiners.[16] As everyone knows, gems, precious stones, and jewels are very portable, hard to detect or track (easy to smuggle), high net worth assets, making them ideal for clandestine and illegal operations. In fact, diamonds have been linked to terrorist operations involving al Qaeda, and the more well-known "blood diamonds" are often used to finance military activities to procure arms and weapons as well as to support insurrections, conflicts, and wars.

There is even some consideration given to regulating telecommunication companies[17] under BSA laws because new technologies allow them to act as a money transfer service[18] using short message service (SMS) to transact funds. The phone value transfer service offered by many telecommunication companies in countries outside the United States is an ongoing concern for many governments[19] and is being addressed by enacting new laws, regulations, and processes. This type of service is also proved to be a cheaper, faster, and more reliable alternative to wire remitter and traditional banking services. It is very easy for someone to "charge up" an account with money and use the value transfer service to send money to other receivers. In fact, a number of retail outlets and store merchants are now accepting payments made from these types of value accounts.

Additionally, there has long been a concern about retail organizations and their gift cards, also referred to as stored value cards,[20] being used as an avenue to launder money. The cards can be purchased (and often reloaded) and used to make purchases or be cashed out. The more popular prepaid cards are offered through banking channels (e.g., Visa and American Express) and can be used at ATMs (automated teller

---

15 "Precious metal" means gold, silver, and the platinum group of metals, when it is at a level of purity of 0.500 (50 percent) or greater, singly, or in any combination—31 CFR §103.140(a)(3). "Precious stone" means inorganic substances that have a market-recognized gem level of quality, beauty, and rarity—31 CFR §103.140(a)(4). "Jewel" means organic substances that have a market-recognized gem level of quality, beauty, and rarity—31 CFR §103.140(a)(2). http://www.fincen.gov/statutes_regs/guidance/faq060305.pdf.

16 Businesses that export refined materials processed from imported raw materials; usually based on the recovery of scrap or waste metals that are cleaned to remove impurities and other contaminants and then recycled.

17 Matt Squire, "U.S. Falling Behind in Technology War with Money Launderers, State Department Says," *MoneyLaundering.com*, March 3, 2008.

18 "Kenyans to Transfer Money Using Cell Phones," *Reuters*, March 6, 2007, http://www.reuters.com/article/technologyNews/idUSL068377620070306.

19 John Forbes, "Effects of Cell Phones on Anti-Money Laundering/Combating Financial Terrorism (AML/CFT) Wire Remittance Operations," *Asian Development Bank*, March 2007, http://www.adb.org/Documents/Others/OGC-Toolkits/Anti-Money-Laundering/documents/Working-Paper-March2007.pdf.

20 http://www.ustreas.gov/offices/enforcement/pdf/mlta.pdf.

machines) to withdraw cash. Cards are easily transported, have defined value, are easily sold to other parties, and generally keep their owners/users anonymous.

The use of prepaid cards is common in the "unbankable" community where there are estimates of more than 80 million people using this form of digital currency with values already exceeding $113 billion (2007); however, it is also becoming a mainstream form of payment due to its ease of use and better security than, say, traditional checking accounts. In fact, large retailers such as 7-Eleven, Inc. recently began accepting[21] Visa ReadyLink™ at its 5,300 stores throughout the United States. Of course, all of this convenience and anonymity opens up new avenues to launder money. Recently it was reported[22] that prepaid cards were being used at some high-end escort businesses as a "preferred" method of payment, allowing the madam to easily collect the money from her clients and distribute the payments to her workers. These types of usage are becoming commonplace and will continue to expand as an alternative financial instrument as it becomes further accepted by the general populace and retail community.

More recently, there have been discussions regarding online auction houses[23] (e.g., trade-based, such as eBay, Amazon, et al.), an industry that is expected to exceed $65 billion by 2010[24] due to the limited controls and oversight, buyer/seller anonymity, and access to an international marketplace. Items sold in this fashion can be undervalued, overvalued, or may not even exist at all; thus, someone could sell a lump of coal for a million dollars, get paid with illegal funds (e.g., drug money), and technically justify the transaction. There is currently very little AML regulation or oversight in this type of market, although PayPal is technically registered as a money service business (MSB). There is still a lot of room for improvement in this market.

Other industries that are also being considered for AML compliance include real estate brokers and developers.[25] Recently, Canada[26] amended its laws that require new home builders and developers to have customer

---

[21] "7-Eleven, Inc. to Implement Visa ReadyLink™ in Its U.S. Stores," http://corporate.visa.com/md/nr/press683.jsp.

[22] Ben Levisohn, "Prepaid Cards: The Cleanup, New Industry Guidelines Aim to Crack Down on Money Laundering," *BusinessWeek*, February 21, 2008, http://www.businessweek.com/magazine/content/08_09/b4073032428110.htm.

[23] Brian Orsak, "Online Auctions, Beyond Scope of Financial Regulators, Pose Money Laundering Threat," www.moneylaundering.com, December 3, 2007.

[24] Carrie Johnson and Brian Tesch, "US Online Auction Sales, 2005 to 2010: A Forecast and Analysis of US Action Sales to Consumers," *Forrester Research*, October 4, 2005.

[25] http://www.fintrac.gc.ca/re-ed/real-eng.asp.

[26] Financial Transactions and Reports Analysis Centre (FinTRAC), http://www.fintrac.gc.ca/.

identification, record-keeping, and transaction-reporting programs.[27] Thus, the government proposes to require accountants, accounting firms, and real estate brokers or sales representatives, when engaged in real estate transactions, to verify the client's identity using a government-issued identity document. They will be required to take reasonable measures to obtain the name, address, and principal business or occupation of any third party on whose behalf a transaction is carried out, and record any beneficial owners of any entity involved as well as their relationship to the originator of the transaction. Canadian laws explicitly define terrorist property to mean any type of real or personal property, which includes any deed or instrument giving title or right to property, or giving right to money or goods. Additionally, Japan has started to require nonfinancial industries, such as real estate agencies, jewelry dealerships, and accountants to comply with the AML requirements.[28]

To be compliant with the BSA filing statutes in the United States, the filing institutions submit their reports via magnetic tape, on hard copy, or through electronic filing (e-file). For CTR forms, an institution has 15 days (25 days if filed electronically) following the date of the transaction to submit the report. These reports are uploaded directly into the Currency Banking and Retrieval System (CBRS) database located at the IRS Detroit Computing Center (DCC). Each document in CBRS is assigned a unique document control number (DCN), which provides some basic description about the report. As shown in Figure 5.2, the DCN consists of 14 numbers banded into groups to convey information about the report.

The first four numbers define the year the report was entered into the system. This can sometimes cause a little confusion because a 2007 DCN might describe transactions that occurred in 2006 because the year reflects when the report is received by the government and recorded into CBRS. The next three numbers represent the Julian date (day) of the

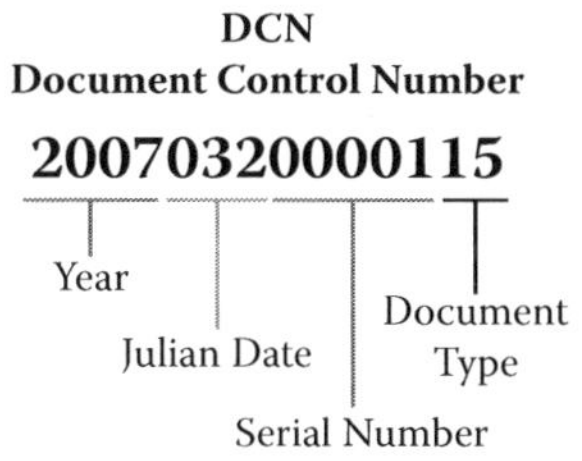

Figure 5.2 Structure of a document control number.

[27] Matt Squire, "Canada Expands Anti-Money Laundering Rules to Cover Real Estate, Gambling Industries," *MoneyLaundering.com,* February 15, 2007.

[28] Brian Moore, "Japan Calls on Non-Financial Sectors to Adopt AML Procedures by March 1," *MoneyLaundering.com*, February 25, 2008.

report, which simply defines the number of days from the beginning of year when the report was filed. For example, a Julian value of 032 corresponds to February 1st and a Julian value of 334 is November 30th (335 in a leap year). The next five numbers are a serial number that uniquely identifies each filing for that particular day. The final two numbers define the form that was submitted. Table 5.2 defines how these numbers are used.

Associated with these forms is a considerable amount of detail stored in the database. Simply reviewing any form will define the type of information collected, which includes the name of the filing organization (e.g., bank, casino, car dealership, etc.), contact information, related dates, transaction amounts, law enforcement referrals, and, where required, detailed descriptions of the nature of the transaction. Every filing is unique and its information represents a piece of a larger puzzle that must be put together—with potentially thousands of pieces.

Depending on the BSA form being reviewed, the specific detail may include the names of the *Subjects* involved (e.g., senders, receivers, payers, payees, etc.) and any other identifying data including *Addresses, Accounts, Phones, SSNs,* and *ID Numbers* (e.g., alien registration, driver's licenses, passports, etc.). Figure 5.3 is representative of data derived from BSA data that would be created for an analytical data model.

A single financial transaction can often be associated with multiple *Subjects* which, in turn, can be connected to multiple *Addresses, ID Numbers, Accounts,* and *Phones.* A *Subject* listed on any one particular

Table 5.2 Definition of the Final Two DCN Numbers

FORM	*NUMBERS*
SAR	10, 11, 13, 14, 15
SARM	16, 17
SARS	18, 19
EXEMPT	20, 21, 22, 23, 24
RMSB	25
CTR	30, 31, 32, 33, 34, 35
CASINO	40, 41, 42
SARC	45, 46
8300	50
FBAR	60
CMIR	70
EXCISE	80
FCF	90

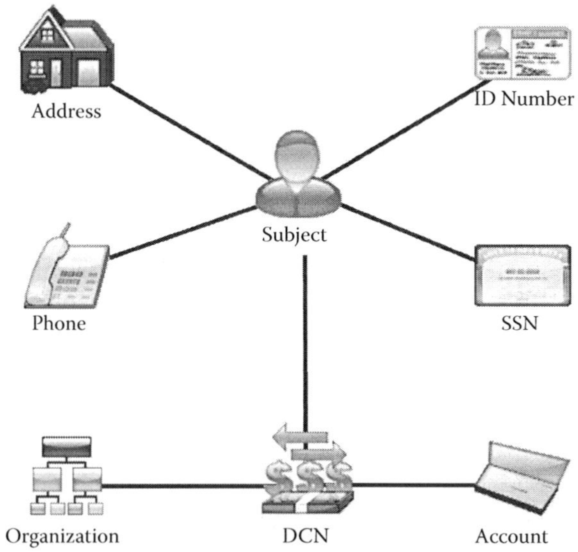

Figure 5.3 Sample analytical data model derived from a BSA report.

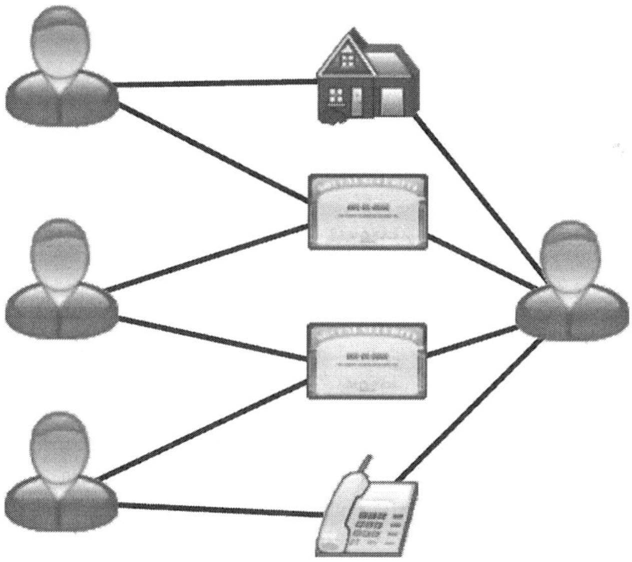

Figure 5.4 Unexpected commonality.

report is usually not very interesting in isolation; however, when the same or similar information begins to appear on different forms, investigators want to know when certain behaviors are being exhibited.

One such pattern is based on ***unexpected commonality,*** where certain entities should never be shared among different *Subjects*. In Figure 5.4, there are a number of different entities with certain common connections that should raise immediate concern. In this case, the *SSNs* are being used by multiple *Subjects* and there are also *Subjects* using multiple *SSNs*. These kinds of situations most often occur because of typos, misspellings, and other poor data collection controls; however, they may also indicate a possible misrepresentation or intentional falsification of data on the forms as a means of avoidance.

In other examples, there can be too much commonality among the *Subjects*. Many patterns are exposed due to repeated behaviors and too many entities in common may indicate some type of organized behavior. In Figure 5.5, two *Subjects* are connected through eight different accounts. Under normal circumstances, one might expect to see people sharing a checking and/or savings account or some other financial instrument, but when the frequency of commonality exceeds a reasonable threshold, it becomes questionable and should be reviewed in more detail. In this case, the *Subjects* might be perpetrating the same crime at different financial intuitions, which is why there are so

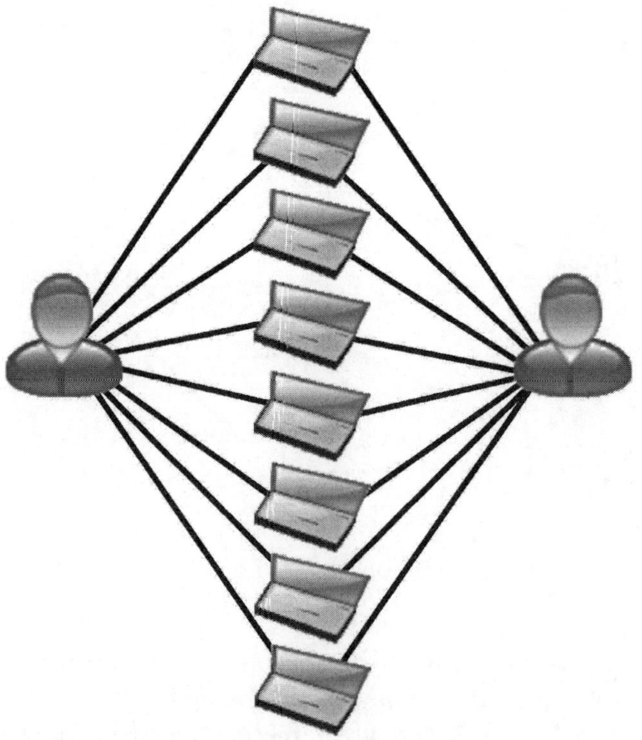

Figure 5.5 Too much commonality.

many accounts (i.e., a different account is submitted by each financial institution).

Finally, other patterns will emerge as accumulated through their individual behaviors. Each unique transaction or filing may look legitimate, but when taken collectively and shown all together, the large number of discrete actions forms the basis for the larger pattern. In Figure 5.6, a single *Subject* is connected through individual transactions to seven other *Subjects*, indicating that the primary target may be trying to avoid detection by diluting the frequency of association with other persons. This type of pattern may reveal human-smuggling organizations, bookies/gambling operations, and even terrorist-financing activities.

Over a period of time, the information derived from these forms becomes cumulative and starts to tie together different operations, groups, and networks cooperating to launder money, as shown in Figure 5.7. Often, people committing financial crimes try to vary the way their personal data is represented and typically will use name variations, alternative spellings, and other misleading information. Detecting this is fairly routine with the support of advanced analytical tools. Following are examples showing different configurations and interpretations of data

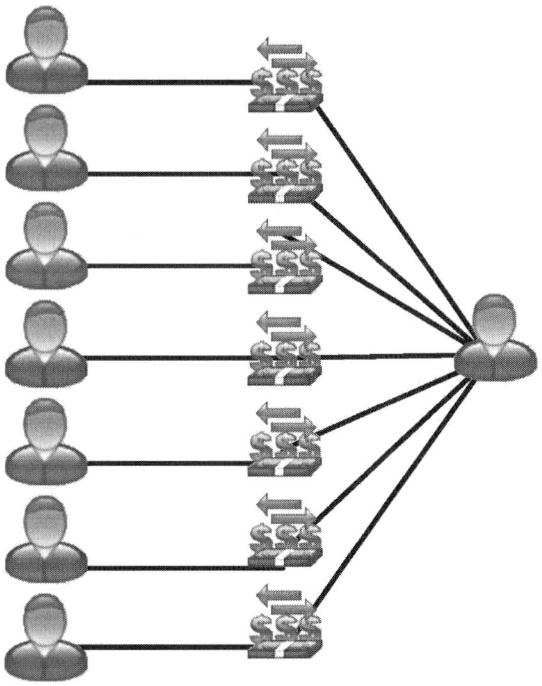

Figure 5.6 Accumulated behaviors.

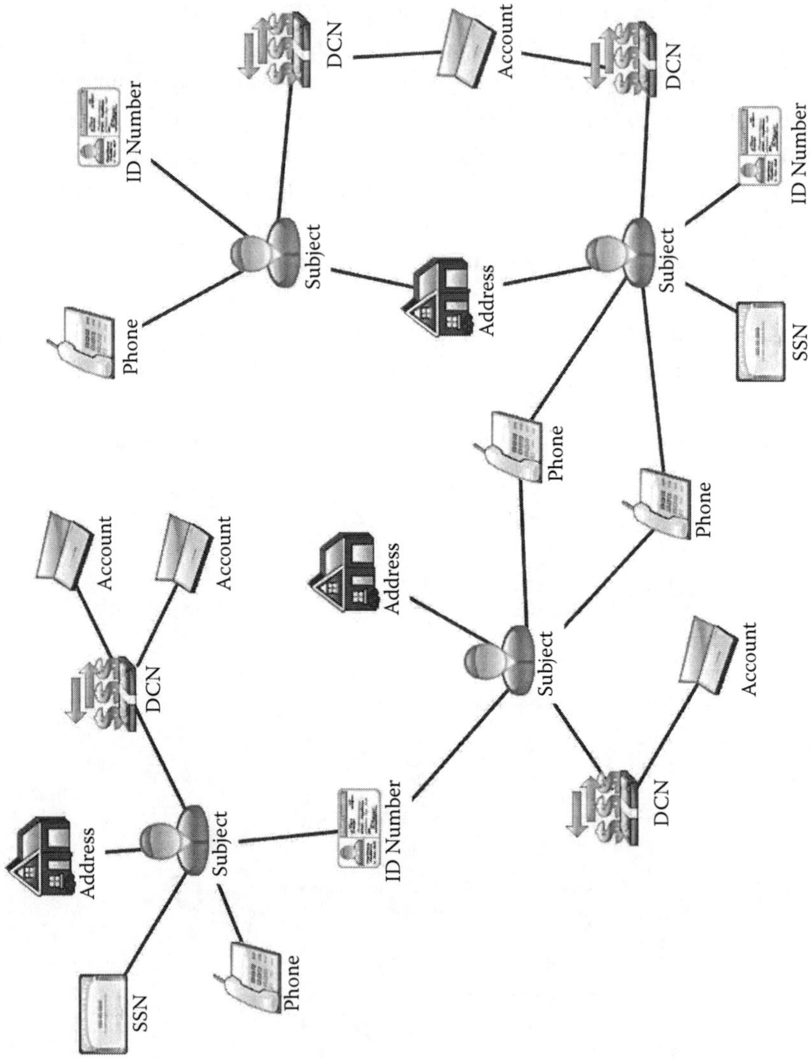

Figure 5.7 Connections among BSA data elements.

that indicate "well qualified" patterns from which to pursue more detailed analyses and/or investigations.

Suspicious Activity Reports

In April 1996, SARs were introduced as a core filing requirement for the banking community. In a nutshell, financial institutions are required to submit SARs within 30 calendar days after the date of initial detection of transactions[29] aggregating $5,000 or more if the bank knows, suspects, or has reason to suspect that the transaction:

- Involves funds from illegal activities or is conducted to hide illicit funds or assets in a plan to violate or evade any law or regulation or to avoid transaction reporting requirements under federal law.
- Is designed to evade any of the BSA regulations.
- Has no business or apparent lawful purpose or is not the sort in which the customer would normally be expected to engage, and the bank knows of no reasonable explanation for the transaction after examining available facts, including the background and transaction purpose.

The interpretation of these regulations is somewhat ad hoc and extremely subjective. There is a lot of speculation around determining what is truly considered "suspicious" with respect to a financial transaction. Many financial institutions have implemented a number of AML systems and internal controls[30] to help assess their risks and try to minimize their exposure to fraud, terrorist financing, money laundering, and noncompliance. Many of these systems rank their results based on a simple scoring factor. Certain official references[31] provide examples of questionable behaviors and activities that should be considered for filing a SAR, including:

- Deposits followed by lump-sum wire transfers.
- International wire transfers to known money-laundering havens.
- Use of loan proceeds in a manner inconsistent with the stated loan purpose.

[29] To include any deposit, withdrawal, transfer between accounts, exchange of currency, loan, extension of credit, or purchase or sale of any stock, bond, certificate of deposit, or other monetary instrument or investment security, or any other payment, transfer, or delivery by, through, or to a financial institution.

[30] Bank Secrecy Act Anti-Money Laundering Examination Manual, Federal Financial Institutions Examination Council, July 2005.

[31] Bank Secrecy Act/Anti-Money Laundering, Comptroller's Handbook, Consumers Compliance Examination, September 2000.

- Deposits of money wrapped in currency straps stamped by other banks.
- Substantial deposits using numerous $50 and $100 bills.
- Transfers routed through multiple foreign or domestic banks.
- Deposits or wire transfers with large, rounded dollar amounts.
- A business or new customer asks to be exempted.
- Residence is outside of the bank's immediate service area.
- Purchases numerous money orders, traveler's checks, or cashier's checks.
- Transfers money between numerous business accounts.
- Deposits of sequentially numbered money orders.
- Frequent exchanges of small dollar denominations for larger denominations.
- Casinos identifying Large Buy-Ins with Minimal Play (see sidebar).

Casino Pattern

In the gaming industry, which is also regulated by BSA statutes, casinos must submit CTRs (referred to as CTR-C) when players are involved with transactions over $10,000, and they are also required to submit SARs[32] (referred to as SAR-C) for any kind of questionable behavior. The types of activities experienced by casinos that trigger a SAR run the gamut, including people refusing to give their names or provide proper identification, people trying to commit frauds against the casino (e.g., bad checks), or people who appear to be involved in questionable sources of money (e.g., wire transfers to/from known money-laundering havens). There is, however, one well-defined pattern that almost automatically results in the casino's submission of a SAR, called *Large Buy-In with Minimal Play.*

This pattern occurs when the total buy-in (the amount of money transacted at the cage or table in exchange for chips) is greater than or equal to $5,000,[33] the length of play is less than 30 minutes, and the amount won or lost is less than 5 percent of the buy-in or the average bet is less than 2 percent of the buy-in. Thus, if someone arrives at a casino, exchanges $25,000 in cash for chips, goes to the blackjack table and bets $100 each hand, and then decides to close out after 20 minutes of play, they will most likely have a SAR filed on them for uncharacteristic player behavior. Of course, the actual parameters and thresholds can vary among the individual casinos.

[32] Casinos have 30 calendar days to file a SAR-C after the date of initial detection of any suspicious transaction.

[33] Some casinos use a $3,000 threshold for the buy-in amount.

Similar to the land border targeting system previously discussed, there are both physical and logical (e.g., data) indicators that can be spotted. Obviously, the physical indicators must be observed by bank personnel (e.g., the tellers, loan officers, etc.) and brought to the attention of the compliance officers. The logical indicators can be detected within the databases maintained by the bank and the AML systems used to discover and expose those high-risk activities. Whichever way, once a financial institution determines there is a questionable situation, a SAR can be filed with the appropriate authorities. There are really no hard-and-fast rules to follow, but rather, only the procedures enacted by the financial institutions and the extent to which their KYC (Know Your Customer) programs are implemented. Eventually, all of the SARs are collected and reviewed by an FIU.

Now the real work begins. The FIU must sift through the collective volume of SARs filed by all the regulated financial institutions—often numbering in the hundreds of thousands or millions. Because each report has already been deemed "suspicious," it is now up to the FIU to determine which ones are "most" suspicious—not unlike finding a needle in a stack of hay, but actually more similar to finding a needle in a stack of needles. The following discussions represent the kinds of incidents encountered by FIUs around the world on a daily basis. The interpretation of these situations and circumstances does not represent any official agency policy, procedure, or process; rather, there can be different meanings, conclusions, and actions taken based on the scenarios presented and the laws enacted within the countries where the violations takes place.

Structuring Transactions

Many people are aware that governments throughout the world require that certain types of information be reported when large quantities of cash are moved into or out of financial institutions (e.g., banks, savings and loans, credit unions, etc.). This is somewhat unsettling to many people because they believe the government is behaving like "big brother" and is using the data to directly track their assets or identify unreported money for additional income taxes or even hiding assets due to a pending divorce. Many people simply don't want a record of the transaction to be documented and sent to the government.

Often, people conducting high-value financial transactions will ask the bank teller, "What is the dollar amount required to file a report with the government?" In the United States, the response is that a Cash Transaction Report (CTR; IRS Form 4789/FinCEN Form 104) is required to be filed for any amounts cumulatively exceeding $10,000 for a single day. Once informed, customers often lower the amount of the transaction to less than $10,000.

Generally, the new amounts deposited or withdrawn reflect values such as $9,900, $9,800, or $9,500. However, once the change in amount is made, the financial institution is obligated to file a SAR (TD F 90-22.47), without notifying the customer of this fact. The reason for this is that "structuring" deposits or withdrawals to avoid detection is a money-laundering technique and a violation of federal law, regardless of the intention.[34] Structuring financial transactions to avoid filing requirements is a form of money laundering and subject to penalties and forfeitures under current laws and regulations. In fact, many of the SAR submissions are based on people behaving in this fashion, and this example reflects such a case.

The specific *Subject* was identified based on her occupation as a *dentist* along with a high frequency of SAR filings. This type of occupation tends not to be a high-cash business because most payment is made through checks, credit cards, or via insurance claims. There are always exceptions to the norm; for example, a dentist might serve an unbanked community (e.g., in remote country settings or in poorer, urban neighborhoods), but those conditions do not apply in this scenario.

The immediate network of SAR transactions on which the *Subject* was reported is shown in Figure 5.8. The diagram depicts 10 individual SARs that are split into different columns based on their filing year. The first column shows four SAR filings in 2006 and the second column shows six filings in 2007. The specific dates for her SAR filings are somewhat sporadic, generally not reflecting a legitimate or regular business practice[35] as defined by the *Subject's* stated occupation. Also shown in the diagram is a single account used for all of these SAR transactions.

Each SAR supports a "narrative," which represents a detailed description, provided by the financial institution, describing the nature of the suspicious activity. For this *Subject,* each SAR narrative similarly stated the following:

> This customer has been previously reported for making large cash withdrawals just under the CTR reporting limit. This is unusual activity and may imply that the customer is attempting to avoid CTR filing requirements. The bank reported that the customer intended to make a cash withdrawal for over $10,000; however, once informed of the CTR filing requirements, the customer lowered the amount to below $10,000.

---

[34] This type of activity contributed to the high-profile downfall of New York Governor Elliot Spitzer in March 2008 when his payments to a front company for an adult escort business were deemed suspicious because they were being structured to avoid detection (http://www.thesmokinggun.com/archive/years/2008/0310082spitzer1.html).

[35] There would be a general pattern based on weekly, monthly, or quarterly filings and the amounts of the transactions would be more consistent.

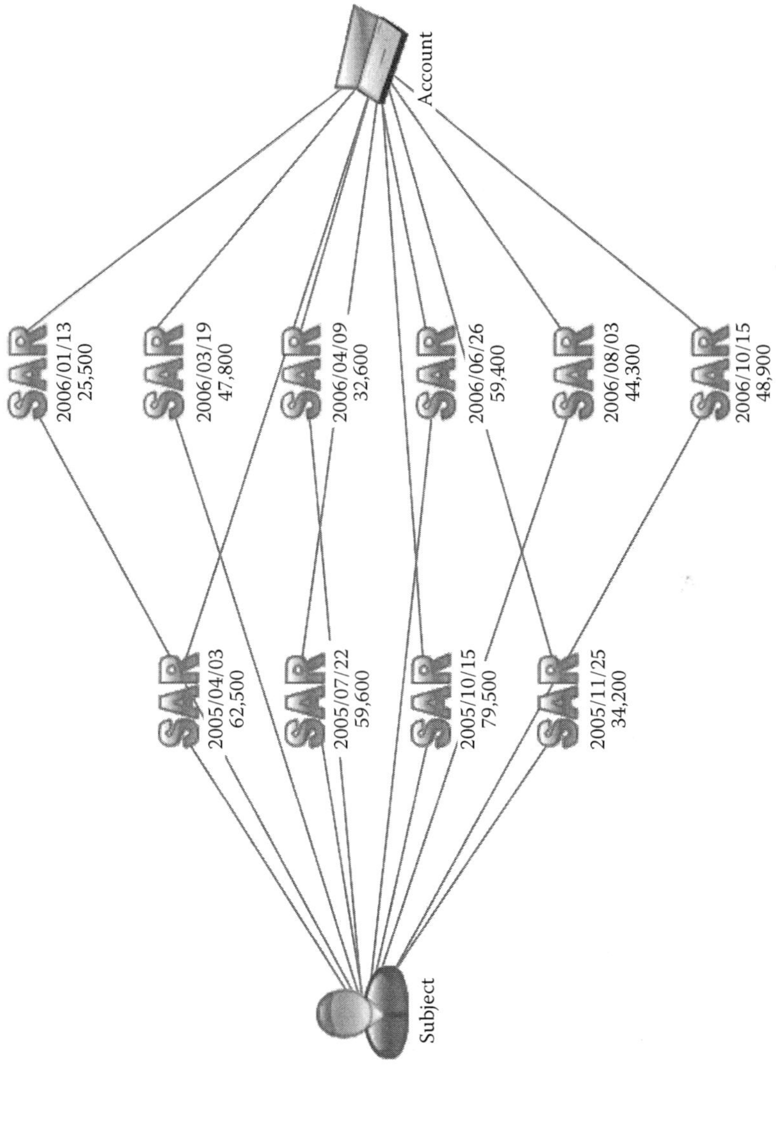

Figure 5.8 Structured SAR transactions for subject.

As was previously discussed, this type of behavior is illegal and constitutes "structuring" on behalf of the *Subject*. At this point in the analysis, additional information from the SARs is presented in the diagram, as shown in Figure 5.9, including *Addresses, Phones,* and *SSNs*.

The thicker lines to each of these objects indicate they were routinely referenced in each of the *SARs*. The fact that these objects, along with the *Account,* have been consistently represented tells investigators that she is not actively trying to "cover her tracks" by varying spellings or information provided to the bank. Keep in mind that the *Subject* does not know that these *SARs* are being filed on her, and the consistency can be largely attributed to the bank's reporting procedures. The next diagram, shown in Figure 5.10, brings in other entities connected to the *Addresses, Phones,* and *SSNs*.

Only a single object is returned—an additional *Subject*. What investigators discover is that this new *Subject* is actually an organization that has the name of the medical practice for this doctor. The investigators interactively change the icon to an *Organization* to more accurately convey the contents of the analysis. At this point, the investigators know that additional *SARs* will be exposed[36] once the links to the *Organization* are expanded.

As shown in Figure 5.11, there are three additional *SARs,* filed in 2007, using the same *Account* connected to the other *SARs*. The investigators determine that this change in behavior is a result of the *Subject* trying to layer her transactions through the medical practice so her activities appear more legitimate and, potentially, less "exposed" to government observations. Needless to say, these types of situations provide the investigators and analysts more insight to their targets.

Additional searches in the SAR database do not reveal any more data for any of these objects. However, as shown in Figure 5.12, the investigators check the CTR database and discover a single transaction that occurred in the year 2004. It is likely this was the event that "tipped" her off that the government required forms to be filed for amounts exceeding $10,000. From that point forward, all of her financial transactions were reported as SARs.

This multistep, multisource analysis clearly shows how people try to structure their transactions to avoid CTR filing requirements. If large volumes of cash are derived legitimately (e.g., from restaurants, bars, churches, etc.), there should be no concern about depositing or

[36] All primary entities, such as *Subjects* or *Organizations,* are always connected to transactions (e.g., *SARs*). Properly represented data will never produce a *Subject* or *Organization* (or *Account*) without a corresponding *SAR*. Therefore, expanding the *Organization* in this diagram will produce at least one *SAR* and, most likely, multiple *SARs* due to the thickness of the linkages connecting the *Organization* to the *Address, Phone,* and *SSN*.

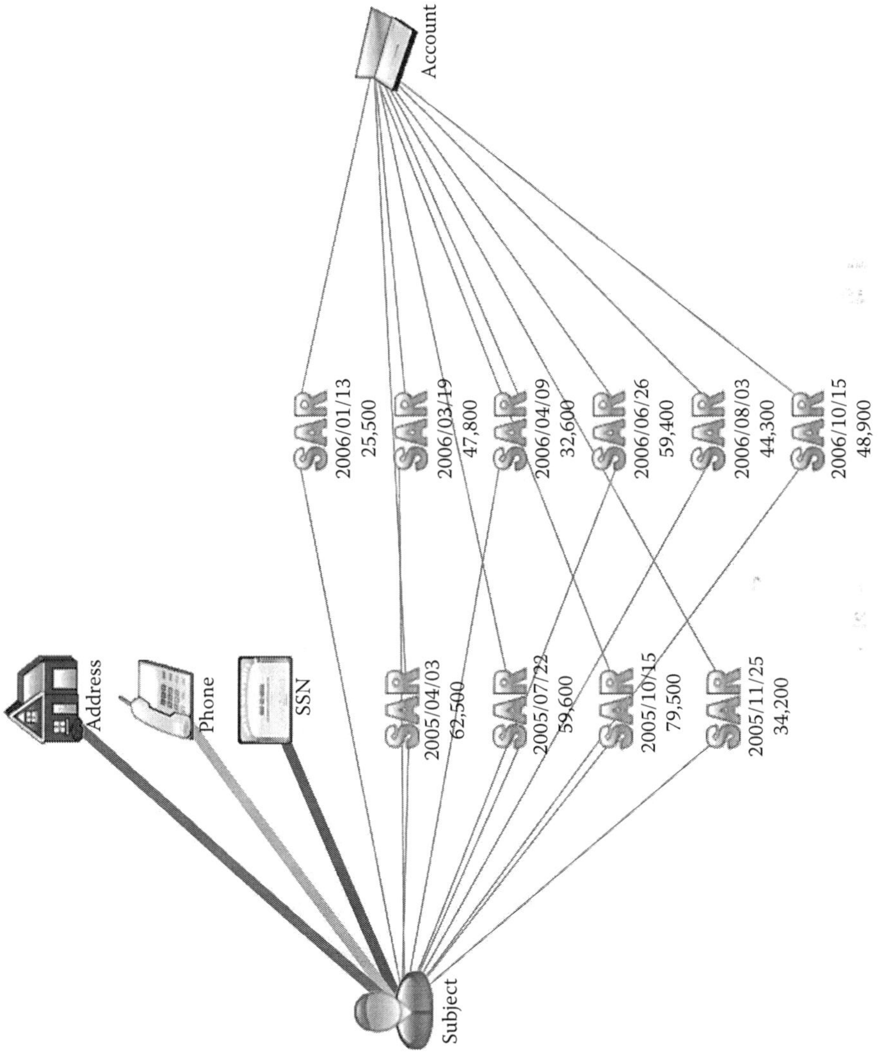

Figure 5.9 Structuring network expanded.

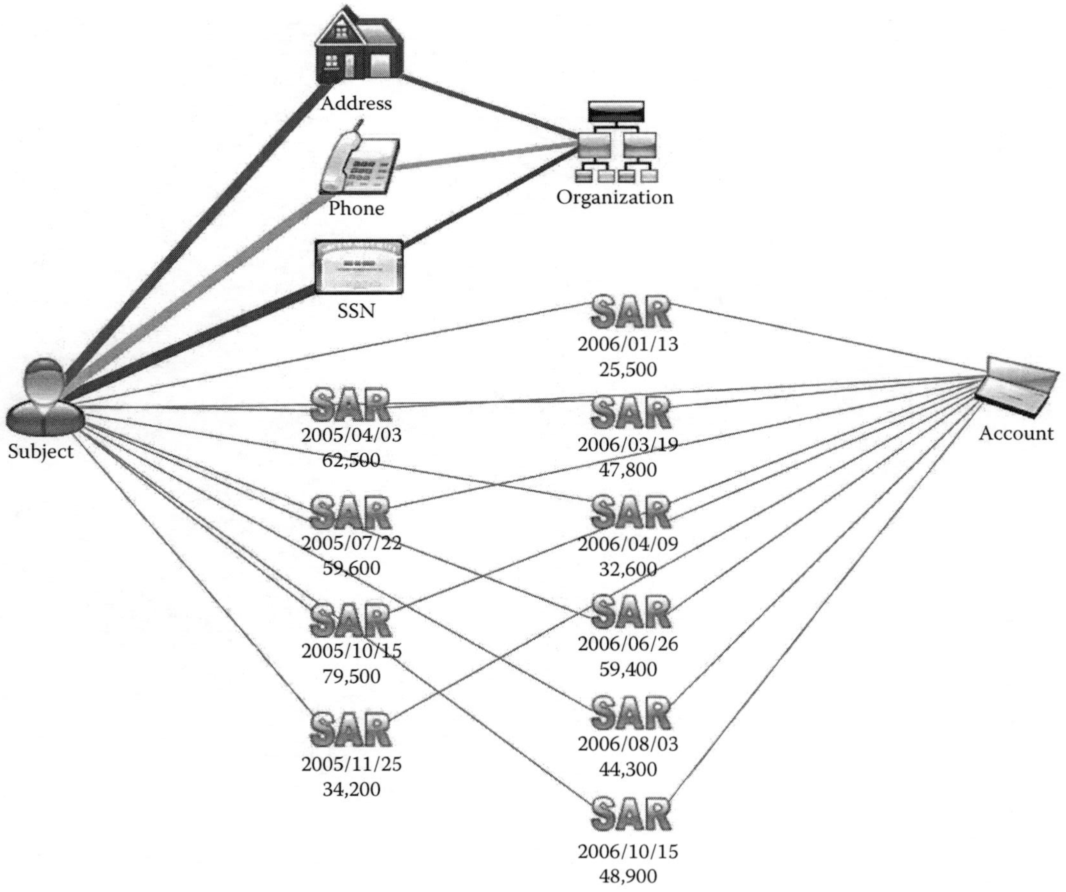

Figure 5.10 Introducing an organization into the structuring network.

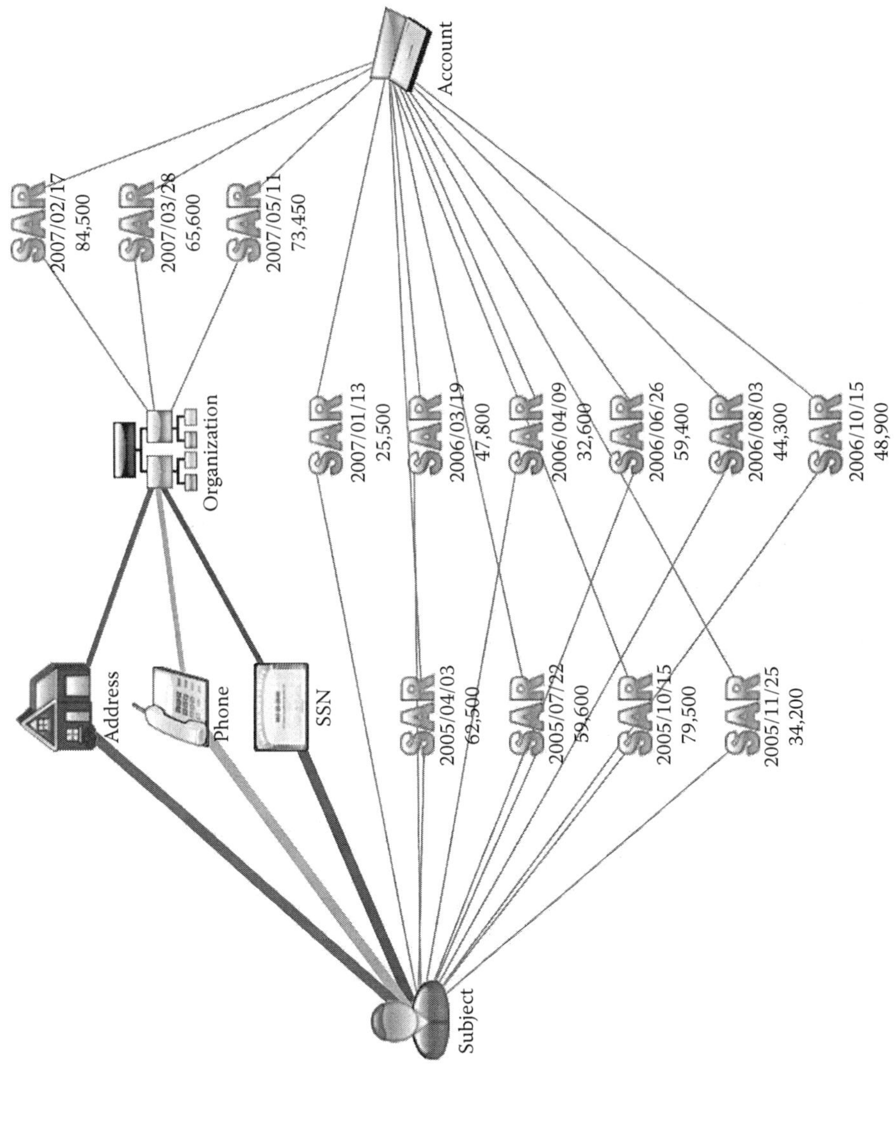

Figure 5.11 Additional SAR transactions show more structuring.

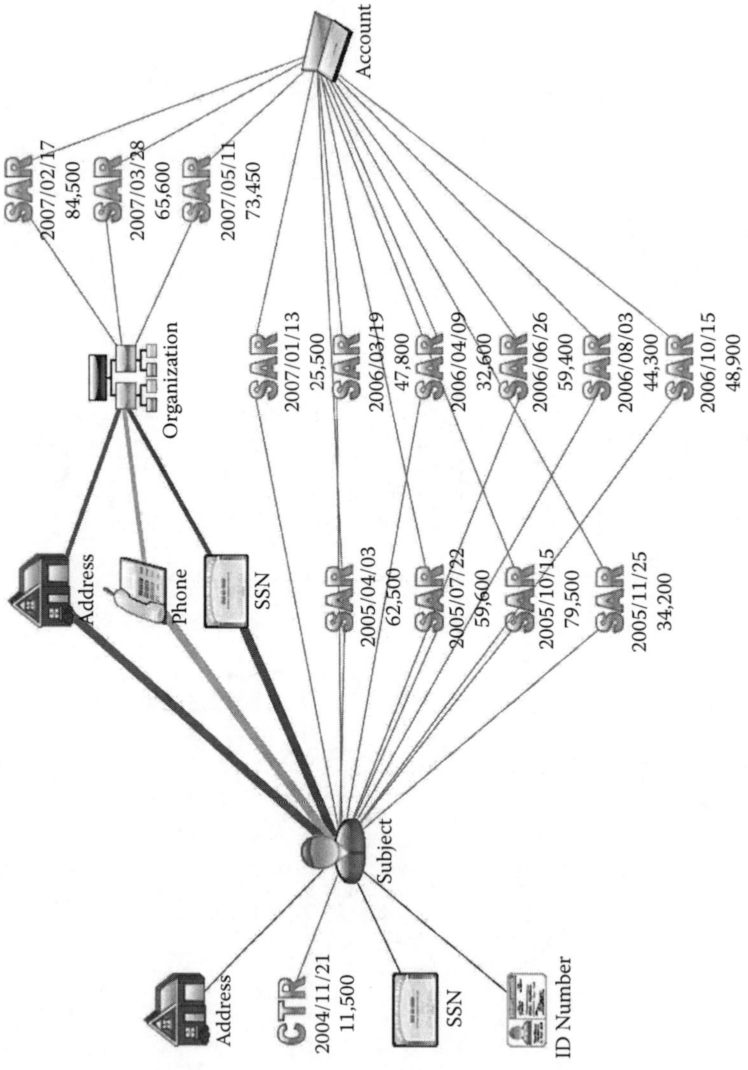

Figure 5.12 A CTR transaction in the network.

withdrawing the money. The CTR forms are generally not currently used for tax purposes or any other government oversight other than to help detect and expose money-laundering activities. Structuring transactions, providing false information, or trying to avoid CTR filings will result in SAR filings, which are highly scrutinized by governments throughout the world.

Bust-Out Schemes

This pattern is based on the submission of SARs filed by banks and financial institutions based on a "bust-out scheme" pertaining to credit cards and checks. Although a bust-out scheme is really more of a fraud than a true money-laundering[37] operation, it still has major implications for the financial sectors and represents unlawful activity. The stolen money can be used by radical factions (e.g., financing for terrorist groups) or by organized crime rings. Often, the FBI, Secret Service, and state-level law enforcement agencies cover these types of crimes.[38]

A bust-out scheme is generally defined[39] as a situation where a corrupt merchant is involved with processing unauthorized credit cards. A business is set up to process credit cards and a merchant account is established with the bank. Initially everything appears fine—cards are being processed, payment is being made, and there is nothing to question about the legitimacy of the operation. After a period of time has passed, and the merchant shows that they are fairly consistent and reliable in their card processing and the bank has established a track record for making payments to cover the charges, the trouble starts.

Basically, the merchant obtains credit card numbers that are either stolen or provided by other individuals involved in the scheme, who know they are not "liable" for any unauthorized charges made on the cards. The merchant quickly maxes out the cards with fictitious charges. Unaware that the outstanding charges are bogus due to the grace periods that are given to card holders to make payments, the credit card (bank) transfers the funds to the merchant's account once the transaction is authorized. After some time, the card holders see the fraudulent charges appear on their statements and then initiate a dispute to have them removed. Because

[37] "FinCEN's SARs Assist in Bankruptcy Bust-Out Scheme Investigation," http://www.fincen.gov/law_enforcement/ss/html/085.html.

[38] "The FBI's Greed Is '"Busting Out"' All Over: Credit Schemes Lead to Guilty Pleas," http://www.fbi.gov/page2/oct03/bust102003.htm.

[39] Mary Beth Guard, "What Are Bust Out Schemes?" *Bankers Online,* November 4, 2002, http://www.bankersonline.com/security/gurus_sec110402a.html.

they are unauthorized charges, the merchant is then hit up with "charge-backs," which are basically debits against their account for these disputed amounts. Many times the merchant will declare bankruptcy or simply "disappear" to avoid paying back the money collected.

Sometimes this happens to a legitimate business—when a "broker" requests use of a merchant's account to process charges for special deals they have arranged and promises to pay a premium fee (e.g., 10 percent or 25 percent of the charges). The fraudulent charges are made to the credit cards, the merchant takes its 25 percent cut, and then passes the remaining money to the broker. At face value, it seems like a decent deal for the merchant; however, when the bank catches improper charges, they are charged back to the merchant to re-collect the full amount. The merchant is ultimately liable for these charges and the broker is nowhere to be found. The merchant paid the broker their money and now is also responsible for the charge-backs—a double whammy. There are many variations to participating in the bust-out scheme, including using family members, targeting certain ethnic groups, or through blatant criminal activities.

In this example, the data extracted was based on those SSNs that appeared in SARs filed in multiple states (based on the branch location of the filing institution). This approach was based on the knowledge that the SSNs utilized by corrupt merchants tend to be used in multiple schemes because the credit scores are good (prefraud). Thus, they can move around very quickly and set up similar bust-out operations at different banks. For this analysis, the data extracted from the system was based on the same SSN being used at financial institutions in at least six different states. There are several dozen occurrences of this pattern in the SAR database, each one containing an explicit bust-out scheme and often extended to a number of other *SARs, Addresses,* and *Suspects.*

The results returned from the query contained some typical "garbage" results—specifically the use of a NULL value for the SSN, which occurred in 74 different states.[40] The second-largest occurrence reflected an SSN value of 999999999, which was therefore discarded. The next value, with a count of nine unique states, is shown in Figure 5.13. Although there are 11 SARs shown in the diagram, they actually represent 7 distinct states because DE (Delaware) is repeated in 2 of the SARs and 3 have a nonstate value; the rest include NY (New York), GA (Georgia), AZ (Arizona), NV (Nevada), MI (Michigan), and CA (California).

The labels show various violation types including check kiting, check fraud, and credit card fraud. Notice that the dates for each of these

[40] As with all data sources, not all values are entered properly into their respective fields and the number of different state abbreviations in this data set, for the defined parameters, indicates there are other problems with the quality of the source data.

Figure 5.13 Bust-out scheme using 11 SARs.

transactions occur over a very short time period, which corresponds to a full billing cycle for the bank to process the credit card charges. There is approximately $250,000 worth of fraud depicted in these 11 SARs. There is a good chance there are additional banks that this *Subject* has defrauded where a SAR may not have been filed; it depends on the policies of the filing institution and how they deal with these types of situations.

In Figure 5.14, the SARs are expanded one level to show the primary *Subject* associated with each transaction. The names of the two *Subjects* shown in the figure are basically the same with some minor spelling variation and are treated as a single target. Additionally, the banks reporting these SARs were each affiliated with several credit card companies as reflected in the account numbers presented—indicating that this was not a localized bust-out scheme.

Expanding the network (not shown) an additional level reveals the SSN originally used to expose this bust-out scheme and there is a very large fan-out, with connections to almost 50 additional SARs. The network was further expanded to reveal that each of the SARs was connected to other *Subjects* and *Accounts,* indicating this is a very extensive bust-out scheme. One interesting observation is that all of the *Subjects* displayed in this level have similar ethnic names. The SAR narratives consistently discuss bounced checks, insufficient funds, and other nonpayments.

The next entry in the original query results, shown in Figure 5.15, represents a bust-out scheme that occurred in eight states: DE (Delaware), UT (Utah), AZ (Arizona), CA (California), OH (Ohio), KY (Kentucky), NV (Nevada), and WI (Wisconsin), represented by each of the unique SARs.

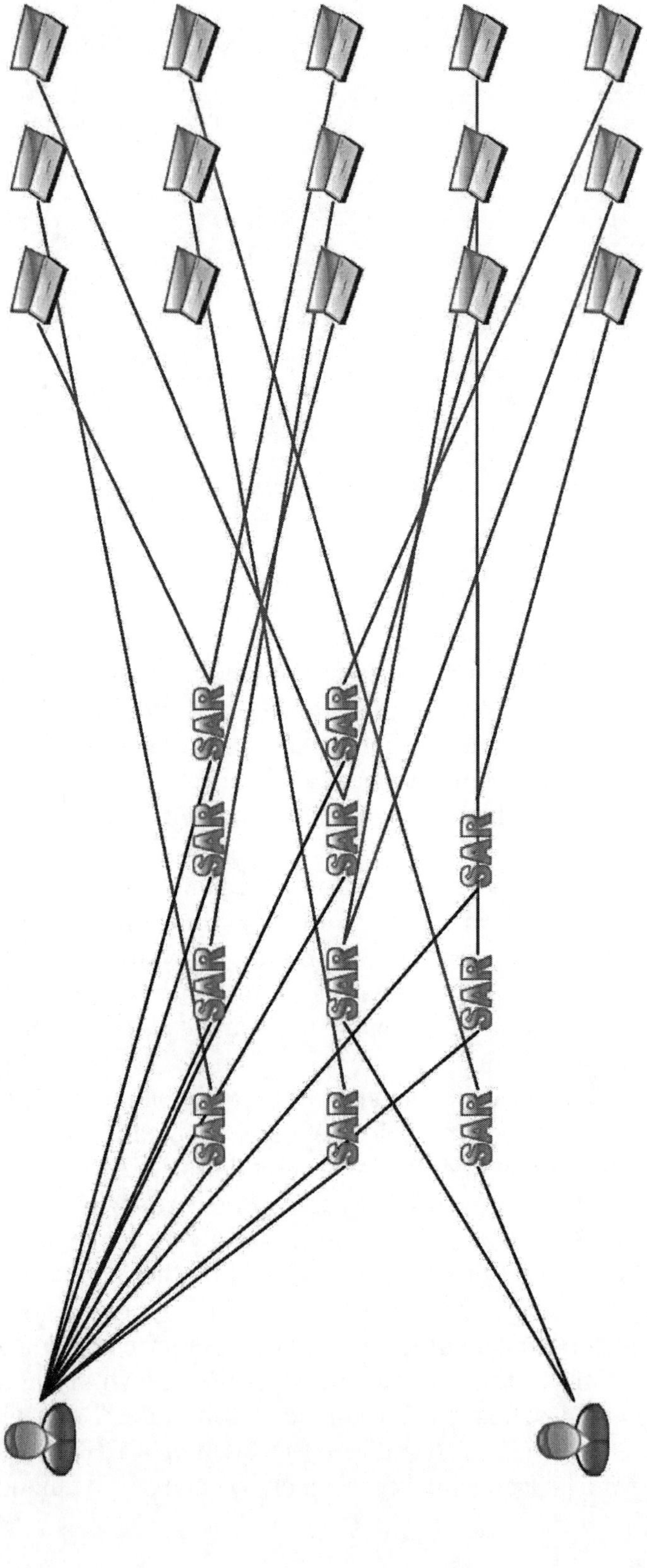

Figure 5.14 Next level of bust-out scheme.

Figure 5.15 Another bust-out scheme pattern.

The filing dates are fairly close, indicating the same type of nonpayment period as seen in the last example. The individual dollar amounts tend to vary quite a bit, but adds up to almost $150,000.

Expanding the network several levels reveals that this pattern is structurally identical to the previous example. Again, the dates reflect that the frauds occur over a very short time period (a single billing cycle). Considering that each SAR is submitted from a separate financial institution, the collective behavior clearly shows the bust-out pattern. However, the individual banks have no knowledge of the other banks involved in the scheme; however, it is fairly easy to spot at a federal level.

Unfortunately, these types of events net their operators some quick money and impact the rest of the financial industry through increased fees, premiums, and other operational inconsistencies. Getting a better handle on the indicators of the pattern can help banks expose the scheme earlier to minimize losses. Additionally, it can help law enforcement pursue and prosecute these schemes with greater success.

A Consumer Bust-Out Scheme

Another example that exhibits a pattern similar to a bust-out scheme is also a form of credit card fraud, mixed in with some check kiting. The example shown in Figure 5.16 was identified when the *SSN* for the *Subject* appeared in multiple SAR reports, filed by at least five different financial institutions. It is important to note that each institution has been compromised with some type of fraud and each files a SAR report based on the perceived wrongdoing of the *Subject*. What is not known by any institution is that the *Subject* is also defrauding other institutions. This pattern can only be seen at a federal/national level because of the filings of multiple institutions.

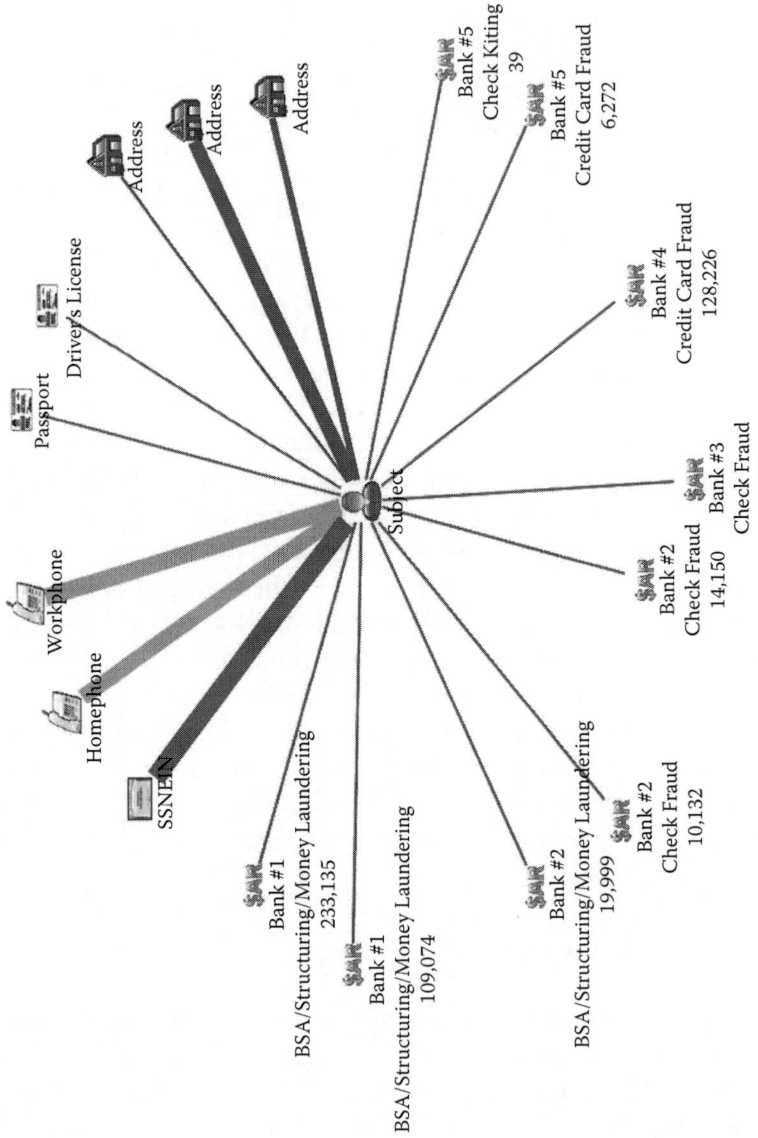

Figure 5.16 Consumer bust-out scheme across multiple institutions.

In the diagram, the transactions are arranged according to which financial institution submitted the SAR. One of the institutions cited that the *Subject* applied for multiple credit cards at a department store where they offer instant credit. In this case, the *Subject* opened up four accounts with three of the cards at a single store, each time providing consistent information regarding his *Address, Phone,* and *SSN*. He ran up the charges on the accounts through purchases and cash advances and then paid with a bad check (nonsufficient funds). This behavior is similar to the other SARs filed and differs from a merchant bust-out scheme because it is being done at the consumer level. Nevertheless, it is still costly for the intuitions and the amount of loss across the nine SARs exceeds $500,000 over approximately a six-month period.

The information provided in the diagram is fairly consistent with this type of situation. Surprisingly, the name, which is Middle Eastern, was consistently represented[41] along with the date of birth (not shown). Based on the link thickness, it can be quickly verified that the *SSN* and *Phones* (home and work) were also accurately provided to each of the filing institutions. Even though there are three unique *Addresses* in the diagram, they all represent the same location, which is an apartment in a large metropolitan city (this type of variation is expected, especially with five different filing institutions submitting data). The only item that stands out is the use of both a driver's license and a passport. The passport confirms the Middle Eastern origins of the *Subject* and the driver's license is verified based on the address provided.

Busting and Kiting

There are many examples of these types of schemes across the world. What works well in one country is often refined and emulated in other countries. In this next example, the pattern is basically the same, but some of the conditions and factors surrounding the data are a bit different. Again, the initial parameters used to identify the dataset were based on the SSN being used at multiple financial institutions. As shown in Figure 5.17, there are eight SAR filings reported on a single SSN and each of the SARs was filed by a different bank with the total amount exceeding $2.25 million. All of these activities occurred over a two-month period.

[41] Often, foreign names entered into these types of data sources tend to have an inordinate amount of variation in their spelling, ordering (first/last), and format (spaces/dashes).

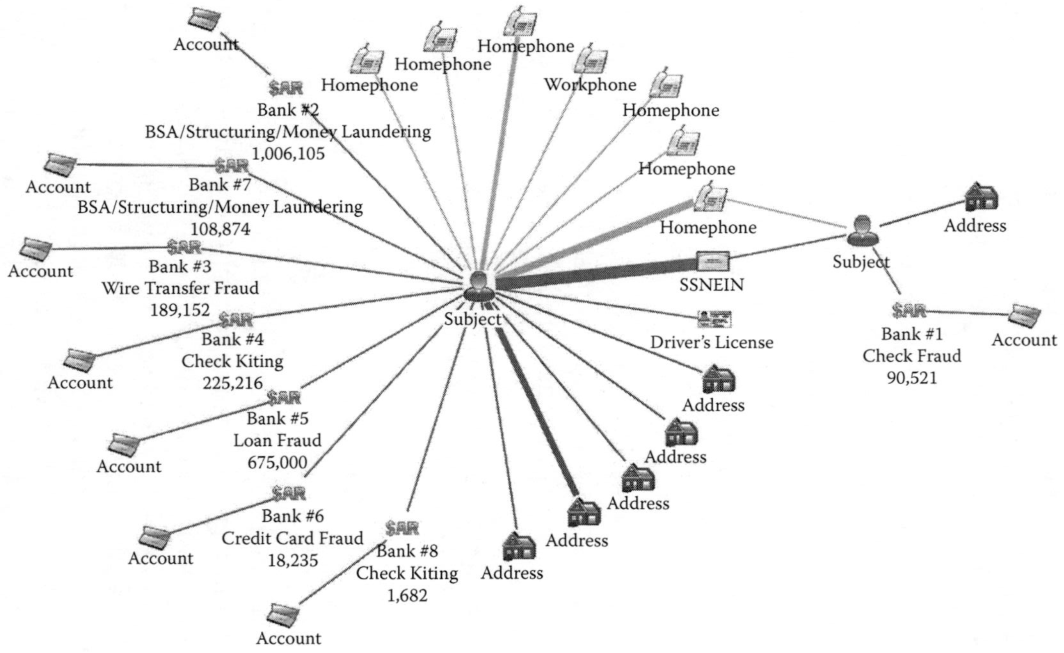

Figure 5.17 High-value busting and kiting.

The two *Subjects* listed are determined to be the same based on the spelling of their names and the degree of commonality shared between them. In terms of the six *Addresses* displayed, three are the same, which means a total of four different addresses were used by the *Subject* when establishing his accounts. The thicker link to one specific address shows it was used in at least three of the SAR filings. Upon reviewing the *Phone*s, the diagram shows almost a one-to-one mapping to the *SAR* objects. A more in-depth examination of some of these numbers show they map back to a fax number at a real estate company, a fax line to a travel agent, the main number to a high-end hotel, the main number to a catering service, numbers listed to other people with similar ethnic names, and several that could not be resolved. As expected, there are also eight unique *Accounts* because each SAR was filed by a different bank. The overall number of unique entities displayed as a factor of the number of SARs filed shows that there is intentional misrepresentation of the data. It is also typical of this type of pattern.

Many of the SARs were filed because there were returned payments made on the *Accounts* held by the *Subject.* A number of these accounts appear to have been defined as commercial merchant accounts and there are numerous references to "UNAUTHORIZED ACH[42] WITHDRAWALS" and "CUSTOMER DID NOT AUTHORIZE CHARGES." One stream of activity shows dozens of returned payments from jewelry stores. In fact, it was known to the bank that one of these jewelers was previously involved in check-kiting activities. This type of behavior imitates the standard protocol for bust-out schemes. Other SAR references indicate misrepresentation of assets, undisclosed debts on loan applications, and rapid utilization of charges. As with any pattern, the results always need to be validated; however, detecting bust-out schemes is fairly straightforward and can prevent the large losses to the financial institutions the schemes target.

Identity Fraud

There are many different types of patterns to expose in financial data sets. Every value of every field of every form of the BSA data set plays a role in exposing new and important patterns; it is simply a matter of finding, interpreting, and verifying the patterns of interest. This next example

[42] ACH stands for Automated Clearing House and is used for interbank clearing of electronic payments. Most people see the ACH references on their bank statements for payments for mortgages, loans, credit cards, and utility bills.

addresses a common worldwide problem that affects millions of people each year—identity theft. In fact, it is one of the fastest-growing crimes and already accounts for almost $50 billion in losses per year. Taking the same basic parameters used in the bust-out and check-kiting patterns previously described, the network shown in Figure 5.18 was uncovered. It is entirely focused on a form of identity fraud.

One immediate observation made about this network is the number of objects present in the display (compared to the previous examples). There are 26 SAR transactions that were submitted by 22 different filing institutions. In this example, the total dollar amount (not shown in the labels) was only $150,000 and occurred over an 18-month period of time. Initial interpretation of the network appears to be fairly complicated due to the number of objects present, but there are a lot of repetitive entities that can be easily cleaned up and disambiguated to generate the network shown in Figure 5.19.

In this example, the underlying data supporting the representation of the *Subjects* clearly points to the same person. In this case, the name variation can be attributed to the large number of different filing institutions slightly abbreviating the name and related data rather than any type of intentional misrepresentation. He has consistently listed his occupation as a Shopping Cart Pusher or a Bag Clerk and has tried to justify a base salary of over $70,000 to $80,000 annually, an excessive amount by any standard for the position defined. Second, all of the *Address* objects reflect the same location—again with small variations in their spelling and formatting. The resulting network is a starburst focusing on a single entity with a large fan-out of *SAR* transactions.

In this case, the *Subject* is trying to get credit from a number of different banks in the form of loans and credit cards. Perhaps the biggest red flag identified by most of the institutions filing SARs was the number of inquiries made on his credit history. For the SSN submitted, there were close to 100 credit bureau checks performed over the past year. In fact, one institution reported that there were more than 400 inquiries[43] on his credit report from numerous financial institutions and almost 30 new accounts established in less than a six-month period.

This type of behavior is typical of what is seen with identity theft scenarios—except in this case it appears that the *Subject* is directly responsible for the volume of applications being submitted, rather than someone else assuming his identity. However, there are other inconsistencies in the data reported. The *Subject* has also submitted multiple applications to several of the institutions, and although he is fairly consistent in the

[43] One institution made note that his credit report was more than 50 pages in length.

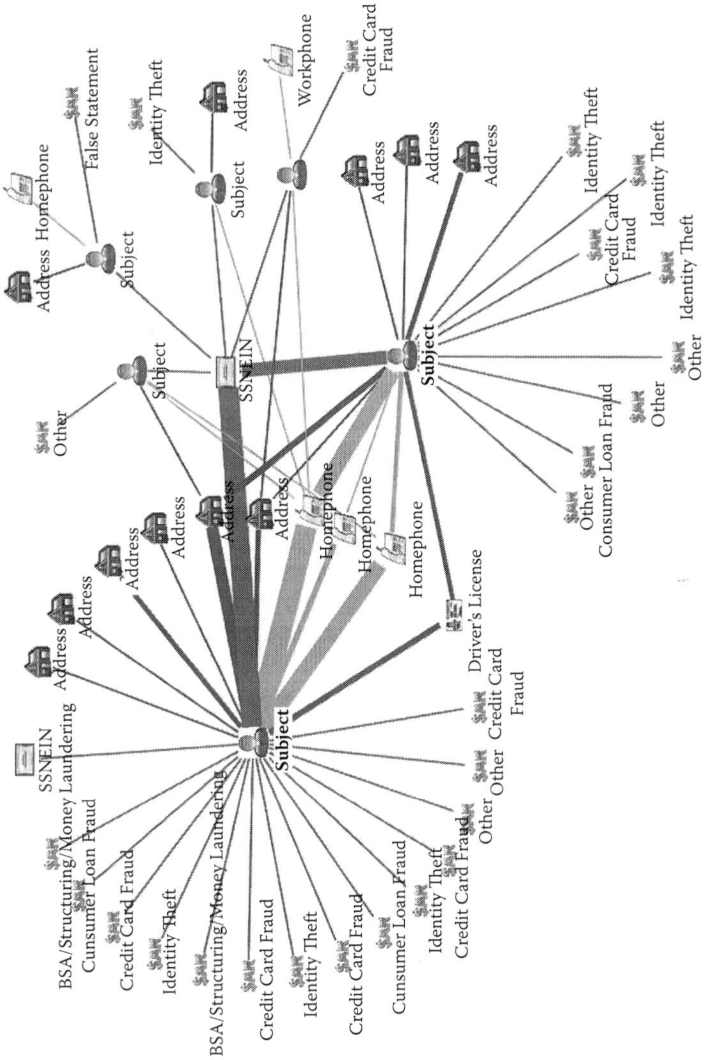

Figure 5.18 Identity fraud network.

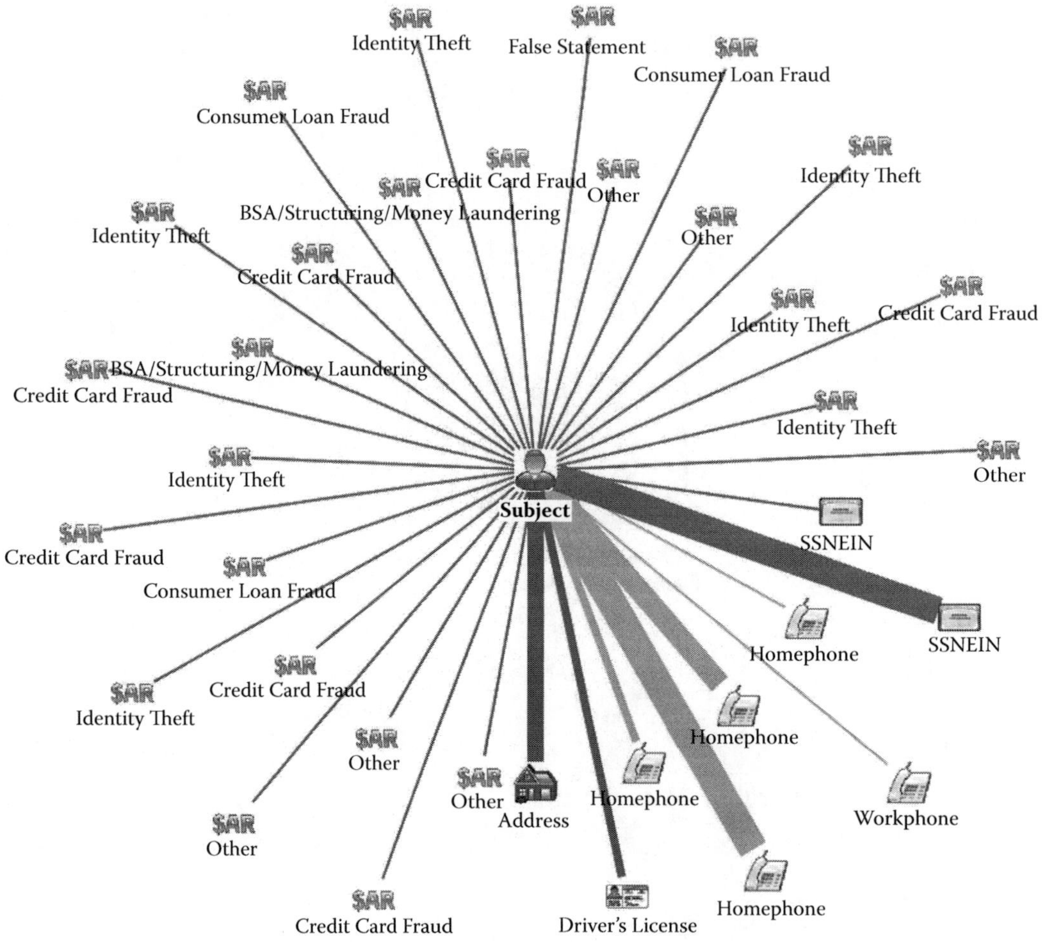

Figure 5.19 Merged identity fraud network.

information he provides, there is strong evidence he has tried using different SSNs on prior applications. The *SSN* (the one shown with a thin link) resolved to more than 200 open credit accounts. Clearly, this type of behavior is excessive and evidence of someone committing fraud. Other public records checks showed over 15 different prior addresses listed for the *Subject,* many with overlapping dates of residency. Additionally, skip-tracing inquires showed the listed phone numbers on many of the applications did not match the address he provided—potentially indicating some type of identity theft or fraud.

Large Connections

Many times, the most obvious of patterns appear to be those with large numbers of connections; for example, a *Subject* with dozens of *SARs,* or *Addresses* connected to numerous *Subjects,* or *SSNs* used by multiple *Subjects.*[44] While sometimes this pans out, many times it just reveals errors or bad data. There should be some type of rationale based on the parameters used to extract the data. At a high level, it is hard to tell what is important. As show in Figure 5.20, there are a number of different network configurations pulled from the data. Simply looking at the structure of the networks, it is hard to decipher exactly what type of content is being displayed and which networks are of a high value—especially without any of the icons or labels being displayed.

There are some basic clues provided from the visual parameters shown in the network, namely the color of the links, the interconnections of the objects, and the overall structure of the individual networks. When viewed, the dark gray links represent connections between *SARs* and *Subjects,* and light gray links between *SARs* and *Accounts.* Although color is a good mechanism to help differentiate values, it represents only one dimension in the overall network and does not help much when objects and links are of the same type. Those networks that appear as bull's-eyes are very entity-centric, meaning there are significant connections between a single object (e.g., a *SAR* or a *Subject* or an *Account*) to a larger number of *SAR* transactions. The question is*: Which network structure is of most value to the investigator?*

To answer this question, the specific details of each network must be exposed to understand exactly what is occurring in the underlying data set. The top row of this diagram shows two object-centric networks that appear identical in structure. However, their content and value are vastly different. Upon closer inspection, the detail of the top-left network is shown in Figure 5.21 and clearly depicts a *SAR* connected to a significant number of *Subjects*—42, to be exact. While this type of structure looks quite impressive, it tends to reflect more of a "fraud" against the bank rather than a bona-fide money-laundering target.

This is not to say that the pattern does not have any value or that it does not represent an actionable event for law enforcement, but rather that it tends to be less critical than detecting, for example, terrorist-financing operations. Usually, this type of situation occurs when someone steals a checkbook and makes payments to unauthorized persons. It is often tied

[44] *Subjects* tend to be of primary interest to law enforcement because they can be arrested for criminal activity and *Accounts* also are targeted because they can be seized.

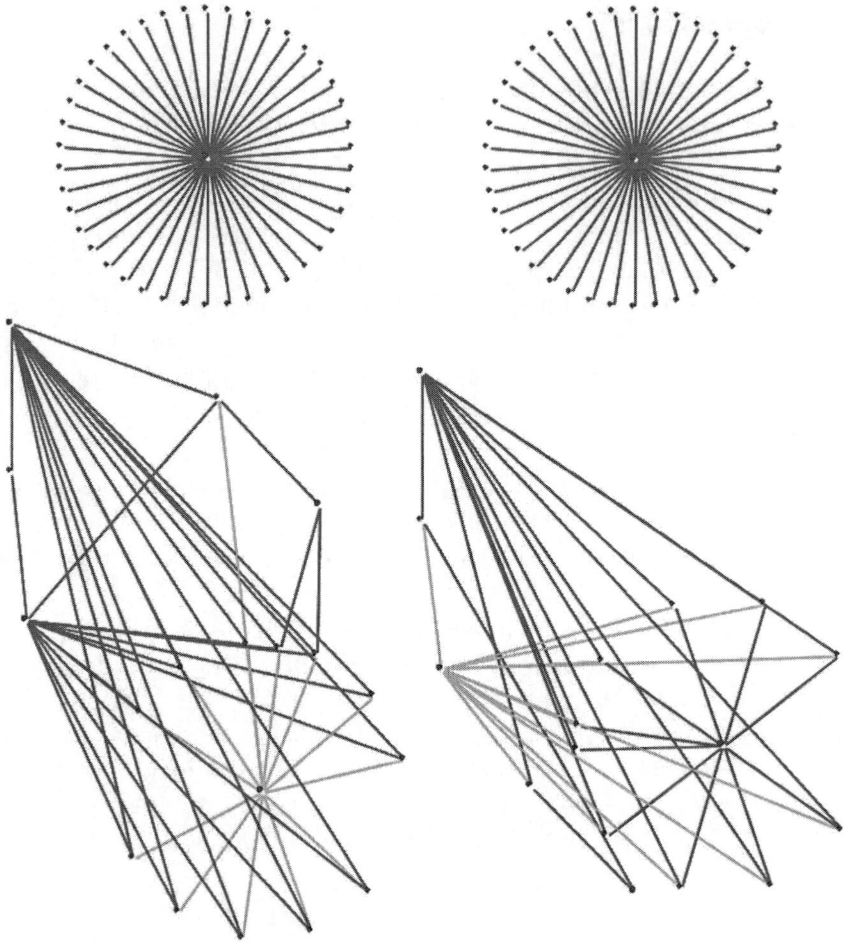

Figure 5.20 Determining high-value network patterns.

to fraudulent loan (e.g., mortgage) applications or, many times, appears for businesses operating a Ponzi or pyramid scheme.

Figure 5.22 shows a more complete network diagram of this type of structure, including *Addresses, Phones,* and *SSN/EIN*[45] entities that were related to a bankrupt investment company with outstanding cease-and-desist orders from government regulators for selling units/ownership shares in various oil and gas drilling operations. Notice that there is only one *SAR* at the center of this network and each of the *Subjects* represents a different incarnation of the fraudulent organization (as a limited liability corporation)

[45] Several SSN/EIN objects show an X over their icon because they matched an entry in the Social Security Death Master Index. This type of situation is generally ignored when the SSN/EIN is tied to an organization or business.

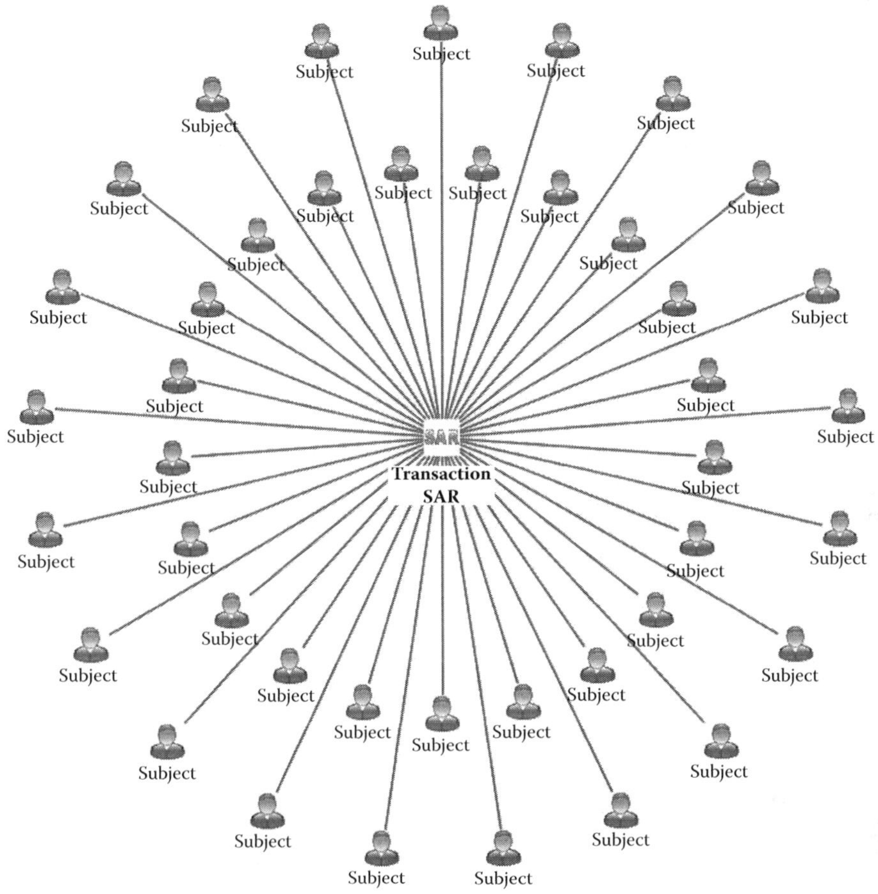

Figure 5.21 SAR connected to large number of subjects.

or one that had previously transferred funds to the organization. Typically, the narratives associated with these *SARs* tend to be quite long, detailed, and extensively documented. An additional example depicting a SAR-centric network is shown in Figure 5.23 where some commonality exists among the *Subjects* based on their *Addresses, Phones,* and *SSNs.*

The upper-right network, in the top row of Figure 5.20, contains the same *SAR* and *Subject* object types and is basically a mirror of Figure 5.21. However, as shown in detail in Figure 5.24, there is a single *Subject* connected to 42 *SAR* transactions. This type of structure provides a well-qualified target of interest (e.g., the *Subject*) because the repeated activities (e.g., the *SARs*) are used to establish the criminal behavior. At this point the interpretation of the *SARs,* their narratives, and all the supporting details can be used to understand the suspicious activities.

One feature that distinguishes this type of network is the repeated use of an *Account* object. If the same filing institution is responsible for

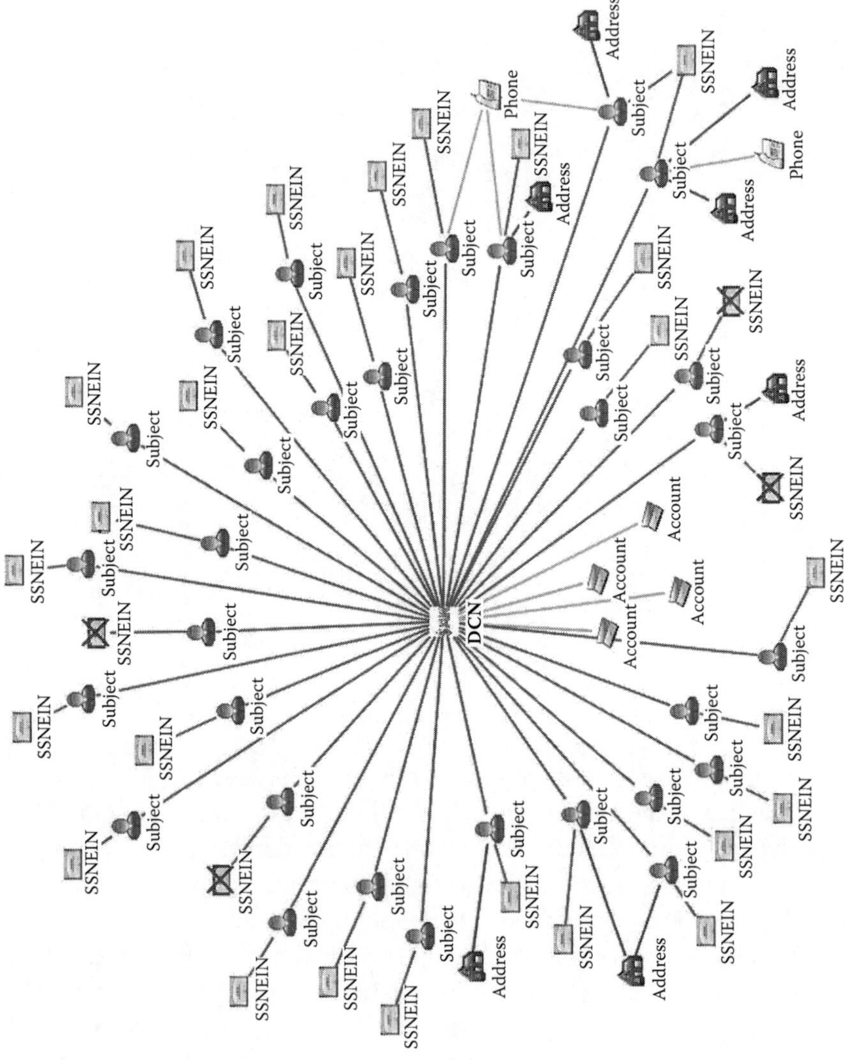

Figure 5.22 Expanded network with a central SAR transaction.

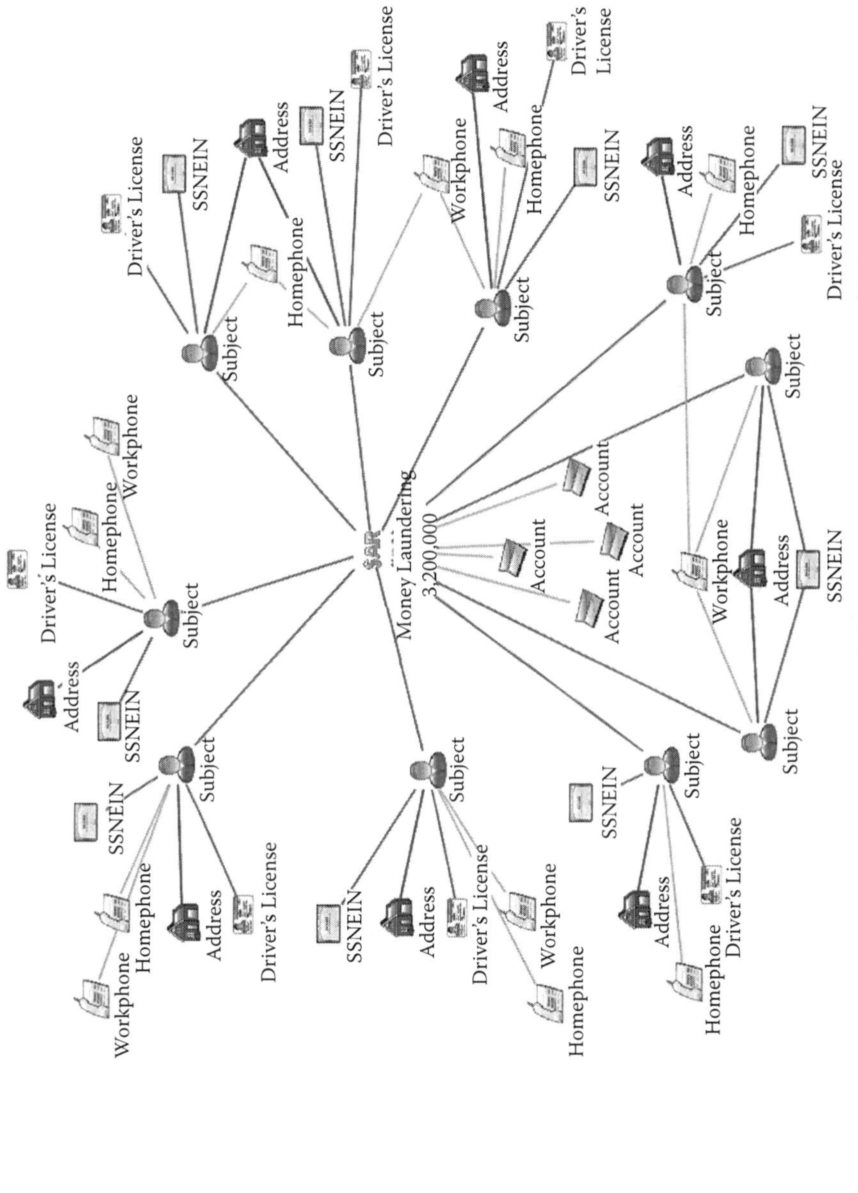

Figure 5.23 A second SAR-centric network.

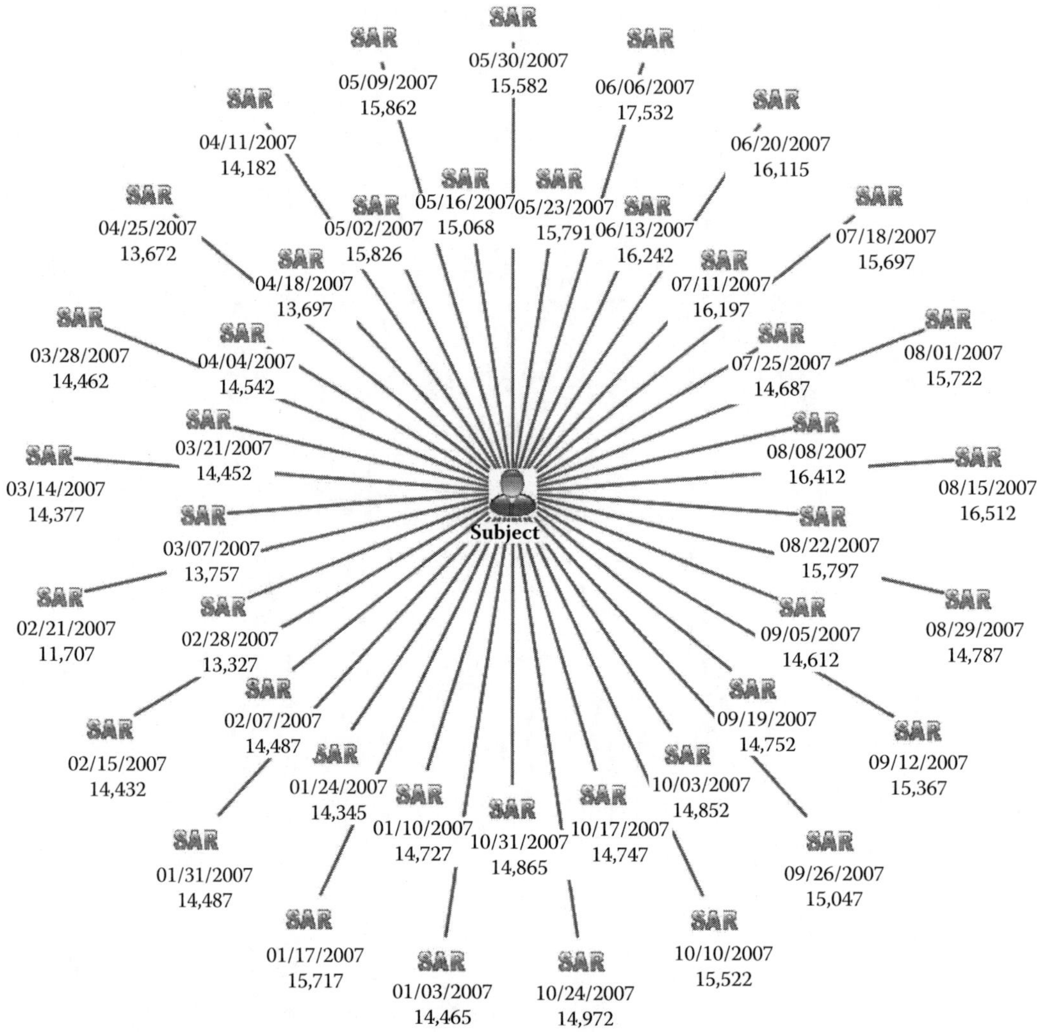

Figure 5.24 Single subject with multiple SAR transactions.

submitting all of the *SARs,* then the related *Account* will be referenced and it often looks like a double-rooted network, where the same number of connections to the *Subject* also appears for the *Account.* This is a bit harder to represent without having lines cross, especially with larger numbers of *SAR* entities. Figure 5.25 depicts this type of network, shown in a somewhat nontraditional format, where 45 *SAR* objects are connected to the same *Subject* and *Account.* Additionally, the thick lines for the *ID Number, Address, Phone,* and *SSN/EIN* show they were consistently represented by the filing institution on each *SAR* submitted.

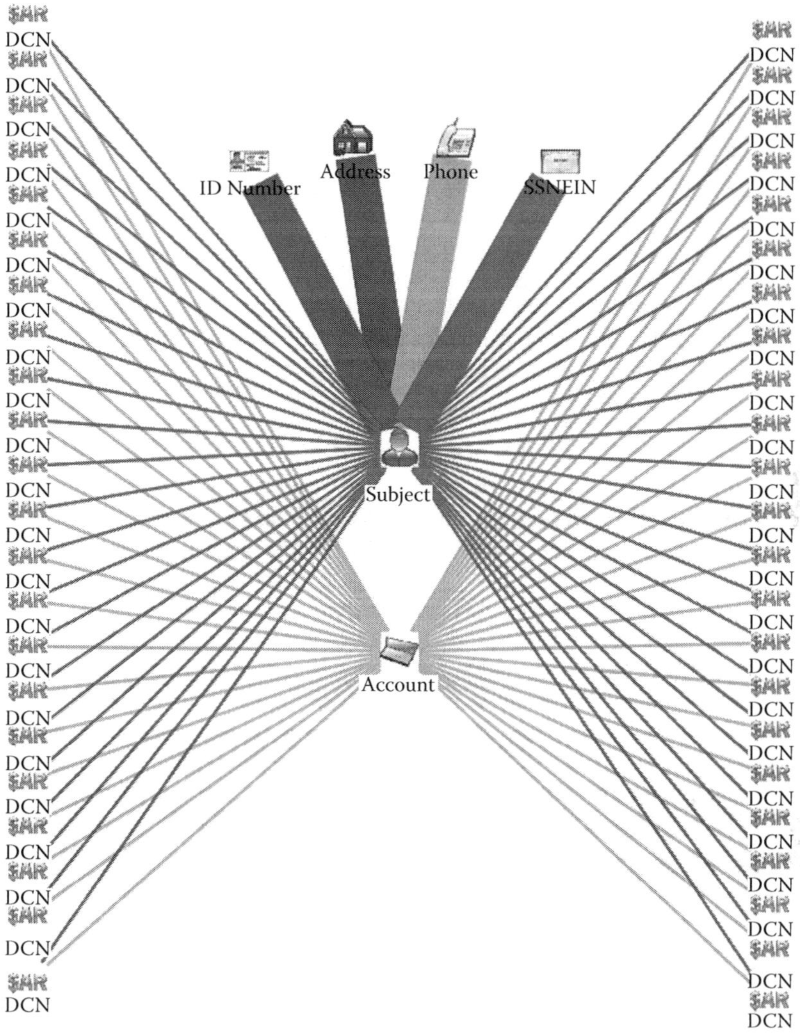

Figure 5.25 Double-rooted network for subject and account.

As previously mentioned, the "behavior" of the suspicious activity can be better understood using this data because each individual transaction has its own unique characteristics including a violation amount and a filing date. In this example, the 45 *SARs* represent more than $200,000, with an average transaction value of $4,600, and were reported for a *Subject* cashing large checks issued from a parent company and then converting them into money orders made out to "cash"—supposedly for distribution to the employees. The occupation of this *Subject* is listed as a courier. The filing date can be used to map the transactions onto a temporal grid to see when the activities occurred to help establish the pattern.

Figure 5.26 shows two grids representing the years 2006 and 2007, from left to right. Each grid is arranged with the day of the week across the *x*-axis and the week of the year down the *y*-axis.

The first reported filing occurred in mid-October of 2006 and repeats through early September of 2007. All of the transactions were conducted on a Thursday as is evidenced in the diagram. The gap in late 2006 coincided with the Thanksgiving holiday (third Thursday of November) and the missing day in 2007 occurred in mid-July—perhaps the *Subject* was on a vacation. This particular temporal pattern is extremely consistent (e.g., predictable) and could be used to target the individual should any type of investigation or follow-up be required.

The main point made in this discussion, and for the networks presented in Figure 5.20, is that there appear to be structurally equivalent networks. Try to determine which ones result in the greatest value to the agency conducting the analysis. The bottom two networks in this diagram show a much more diverse set of connections and will generally be a hybrid of the scenarios just presented, meaning that either of these networks will produce some reasonable targets.

Attorneys and Law Firms

There are many different avenues to laundering money throughout the banking systems and one particular method involves the use of Interest On Lawyers' Trust Account (IOLTA),[46] a well-intentioned program that operates without taxpayer support, designed to help provide civil legal services to the indigent, poor, and other underserved communities such as the elderly or disabled. The IOLTA program issues grants to nonprofit, legal aid providers, and advocates helping low-income families with landlord/tenant disputes, child custody and abuse issues, and many other legal matters. It can also, unfortunately, double as a vehicle to help launder money and hide proceeds of unscrupulous and corrupt lawyers.

The IOLTA program uses the interest generated from "qualified funds," typically escrow payments, court fees, or settlement checks received by the attorney or law firm from a client where the amount is too small or the length of time too short (generally defined to be less than $150 worth of interest) to make it worth the time required to set up and administer a separate account for the benefit of the client. Modeled after programs already established (circa 1960s) in Canada and Australia,

[46] http://www.iolta.org/.

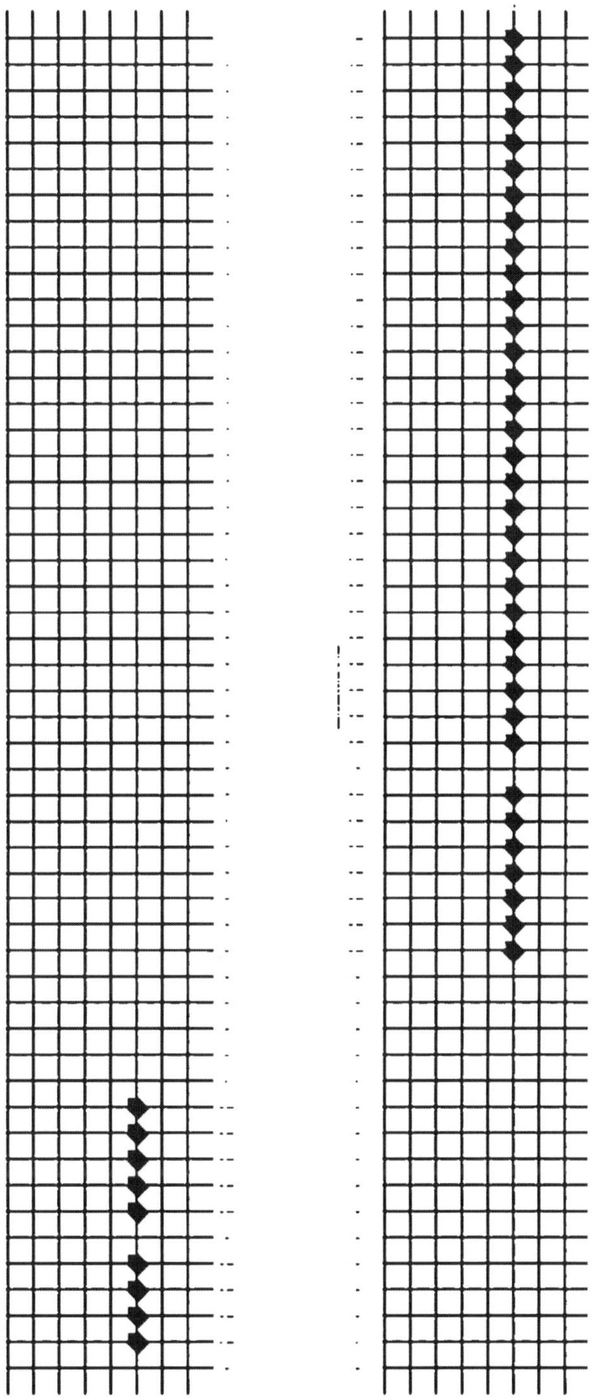

Figure 5.26 Temporal grid of SAR reports.

virtually every state[47] in the United States has an IOLTA program with somewhat different regulations, requirements, or rules.

Many banks participate in the IOLTA program and the accounts are easily established using a simple application form. The interest earned on an IOLTA account is redirected on a monthly or quarterly basis by the bank and sent to the primary state IOLTA fund where it is accumulated—with the interest payments made from all the other state IOLTA bank accounts—to the tune of more than $133 million[48] annually (across all states).

The spin on this situation is that the tax information number (TIN) on all IOLTA accounts bears the number of the IOLTA fund for their respective state. Thus, the state of New York is #13-3246797, the Texas Equal Access to Justice Foundation is #74-2354575, and the State Bar of California (Trust Fund Program) is #94-6001385, so the taxes related to the interest earned are not imposed on the lawyer, but are exempt through the IOLTA fund. Because the IOLTA accounts basically act as a pool for all the deposits made on behalf of the attorney or law firm,[49] it becomes difficult to track who actually owns the money and its intended purpose. The attorney or lawyer essentially becomes a front man and acts as a buffer that shields the client from any type of financial disclosure or exposure. It is ultimately the responsibility of the individual lawyer or law firm to separately account and track for each client's money, essentially amounting to a secondary set of bookkeeping.

The network shown in Figure 5.27 is typical of an IOLTA-related structure where the *Subjects* exclusively represent attorneys and law firms who are related through a common *SSN* (e.g., the TIN) for their respective IOLTA state fund. Thicker lines indicate more numerous SARs for the associated *Subject,* obviously establishing a less than credible pattern for this esteemed community, presumably well versed in the jurisprudence of financial crimes.

The types of activities reported in the SARs run the gamut and include such behaviors as lawyers issuing sequentially numbered checks to their clients in various amounts (under $10,000 to avoid CTR filing requirements); making large cash deposits (hundreds of thousands of dollars) based on money supposedly provided by their clients; funds being wired to known tax havens; various embezzlement and misappropriation allegations; the use of IOLTA accounts for personal expenses (e.g., payroll, video

[47] http://www.abanet.org/legalservices/iolta/ioltdir.html.

[48] http://www.iolta.org/grants.cfm.

[49] Of course, there are protections in the various laws that state "no attorney or law firm shall be liable for damages nor held to answer for a charge of professional misconduct because of a deposit of moneys to an IOLTA account pursuant to a judgment in good faith that such moneys were qualified funds."

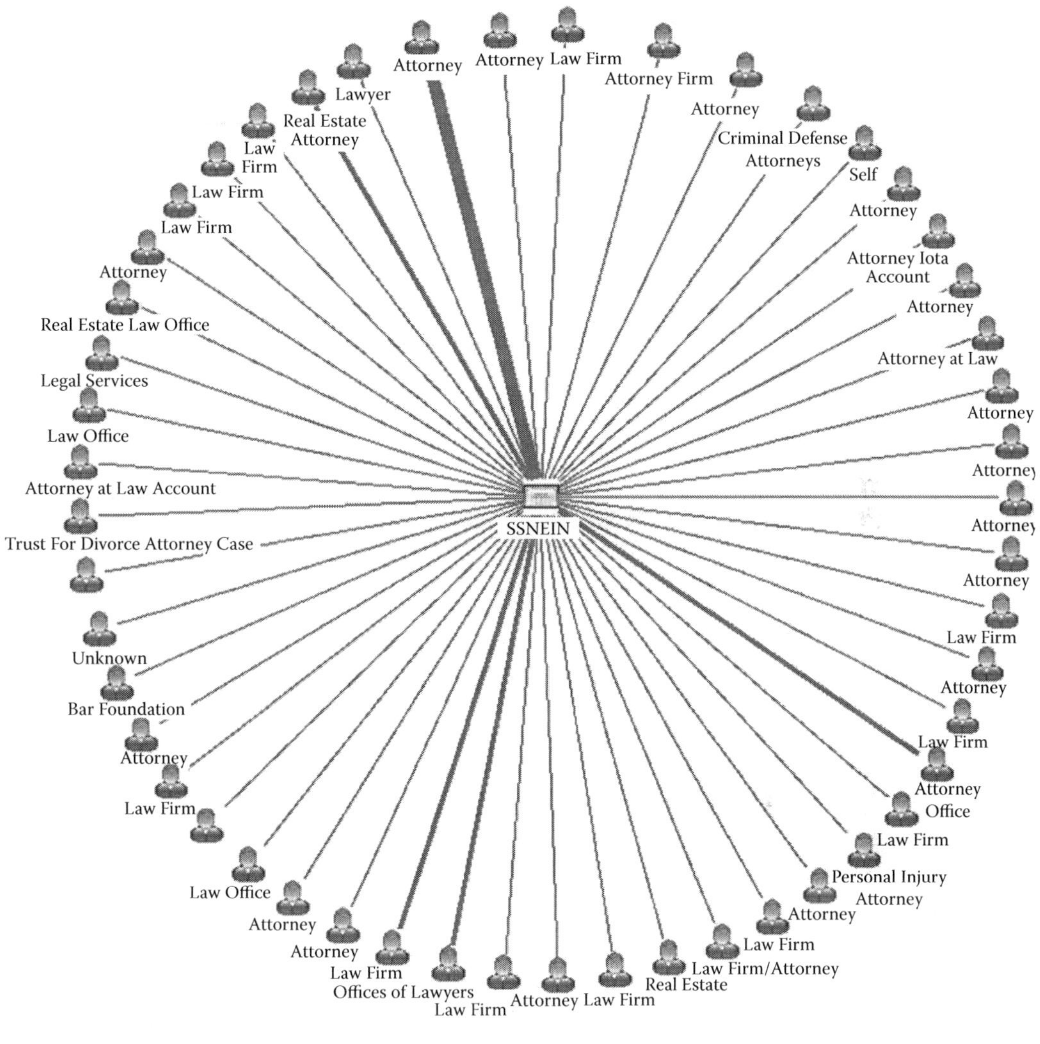

Figure 5.27 An IOLTA network.

rentals, electronic purchases, restaurant charges, and grocery store bills); various check frauds; and a number of other questionable behaviors.

Cheap Motels

There are actionable situations contained throughout the SAR datasets across all the countries capturing this type of data—it is just a matter of digging around and finding scenarios that are worth pursuing. This next example is the epitome of the run-down motel you would see in a Hollywood movie, located at the side of an interstate highway—or, in this case, on a four-lane road located in a mixed residential/commercial neighborhood near an industrial complex. The motel is a single-story structure with a main office/lobby and offers no restaurant, coffee shop, or bar. There are only 25 rooms, you park directly in front of your door, and the room rates range from $35/daily to $150/weekly—not exactly on par with the Waldorf Astoria.

As shown in Figure 5.28, there are numerous SAR reports filed against this establishment. Upon seeing this network structure, being

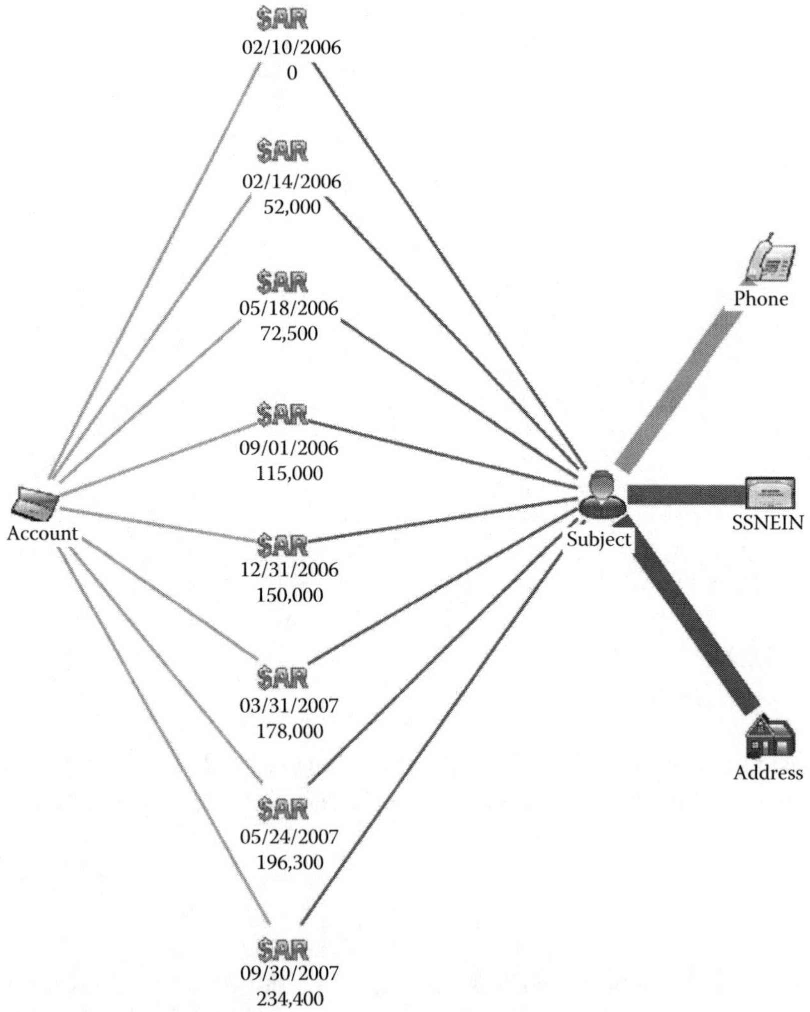

Figure 5.28 Repeat SAR filings on same hotel.

one of the most consistent in terms of its representation (e.g., *Subjects, Addresses, SSN/EIN,* and *Phones*) and using only one *Account* number, it can be determined that a single filing institution generated these eight SARs. Knowing this fact means that care must be taken with respect to interpreting the results of these filings because there are particular characteristics about how SARs are completed by their respective filing institutions that can impact the overall results and analytics that can be performed.

Specifically, the SAR form[50] has a field (Part III, Line #33) called "Date or date range of suspicious activity" used to record the start/end dates of the reported activity. All eight of these SARs have the same "From" date defined (not shown in the diagram), which implicitly means that they are reporting the same suspicious activity multiple times at different date intervals. The "To" date represents the last incident recorded by the bank, which is what appears as the date in the labels of the SAR objects presented in the network and which is occurring approximately every three to four months. Remember, a SAR is used to report behavior (i.e., the activity) over a period of time and does not necessarily reflect each individual transaction made by the *Subject* of interest.

The SAR objects have been arranged based on the "To" date and, as seen in the figure, the violation amounts start at $0 and go up to $234,000. Without understanding how the SARs were filed, one might mistakenly calculate this network to be worth almost a million dollars, if all of the violation amounts were added together. However, because the SARs are all from the same filing institution, reporting on the same suspicious activity, and all starting on the same date, it means that the violation amount reported on any SAR is the cumulative amount since the suspicious behavior was initially detected. So, the total violation amount for this network is actually $234,000.

In this situation, a motel representative comes into the bank every week or so to make a deposit consisting of stacks of $20 bills, with no other denomination values ever being deposited. Monthly totals routinely exceed $10,000 for this account and bank employees can't justify a legitimate basis for the volume of cash generated from this establishment. Bank tellers have heard that the motel has a "reputation" for drugs and prostitution, which would help explain the amount of cash they are depositing. Of course, one question to ask is why law enforcement (state or federal) has not interdicted or investigated this operation considering it has been officially reported for almost two years.

[50] http://www.fincen.gov/forms/files/f9022-47_sar-di.pdf.

Location, Location, Location

The following analysis was conducted based on a recent investigation involving the filing of SARs located within Howard County, Maryland. Over a two-year period, approximately 300 SARs were filed by banks operating in this particular region. Although not a large number by any means, the SARs did provide interesting observations regarding the movement of money within the region.

Howard County is an affluent region within the Baltimore/ Washington, D.C., metropolitan area that is home to a number of corporate executives, doctors, lawyers, and other business professionals. Not only does it provide a convenient locale for those working in either Baltimore or Washington, DC, but it is also a hub for many employed at the National Security Agency (NSA) and Fort Meade. Additionally, it is situated along Interstates 95 and 70, which are known drug corridors.

Howard County is quite diverse, made up of various farmlands, equestrian estates, and ever-expanding residential areas including Columbia, one of the first "planned" communities in the United States. Additionally, the historic district of Ellicott City provides a wide range of antique stores, shopping boutiques, a brewery, and several restaurants.

The population of Howard County in 2006[51] was approximately 272,000 and growing strongly. Additionally, Howard County is the wealthiest county in Maryland with an average household income of over $83,000 and a per capita income of almost $35,000. Howard County is also one of the smallest counties in the state with a total of 252 square miles.

Table 5.3[52] provides a breakdown of the number of SARs filed from banks operating branches within the county. The DCN was used to uniquely identify each SAR. The results are grouped by the city/ state of the addresses listed on the SARs for each of the corresponding *Subjects*. Sorting by this count, the investigator quickly sees that the majority of the filings occurred in the city of Columbia, with 90 SAR filings. The next grouping shows that there are 50 SARs without a listed city or state—obviously, a problem in the data collection process and perhaps an indicator that several of the banks need to retrain their tellers or compliance officers to ensure that the SAR forms are filled out completely.

Instead of using a link analysis diagram to present the data, all the SARs for this data extraction were plotted onto a geographic map as shown in Figure 5.29. The coordinates were derived from the ZIP

[51] http://quickfacts.census.gov/qfd/states/24/24027.html.

[52] Only those city/state combinations with five or more SARs represented are shown.

Table 5.3 Breakdown of SAR Filings by City/State

DCN COUNT	*CITY*	*STATE*
90	COLUMBIA	MD
50	—	—
40	BALTIMORE	MD
35	ELLICOTT CITY	MD
20	ELKRIDGE	MD
18	LAUREL	MD
12	SYKESVILLE	MD
10	WOODSTOCK	MD
8	JESSUP	MD
8	UPPER DARBY	PA
8	WARRINGTON	PA
8	WASHINGTON	DC
8	WOODBINE	MD
5	CATONSVILLE	MD
5	ELDERSBURG	MD
5	ROCKVILLE	MD
5	WESTMINSTER	MD

code of the address contained on the SAR. In those systems that do not perform roof-top encoding of addresses, a "centroid" (e.g., generalized central location) for the ZIP code can provide the latitude and longitude values. This type of approach is invaluable for quickly determining the location of any address based on its associated ZIP code.[53] For the purposes of this investigation, the centroid provides the best high-level view of the data.

Reviewing the map shows that there is a heavy concentration in and around the Baltimore/Washington, D.C., corridor. Additionally, as is clearly shown, a number of SARs were filed on people near Philadelphia, Pennsylvania, as well as Dover, Delaware. These outliers are checked to determine the nature of the suspiciousness. Attribute-to-attribute comparisons can be performed to find these types of situations by looking for the Branch-State of the filing institution not equal to the Address-State of the *Subject*.

At this step, the investigators wanted to look at "high-value" targets, and defined the minimum value of the SAR to be $100,000. Keep in mind that a SAR can represent numerous transactions occurring over a period

[53] There are more than 45,000 ZIP codes in the United States, about 850,000 postal codes in Canada, and approximately 28,000 postal codes in Mexico.

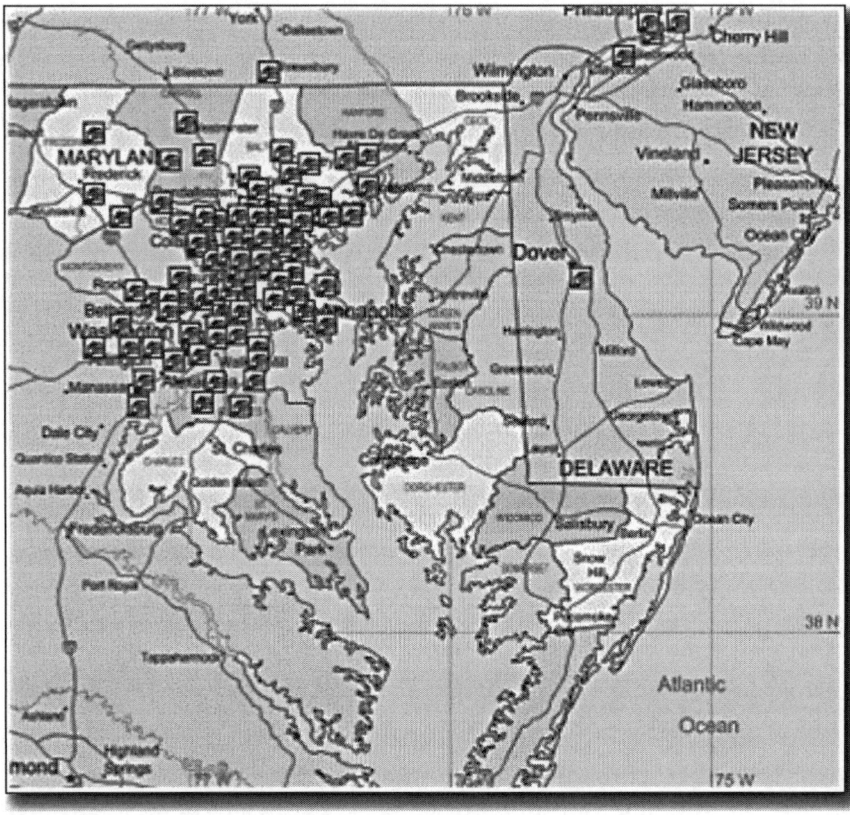

Figure 5.29 Geospatial mapping of SAR filings.

of time. Thus, the resulting SARs often depict a number of individual transactions rolled up into a single report, and their accumulated value is what will exceed $100,000. Figure 5.30 now shows the 30 addresses that are associated with SARs meeting this condition. Immediately, the investigators noticed that the intensity of addresses around their original target area was no longer supported with the $100,000 filter condition. The concentration appears mostly along the I-95 corridor and areas south of Howard County.

The investigators take a closer look at the map in the area where the remaining addresses are shown, as presented in Figure 5.31. It becomes much clearer that the high-value transactions are being conducted within Howard County from addresses outside the immediate area. In fact, many exceed 10 to 25 miles. To emphasize this pattern, the map uses a transparent highlight to emphasize the Howard County area. From this, investigators

Figure 5.30 Only SAR transactions over $100,000.

can quickly see that only several of the 30 transactions over $100,000 were actually conducted by people living within Howard County.

The investigators[54] find these circumstances to be of interest because several *Subjects* crossed state lines (Virginia and Pennsylvania), many traveled at least 25 miles to conduct the transactions, and most were not from as affluent communities as Howard County. Drilling down on the narratives associated with the SARs for the Howard County addresses showed that many of the *Subjects* involved in these transactions were foreign nationals. Additionally, the main violation type was some type of "structuring" where the money was layered into different account(s).

[54] The patterns exposed are just one particular viewpoint of the data with respect to identifying questionable actions and behaviors. The investigators identified well-qualified leads to pursue to determine if any actual wrongdoing has occurred.

Figure 5.31 Closer view of SAR activity.

Individual Taxpayer Identification Number

An Individual Taxpayer Identification Number (ITIN)[55] is a tax-processing number issued by the Internal Revenue Service (IRS) to foreign nationals or other persons with a tax-filing obligation that are not eligible for an SSN. Although very similar to an SSN, with a nine-digit number, the ITIN begins with the number 9 and has a 7 or 8 in the fourth digit (for example, 9XX-7X-XXXX or 9XX-8X-XXXX). making it easy to recognize and identify as an ITIN.

The IRS issues ITINs to individuals not eligible to receive an SSN but who need a way to be recognized for federal tax-reporting requirements because they have some form or obligation of a tax (debit or credit). The assignment of an ITIN to an individual does not change their immigration status, provide entitlements to Social Security benefits, or provide the right to work in the United States. The types of people who need an ITIN generally include resident and nonresident aliens (who are not eligible for an SSN), their dependents, or their spouses, who are required to file a

[55] http://www.irs.gov/individuals/article/0,,id=96287,00.html.

U.S. tax return because they either have payment responsibilities or are entitled to some form of refund.

According to the IRS, the ITINs are only to be used for federal tax-reporting requirements and are not intended to serve any other purpose, especially as a generic form of identification for obtaining a driver's license, lines of credit (e.g., credit cards, mortgages), or other nontax purposes. Most important, the ITIN should not be relied on as an official means for verifying the identity of a foreign national.[56] Acquiring an ITIN is a simple process of filing a W7 form, which does not require an extensive number of background checks.

Various forms of identification can be used to apply for an ITIN including foreign driver's licenses, foreign voter's registration cards, foreign military identification cards, and even medical or school records. Of course, many of these documents are easily forged or counterfeited; therefore, the issuance of an ITIN is extremely susceptible to fraud and misrepresentation. In fact, the IRS has issued more than 5 million ITINs with approximately 1 million new applications received each year;[57] however, only 1.5 million ITINs were actually used on tax returns filed in the year 2000, which means more than 3.5 million are inactive or are being used for nontax situations and circumstances.

Once an ITIN is acquired, it can then be used by a growing number of banks[58] and financial institutions,[59] which have recently begun to court the unbanked community, which consists largely of undocumented or illegal aliens. Naturally, this increases the exposure and liability for money-laundering activities because the background checks conducted on an ITIN may not adequately disclose a person's true identity. Thus, one of the higher-profile targets to review in the BSA data is the utilization of ITINs as a form of identification, especially when it has been reported in a SAR filing.

A general observation regarding ITINs is that they tend to have multiple *Subjects* associated with the SAR, meaning that the filing institution listed more than one *Subject* as being involved or perpetrating a suspicious activity. Many times, they also link it to a business identity (DBA or doing business as). As would be expected in these types of filings, often the related *Addresses* come back with an overseas reference (e.g., Mexico, Brazil, Indonesia, etc.).

---

56 http://www.treasury.gov/press/releases/reports/sec326breport.final.pdf.

57 Ibid, p. 23 (also see http://iblsjournal.typepad.com/illinois_business_law_soc/2007/02/loophole_in_the.html).

58 Dilip Ratha, "Workers' Remittances: An Important and Stable Source of External Development Finance," in *Global Development Finance* (New York: World Bank, 2003), 167.

59 William Edwards, "B of A loosens its policy on credit cards," *Bloomberg News*, February 14, 2007. Retrieved from http://seattlepi.nwsource.com/business/303574_bofacreditcards14.html?source=mypi.

Figure 5.32 and Figure 5.33 show sample diagrams where an ITIN value was used to identify a SAR filing and its immediate network. The actual ITIN is depicted using an *SSN* icon with a marker flag. The value of YES or NO under the *SSN* icon in these diagrams is based on its value passing a Social Security validation check, which ITINs will routinely fail because they are not technically a valid SSN. Furthermore, the thicker lines between a *Subject* and an *SSN* indicate there are multiple SAR violations—thus the network will further expand to include other SAR filings. Most violations involving an ITIN appear as simple structuring violations or frauds.

SAR Versus STR

There are upwards of 100 countries with established FIUs, and this number continues to grow every year as more and more pressure is exerted from the global marketplace to help stem the tide of criminal enterprises and terrorist-financing activities operating within their respective jurisdictions. However, there is no master blueprint, no standard operating

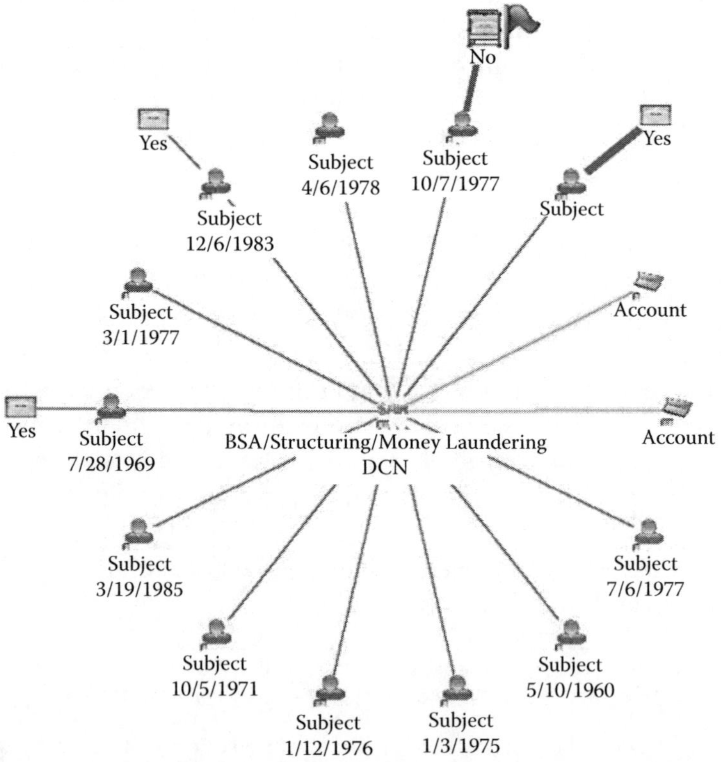

Figure 5.32 Example of an ITIN network.

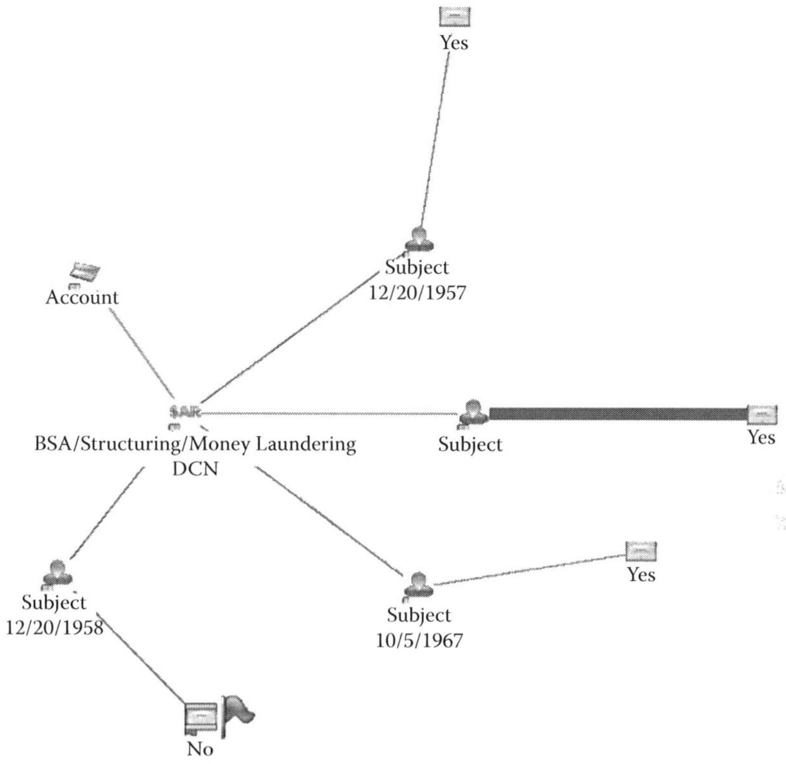

Figure 5.33 Another ITIN network.

procedure, and no handbook to consult when establishing the day-to-day operations of an FIU. Although governments throughout the world are in agreement that money laundering needs to be stopped, their laws, violations, fines, and punishments vary dramatically. One primary difference is in the filing of suspicious reports themselves.

Within the United States, the Department of the Treasury has defined the use of SARs as the primary interface between the filing institutions and the government. When these reports are filed, they can cover multiple individual transactions during a 30-day period from the date of the initial detection of the questionable behavior. In virtually every other country, the FIUs require separate Suspicious Transaction Reports (STRs), where each and every transaction must be individually detailed and filed.

It is a somewhat subtle difference, but has a large impact on the types of analyses that can be performed. In particular, using SARs, if there are multiple transactions, the details of the individual transactions are lost because they are usually documented in a textual format within the narrative of the SAR (as is depicted in Figure 5.34). What this means is that

SAR Report

This Customer Has Been Previously Reported For Large Checks Being Cashed against the Account Just Under the CTR Filing Limit. This Type of Cash Activity May Imply That the Checks Are Being Written to Avoid CTR Requirements. Cash Withdrawals Reviewed Since the Last SAR Filing Include: Account Date Amount Branch.

0007654321 03/24/2005 $10,000.00 BR #153 0007654321 03/24/2005 $10,000.00 BR# 223 0007654321 03/25/2005 $10,000.00 BR# 223
0007654321 03/25/2005 $10,000.00 BR# 198 0007654321 03/25/2005 $10,000.00 BR# 223 0007654321 03/25/2005 $10,000.00 BR# 150
0007654321 03/25/2005 $10,000.00 BR# 153 0007654321 03/25/2005 $20,000.00 BR# 223 0007654321 03/28/2005 $10,000.00 BR# 223
0007654321 03/28/2005 $10,000.00 BR# 223 0007654321 03/28/2005 $10,000.00 BR# 198 0007654321 03/28/2005 $10,000.00 BR# 223
0007654321 03/29/2005 $10,000.00 BR# 150 0007654321 03/31/2005 $10,000.00 BR# 223 0007654321 03/31/2005 $10,000.00 BR# 223
0007654321 04/01/2005 $30,000.00 BR# 223 0007654321 04/01/2005 $10,000.00 BR# 150 0007654321 04/01/2005 $10,000.00 BR# 198
0007654321 04/01/2005 $10,000.00 BR# 223 0007654321 04/01/2005 $10,000.00 BR# 223 0007654321 04/01/2005 $10,000.00 BR# 150
0007654321 04/01/2005 $10,000.00 BR# 223 0007654321 04/04/2005 $30,000.00 BR# 223 0007654321 04/04/2005 $10,000.00 BR# 153
0007654321 04/04/2005 $10,000.00 BR# 223 0007654321 04/04/2005 $20,000.00 BR# 223 0007654321 04/05/2005 $10,000.00 BR# 223
0007654321 04/06/2005 $10,000.00 BR# 223 0007654321 04/07/2005 $10,000.00 BR# 198 0007654321 04/07/2005 $10,000.00 BR# 150
0007654321 04/08/2005 $10,000.00 BR# 150 0007654321 04/08/2005 $30,000.00 BR# 223 0007654321 04/08/2005 $10,000.00 BR# 150
0007654321 04/08/2005 $10,000.00 BR# 223 0007654321 04/08/2005 $10,000.00 BR# 198 0007654321 04/11/2005 $10,000.00 BR# 153
0007654321 04/11/2005 $10,000.00 BR# 223 0007654321 04/11/2005 $10,000.00 BR# 150 0007654321 04/12/2005 $10,000.00 BR# 150
0007654321 04/12/2005 $10,000.00 BR# 153 0007654321 04/12/2005 $10,000.00 BR# 150 0007654321 04/13/2005 $10,000.00 BR# 150

Total: $500,000.00

Figure 5.34 A SAR with multiple documented transactions.

the analyst has to read each narrative to understand the true behavior that prompted the SAR, which is an extremely time-consuming job and one fraught with errors and inconsistencies due to the volume of material that has to be reviewed. So in reality a *Subject* with, say, four or five reported SARs may actually have hundreds of individual transactions, making it harder to spot patterns and obscuring the true behavior.

In this figure, there are 42 individual transactions reported under a single SAR with a total accumulated value of \$500,000. The account, date, amount, and branch are broken down into three separate columns, which basically look like a bunch of indecipherable numbers. The time period covers a mere 21 days, with four distinct branches involved and only a single account. In this format, it is hard to understand when the transactions occurred and if there is any type of pattern associated with this person's behavior. Figure 5.35 provides a different interpretation of this data using a date grid visualization.

The grid is structured, in this example, to support a 7×52 format. The x-axis is defined to show the seven days of the week (Sunday through

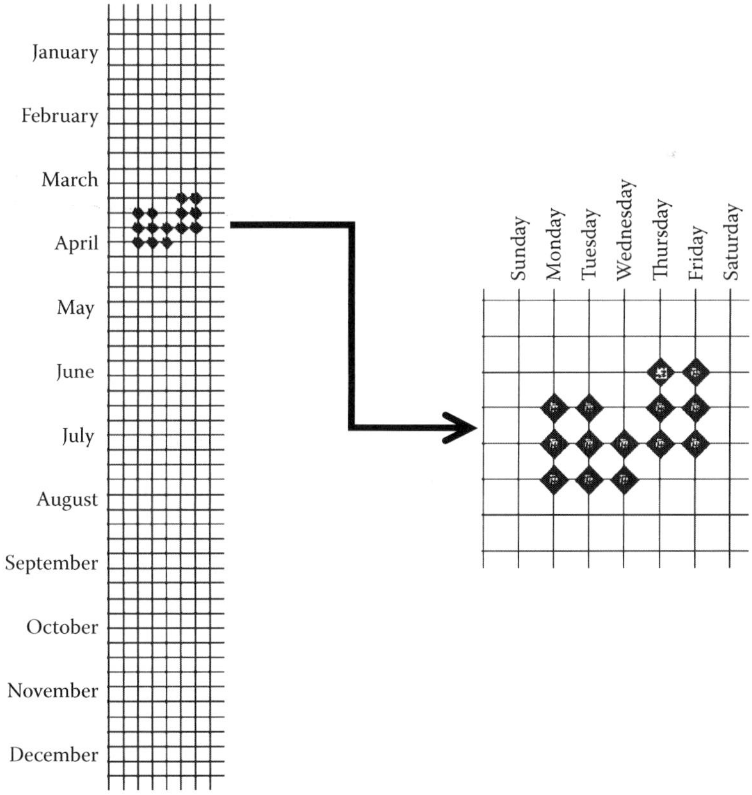

Figure 5.35 A date grid for the transaction details.

Saturday) and the *y*-axis is set to show the 52 weeks of the year. When the transactions are placed on the grid at their appropriate date location, it reveals that the activity took place between late March and mid-April. It is easy to see that no activity occurs on the weekends (Saturday/Sunday) and a transaction happened every weekday except the first Wednesday of the first week. The most active day of the week appears to be Friday (due to the lighter-colored indicators), which is confirmed in Figure 5.36, when the grid is slightly turned using a three-dimensional placement.

All three Fridays (March 25th, April 1st, and April 8th) have the largest number of transactions with six, seven, and five occurring respectively—giving new meaning to the word *payday.* From here, a few additional data dimensions can be checked, such as which branches were conducting the transactions. To keep the date grid perspective and show the branch information, the color of the objects (depicted as different grayscales) is set to the branch reference. As is shown in Figure 5.37, almost every day involves at least two branches, clearly exposing the intentional "structuring" of these transactions.

Depending on the analytical software being used, additional dimensions could easily be applied, including sizes and shapes and groups for

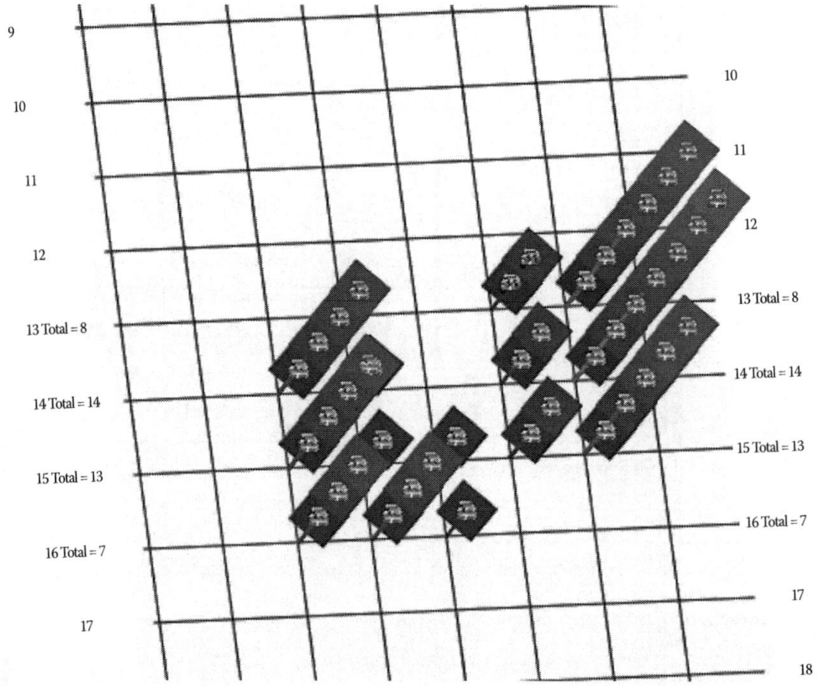

Figure 5.36 Date grid rotated showing multiple transactions on the same day.

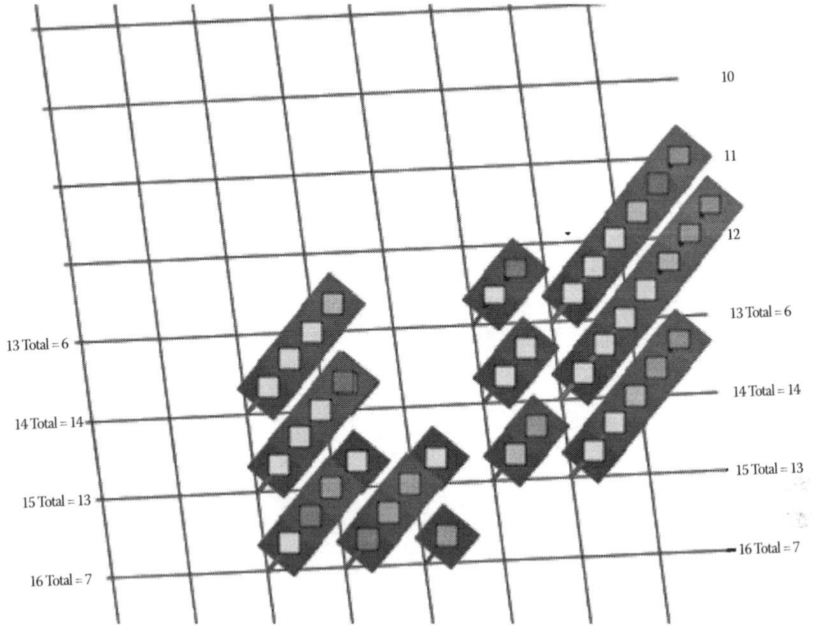

Figure 5.37 Date grid using different shades of gray to show branch references.

the objects. Alternatively, different grid configurations, including week of the month, day of the month, and time configurations, where applicable, can be used (e.g., hour of the day, minute of hour, etc.).

Timing Is Everything

The previous example introduced the concept of a date grid for showing when financial transactions occur for a person of interest. Keep in mind that the focus can be any value contained in the transaction (e.g., CTR, SAR, etc.) including people, accounts, phones, addresses, identification numbers, or any other field values provided on the forms. This type of visualization allows the analyst to see when things are happening and, equally as important, when things are *not* happening—also referred to as an absolute temporal reference. Seeing this type of information explicitly represented in a date grid allows the user to understand the behavior of the target entity and potentially predict future activity. The following examples show how date grids can help investigators better understand the filing behavior associated with a target entity.

The first, shown in Figure 5.38, presents a very consistent pattern of 11 SAR transactions. These filings occur about four or five weeks apart,

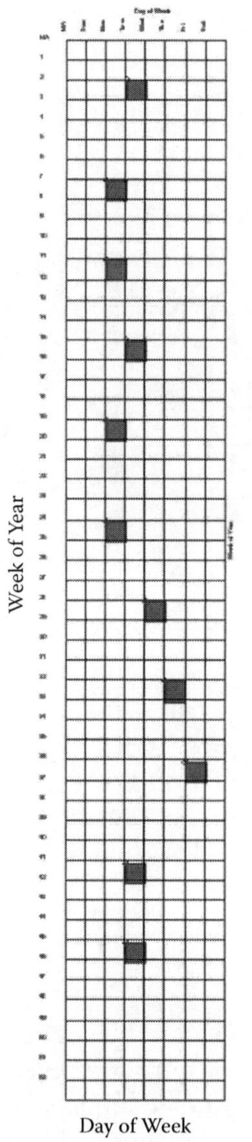

Figure 5.38 Regular SAR filings each month.

or approximately once a month except for December. During the first six months, the reports are generally filed at the beginning of each week (i.e., Monday and Tuesday), and after July the filing day jumps around a bit. So, what does it all this mean? How should it be interpreted? Unfortunately, this does not represent a big conspiracy or hidden terrorist network; rather, it directly portrays the filing behavior of the financial institution because they are required to submit SARs within 30 days of detecting any questionable activities. Thus, this particular individual is doing some common structuring of his deposits, which is occurring multiple times throughout a month, but the bank accumulates them into a single SAR filing. Therefore, the pattern being observed reflects that of the bank as a by-product of the individual. The true behavior of the individual is still unknown, except something or some number of events is happening every month.

The next example shown in Figure 5.39 comes from a collection of SARs filed by different casinos on a particular individual who travels between multiple districts and states to gamble. The most noticeable features of this visualization clearly show the individual's preference for weekends to conduct his gambling. The first filled column represents Sundays and most of these are paired with the last column from the

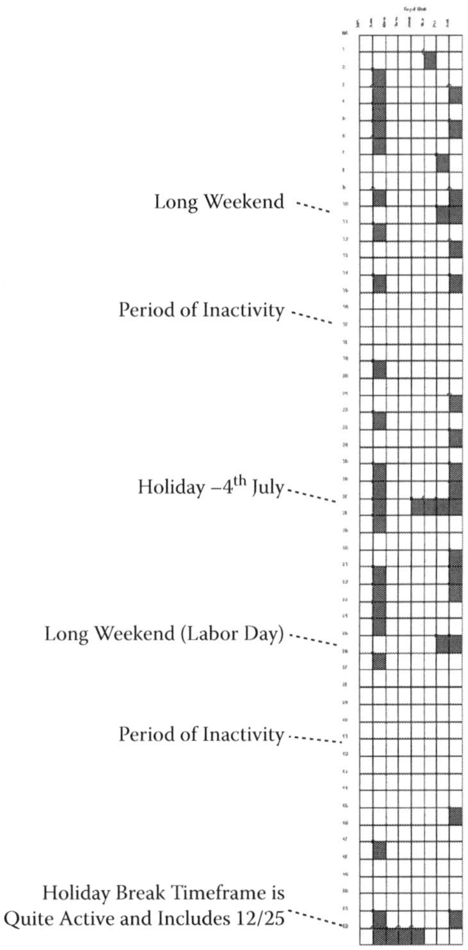

Figure 5.39 Casino SAR filings showing a well-defined pattern.

preceding week (e.g., row) representing the corresponding Saturdays. Remember, these are SAR (SAR-C) filings and not every gambling event results in a report, so there are bound to be some gaps or holes in the display. There are several examples of long weekends and holidays, including Independence Day (July 4th), Labor Day (which falls on the first Monday in September), and Christmas (December 25th). The periods of inactivity also correspond to time frames when people are typically not vacationing. Therefore, based on all of these indicators, it is a safe bet to conclude that this individual is gainfully employed. Additionally, his past trends are a good indicator of his future behavior and it would not be hard to find this person at one of his favorite haunts should law enforcement decide to take action against him.

The next temporal pattern looks somewhat similar to the previous example, except that the filings are performed regularly on Mondays and Fridays rather than on weekends. For this case, the dates are derived from CTR filings for a convenience store owner whose business offers "check cashing" for its clients. Remember, CTRs represent transactions over $10,000 and the volume presented in Figure 5.40 would not be at all unusual for such an establishment. One could reasonably surmise that the focus on Mondays and Fridays is due to their need to cash checks for the weekend (e.g., Friday) and to resupply and have operating capital for the duration of the week (e.g., Monday).

Within the diagram, there is also a period of inactivity, which perhaps represents when the owner was on vacation because it occurs about the time of the Memorial Day weekend (i.e., the last Monday in May) and the kick-off to summer festivities. At face value, everything appears in order for this business, based on the information presented in the diagram, except the flow of the money is shown as deposits rather than withdrawals at the bank. This begs the questions: How are they cashing checks without pulling money out of the bank and where is the cash for all the deposits coming from? They might simply be a very successful store or potentially a front for laundering cash. Finally, for some unknown reason the pattern abruptly stops at the end of summer, which may represent a compliancy issue with the bank or, perhaps, the business shut down or changed ownership.

The next example, also based on CTRs, presents the related transactional behavior from an auto parts retail store. Overall, everything appears fine with this business; deposits are reliably made every other Friday, except for two times when they were diligently made the following Monday; the amounts are between $10,000 and $45,000 with an average deposit somewhere in the midteens; and cross-checks against the

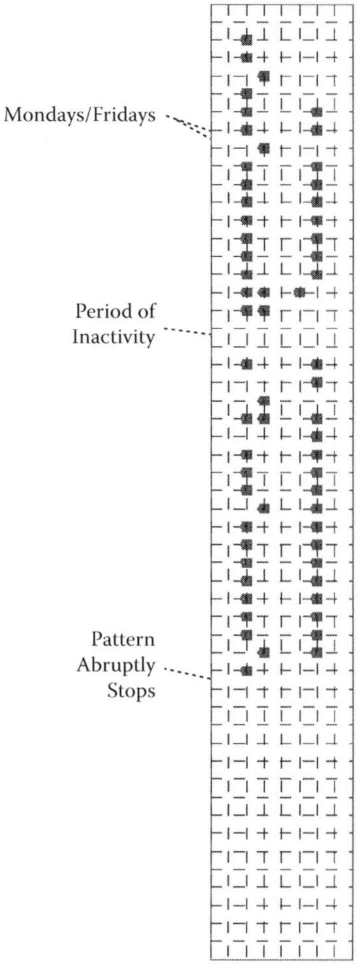

Figure 5.40 CTR convenience store deposits.

name, SSN, and address into the SAR database reveal no additional filings. So what could possibly be wrong with this picture? As shown in Figure 5.41, the diagram on the left depicts the filing behavior associated with the business; however, there can be instances where there are multiple CTR filings on the same day (in the operational systems, those are depicted using a lighter shading for the box-fill cover). The same diagram is slightly rotated (right side), revealing that there are multiple filings, up to five a day, which would be very unusual for this type of operation. A bit more digging shows there are multiple banks involved. One possible answer could be that there are multiple stores and each frequents a bank close to its operating location, but these CTRs are all reported under the

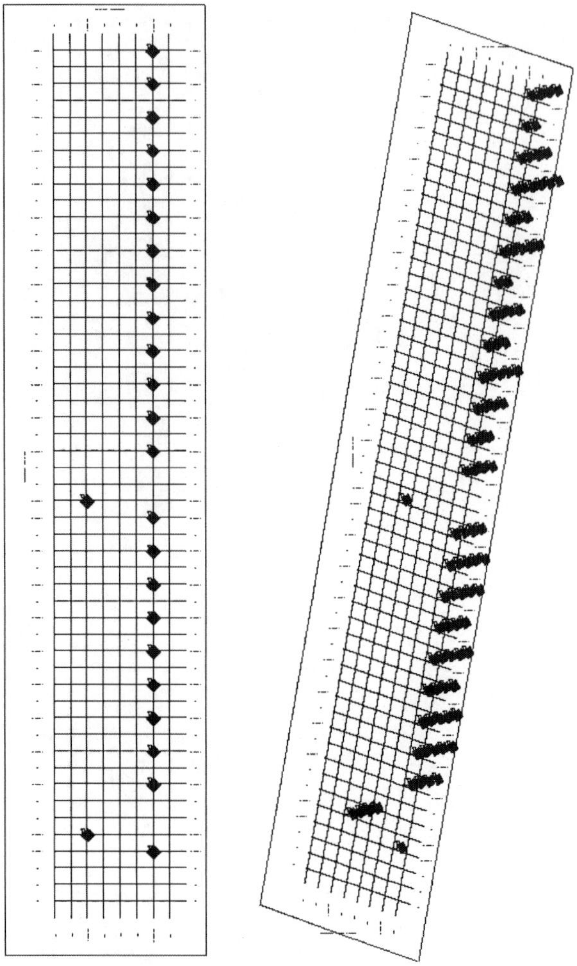

Figure 5.41 CTRs for auto parts retailer.

same EIN/SSN[60] and, therefore, would presumably also use the same bank for their daily business needs. Thus, this presents a situation that requires further investigation by an analyst to determine if there is any wrongdoing.

The next example also shows a very consistent SAR filing pattern for an individual that routinely goes into a bank and exchanges company checks for money orders that are drawn out of his personal account to pay his employees. It is fairly unusual to take business proceeds, mix them with personal finances, and make payroll using a form of a "cash"

[60] One explanation would be that the EIN/SSN referenced is for a parent company and each store simply files their weekly earnings under this number.

method, which is why the bank is filing the SARs in the first place. As is shown in Figure 5.42, the transactions are always conducted on a Thursday, presumably to make payroll on Friday. All of the information contained in the SARs is fairly consistent with respect to his name, address, identification number, and other supporting details. The only major difference is the amount of the transactions, which range from \$2,500 to upwards of \$6,500 a week. Thus, even though the bank can roll 30 days' worth of transactions into a single SAR, they have opted to report on each occurrence, thereby providing much more detail into the activities of this particular individual. Otherwise, it would have looked like the Figure 5.38.

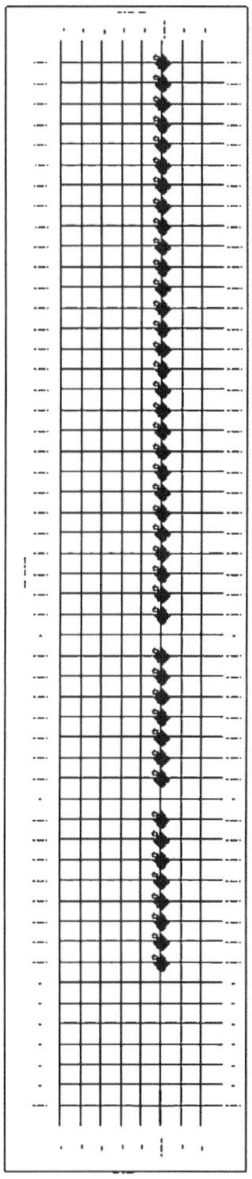

Figure 5.42 Transferring business proceeds through a personal account.

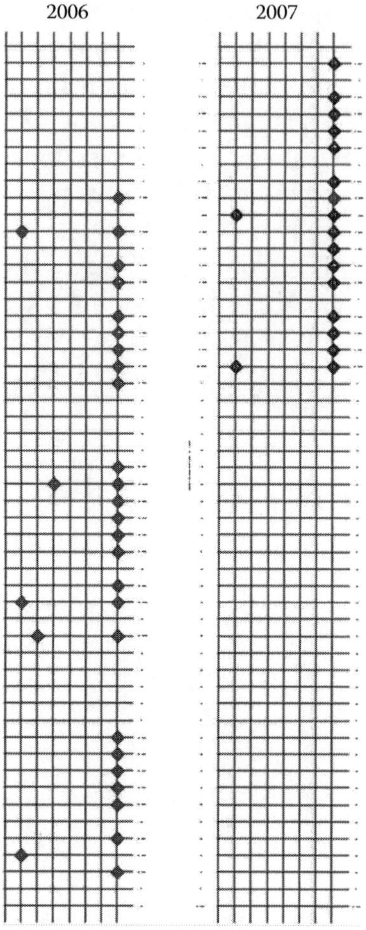

Figure 5.43 Using slots to launder money.

Another very well-defined pattern is shown in Figure 5.43, and is again based on the SARs filed by a casino—a Tribal Licensed Casino.[61] In this example, there are actually two columns presented to show multiple filing years, 2006 and 2007, respectively, from left to right. Literally, all of these violations occurred on Saturdays (predominantly) and Sundays with the exception of two dates in 2006 that correspond to July 4th (Independence Day) and September 4th (Labor Day). Furthermore, all 50 of these SARs were filed by the same casino for a total amount approaching $600,000, where the smallest filing was about $2,000 and the

[61] http://www.law.cornell.edu/uscode/html/uscode25/usc_sup_01_25_10_29.html. The Indian Gaming Regulatory Act (Pub.L. 100-497, 25 U.S.C. § 2701 et seq.) created in 1988 establishes the laws, regulations, and jurisdictional framework that governs Indian gaming establishments.

largest a little over $11,000—therefore, averaging approximately $6,000 per incident.

This particular individual is an 80-year-old man who regularly comes into the casino to play the slot machines. His modus operandi is to pick a machine that accepts cash and then proceed to insert a number of $100 bills to initiate play. He then plays a few rotations (e.g., minimal play) and keeps adding more money until there are several thousands of dollars of credits on the machine.[62] In addition to accepting cash bills up to $100, many modern slots use a technology called Ticket In/Ticket Out (TITO), a method where the slot prints out a bar-coded slip of paper (e.g., a voucher) that can be used to play other TITO-enabled machines, or be paid out by casino cashiers. Once enough money is credited on the machine he is playing, this individual then prints his vouchers and cashes them out; most often, he is paid in large bills (e.g., $100s), but also sometimes requests $50 bills. The reason for the sudden drop-off in SAR filings in 2007 was because the casino decided to mitigate their exposure to any money-laundering activities associated with this person and permanently banned him from entering the casino property.

False Temporal Patterns

There are also cases presented in the SAR data where specific temporal patterns turn out to be false positives or not qualified. When scanning the databases, there are spikes occasionally encountered where a particular account or subject has a large number of filings against them in a predetermined time period. In this example, an individual was identified with dozens of SAR filings with a fairly high dollar value. When these transactions are presented in a date grid (Figure 5.44), it shows five distinct dates with one date being significantly more popular than the others. In this case, the large number of filings actually correlates to a "resubmission" of previous SARs by the bank due to corrections[63] made to improperly coded field values that were identified by government regulators. This is not an uncommon event and happens less frequently as financial institutions become more experienced with how the forms should be submitted. However, these new SARs are now duplicated in the database, so

[62] The maximum amount of cash these machines would accept was set at $8,000.

[63] Resubmissions are requested for a variety of reasons including the reporting of missing field values, incorrectly filled-out forms, or additional detail on certain events. There are even cases reported where automated AML software used by the financial institutions to submit SAR reports has improperly mixed up field values where, for example, dates were reported as violation amounts—resulting in some very large and erroneous filings.

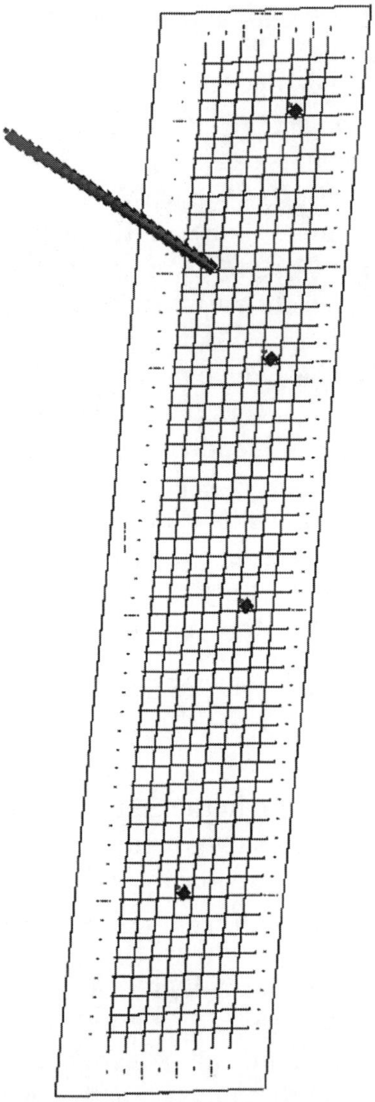

Figure 5.44 Resubmission of SAR form to correct a submission problem.

additional measures need to be put into place to help minimize this kind of duplication.

The previous date grids presented some very well-qualified patterns that were easy to grasp. However, many times there are no easily discernable patterns contained in the transaction data. The date grids presented in Figure 5.45 are to provide examples of those more common situations where no tangible pattern immediately stands out. It is not to say that given enough context and understanding of the underlying data something will

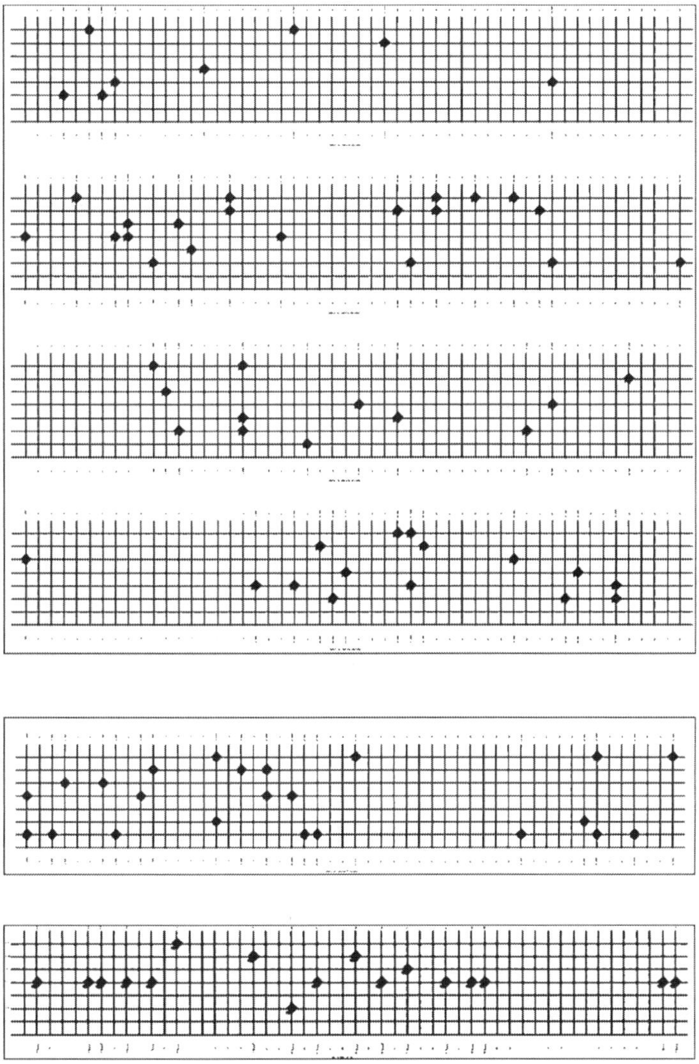

Figure 5.45 No explicit date grid patterns.

eventually be found, but rather, when performing a cursory review there are no revelations or new findings encountered.

A Final Note

Over the years of reviewing thousands upon thousands of SAR narratives, from dozens of different FIUs from around the globe, there are some highlights that stand out and are personal favorites. There are many reasons for filing a SAR and the narrative section is important because it describes the primary reason why the financial institution believed the actions or behavior of the individual were suspicious. On the U.S. forms,[64] the following instructions are provided to help guide the compliance officers on how to best describe the events and justify submitting the form:

> This section of the report is critical. The care with which it is written may make the difference in whether or not the described conduct and its possible criminal nature are clearly understood. Provide below a chronological and complete account of the possible violation of law, including what is unusual, irregular or suspicious about the transaction, using the following checklist as you prepare your account. If necessary, continue the narrative on a duplicate of this page.

- Describe supporting documentation and retain for 5 years.
- Explain who benefited, financially or otherwise, from the transaction, how much, and how.
- Retain any confession, admission, or explanation of the transaction provided by the suspect and indicate to whom and when it was given.
- Retain any confession, admission, or explanation of the transaction provided by any other person and indicate to whom and when it was given.
- Retain any evidence of cover-up or evidence of an attempt to deceive federal or state examiners or others.
- Indicate where the possible violation took place (e.g., main office, branch, other).
- Indicate whether the possible violation is an isolated incident or relates to other transactions.
- Indicate whether there is any related litigation, if so, specify.
- Recommend any further investigation that might assist law enforcement authorities.

[64] All SAR forms (Depository Institutions, Casinos and Card Clubs, Money Services Businesses, and Securities and Futures Industries) require a narrative to be submitted as part of the report.

- Indicate whether any information has been excluded from this report, if so, why?
- If you are correcting a previously filed report, describe the changes that are being made.

Investigators consistently find the narratives to be one of the most useful sections of a SAR submission and many agencies have teams of staff dedicated to reading their content. Some are very long and detailed, yet others are short and to the point. The following narratives are restatements of those of unusual interest, mostly for their entertainment and humorous content. Keep in mind, there are no hard-and-fast guidelines for what is considered suspicious, so everyone has a different interpretation.

The simplest narrative ever encountered is represented by these two words: SEE ATTACHMENT. Basically, all of the guidance presented for writing a narrative is ignored and provided on supplemental forms, attachments, and via other documents. Although their intentions are good, the filing institution does not realize that those "attachments" never make it into the databases for review by the analysts, rendering the SAR fairly useless. Of course, government regulators can request that the filing institution resubmit these types of filings with appropriate narrative content.

Another favorite is THE MONEY SMELLS LIKE "XYZ" and is reported in narratives more often than one would generally imagine. Depending on the circumstances, the smell is FISH, MUSTY, DIRT, PERFUME, or DRUGS. These types of submissions are usually not for just a few bills being transacted but often for larger volumes of money. There are also references to THE MONEY WAS WET (OR DAMP). One can only imagine where the money was acquired or how it was stored.

One SAR involved a mentally challenged man who was well known and liked by the bank's employees. He would regularly come into their branch and try to cash checks for a billion dollars. The checks were created at home, drawn with a pen on lined notebook paper, and colored in with crayons. The employees were aware of his limitations and generally put up with his behavior. However, on one occasion he came in to deposit a check for $750,000,000. The check was drawn on a computer and printed on 8.5″ × 11″ paper. It was clearly an unofficial check and a very simple and unsophisticated design. However, since it was generated using a computer, it could be considered counterfeit and, therefore, the bank filed a SAR to document the incident and cover their assets.

In another SAR, a customer came into the branch with $5,000 in cash, all $20 bills tied together with rubber bands, placed in a brown lunch bag, with deposit instructions written in crayon. Astute tellers thought this was unusual and filed a SAR on this individual. There are actually numerous examples involving the use of crayons in a wide range of banking transactions. Of course, this situation could be considered a ***defensive filing***,[65] where the smallest indicator of suspicion or risk based on the underlying conduct of the customer will trigger the filing of a SAR. This occurs because FIUs and governments around the world have stepped up their oversight and regulation of different financial industries. A fundamental issue being addressed is the compliance of these regulated institutions to properly, timely, and accurately submit the required information.

Recently, in the United States there has been a heavy crackdown, across the board, on different violations including failure to monitor accounts, failure to file reports, inadequate AML procedures to detect and report suspicious activity, failure to designate a compliance officer, and failure to implement a client identification program. The stepped-up oversight, compliance, and regulations have resulted in large penalties. Table 5.4 provides an example of some fines imposed.

There have been serious concerns raised throughout the financial industries regulated by the various governments involved in AML operations to remain compliant with respect to the required filings. In fact, a new wave of defensive filings has flooded many FIUs because the institutions

Table 5.4 Example of Noncompliancy Fines

Name of Bank	*Year Fined*	*Fine Amount*
American Express Bank Intl (Miami)	2007	U.S.$65M
Union Bank of California	2007	U.S.$31.6M
Bank of America	2006	U.S.$7.5M
Israel Discount Bank (New York)	2006	U.S.$12M + US.$8M
Arab Bank PLC (New York)	2005	U.S.$24M
ABN AMRO Bank, N.V.	2005	U.S.$80M
Bank of New York	2005	U.S.$38M
Riggs Bank (Washington, DC)	2004	U.S.$25M + U.S.$16M
AmSouth Bancorp (Alabama)	2004	U.S.$40M + U.S.$10M

[65] Testimony of Megan Davis Hodge on behalf of the American Bankers Association before the Subcommittee on Oversight and Investigations Committee on Financial Services United States HouseofRepresentatives,May10,2007.http://www.house.gov/apps/list/hearing/financialsvcs_dem/hthodge051007.pdf.

want to cover any item that may be of concern. Many of these defensive filings are not appropriate,[66] but the institutions do not want to be liable for criminal penalties or fines that could easily reach millions of dollars.

Additionally, in the United States, due to strict Patriot Act requirements, including Section 312, many financial institutions are dropping correspondent accounts and private banking clients or even complete industry classes (such as money service businesses) to avoid exposure to compliance or reporting deficiencies.[67] The closing of these accounts by the institutions to prevent these penalties is often based on broad-reaching and generic guidelines rather than specific issues, violations, questionable behaviors, or unusual activity.

Now, back to discussing SAR narratives (and defensive filings). This next example was actually filed by a bank supervisor on one of his own employees. The employee was caught removing a disk drive from a desktop computer owned by the bank without receiving proper authorization and, when subsequently questioned about the incident, denied knowledge of the missing equipment. After being informed of the security tape recording his actions, he admitted to removing the disk drive (which was later returned to the bank), at which point his employment was promptly terminated. The bank then went above the call of duty to submit a SAR on this individual. Generally, many banks will submit SARs when tellers steal money, manipulate client accounts without prior approval, or are involved in some type of organized ring/conspiracy to defraud the bank. In this case, however, one could question the rationale behind submitting a SAR for a nonfinancial incident.

The next example is one of the strangest ever seen and has to deal with an individual who thinks the bank is using spies and people wearing masks and disguises to try and steal his patents and copyrights for his time travel and various flying saucer technologies. He also references contacting the U.S. Congress to report the bank for being involved in organized crime and for falsely imprisoning him in an attempt to steal his secrets. It is really not clear how this SAR got into the system,[68] but it represents one of the more extreme narrative contents encountered.

---

[66] There are really no minimum standards defined for submitting (or not submitting) SARs and there is currently very limited feedback from government agencies or law enforcement organizations with respect to those that are actually filed.

[67] In February 2008, Dutch bank ABM AMRO dropped all U.S. customers with passport and trading accounts. These actions are believed by some to be related to the stringent compliance requirements (regulations and liabilities) imposed by the U.S. government.

[68] Technically, anyone can submit a SAR to the IRS-DCC in a hard-copy format without any type of oversight or review. In fact, prisoners have been known to fill out fictitious SARs and try to submit them on people they dislike.

Another SAR narrative describes the level of diligence involved in KYC (Know Your Customer[69]) for one very dedicated and committed bank employee. In this case, the employee (a branch officer) had concern over the legitimacy and nature of the funds being deposited by a female customer. He therefore initiated a visit to her place of employment, an adult nightclub, where he noted about 20 patrons and 5 exotic dancers. One of the dancers asked him to donate $150 for receiving a special service offered in one of the rooms located in the back of the establishment. Based on the frequency of the customer's transaction history, the volume of funds involved, and the apparent unlawful activity of the business, the bank believed that the customer tried to evade reporting requirements and filed a SAR on her. However, the narrative never did say whether the employee accepted the offer for the special services offered.

In this last example, anyone with an e-mail account, including bank representatives, has received an offer from various foreign correspondents (many from Nigeria) who claim they need help moving millions of dollars of unclaimed funds, inheritances, government contracts, or other sources of funds. These scam e-mails come in all flavors and basically state: "I SOLICIT YOUR STRICTEST CONFIDENCE ABOUT RECORDS OF UNCLAIMED FUNDS OF TOTAL SUM £9.5 MILLION THAT I DISCOVERED DURING ONE OF MY ROUTINE CHECKS IN MY DEPARTMENT WHICH BELONGED TO A RICH INDUSTRIALIST WHO DIED AS A RESULT OF A CAR ACCIDENT LAST YEAR. THERE WAS NO RECORDS OF NEXT OF KIN OR HEIR MENTIONED IN THE DATA FOLDERS OF THIS BANK ACCOUNT..." Unfortunately, when these e-mails first came out, a number of them were submitted into the SAR database because they were received by bank personnel and were financially oriented. They are less prevalent now, but the data is usually held for 10 years, so they continue to waste the valuable time and resources of the agencies tasked with combating financial crimes.

Conclusion

The number of patterns contained in financial data sets is virtually unlimited. With more than a 100 variables captured by each form regulated under the BSA governances and laws, there are thousands upon thousands

[69] A policy enacted under the BSA and Patriot Act to confirm customer identifications and sources of funds.

of combinations that can potentially expose criminal behavior. The trick is in interpreting the data and understanding the context under which the forms were filed. This means ensuring the analysts have the skills and experience necessary to prioritize the patterns identified to minimize the investigatory resources required to follow up on and initiate a case, while maximizing the potential criminal charges that can be applied.

Some FIUs act merely in an intelligence role, conveying results to external organizations for follow-up, while others are chartered with law enforcement responsibilities to arrest people, seize assets, and disrupt money-laundering operations. The justice systems for those countries involved in combating financial crimes must also keep pace with current practices and trends to ensure there are new laws and regulations imposed on different industries susceptible to money laundering. Additionally, these laws must address emerging technologies that can be used to help conceal the proceeds of crimes by helping to circumvent detection and avoid discovering or exposing the origin(s) or targeted destination(s) of the money. Over the next several years, there will be many more changes and regulations imposed by our collective governments, especially on those businesses where money, financing, or funds can be used to help support terrorist activities, organized crime operations, or any type of illegal operation.

Chapter 6

Money Service Businesses

Introduction

This chapter provides an overview of how money service businesses (MSBs) are used by criminal elements throughout the United States to launder money derived from human smuggling and narcotics trafficking. There is considerable attention given to the U.S. Southwest border, specifically Arizona, in detailing how these operations are conducted and many of the related dimensions associated with this illegal industry. The scenarios and circumstances presented here are played out numerous times each day in this never-ending game of cat and mouse between law enforcement and the smugglers they are trying to stop. Each side continually adapts and evolves according to necessity, survival, and environmental demands.

What Is a Money Service Business?

According to the U.S. Department of the Treasury,[1] a money service business is defined as a money transmitter or issuer, or seller or redeemer of money orders or traveler's checks (which also includes the U.S. Postal Service), currency exchange, check-cashing business, or a stored-value instrument. The amount transacted by the MSB must exceed $1,000 in one or more transactions on any particular day. Perhaps the most well-known wire remitters include Western Union and MoneyGram, with their many locations around the globe designed to provide a fast and easy way to send money.

However, MSBs come in all shapes and sizes. There are over 36,000[2] MSB companies registered with the federal government—and that number grows monthly. The list includes virtually every type of establishment, including supermarkets, delis, dry cleaners, pharmacies, gas stations, investment houses, travel agencies, and proverbial liquor stores. Each registration defines the type of money service offering made by the company to include issuance/redemption of traveler's checks, money orders, currency dealer/exchanger, check cashing, and money transmission. Unfortunately, not all businesses that qualify as an MSB are properly registered with the government. As with all financial-oriented institutions, there are government regulations designed to track the abuses and illegal activities associated with this industry.

---

[1] http://www.msb.gov/msb/index.html.

[2] As of July, 2008, based on reference: http://www.msb.gov/pdf/msb_registration_list.pdf.

Why Wire Remitters?

Jobs in the United States pay a substantial amount more when compared to similar types of employment in places like Mexico, El Salvador, and Guatemala. In fact, the pay can be up to five times as much as that in an immigrant's home country, making the United States an attractive destination for those wanting to better their lives and generate more income for their families. Currently, Latinos represent more than 41 million residents and account for one of every four births in the United States.

Generally, an immigrant will send a portion of his earnings back to family members in his home country in what are called "family maintenance wires," used to help supplement their daily needs for food, fuel, medicine, and clothing. These types of transfers are perfectly legitimate and are fairly commonplace—to the point that entire economies are built upon this type of benevolence.

The United States and Saudi Arabia support the largest number of worker remittances to developing countries, with the top remittances going to India, Mexico, and the Philippines.[3] According to several studies,[4] the average Mexican immigrant earns approximately $21,000/year in the United States, and is typically employed in low-cost, manual industries, such as construction, hospitality (e.g., housekeepers, busboys, kitchen support), landscaping, food processing (e.g., poultry- and meat-packing plants), and manufacturing (e.g., textiles).

Immigrants usually send home remittances, on average, between 12 to 13 times a year, for approximately $150 to $250 (with $240 being the national average[5]) or almost $3,000 a year. These numbers rise as economies change the demands for labor (e.g., housing booms and new agricultural demands). These maintenance transactions are usually easy to spot in data because the information used is typically very consistent in terms of how names are represented (many also share the same last name); and addresses, phone numbers, and ID numbers are always consistent. The time periods between transactions are very predictable as they are most often conducted monthly (or biweekly) to correspond with a paycheck. Perhaps most importantly, the amount wired is typically below $500. The consistency, frequency, and regularity of

[3] Dilip Ratha, "Workers' Remittances: An Important and Stable Source of External Development Finance." Washington, D.C. World Bank, 2003.

[4] Douglas Woodward, "Mexican Immigrants: The New Face of the South Carolina Labor Force." Columbia: University of South Carolina, Moore School of Business, March 2006.

[5] "Sending Money Home, The First State-by-State Analysis of Remittances from the U.S. to Latin America." Washington, D.C. Inter-American Development Bank, 2004.

these transactions give them a low probability of being a front for money-laundering operations.

Wire remitters are the preferred avenue used to transfer money among the immigrant population because of the strict rules and regulations traditionally associated with the banking industry, concerns over acquiring official identification numbers, such as Individual Taxpayer Identification Numbers (ITINs) and Social Security numbers (SSNs), and sometimes even the legality of their stay in the United States. The services offered by wire remitters allow the immigrant population a fairly safe and secure method to transfer money across international borders while keeping a low profile with respect to their financial interests.

Steps of a Wire Remittance

The general process associated with making a wire remittance[6] is fairly simple and can be done in a matter of minutes from a number of locations.[7] An individual wishing to send money to another person can do so with a fair amount of anonymity and with limited background checks. Generally, a "send form" is filled out by the individual initiating the transfer. This form requires some basic information, such as the sender's full name (first/middle/last), complete address (street/city/state/ZIP), phone and/or e-mail, and the receiver's name (first/middle/last/second last) and address (city/state/country). However, the consistency of the information recorded on the form can vary dramatically, especially when someone is trying to avoid detection. Figure 6.1 shows an example of the Send and Receive forms for both Western Union and MoneyGram.

Formal identification is generally not required to conduct financial transactions for smaller dollar amounts. Credentials are usually presented to the agent to verify that the sender/receiver is who they say they are, but the information is not recorded on the form. However, if the transaction exceeds $3,000, then, based on the Bank Secrecy Act (BSA) regulations as well as several state laws, additional information is recorded, including occupation and date of birth along with a valid SSN, alien registration number, or passport number. This applies to both the sender and receiver in these high-dollar transactions. Generally, money transmitters require identification for transactions over $1,000 based on internal policies to protect themselves from fraud.

[6] Supplemental Declaration of Steven Nasalroad, Superior Court of the State of Arizona, Maricopa County, No. SW 2006-002213, November 27, 2006.

[7] One of the largest remitters, Western Union, advertises that has more than 245,000 agent locations in over 200 countries.

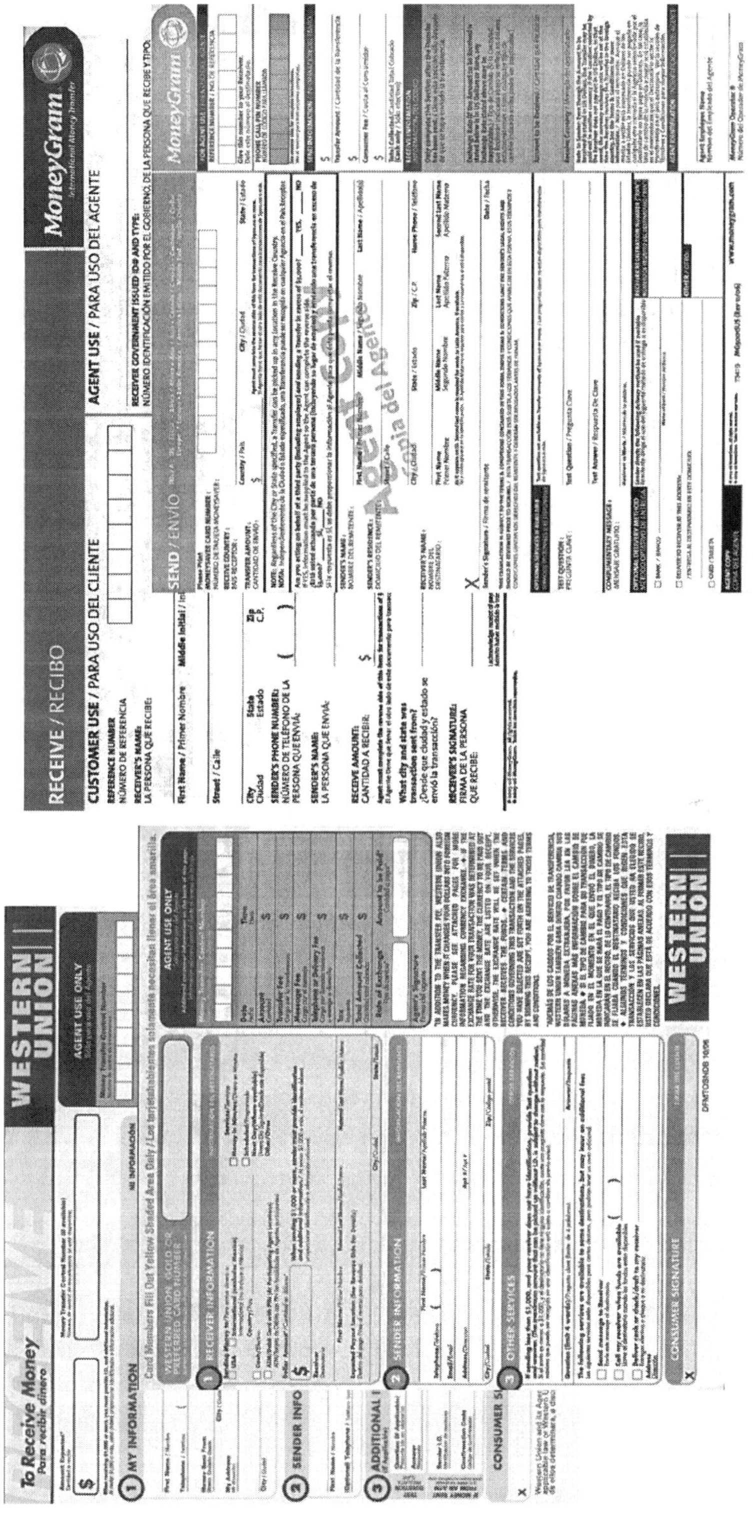

Figure 6.1 Send and Receive forms for Western Union and MoneyGram.

The sender then provides the transfer amount to the clerk (agent representative) in cash, along with the payment fee associated with the wire. Depending on the remitter, the fees are usually calculated on a sliding scale, typically starting at approximately 8 to 10 percent of the transmitted amount. Once initiated, the sender receives a transaction reference number as part of their receipt. At places like Western Union, these are referred to as a Money Transfer Control Numbers (MTCNs) and at MoneyGram, they are called Reference Numbers. Often, this number is sent to the receiving party, as a convenience, to help the receiving agent locate the transaction and speed up the overall process.

The receiver then goes to a designated agent representative and fills out a "receive form" to initiate collection of the wired funds. The same standard information is required on this form, including the receiver's name (first/middle/last), address (street/city/state/ZIP), and phone. Additionally, the form typically includes the sender's name, phone, address (city/state), and the amount sent. The MTCN or Reference Number is not required to receive the wire, but it does help in expediting the payout of the transaction.

A separate receive form is required for each individual wire being collected. Once the information is verified, the transaction is authorized for payment and the agent prints remittance drafts or checks made payable to the receiver. These checks can be cashed at a later time or at other locations, but almost all receivers endorse the checks back to the issuing agent and then receive the allotted cash payment.

For brevity, not all details or laws related to wire remitters were covered in this discussion; however, it does shows the relative ease with which money can be transferred, both domestically and internationally. This process, however, is also fraught with considerable flaws that can be used to bypass anti–money laundering (AML) laws and enable criminal activity, specifically human smuggling and drug trafficking, to flourish fairly unhindered by law enforcement. Fortunately, there are resources being applied to this area to help stem the abuses and criminal activity rampant throughout this industry.

Structure of a Wire Transfer

The data schema associated with wire transfer data varies among the different companies that offer such a service. However, the overall structure is fairly simple; there is a sender and a receiver of a specified amount of money that is transmitted on a certain date, at a certain time. Depending on rules, regulations, and requirements surrounding the MSB, there are potentially other types of data required to be collected.

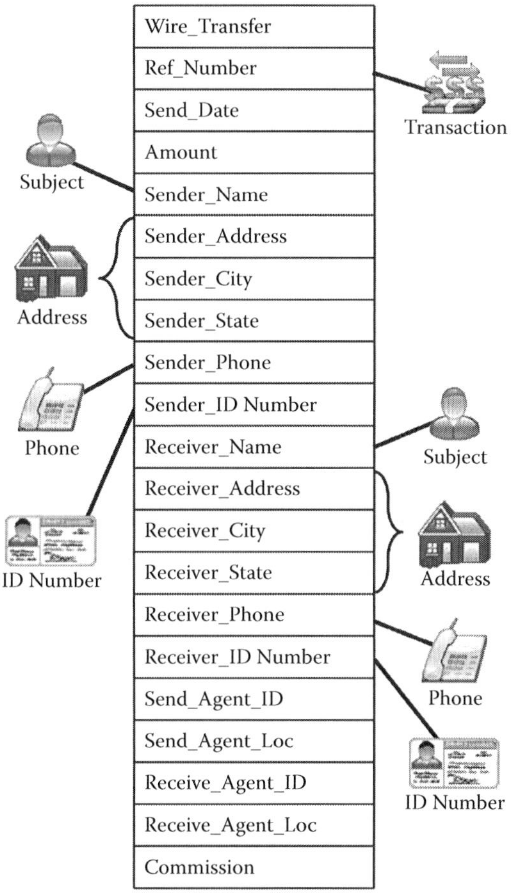

Figure 6.2 Standard wire remitter structure.

Figure 6.2 shows a fairly basic wire remitter schema that depicts the primary data elements, including the *Transaction*, *Subject*, *Address*, *Phone*, and *ID Number*.

What is important to note in this diagram is that there are two Subjects—one each to represent a sender and a receiver, which means that the direction of the association is important to the flow/direction of money. Link direction tends to be analytically important only when objects of the same type are related by some event (e.g., a wire transfer, a phone call, network traffic, etc.). The rationale for using this methodology is to ensure that all of the associations for an object, regardless of its role in the transaction, are clearly depicted—otherwise, there would be numerous objects (e.g., sender or receiver) with the same values (e.g., name). This would require analysts to submit multiple queries to find targets of interest and interpret several different diagrams to understand the interactions, and would generally complicate the overall analysis, potentially leading to incomplete or inconsistent results. As was discussed in Chapter 3 under "Generic Data Types," distancing the "role" of the object in a transaction from its real-world type is always recommended, especially when dealing with "like" objects. Figure 6.3 shows the most logical analytical model derived from this schema.

Due to the common use of names, intentional misrepresentation (typos and misspellings included), and other factors involved in recording wire remitter data, there must be better and more accurate methods to track and correlate how people send money to each other. For example, simply using the lowest common denominator—just a name—makes it impossible to track the transfer activities for someone named John Smith due to the large number of people associated with such a common name. Although including related data, such as the address (street/ZIP code), improves the uniqueness, that type of data is not always reliable and is sometimes not collected on the forms. Therefore, a different analytical tack must be considered.

One of the better approaches for using an alternative representation of the Subject presented in the data schema is to extend its structure to also include the respective sender or receiver Agent ID as part of its encoding (e.g., as its primary key). Every agent registered in a network for, say, Western Union or MoneyGram, has a unique identification number. Due to the large number of agent providers in these networks, and the fact that each transaction consistently records the proper Agent ID, more detailed

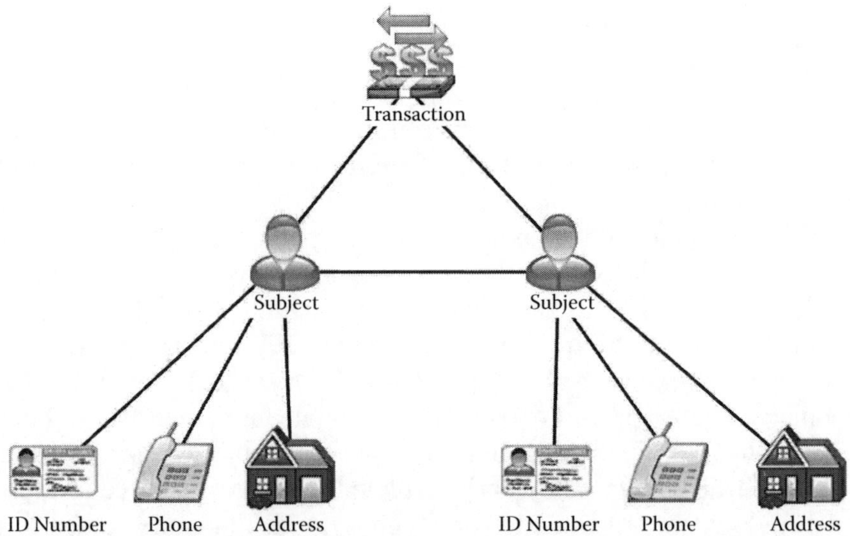

Figure 6.3 Analytical model of wire remitter structure.

analytics can be conducted using a combination of the subject's name and the agent's ID as the unique identifier for the Subject. Although not foolproof, because two or more people with the same name can use the same agent location, it does reduce the overall number of false-positive matches that are encountered in the data. Also, while it is true that this would cause an individual going to different agent locations to be represented as multiple people within the analytical networks, he or she would be easily spotted by connections to common addresses, phone numbers, or identification numbers and, many times, by the same senders or receivers.

There are literally millions of wire transfers conducted every year that are used as the foundation for forming networks of connections based on the parties involved. Analyzing these networks helps reveal patterns of activities (including criminal) and helps investigators to understand the flow of the money. Figure 6.4 shows a fairly standard wire remitter

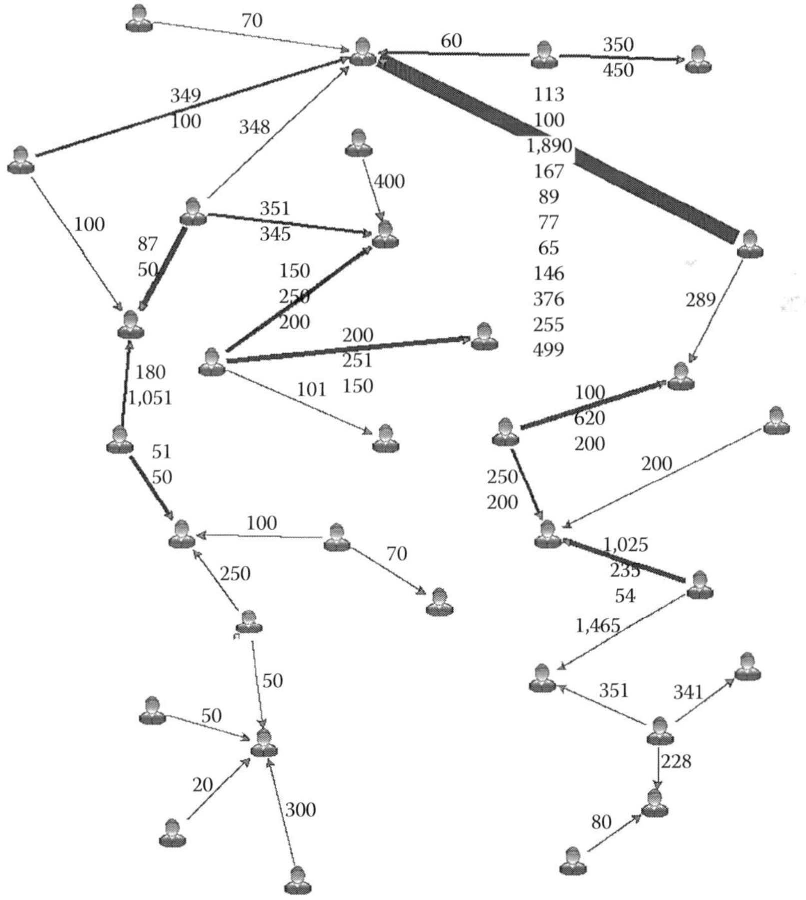

Figure 6.4 A typical wire remitter network structure.

network consisting of 32 individual subjects. The wire amounts (lowest = $20, highest = $1,890) are shown on the links revealing the amount of money transferred during each transaction. The thicker lines (proportionally) indicate multiple transactions among the parties and the link arrows show the direction or flow of the money.

Although these networks may look complex, they are actually very easy to interpret. Many times the number of Subjects presented in a network is significantly inflated due to the extensive name variations reflected in the data. To make this point, Figure 6.5 shows another remitter network consisting of 14 Subjects whose names have been adjusted to reflect their real-world counterpart using an alphabetical index (e.g., DAVID-a, DAVID-b, DAVID-c, and DAVID-d are all the same person).

Upon closer examination of the names in this network, it becomes clear that there are several variations of three primary names: Edison, Maria, and David. Using some simple consolidation (e.g., entity resolution)

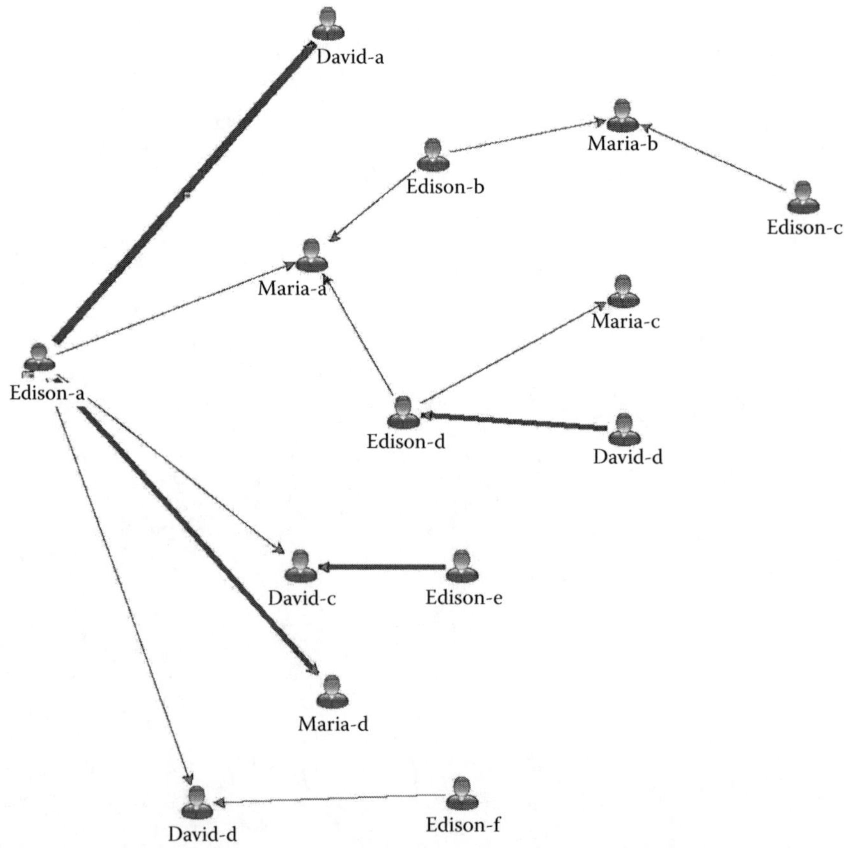

Figure 6.5 Sample remitter network showing name variation.

techniques, the network is collapsed by merging the similarly named objects together. The resulting network is shown in Figure 6.6.

It is now very easy to tell the nature of the relationships among the networked entities; Edison and David are heavily connected with mutual levels of funding between them; David and Maria have no direct wire transfers; and the transfers between Edison and Maria are always sent from Edison to Maria. Additional analytics could also be performed on the transactional activities (e.g., the wire transfers) using a temporal grid (not shown). This would expose when the remittances are occurring and if there are any temporal dependencies or sequences among members of this network. It would also help establish any patterns for the level of money being transacted (e.g., David receives only high-value transfers). Regardless of the type of analysis being performed, it is more understandable when the duplicate information is consolidated.

Generalizing the overall interpretation of networks, especially using the model previously presented in Figure 6.3, a number of different analytical scenarios can be construed based on how the objects are interconnected. For example, take the network depicted in Figure 6.7, which shows only Subject to Phone connections.

This specific network represents one of the thousands typically found in wire transfer data sets and it depicts several interesting structures. The Subject at the center (1) has used six different phone numbers, which is somewhat unusual; the Phone in the middle (2) acts somewhat like an articulation point connecting two discrete subnetworks together; and one Phone (3) was used by three different subjects, perhaps as a business line.

Reviewing network connections between subjects and phone numbers also helps to expose a number of interesting details about the

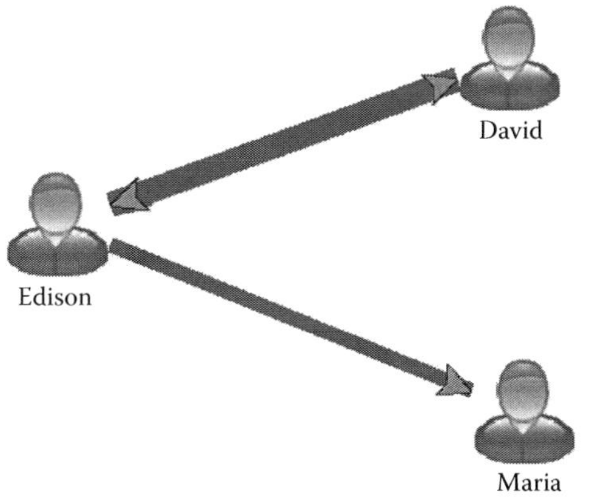

Figure 6.6 Similar objects merged together.

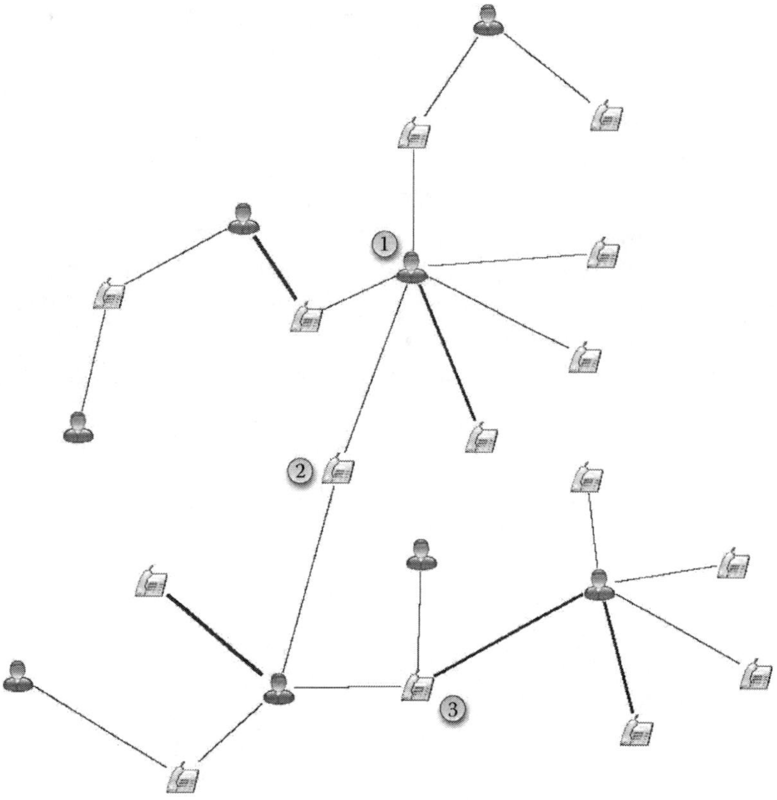

Figure 6.7 Subject and Telephone network connections.

network, including alternative name spellings for a subject using the same phone (including intentional misrepresentations), identification of business lines, exposure of potential "safe house" phones, and collusive networks of individuals. These types of details can also be seen when reviewing networks of Subjects and Addresses as depicted in Figure 6.8.

As a rule of thumb, addresses are one of the most inconsistent values in most data sources, and wire remitter data is no exception. Small variations can cause large network fan-outs (many-to-one relationships), resulting in complex-looking networks. Other factors related to addresses that complicate analysis include locations, such as apartments or common housing areas that may show (falsely) many people living at the same place. Of course, there are automated methods that exist to help clean up and standardize addresses to help resolve these types of issues. Figure 6.9 shows a simple example of three distinct address objects that obviously all refer to the same place, but because the data was not entered consistently, three distinct objects are presented in the display. It is not uncommon to find addresses in wire remitter data with dozens of variations.

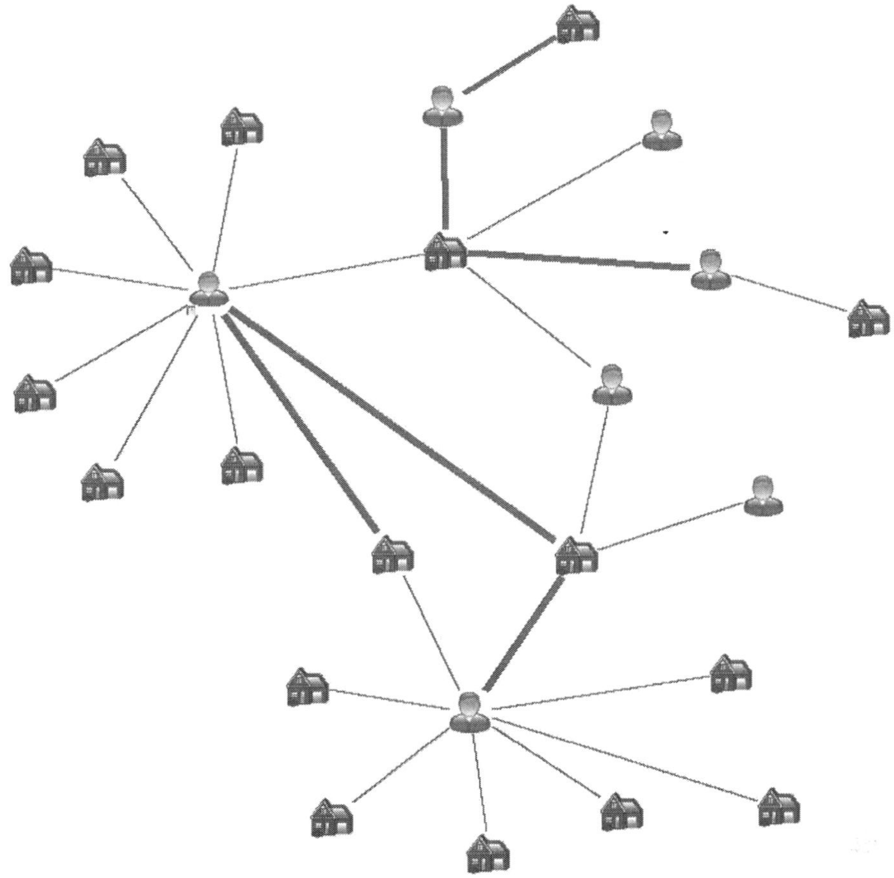

Figure 6.8 Subject and Address network connections.

Paying attention to the structures, connections, frequencies, link directions, and general format of the networks formed using wire remitter data can help identify and expose various types of behaviors. The key is in interpreting the data within the context of the analysis being performed. For example, given the following three diagrams (Figure 6.10 to Figure 6.12), each of the network structures is vastly different from each other and each clearly indicates a different type of activity.

Figure 6.10 depicts a highly centric network that shows source objects where money emits from a single entity, and sink objects, where money is consumed by (flows into) the entity; these kinds of behaviors tend to exhibit strong influence and control over the network. This type of network is vulnerable and easy to detect, monitor, and, ultimately, seize. Generally, this network configuration indicates alien smuggling or various other fraudulent activities (mortgage loan frauds, bust-out schemes, etc.). Figure 6.11 shows more interconnected nodes, which naturally provides

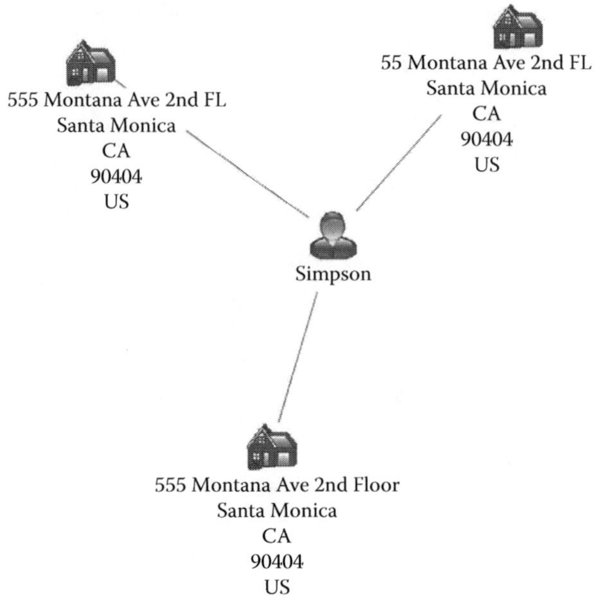

Figure 6.9 Address variations in wire remitter data.

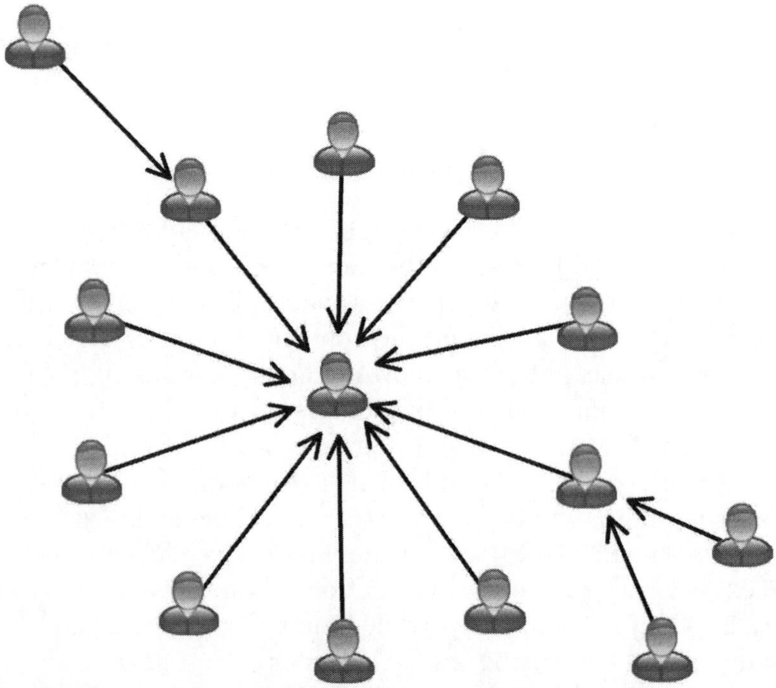

Figure 6.10 Human smuggling pattern.

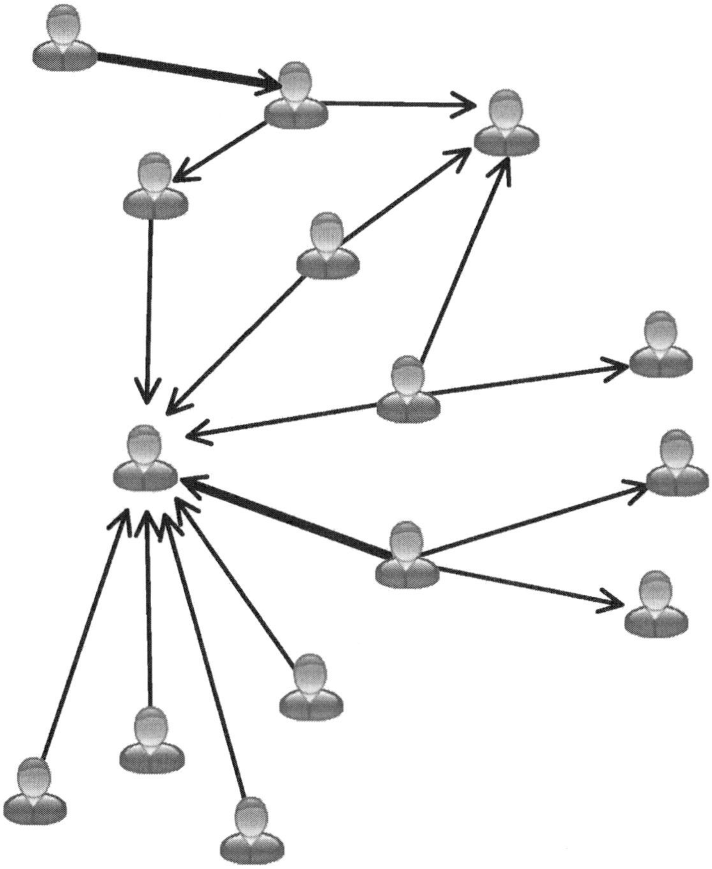

Figure 6.11 Narcotics trafficking pattern.

less overall control in the network. Multiple players act in a distributed fashion to add complexity and some redundancy, making it more resource-intensive to monitor or disrupt due to the multiple targets of interest. These types of networks may be related to narcotics trafficking or gambling operations. Finally, Figure 6.12 displays a highly distributed structure, which results in limited control or oversight across the network. There is no single control point and, therefore, the network can easily reconstitute using alternative entities. This type of structure is hard to trace and track and, thus, is ideal for terrorist financing related activities.

There are many different types of network patterns contained in wire remitter data and the key to exposing criminal activities is in knowing what to look for. Fortunately, there are a number of law enforcement organizations that have performed extensive amounts of analysis on wire remitter data and understand how to interpret and classify the resultant networks. More importantly, they know how to use the data to defeat the

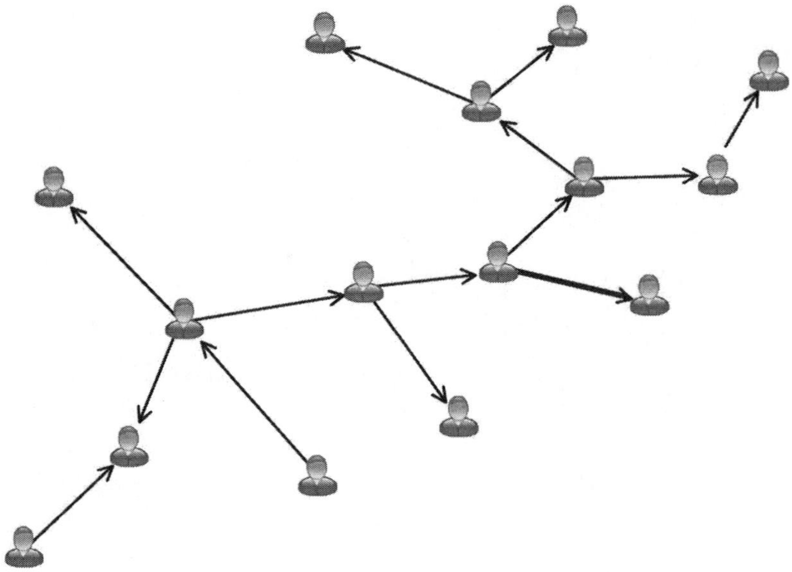

Figure 6.12 Terrorist financing pattern.

criminal activities involved in laundering money associated with human smuggling and narcotics trafficking.

Combating Human Smuggling

The Arizona Office of the Attorney General (AZ AG), Financial Remedies Section (FRS) established the Financial Crimes Task Force (FCTF) in October 2000 to interdict money transfers and disrupt the operations associated with human-smuggling and narcotics-trafficking organizations. The FCTF is responsible for acquiring and analyzing data from wire remitters, banks, and other financially oriented businesses operating in the state of Arizona. All of this data is used to help enforce state laws, rules, and regulations. The FCTF is comprised of detectives from the Arizona Department of Public Safety, special agents from the Arizona Attorney General's Office, detectives from the Phoenix Police Department, and agents from the U.S. Customs and Border Protection and the Bureau of U.S. Citizenship and Immigration Services (formerly the Immigration and Naturalization Service), both now part of the U.S. Immigration and Customs Enforcement (ICE) under the U.S. Department of Homeland Security.

A substantial amount of resources are expended every year by the state of Arizona to help combat the criminal organizations involved in these operations because the smugglers pose a major threat to public safety through related assaults, homicides, kidnappings, auto theft,[8] identify theft, and other crimes associated with their illegal dealings. The AZ AG has been on the forefront of combating financial crimes since the early 1990s and has cleverly adapted its approaches, techniques, and technologies to keep pace with its adversaries.

Since its inception, the FCTF has run a number of targeted operations (i.e., warrants for seizure) against several high-volume money remitters operating in the region. In fact, over 15 seizure warrants have been executed since 2001, each being carefully crafted and updated to target very specific patterns of illicit behavior, primarily targeting human and illegal drug smuggling.

According to various transcripts, affidavits, and court documents, provided to the Superior Court by the FCTF, there is strong evidence of very lax compliance with respect to collecting accurate data regarding the persons involved in the wire transfers. The names, addresses, and identifications of the receiving parties are allowed to vary significantly, often observed when transactions are received during a short time period (e.g., minutes apart)—potentially indicating criminal collusion with the representative agents. The names of sending and receiving cities are abbreviated, misspelled, or varied to help cloud the understanding of the money flows and to defeat the internal compliance-monitoring systems. These are classic techniques used by criminal elements to frustrate law enforcement operations. However, they are also the type of indicators that clearly designate that unlawful—and evasive—activities are occurring.

Identification of corrupt remitter agents is a serious factor to contend with in such a large enterprise. In fact, Western Union[9] was ordered to cease and desist doing business with eight locations permanently, and another six until they could demonstrate their compliance processes were improved and working adequately—which ultimately cost them $3 million in related fines and penalties. Some of the violations included failure to maintain appropriate training materials; submitting forms with smudged, illegible, or unusable fingerprints; failure to record customers' identities or acceptance of invalid or missing signatures; identification/name mismatches on forms; and even failure to file forms with the designated authorities.

Based on analytics performed by the FCTF, it was determined that one agent location in Mexico received more than five times the number

[8] Phoenix has ranked in the top five cities nationally from 2001 through 2006 for the highest vehicle theft rates.

[9] Arizona Department of Financial Institutions, Consent Order No. 07F-BD 020 SBD against Western Union Financial Services, Inc. (Respondent) dated August 17, 2006.

of transactions than its nearest competitor—an obvious indicator that the agent is collusive with the smuggling industry. It is not unusual for an agent to become a clearing center for supporting money laundering by being lax in their diligence and compliance. In fact, there are documented instances of agents knowingly allowing money launderers to use false IDs, change their names,[10] structure the transactions into multiple parts to avoid reporting requirements, and alter and adjust their names to circumvent the compliance software. Fortunately, these "facilitating" agents[11] are easy to spot in the transaction datasets because these high-volume and high-value customers do not reflect the industry standards.

Often wire remitter employees, and even the representative agent (e.g., the owner), will accept bribes, commonly referred to as "tips," to help facilitate the transactions, even though they are fully aware the money is used for unlawful purposes. It would not be uncommon to receive a $100 tip for transacting a few thousand remittance dollars. Obviously, these tips significantly subsidize the agents' or owners' monthly living expenses for rent, car payments, and other household necessities. Undercover operations and surveillance tapes show how blatant the tipping process has become in these types of operations. It has even been reported that some corrupt agents maintain a stack of false identification cards to help hide the identity of the recipient.

A majority of smuggling (human and drug) operations occur along the Arizona border, which accounts for more than 50 percent of the illegal immigrant arrests (in 2004). It is estimated[12] that between 3,000 and 4,000 illegal crossings occur each and every day along the Arizona border. Therefore, the FCTF must remain responsive to understanding how their adversary is adapting to their interdiction techniques and adjust accordingly and frequently. The FCTF has come up with new and ingenious ways to deal with these situations. The following is an overview of the smuggling process and why the FCTF's role is so vital in disrupting these organizations.

The Smuggling Process

As stated previously, the amount of money to be made working in the United States far exceeds the risks it takes to enter the country. As could

[10] According to court documents, a woman from Douglas, Arizona, had 63 different spellings of her name in the database.

[11] Some estimates place the volume of criminal business at 80 percent for facilitating agents.

[12] Donald Barlett and James Steele, "Who Left the Door Open?" *Time Magazine*, March 30, 2006. http://www.time.com/time/magazine/article/0,9171,995145,00.html.

be expected from this imbalance, an entire community, ranging from transportation and housing to financing and enforcement, has emerged around supporting the illegal smuggling of humans across the border, which now represents a multibillion-dollar industry.[13] Keep in mind that these are criminal activities, and the people conducting human smuggling, as well as those being smuggled, violate numerous federal and state laws. Even though the government spends billions of dollars protecting its borders, it remains fairly easy to enter and remain in the United States as proven by the millions of illegal aliens permanently living within our borders.

A "coyote" or "pollero" (chicken handler) is a term applied to the individuals involved in the smuggling operations and can be someone who picks up the undocumented aliens (UDAs), guides them across the border, manages the safe house (also called a drop house), or collects payment. There are also a host of additional support roles,[14] ranging from stagers and managers to drivers and enforcers. A UDA, also referred to as a "pollo" (chicken) by the coyotes, is the person trying to gain illegal entry into the United States. The UDA's sponsor is most often a family member or friend already in the United States, or occasionally an employer who requires the labor resource and is paying the "fee" directly to the coyote.

Arizona shares more than 480 miles of border with Mexico, all with Sonora (a state within Mexico). To illegally cross the border into Arizona, UDAs migrate their way across Mexico, as shown in Figure 6.13, using buses or trains to arrive at various staging areas in Sonora, which are usually no more than one hour's drive from the border, with several actually being border towns themselves. The largest influx of crossings tends to occur between January and April, when the seasonal temperatures[15] are still bearable in the Arizona deserts.

According to authorities, one of the primary crossing locations is the Caborca/Altar corridor. In Figure 6.14, the map on the left depicts Sonora, Mexico, with the primary staging towns indicated by circles. For reference, the distance between Phoenix and Hermosillo (the capitol of Sonora, Mexico) is approximately 310 miles; to Nogales, 187 miles; and to San Luis Rio Colorado, a bit over 200 miles. The map on the right in Figure 6.14 shows the secondary staging towns used for smuggling, indicated by squares.

---

[13] Estimates show that approximately $1.7 billion to $2.5 billion annually is routed through Arizona for undocumented aliens (UDAs)—with more than $28 billion across the entire Southwest border (including drug money).

[14] http://www.azcentral.com/specials/special42/articles/0720Online-Drophouse-Terms.html.

[15] Summertime high temperatures can easily reach 120°F (48.8°C).

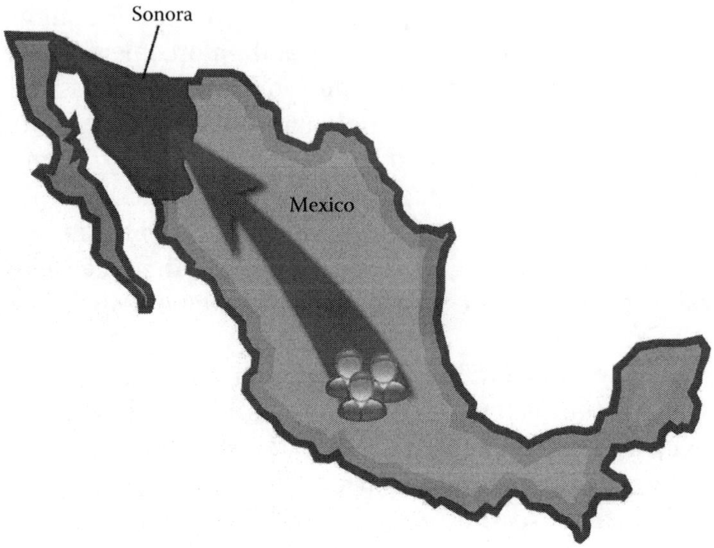

Figure 6.13 Migrating across Mexico to Sonora.

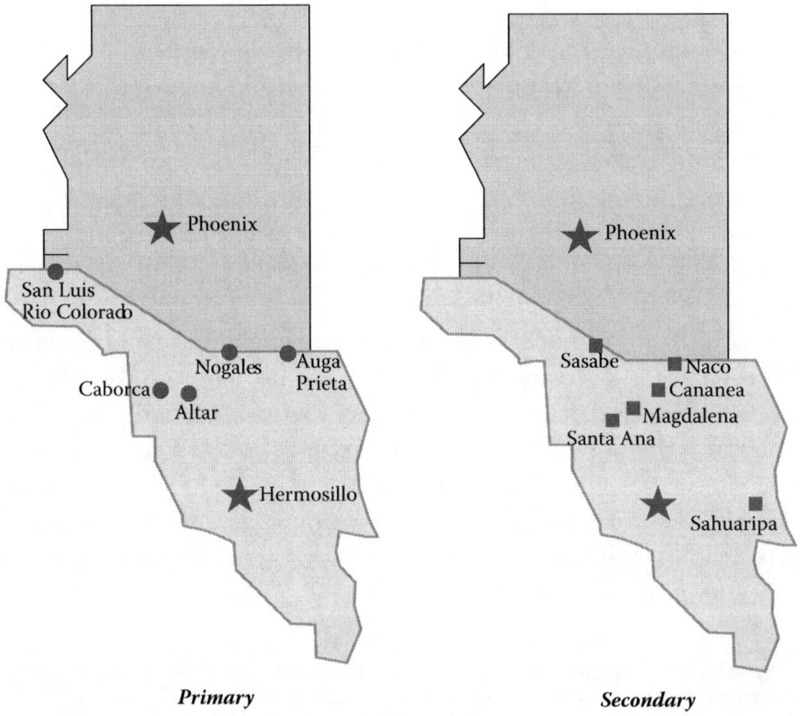

Figure 6.14 Map of primary/secondary staging towns in Sonora, Mexico.

Upon arrival, the UDAs are quickly met at the bus terminals by smugglers looking for new clients (similar to the way taxi drivers solicit fares at unregulated airports). Once contact is made between a UDA and a smuggler, a price is negotiated and the process begins. Traditionally, Mexican authorities have done little to interdict or combat the flow of UDAs, such as targeting the coyotes at their source,[16] and bribery and corruption are rampant within the Mexican police force.[17]

There are specific crossing areas selected along the border, and borders are usually crossed during evening hours when it is cooler, and more important, when the U.S. Border Patrol is getting ready for a shift change—usually around 7:00 p.m. and then again at 3:00 a.m.—when enforcement and surveillance levels are minimized. The coyotes are also aware of numerous border sensors, lookout points, patrols, and other deterrents that would result in the capture or delay of their human cargo. It is estimated that for every apprehension made by Border Patrol, at least three more make it through to safety.

UDAs do not have many personal possessions when they cross the border, nor do they travel with any significant amount of cash. It can take the UDAs up to four to five days to cross the desert, usually not under ideal circumstances. Not only are the rough terrain and harsh environment threats to the UDAs, they also need to be aware of others who may try to rob them. UDAs have limited supplies of water and food and tend not to have much shelter in which to sleep. Unfortunately, there are numerous deaths of UDAs in the desert reported each year due to the extreme heat, lack of water, or other careless behaviors of the coyotes.

Those lucky enough to make it across the border, as depicted in Figure 6.15, are then picked up and delivered to a drop house, where they are held until their crossing fee is paid. The drop houses are usually rented houses, apartments, or even hotel rooms, and in some cases, can have dozens of UDAs waiting for transfer to their final destinations pending payment of the coyote fees. The drop houses are cramped, sparsely furnished, and often dirty; the windows are boarded up or barred to prevent escape; and the UDAs are routinely tied up or handcuffed (many times their belts and shoes are also confiscated), essentially prisoners until the coyotes are paid their fees.

---

[16] La Crónica (Méxicali), June 27, 2001. Articles by Carlos Lima and José Manuel Yépiz. Also found at http://www.nmsu.edu/~frontera/jul01/immi.html.

[17] Marjorie Lilly, "On the line", *Desert Exposure*, August 2005. http://www.desertexposure.com/200508/200508_line.html.

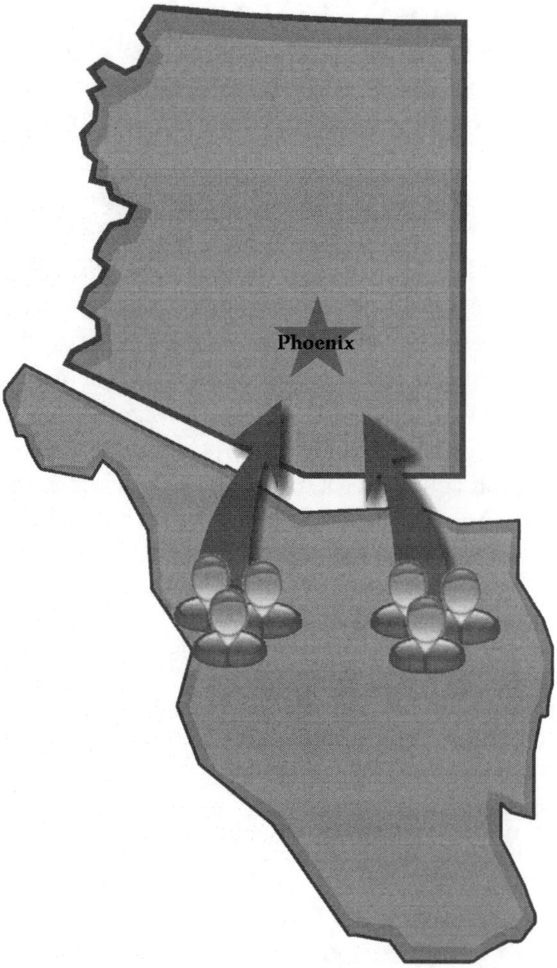

Figure 6.15 Crossing the border from Mexico into Arizona.

Sadly, the coyotes abuse[18] many of the UDAs by beating them, withholding food/water, and often raping or sexually abusing the women. In extreme cases, such as when a UDA argues with a coyote or a payment is

[18] An excerpt of a letter dated April 14, 2004, between the AZAG-FRS and FinCEN: "Phoenix Police Department statistics show that, from January through October 2003, Phoenix experienced 216 homicides, compared to 149 for the same period in 2002, a 45 percent increase. In fiscal year (FY) 1998, there were 96 home invasion crimes committed in the Phoenix area. By FY 2002, the number of home invasions increased to 490. There were 61 coyote-related homicides in Phoenix from 1/1/03 to 9/30/03, in addition to a series of almost a dozen executions in surrounding Maricopa County. This constitutes over 50 percent of all homicides. Over the last few years, the number of incidents involving extortion, kidnapping, and home invasions has risen rapidly. In 2002-2003, there were 623 such incidents, 75 percent of which were the result of human smuggling-related activity. Sexual exploitation of undocumented immigrants is also rising. It takes the form of sexual assault on immigrants in transit, forced prostitution, and even child prostitution involving immigrants from around the world transiting Arizona's particularly open border."

not made, the UDA is executed. See the sidebar on two cases conducted by the Phoenix Police Department, Case #2007-70098392 (Homicide) and Case #2004-40661282 (Homicide/Rape), that detail the violence and degradation associated with this industry.

Once the UDA has arrived in the drop house, he or she will give the coyote the name and phone number of the sponsor. At this point, the coyote contacts the sponsor and provides instructions on how to send the money, as in shown in Figure 6.16. Wire remitters, such as Western Union and MoneyGram, are used to transfer money because the coyote requires cash in hand before the UDAs are released and sent on to their respective sponsor. In this business, there are no credit lines, merchandise exchanges, or refunds available because of the anonymity associated with human smuggling. In fact, when the coyote contacts the sponsor, typically the only information given is the amount to send and the receiver's name, city, and state. A contact phone number is almost never supplied by the coyote[19] in order to keep the transactions anonymous and make it more difficult for law enforcement to track. As opposed to more traditional banks, wire remitters have a very expansive network of agents and locations from which to initiate and receive the transaction and tend to require minimal background checks, regulations, or questions for the parties involved, making them the preferred choice for sending money.

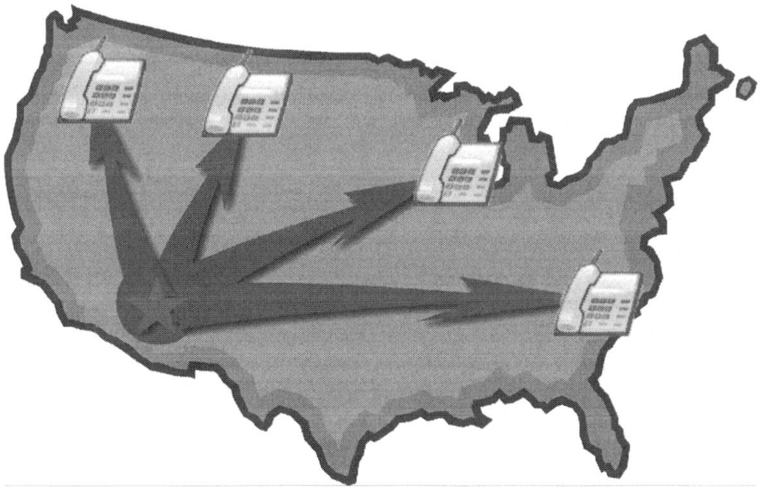

Figure 6.16 Calling the sponsor.

[19] Results from seizure warrants show that more than 75 percent of transfers associated with smugglers do not list a receiver phone number.

Case #2007-70098392

Case #2007-70098392 (Homicide). Excerpt from a Declaration made by Detective John Shallue of the Phoenix Police Department:

"This case was initiated from a 911 call of unknown trouble at the location of 4000 block N. 63rd Avenue, Phoenix on 04/21/2005 just before 5:00 p.m. About 20 undocumented aliens (UDA) were being held at this residence by approximately four to six armed human smugglers. Several neighbors called 911 when the UDAs ran from the residence into the neighborhood, after shots were fired. Police responding to the scene detailed as many of the UDAs as they could find.

I was involved with the interviews of the UDAs at the scene and later at police headquarters, 620 W. Washington. The UDAs said that they had contracted with a human smuggler in Caborca, Sonora, Mexico to bring them into Arizona and beyond for U.S.$800.00. They walked across the desert north of the Altar/Caborca area in different groups with guides, some for as many as five days. When they were brought to the N. 63rd Avenue address, the smugglers demanded approximately double the agreed upon fee.

The victim, Javier, stood up for himself and for all of his fellow UDAs and argued with the smugglers over the extortion that was taking place. One coyote told another they had a trouble-maker. Javier told them that he was going to call the police. The coyote told him that if he did, that he would be shot. When Javier continued to protest, a smuggler escorted Javier to a hallway where he was allowed to call his brother in Pennsylvania. The argument continued in the hallway. One of the smugglers then executed Javier, by shooting him in the head, testicles, and mid-section. It appeared that Javier had been sitting down at the time he was shot, because he was found sprawled and entangled with a chair and because one of the bullets passed through him and hit the back of the chair. After the shots, the smugglers fled from the scene in their van, leaving Javier bleeding to death on the floor. He died about 9:40 p.m. in the hospital. The other UDAs panicked and ran. When the UDAs fled, the neighbors called 911 after seeing a larger number of people running through their yards. No smugglers were found. Javier's brother began calling Phoenix area hospitals, looking for Javier, due to the nature of the argument he had heard over the phone and how the phone call was cut off suddenly. He believed that something terrible had happened to his brother. Javier's brother and Javier's wife were aware that Javier was on his way to join them in Pennsylvania from Mexico. He was 36. His brother came to Phoenix to care for his remains.

Human smuggler ledgers (pollo books) were found inside the residence, in close proximity to where the victim was murdered. An examination of these polo books revealed that at least over one hundred UDAs had been smuggled by these smugglers. On several pages of these books were the

Money Transfer Control Numbers (MTCN), names of the persons receiving the funds, names of the person who sent the funds and from which states and contact names and telephone numbers. Several of the people interviewed on the day of the murder were listed on the books. Their names had been taken as they arrived but they had not yet been paid for."

Case #2004-40661282

Case #2004-40661282 (Homicide/Rape). Excerpt from a Declaration made by Detective John Shallue of the Phoenix Police Department:

"This case was initiated on 02/19/2004 by Maria, a Mexican National who was illegally residing in the United States. Maria had been smuggled into the United States, via Altar, Sonora, and held at a stash house located at 7000 block W. Monte Vista Rd. in Phoenix.

Maria reported that she had been gang raped by the smugglers during the course of her stay there. She also witnessed two other fellow aliens victimized in the same way. Maria watched one smuggler beat and then execute a Guatemalan man because he could not pay his smuggling fee. She was made to clean up the bloody mess that was left behind after the execution and removal of the body. The body was never recovered. Several smugglers were identified but the rapes and homicide have yet to be charged.

Maria said that she was taken by the smugglers to a Western Union store, located in Phoenix, Arizona. There, she was made to produce her identification and to put her fingerprints on many different Western Union receiver forms in plain view of the Western Union agent. Maria did not know who the smugglers were receiving the money from or for what other aliens. Western Union data confirms that Maria was a receiver in 11 transfers dating from 10/31/03 to 11/09/03 totaling U.S.$16,300.00. Maria did not receive any of this money for herself and did not get any for her smuggling fee. The transfers were from all over the United States to Phoenix, Arizona. Maria did not fill out the Western Union forms herself. The coyotes supplied a bogus social security number and a bogus address and other personal information. Maria escaped from her smugglers after approximately one week of sexual abuse and forced labor.

Surveillance was conducted on the residence Maria identified. Traffic stops were made and it was determined that individuals were continuing a smuggling operation at that location. A search warrant was served on the residence on 05/24/04. It was discovered that several undocumented aliens (UDAs) were being held there and four smugglers were arrested. One UDA had been beaten because he was not able to find anyone to pay for his smuggling fee. He was also threatened that if he could not pay, that they would execute him and dispose of his body in the desert. The windows to the room where the UDAs were being kept were boarded up with plywood to prevent their escape. Western Union receipts were found at the house and in the organization's vehicles. Several suspects of the initial crimes were identified through information sources and police records, but were not arrested due to lack of corroborating evidence (no body has been found)."

The coyotes are fairly organized with respect to their activities, especially tracking the finances involved in their transactions and managing their cargo. Many coyotes are part of a much larger criminal organization, which is able to coordinate, maintain, and control all levels of the operation. To properly account for their merchandise, the coyotes maintain detailed lists, called pollo lists, of their transactions. These lists record the name of the UDA, the phone number, the city/state, and name of the sponsor, amount of the fee charged, the tracking number (e.g., MTCN or Reference Number) of the wire transfer, and the date of transfer.

Once payment has been received, as shown in Figure 6.17, the debt is settled between the coyote and the UDA. It is at this point that the coyote will send the UDAs along to their final destination, as depicted in Figure 6.18. Eventually, the monies collected by the coyotes will make their way back to the larger smuggling organizations located in Mexico, as shown in Figure 6.19, so the cycle can begin all over again.

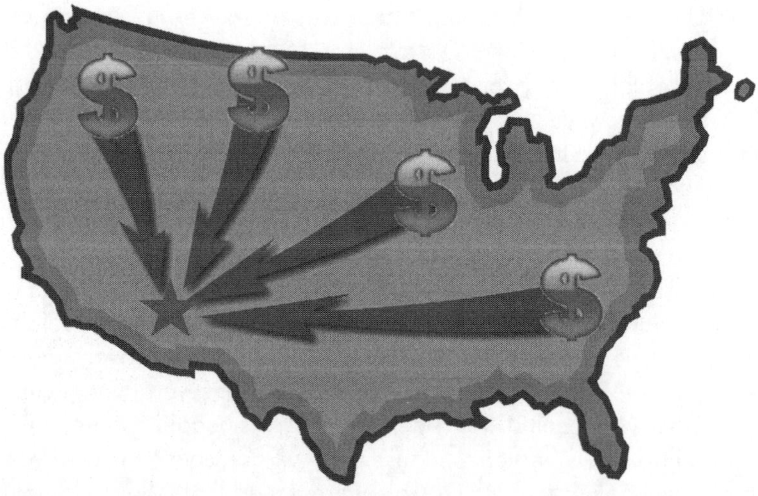

Figure 6.17 Sponsors pay the coyote's fee.

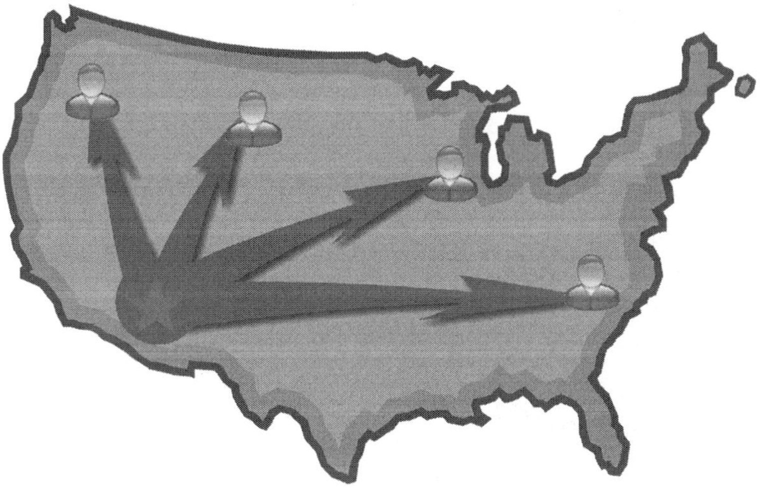

Figure 6.18 UDAs are sent to their final destination.

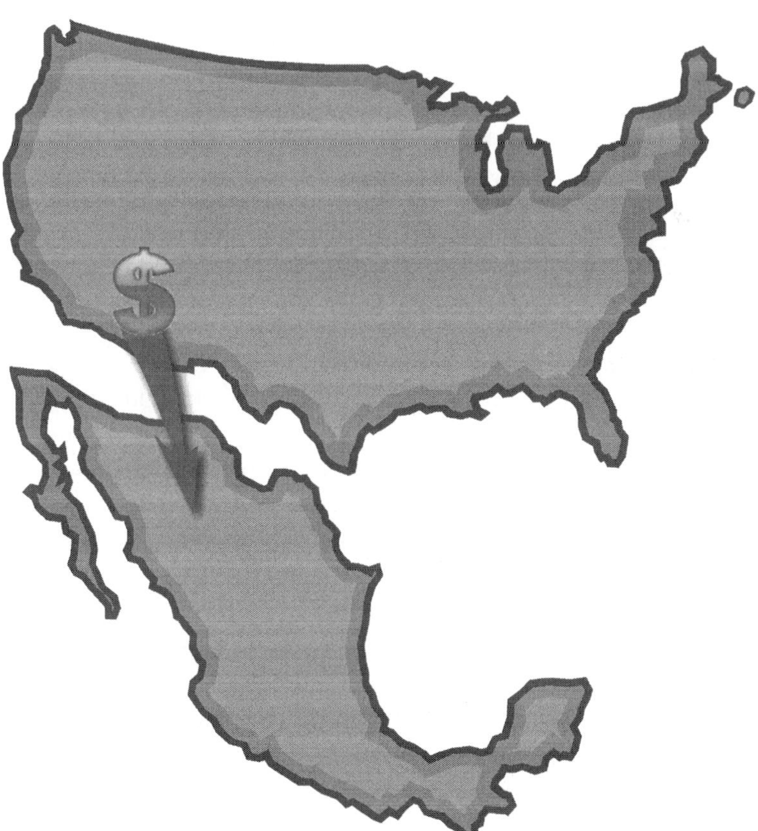

Figure 6.19 Money transfers into Mexico.

Changing the Rules

The aggressive enforcement conducted by the AZ AG has changed the way UDAs are managed, especially from the finance and transportation aspects of the smuggling operations. As more restrictions, rules, and regulations are imposed on the money services industry, the behavior of the criminals adjusts and adapts to follow suit. Recently, the coyotes learned that many of the seizure targets were identified by the repeated use of their names in the transaction data. To counteract this situation, the coyotes started to use the names of their "pollos" when filling out the receiver forms to help avoid detection in the databases.

Other countermeasures included breaking the transaction amount into multiple, smaller denominations to make it harder to detect. Typically, the amount charged by a coyote for transporting a UDA into the country runs between $1,600 and $2,200. Accordingly, law enforcement will target these ranges for additional scrutiny, review, and ultimately seizure. Therefore, the coyotes now request that payments be broken up into multiple $400, $500, and $600 transactions to help conceal their activities by making them look more like legitimate maintenance remittances while also minimizing their exposure to seizure losses.

Additionally, coyotes have even moved their financial operations due to the pressure exhibited by law enforcement. In fact, one sweeping change occurred when Western Union restricted any transactions over $450 into Arizona. As a result, the coyotes have transitioned their financial remittances away from Arizona and have tended to moved them south into Sonora, Mexico, where there are very few controls and limited oversight imposed by the Mexican government.

This fairly recent initiative has led to a new type of pattern called "triangulation," because the coyote, in Arizona, instructs the sponsor, who is located in another state, to remit the funds to an associate, who is located in an area outside of Arizona—such as Sonora, Mexico. Once the funds are received by the associate, the coyote is notified the payment has been made in full and the UDA can be transitioned to their final destination. Figure 6.20 depicts this simple scheme where the coyote, sponsor, and associate represent different points of the smuggling triangle.

During the peak smuggling season, there are literally hundreds of vans and trucks loaded up with UDAs to be transported (e.g., driven) across the country. The smugglers have started to utilize the resources and infrastructure in Nevada as a secondary hub for transporting UDAs, specifically near Las Vegas because there is less surveillance and scrutiny applied to UDAs in this area. In fact, a subsidiary market has emerged in the Phoenix area (variations of this are also seen in Los Angeles) where

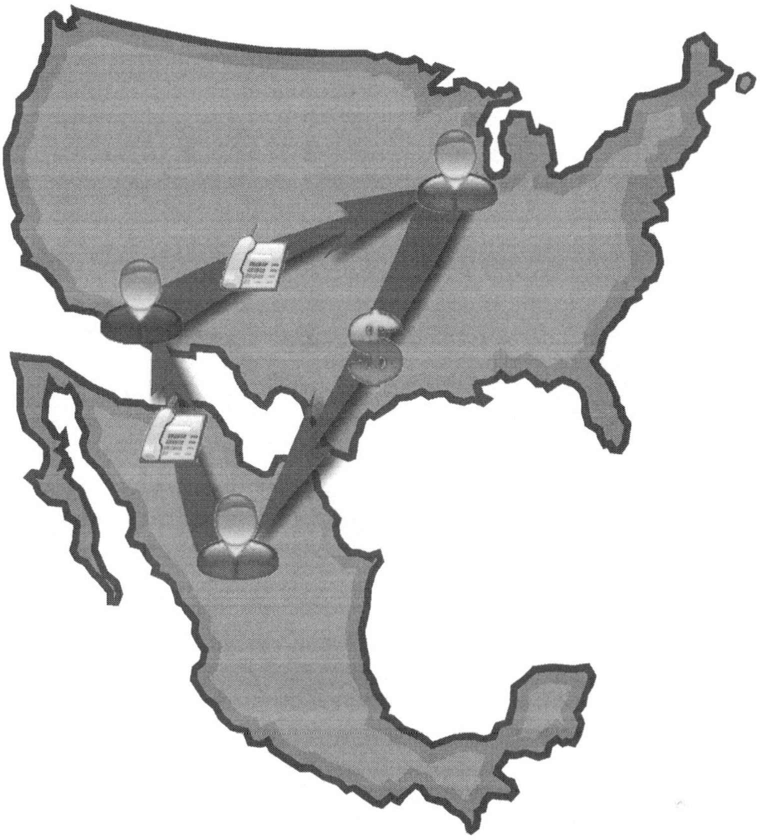

Figure 6.20 Smuggling triangle.

travel agents are booking one-way tickets to various locations around the United States from McCarran Airport located in Las Vegas, which is about 300 miles away from both the Sky Harbor Airport in Phoenix and the Los Angeles International Airport.

The travel agents[20] admit that they are aware that the majority of their customers are suspected of being involved with human smuggling, and often the same customers repeatedly book flights for other people (i.e., the name of the person booking the flight is not the name of the person flying). Area law enforcement in Las Vegas also admits that they have no jurisdiction over illegal immigrants, and federal support has been slow in responding to their needs. Furthermore, there is a corresponding increase in the use of money remitter agents within the Las Vegas area.

[20] One travel agent under indictment headquartered in Phoenix with no branch offices in Las Vegas was shown to have purchased more than 12,000 one-way tickets from the Las Vegas McCarran Airport with an additional 2,500 tickets (from an independent airline) directly tied to the owners of the business.

Although these avoidance techniques are clearly an attempt to circumvent law enforcement efforts to disrupt the smuggling operations, the primary activities are still conducted in, facilitated by, and transitioned through Arizona, and, therefore, fall under the auspices of the AZ AG to follow up and prosecute. The following bullet points summarize several of the more obvious violations:

- The agreement between the coyote and the UDA is made/conducted in Arizona.
- The agreement between the coyote and the sponsor is conducted in Arizona.
- Interstate communication between the coyote and sponsor is conducted in Arizona.
- Interstate communication between the coyote and the associate is conducted in Arizona.
- Detention/housing of the UDA occurs in Arizona.
- Transportation of the UDA takes place in Arizona.
- Financial remittance is made in Arizona (although declining).
- Maintenance payments are made by organizations to the coyotes operating in Arizona.

Under any one of these circumstances, Arizona can claim jurisdiction[21] over the crimes and can utilize whatever resources are necessary to stem the flow of UDAs through Arizona, including the subpoena of data involving other states and countries. This has recently become a mainstream debate[22] among the different parties, jurisdictions, and facilitators involved in or affected by these illegal smuggling operations. Arizona has been a leader in this field and has expanded the boundaries that law enforcement can use to combat this illegal trade and related criminal activities.

Seizing Assets

To confiscate the proceeds of the criminal activity, a damming seizure warrant[23] is issued by a judge who authorizes the actions requested by law

---

21 Smuggling-related wires from sponsors in other states potentially constitutes racketeering felonies in Arizona.

22 Dennis Wagner, "Suit Filed Over Wire Transfers: Immigrant Group Says Ariz. Official's Crackdown on 'Coyotes' Also Seized Innocent People's Money," *The Arizona Republic*, October 19, 2006. Also found at http://www.azcentral.com/specials/special42/articles/1019immigrant-suit.html.

23 It is called a "damming" seizure warrant because it "blocks" the flow of illegal funds to disrupt criminal operations.

enforcement. The FCTF must clearly define the types of data that constitute a violation, and the authorized warrant allows them to make seizures for a fixed period of time (e.g., all transactions over a certain dollar amount from specific originating locations to a specific destination region). These conditions are also prevalidated for their accuracy, using random samples of data (e.g., test runs) that are manually verified by the investigators to prove to the judge that the requests will yield results that are not speculative.[24]

Seizure warrants are authorized for 10 days, at which time they come back up for review and the judge can extend them for an additional 10-day period. In addition, the FCTF takes additional steps to help mitigate the disruption and concern the seizure actions might have on those involved in legitimate transactions by providing a phone bank of 800 numbers that the involved parties can call into once they have been notified their monies have been seized. The service operates under the following guidelines:

- Staffed with bilingual officers (Spanish/English) to ensure that all questions can be properly answered in a timely fashion.
- Operates 24/7 for the convenience of those affected by the seizures.
- Strict procedures to maintain the highest level of professionalism.

When a seizure warrant is active at a money remitter, the funds are actually routed into a seizure account that is later transferred to the Clerk of the Court by court order. When the receiving individual goes to collect their funds, they are notified by the agent that their money was seized by law enforcement; at which point they are given a phone number to call to try and resolve the issue. The number provided is actually operated by the FCTF, and once contacted, the parties are interviewed regarding the nature and origin of the money, the rationale for the transfer, and other pertinent questions. If the questions are answered truthfully and do not constitute any type of illegal behavior, the funds are released by law enforcement, otherwise the funds are held for forfeiture.

If there is any doubt regarding the nature of the transaction, the officers are trained to release the money. According to the affidavits provided from the FCTF, there have been very few complaints[25] and the operating center is based on an open setting so that all conversations and discussions

[24] FCTF estimates that the average hit rate for their seizures exceeds 90 percent accuracy and some approach 97 percent.

[25] Declaration of November 22, 2006, from Ann Marie Barrett, a Customer Support Manager at Western Union, in response to a seizure warrant (SW2006-002213) for removal of funds from interstate and foreign commerce indicated that customers were upset and stated that "officers had interrogated them and had directly accused them of fraud, selling drugs, and of being liars." Other complaints ranged from blocked Caller IDs, late-evening phone calls, use of poor/broken Spanish, and the "interrogators were impatient, unresponsive, and threatening."

are held in front of supervisors and other law enforcement officers. If a transaction is released, officers call a hotline set up at the wire remitter, which authorizes the transfer of the money.

If the remittance is determined to be related to money laundering or other illegal purposes, the funds remain seized, at which point, an official notice is mailed from the state to the address on record (or acquired through the phone call) advising the individuals of their legal rights and recourse for challenging the seizure in a court of law. Many times, the letters are returned to the state because the addresses do not exist because they were fabricated by the coyotes to avoid detection.

When the FCTF requests the court to issue these damming seizure warrants, they result in a number of individual seizures approximating anywhere from a few thousand dollars to upwards of several million once all the disputes and challenges are resolved. Additionally, over the years, they have been instrumental in the arrests of hundreds of drug dealers and coyotes, the confiscation of numerous weapons, the interdiction of thousands of UDAs, the forfeiture of businesses (wire remitter locations, used-car lots, travel agencies), the exposure of a number of stash houses, and the seizure of over $15 million. Even with these impressive statistics, it is estimated that only one-tenth of the actual flow is affected in any way.

Corridor States

The FCTF has done considerable analysis on the types, flows, and nature of the transactions that are received within Arizona, with a specific focus on where the funds originate. In their findings, it became clear that there were extreme variations in the amount of funds flowing into Arizona versus being sent out to other states. These transaction imbalances are direct evidence of smuggling activities and provide the investigators with criteria from which to target their seizures.

The data[26] used to construct Table 6.1 is based on person-to-person transactions exceeding $500 for the time frame January 1, 2005, through November 15, 2005. The FCTF is primarily interested in only the person-to-person transactions for a money remitter and does not typically review the person-to-business transactions because those tend not to harbor criminal activity and mostly reflect the payment of car notes, mortgages, and utility bills. This also cuts down on the amount of data that must be reviewed, making it easier to spot illegal activities and patterns.

---

[26] From a declaration made by Daniel Kelly, Arizona Department of Public Safety, July 24, 2006.

Table 6.1 Corridor State—Imbalanced Transaction Amounts

#	State Abbr.	State Name	Transferred	Received	Ratio	%
1	AL	Alabama	$3,412,392	$160,802	21:1	95%
2	CT	Connecticut	$1,782,326	$60,125	30:1	97%
3	DC	Dist. Columbia	$423,236	$23,704	18:1	94%
4	DE	Delaware	$1,369,131	$22,795	60:1	98%
5	FL	Florida	$19,014,057	$905,888	21:1	95%
6	GA	Georgia	$13,485,128	$535,351	25:1	96%
7	IA	Iowa	$962,920	$117,179	8:1	88%
8	IL	Illinois	$13,260,562	$772,165	17:1	94%
9	IN	Indiana	$3,782,382	$220,753	17:1	94%
10	KY	Kentucky	$2,135,889	$182,522	12:1	92%
11	MA	Massachusetts	$2,015,666	$124,480	16:1	94%
12	MD	Maryland	$3,536,755	$160,452	22:1	96%
13	MI	Michigan	$3,522,072	$437,346	8:1	88%
14	MN	Minnesota	$1,825,869	$125,947	15:1	93%
15	MS	Mississippi	$1,060,887	$106,015	10:1	90%
16	NC	North Carolina	$9,465,467	$268,390	35:1	97%
17	NE	Nebraska	$1,116,562	$108,036	10:1	90%
18	NJ	New Jersey	$9,029,341	$294,749	31:1	97%
19	NY	New York	$17,233,091	$851,683	20:1	95%
20	OH	Ohio	$3,521,945	$351,935	10:1	90%
21	OR	Oregon	$2,287,586	$278,732	8:1	88%
22	PA	Pennsylvania	$4,346,601	$237,252	18:1	95%
23	RI	Rhode Island	$300,452	$20,790	15:1	93%
24	SC	South Carolina	$4,248,434	$111,197	38:1	97%
25	TN	Tennessee	$4,271,416	$242,963	18:1	94%
26	UT	Utah	$1,747,418	$214,144	8:1	88%
27	VA	Virginia	$5,283,817	$221,048	24:1	96%
28	WI	Wisconsin	$1,994,813	$158,553	13:1	92%

The states listed (in alphabetical order) are those with at least an 8:1 ratio of sending volume versus receiving volume, the highest being Delaware with a 60:1 ratio. These imbalances are so considerable that these states are selectively chosen as part of the seizure warrant conditions issued by the FCTF and are commonly referred to as "corridor states" due to their high volume of transactions into Arizona and Sonora, Mexico. These states are also highlighted in dark gray on the map shown in Figure 6.21.

More detailed analysis by the FCTF revealed that the transaction data for one specific smuggler showed that they received 45 wires sent by

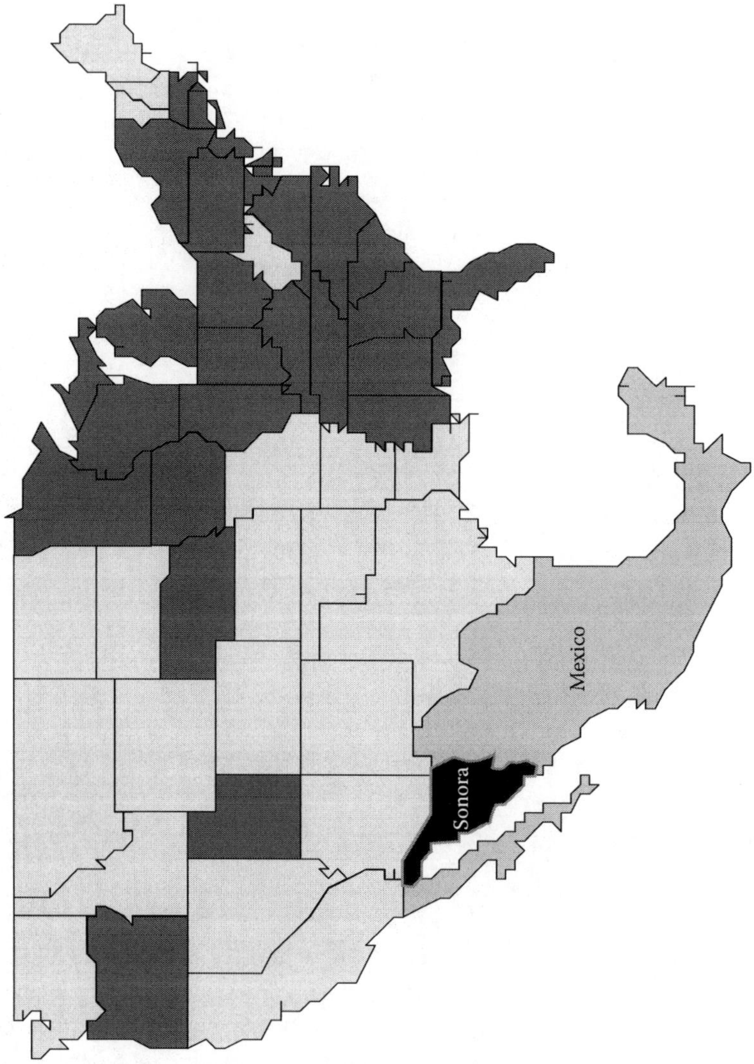

Figure 6.21 Corridor state map—imbalanced transaction amounts.

43 different people from a number of different states other than Arizona over a two-month period of time. There are hundreds of identical scenarios played out in the data, helping confirm that there are illegal transfers being sent to Arizona.

Based on these types of situations, the extensive research conducted by the FCTF, and the years of experience gained by conducting investigations, interviews, and analysis of the databases, a well-defined set of conditions used to expose high-volume alien smugglers has emerged as defined below:

- Uses a limited number of agent locations frequented by other high-volume smugglers.
- Uses different identification numbers, often invalid or stolen.
- Varies the spelling and format of their names.
- Contact information, such as phones/addresses, is not provided (Figure 6.22).
- Receives transactions from multiple "corridor" states (Figure 6.23).
- Transactions tend to be over $500 each or larger (Figure 6.24).
- Senders have different last names; appear unrelated to receiver (Figure 6.25).
- Receives multiple wires on the same day within a short time period (Figure 6.26).
- It is not unusual for dozens of wire transfers to be sent over a few weeks to the same receiver, where the amounts can easily total tens of thousands to hundreds of thousands of dollars.

In the following diagram (Figure 6.27), a slightly different display paradigm is presented to help convey additional dimensions contained in the wire transfer data. All of these 36 icons represent individual Transactions received by a specific Subject. They are grouped and ordered according to the transfer date, resulting in nine discrete clusters arranged in chronological order (one for each unique date). Each transaction is shaped by the Agent ID used to receive the transaction. It is fairly obvious that one particular agent (circle) is preferred by this Subject. What is perhaps of most interest in this diagram is the consistent utilization of multiple, different agents on the same day, with as many as five shown in the cluster located at the 3:00 position as well as the larger band at the 7:00 position. This type of behavior is not typical of an individual involved in legitimate financial activity and most likely indicates some type of criminal behavior—specifically, human smuggling.

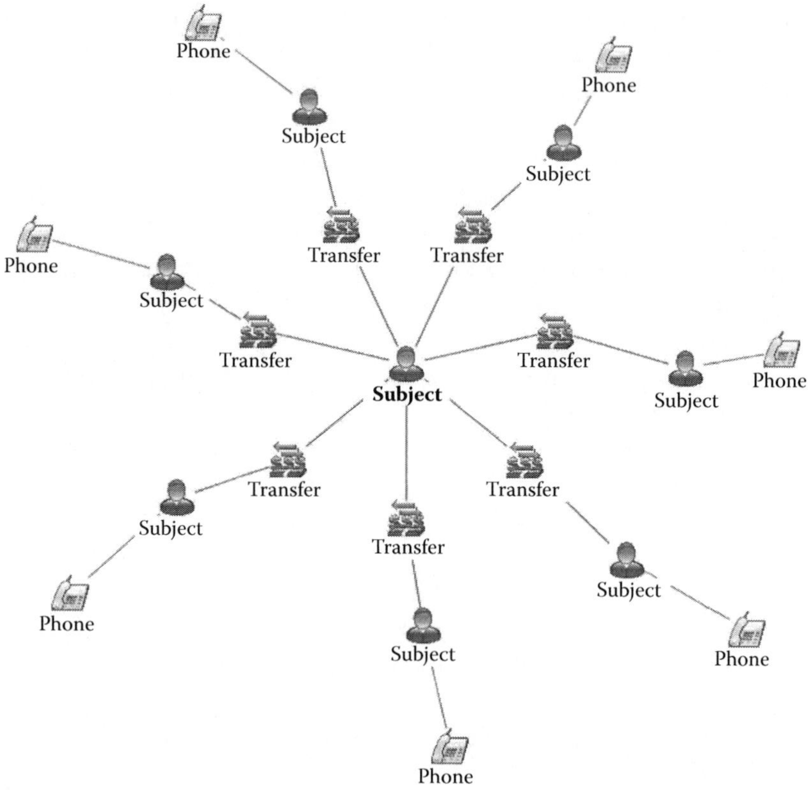

Figure 6.22 Receiver has no contact phone number.

Drug Dealers

Up until now, there has been limited discussion of the patterns that apply to exposing drug dealers as opposed to human smugglers. The major difference lies in the trust relationships between the buyers and sellers, which imply repeat business, and, therefore, the frequencies of the connections among the various party members will be stronger and replicate themselves. As such, investigators will look for situations where repeated transactions exist among a core group of suspects—typically with the buyers being out of state (e.g., outside of Arizona).

Perhaps one of the easiest ways to track down a drug network is to start with a known perpetrator. Occasionally, when reviewing transaction data, a familiar name will appear to the investigators and they can grow their networks to find other dealers and distributors. For example, the following is a subject known to law enforcement for being involved with narcotics trafficking. The diagram presented in Figure 6.28 shows the network that forms and exposes other suppliers, financiers, and distributors—each of which can be rightfully targeted for additional investigation.

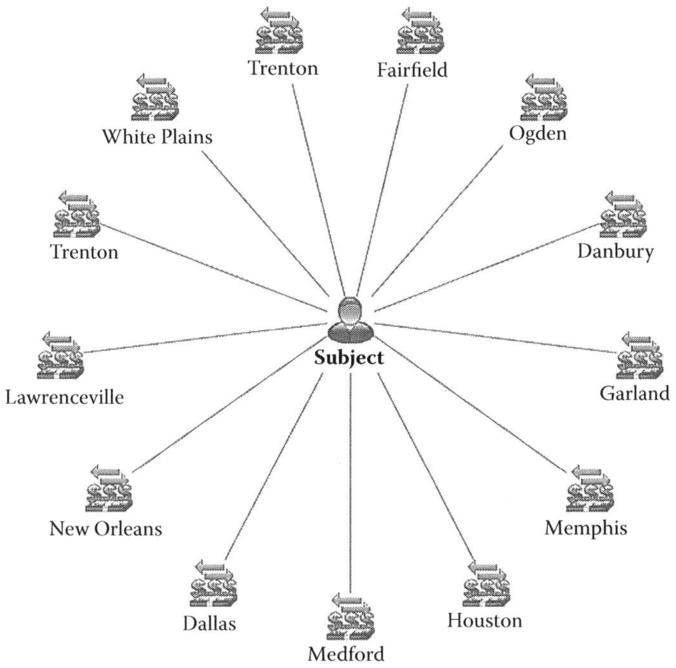

Figure 6.23 Transactions from multiple city/state locations.

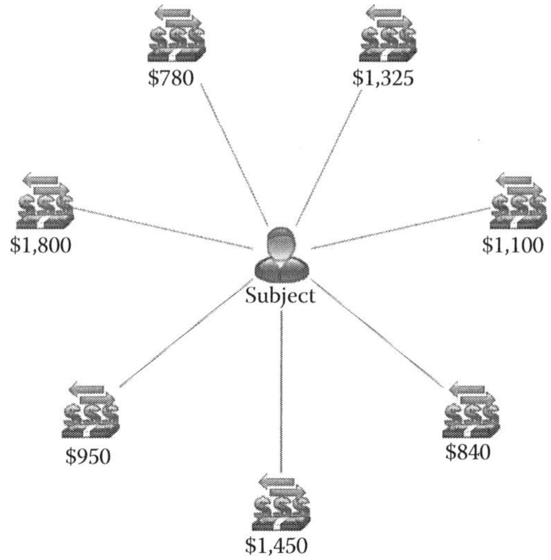

Figure 6.24 Multiple wires over $500.

In a slightly different scenario, more subtle details embedded in the transaction data can help expose drug dealer patterns. In these situations, there are no "direct" relationships among the subjects involved with the transaction and no sharing of related details, such as phones, addresses, or identification numbers. The pattern is based directly on

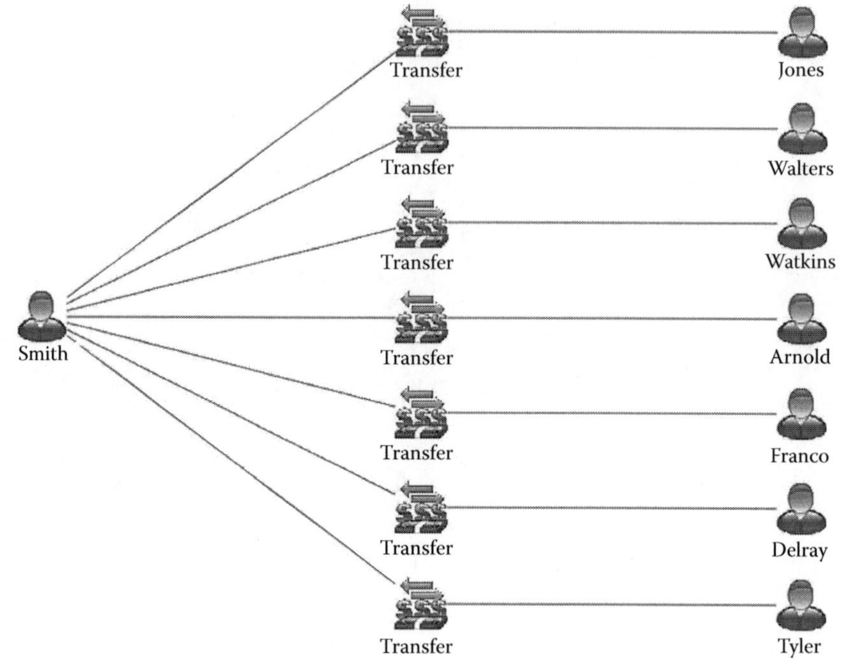

Figure 6.25 Senders have different last names.

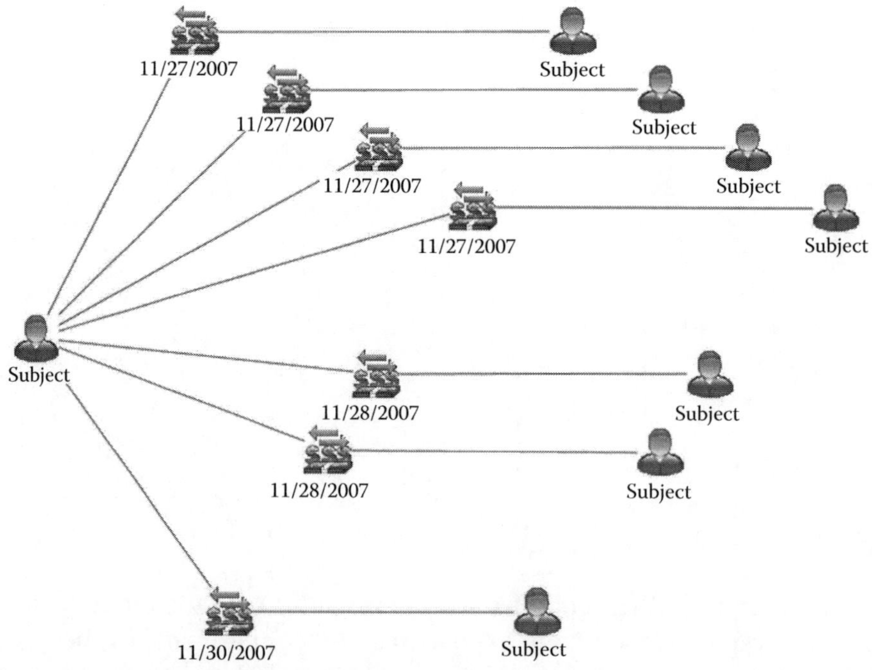

Figure 6.26 Receive multiple wires on same day.

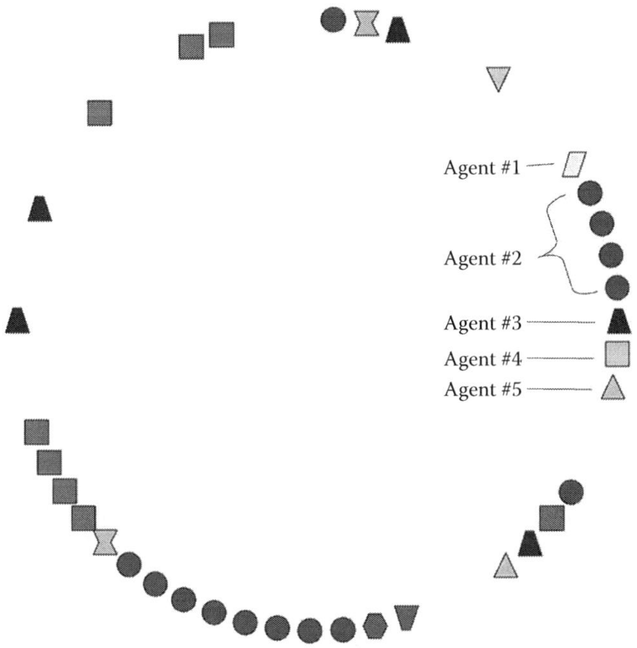

Figure 6.27 Multiple transactions on same day using different agents.

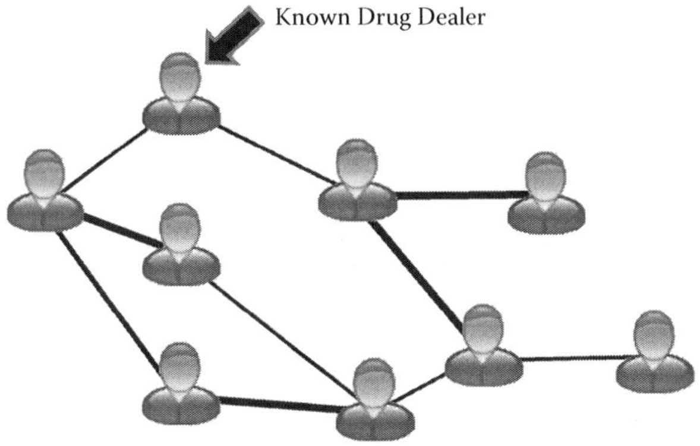

Figure 6.28 Drug dealer network.

the time and location associated with money being sent and received. For example, tracking a Jamaican drug gang can be done by observing a series of, say, eight wire transfers that are made by eight different people from eight different locations all sent from the Bronx, New York, on a single day. All eight of these transactions were then picked up at a single location in Phoenix within a very short time period (e.g., minutes), and all were for similar dollar amounts going to different people.

Mapping the sending locations in the Bronx shows a sequence similar to a circle, or a loop, where the senders drove around the neighborhood and stopped at various remitter locations, ranging from the Caribbean Food Store to the Reggae Music Shop, where the smurfs[27] would conduct the transaction. Figure 6.29 shows the ring of locations associated with the transmittal of the funds. This clearly shows a distinctive financial pattern for narcotics trafficking versus human smuggling.

Suspicious Activity Reports

The examples provided clearly show that there are indicators in the wire remitter data that relate to unlawful activity. By law, MSBs are required

Figure 6.29 Ring of transmittal locations for narcotics trafficking.

[27] Smurfs are a term used to describe low-level grunts (generic, vanilla drones) doing the busy work in a drug organization in much the same way that the term coyote is used in human-smuggling organizations.

to constantly review their data and identify questionable transfers, expose unusual behaviors, check watch lists for name matches, and be diligent in their AML operations. If any activity appears to be an illegitimate form of transfer, the MSB is required to submit a Suspicious Activity Report (SAR) within 30 days by filing a SAR-MSB form when a transaction (or series of transactions) appears suspicious and exceeds $2,000. The SAR-MSB form[28] is used to collect the details of the transaction and report them to the government. According to government definitions, a suspicious transaction:

- Involves funds derived from illegal activity or is intended or conducted in order to hide or disguise funds or assets derived from illegal activity.
- Designed to evade the requirements of the Bank Secrecy Act, whether through structuring or other means.
- Serves no business or apparent lawful purpose, and the reporting business knows of no reasonable explanation for the transaction after examining all available facts.

An MSB must register with the federal government and update this registration every two years. There is actually a public list[29] of registered MSBs that can be viewed online and is organized by state. This list is maintained by the Financial Crimes Enforcement Network (FinCEN). The basic business process of money transmitters is to transfer money within a network of authorized agents. There is always a sender and a receiver of the money and reviewing the flow of money between the actual participants (e.g., the Subjects) in the network is the basis for performing money-laundering investigations. However, it is also a duty of the MSB to monitor the individual agents to ensure they remain compliant with their reporting requirements and are not trying to circumvent any controls within the system.

Figure 6.30 shows a SAR-MSB form (three pages) and the objects used to analyze its contents. Figure 6.31 shows a typical analytical model used to relate and understand the contents of the remittance. Similar to other financial forms, the same standard types of data are collected, Subjects, Addresses, ID Numbers, Phones, and SSNs (where appropriate). For any SAR-MSB there can be multiple Subjects identified as part of the suspicious transaction, and, in fact, there are quite a number filed with dozens and dozens of Subjects listed on a single form.

[28] http://www.fincen.gov/forms/files/fin109_sarmsb.pdf.

[29] http://www.msb.gov/guidance/msbstateselector.php.

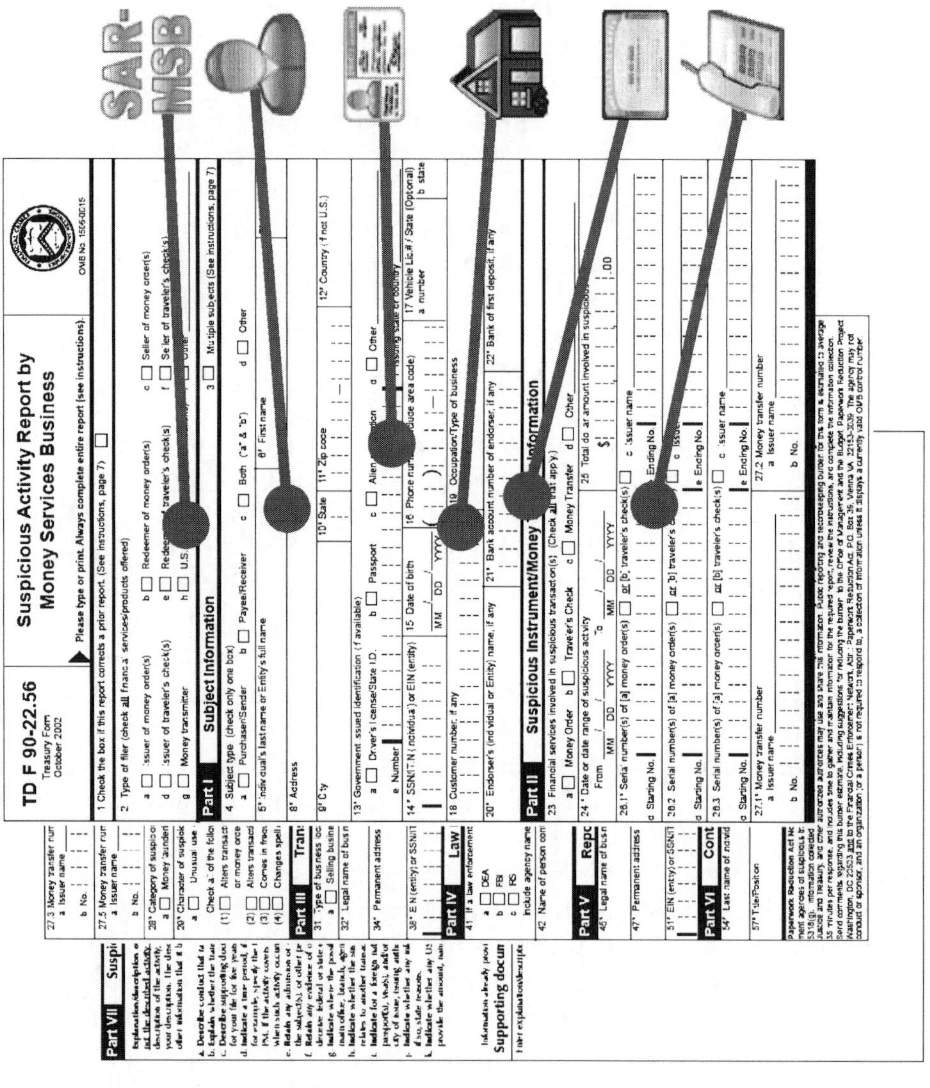

Figure 6.30 SAR-MSB form with entity types.

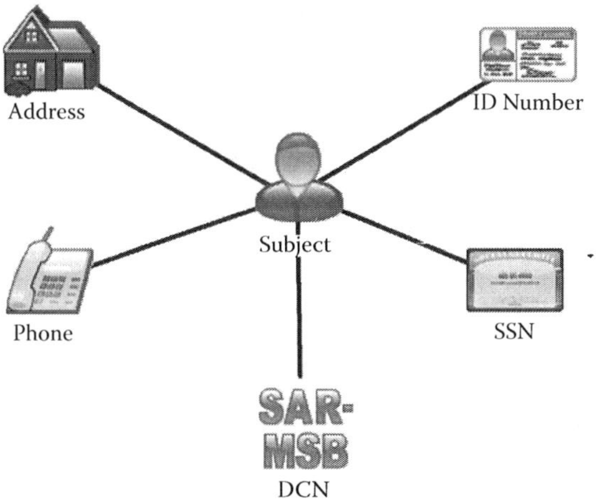

Figure 6.31 SAR-MSB analytical model.

Table 6.2 Annual Counts for SAR-MSB Filings

Filing Year	*Transaction Count*
2003	209,512
2004	296,284
2005	383,567
2006	496,400
2007	581,307

The SAR-MSB form also has a narrative section where the remitter describes the nature of the suspicious behavior and any other pertinent details regarding the transaction. The amount of data reported by MSBs is increasing every year as more filing requirements and compliancy laws are being enacted to help combat financial crimes. Table 6.2 represents the counts of the SAR-MSBs for the past several years, according to official reports.[30]

The following examples provide an overview of the many different types of patterns that can exist in the SAR-MSB data. By no means is this an exhaustive list, or the only categories of patterns that exist within the SAR-MSB dataset, and these patterns are a subjective interpretation[31] of the collected data. Every day, new types of schemes, patterns, or situations are discovered that warrant additional investigations or further analysis. Those involved with laundering money are always trying to

[30] http://www.fincen.gov/news_room/rp/files/sar_by_numb_07.pdf.

[31] A good reference for subjective interpretation of data: David Leinweber, "Stupid Data Miner Tricks: Overfitting the S&P 500" (Pasadena: California Institute of Technology, 1995), http://nerdsonwallstreet.typepad.com/my_weblog/files/dataminejune_2000.pdf.

avoid detection and are constantly changing their routines to adapt to the new rules and regulations.

Elder Abuse Pattern

This type of pattern is a bit harder to spot in SAR-MSB data than it is in the original transaction data because it is up to the discretion of the remitter agent to flag the transaction as suspicious. Luckily, there are still some good-hearted agents who watch out for the elderly members of their communities and try to dissuade them from transmitting money when fraud is suspected. There are literally hundreds of scenarios played out in wire remitter data that are all based on the same scheme—an individual has promised to pay out a large sum of money based on a lottery winning, sweepstakes award, or an inheritance, but requires the prepayment of taxes, attorney fees, or some other false justification for sending the money.

The predators in this case target elderly people because they tend to be a bit more vulnerable in believing the fraud—thus, spotting the pattern is straightforward because it requires only a simple query and sort based on the date of birth (DOB) of the person sending the money. The majority of the data retrieved from queries looking for any DOB < 1930 will result in some form of elder abuse pattern. Figure 6.32 shows some samples of SAR-MSB details exposing the violation descriptions, suspect (e.g., fraud victim) date of birth, and transaction amounts.

Although the specific details regarding the SAR-MSB are not shown in this figure, there are many instances where individuals are making multiple transactions based on the repeated data. Furthermore, after reviewing the narratives, they explicitly state that the agents try to warn these elderly people that the transfer is most likely based on a fraud or a scam—but the victims appear scared that the recipient (i.e., the perpetrator) will be angry or upset with them if they don't send the money. Many times, the perpetrator will instruct the victim about how to answer any questions that might be raised by the agents, such as saying that the money is being sent to a friend who is sick, or a friend trying to get back into the country, or a grandson for school supplies. Many of the wire transfers appear to be heading out of the country, to places such as Jamaica, Canada, Netherlands, England, and, of course, Nigeria.

Additional details are shown in Figure 6.33, and as these networks expand it is easy to spot those sending multiple payments to their perpetrators. One note of interest is that these people also are very diligent about providing accurate details in their transaction data so the addresses,

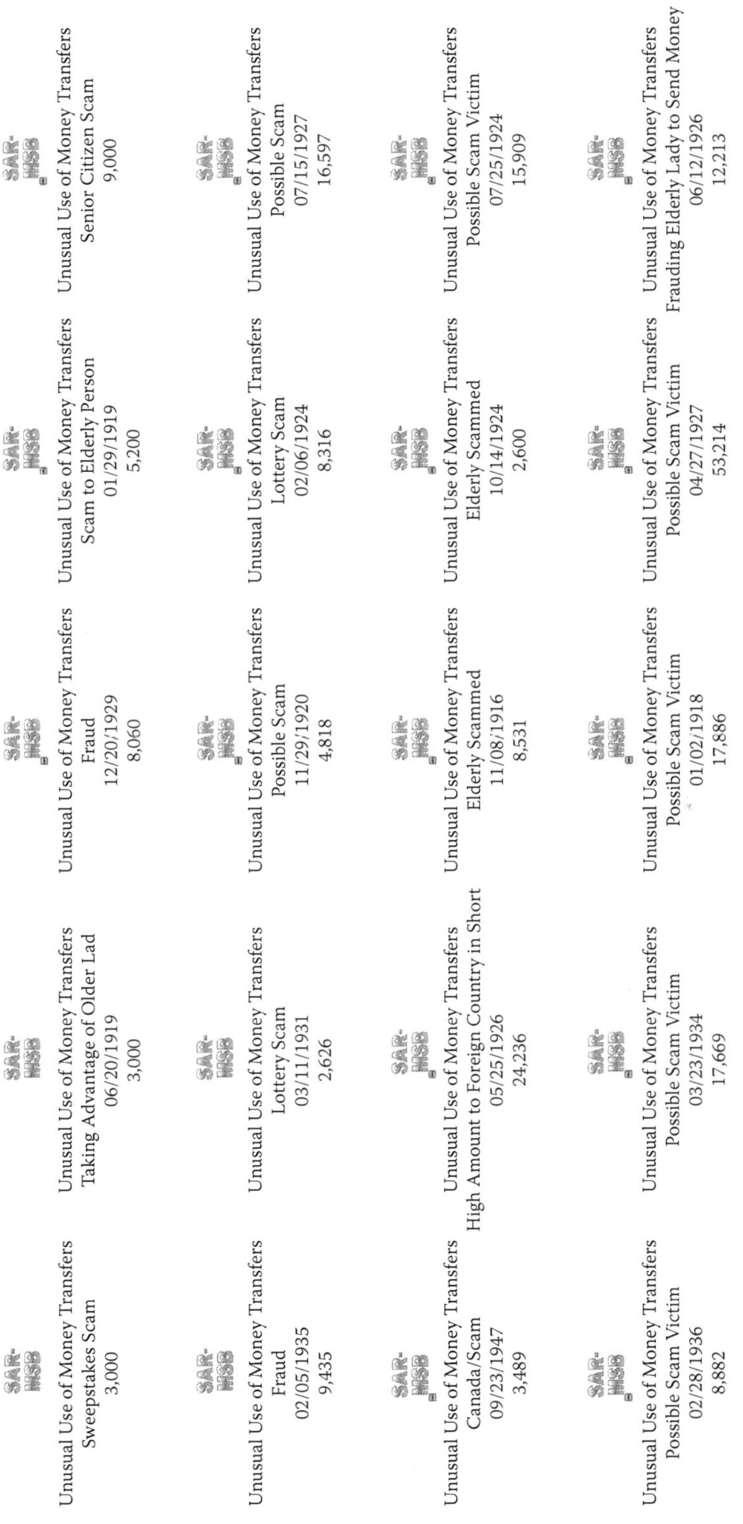

Figure 6.32 Elder abuse pattern.

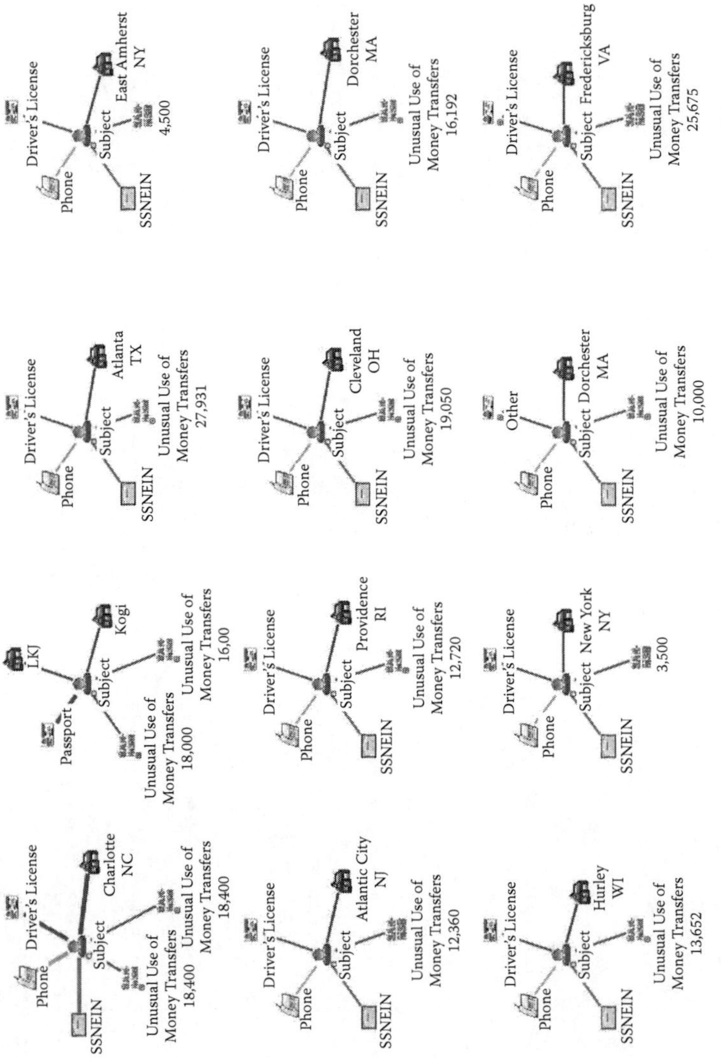

Figure 6.33 Elder abuse network first-level connection.

phones, and identification numbers tend to be complete and truthful in their representations. Therefore, once the fraud is detected or there is any type of follow-up by law enforcement, these victims are easy to contact and find.

Ornery Old Man

This example represents a fairly standard type of pattern found in the SAR-MSB data. Originally, this individual was exposed when looking for elder abuse patterns; in this case, however, he was not the victim but rather the perpetrator of a different scheme. When scanning the data for a larger frequency of filing occurrences for dates of birth between 1920 and 1930, this individual ranked high on the output results due to the consistent filings using the same ID Number reference (in this case a driver's license). In fact, this suspect was 76 years old.

This man had 55 unique SAR-MSB filings, as shown in Figure 6.34, using the same ID Number. The heavy, thick lines appearing at the right side of this diagram show connections between the Subject and his related SSN, Address, ID Number, and Phone because each was represented consistently by the MSB submitting this SAR form. Usually, this level of consistency indicates that the MSB is using some automated system (e.g., a customer relationship management tool) to help generate their SAR-MSB submission, which certainly helps investigators perform the analysis and produce much more reliable and accurate results.

Reviewing the details of the transaction shows that the narratives for the SAR-MSBs state that the "CUSTOMER PURCHASES MONEY ORDERS TOTALING LARGE AMOUNTS VERY FREQUENTLY," or "CUSTOMER NEEDS THEM FOR PAYROLL FOR EMPLOYEES," and "CUSTOMER OPERATES AN INSURANCE BUSINESS." There was other mention in the narratives that the customer was cantankerous, irritable, and not very forthcoming with his information. Based on the number of filings made on this man, more than $400,000 worth of wire transfers were made over a five- to six-month period. Figure 6.35 shows a temporal breakdown of the transactions, and it is clearly shown that he averages two to four transactions per week, with a heavy emphasis on Mondays and Wednesdays.

When reviewing this data, there are a number of factors that do not add up with respect to the situation. Generally, a legitimate business that needs to make payroll on a regular basis will use some type of payroll service, and not a high-commission/fee MSB. It does not make good business sense nor is it financially practical to use the services of an MSB

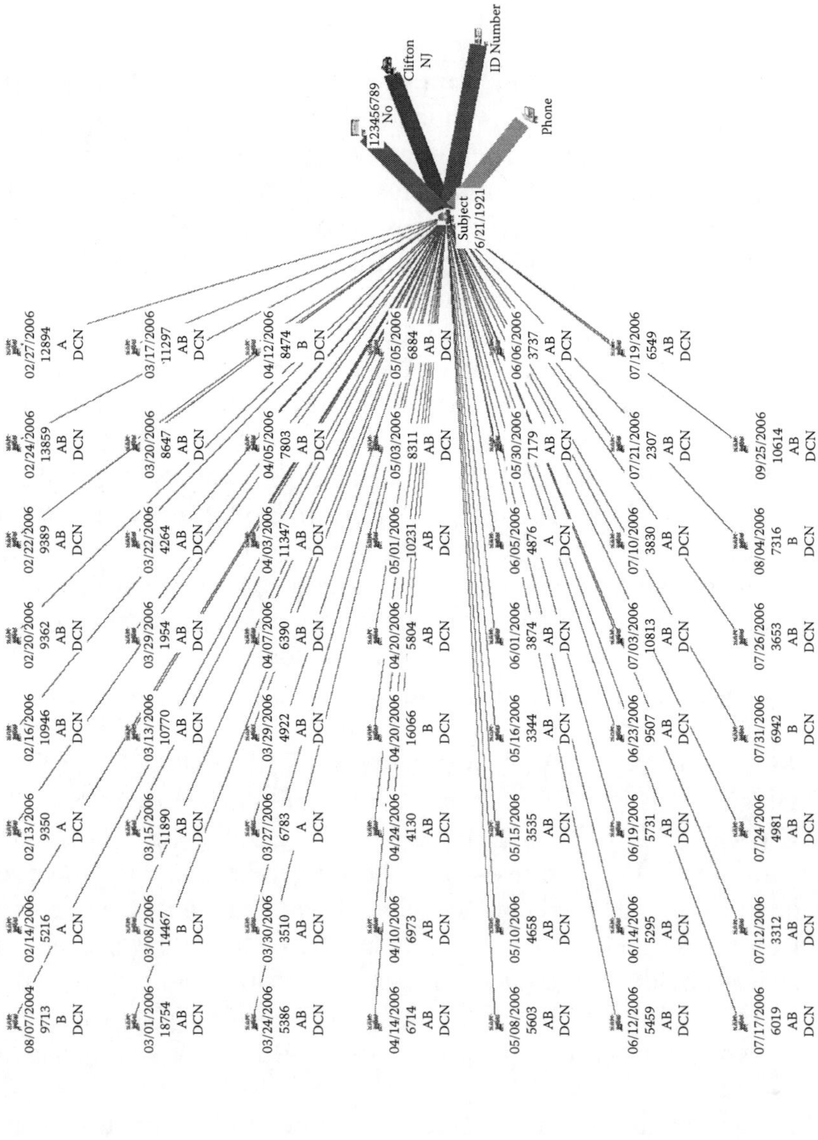

Figure 6.34 Ornery old man.

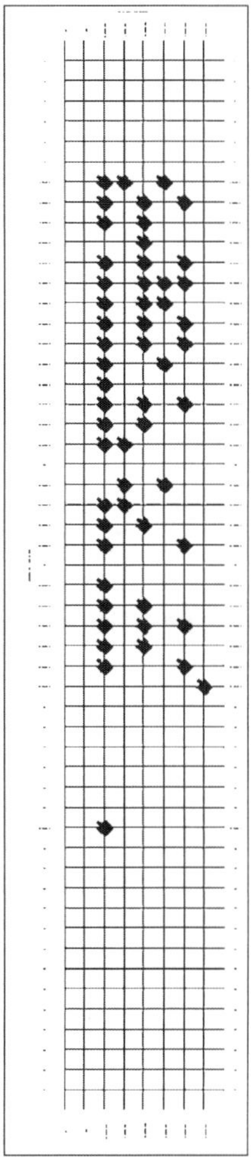

Figure 6.35 Temporal grid of SAR-MSB transactions.

on a regular basis to conduct this type of business because there are more economical (and automated) methods widely available in the marketplace for businesses to utilize. Second, payroll for a legitimate business is usually made monthly or biweekly, not multiple times a week as is evidenced in the diagram. Unless there are multiple offices for which his "payroll" is being sent, which there are not, this type of behavior does not make much sense and is hard to justify. Finally, insurance businesses typically are not a "cash" business because premiums are usually paid with a check or some type of automated withdrawal, and certainly making "payroll" using cash is highly unusual—especially because the requisite taxes (state/federal) are not being properly addressed. All things considered, the entire situation is highly suspicious and requires further investigation.

Other MSB Patterns

The nature and types of patterns that can be found in the SAR-MSB data are virtually limitless and many times questionable situations can be found just by perusing the data to see what particular patterns stand out. The following are several interesting scenarios based on different circumstances and combinations of data.

Multiple Locations

This first pattern was exposed when the same Social Security number/Employer Idendification number (SSN/EIN) was seen being used at multiple agent locations—a classic indicator of someone trying to avoid detection. In these cases, the subjects figure that if they can go to many different agent locations, they will just appear as background noise because no one will be likely to remember them and they won't really stand out—as opposed to performing multiple, high-value transactions at a single location. This is also a tactic often used at banks to avoid the filing of cash transaction reports for amounts exceeding $10,000 (cumulative).

As shown in Figure 6.36, the SSN/EIN icon at the center ties together three different Subjects, which in reality represent the same person, albeit with slight variations of the name. According to the agents filing the SAR-MSBs, this person has intentionally changed her name in sequential transactions by interjecting a different spelling or using a middle name. Each representation of the person is in turn connected to one or more SAR-MSB transactions. In this example, there are at least a half dozen different agent locations represented among the 17 distinct SAR-MSBs. The majority of the Addresses depicted in this network are also considered the same because they are permutations of the same address, with slight spelling variations, abbreviations, and other small dissimilarities. The most common violation description for this subject shows "Frequent Purchase Under $3,000," which means they don't want to provide additional detail (identification), which is mandatory for transactions over $3,000—and further validates that they are most likely structuring their transactions to avoid the $10,000 reporting limits.

Finally, the violation amounts tend to be quite high with respect to these types of transactions. Keep in mind, the SAR-MSB represents the cumulative "activity" for a suspect over a period of time (usually 30 days). Thus, when reviewing the narratives of each SAR-MSB, there are potentially dozens of individual transactions rolled up into the SAR-MSB. In this case the amounts range from $1,200 to $3,000, which indicates she is

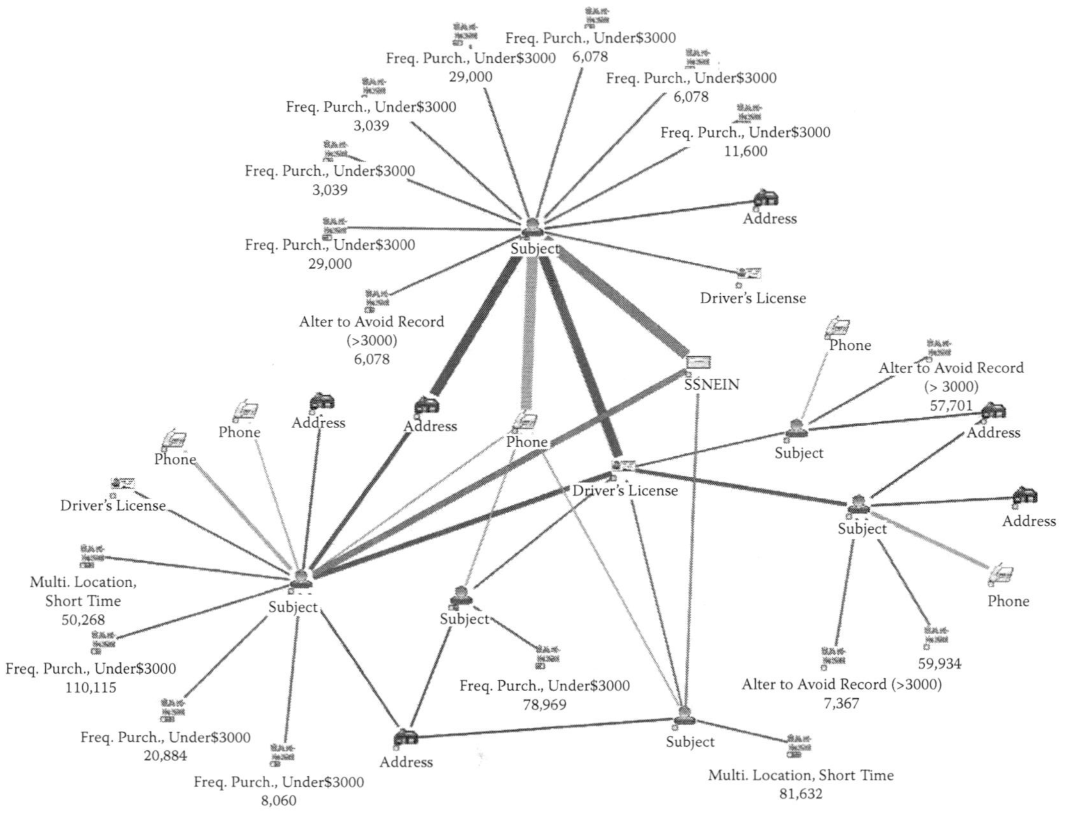

Figure 6.36 Using multiple locations to structure SAR-MSB transactions.

trying to circumvent the filing requirements and is minimizing the information she is required to provide for conducting her transactions.

Minimal Overlaps

The next example, shown in Figure 6.37, is of interest due to the hierarchy of connections based on Subjects and SAR-MSB relationships. Although the same name does appear several times in the chart, none of the connecting Subjects are exactly the same. In fact, they appear to be variations of different family members conducting the transactions. The nature of the violations, similar to what was shown previously, is based on trying to avoid additional filing requirements (e.g., Cash Transaction Reports) and visiting multiple locations within a short time period. The dollar amount of these SAR-MSBs is fairly high, almost $750,000 in transfers, and is not indicative of legitimate business dealings. Also, the flow of the diagram with respect to the column placement is not arranged by date, but rather based on connections and minimal line crossings. The 14 SAR-MSBs shown in this figure were all conducted during a four-month period.

It is clear from reviewing the narratives associated with this chart that there is a large amount of money flowing to The Netherlands and some moving into Great Britain. In one specific transaction, a Subject disclosed to the compliance officer for the remittance company that the money was being used to repay a loan made from a friend. After being presented with this information, the company declined to do further business with the Subject and rejected any future transactions made by this individual. This is an important fact to note because wire remitters are bound to industry standards and specific levels of diligence to help thwart money laundering and financial crimes. Although only one remitter acted on this fact, it is an important piece of the puzzle to see when looking at the “big picture” of all the related transactions associated with this group of subjects; it helps set a precedence of questionable activities and lays the foundation for additional investigations.

Official Deposits

Working with SAR-related data can be enlightening and quite interesting based on how people behave and structure their financial transactions. Every data value in the underlying sources is fair game to use in exposing

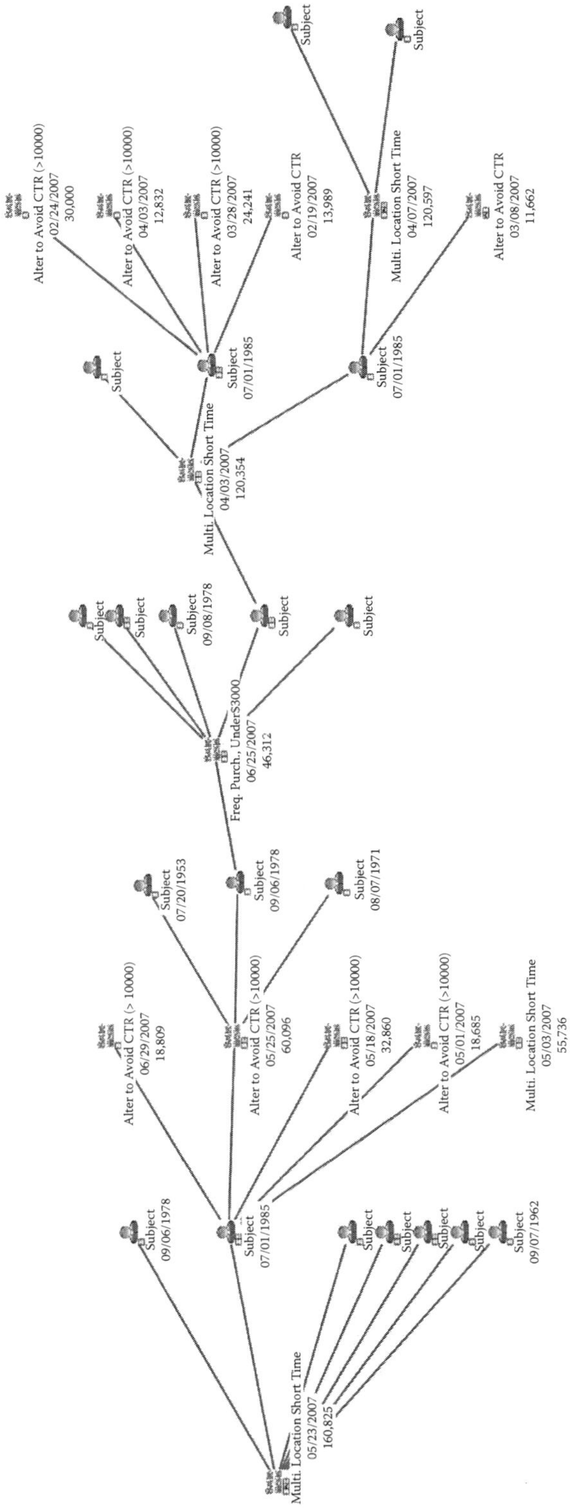

Figure 6.37 Hierarchy of SAR-MSB transactions.

new patterns because these transactions are reported as suspicious or unusual as determined by the filer. In the following examples, those individuals whose occupation was listed as a "police officer" were queried and their immediate connections (first level) displayed.

The structure shown in Figure 6.38 is fairly basic and shows an individual (e.g., the police officer) with four SAR-MSBs for varying amounts. There are two different addresses associated with this person that are about five miles apart and, as can be seen by the thicker link line, one address was listed in three of the four transactions. A reverse lookup of the phone numbers shows that one is "unlisted," which would be unusual if it represented the precinct where he worked, but could be part of an undercover operation. Of course, we are not exactly sure what phone numbers (e.g., work or home) are represented in these transactions because this level of detail is not delineated on the forms. The other phone number actually resolves to the name of the person listed on the SAR-MSB and confirms the city presented in one of the addresses, so we have some confidence regarding the accuracy of the data presented within the system using third-party references.

Interestingly, the form of identification used by this subject is defined as "other," which means it was not a driver's license, passport,

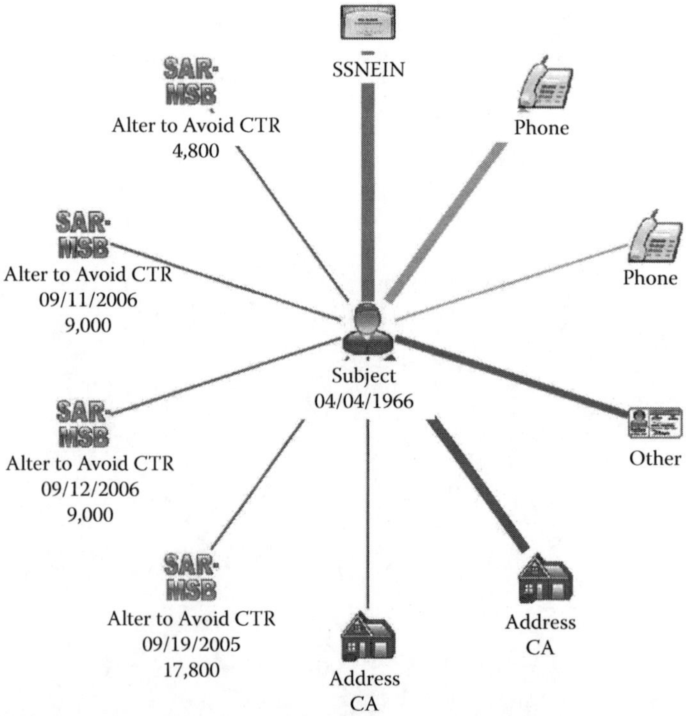

Figure 6.38 Multiple transactions using high-denomination bills.

or alien registration. Based on the number given, it is hard to determine the exact nature of the identification, perhaps a state-issued ID number or even his police credentials. Regardless, it was consistently used in the transactions based on link thickness and related details. However, what is of most importance in this network is the nature of the SAR-MSB transactions; all of the money deposited in these transactions were $100 bills and were made to a "credit union" facility. So, one must ask the question: Why is a policeman making large deposits into an account using $100 bills over the course of a single week? There is obviously some type of questionable activity—but is it an officially sanctioned endeavor, an undercover operation, or simply a corrupt officer? This represents a situation that must be followed up on and verified by the analysts and the investigating agencies to determine if there is a serious crime being perpetrated.

In this next example, the diagram shown in Figure 6.39 looks almost structurally identical to the last network insofar as there is a single (male) subject and four SAR-MSB transactions. However, the interpretation of this situation is vastly different from the previous example. The biggest disparity is that there are three addresses listed in this network, and a review of their details indicates that they represent the same address (an

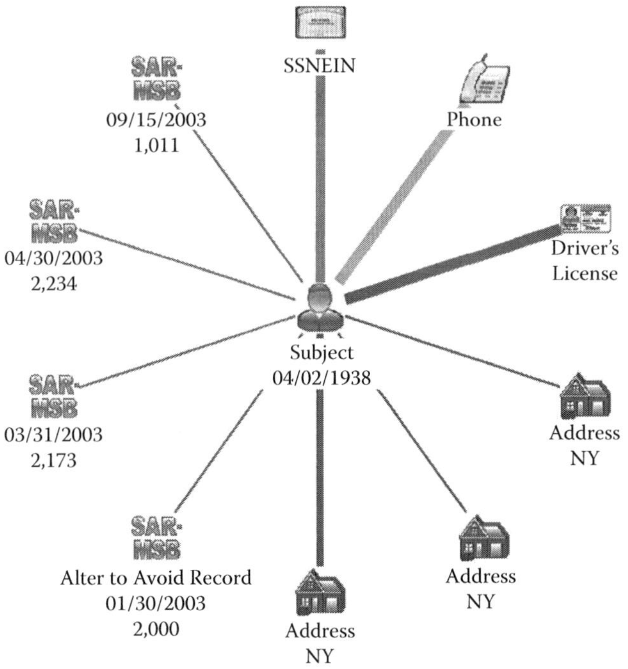

Figure 6.39 Mail-order bride.

apartment building) with only slight variations in their spelling. This is typical for SAR-related data, and in this case does not appear to imply anything underhanded, only careless data entry by the remittance agents. There is also a valid driver's license used for each of the transactions and the phone number was consistently provided. A slight anomaly exists for this phone number when a reverse lookup is performed in the public records—it is registered to a Hispanic-named woman and our subject has a male Indian name. Additionally, the addresses listed for the subscriber of this phone number, although close (at about 1.4 miles apart) in the same city, are different nonetheless.

When reviewing the narratives, the remitter agents state that this individual makes a large number of transactions[32] and that they are for just under $1,000 each. There is also reference to a "young lady" involved in receiving this money. Looking at the filing dates, the age of this individual (born in 1938), and the amounts of the transactions, it appears to be some sort of "mail-order bride" scam where an individual sends money to a needy lady (typically a Russian woman) who promises marriage but needs money to cover her expenses (e.g., visa applications, wedding dress, airfare costs, doctors bills, and all sorts of miscellaneous debts). Every few weeks, there is another sob story, another excuse, and another reason to send more money. This person is a retired police officer and is seeking some type of companionship later in his life, and although sending money under these circumstances is technically not illegal on his part, the subject needs to ensure he does not affect the nature of the transactions so as to avoid any paperwork or structure the amounts so they are not reported.

Heavenly Offerings

Another category of subjects, whose occupation is "priest," was pulled from the data source and one of the immediate observations was that many of the remittances were being sent overseas to a variety of individuals in a number of different countries (India, Hong Kong, Mexico, Nigeria, etc.). There has been a lot of concern about "charitable" organizations acting as fronts for terrorist groups, making these types of scenarios important to review and understand to see if there is anything suspect.

[32] Remember, a SAR represents the cumulative activity for a period of time; therefore, the dollar amounts shown on the label of the SAR are the total for that filing and do not reflect the individual transactions.

One particular network of interest is shown in Figure 6.40, which consists of four Subjects with five Transactions. The names of the subjects appear to represent three different people with two subjects sharing the same date of birth as well as SSN and Driver's License numbers. There is a lot of variation in this diagram for such a small number of transactions. The two Addresses are virtually the same and everyone appears to use a common Phone Number, which is confirmed to be registered to one of the Subjects.

The narratives indicate that the money is always sent to two different people, the individual conducting the transaction does not have a wallet and carries large-denomination bills of cash in a "giant plastic Ziploc® bag," and the individual is known to change his name between transactions. This type of situation appears highly unusual for someone acting as a priest and should be subjected to more detailed analysis. There are also other examples where priests are sending fairly large amounts of money to other people, claiming they are helping to subsidize sick people. In these cases, the same person is being sent thousands of dollars each week,

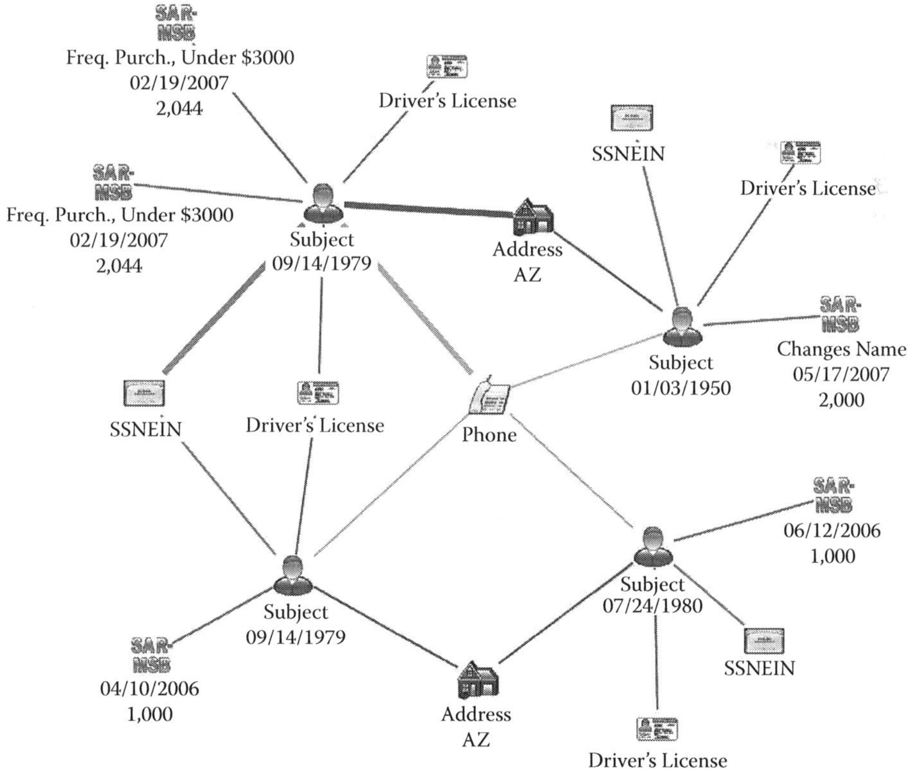

Figure 6.40 Out-of-Country Transactions.

converting large-denomination Swiss francs, utilizing multiple agent locations, having money sent to pharmacies and restaurants, and structuring transactions to avoid additional identification and documentation.

Dirty Dancing

We now turn our focus to a different industry, one that is typically heavily "cash" oriented—namely, exotic dancers. After sorting through names like Brandi, Barbie, Cherri, and Tiffany, there was a network exposed where a large number of variations were present in the context of the addresses, phones, and identification numbers. Overall, the two individuals presented in Figure 6.41 have a relatively limited number of SAR-MSBs—a total of six with two referencing both subjects working together.

The subject at the top of the diagram has five transactions that result in five different addresses, five different phone numbers, three SSNs, and three driver's licenses. It is important to note that each of the addresses was a distinct and different location—not just a variation due to a data transposition error and each of the phone numbers is also unique. This person is clearly trying to avoid detection by varying the type of information presented to the remittance agent. Additionally, the transactions are based on small denominations, mostly twenties, tens, fives, and lots of ones. The narratives reveal that these individuals send multiple transactions, several times a week, for about $2,800 and $2,900 each—just under the limits requiring additional identification to be presented.

The subject at the bottom of the diagram also exhibits an identical pattern of trying to avoid detection by varying her addresses, phones, and identification numbers. The five transactions, reported over a six-month period, totaled almost $80,000, which is quite a hefty sum of cash to share with other people, especially in their line of business. The receiving agents are also varied and the recipient's name also changes among the different transactions. Generally, this type of pattern appears to be some type of large-scale escort business where payments are being made back to a home office.

Conclusion

The utilization of money remitters traditionally conjured up the image of family members quickly responding to someone in need of emergency funds, such as a starving college student trying to purchase his textbooks

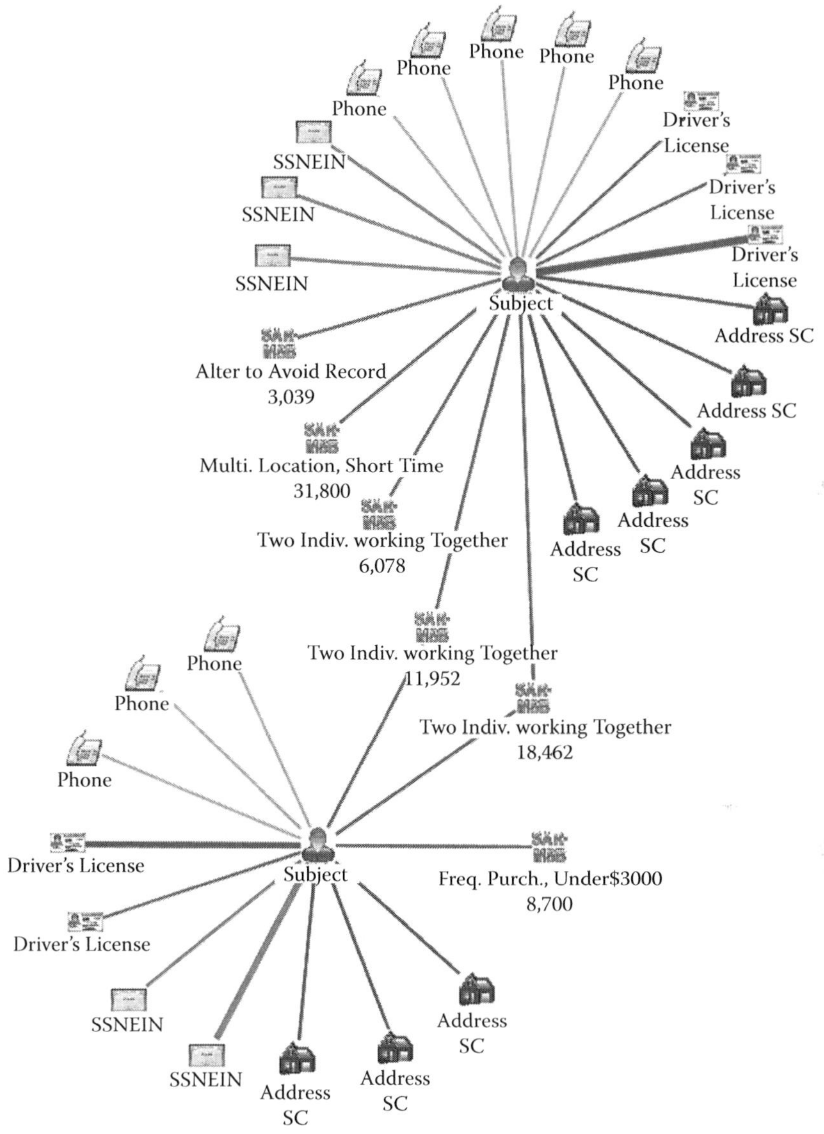

Figure 6.41 Large variation in supporting transaction details.

for the semester or someone whose car just broke down and needs to get it fixed. However, in recent years, the use of money remitters has become a much more commonplace service and is regularly used by a large number of people, especially in the unbanked community, to pay their bills (utilities, car payments, etc.) or send family maintenance payments home when they are working abroad.

The industry has created a fairly safe and secure method to send practical amounts of cash in a very convenient and timely manner. Part of the allure for using money remitters is the relative ease and anonymity it offers its customer. This underpinning for the industry's success is also its Achilles' heel, because it has inadvertently facilitated a product/offering that is susceptible to wide-scale abuses that has enabled criminal enterprises to flourish, especially human trafficking and drug dealing. At the end of the day, it is not just about transacting some money; rather, it is about impacting people's lives, families, and society as a whole.

The rules and regulations defined for the industry are evolving and are still somewhat easy to circumvent. Legitimate MSBs are reasonably diligent in their compliance and oversight and try to minimize the exploitation of their business for illegal and/or criminal transactions. Fortunately, there are proven methodologies (and technologies) defined to help combat these offenses by better understanding the nature of the data (i.e., origin, destination, composition, etc.). This emerging marketplace continues to pose challenges for both domestic and international governments to address. Over the next several years, there should be some dramatic reforms seen within the MSB sector.

Chapter 7

Fraud Analytics

Introduction

Fraudulent activities account for billions of dollars lost in the insurance, banking, healthcare, retail, transportation, manufacturing, and communications industries each year. Likewise, fraudulent activity riddles our federal and local governments; virtually every industry is vulnerable to fraud.

The U.S. General Accountability Office estimates[1] that $1 out of every $7 spent on Medicare is lost to fraud and abuse.[2] Depending on the reference, each year Medicare loses up to $20 billion dollars[3] to fraudulent or unnecessary claims. The insurance industry (e.g., covering property/casualty, medical, life, and automobile) estimates that about 25 percent of each premium dollar is spent on covering fraudulent or inflated claims, putting the yearly costs at an estimated $30 billion nationally. In a more highly publicized type of fraud, the identity theft epidemic affects approximately 10 million people and it is estimated that over $50 billion is lost to identify theft each year.[4] To put these numbers into perspective, consider that only 82 of the 183 countries ranked by the World Bank in 2006[5] had a gross domestic product (GDP) over $20 billion. In other words, the losses from fraudulent activity in the U.S. insurance market alone exceed the GDP for more than half of the world's countries.

These numbers are staggering, especially considering that they are largely paid for by the consumer. More effective methods must be deployed to minimize these losses. Industry experts estimate that for each dollar spent on combating fraud, $5 to $15 is saved, depending on the industry being served. This return-on-investment is cumulative because it minimizes future losses for the same fraudulent activities.

Flexibility remains a critical aspect for quickly responding to changing fraud patterns. It is crucial to dynamically expose new patterns of fraud without having to reprogram, retrain, or reinvent the underlying systems. Most important is to expose the fraud before it impacts the operations or business foundations. Keep in mind that before patterns are classified they first have to be discovered. Discovering insurance fraud

[1] Stephen Barrett, "Insurance Fraud and Abuse: A Very Serious Problem," February 15, 2005, http://www.quackwatch.com/02ConsumerProtection/insfraud.html.

[2] Charging for services not performed, double billing, unbundling claims, miscoding and upcoding procedures.

[3] In 2006, Medicare benefit payments totaled $374 billion (13 percent of the $2.65 trillion in federal spending). *Medicare: A Primer* (San Francisco: Henry J. Kaiser Family Foundation, March 2007).

[4] Mary Monahan, "2007 Identify Fraud Survey Report," *Javelin Strategy and Research*. February, 2007.

[5] http://siteresources.worldbank.org/DATASTATISTICS/Resources/GDP.pdf.

is not really any different from exposing money launderers, terrorists, smugglers, embezzlers, or entities involved in elusive behaviors.

The data associated with workers' compensation, property and casualty, personal injury, and other types of insurance-related matters can be viewed in its most basic form—as interrelated objects. Generally there will be a subject (policy holder, claimant, injured party, lawyer, doctor, etc.), addresses, phone numbers, accounts (policies), and, of course, the claims themselves. How the objects are related is based on the nature of the claims submitted, and behaviors can be exposed through repeated claim submissions. It is this repeated behavior, connecting the different objects, that provides the patterns of interest. Figure 7.1 shows an example of a basic network derived from insurance claim data.

The focus is on finding anomalies in the construction of these networks where the frequency of connections and the commonality among the entities show patterns of interest. It could be something as simple as two people sharing the same phone number to something more complex, such as network of physicians and lawyers in a conspiracy, with a ring of perpetrators to inflate the damages and losses incurred. It might include a corrupt body shop providing kickbacks, padding the estimates, or not even performing the repairs. Figure 7.2 depicts and abstraction of a collusive network of entities that emerges across multiple accident claims.

There have been a multitude of new technologies introduced into the antifraud marketplace over the past several years, including link analysis and other systems for detecting nonobvious relationships and associations. Perhaps even more important are the refined analytical methodologies that help to interpret the complex networks and patterns presented by these technologies. Better understanding of the data will inevitably lead to better pattern detection, and ultimately, lower fraud incidence. Once a pattern has been exposed, it is up to the affected company to act on that knowledge by changing business processes to flag related or similar

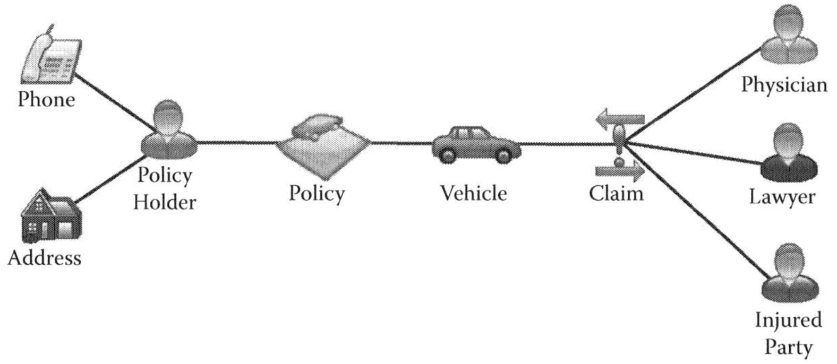

Figure 7.1 Sample insurance analytical model.

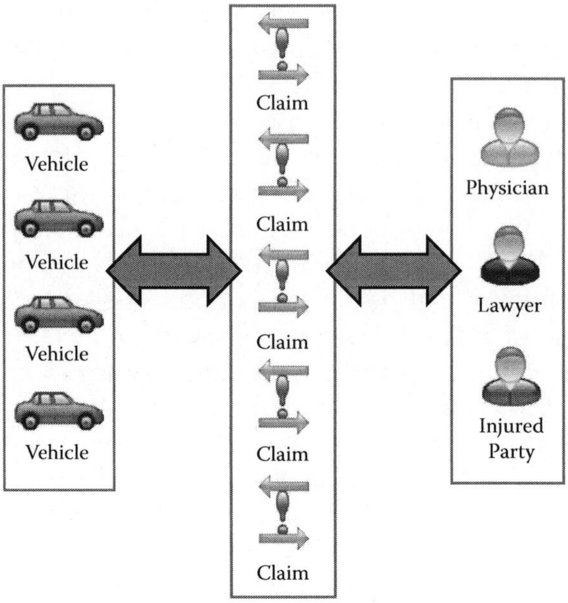

Figure 7.2 A collusive network of entities.

occurrences of the pattern. Remember that there are always exceptions to the rule, and there are exceptions to the exceptions.

Warranty Fraud Anecdotes

Warranty fraud comes in all flavors and covers a wide number of industries ranging from computers to home appliances. It comes from a mixture of consumers wanting to cover or minimize their repair costs to the authorized service representatives blatantly submitting false warranty claims. In fact, one of the largest technology providers, Hewlett Packard (HP), spends approximately $1.8 billion a year on warranty claims[6] and has determined that 6 to 8 percent is fraudulent.[7] HP estimates that the loss of $140 million to warranty fraud would be equivalent to the profit generated on the sale of an additional 15 million printers.

In HP's case, the fraud is committed in a variety of ways, including swapping new units for refurbished models or simply manufacturing false repair orders and submitting fabricated claims. In one particularly

[6] Top 100 Warranty Providers, *Warranty Week*, January 10, 2007, http://www.warrantyweek.com/archive/ww20080110.html.

[7] http://www.warrantyweek.com/archive/ww20050419.html.

shameless scenario, HP's warranty process and systems manager[8] said, "Companies sent staff into computer retail storefronts in search of floor models from which they could copy down the serial numbers. Worse, each seemed to share the serial numbers they gathered with the other company. Over a span of 12 months, these scammers cost HP an estimated $2 million."

Perhaps the biggest and most costly warranty repairs stem from the automotive industry. In the first nine months of 2007, Ford Motor Co. spent over $2.8 billion (2.5 percent of product sales) and General Motors almost $3.4 billion (2.6 percent) in warranty claims. Based on industry estimates that an average of 6 percent of revenue is lost to fraudulent activity, the amount of warranty fraud losses for just these two companies would be $168 million and $204 million, respectively. Any improvements in fraud detection help impact these numbers in a positive fashion and can result in significant savings to the manufacturers.

Automobile Warranties

This discussion describes a scenario where the auditing department of a foreign automobile manufacturer was concerned that they had fraudulent warranty claims being submitted by their affiliated dealerships. They were not sure where it was or what it looked like, only that they knew it was there. As with all car manufacturers, they pay dealerships to perform maintenance warranty repairs (e.g., three years, 36,000 miles, bumper-to-bumper) on its cars to fix vehicle problems and satisfy customer complaints. The charges that are incurred by the manufacturer reflect the costs for parts, labor, sublets (outsourced work), and miscellaneous expenses (see sidebar on dealership charges). With more than 1,200 dealerships in North America, the amount paid out annually by this particular manufacturer for warranty repairs exceeded $350 million at the time the analysis was performed. Because dealership mechanics are paid based on the amount of work they generate (see sidebar), there is a potential for some repair orders to be padded with extra costs for work that has not been performed or are considered inappropriate charges. Even small percentages of fraud result in significant losses when scaled to this type of industry.

This particular manufacturer had established a progressive warranty audit team that was chartered with identifying unallowable charges and patterns of noncompliant claims. The team recognized

[8] William Fung, PC & Appliance Warranty Fraud Panel, *1st Annual Warranty Chain Management Conference*, San Francisco, March 3, 2005.

Dealership Charges

In many repair shops, including car dealerships, mechanics are typically paid[9] on a flat rate (also called a book rate) that represents the average time required for performing a specific repair. The flat rates are published by the manufacturers as a way to ensure consistency and reasonableness in the time that is allowed to be charged for completing the repair. Say the flat rate for completing an oil change is set at 15 minutes; this is the total amount of labor time the mechanic will be paid regardless of whether it takes 10 minutes or an hour to finish the job. Examples of published manufacturer flat time rates include: 3.2 hours[10] to replace a water pump on a 1989 Chevy G20 Van with a 6.2 liter diesel, 2.6 hours[11] to replace the oil pan gasket on a 1993 Ford Ranger 3.0 v6 with an automatic transmission and two-wheel drive, and 1.5 hours[12] to replace the latch assembly on a roll-up door for a Trainmobile trailer.

The more jobs a mechanic can get done in a day, the more he or she will be paid. In fact, it is possible for decent and experienced mechanics to log more than eight hours of book time (e.g., 12 or even 15 hours) in an actual eight-hour day. This can lead to a nice, plump paycheck for the mechanic, and there is some debate as to whether or not the use of flat rates leads to rushed jobs that are not properly completed, inevitably requiring the same job to be redone multiple times. This situation is further compounded because many service advisers are paid by the number of labor hours they sell, and of course the dealerships are also paid an overhead cost plus additional fees to process the warranty claims. Everyone makes a cut on the warranty repair. As a side note, some manufacturers use the concept of a "warranty time" to further reduce the flat-rate time required to complete a repair.

---

9 http://wiki.answers.com/Q/How_much_money_does_an_auto_mechanic_earn.
10 http://autorepair.about.com/library/faqs/bl983e.htm.
11 http://www.autoqna.com/Maintenance-Repairs/1024-2-autoqna-3.html.
12 http://www.trailmobile.com/site/files/638/54471/213436/285691/TMFlatRateMaintenance.pdf.

the need for using advanced technologies and analytical techniques to help with processing the almost 2 million warranty repairs that are performed each year by their authorized dealerships. They wanted to become proactive in their audits so that they could effectively seek out and discover the fraudulent claims. They realized it would require an analytical system that could support a number of parameters ranging from dealership regions and repair types to car models and/or mechanic training, where virtually any one of the hundreds of variables contained within their datasets was fair game. In this example, a number of different data sources were identified for analysis including warranty repair orders, customer complaints, technician training, and customer satisfaction survey data.

The patterns exposed can be generally broken down into four different types of categories,[13] which are outlined below:

- **Routine and Known:** These types of warranty activities occur based on known risks and probabilities. The exceptions are "flagged" as being outside of standard parameters. For example, the manufacturer will allow the dealerships to use only certain parts and if a part is submitted that is not found in the standard parts list, the system will reject the entry. This represents standard business operations and procedures.
- **Routine and Unknown:** The nature of these warranty repairs is based on taking advantage of situations where existing systems have limited detection capabilities. The size and scope of these activities are left to be uncovered through alternative methods. For example, a dealership performs routine transmission repairs, but does not employ technicians trained at the required levels.
- **Nonroutine and Known:** The warranty repairs slotted into this category are based on discontinuous patterns. The circumstances occur based on unfamiliar sequences of activities. For example, the warranty repairs for a particular dealership are above average because the time of year for that geographic region or zone has fewer COD clients (i.e., nonwarranty-covered repairs), requiring the technicians to make up their extra pay through increased warranty work.
- **Nonroutine and Unknown:** This is the most damaging situation directly affecting the manufacturer. The models used here help identify unknown patterns and practices, detect covert/unexplained practices, and have the capability of exposing organized activity. The types of behavior that occur in this category are yet to be discovered and are of most interest and value to the manufacturer.

One of the most notable patterns found in this manufacturer's warranty database was based on an initial query looking at claims involving vehicles with less than 100 miles on the odometer. Generally, this is a somewhat unrealistic mileage for performing warranty work. Unless the defect renders the car unusable, such as a broken starter motor, or makes it annoying or uncomfortable (e.g., squeaking brakes or a broken A/C unit), most people won't report the issue until they bring the car in

[13] Christopher Westphal and Teresa Blaxton, *Data Mining Solutions: Methods and Tools for Solving Real World Problems* (New York: John Wiley & Sons, 1998), 62.

for its first oil change around 3,000–5,000 miles. Therefore, the resultant set of claims basically reflected new vehicles that were most likely still located on the dealership lot and had not yet been sold. Additionally, the data extraction used for the analysis was set to remove any part replacement codes—showing labor-only repairs (e.g., like soft-tissue injuries in insurance fraud claims) exclusively. These claims are based entirely on a mechanic's time under the hood where no parts were replaced (and, therefore, not traceable) and no work was outsourced to any external or third-party entity (e.g., radio repairs).

The results of the query were subsequently presented using visual-clustering techniques. When the "repair type" was used for grouping the claims, it became explicit that there was a dominant group (i.e., a specific type of repair) represented in this data. Surprisingly, the most prevalent group in this set was *cigarette lighter* repairs and each claim had a single hour of labor time charged that, depending on the dealership rates, was between $45 and $65. After reviewing the pattern with the audit group, it was obviously clear—when people test-drive cars, the cigarette lighter is often removed (i.e., stolen), and because it is both a functional as well as cosmetic component in the car, the dealerships were charging an hour of labor to recover the cost of replacing the part. The general flow of this pattern is depicted in Figure 7.3.

Needless to say, this was not a circumstance that the manufacturer was required to cover under warranty. In fact, the manufacturer could go back, up to three years, to deny any paid claims. For the time period reviewed, the number of dealership franchises that existed, and the number of claims made of this type, this was a multimillion-dollar fraud. Nowadays, to help deal with this situation cigarette lighters are packed in a welcome kit that comes with the vehicle—often encased in a plastic binding that is unpackaged once the car is prepped after the sale is made. Generally, cigarette lighters have been repurposed into power ports to

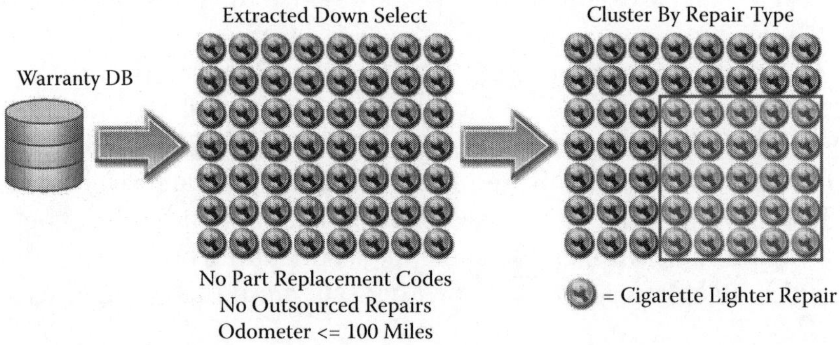

Figure 7.3 Cigarette warranty claim repairs.

run modern electronic devices, such as radar detectors and GPS satellite navigation systems. For some manufacturers, it has become an option that costs extra.

Other types of warranty patterns were also identified in the dataset. One particular make and model distributed by the manufacturer had a faulty paint job, such that the paint flaked off certain areas of the car (e.g., hood, roof, and trunk), for a period of approximately two years. This was a situation known by the warranty team, but was immediately spotted within the data. What came to light was the range of costs associated with this type of repair. Generally, the claims were between $400 and $800 to repaint the affected areas. However, unknown to the auditors was that there were quite a number of claims exceeding several thousands of dollars. The only justification for those claim amounts would be an entirely new paint job and/or body work.

Other patterns included repair "itises" (where certain types of claims are always done together even though the problems are unrelated), duplicate repair submissions, having the same problem fixed multiple times, and even tracking customer complaints and issues before they reach a boiling point (i.e., customer will never buy another car from this manufacturer again). Below is a simple list of other repair patterns that were reviewed along with their colorful name definitions in brackets.

1. Look for commonality among dealerships based on customer name, VIN, address, telephone number. [Merry-Go-Round] (Similar to the HP example discussed previously.)
2. The warranty repairs for a dealership exceeded the zone average.
    a. Dealership charges excessive warranty repairs to lot cars based on problems indicated during a test drive. [Bait & Switch]
    b. Service adviser is observed authorizing additional time expenses exceeding preset time allotments for repairs. [Padding]
    c. Technicians spend a majority of time working on nontraceable repairs (e.g., rough engine) to inflate warranty charges. [Soft Repair]
3. Vehicle requires multiple "remove and replace" repairs. [R&R]
4. Customer invoice indicates repair X and the manufacturer invoice shows repair X, repair Y, and repair Z. [Creative Repair]
5. Car is brought in for a specific problem and the dealership identifies several additional "nonsafety" repairs. [Ambitious Technician]
6. Repair technician has been trained to a certain level (A–E) and repair order indicates problem skill is above certification level of technician. [Brainiac]
7. Dealership charges the customer for a repair and then submits it to the manufacturer as a warranty claim. [Double-dipping]

There are also reports of dealerships initiating warranty claims, forging signatures,[14] and rolling back the odometers to qualify for warranty work.[15]

Traditional methods limited manufacturers to only a few detailed audits each quarter. With the help of more automated systems, they have the capability to review and audit hundreds of dealerships by focusing on the anomalies that present themselves within the warranty data. Through development of the system, the manufacturer also has the ability to effectively identify and detect unallowable warranty repair orders. This allows them to deny and directly charge the costs back to the dealerships. Those mechanics, service advisers, or dealerships that have an excessive or recurring denial of claims can often be traced back to a misinterpretation of established manufacturer policies and procedures. The audit department, through close association with the training department, can recommend that corrective processes be initiated in these cases.

Hurricane Katrina

Pre-9/11 the big concern was counter-*narcotics,* and post-9/11 it is counter-*terrorism* (ironically, both are nine-letter words). After the attacks there was massive spending to ensure that public services personnel, including police, fire, and emergency workers, could communicate with one another; there were large quantities of anthrax antidotes, biohazard suits, and gas masks stockpiled throughout the country; and huge numbers of personnel including Transportation Security Administration (TSA) inspectors, air marshals, and special agents were hired to help battle this new and emerging threat. Although critical, it represents a significant amount of additional investment to deal with situations after they have occurred. Is the United States, or the world, a safer place? By all accounts it is, but that is largely based on how one defines "safer."

Regional emergencies, such as Hurricane Katrina,[16] certainly showed that there is still a lot of room for improvement with respect to how data is used to better manage situations, services, and operations. The GAO has reported[17] that there has been at least $1.4 billion in fraud,

[14] http://scholar.lib.vt.edu/VA-news/VA-Pilot/issues/1997/vp970807/08070482.htm.

[15] http://www.usdoj.gov/usao/eousa/foia_reading_room/usam/title4/civ00159.htm.

[16] "Waste, Fraud and Abuse in Hurricane Katrina Contract," United States House of Representatives, Committee on Government Reform—Minority Staff, Special Investigations Division, August 2006, http://en.wikipedia.org/wiki/Hurricane_Katrina.

[17] Gregory Kutz and John Ryan, "Hurricanes Katrina and Rita Disaster Relief: Improper and Potentially Fraudulent Individual Assistance Payments Estimated to be between $600 Million and $1.4 Billion," GAO-06-844T, June 14, 2006, http://www.gao.gov/new.items/d06844t.pdf.

misrepresentation, and theft from the coffers that were put in place to aid the victims of Katrina, and there are billions[18] more in overcharges and mismanagement by contractors providing relief and recovery services, often awarded without a competitive bidding process. Certainly the aid provided was desperately needed by many people and used for the appropriate purposes, but without any type of oversight or controls in place to properly manage this process, the government doled out much more money than was required for this crisis.

After the hurricane hit, the levees burst, and the damage was done, the Federal Emergency Management Agency (FEMA) offered $2,000 in disaster assistance through the use of prepaid debit cards to those people in need to help cover immediate food, shelter, clothing, and basic living necessities. To be eligible, recipients had to have a primary residence in an area damaged by the hurricane. Additional funds, including disaster unemployment assistance, were also made available from the Louisiana Department of Labor (LDOL) as well as other state and local agencies. Other benefits[19] included housing assistance (e.g., manufactured housing and mortgage and rental assistance), individual and family grants, and a number of funding avenues to help offset the massive losses encountered during this crisis. In total, over 2.5 million applications requesting disaster assistance were received by FEMA.

Unfortunately, the management of the crisis was not handled well by FEMA officials and proper oversight and controls were largely lacking from their assistance programs. As such, there are numerous reports[20] of people receiving duplicate aid payments from FEMA, and other questionable expenditures, such as purchases of alcohol, prostitutes, tattoos, weapons, and the paying of gambling debts, traffic fines, and adult club fees. There was even one report[21] of a person giving the address of a cemetery for their claim information. The true nature of the abuses will never be fully realized because a significant amount of the aid provided through the distribution of the debit cards was converted to cash and, is therefore, untraceable.

In one particularly shameless case of fraud,[22] an individual who lived in an area located a short distance from downtown Atlanta, Georgia, and some 450 miles from New Orleans submitted more than 50 fraudulent

[18] http://oversight.house.gov/Documents/20060824110705-30132.pdf.

[19] http://katrinalegalrelief.org/index.php?title=FEMA_Benefits.

[20] Gregory Kutz, "Expedited Assistance for Victims of Hurricanes Katrina and Rita: FEMA's Control Weakness Exposed the Government to Significant Fraud and Abuse," GAO-66-403T, February 1, 2006, http://www.gao.gov/new.items/d06403t.pdf.

[21] Frank Bass, "FEMA Wants More than $300 Million in Hurricane Aid Returned," *Associated Press*, February 6, 2007.

[22] http://www.usdoj.gov/katrina/Katrina_Fraud/pr/press_releases/2006/jan/01-20-06whittakerindicted.pdf.

applications for disaster unemployment assistance. Basically, he fabricated a number of names, all sharing the same date of birth, using one of two common last names and false Social Security numbers (SSNs) that were very similar to each other (e.g., one or two of the middle digits of the SSN were changed in an incremental numbering fashion). He claimed that these people lost their jobs as a result of the hurricane and then received dozens of debit cards that were all mailed to the same post office box in Georgia.

He was eventually caught because automated methods within the LDOL computer systems flagged that multiple claims/payments were being made to the same address. What is particularly interesting about this case is that on September 16 (2005) he filed a claim using his own name, and then on September 27 filed a new claim using a completely different name. Presumably, after receiving payment without additional follow-up, questions, or any type of red flag being raised by FEMA or the LDOL, he decided to take advantage of the circumstances. His next set of claims came on October 27, when seven claims were filed under different first names using a common Latin surname, each with a slightly different SSN and all with the same date of birth and same address. The next day, on October 28, he filed another 32 claims using a similar configuration of the same surname (different first names), date of birth, and address. Finally, a few days later on November 1, an additional 10 claims were filed using a different last name (also a very common Latin name) with the same date of birth and address as the claims filed the previous week. An abstraction of this data is presented in Figure 7.4.

To the credit of the government personnel involved, this case was sent to the U.S. Attorney's Office on November 7 for prosecution and the last 10 payments, for the November 1 claims, were stopped before payment was disbursed. In fact, all the debit cards were electronically zeroed out once it was determined there was a potential fraud. Once the fraud pattern was detected, it was acted upon and shut down in fairly short order helping to minimize the damage and losses of money to fraud.

The LDOL normally has a number of safeguards in place to help minimize the risk of fraud, but based on the mitigating circumstances, many of these safeguards were removed for the first 12 weeks to help expedite the claim processing. Under normal operating conditions the standard process requires all recipients to call in each week to request money and answer specific questions about their accounts; however the phone systems were down because of the widespread damage inflicted by the hurricane and the proper follow-ups could not be conducted. It was decided that debit cards would be used to fund the employment benefits because the postal system was also devastated by the hurricane and

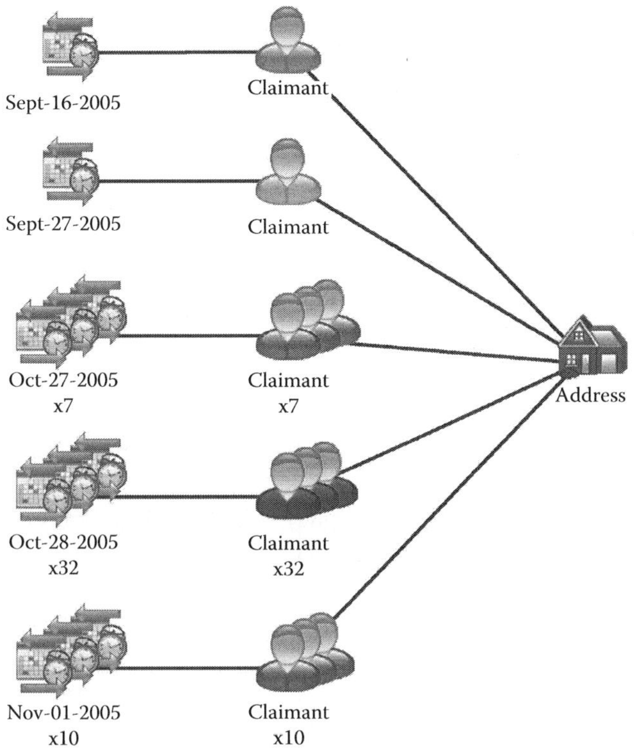

Figure 7.4 Fraudulent Katrina benefit claims.

not operational in many areas, further compounding the situation and resulting in more delays or potential nonpayment to many needy persons. Therefore, electronic funds passed via a debit card were the most logical alternative to ensuring people received their benefits in a timely manner. The individual in question eventually pleaded guilty,[23] was sentenced to 27 months of prison, and ordered to pay restitution.

Other patterns of fraud were discovered when the investigators saw an influx of applications coming from a specific street, apartment complex, or area not affected by the hurricane. Typically, someone would file a fraudulent claim, receive payment, and brag about it to their neighbors and friends, prompting others to start filing fraudulent claims to receive debit cards. Many of these cases were exposed by the tip line established for people to report suspected wrongdoing and fraud. Once the applications got pulled up for review, the investigators quickly saw the pattern and were able to deal with the situation accordingly.

[23] http://www.usdoj.gov/katrina/Katrina_Fraud/pr/press_releases/2007/jul/07-05-07 whittaker.pdf.

Disturbingly, there were also instances of government employees from FEMA arrested for soliciting bribes as public officials. Several FEMA individuals[24] running base camps located in Louisiana inflated the head counts for the meal services being run from their facilities in return for kickbacks from the contractor supplying the meals. Still other officials, from both the federal and state governments including police organizations, were charged with theft of property, filing false claims, and even overcharging for labor and vehicle use. One large-scale incident[25,26,27] involved a call center operated by the Red Cross located in Bakersfield, California. The volunteers staffing the call centers filed fraudulent claims for themselves, family, and friends due to the minimal amount of data required to issue a claim number to collect the funds. One person went to the same Western Union office on three different occasions to collect payments, which aroused the suspicion of store employees who reported the incident to the Red Cross. This led the investigators to follow the thread, which ultimately led to more than 80 prosecutions within the Eastern District of California resulting from this scheme. There are many references[28,29] in the open-source reports to a wide variety of fraud associated with this disaster.

On September 8, 2005, within two weeks of the hurricane landfall, the Hurricane Katrina Fraud Task Force[30,31] was set up by the U.S. Attorney General with the expectation to address the frauds and abuses associated with the aftermath of disasters. Within the first six months[32] of the establishment of the task force, there were more than 200 people charged with fraud-related crimes. After a full year,[33] there were over 6,000 fraud-related tips and more than 400 people charged with fraud crimes from hurricanes Katrina, Rita, and Wilma. Unfortunately, trying to re-collect the money once it is distributed is a much harder task than being more diligent when processing the aid requests in the first place. Of course, due to the severity of the situation, some of these cases were unavoidable.

It must also be pointed out that not all of the fraud reported in the press and news is due to incompetence or the inability of the government

[24] http://www.usdoj.gov/katrina/Katrina_Fraud/pr/press_releases/2006/jan/1-27-06USAOEDLA.pdf.

[25] Kareen Wynter, "Dozens Indited in Alleged Katrina Scam; Red Cross Workers Accused of Filing False Claims," *CNN,* December 29, 2005. http://www.cnn.com/2005/LAW/12/28/katrina.fraud/index.html.

[26] http://sacramento.fbi.gov/dojpressrel/pressrel06/katrina_fraud070306.htm.

[27] http://www.usdoj.gov/katrina/Katrina_Fraud/pr/press_releases/2006/mar/03-17-06eight indicted.pdf.

[28] http://www.publicintegrity.org/katrina/filter.aspx?cat=14.

[29] http://www.usdoj .gov/katrina/Katrina_Fraud/pr/press_releases/.

[30] http://www.usdoj.gov/katrina/Katrina_Fraud/.

[31] http://www.usdoj.gov/opa/pr/2005/September/05_ag_462.htm.

[32] http://0225.0145.01.040/katrina/Katrina_Fraud/docs/katrinarerportfeb2006.pdf.

[33] http://www. usdoj.gov/katrina/Katrina_Fraud/docs/09-12-06AGprogressrpt.pdf.

to detect these schemes. There are many restrictions, due to privacy laws, that make it hard to deal with these situations. It becomes a balancing act between exposing criminal behavior and protecting an individual's privacy. The Computer Matching and Privacy Protection Act of 1988 (5. U.S.C. 552a), an extension of the Privacy Protection Act of 1974,[34] defines the regulations for record keeping, disclosures, and sharing of data. These laws put a number of limitations and restrictions on what different agencies can do with respect to their use of data sources. Civil liberty rights groups have long espoused their concerns regarding the potential abuses involved with collecting and combining data from multiple sources and were instrumental in the downfall of the Total Information Awareness (TIA[35,36]) program sponsored by the Defense Advanced Research Projects Agency (DARPA) back in 2003.

Before the hurricane, there were no Memorandums of Understanding (MOUs) in place between FEMA and the Social Security Administration (SSA) and, therefore, many reported identities could not be verified. Even after the establishment of the Task Force, access to the National Emergency Management Information System (NEMIS) operated by FEMA (used to enter and manage all information regarding disaster assistance from registered applicants) remains tightly controlled. An official MOU was executed between the Task Force and FEMA with access granted only to approved staff members and only for use checking a specific allegation or fraud under the premise of law enforcement protocols. This ensures that there are no fishing expeditions or witch hunts being conducted by the government.

To be fair, it should be recognized that the $1.4 billion estimate made by the Government Accountability Office (GAO) is an extrapolation from a sampling of claims and includes losses from both fraud and mismanagement. This number includes applications that were filed where the information did not properly or adequately support the claim being made and technically should not have been paid. This occurred, for example, in about 2,300 applications where a post office box was listed as the physical address of the property damaged. In a high percentage of these claims, investigators were able to confirm, through the postal databases, that the victims actually had real property and residences located within the affected areas damaged by the hurricane. This type of filing happened so frequently because the physical property no longer existed and the applicants mistakenly or inadvertently put the contact address into the wrong

[34] http://www.usdoj.gov/oip/04_7_1.html.
[35] http://en.wikipedia.org/wiki/[nformation_Awareness_Office.
[36] http://www.epic.org/privacy/profling/tia/.

part of the application. Therefore, the value for the entire lot of claims was deemed unacceptable and included into the baseline losses reported by the GAO, which skews the total number.

Corporate Frauds

In the commercial world, there are innumerable ways in which to conduct internal frauds against a corporation, including improper billing practices, padding expense reports, filing duplicate invoices, submitting fictitious receipts, tampering with checks, or voiding cash entries—the list is virtually endless. Frauds can be perpetrated throughout the corporate hierarchy, from top management officials involved in complicated investment scams all the way down to the mailroom clerk stealing from the petty cash drawer. Generally, the amount of loss incurred by the business community in the United States is estimated[37]at approximately 5 percent, which translates to over $650 billion in fraud losses for 2006, and this number is expected to continue to rise.

Fraud is basically a theft against the organization and is performed in a concealed or stealthy manner so as to avoid detection. Fraud has many different names, including embezzlement, bribery, kickbacks, forgery, falsification, and conflicts of interest, to name a few. One particular conflict of interest comes in the form of procurement fraud, where purchasing agents earmark contracts for a favored or preferred vendor without requiring competitive bids. This situation can also manifest itself in a pattern of employees also acting as vendors of the corporation—where they might have inside knowledge regarding the budgets, specifications, or competition bidding for the work.

Employees as Vendors

Some very basic and fundamental checks can be performed on company data sources to check addresses or phone numbers from an employee master file against the vendor master file to expose any potential commonalities. For example, the fax number listed for a company turns out to be the same as the number listed for the emergency contact information of an employee. An illustration of this is shown in Figure 7.5. Although simple, it does occasionally expose some questionable

[37] 2006 Report to the Nation on Occupational Fraud and Abuse. *Association of Certified Fraud Examiner, Inc.*, http://www.acfe.com/documents/2006-rttn.pdf.

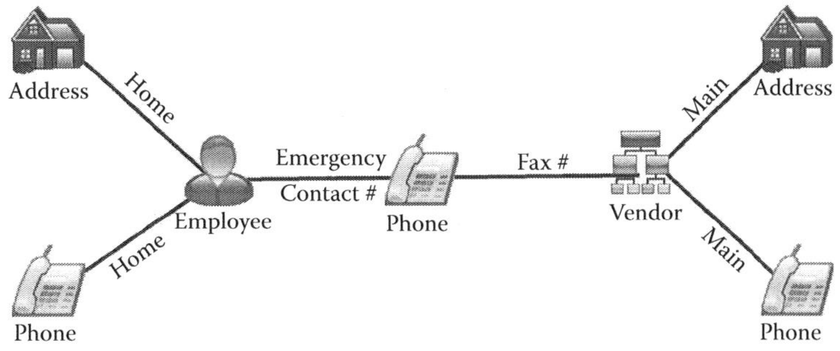

Figure 7.5 Employee linked directly to a vendor.

relationships within the operations of a business, especially some of the larger entities.

In other cases, there could be less obvious connections that require the incorporation of additional sources of data. Many times corporations are run or influenced by a cadre of people including owners/founders, senior management, and board directors. Often, these people also have similar roles in other corporations. Therefore, knowing the chain of command often helps in understanding how decisions can be influenced. For example, the diagram[38] in Figure 7.6 depicts a large, well-known U.S. retailer at the center of the network and all of its directors as its immediate linkages, shown as male or female person icons. A number of these board members are also affiliated with other large companies addressing a wide spectrum of business offerings, including equipment manufacturing, computer sales, cloths retail, news media, insurance, investment and financing, communications, restaurant, banking, and others. As the diagram shows, several are also in common to multiple companies, showing how a select few can have large impact across a number of different industries. Of course, each of these businesses can be further expanded thereby extending the network of influence even more.

A second example of this is shown in Figure 7.7. This information[39] is more directly based on corporate ownerships and which companies own other companies. Each company will have a president or a CEO that will act as the official figurehead and there will be a multitude of senior executive vice presidents and others not explicitly listed. Some individuals can prove to be quite active and represent multiple companies or subsidiaries at the same time, as is shown in Figure 7.8. These just represent other avenues where improper procurement practices could be encountered due to the indirect nature of these kinds of relationships.

[38] Generated from *http://www.theyrule.net* using data circa 2004.

[39] Can be derived from sources like Dun & Bradstreet.

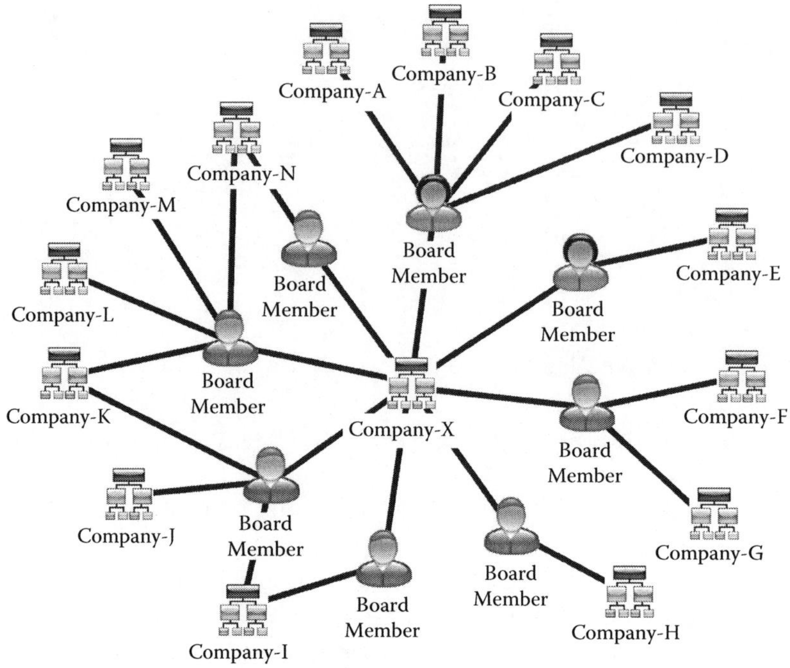

Figure 7.6 Corporate board member intrarelationships.

Vendors as Vendors

As was introduced in the previous section, companies can operate in an official capacity and subsume, control, purchase, own, and influence other companies. There are also more cozy and comfortable relationships that are forged where a company (e.g., vendor) is indirectly associated with other vendors, potentially doing similar work. There is concern about these types of situations because a vendor might act as a front company, submitting unreasonably high quotes for a job only to make another vendor look more favorable, yet both companies are owned or controlled by the same entity. Figure 7.9 shows an example of two companies using the same phone numbers for both their main call-in lines and fax numbers.

The same circumstances also exist when the organizations share a common address. Figure 7.10 provides a depiction of this type of network. There may be legitimate reasons for such activity, including, for instance, when the facilities represent a large, shared warehouse space and a distributor handles the related processing originating from the same place. This is somewhat of a stretch and, in reality, the CFO of the agency should investigate why such conditions exists.

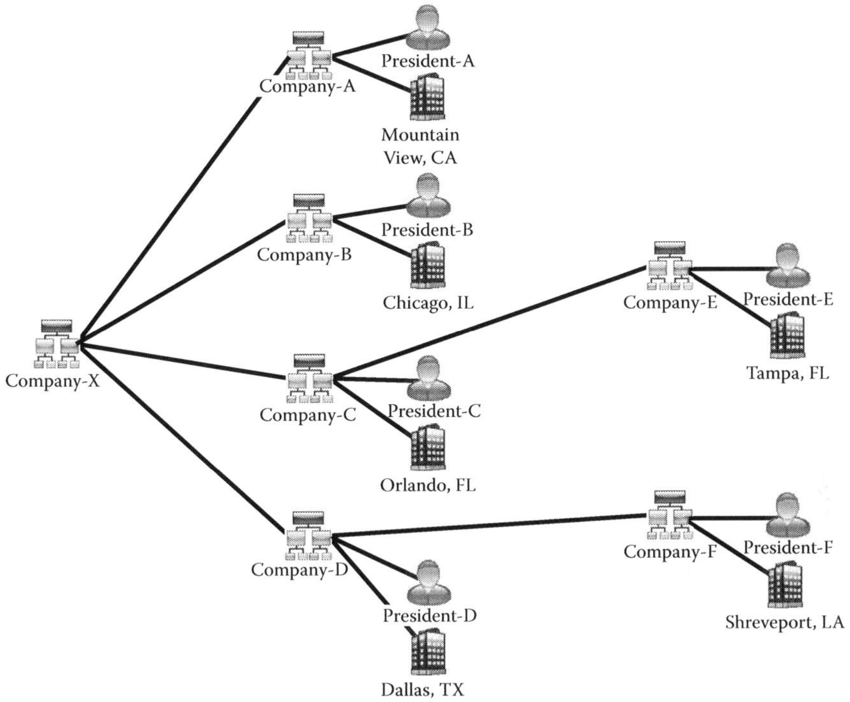

Figure 7.7 Corporate ownership networks.

Expanding on this concept, the use of common phones and addresses is one way to help identify inconsistencies in the underlying data and potential areas of fraud against the corporation. The diagram shown in Figure 7.11 presents an address with three related vendors, all with similar names. The number below the vendor name represents the vendor ID code assigned in the accounting system. To the system, there are three entirely separate vendors capable of doing business with this corporation. Most likely, this situation exists because the procurement staff did not take the time to see if an existing entity was already present in the data, or their search was unable to return an exact match. Not knowing the duplications that are present in the data can complicate accounting matters because there is never a true accountability of how much money has been spent with the vendor overall. One or more of the vendors could also be a front for special pet projects or kickbacks. Regardless, it represents circumstances that should be investigated.

A variation of this is shown in Figure 7.12 where the vendor ID appears in sequential order. What is interesting to note in this case is that the middle entry is the only valid value. One would have to question why this sequence was entered into the system, why the last entry made

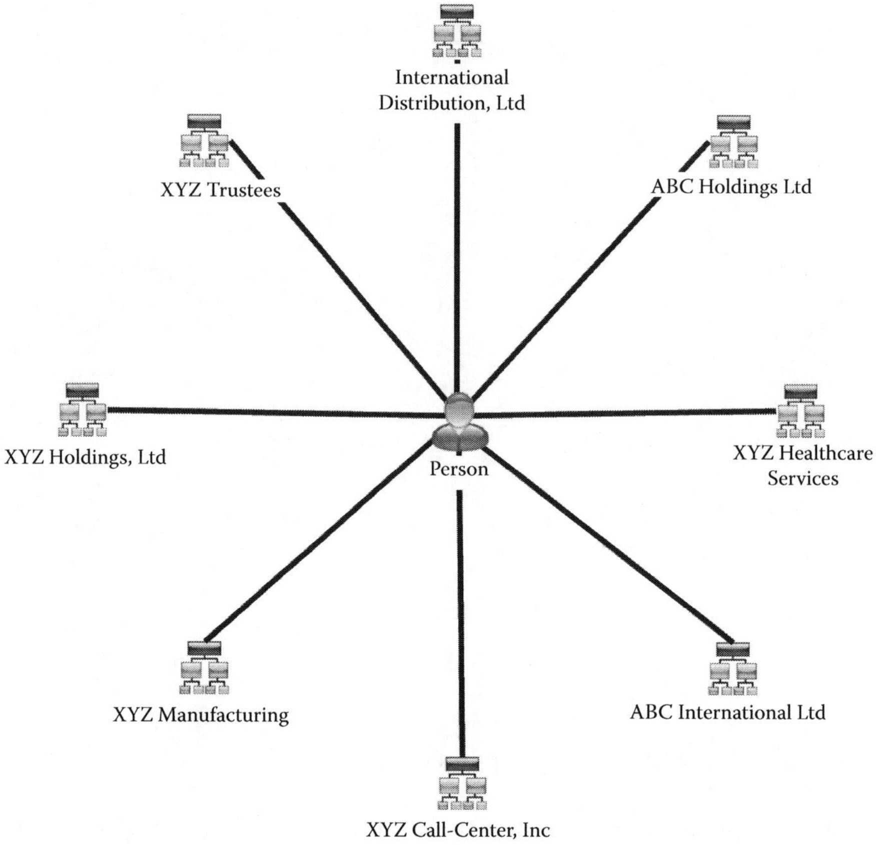

Figure 7.8 Individual with large corporate influences.

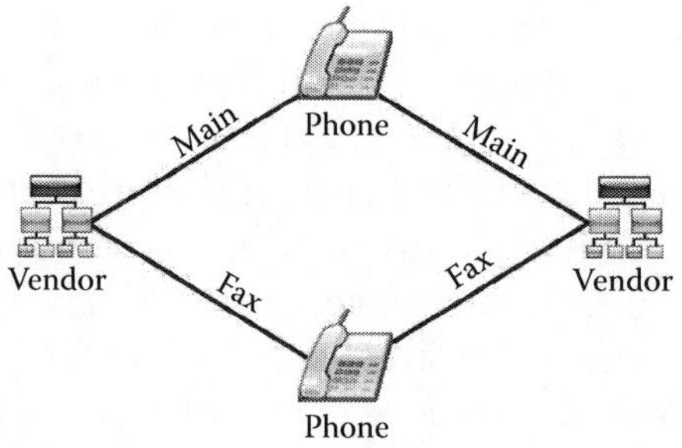

Figure 7.9 Common use of same corporate phone numbers.

is invalid, and if the two vendors are actually invalidated or if the system treats them as active vendor ID codes. Again, this situation needs to be brought to the attention of management and audits run against the system to determine if there are any improper procurements or

Figure 7.10 Common use of same corporate address.

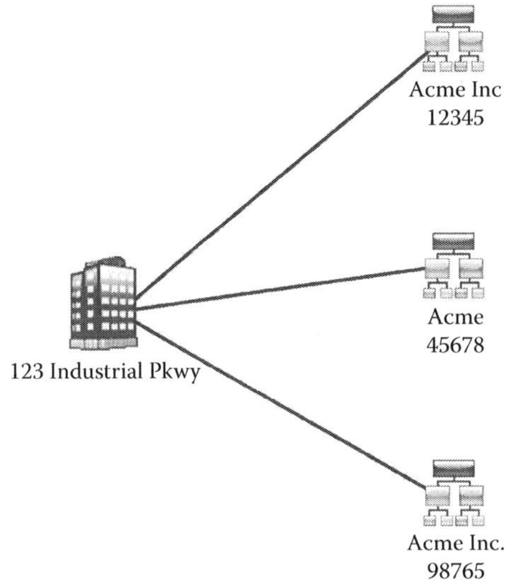

Figure 7.11 Multiple vendor ID codes assigned to the same vendor.

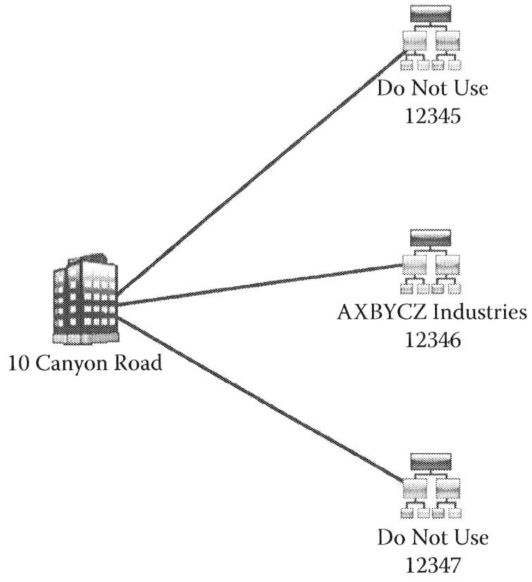

Figure 7.12 Improper vendor ID codes assigned to a single vendor.

invoices associated with these codes. Ideally, they should be deleted from the system so this condition does not represent a risk to the corporation.

To further exemplify how inconsistencies impact the overall reliability and integrity of procurement systems, very large networks can be produced from just the different variations present in the data. They do not always reflect any type of fraud, but often poor controls in the accounting and procurement systems that, if allowed to persist, make it harder to differentiate legitimate activity from fraud. A sample of the vendor information contained in an invoicing system for a property management firm is shown in Figure 7.13, depicting a popular company that offers bath and body gifts, fragrances, and skin care products. Even if the spelling of the company name is identical, each object represents a different client ID (e.g., vendor ID) showing a total of 11 different entries for one company, plus a number of variations on the payment address. Clearly, some better internal controls need to be employed by the management firm because this degree of repetition could easily lead to duplicate invoicing and other improper posts or ledger errors.

Corporate Expenses

This next round of examples is based on some fundamental processes common to all businesses large and small, from around the globe—namely, expense reimbursements. They are one of the necessary tribulations associated with doing business, especially when travel is involved. There are many ways in which to "embellish" an expense report, which is just another form of stealing from a company through padding costs, fabricating expenses, and bait-and-switch expenditures. Often it can help supplement the salary of a disgruntled employee and will tend to repeat itself over and over. It is also a nice loophole for earning money as a form of nontaxable income.

In one scenario,[40] large computer hardware manufacturing company was concerned that there were employees embezzling money through various loopholes in their expense-reporting systems. The security office had excellent physical measures to keep their equipment from being stolen from their facilities and warehouses, but they had little control of or insight into how the employees were expensing their travel costs. The company's main interest was in determining whether there were any

[40] Updated from the previous work described in: Westphal, Christopher and Blaxton, Teresa, *Data Mining Solutions: Methods and Tools for Solving Real World Problems*, (New York: John Wiley & Sons, 1998) 53.

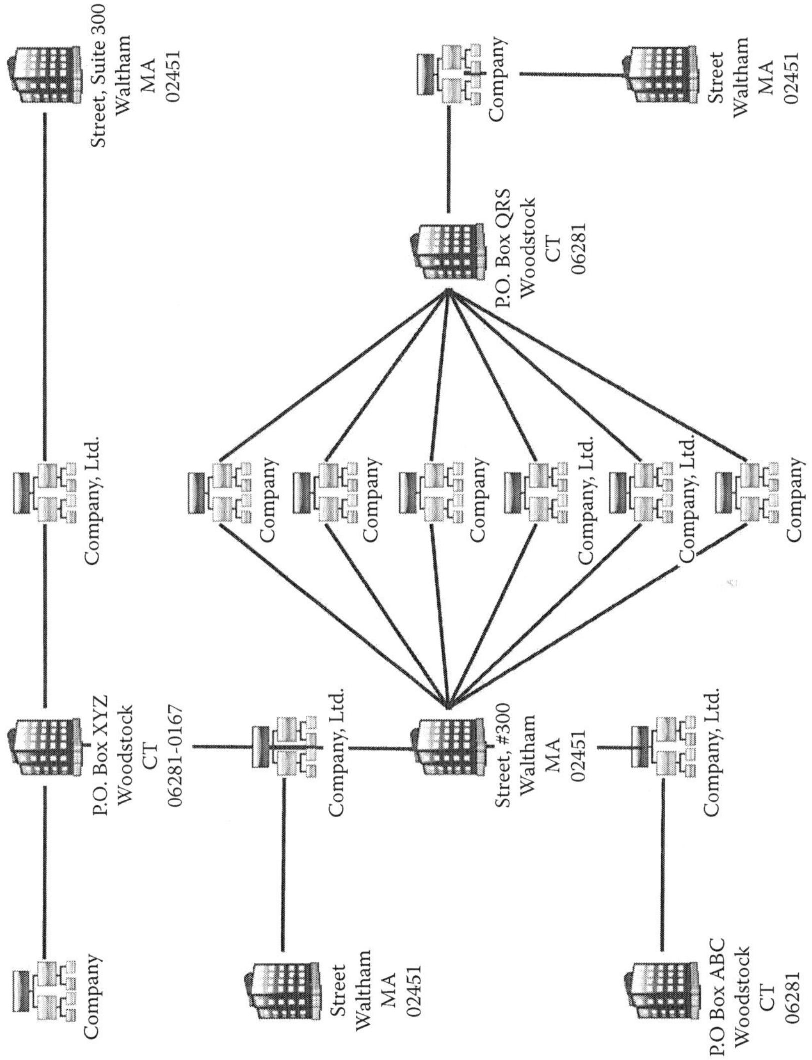

Figure 7.13 Large variations on a single company profile.

patterns of theft that could be detected without too much room for ambiguity with respect to the nature of the activity.

In this particular application the patterns were derived from two electronic data sources. The first was an online expense-reporting system developed for internal use, which contained employee reports of business expenses, out-of-pocket charges, and travel reimbursements. The second data source contained actual charges incurred on the company-owned credit cards (American Express) issued to company employees. Each data source was mined individually to detect intradomain patterns indicating personal use of the credit cards for purchases in liquor stores, home furnishings, and women's lingerie shops, and for questionable business expense reimbursements, such as large phone call charges, hotel services charged back to a room, or cash advances.

At the time, the company had strict policies on air travel bookings. They required that all air-related travel be handled through their appointed travel agency. The travel agency could find better travel rates, manage flight changes, and properly address all the related travel logistics. Naturally, one of the first queries made into the system was for all credit card purchases involving an airline carrier, as shown in Figure 7.14. Surprisingly, there were a significant number of airline ticket references that were identified.

In continuing with defining the pattern, the next logical step was to extract all travel expense reports with an associated airline ticket purchase. Most of the expense reports flagged looked fairly typical and included airfare, meals, lodging, and local transportation, such as cab fare or rental cars. A depiction of this is shown in Figure 7.15. At this point it was easy to spot those employees that traveled frequently, those who had high-dollar reports, and those who were more compliant with submitting their reports and properly breaking down each expense.

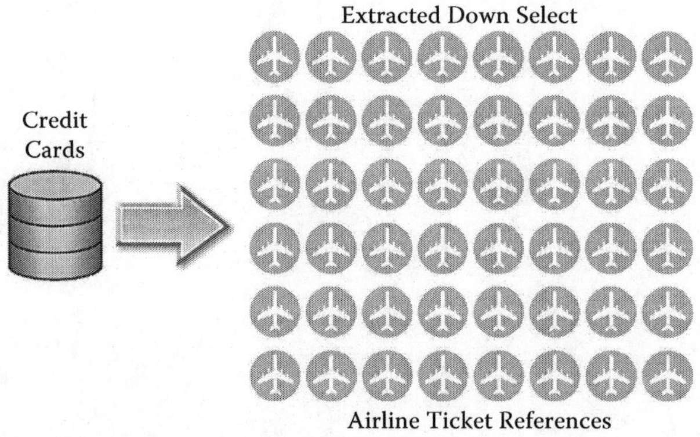

Figure 7.14 Credit card ticket references.

The online expense report and credit card data were correlated showing all reimbursements for air travel during similar time periods, as shown in Figure 7.16. In most cases there was a one-to-one correspondence of credit card charges and expense report reimbursements, exemplified by EMP #1, indicating that employees submitting airplane ticket charges to the online expense reimbursement system were automatically compensated for their charges. All that was required was a copy of the receipt for the ticket.

However, when the color/style of the credit card transaction was changed to reflect whether the charge was a credit or a debit, a whole new pattern emerged. For several particular employees (EMP #2 and EMP #3), it was apparent that they were buying full-fare, fully refundable airplane tickets on the corporate credit card (upward-facing airplane), submitting

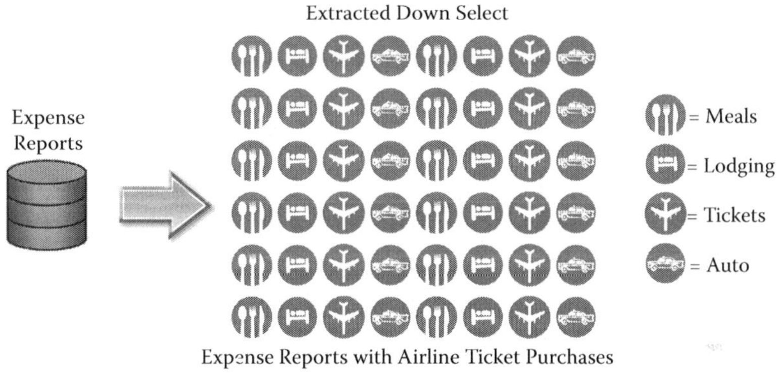

Figure 7.15 Expense reports with airline ticket purchases.

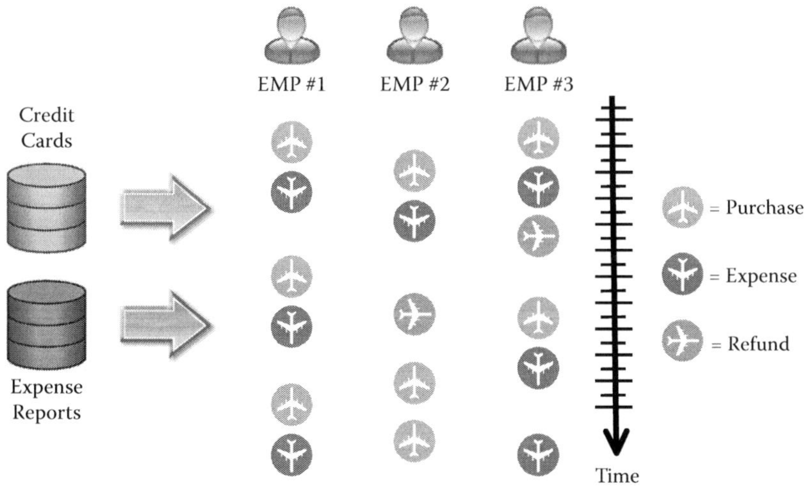

Figure 7.16 Combined data sources showing air travel expenses.

for a reimbursement through the online expense system (downward-facing airplane), and then returning the unused tickets to the airlines for a credit back on their charge accounts (sideways-facing airplane). The net result was that they were pocketing the cost of the ticket at the expense of the company. Some of these fares were quite expensive, especially a full-fare, round trip from the West Coast to the East Coast.

Another pattern that was observed occasionally showed a ticket expense without any correlating credit card debt, also shown by EMP #3 as two downward-facing airplane icons in a row, which implies the ticket was probably purchased on a personal credit card. This tends to be out-of-the norm because most employees don't want to float the cost of corporate travel expenses on their personal accounts. There could certainly be special circumstances causing this type of event to occur; however, it should be evaluated and reviewed by the internal accounting staff to ensure it is legitimate.

Duplicate Payments

There are many ways to detect fraud and some approaches are quite simple. Basic list sorting, accumulating values, and other combinations of data can help expose situations that should be reviewed and justified by auditors. Using traditional online analytical processing (OLAP) approaches is one of the quickest ways to get a breakdown of various data fields, such as payments, amounts, dates, and other content where multiple (repeating) instances of the values is considered questionable behavior. OLAP-like approaches are often used for understanding transactional behaviors, such as payment and invoicing frauds.

The results from this analysis are based on the payments made from a medical company over a period of one year. Figure 7.17 shows the top 10 payments, in terms of frequency ("# Payments"), in the system queried on the vendor master file. Each row in the results table presents the total number of payments made to a specific vendor for a specific dollar amount.

Upon closer inspection, there are a few items that stand out as "questionable" and require further evaluation. What is immediately revealed is that the top entry, Employee #123, has 64 checks[41] issued to her for the exact amount of $96.15. The nature of her business is unclear; however, basic breakdowns for monthly or weekly reimbursements do not correlate to any type of known payment frequency (e.g., monthly parking, Internet fees, meals, mileage reimbursement, lease or rental costs, etc.). In fact, when the checks are presented using a date grid shown in Figure 7.18, there are several items that appear problematic in terms of when some of these checks were issued.

[41] The Company records payments made by check to employees as vendor payments.

#Payments	Amount	Check Recipient
62	$96.15	**Employee #123**
26	$5,984.55	Lease/Rent Payment
24	$1,527.22	Audit/Accounting Fees
19	$35	Transportation Services
19	$236.22	Uniform Rentals
19	$1,710.83	Medical Supply
18	$97.98	Printer Lease
18	$192.3	**Employee #123**
16	$250	Employee Assistance Services
16	$136.75	Pest Control

Figure 7.17 Table showing payment by frequency.

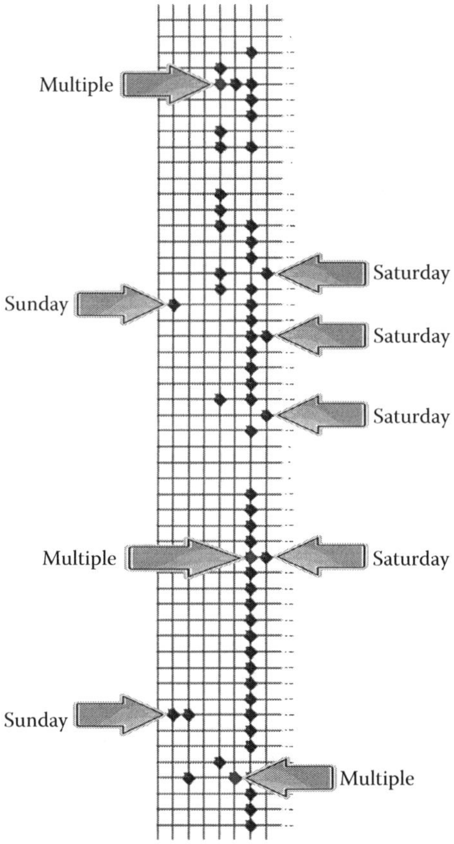

Figure 7.18 Date grid for the 64 check payments.

Quite clearly, the scheduled check-cutting day for this company appears to be Friday; however, there are also a number of Saturday and Sunday check issue dates, which raises flags as to why anyone from the accounting department was working over the weekend to issue checks. It would not be inconceivable to work over certain weekends to get a backlog of work cleared out; however, it represents a highly unusual situation that should be reviewed. Furthermore, there are at least three instances of multiple checks being cut on the same day, and as can be seen in the diagram, there are weeks when two and even three checks are issued to Employee #123, which begs the question of why these were not rolled up into a single check.

Looking further down the table presented in Figure 7.17, there is a second entry for Employee #123, showing 18 payments of $192.30, which is exactly double the $96.15 payment amount ($96.15 × 2 = $192.30). This can be considered an additional 36 payments of $96.15, which conceptually brings our total up to exactly 100 payments of $96.30. These payments are shown in Figure 7.19. Furthermore, there are no other payment amounts for this vendor in the data, only these specific amounts.

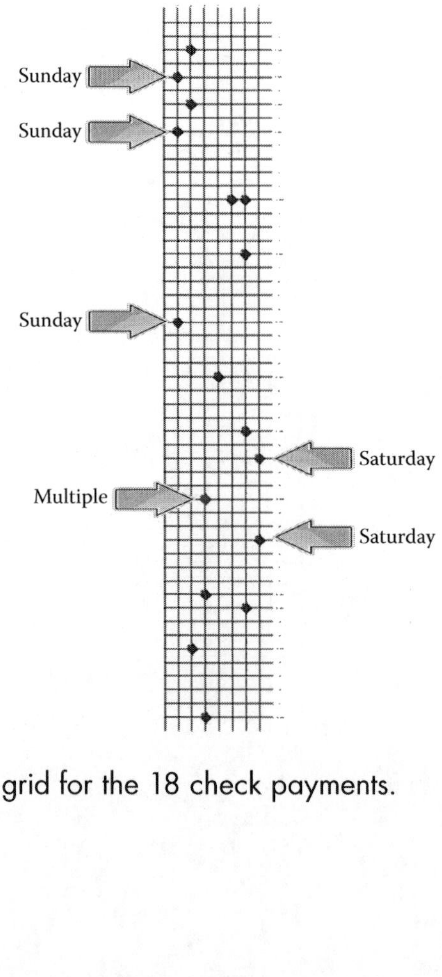

Figure 7.19 Date grid for the 18 check payments.

Why did the company not roll many of these into bundled payments? There is a lot of extra overhead and resources going into processing those checks each and every week. Figure 7.20 presents a final image with the two date grids combined where the $192.30 checks are shown marked with an arrow. This situation raises a lot of questions; however, it does not necessarily mean that any wrongdoing has occurred. As with all patterns the truth must be established and the internal auditors need to review the expense statements to see if they represent appropriate and legitimate cost expenditures for the company. Until this final step is performed, the pattern remains high value but unconfirmed.

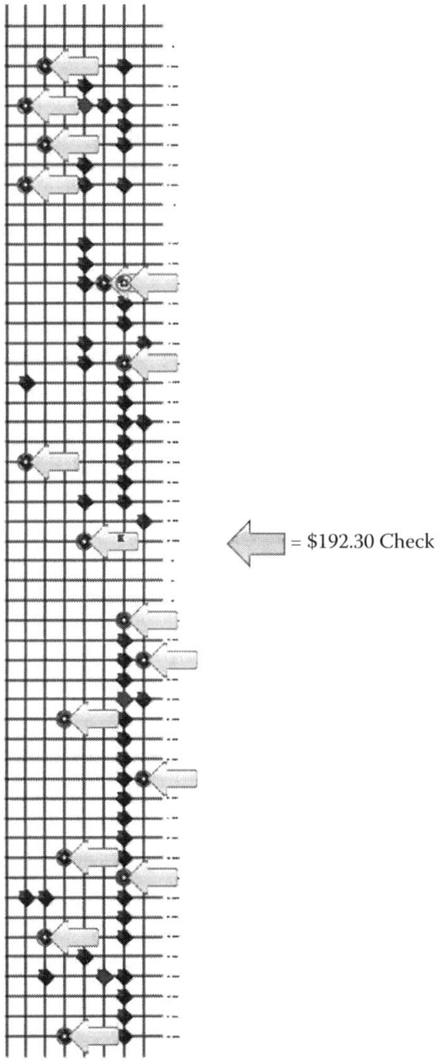

Figure 7.20 Date grid for the combined check payments.

# PAYMENTS	AMOUNT	CHECK RECIPIENT
3	$122,281.71	CIRCUIT MANUFACTURER, CO.
3	$119,298.62	CIRCUIT MANUFACTURER, CO.
2	$56,233.5	COMMUNICATIONS, CO.
2	$52,500	HEARING AID DEVICES, CO.
2	$43,053.33	FLUID DISPENSING, CO.
2	$39,069.15	HEARING RESEARCH, CO.
2	$39,068.35	HEARING RESEARCH, CO.
2	$38,766	CIRCUIT MANUFACTURER, CO.
2	$31,813	COUNTY TREASURER
4	$30,028.5	INTEGRATED CIRCUITS, CO.

Figure 7.21 Table showing payment by amount.

In expanding on these concepts, the results of the previous database query are now re-sorted using the Amount column, shown in Figure 7.21, to expose the highest payment amounts with multiple checks. The light arrows show a particular vendor receiving some of the largest duplicate payment amounts recorded. The concern here is to determine if the payments are part of a financing plan (e.g., equipment, construction) or if the payments potentially represent duplicate payments for the same invoices. It is somewhat unusual for a vendor to receive three payments for $122,281.71 and another three payments for $119,298.62. A check on the actual details shows that these checks were all cut and paid within three weeks of one another. The dark arrows show the payments for a different company where a similar type of pattern seems to exist, except with only two payments for each. Each of these vendors also has quite a number of additional payments for various amounts; however, these particular entries appear "questionable" and need to be further investigated.

When performing these types of reviews, there are also checks made to see if any of the amounts tend to be more "rounded" (whole numbers, no cents) and "clustered" around the same range. In this dataset, there are numerous payments (not shown) clustered around the $30,000 range, which might be an attempt to circumvent the signature levels for purchase authorizations by unbundling the costs into multiple payments. Also, there were several dozen payments made to specific vendors where the invoice amounts did not match the payment posted such that they were off by a considerable amount; in some cases, up to several thousands of dollars. The companies in question are large organizations (e.g., overnight delivery, travel agencies, temporary staffing) and therefore no fraud is probable, but rather there is more likely a flaw in the accounting software someplace. Additional review of these payment scenarios was initiated to determine the nature of these payments.

Human Resources

The cliché "good help is hard to find" applies throughout all levels of business. Periodically reviewing the indirect relationships among employees can help to spot trouble areas that may lead to future problems, especially when an employee is terminated. The indirect relationships can be established through e-mail networks, interoffice phone calls, and personal residences. In this next example, all of the employees of the organization were tracked in a human resources (HR) database and given a status indicating whether they were "active" (A), "terminated" (T), or "leave" (L), as presented in Figure 7.22.

There are a total of 191 employees represented in the database with 163 active employees, 127 terminated staff, and 1 out on leave (maternity leave). As it turns out, there are also six people listed in the database with both an "active" and "terminated" status code, which is logically impossible and indicates some type of data inconsistency in the HR database. For reference, these people are considered terminated. At this point, the data is expanded to show the home addresses associated with each employee, shown in Figure 7.23.

As expected, the majority of these networks represent a one-to-one relationship between an employee and their home address. The eight networks highlighted in the upper-left corner of this diagram contain larger numbers of entities, indicating there is some type of shared asset—either an employee with multiple addresses or an address with multiple employees, with the latter being more common. A closer look at these eight networks is displayed in Figure 7.24.

The first network (#1) shows that there are three employees, one active and two terminated, with the same last name living at the same address. From the information provided, the relationships between these persons are not known, insofar as whether they are siblings, cousins, or some combination of parents, spouses, and children. Regardless, this situation should concern HR representatives because depending on what the reasons[42] were for the terminations, it could directly impact the working attitude and ability of the active employee.

[42] If they were terminated for cause for stealing, tardiness, or incompetence, it would not reflect well on the reamaining employee. If they left to return to school, it would not be a material reason to be concerned.

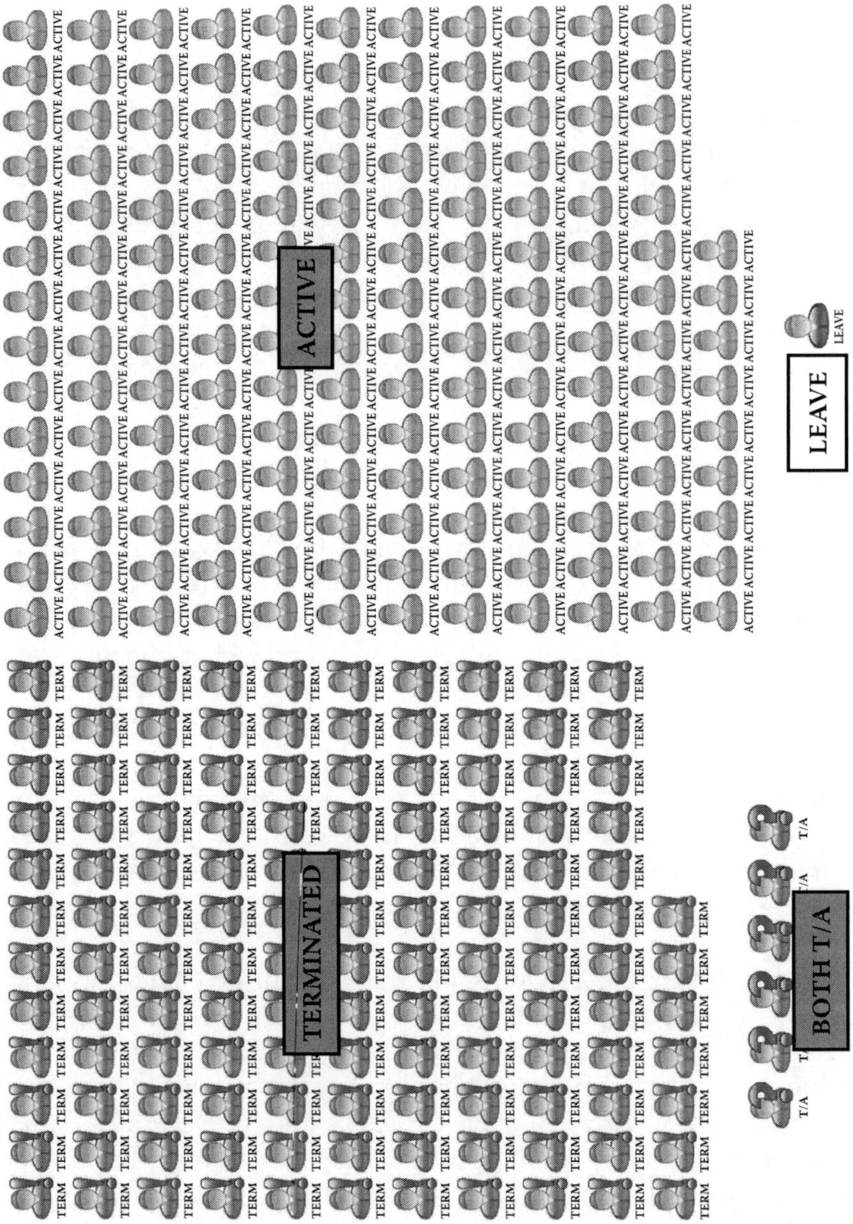

Figure 7.22 Employment status based on HR database.

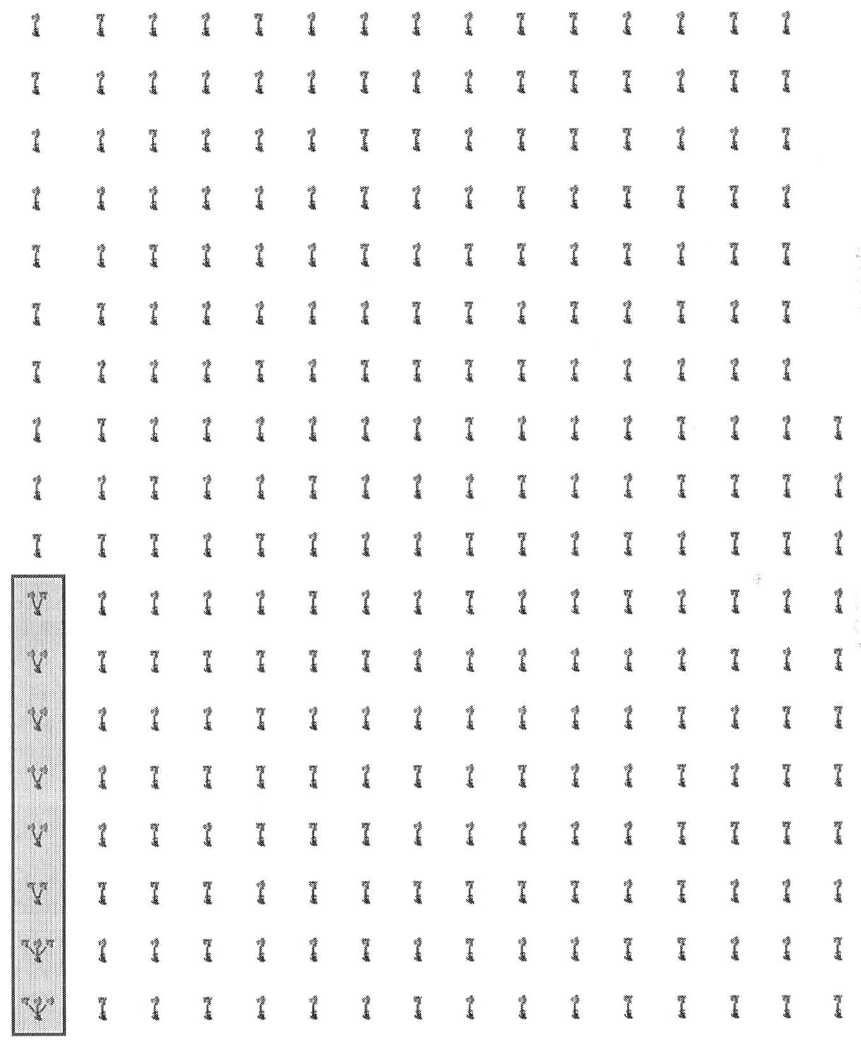

Figure 7.23 Network of employees' home addresses.

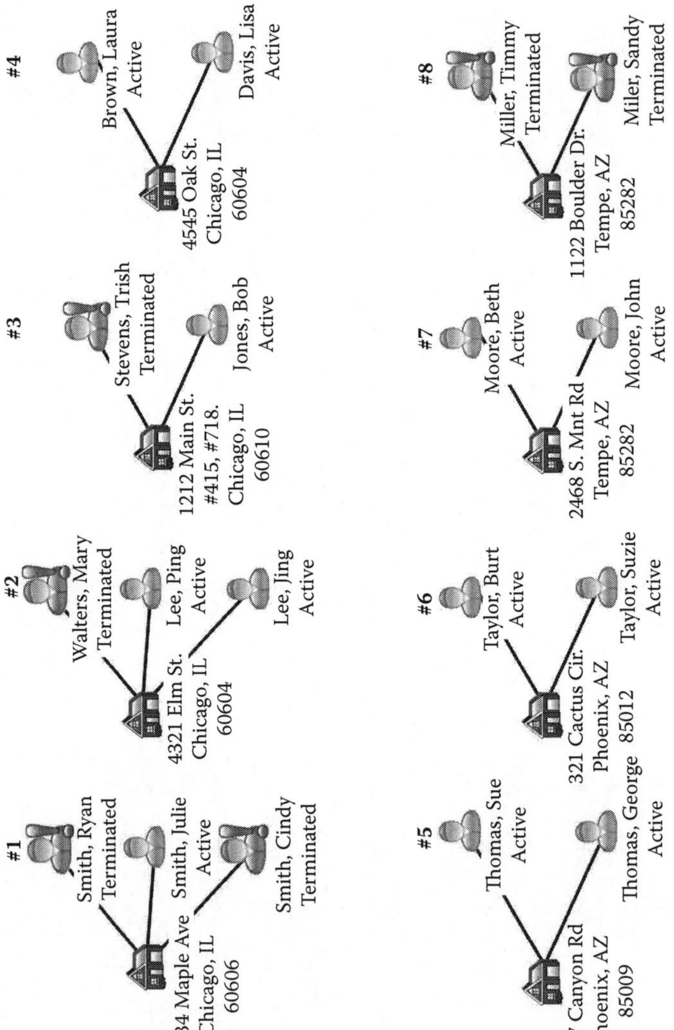

Figure 7.24 Many-to-one connections between addresses and employees.

Network #2 shows a terminated employee living with two active employees who share the same last name—perhaps husband and wife or brother and sister. Because the couple can be influenced negatively by the terminated employee, there should be some type of follow-up or review to see if there are any problems or questionable behaviors.

Network #3 is of less concern because the address depicted is really an apartment building and the apartment numbers show that these employees are living on different floors. Thus, even though this is a close match, it is not a direct relationship. The employees may have known each other and perhaps even carpooled into the office together, but the influence of the terminated employee is of less concern than if they had been living together. Networks #4, #5, #6, and #7 are virtually identical and are not of any importance at this time because both employees are active. Finally, the last network, #8, does not set off any alarms because both employees are terminated and no longer with the company.

Reviewing these types of networks can help gain insight into the relationships among employees and how changes, such as termination, can affect and impact other employees. Although this company had less than 200 employees, you can imagine the delicate networks and cross-relationships that exist in larger organizations. This is also where social network analysis (SNA) can come into play to help better understand advice, trusts, and influence networks within an organization. Although a detailed discussion of SNA is outside the scope of this book, there are a number of government agencies that use SNA approaches to help understand, prioritize, and apply confidence to the networks that exist within their data sources.

Gift Card Fraud

What do you get someone for a birthday, graduation, or holiday gift? Many people are now turning to giving gift cards because they allow the recipient to get exactly what they want. Many retail stores and restaurants offer their own brand of cards and virtually all credit card companies also offer gift cards. The cards are convenient to use and can be refunded or replaced if they are ever lost or stolen. The National Retail Federation estimated that consumers spent $26.3 billion on gift cards during the 2007 holiday season. As with any financial instrument that has a monetary value or worth, it is subject to various types of fraud[43] and scams.

---

[43] http://www.snopes.com/fraud/sales/giftcard.asp.

This next example provides a snapshot of a scenario that was analyzed when stolen credit cards were used to purchase gift cards from a national hardware retailer. Typically, a criminal will use a stolen credit card to purchase in-store gift cards, which in turn, can be easily resold for cash. Usually stolen credit cards are reported within a short amount of time and are shut down very quickly. Purchasing gift cards gives criminals more time to act because it can take days or weeks for authorities to track down the individual cards and deactivate them. According to one source,[44] "the group used the increasingly common tactic of using the bogus credit cards to purchase gift cards and then cashing them at Wal-Mart and Sam's Club stores. The group usually purchased $400 gift cards because when the gift cards were valued at $500 or more, they were required to go to customer service and show identification."

Depending on the type of gift card being compromised, there are different approaches and amounts that are used to commit the fraud. Overall the process involved is fairly straightforward. The template shown in Figure 7.25 depicts a stolen credit card on the left that is used to make a purchase (e.g., the transaction in the middle) at a specific store location, on a specific date, for a gift card of a specific amount. If there are multiple purchases made, then multiple transaction objects will appear in the network, which can be used to view the temporal behaviors of the perpetrators.

In the next example, the stolen credit card was used at the same store location to purchase five gift cards, worth $500 each, on the same day. The charges initially went through; however once the card was reported as stolen to the merchant, the gift cards were automatically shut down and voided from future use. Figure 7.26 provides a representation of this particular network. In this case the quick reaction of the store manager limited the losses incurred by the merchant. Obviously, these types of conditions (e.g., patterns) can easily be encoded into a series of rules or alerts or be used as the inputs to a predictive analysis system.

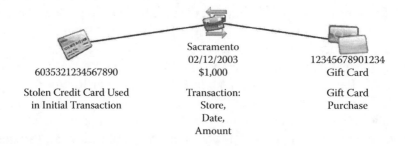

Figure 7.25 Gift card purchase using a stolen credit card.

---

44 http://www.bestsecuritytips.com/news+article.storyid+205.htm.

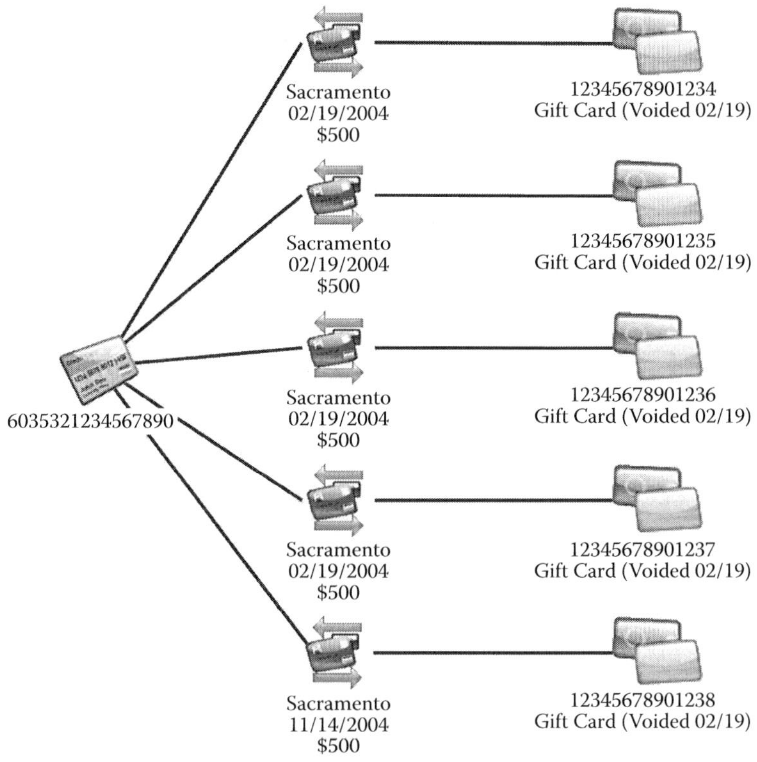

Figure 7.26 Multiple gift cards purchased at same merchant location.

The next example, shown in Figure 7.27, is virtually identical to the previous example, except that the stolen credit card was used at different stores throughout a region. In this case not all the stores identified the gift cards purchased with the stolen credit card and therefore not all gift cards were voided. Only after a broader analysis was done by the merchant was the card shown to connect purchases among the different stores. As a potential safeguard the merchant could consider enacting additional audit rules pertaining to the scope and scale of the gift cards purchased by a single credit card.

Based on the analysis performed for this merchant, the transactions associated with purchasing gift cards were arranged according to their amount, ranging from $25 up to $5,000. The distribution, shown in Figure 7.28, depicts both a circular and linear placement of the transactions, where those cards having the same face value appear as clusters in each format and the single instances represent unique dollar amounts. There are a few items to note in this figure, including that most cards purchased were based on "rounded" amounts such as $500, $1,000, and $2,000. There is also an anomaly where three gift cards were purchased at the same store for $1,072.85, which is a very specific and unusual amount.

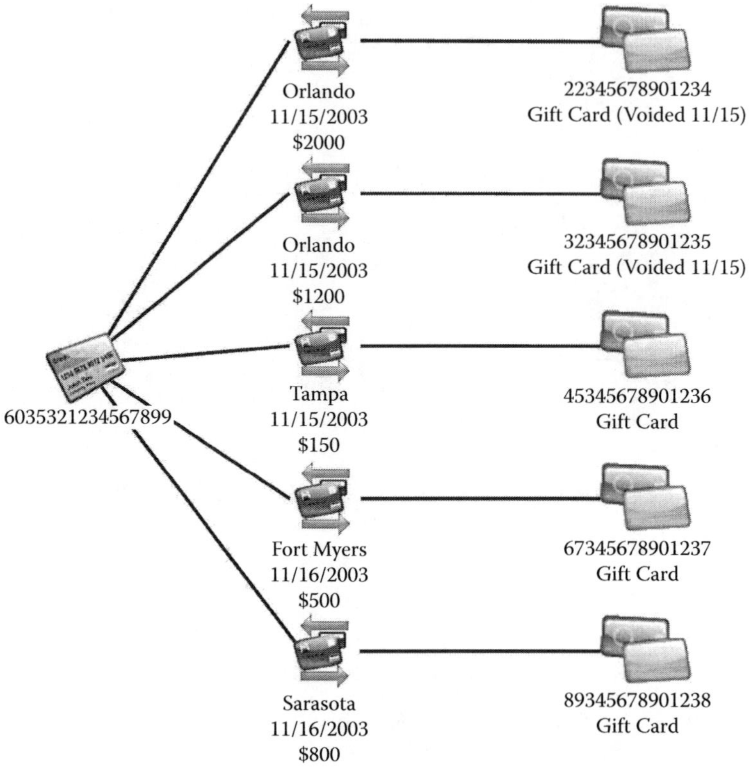

Figure 7.27 Multiple gift cards purchased at different merchant locations.

Taking a broader look at the gift card purchases shows that there are a variety of different network sizes and shapes, as presented in Figure 7.29. In this diagram, representing only a subset of the entire data, the transaction object is removed and the credit card is linked directly to the gift card. The direct relationship implies the stolen credit card was used to purchase the gift card. Most of the network structures are fairly common, where one or more gift cards were purchased.

Upon closer examination the two networks in the lower left show something slightly different. One of the gift cards purchased with the stolen credit card was subsequently used to purchase additional gift cards. Essentially they appear to be layering the transactions, making them harder to track. When reviewing larger samples of this merchant's dataset, the gift-card-to-gift-card purchases never went more than one level deep and tended to be only for one or two other gift cards.

Selecting one of these networks and expanding it to show all of its related transactions reveals a much more complicated network, as shown in Figure 7.30. In this diagram purchases made by the credit card (shown

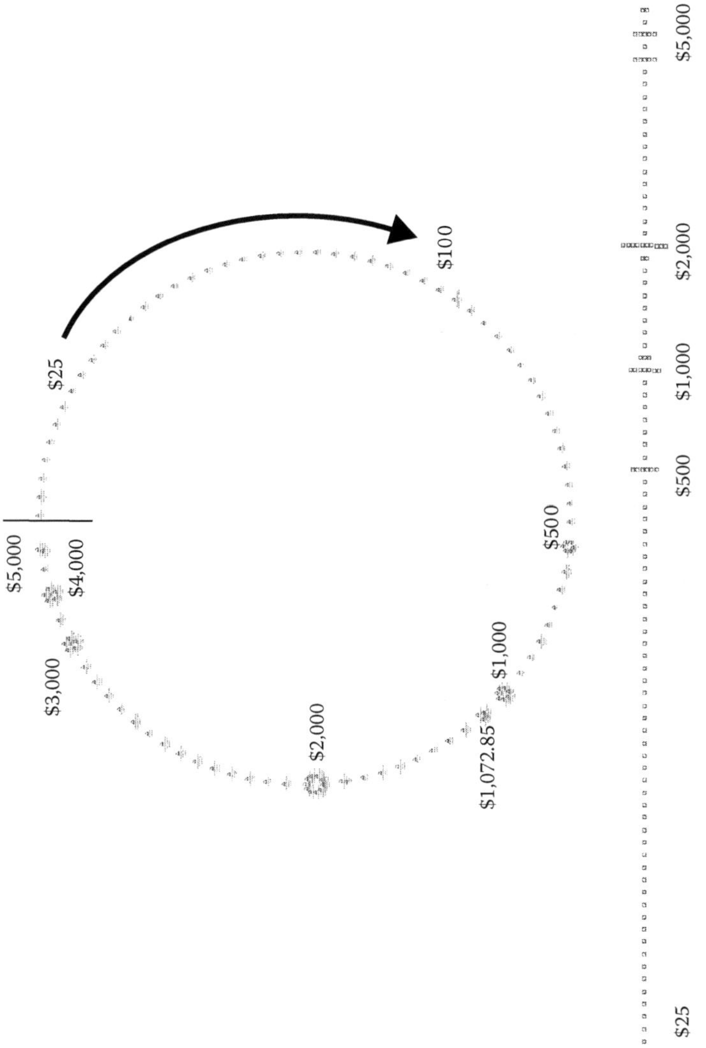

Figure 7.28 Distribution of gift card value.

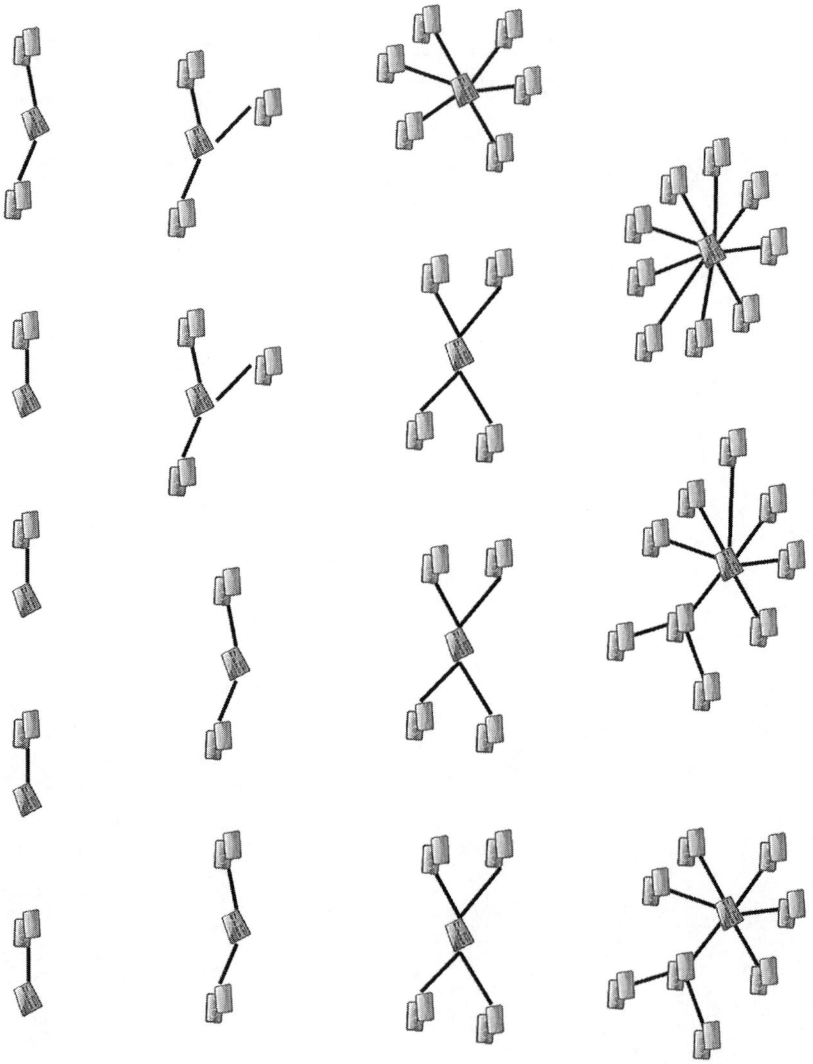

Figure 7.29 An overview of the network structure.

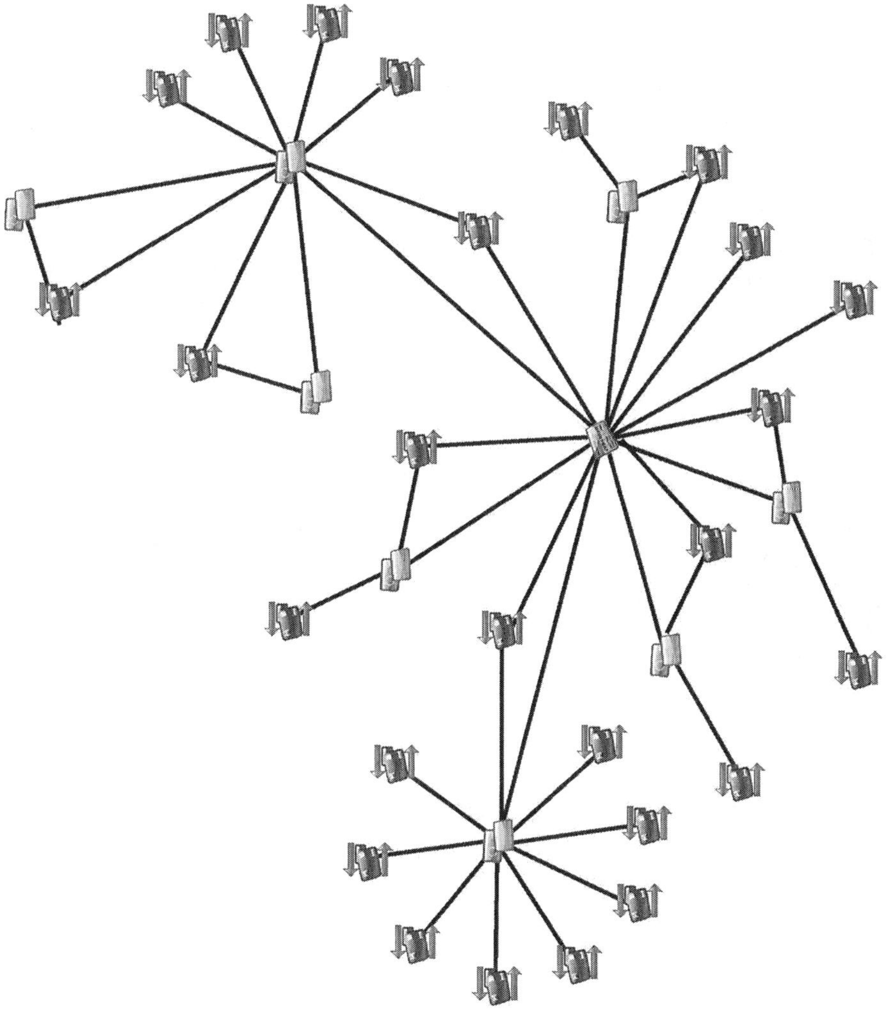

Figure 7.30 Full transaction details stemming from a single credit card.

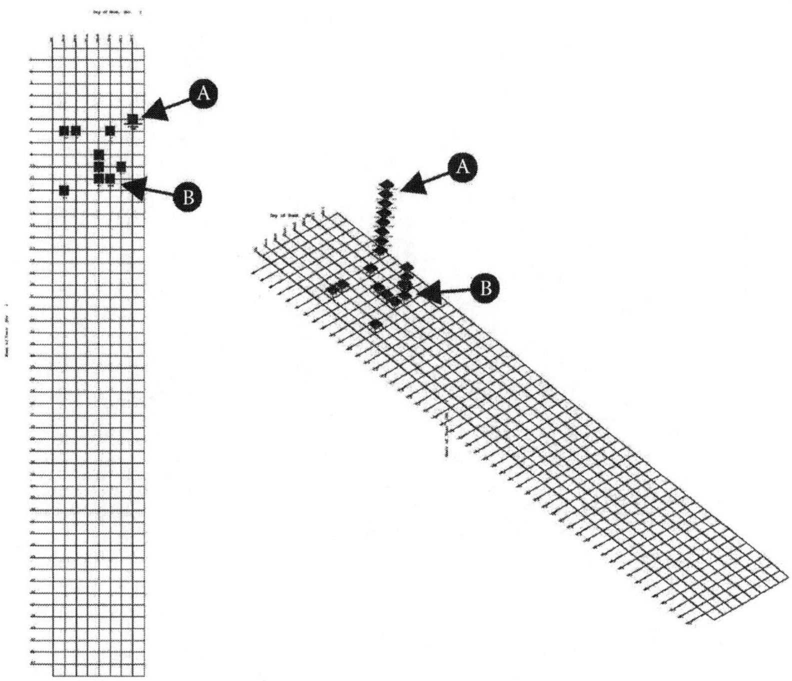

Figure 7.31 Date grid for card transactions.

near the center) or any of the gift cards are displayed as a transactional object and it becomes clear that the gift cards are being drawn down in value by additional purchases of merchandise; where some have only a few purchases, others have many purchases.

Taking advantage of the date information contained in the transactional objects, a date grid is generated to show the exact behavior in this situation (presented in Figure 7.31). These transactions all take place over a one-month period, in the March time frame. The activity starts on a Saturday with a large number of purchases, indicated by the (A) arrow, that continue into Sunday and Monday. There is then a three-week period where transactions occur on Wednesdays and, just before finishing, the perpetrators executed multiple transaction on another day, Thursday, indicated by the (B) arrow.

Additional Examples

There are too many different industries and fraud scenarios to cover in this section; however, understanding the parameters, boundaries, and relationships goes a long way in uncovering patterns and trends. Generally, the types of patterns found in one domain can typically be abstracted and used in other domains because the structure of the patterns is often similar in terms of connections, frequencies, and sequences of activities. The following quick examples simply show the concept of employing visualizations to better understand novel patterns.

Pharmaceutical

The medical and healthcare industries are prime candidates for data analysis and visualization tools. There are a myriad of practical applications of such tools in these industries. The ability to access and analyze data related to illness, injury or disease occurrence, frequency, and prognosis allows for accurate tracking and cause resolution of outbreaks. Pattern analysis can also contribute to the medical community's ability to prepare for and respond to uncommon illness, injury, or disease occurrences. Additionally, thorough data analysis can help uncover fraud, both by and through a medical practitioner. Data analysis exposes such fraudulent situations as unbundling, upcoding, pharmacy fraud, and use of ghost patients. Figure 7.32 shows an example of how prescription utilization and pharmacy compliance can be reviewed using visualization techniques.[45]

Notice that in the area above the patient icon there are clusters of similar prescriptions that are filled multiple times for Zofran,[46] sodium chloride, Dexamethasone,[47] and Kytril.[48] The label of the claim shows us the medication, pharmacy, date filled, cost, and number of days supplied. This individual is most likely being treated for cancer and related symptoms. This approach can help spot pricing anomalies, issues with refilling prescriptions before the prescribed supplies are used up, and other types of anomalies that may cause concern.

Phishing/Click Fraud

Another example comes from cyberspace, where fraud and deception are commonplace in a number of online resources. Everyone is familiar

---

[45] Several prescription drug names were referenced in the dataset and several represent registered trademarks including the following. Duragesic® (Ortho-McNeil) and Dilaudin® (Abbot Laboratories).

[46] Zofran® (GlaxoSmithKline) is an ondansetron that is used to prevent nausea and vomiting assoicated with chemotherapy and radiation.

[47] Dexamethasone (Decadron® Merck & Co.) is a class of drugs also referred to as steroids typically used to help reduce swelling.

[48] Kytril® (Roche Pharmaceuticals) is another medication used to control nausea and vomiting from chemotheray and radiation treatments.

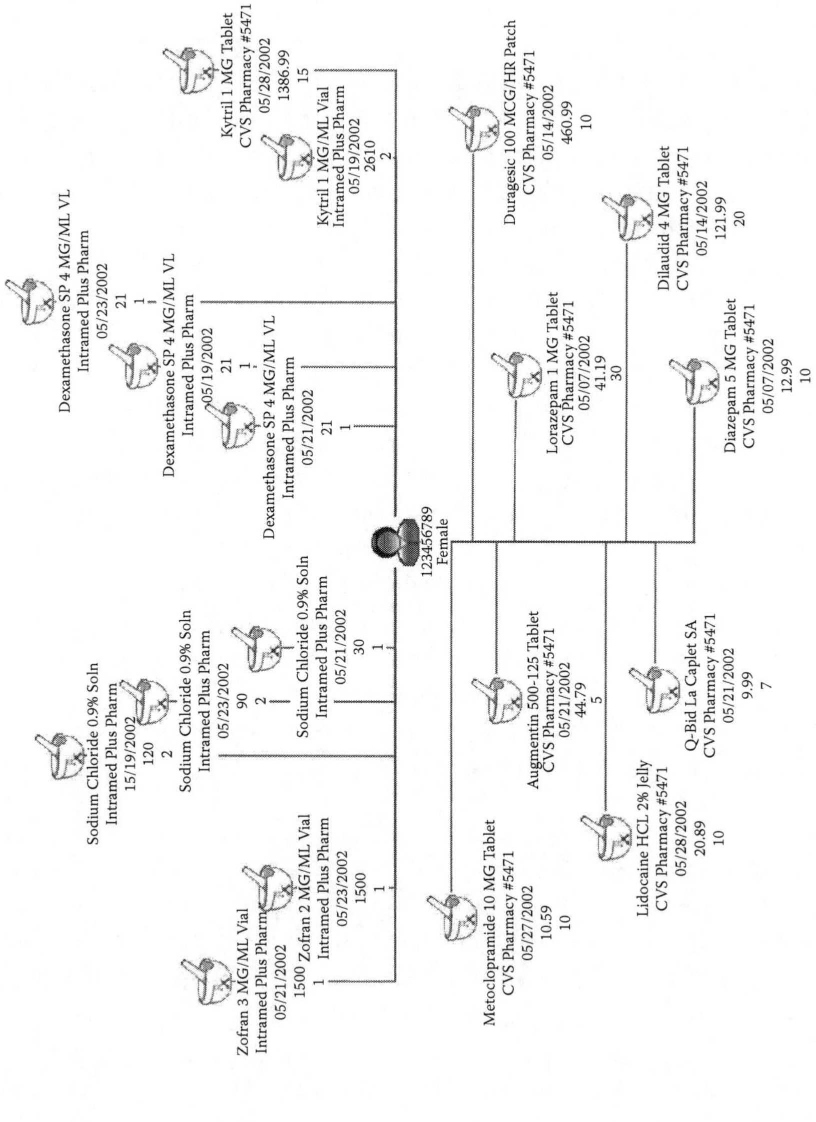

Figure 7.32 Prescription claims filed for patient.

with the spam e-mails they receive for every type of male enhancement pill, insider stock pick, and winning lottery scheme. A lot of spam also comes in the form of phishing where a legitimate-looking e-mail from a bank, a retailer, or some other industry tries to acquire personal information under false pretenses stating that one's account will be suspended or closed. Webopedia[49] defines *phishing* as:

> *(fish´ing) (n.) The act of sending an e-mail to a user falsely claiming to be an established legitimate enterprise in an attempt to scam the user into surrendering private information that will be used for identity theft. The e-mail directs the user to visit a Web site where they are asked to update personal information, such as passwords and credit card, social security, and bank account numbers, that the legitimate organization already has. The Web site, however, is bogus and set up only to steal the user's information.*

The most common phishing attacks have come from sites posing as eBay or PayPal. Figure 7.33 shows an example of a false eBay and PayPal phishing e-mail. Notice that the embedded URL for the eBay message does not actually point back to eBay, but rather some farce site with a registrant in France. Many times the e-mail will mask the URL so it appears as a legitimate address until it is selected.

Using the log files of a Web server and some domain name service (DNS) lookup utilities, some insight can be gained to develop an approach to detecting the originating IP addresses from which phishing attacks are launched. The goal is to cause as much disruption as possible to perpetrators of phishing attacks through a process that may also assist with the prosecution of the offenders. One approach to tracking phishing attempts is to reference each URL to a traced host name and IP address and isolate the host IP or host name for each URL. This can then be related to show a Host, Page, and Visitor as shown in Figure 7.34.

As all the data is pulled into visualization, a larger-scale network starts to form, as shown in Figure 7.35. From here, Visitor commonalities can be exposed as well as more active Pages and Hosts. Interpretation of the results can vary depending on the tasks at hand. These approaches are not too dissimilar to click-fraud techniques where the behavior, origin, and frequency of the clicks can be interpreted and classified into questionable activities.

---

[49] http://www.webopedia.com/DidYouKnow/Internet/2005/phishing.asp.

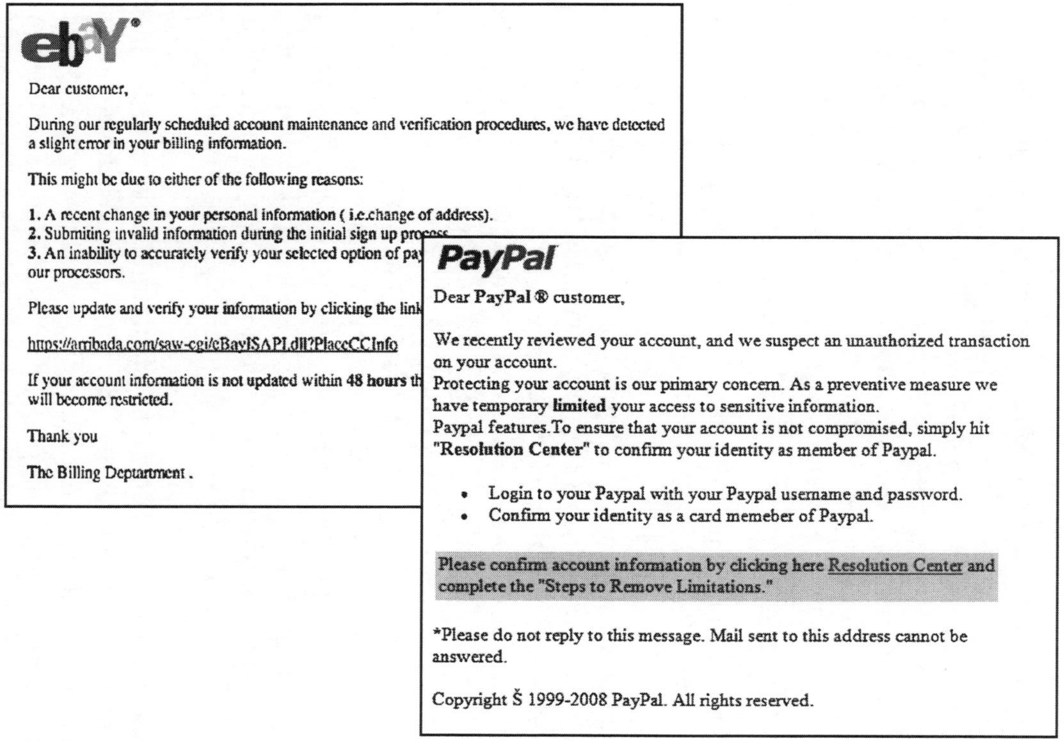

ebay
Dear customer,
During our regularly scheduled account maintenance and verification procedures, we have detected a slight error in your billing information.
This might be due to either of the following reasons:
1. A recent change in your personal information (i.e.change of address).
2. Submiting invalid information during the initial sign up pro
3. An inability to accurately verify your selected option of pa
our processors.
Please update and verify your information by clicking the lin
https://arribada.com/saw-cgi/eBayISAPI.dll?PlaceCCInfo
If your account information is not updated within 48 hours t
will become restricted.
Thank you
The Billing Deptartment .
PayPal
Dear PayPal ® customer,
We recently reviewed your account, and we suspect an unauthorized transaction on your account.
Protecting your account is our primary concern. As a preventive measure we have temporary limited your access to sensitive information.
Paypal features.To ensure that your account is not compromised, simply hit "Resolution Center" to confirm your identity as member of Paypal.
• Login to your Paypal with your Paypal username and password.
• Confirm your identity as a card memeber of Paypal.
Please confirm account information by clicking here Resolution Center and complete the "Steps to Remove Limitations."
*Please do not reply to this message. Mail sent to this address cannot be answered.
Copyright Š 1999-2008 PayPal. All rights reserved.

Figure 7.33 Sample phishing email.

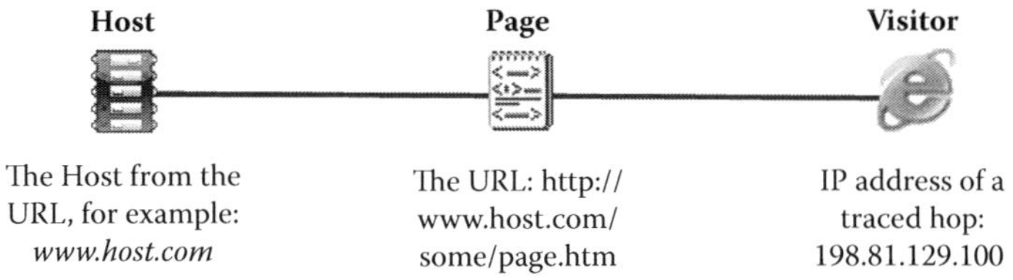

Figure 7.34 Sample phishing representation.

Tax Evasion

Finally, tax evasion is a type of fraud against the government and its taxpayers where individuals and corporation try to structure their earnings and losses in a way as to maximize their savings. Unfortunately, many resort to blatant misrepresentations, undervalued reporting, and other fabricated values and figures to justify their tax returns. Every year in the United States, over 230 million tax returns are filed[50] with the IRS. For corporate returns, it is important that the IRS identifies abusive schemes and illegal offshore tax shelters. Many of the companies of concern fall into one of three categories, a 1065 (partnership income), a 1041(estates and trusts), or an 1120S (S corporations). The following provides more detail for each:

1. Form 1065—Partnership Income[51]
   a. Form 1065 is an information return used to report the income, deductions, gains, losses, etc. from the operations of a partnership. A partnership does not pay tax on its income but "passes through" any profits or losses to its partners. Partners must include partnership items on their tax returns. A partnership is the relationship between two or more persons who join to carry on a trade or business, with each person contributing money, property, labor, or skill and each expecting to share in the profits and losses of the business whether or not a formal partnership agreement is made.
2. Form 1041—Estates and Trusts[52]
   a. The fiduciary of a domestic decedent's estate, trust, or bankruptcy estate uses Form 1041 to report:
      i. The income, deductions, gains, losses, etc. of the estate or trust.
      ii. The income that is either accumulated or held for future distribution or distributed currently to the beneficiaries.

[50] http://www.irs.gov/pub/irs-soi/12proj.pdf.
[51] http://www.irs.gov/pub/irs-pdf/f1065.pdf.
[52] http://www.irs.gov/pub/irs-pdf/f1041.pdf.

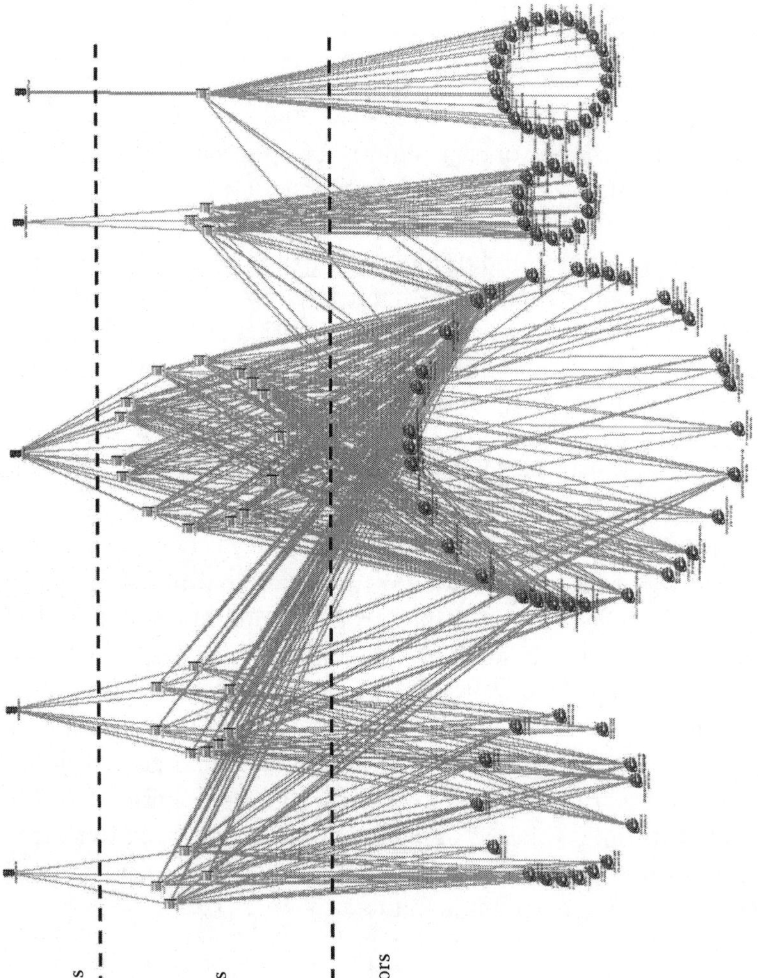

Figure 7.35 Larger phishing network/click-fraud network.

   iii. Any income tax liability of the estate or trust.
   iv. Employment taxes on wages paid to household employees.
  b. Abusive Trust Arrangements—Certain trust arrangements purport to reduce or eliminate federal taxes in ways that are not permitted under the law.
3. Form 1120S Corporation[53]
  a. Form 1120S is used to report the income, gains, losses, deductions, credits, etc., of a domestic corporation or other entity for any tax year covered by an election to be an S corporation. Generally, an S corporation is exempt from federal income tax other than tax on certain capital gains and passive income. On their tax returns, the S corporation's shareholders include their share of the corporation's separately stated items of income, deduction, loss, and credit, and their share of nonseparately stated income or loss.

The type of information collected on each form varies somewhat, but each collects standard information, such as name, address, Employment Identification Number (EIN), year of filing, and backup information regarding deductions, income, payments, dividends, etc. Naturally, companies are owned by other companies or individuals and the income and the tax liabilities can pass through to these other taxpayers. Therefore, networks of connections among these companies exist and the monies can be tracked to see where the profits are skimmed off and the losses pass through to the owners—resulting in a nice write-off. The shareholders of these companies receive a Schedule K-1 form, which defines the specific income, deductions, credits, and other items.

Figure 7.36 shows an example of a fairly simple and well-bounded network where an 1120S-declared company makes three distributions to its core owners, shown as SSN icons. Schedule K-1 of Form 1120S is used to report each shareholder's prorated share of net income or loss from an S corporation. In this case, the corporate ownership can be understood because two of the distributions are the same at $25,000 payout while the third is doubled at $50,000 (ordinary business income in this case). The arrow heads indicate the flow of the money.

While this network is fairly basic, they can get more complex and much more seasoned analysts are required to fully understand the dynamics and interactions among the companies. Large, intertwining corporate networks, such as Enron, are almost impossible to fully understand because of all the layering, numbers, and sheer volume of filings. In Figure 7.37 a slightly

[53] http://www.irs.gov/pub/irs-pdf/f1120s.pdf.

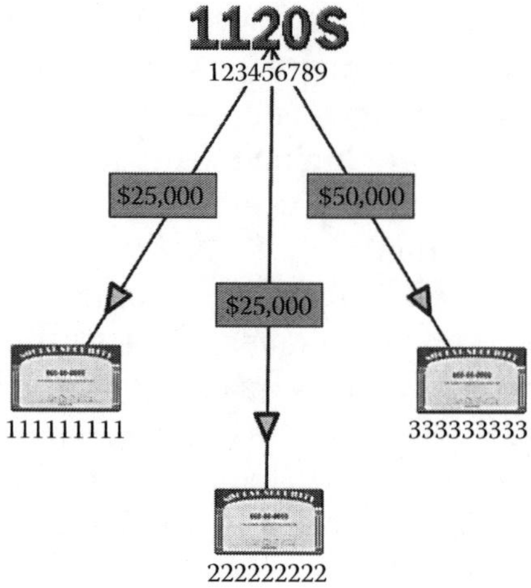

Figure 7.36 Example of 1120S K1 distributions.

more complex distribution network is depicted where the two 1065 companies located at the top of the diagram have generated substantial earnings reported as ordinary corporate income. The total, $62 million ($28 million + $34 million), flows into the middle 1065 company where somehow it is converted into two identical losses of $31 million, each of which flows down into the individual owners, but also manages to lose an additional $38 million, which passes into a flow-through entity (FTE) for distribution to the same two shareholders. All- in-all, a $64 million profit was somehow turned into a $100 million loss by this particular enterprise or collection of partnerships.

The schemes identified and encountered in these datasets are virtually endless, and require astute analysts who fully understand the tax codes and know why certain combinations of values, and how the entities relate together, are important. Remember, there are no right answers and no wrong answers, only situations that appear questionable and require further evaluation and review before passing a financial decision. In this case, the result would be to open a tax case against the perpetrators of the scheme/fraud; other times, it might be to try and identify more details of a criminal enterprise. Ultimately it is up to the investigating agency to determine how to respond to what has been identified.

Medicare Claim Fraud

Some approaches to identifying fraud and other questionable patterns contained in transactional data sets use the entity uniqueness as a ratio of the related transactions. Depending on the circumstances, the interest can focus on high ratios or low ratios. For example, when reviewing claims

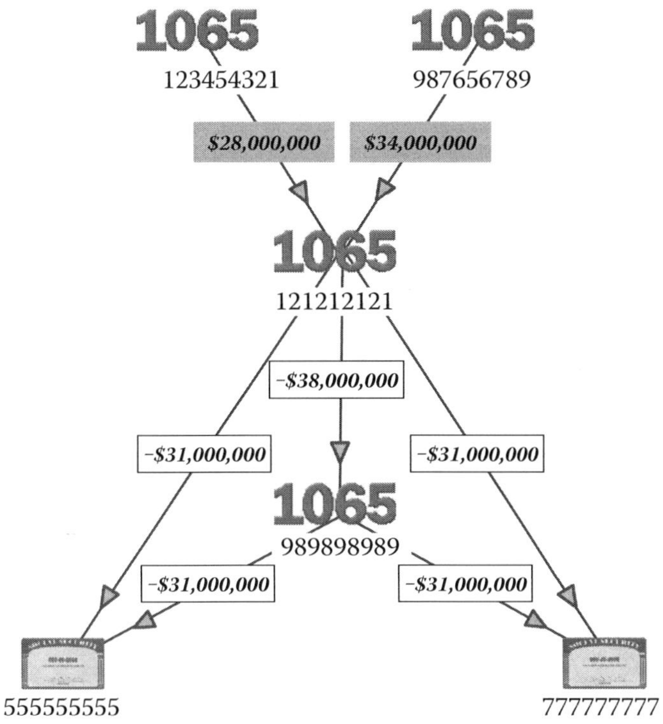

Figure 7.37 Example of 1065 K1 distributions.

submitted by medical practitioners to insurance companies, Medicare, or other governmental services, there is an interest in looking at high-ratio filers as a factor of the number of claims submitted versus the number of patients served. The justification for this review is that prescribing more procedures per patient helps drive up the overall cost of the services performed. Therefore, instead of pushing more patients (high volume) through the system, the goal is to increase the unit cost of a smaller number of patients. There are reported incidents where the number of claims per patient has exceeded hundreds.

The following shows a sample of medical data focusing on the ratio of the number of claims provided for each participating member based on the International Classification of Diseases (ICD) description (see boxed text) submitted by the provider. The table in Figure 7.38 shows four columns corresponding to each of the variables used in the query (claims, members, ICD, and provider). For each unique combination of the provider number and the ICD code, a count was performed to summarize the total number of claims and the total number of unique members who received that particular service from the provider. The table is sorted by the number of claims made, from highest to lowest. This data sample shows that the top provider submitted 3,360 claims for 275 different members (e.g., the insured party) for basic "laboratory examination," which represents a modest ratio of 12:1.

#Claims	#Members	ICD Description	Provider Key
3,360	275	Laboratory Examination	PRV0062230
819	65	Routine General Medical Examination	PRV0062230
680	62	Other And Unspecified Hyperlipidemi...	PRV0062230
658	61	Diabetes Mellitus without Complicat...	PRV0062230
624	8	Generalized Anxiety Disorder	PRV1754997
576	9	Diabetes Mellitus without Complicat...	PRV3273933
534	71	Laboratory Examination	PRV4120896
485	54	Pure Hypercholesterolemia	PRV0062230
459	9	Malignant Neoplasm of Prostate	PRV1251458
448	8	Lumbago	PRV2305050

Figure 7.38 Top claim and member counts for ICD and provider.

ICD Codes

The International Statistical Classification of Diseases and Related Health Problems, commonly referred to as ICD (International Classification of Diseases), are international standard codes (up to six characters) used to classify diseases, symptoms, and other health problems. Classification of diseases, more specifically, causes of death, originally started back in the 18th century[54] and steadily evolved over the next 150 years until a Frenchman named Jacques Bertillon (1851–1922) was credited for establishing one of the first international standards for uniformly classifying the causes of death. Generally, these classifications became more refined, improved, and consistent as more governments and health organizations adopted their use and started to standardize their reporting needs. Eventually, around 1945, it was decided that the causes of morbidity and mortality were closely related to the classification of sickness and injury and the reporting codes were updated to include diagnostic terms as well. This was also when the United Nations was formed and discussions were had about creating a World Health Organization (WHO), which was chartered in 1948 and given the responsibility for overseeing, revising, and supporting the list, which became known as the ICD. Over the years, the list has been refined and updated; the United States is currently using the ICD-9 standard, published by the WHO in 1977, which became the standard for reporting Medicare- and Medicaid-related services. Most other countries have since adopted the ICD-10 standard, which was completed in 1992. ICD-11 is currently under development and is expected to be implemented by 2013.

[54] History of the Development of the ICD, (http://www.who.int/classifications/icd/en/).

Rows 2, 3, and 4 also have similar ratios (12:1, 10:1, and 10:1, respectively). However, row 5, with 624 claims filed on eight members for ICD code "Generalized Anxiety Disorder" (ICD #30002), has a 78:1 ratio, warranting further investigation into why there are so many claims being filed for this group of patients by a single provider. The specific information is pulled from the underlying database and presented using a date grid as shown in Figure 7.39. The diagram shows a separate grid for each patient (e.g., unique member #) and is arranged to show the day of the week on the *x*-axis and the week of the year on the *y*-axis.

There appears to be one overwhelming pattern for all eight patients—they receive treatment literally every week from this provider and their treatment schedule is very regular. For example, patient P1 tends to prefer Friday and Saturday visits, while patient P2 prefers Sunday and Monday sessions, P6 has visits on Saturday and Sunday, and patient P7 is treated on Wednesdays and Thursdays. One slightly misleading fact about this display is that each grid shows treatments over a four-year period and the apparent "double" visits per week are actually across multiple years. This is clarified in Figure 7.40 where only claims pertaining to patient P1 are presented and the grids are grouped according to the year.

Interpreting this diagram is fairly straightforward. In late 2002, the patient (e.g., member) started seeing this particular provider for Friday appointments. This continued throughout all of 2003, except for a few weeks where service was not rendered (i.e., a claim was not submitted). In 2004, the regular day of therapy changed to Saturday and remained consistent until the end of the year. The services were apparently then discontinued, with only an occasional visit or two in 2005. Generally, one could argue that the nature of these claims, their frequency, and their temporal pattern would be consistent with behavioral health claims made by a psychiatric doctor providing psychotherapy sessions (e.g., 45 to 50 minutes) for his or her patients.

A final check can be done on the temporal patterns associated with the cumulative number of claims made by the provider. Figure 7.41 presents the same data presented in Figure 7.39; however, this diagram is grouped according to the year the service was rendered. The majority of the weeks show that the provider worked five of seven days, with an occasional six-day workweek. In 2003, the nonworking days are shown as Monday and Tuesday and, in 2004, they are Tuesday and Wednesday. With little variation around the summer months, there appears to be no time taken off for a holiday or vacation. Thus, one might ask if all of these claims truly represent services rendered.

Returning to the original result set presented in Figure 7.38, the next item on the list shows 576 claims for nine members receiving

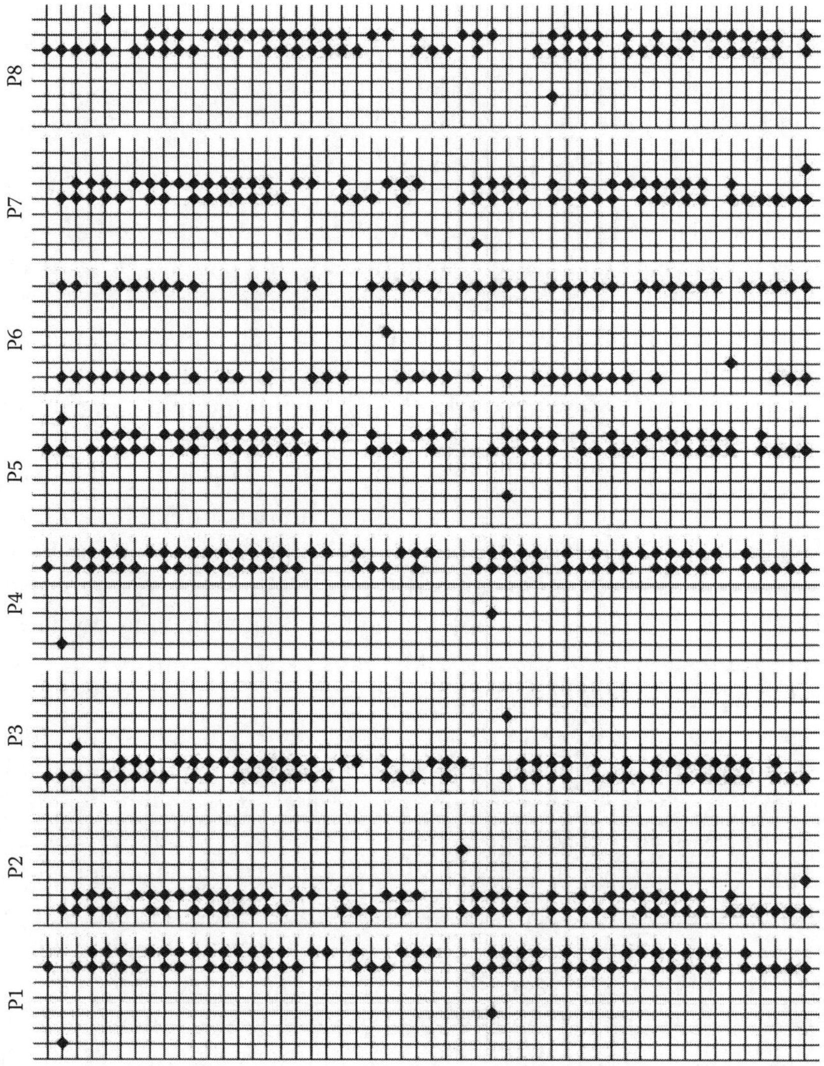

Figure 7.39 Date grid for ICD code = 30002.

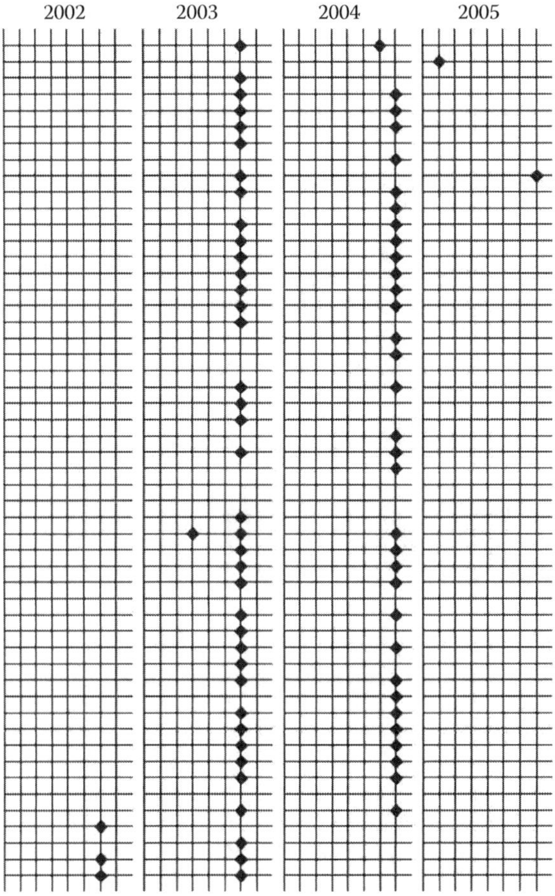

Figure 7.40 Claims for patient P1 grouped by claim year.

treatment for "Diabetes Mellitus without Complication Type I" (ICD #25001). This represents a 64:1 ratio for this provider.[55] Diabetes is certainly a more involved process of diagnosis and treatment, and, therefore, it could be expected that the claim ratio might be elevated. However, this must be verified by looking at the patterns contained in the database. Figure 7.42 shows all of the claim detail presented as a temporal display grouped according to the nine patients (e.g., members) identified by the summarization.

A very distinct pattern is exposed and is repeated for each group: an initial claim is made; exactly four weeks later another claim is filed; followed by another claim three weeks and one day later; then two more claims about two weeks later; followed by another claim made a week

[55] This same ICD was reported by another provider with only an 11:1 ratio.

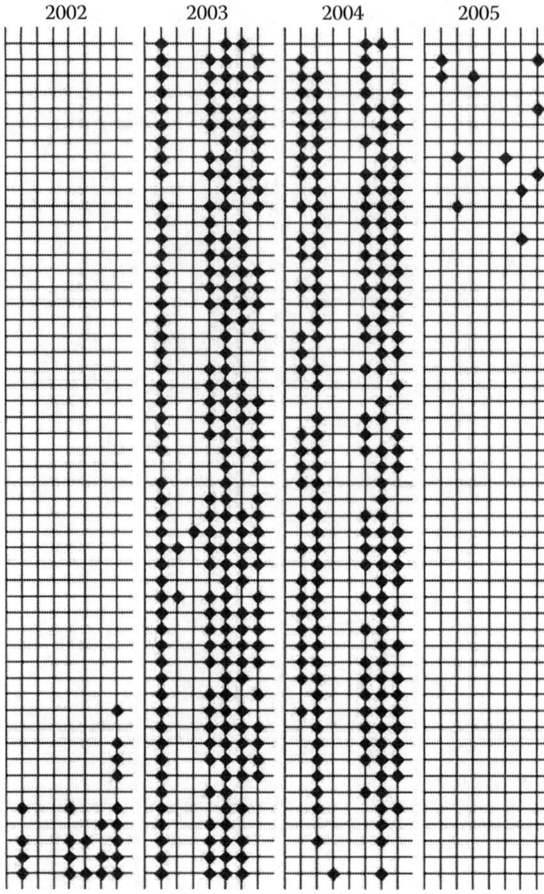

Figure 7.41 Temporal display for ICD code = 30002 grouped by year.

later; eight weeks beyond, another claim is made; and finally, six to seven weeks later, a last claim is made. Using a slightly modified and condensed layout with a manual overlay, the pattern becomes very explicit, as presented in Figure 7.43. Obviously, the treatment regimen prescribed by this provider (a physician of internal medicine) is very consistent.

Upon further evaluation of the diagrams, each patient (pattern) has eight unique claim dates shown in the temporal display. However, there is a 64:1 ratio for this data, meaning that each date must represent multiple claims. Drilling down on the diagram confirms this fact. Figure 7.44 shows the same data from a rotated perspective, where each column corresponds in height to the number of claims submitted. Each date supports multiple claims because every visit, test, and procedure is submitted as a separate Current Procedural Terminology (CPT) code, a convention defined by the American Medical Association to describe medical, surgical, or

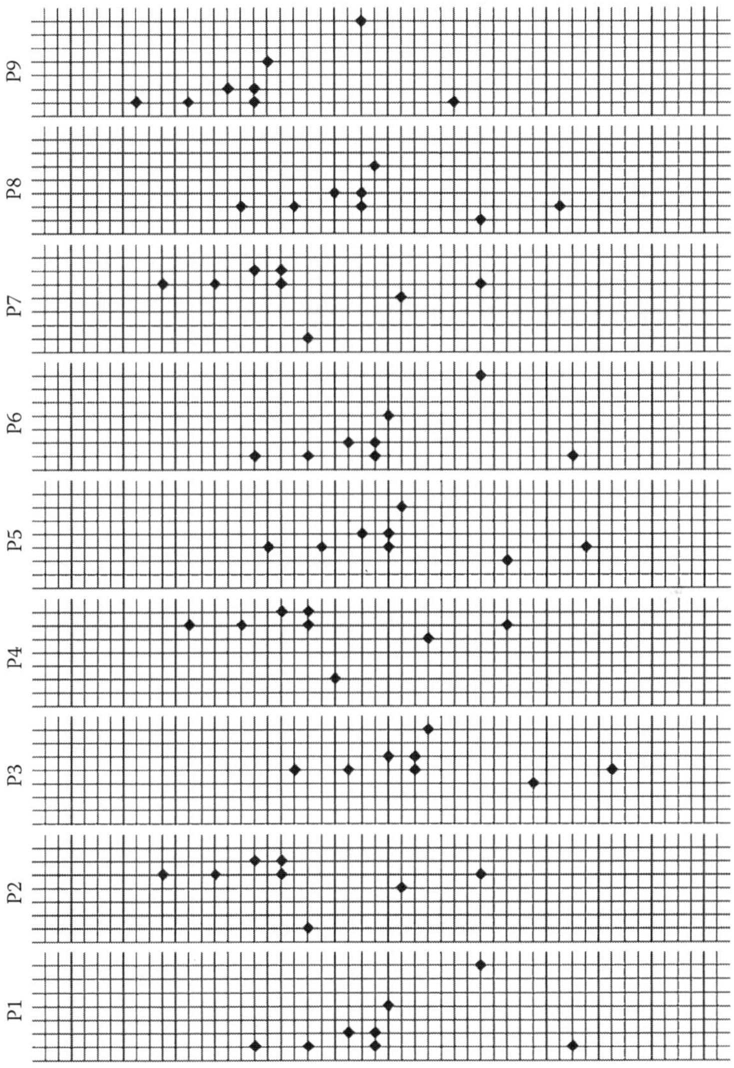

Figure 7.42 Temporal display for ICD code = 25001.

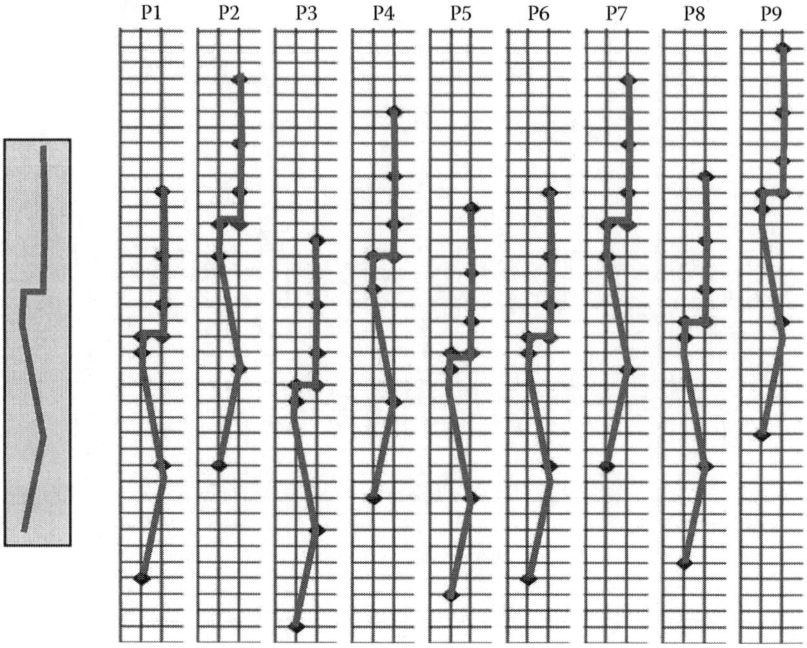

Figure 7.43 Pattern emphasized for ICD code = 25001.

diagnostic services. For example, the following are some codes reported for one of the claim dates: 99213 = Office visit, 83036 = Hemoglobin; glycosylated, and 81001 = Urinalysis.

Finally, a single patient (P#1) is extracted and temporally regrouped on the claim year. The actual pattern exposed for this physician for the ICD code becomes more explicit, as shown in Figure 7.45, and forces a reinterpretation of the original sequence of claims previously defined. The initial diagnosis occurs (1:11) with 11 claims; a week later a follow-up is conducted (2:3) with three more claims; 14 weeks later an additional office visit occurs (3:8) with eight claims; the following year the fourth visit occurs (4:8) with the same identical eight claims made on the previous visit; the fifth claim occurs exactly four weeks later and represents just a single office visit (5:1); and the sixth (6:8), a few weeks later, is again a repeat of the same eight claims performed previously; two weeks later the seventh (7:17) and largest number of claims submitted, at 17, occurs; and finally, after two more months the last claim (8:8) repeats the same eight claims made previously.

The importance of this level of detail allows the investigator to see what is actually occurring and to determine if the process of treatment

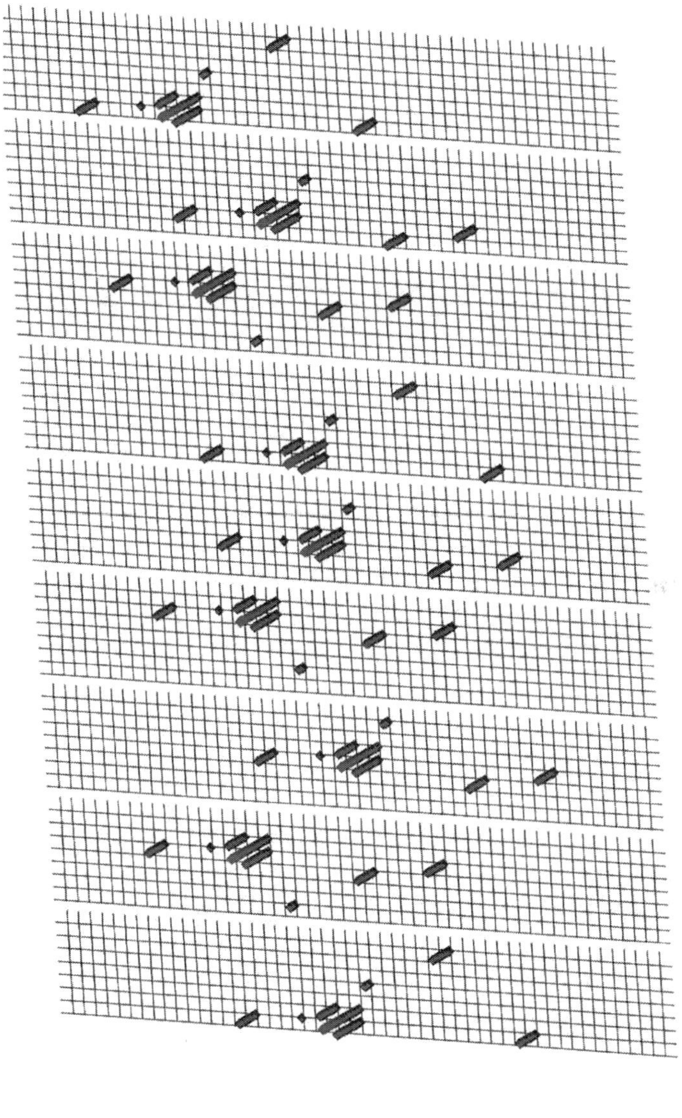

Figure 7.44 Temporal display showing multiple claims.

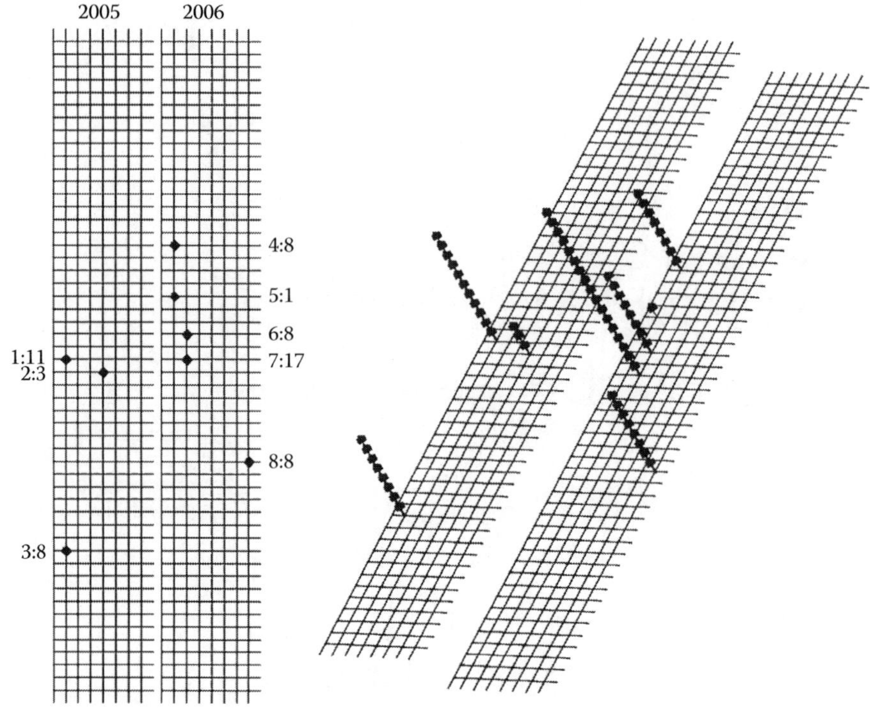

Figure 7.45 Multiyear claim Review for P#1.

is within normal operating parameters, if something needs to be flagged for additional review, or if there is obviously an error present. This can lead the insurer to deny or reduce payments for claims that are questionable or miscategorized,[56] and occasionally, albeit infrequently, it results in the provider receiving additional payments. More important, it provides a method to quickly review a large quantity of data and form an opinion without an overly complicated or extensively computational process, providing a means to adapt, refine, and update a knowledge base of patterns.

This type of high-ratio, transaction-to-entity pattern not only applies to medical claims review, but can also be used to describe activities involving credit card frauds. In the case of those kinds of fraud, if the number of entities (e.g., unauthorized or stolen credit cards) has a high ratio compared to the total number of overall transactions conducted on a merchant account, it would be an indication that the behavior was suspect. This type of situation is common for the bust-out scheme patterns previously discussed. For example, if a merchant conducted, say, 100 transactions

[56] "Appeal That Claim: Be informed, Be Approved," *American Medical Association*, 2007, http://www.amassm.org/ama1/pub/upload/mm/368/appeal-that-claim.pdf.

on 90 unique card numbers in a single day, it would be considered normal business activity. However, if those 90 card numbers comprised, say, 50 invalid numbers (e.g., stolen, counterfeit, unauthorized use, etc.), then the 90:50 (almost 2:1) ratio for this merchant would be of serious concern to the banks underwriting those accounts. For this pattern, the ratio is much lower than the medical billing example; however, the same overall process is invoked to expose questionable behaviors. Obviously, the use of ratios is only a single dimension or viewpoint on the data that can often result in identifying qualified targets of interest.

To expand on the medical discussions, once a "target" entity (e.g., a provider) has been identified for, say, improper billing, code bundling, misclassifying diagnoses, or some other error, further checks can be performed on related entities. If errors were found for one member of a medical practice, there is reason to believe that similar types of "inconsistencies" might be found among the other members of the practice. In the data set there is relevant contact information for the provider, including phone numbers, faxes, and correspondence addresses. Figure 7.46 shows the direct relationships between the provider, an address and a fax number. The thickness of the links is indicative of the 576 claims submitted because each consistently listed the same address and fax number. In reality there are 772 links because this provider also submitted other claims for different ICD codes not covered in the immediate investigation.

Expanding the network reveals that there are additional linkages contained in the database, as shown in Figure 7.47. For this example there are three additional providers connected to the same address as our target entity and no further connections stem from the fax number. Two of the providers shown in this diagram are ophthalmologists and have few claims submitted and are therefore of little "value" to the

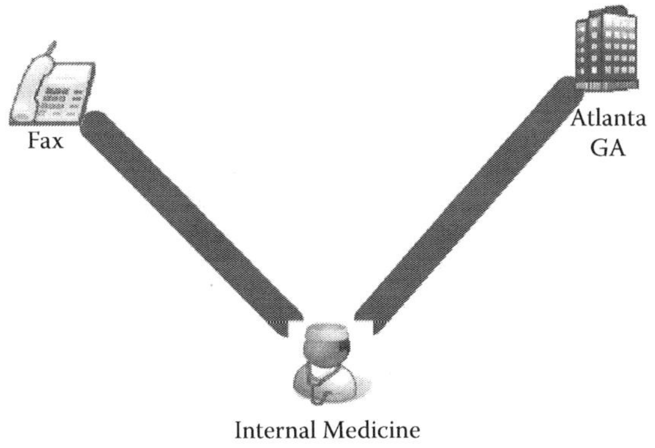

Figure 7.46 Direct connections to provider showing address and fax.

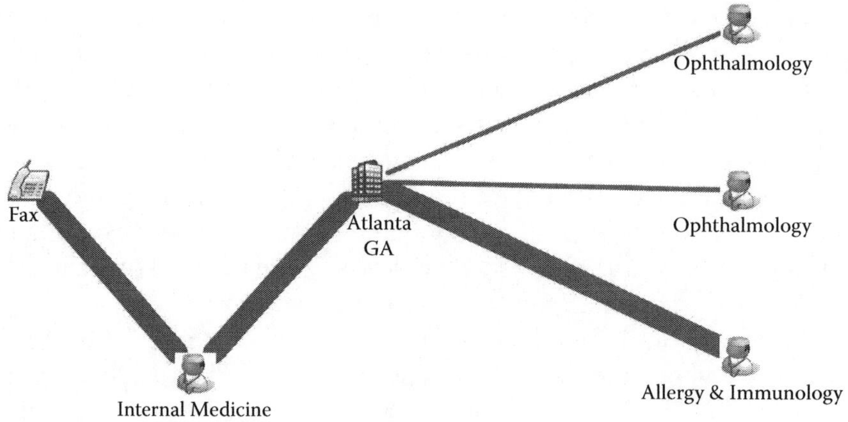

Figure 7.47 Indirect connections to provider via an address.

investigator. The third provider deals with allergies and immunology, and based on the link thickness, has a considerable number of claims submitted. Thus, a drill-down of this provider's claim detail could be performed to determine if everything appeared legitimate and aboveboard. The network can be expanded for as long as the data supports connections and the investigator feels continued analysis is warranted.

One final point to make on this type of analysis is that virtually any dimension contained in the data can be used to help expose anomalies. Many times, some type of metadata extraction or referential source can be used to add value to the core analytical data. Using the address of the providers and the members is one such dimension where distance calculations can be made using the centroid of a ZIP code, or more accurate, street-level geo-coding can be performed. This allows investigators to target providers based on their geographical proximity to the member addresses. As shown in Figure 7.48, if the provider's business is more than a certain distance away from their member's residential addresses, and assuming the provider is not a "specialist" per se, then one might question why the members would not seek out medical attention closer to their homes. This type of situation might be an indicator of a fraud where the provider solicits business from underserved populations, as was shown when several hospitals and medical centers in the Southern California area were accused of submitting claims on indigents and defrauding Medicare and the Medi-Cal systems of millions of dollars.[57]

[57] Cara Mia DiMassa, Richard Winton, and Rich Connell, "3 Southern California Hospitals Accused of Using Homeless for Fraud," *Los Angeles Times*, August 7, 2008. http://www.latimes.com/news/local/la-me-skidrow7-2008aug07,0,6,5921372.story.

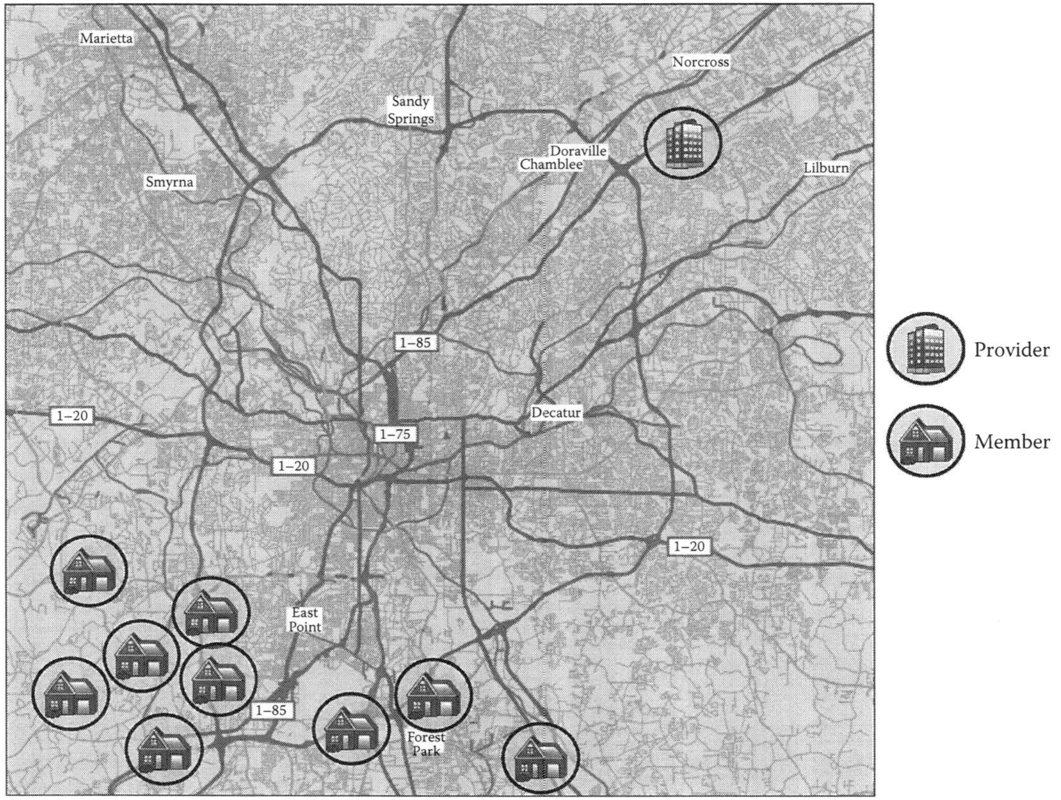

Figure 7.48 Large distances between provider and member addresses.

Conclusion

A number of fraud-centric patterns were discussed and presented in this section, often enhanced through the use of visualization diagrams. Of particular importance is defining the protocols, parameters, and conditions that go into exposing the anomalies. In many of the cases presented, there was no clear-cut right or wrong answer, rather an irregularity in the data, a variance in the values, or an inconsistency in the expected results that stood out as unusual. The majority of the patterns are not particularly complicated to discover and often there are many instances from which to choose and review. Eventually, the data involved in these patterns must be manually reviewed to determine if actual fraud exists. This is analogous to a metal detector signaling an alert that there is something hidden under the surface, and not until the object is dug out of the ground and closely inspected can its true value be determined.

Fraud is a very dynamic entity and is constantly changing, adapting, and morphing itself to take advantage of vulnerabilities and flaws within the oversight and control systems that are established to minimize their presence. For example,[58] a South Carolina parts supplier found a flaw in a purchasing system used by the U.S. Department of Defense, and was able to charge almost $1 million for shipping two 19¢ washers (slated for priority deliver to military operations in Iraq and Afghanistan). The automated system was not outfitted with any type of boundary parameters or internal checks to limit or detect discrepancies in the amounts charged for shipping items that had a "priority" status. The pattern was actually discovered through a manual review when a purchasing agent saw the excessive amounts being charged and rejected the claim.

These types of situations are prevalent throughout many systems and processes. Ultimately, their detection, interpretation, and resolution are up to the customer; they are the ones that determine the tolerance on how much fraud is acceptable and eventually bear additional costs in trying to minimize their losses. Approaching the problem space from different angles, from new starting points, and with nontraditional methods will most likely yield a better return on investment. Additionally, applying analytical techniques from different industries can help increase yields. The trick is in recognizing where and when they should apply.

[58] Tony Capaccio. "Pentagon Paid $998,798 to Ship Two 19-Cent Washers," *Bloomberg.com*, August 16, 2007, http://www.bloomberg.com/apps/news?pid=newsarchive&sid=a_pIZ20xQxeU.

PART 3

INFORMATION SHARING AND FUSION CENTERS

During a routine traffic stop, a car is pulled over for a broken taillight. The officer runs[1] the license plate and it comes back registered to a male subject. This name is automatically cross-referenced against various arrest databases, prison records, sex offender registries, and watch lists. The results show that the owner has been involved in prior assaults, including domestic violence and weapons charges, and even has a prison record for various narcotics violations. The registered address is also checked for prior incident reports and comes back with several related shootings at or near the location. Additionally, there are other people associated with the address listed, including several with outstanding warrants and others with gang affiliations. The officer approaches the vehicle cautiously, armed with the information the system has provided.

This scenario is being played out across law enforcement jurisdictions around the country every day. Officers are being equipped with more information from which to make decisions, ultimately providing them more safety while performing their jobs. The ability to access multiple data sources and obtain a more complete and detailed understanding of the situation is invaluable. Since 9/11, a number of protocols and systems have been defined to help set standards for integrating and sharing data sources. These have been steadily gaining acceptance and growing in capabilities and deployment throughout the United States—as well as the world.

Perhaps some of the more successful approaches embraced within the law enforcement and intelligence communities are based on a "hybrid"

[1] Brad Flora, "What Do the Cops Have on Me? What Turns Up When a Police Officer Punches Your Name into the Computer?" *Slate.com,* December 4, 2007, http://www.slate.com/id/2179180/.

approach to performing federated searches. Generally, these represent systems that offer a single point of access for querying (processing) multiple data sources, including relational databases, unstructured sources (e.g., documents, cables, URLs), and e-mail. This approach to information sharing has several advantages over traditional, centralized, data warehouse techniques including:

- Data is always up-to-date when queried because it is never copied or moved out of the original source.
- Control of the data is maintained by the original owners who define how it is accessed (who has permission, when it can be used, how many results can be returned).
- There is no costly translation, fixed schema, or data transport (as is required by a physical data warehouse or other approaches).
- There is flexibility to rapidly add new data sources and adapt to changes in existing data sources.
- It is more fault-tolerant should a system go offline or become unavailable (a single failure does not bring down the entire system).

Overall, this was, perhaps, one of the more difficult sections of the book to write due to the dynamic nature and fast pace of this emerging marketplace. There are several standards being implemented and dozens upon dozens of systems being deployed. Thus, this section is meant to act as an introduction to several of the more accepted data-sharing standards and protocols. It also provides a high-level overview of various fusion center initiatives and regional information-sharing systems. The information is inherently dated, and therefore the reader is encouraged to continue researching and reviewing more updated materials as they are made available by the various industries, organizations, and agencies that have sponsored their development.

Chapter 8

Information-Sharing Protocols

Introduction

Terrorism, as well as other forms of asymmetric threats, represents a broad topic area that encompasses an extremely wide range of concepts from security to logistics, including finances, recruitment, and operations. Terrorism is a global concern that is designed to influence the attitude and behavior of a target group (e.g., the public, governments, etc.) by threatening or carrying out devastating actions that can include the use of conventional weapons and biological, chemical, and nuclear agents. A strong offense is needed to proactively target and stop terrorist groups before they strike.

Terrorism is usually viewed as a form of violent actions, such as bombings, shootings, or other forms of devastation. New classifications, such as economic terrorism and information terrorism, are also of significant concern, and this vulnerability expands with society's growing reliance on information technologies. Increased access to information and the centralization of vital components of local, national, and global infrastructure threaten both local and national security.

Individuals, groups, and state-sponsored organizations can formulate and conduct terrorism. Although the majority of their actions will be covert, disguised, or concealed to make it difficult to track them, they still must perform basic "operational" functions in pursuit of their objectives. Many terrorist groups exhibit standard business processes, such as acquiring an assortment of materials and supplies for carrying out their missions, performing travel in conjunction with their objectives, obtaining the finances and financial backing to sustain their operations, and communicating with other group members using phones, e-mail, and text messages.

Financing terrorism is accomplished through weapon sales, narcotics trafficking, bank robberies, or other illegitimate means[1] and, therefore, often leads to money-laundering activities. These "public" operational encounters, where observations can be made and data collected, are when terrorists are most vulnerable and it is where their weaknesses can be exploited. These events can be tracked and analyzed by technologies used for early detection of potential threats and assessment of vulnerability, and can produce recommended courses of action (e.g., force protection and interdiction).

Developing approaches for detection, assessment, and interdiction capabilities can be accomplished only through proper data acquisition, knowledge representation, and information-processing capabilities.

[1] Even charitable donations from sympathetic or supportive persons/businesses provide a funding avenue for certain terrorist groups.

Investigating today's terrorist groups[2] requires interagency communication and collaboration. It is essential that law enforcement agencies and task forces be able to collect and analyze data from multiple sources in order to detect, monitor, and prevent terrorist activity. Terrorism is a premeditated act that requires detectable preparations including money transfers, material purchases, and personnel movement. Intelligence works against terrorism.

A number of significant advances have been made over the past several years with respect to information-sharing initiatives and establishing widely acceptable industry processes and procedures. This trend can be expected to continue, and in fact we can expect several to become mandatory requirements in the not-so-distant future. The following sections are provided to present a *high-level* overview of several information-sharing protocols and systems. It is outside the scope of this book to provide a comprehensive review or detailed tutorial on each, but rather these materials are presented to introduce the reader to the concepts and general approaches offered by each protocol or system. There is a considerable amount of literature available on the Internet should one wish to delve into more detail about any aspect of information sharing. For brevity, some of the concepts addressed are simplified to limit the amount of background understanding necessary to appreciate the power of these information-sharing advances.

One of the key foundations of information sharing is to define the common definition of vocabulary, representation style, and values that are shared. The processes and protocols involved in defining a generic sharing standard have evolved over the past several years and one of the more mainstream approaches comes from the U.S. Department of Justice (DOJ) in the form of the Global Justice XML.

Global Justice XML Data Model (Global JXDM)

Perhaps one of the more successful endeavors achieved since 9/11 has been the deployment of the Global Justice XML Data Model (GJXDM) sponsored by the DOJ, Office of Justice Programs (OJP). GJXDM is not a program, network, or computer system; rather it is a *data reference model* used for defining, representing, and exchanging justice-related information among local, state, tribal, and federal agencies. The focus of GJXDM is not only law enforcement and public safety agencies, but also includes prosecutors, public defenders, courts, correctional facilities, probation and parole departments, and virtually any other agency related to the justice process.

[2] Also useful for criminal enterprises and money-laundering operations.

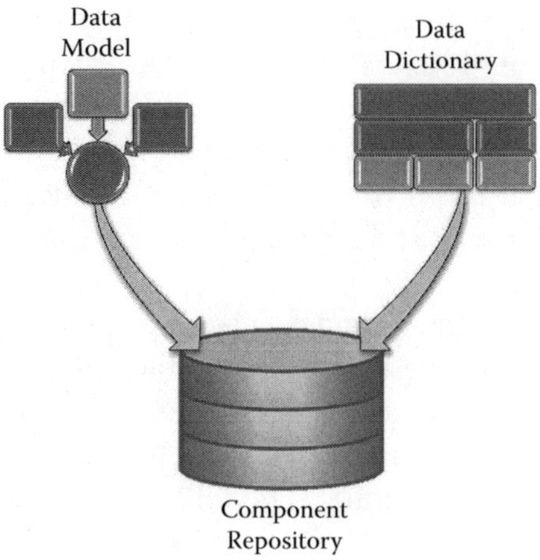

Figure 8.1 GJXDM structure.

The GJXDM concept[3] is based on establishing a hierarchy of classes of different object types leveraging the native power of XML to share data and promote reuse of common definitions. This essentially provides the building blocks for consistently constructing a wide range of different representations needed for encoding, processing, and sharing crime-related data. The structure originally came from a review and consolidation of 35 different data sources in use from various justice and public safety systems and is constantly being refined to address a growing community of users. Overall, the GJXDM structure comprises of three primary elements including the Data Dictionary, the Data Model, and the Component Reuse Repository, as shown in Figure 8.1.

Data Dictionary

The Data Dictionary represents a common vocabulary that allows different agencies and systems to share their data using a standardized structure. The Data Dictionary is simply the GJXDM XML schema types, property names, and descriptions that form the building blocks[4] for representing data in GJXDM. The "primary types" include *Person, Organization, Property, Location, Contact Information, Activity,* and *Document.* Each of the primary types has more specific subtypes, for example, *Property* is further refined or extended into subtypes, such as "Aircraft," "Boat," "Drug,"

[3] http://it.ojp.gov/jxdm/faq.html; http://www.it.ojp.gov/jxdm/faq.html.

[4] Based on the original 35 sources, it was determined that there were 550 distinct types (e.g., people, places, events) and approximately 2,200 descriptive properties called elements (e.g., weight, height, hair color, etc.).

"Firearm", "Jewelry," "Real Estate," and "Vehicle." The properties, also referred to as elements (e.g., people have names), are what describe the primary types and may be assigned values based on their data structure (e.g., dates, boolean, strings, numbers, etc.).

There are 142 different varieties of the PersonType within the current GJXDM[5] and the structure supports more than 100 properties used to describe everything from the name and place of birth to relationships and affiliations. Much of the PersonType gets inherited from other types, including, for example, PersonBiometricsDetails (height, weight, DNA, fingerprints, etc), LocationType (city, street, state, etc.), and DriverLicenseTypes. Table 8.1 contains the first few entries for the PersonType, which is a SuperType defined as a root object in the inheritance hierarchy. Since the Person is made up of over 75 different subtypes, only the part describing the PersonName is shown in Table 8.1 below.

Ultimately, this data dictionary is coupled with the actual data, converted into an XML representation, and transmitted in an information exchange package (IEP). These packages contain routing information, security restrictions, package purpose, database queries, and database results. Essentially, these IEPs are messages (a container with a payload) used for conveying and transferring data among different applications. A sample of some XML code is shown below depicting the encoding of the name of a person with sample data.

```
<DocumentAuthor LanguageText="eng" Source="http://
www.@@@.com/">
      <PersonName>
            <PersonPrefixName>Mr.</PersonPrefixName>
            <PersonGivenName>John</PersonGivenName>
            <PersonSurName>Smith</PersonSurName>
      </PersonName>
<PersonBirthDate>1960-01-01</PersonBirthDate>
</DocumentAuthor>
```

Data Model

The Data Model defines the structure and organization, which is essentially a graphical mapping of the underlying data structures and their relationships and interdependencies. This is very similar to UML (Unified Modeling Language) class diagrams that depict an abstract model of a system. The

[5] JXDM 3.0.3.

Table 8.1 Sample Person GJXDM Definitions

Property	*Type*	*Definition*
Person	PersonType / SuperType	Describes inherent and frequently associated characteristics of a person.
PersonName	PersonNameType	A name by which a person is known.
PersonPrefixName	Text Type	A title or honorific used by a person, e.g., Dr., Judge, General, Ms.
PersonGivenName	PersonNameTextType (TextType)	A first name of a person.
PersonMiddleName	PersonNameTextType (TextType)	A middle name of a person
PersonSurName	PersonNameTextType (TextType)	A last name or family name of a person.
PersonSuffixName	TextType	A component that is appended after the family name that distinguishes members of a family with the same given, middle, and last name, (e.g., Jr, Sr, III), or otherwise qualifies the name (e.g., MD, LLD, PhD).
PersonMaidenName	PersonNameTextType (TextType)	An original surname of a person before changed by marriage.
PersonFullName	PersonNameTextType (TextType)	A complete name of a person.
PersonNameInitials Text	TextType	A first letter of a person's given, possibly middle, and last names.
PersonNameSoundex Text	TextType	A name encoding such that similar sounding names with different spellings appear the same.

data model is considered a high-level interpretation, most often generated by subject matter experts to convey their view of the information available for sharing as well as to maximize the understanding of the model. These models do not have to reflect the actual database schema or be technical in nature; they show only the structure and flow of the information.

The purpose of the data model is to provide a method for properly understanding the relationships among the different data components. As previously mentioned, there are 142 different PersonTypes defined in the current GJXDM schema. Properly interpreting different roles will remove confusion, such as whether someone was, for example, the Victim, Subject, or Enforcement Official in an event. The standard notations used to differentiate relationships in these diagrams are

- "is_a" when a type inherits its properties from another type, and
- "has_a" to reflect the details or elements of the type.

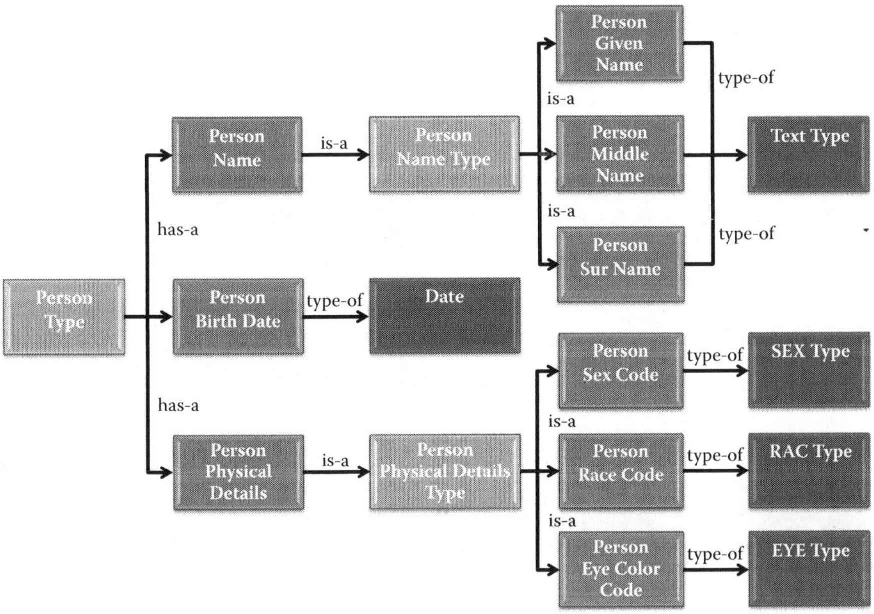

Figure 8.2 Data model sample for PersonType.

For example, a *Victim* "is_a" type of *Person* while a *Person* "has_a" *Date-of-Birth*. Figure 8.2 shows how the GJXDM data model looks for a subset of the PersonType. In this example, the entities are shown in a left-to-right flow where more detail is revealed at each level. The shading of the boxes depicts their structure; light shading = type, medium shading = element or subtype; and dark shading = data type (e.g., string, boolean, date, special reference). Figure 8.3 shows a slightly different layout for a Residence (a subtype of the Person) along with objects that represent SuperTypes in the GJXDM schema.

The structures defined in a data model closely represent those of the data dictionary. An *element* (e.g., a property) is the most fundamental structure and is used to actually store the data values used to share information. *Components* (e.g., types) are used to group elements into logical configurations and are designed so that they may inherit their structures and elements from other components, essentially creating instances of the component that can also be assigned additional elements. *Sections* are even higher-level groupings of information, where there may be multiple components required to define the section. *Associations* are used to relate sections or components together. Finally, the *Document* is what ties all of the sections together and represents the highest level (e.g., a SuperType). An abstraction of this structure is shown in Figure 8.4.

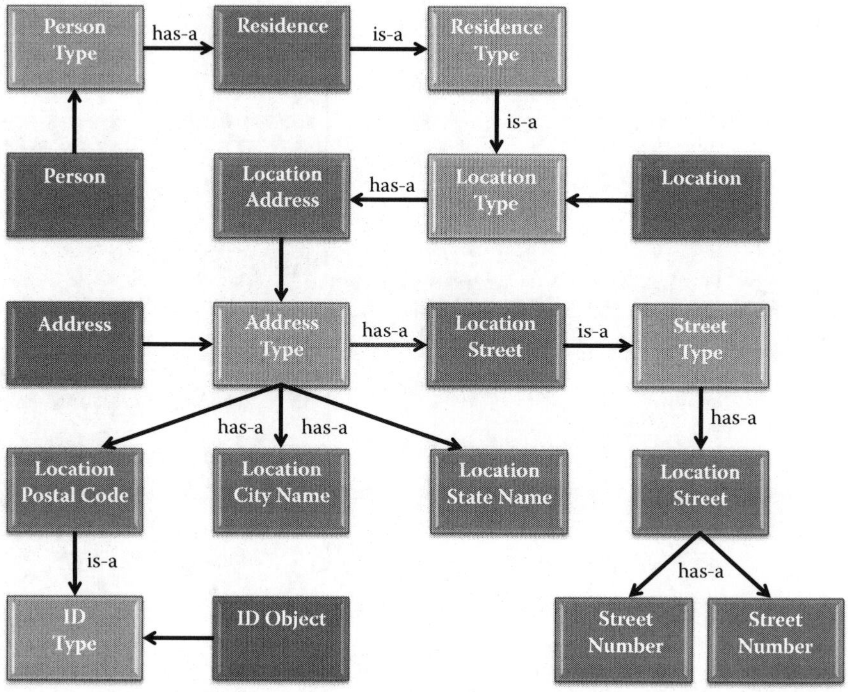

Figure 8.3 Data model sample for ResidenceType.

Component Reuse Repository

The overall structure of the GJXDM strongly promotes the use of inheritance to help standardize representations while providing flexibility to customize and refine those representations to meet specific needs. This reuse saves a considerable amount of time and resources because a common template can be employed and referenced across the user community without having to reinvest the effort to create a new one each time. GJXDM encodes these templates into XML schemas to facilitate sharing by Information Exchange Package Documentation (IEPD), which helps describe the structure and content, metadata, and other artifacts of the information exchange.[6] The IEPD can be stored in a component reuse repository and is used to define the methods for sharing data between disparate computer systems.

A number of common IEPDs have already been developed[7] for common reuse, including Amber Alerts, Field Interview Reports, Charging

[6] http://www.it.ojp.gov/topic.jsp?topic_id=133.

[7] *Case Studies on Information Exchange Package Documentation (IEPD) Development,* GJXDM Users' Conference, Atlanta, GA, June 9, 2005. SEARCH: The National Consortium for Justice Information and Statistics.

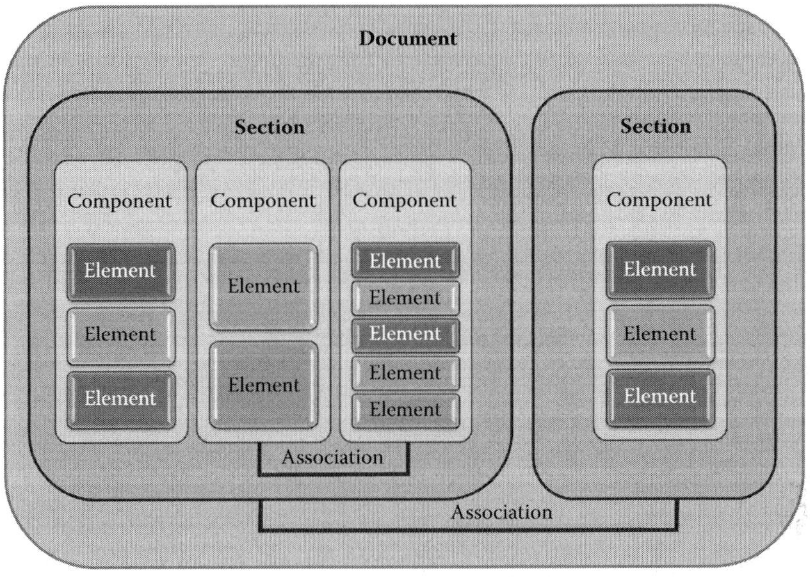

Figure 8.4 Overview of the data model structure.

Documents, Incident Reporting, Uniform Rap Sheets, Booking/Arrest Reports, and Sentencing Orders. Essentially, IEPDs are encapsulated business logic and subject matter expertise rolled into a well-defined package that acts like a road map to help promote discovery, sharing, and integration with other systems. The diagram in Figure 8.5 shows some of the key elements for an IEPD for the Amber Alert system, specifically the Data Model and diagram officially sponsored by OJP to show the necessary structure and relationships. Although the diagram is fairly complex (and potentially hard to read due to the small print), it shows all of the details necessary for the elements, components, and associations to make sense of the data structure.

The larger box in the middle is the core representation for a Person, which is ultimately referenced by the Missing Person (e.g., victim) and any identified Subjects (e.g., perpetrators or suspects). It also relates to PersonPhysicalDetails and provides a reference for a Picture. Figure 8.6 presents a more readable diagram for all of these components, their elements, and related associations.

The mapping of the structures in the data model to the GJXDM is usually defined in a simple spreadsheet format, typically broken into three columns where the first column is the class (e.g., component), the second column represents the properties (e.g., elements), and the third column contains the paths or references to the GJXDM data dictionary, corresponding to the properties. There can also be additional columns added to provide

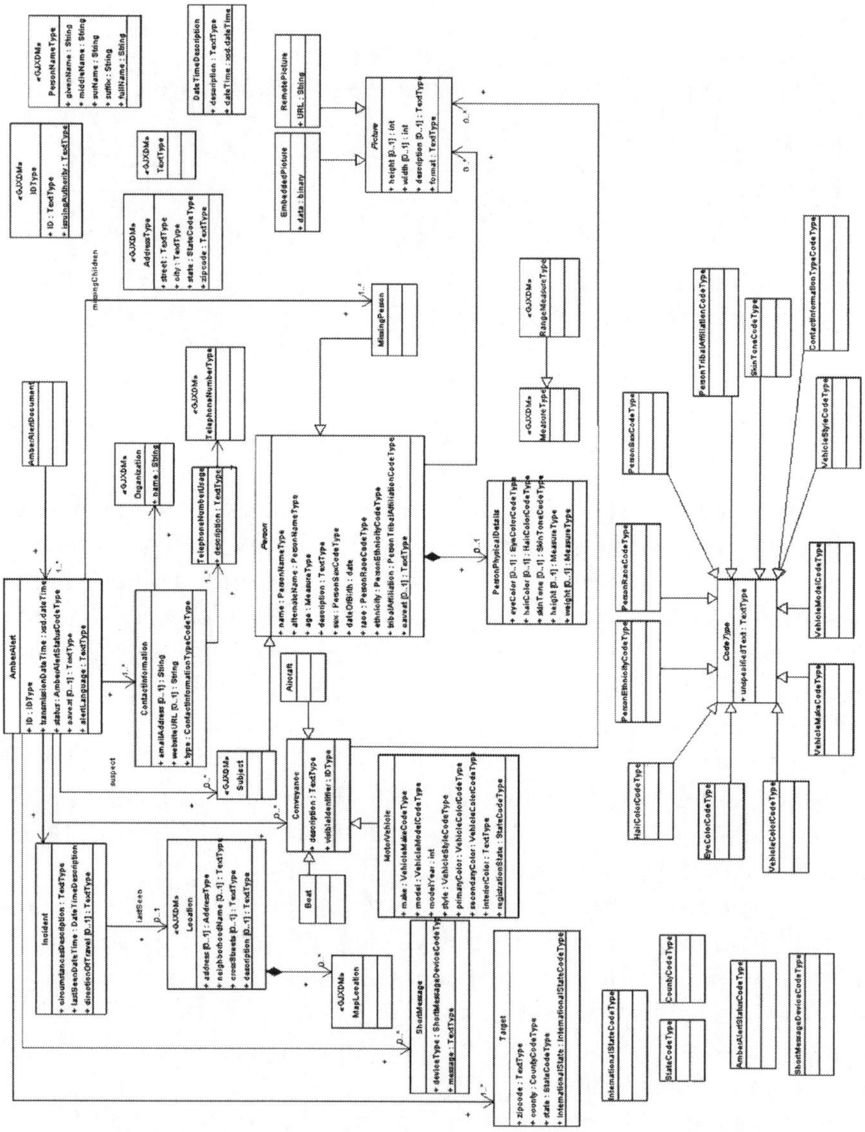

Figure 8.5 Data model for Amber Alerts.

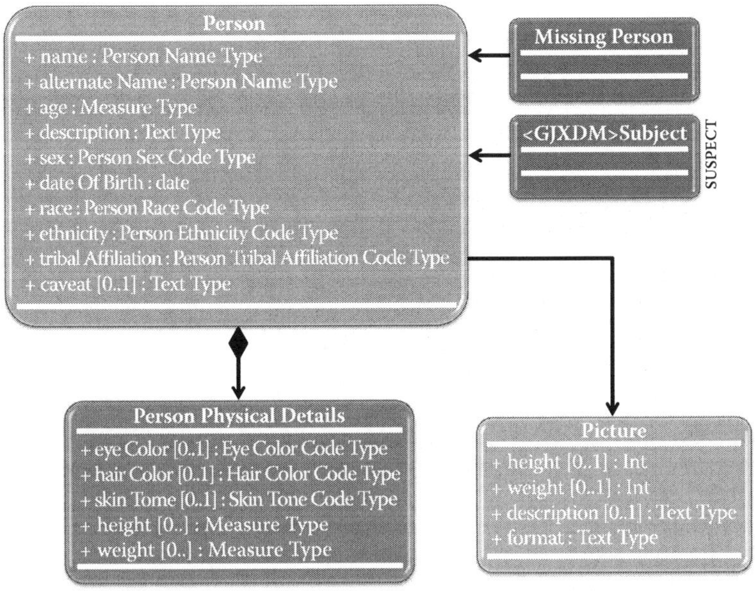

Figure 8.6 Details for Amber Alerts person component.

more details regarding inherited properties, other types, descriptions, and general comments. If a property from the domain is not able to be matched against the GJXDM, then the spreadsheet should indicate that it requires an extension to the GJXDM. Elements highlighted in dark shading usually denote local extensions and no prefix is assigned. Figure 8.7 shows a subset of mappings defined and supported for the Amber Alerts model.

Finally, Figure 8.8 provides a sample of the XML code[8] (Amber Alert, version 2.0) used to represent an example of an Amber Alert with valid data values. There are several components not expanded to allow the data to fit for the purposes of presenting this example. In this case, a seven-year-old female named Jenny Jones, born on January 6, 1997, was abducted by a large, muscular male subject and was last seen heading south in a green SUV.

The use of GJXDM has been fairly widespread, especially in more recent program development efforts involving the integration of DOJ systems among state and federal agencies. Also, a number of commercial Records Management Systems (RMSs) have updated their input/output interfaces to support GJXDM standards. There is a tremendous amount of material available on GJXDM from OJP and their contactors

[8] http://justicexml.gtri.gatech.edu/xstf/doc/amber_alert/2.0/index.html.

Class	Property or *relationship*	GJXDM Path
AmberAlertDocument		AmberAlertDocument
	AmberAlert	AmberAlertDocument/AmberAlert
AmberAlert		AmberAlert
	ID	AmberAlertDocument/DocumentDescriptiveMetadata/DocumentID
	transmissionDateTime	AmberAlert/AmberAlertTransmissionDateTime
	status	AmberAlert/AmberAlertStatus
	caveat	AmberAlert/CaveatText
	alertLanguage	AmberAlert/AmberAlertLanguageText
	ContactInformation	AmberAlert/AmberAlertContactInformation
	MissingPerson	AmberAlert/AmberAlertMissingChild
	Target	AmberAlert/AmberAlertTarget
	ShortMessage	AmberAlert/AmberAlertShortMessage
	Subject	AmberAlert/AmberAlertSuspect
	Incident	AmberAlert/AmberAlertIncident
	Conveyance	AmberAlert/AmberAlertConveyance
ContactInformationType		AmberAlertContactInformation
	emailAddress	AmberAlertContactInformation/ContactEmailID/ID
	websiteURL	AmberAlertContactInformation/ContactWebsiteID/ID
	type	AmberAlertContactInformation/ContactType
	Organization	AmberAlertContactInformation/ContactOrganization
	TelephoneNumberUsage	AmberAlertContactInformation/TelephoneNumberUsage
TelephoneNumberUsage		TelephoneNumberUsage
	description	TelephoneNumberUsage/TelephoneNumberUsageDescription
	TelephoneNumberType	TelephoneNumberUsage/TelephoneNumber
TelephoneNumberType		TelephoneNumber
Organization		Organization
TargetType		Target
	zipcode	Target/LocationPostalCodeID/ID
	county	Target/LocationCountyCode
	state	Target/LocationStateCode.fips5-2Alpha
	internationalState	Target/LocationStateCode.fips10-4International
ShortMessage		ShortMessage
	deviceType	ShortMessage/ShortMessageDeviceType
	message	ShortMessage/ShortMessageMessageText

Figure 8.7 Amber Alerts schema mapping.

```
- <amber:AmberAlert>
  + <amber:AmberAlertID>
    <amber:AmberAlertTransmissionDate>2004-11-15</amber:AmberAlertTransmissionDate>
    <amber:AmberAlertTransmissionTime>09:15:30</amber:AmberAlertTransmissionTime>
    <amber:AmberAlertStatus>Active</amber:AmberAlertStatus>
    <j:CaveatText>Beware of general danger regarding this situation.</j:CaveatText>
    <amber:AmberAlertLanguageText>English</amber:AmberAlertLanguageText>
  + <amber:AmberAlertContactInformation>
  - <amber:AmberAlertMissingChild>
    - <j:PersonName>
        <j:PersonGivenName>Jenny</j:PersonGivenName>
        <j:PersonSurName>Jones</j:PersonSurName>
      </j:PersonName>
      <j:PersonBirthDate>1997-06-01</j:PersonBirthDate>
    - <j:PersonPhysicalDetails>
        <j:PersonHeightMeasure j:measureUnitText="inches">52</j:PersonHeightMeasure>
        <j:PersonWeightMeasure j:measureUnitText="pounds">65</j:PersonWeightMeasure>
        <j:PersonSexCode>F</j:PersonSexCode>
      </j:PersonPhysicalDetails>
    </amber:AmberAlertMissingChild>
  + <amber:AmberAlertTarget>
  - <amber:AmberAlertShortMessage>
      <amber:ShortMessageDevice>SMS-140</amber:ShortMessageDevice>
      <amber:ShortMessage>Little girl, age 7, 4'4", traveling in a green SUV traveling south towards
        Portland.</amber:ShortMessage>
    </amber:AmberAlertShortMessage>
  - <amber:AmberAlertSuspect>
      <j:PersonDescriptionText>Tall, muscular male with handlebar moustache</j:PersonDescriptionText>
    - <j:PersonPhysicalDetails>
        <j:PersonHeightMeasure j:measureUnitText="inches">74</j:PersonHeightMeasure>
        <j:PersonWeightMeasure j:measureUnitText="pounds">245</j:PersonWeightMeasure>
        <j:PersonSexCode>M</j:PersonSexCode>
      </j:PersonPhysicalDetails>
    </amber:AmberAlertSuspect>
  - <amber:AmberAlertIncident>
      <j:ActivityDescriptionText>Girl was last seen walking home from school on Tuesday, then was seen getting into a
        green SUV that proceeded onto Interstate 5 near the school, heading south</j:ActivityDescriptionText>
    - <j:IncidentLocation>
        <j:LocationDescriptionText>8th Street near Lincoln Elementary School</j:LocationDescriptionText>
      </j:IncidentLocation>
      <amber:IncidentDirectionOfTravelDescriptionText>south</amber:IncidentDirectionOfTravelDescriptionText>
    </amber:AmberAlertIncident>
  + <amber:AmberAlertConveyance>
  </amber:AmberAlert>
```


Figure 8.8 Sample XML for an Amber Alert.

and affiliates. Not all aspects or details of GJXDM are presented in this section and those readers wanting more information should follow up on and review the references cited.

National Information Exchange Model

The National Information Exchange Model (NIEM), originally started as a partnership between the DOJ and the U.S. Department of Homeland Security (DHS), launched in early 2005 and is expanding to other agencies and organizations. It is largely based on the use of DOJ's GJXDM[9] and offers the community an automated framework for information exchange using XML-based protocols coordinated through a centrally maintained system. NIEM is not designed as an all-encompassing data normalization and interchange process where every piece of data is available for access. Rather, it is designed to address only those information components that are relevant across system or agency boundaries and can be easily extended to accommodate new or custom properties as needed to fulfill a stakeholder's needs.[10]

There are several domains defined in the NIEM representing justice, intelligence, immigration, emergency management, international trade, infrastructure protection, and information assurance.[11] A domain represents an area of interest or related functions. For example, any concerns related to criminal arrests would be handled under the justice domain where more specialized and specific data components are available to handle these types of representations. Figure 8.9[12] shows a representation of the NIEM domains. The NIEM framework facilitates a central clearinghouse used for the registration, discovery, and reuse of IEPDs that have been certified by authoritative sources and offers predefined templates of reusable objects for building the IEPs.

The primary data components are called *universals* and provide a set of fundamental, standardized, and reusable components that represent those generalized elements found in every federal domain including, for example, people, addresses, and events. There is also a category called *common* that represents items with the same shared meanings across several domains, but are not found in all the domains like the universals. Together, the universal and common types form the foundation of the NIEM core. Additionally, there are specific types that apply only to a

---

[9] GJXDM has become the justice domain of NIEM.
[10] http://www.niem.gov/files/NIEM_Introduction.pdf.
[11] http://www.niem.gov/whatIsADomain.php.
[12] Figure is referenced in http://www.niem.gov/files/NIEM_Introduction.pdf.

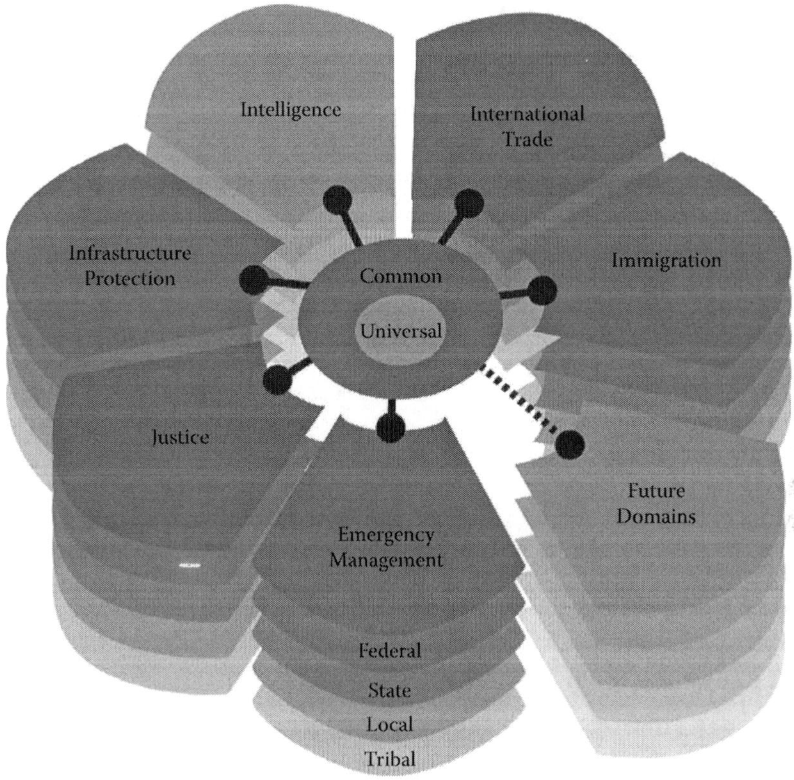

Figure 8.9 NIEM core and domain.

single domain. Overall, there are approximately 4,000 elements and 650 data types available within the current NIEM framework.

Semantic equivalence among the components is key for the NIEM framework to facilitate information sharing. For example, an agency involved with pursuing financial crimes might refer to people involved in suspicious financial transactions as *Subjects* while another law enforcement agency targeting narcotics crimes defines those people it arrests as *Perpetrators*. In this case, both agencies are referring to *People* even though they use different terminology; thus, they can continue to conduct business as usual, without changing any core infrastructure, and still be able to interchange data with one another using the NIEM framework.

Figure 8.10 shows a comparison of a point-to-point configuration among different agencies versus a centralized approach. The point-to-point configuration is somewhat overwhelming with respect to the number of mappings that must be established for agencies to share their information because it complicates the overall management, thereby increasing costs, limits scalability due to the number of mappings that need to be established, and puts the procedure at risk because nonstandard protocols between two or more agencies can inadvertently be introduced without

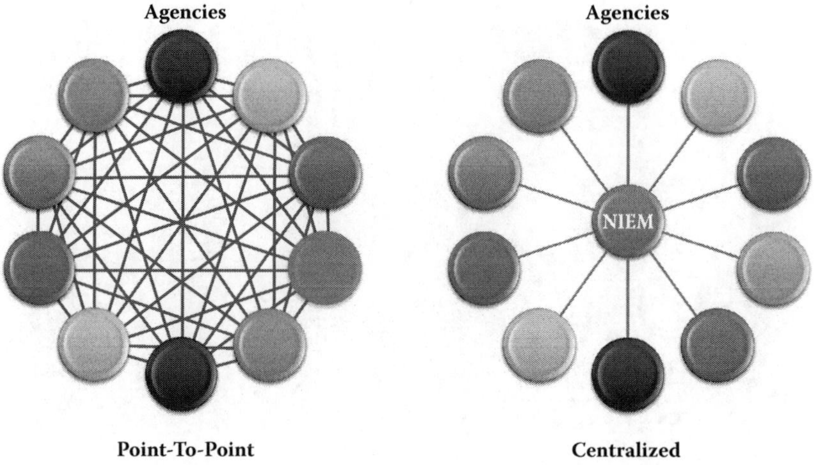

Figure 8.10 Point-to-point versus a centralized configuration.

vetting them to the rest of the stakeholders. The centralized approach for controlling the IEPDs proves to be more advantageous for this type of requirement because it defines all exchanges in one layer instead of having multiple, different interfaces.

The detail on the NIEM provided in this section is somewhat limited because it is largely based on the GJXDM framework and currently undergoing revisions. The intent is to introduce the reader to the fact that the NIEM exists and is growing in acceptance as a national standard for information sharing. Significant advances with NIEM should be observed over the next several years.

28 CFR Part 23

The term "28 CFR Part 23" sounds more like a component used in a repair manual from some complicated machinery rather than a policy to help define how information can be shared among different organizations, especially those that are using funds received from federal grants that are applied to the operations of a criminal intelligence system. There exists a policy titled "28 Code of Federal Regulations [CFR] Part 23" (Executive Order 12291) that applies to all state and local multijurisdictional or multiagency criminal intelligence systems operating under Title I of the Omnibus Crime Control and Safe Streets Act of 1968. The primary emphasis of this guideline[13] is to ensure that the systems are "utilized in

[13] For a good overview of 28 CFR Part 23, see http://www.iir.com/28cfr/FAQ.htm.

conformance with the privacy and constitutional rights of individuals." Basically, this guideline establishes limits on the types of data that can be collected and shared among law enforcement organizations and helps minimize negative perceptions regarding witch hunts and big-brother activities, which are presumed to occur by many in the private sector, by controlling the collection, access, and dissemination of the data.

According to the policy, a *criminal intelligence system* means: "the arrangements, equipment, facilities, and procedures used for the receipt, storage, interagency exchange or dissemination, and analysis of criminal intelligence information." Thus, these types of systems are logically separated from other systems in use by law enforcement organizations and there exists explicit protocols for entering, accessing, and disseminating the data. Furthermore, under the operating principles section of this policy, it states that "a project shall collect and maintain criminal intelligence information concerning an individual only if there is reasonable suspicion that the individual is involved in criminal conduct or activity and the information is relevant to that criminal conduct or activity." Or, to put it in more direct terms,[14] a criminal intelligence file consists of information on:

1. Individuals who:
    a. Are suspected of being involved in the actual or attempted planning, organizing, financing, or commission of criminal acts.
    b. Are suspected of being involved in criminal activities with known or suspected crime figures.
2. Organizations, businesses, and groups that:
    a. Are suspected of being involved in the actual or attempted planning, organizing, financing, or commission of criminal acts.
    b. Are suspected of being operated, controlled, financed, or infiltrated by known or suspected crime figures for use in an illegal manner.

Whether data should be entered into a criminal intelligence system is often likened to the Supreme Court case *Terry v. Ohio,*[15] 392 U.S. 1 (1968)[16] (see the sidebar for more details on the case), typically referred to as the "Terry Stop" (or test)[17] because officers stopped and searched suspects they believed were going to commit a robbery based on observed behaviors

[14] Defined in: http://www.fas.org/irp/agency/doj/lei/app.pdf (p. 210).
[15] http://en.wikipedia.org/wiki/Terry_v._Ohio.
[16] http://supct.law.cornell.edu/supct/html/historics/USSC_CR_0392_0001_ZS.html.
[17] David Carter, *Law Enforcement Intelligence: A Guide for State, Local, and Tribal Law Enforcement Agencies* (Washington, D.C.: U.S. Department of Justice, Office of Community Oriented Policing Services (COPS), 2004), p. 73, http://www.cops.usdoj.gov/Default.asp?Item=1404.

(e.g., reconnaissance) that were consistent with casing a store. Based on the training and experience of the officers, they were able to articulate the rationale behind their actions rather than just stating they had a "hunch" or "gut feeling" that something was not right. The same holds true for intelligence systems. There must be a clearly-defined rationale for entering data—it must be tied to criminal activities and behaviors. This precludes adding people just because they are, for example, sex offenders or ex-convicts, unless they are actively involved in or suspected of new criminal activities.

U.S. Supreme Court—*Terry v. Ohio*

U.S. Supreme Court - *Terry v. Ohio,* 392 U.S. 1 (1968)[18]
Argued December 12, 1967 - Decided June 10, 1968
No. 67 - 392 U.S. 1 - Syllabus

A Cleveland detective (McFadden), on a downtown beat which he had been patrolling for many years, observed two strangers (petitioner and another man, Chilton) on a street corner. He saw them proceed alternately back and forth along an identical route, pausing to stare in the same store window, which they did for a total of about 24 times. Each completion of the route was followed by a conference between the two on a corner, at one of which they were joined by a third man (Katz) who left swiftly. Suspecting the two men of "casing a job, a stick-up," the officer followed them and saw them rejoin the third man a couple of blocks away in front of a store. The officer approached the three, identified himself as a policeman, and asked their names. The men "mumbled something," whereupon McFadden spun petitioner around, patted down his outside clothing, and found in his overcoat pocket, but was unable to remove, a pistol. The officer ordered the three into the store. He removed petitioner's overcoat, took out a revolver, and ordered the three to face the wall with their hands raised. He patted down the outer clothing of Chilton and Katz and seized a revolver from Chilton's outside overcoat pocket. He did not put his hands under the outer garments of Katz (since he discovered nothing in his pat-down which might have been a weapon), or under petitioner's or Chilton's outer garments until he felt the guns. The three were taken to the police station. Petitioner and Chilton were charged with carrying concealed weapons. The defense moved to suppress the weapons. Though the trial court rejected the prosecution theory that the guns had been seized during a search incident to a lawful arrest, the court denied the motion to suppress and admitted the weapons into evidence on the ground that the officer had cause to believe that petitioner and Chilton were acting suspiciously, that their interrogation was warranted, and that the

[18] http://supreme.justia.com/us/392/1/.

officer, for his own protection, had the right to pat down their outer clothing having reasonable cause to believe that they might be armed. The court distinguished between an investigatory "stop" and an arrest, and between a "frisk" of the outer clothing for weapons and a full-blown search for evidence of crime. Petitioner and Chilton were found guilty, an intermediate appellate court affirmed, and the State Supreme Court dismissed the appeal on the ground that "no substantial constitutional question" was involved.

According to policy subsection § 23.20 Operating Principles (2) (g),[19] the data entered must be referenced with a level of sensitivity that defines how it can be disseminated to other people, organizations, or agencies, and it must also have a level of confidence that is used to determine the accuracy or reliability of the data. There are no officially defined standards for these requirements, and different agencies and organizations establish their own levels, verbiage, controls, and release authority. Some common terms include Sensitive But Unclassified (SBU), Law Enforcement Sensitive (LES), Limited Official Use (LOU), and For Official Use Only (FOUO). Generally, many law enforcement circles use the following terms and definitions:[20]

1. **Information Classification**
   a. Sensitive
      i. Information pertaining to significant law enforcement cases currently under investigation.
      ii. Corruption (police or other government officials), or other sensitive information.
      iii. Informant identification information.
      iv. Criminal intelligence reports that require strict dissemination and release criteria.
   b. Confidential
      i. Criminal intelligence reports not designated as sensitive.
      ii. Information obtained through intelligence unit channels that is not classified as sensitive and is for law enforcement use only.
   c. Restricted
      i. Reports that at an earlier date were classified sensitive or confidential and the need for high-level security no longer exists.

---

[19] http://www.it.ojp.gov/documents/28CFR_Part_23.PDF.

[20] David Carter, *Law Enforcement Intelligence: A Guide for State, Local, and Tribal Law Enforcement Agencies*, p. 216, http://www.cops.usdoj.gov/pdf/e09042536_chapter_appendices.pdf.

    ii. Nonconfidential information prepared for/by law enforcement agencies.
  d. Unclassified
    i. Civic-related information to which, in its original form, the general public had direct access (i.e., public record data).
    ii. News media information—newspaper, magazine, and periodical clippings dealing with specified criminal categories.
2. **Source Reliability:**
   a. Reliable—The reliability of the source is unquestioned or has been well tested in the past.
   b. Usually Reliable—The reliability of the source can usually be relied on as factual. The majority of information provided in the past has proven to be reliable.
   c. Unreliable—The reliability of the source has been sporadic in the past.
   d. Unknown—The reliability of the source cannot be judged. Its authenticity or trustworthiness has not yet been determined by either experience or investigation.
3. **Content Validity:**
   a. Confirmed—The information has been corroborated by an investigator or another independent, reliable source.
   b. Probable—The information is consistent with past accounts.
   c. Doubtful—The information is inconsistent with past accounts.
   d. Cannot Be Judged—The information cannot be judged. Its authenticity has not yet been determined by either experience or investigation.

Due to the sensitive nature of the data contained in a criminal intelligence database, there are strict controls on how the information can be accessed, including no direct remote terminal access unless explicitly approved by OJP (when federal funds are involved). There are also requirements to track and record anyone outside of the project who has been given information, the reason for their request, and the date of access. This section also requires that each intelligence project assures that the following security requirements are implemented:

1. Where appropriate, projects must adopt effective and technologically advanced computer software and hardware designs to prevent unauthorized access to the information contained in the system.
2. The project must restrict access to its facilities, operating environment and documentation to organizations and personnel authorized by the project.

3. The project must store information in the system in a manner such that it cannot be modified, destroyed, accessed, or purged without authorization.
4. The project must institute procedures to protect criminal intelligence information from unauthorized access, theft, sabotage, fire, flood, or other natural or manmade disaster.
5. The project must promulgate rules and regulations based on good cause for implementing its authority to screen, reject for employment, transfer, or remove personnel authorized to have direct access to the system.
6. A project may authorize and utilize remote (off-premises) system databases to the extent that they comply with these security requirements.

The period of retention for keeping data in a criminal intelligence system is defined to be five years. At the end of this period of time, the records must be removed from the system unless they are reviewed and the suspects are determined to still be criminally active, which basically resets the clock for an additional five years. Additionally, the data must undergo a periodic review and any information that is misleading, obsolete, or deemed unreliable must be purged. All information retained is justified with an explanation, a review date, and the name of the individual responsible for making the determination to keep the data in the criminal intelligence system. Furthermore, all systems are subject to inspection, audit, and review by project representatives.

To address modern circumstances and technological advances, an addendum to the CFR was defined under a 1998 Policy Clarification[21] stating that criminal intelligence systems may conduct searches across the spectrum of nonintelligence systems without those systems being brought under 28 CFR Part 23. Therefore, sources such as motor vehicle registrations, newspapers, public records, or data found on the Internet would not be required to be brought under 28 CFR 23 regulations.

The statute 28 CFR Part 23 has become increasingly popular and has established widespread use and acceptance partially because it was adopted by the National Criminal Intelligence Sharing Plan (NCISP).[22] Specifically, it states under Recommendation 9: "In order to ensure that the collection submission access, storage, and dissemination of criminal intelligence information conforms to the privacy and constitutional rights

[21] Issued by the Bureau of Justice Assistance (BJA), Office of Justice Programs (OJP).

[22] http://www.it.ojp.gov/documents/National_Criminal_Intelligence_Sharing_Plan.pdf (June 2005).

of individuals, groups, and organizations, law enforcement agencies shall adopt, at a minimum, the standards required by 28 CFR Part 23, regardless of whether or not an intelligence system is federally funded." Thus, this guideline will continue to help define the structures, processes, and protocols of establishing criminal intelligence systems to enable law enforcement to access and share data while protecting an individual's privacy and constitutional rights.

Conclusion

Information-sharing protocols are critical to the future success of many government programs that are dependent on the ability to access and share data among a community of users. Regulations, standards, and protocols are being enacted to help manage the assortment of representations, formats, schemata, and values found in most data sources. New frameworks are being created to help simplify the development and expedite the time required to access and integrate new sources. The natural evolution, once this capability is achieved, is to create centers where larger volumes of data can be accessed, integrated, and analyzed. Fusion centers and information-sharing systems are discussed in the next chapter.

Chapter 9

Information-Sharing Systems

Introduction

There are literally hundreds upon hundreds of systems that have been conceived, designed, implemented, and deployed in various regions, jurisdictions, and agencies across the United States.[1] Each one has served a specific purpose, to meet a specific need, and was implemented in a specific fashion to get the job-at-hand done. Some of these systems are small and simple, serving a single county, while others are much larger and more ambitious, spanning entire states or even being offered nationwide. Regardless of the size of the endeavor, the goal of each of these systems is to improve how law enforcement and intelligence units operate[2] by providing timely access to relevant data sets and necessary resources.

The majority of these systems do not create any new records; they simply provide a more efficient means by which to access, integrate, analyze, and report on existing data contained in records management, computer-aided dispatch, and database systems maintained by various local, state, and federal agencies. Believe it or not, the sharing of data has been commonplace among law enforcement agencies and within the intelligence communities for quite some time. Traditionally, however, it has required a team of people with special access to separately log in and query their respective organization's data sources, taking more time and resulting in less accurate results, which ultimately impacts the safety and security of the general public. Automated methods simply speed up this process and provide a more complete picture of the threats against society and national security.

Creating efficiencies has a big impact on the ability of an agency to respond to its constituents, especially in the law enforcement community. According to 2004 statistics published[3] by the Bureau of Justice Statistics (BJS), there are almost 18,000 independent state and local law enforcement agencies (police, sheriff, etc.) in the United States, representing over 730,000 sworn officers—which does not include the 104,000 federal officers. The largest, the New York City Police Department, had 40,435 full-time sworn personnel as of June 2000.[4] The Chicago Police

[1] Lisa Walbolt Wagner, *Information Sharing Systems: A Survey of Law Enforcement,* Justice Research and Statistics Association, 2006, http://www.jrsa.org/pubs/reports/improving-crime-data/Info_Sharing.pdf.

[2] An important benefit of these systems is to improve the safety and security of the law enforcement personnel so that they have a more complete picture of the environment or persons they are dealing with, especially when it comes to violent offenders.

[3] http://www.ojp.usdoj.gov/bjs/lawenf.htm.

[4] Brian Reaves and Matthew Hickman, *Census of State and Local Law Enforcement Agencies, 2000,* Bureau of Justice Statistics, October 2002, NCJ 194066, http://www.ojp.usdoj.gov/bjs/pub/pdf/csllea00.pdf.

Department ranked second with more than 13,800 sworn officers[5] and the Los Angeles County Sheriff's Department[6] is third with over 9,500 officers.

When looking across the globe, other organizations, such as the Uttar Pradesh Police, located in India, represents the largest police force in the world under a single command with over 206,000 officers.[7] The People's Armed Police in China represents over 1 million personnel, which is essentially an armed defense force that undertakes police duties. Honorable mention also goes out to the New South Wales Police Service[8] in Australia with more than 13,000 sworn officers. These are just a few examples of the sizes of the various policing organizations—and each has similar information-sharing needs.

One can imagine the sheer volume of data, collaboration, and support that must go into facilitating information sharing in these types of organizations. When one looks at the number of systems, processes, protocols, laws, reports, groups, councils, organizations, and so forth available on this topic, it is quite simply *overwhelming*. It is hard to keep track of what is current, what is recommended, what works, what doesn't work, and what is standard. As the cliché states, "The good thing about standards is that there are so many from which to choose." Simply polling the industry, you will find references to systems, protocols, policies, laws, reports, studies, and technologies, with several listed below, in no particular order:

- Global Justice Information Sharing Initiative Intelligence Working Group (GIWG)
- National Criminal Intelligence Sharing Plan (NCISP)
- Global Justice Information Sharing Initiative
- IEM (Information Exchange Model)
- Law Enforcement Information Sharing Program (LEISP) EXchange Specifications (LEXS)
- Markle Foundation Task Force: Creating a Trusted Network for Homeland Security
- 9/11 Commission Report and Recommendations
- Law Enforcement Regional Data Exchange
- Intelligence Community Information Sharing Working Group
- Community Interoperability and Information Sharing Office Policy Board

---

[5] http://www.illinois.com/details/city.php?cityFips=1714000.
[6] http://www.lasd.org/lasd_services/contract_law/municipalsrv1.html.
[7] http://uppolice.up.nic.in/phg.html.
[8] http://www.policensw.com/info/gen/p2.html.

- DOJ-DHS Ad Hoc Working Group on SBU-level Information Sharing Systems
- National Virtual Pointer System Coordinating Committee
- Justice Intelligence Coordinating Council
- Homeland Security Advisory Council Working Group
- National Association of State Chief Information Officers
- Information Sharing Environment Enterprise Architecture Framework

To better organize and address the morass of systems and approaches available within the community, in December 2004, Congress passed the Intelligence Reform and Terrorism Prevention Act (IRTPA) of 2004, seeking improvement in how the intelligence community operates and explicitly calling for the creation of an information-sharing environment (ISE). According to the IRPTA under Section 1016, Information Sharing, the "terms *information sharing environment* and *ISE* mean an approach that facilitates the sharing of terrorism information, which approach may include any methods determined necessary and appropriate for carrying out this section." Additionally, the IRTPA states that the Director of National Intelligence shall:

- Establish uniform security standards and procedures.
- Establish common information technology standards, protocols, and interfaces.
- Ensure development of information technology systems that include multi-level security and intelligence integration capabilities.
- Establish policies and procedures to resolve conflicts between the need to share intelligence information and the need to protect intelligence sources and methods.
- Develop an enterprise architecture for the intelligence community and ensure that elements of the intelligence community comply with such architecture.
- Have procurement approval authority over all enterprise architecture-related information technology items funded in the National Intelligence Program.

The IRTPA calls for the ISE to provide the functional equivalent of, or otherwise support, a decentralized, distributed, and coordinated environment that:

- Connects existing systems, where appropriate, provides no single points of failure, and allows users to share information among agencies, between levels of government, and, as appropriate, with the private sector.

- Ensures direct and continuous online electronic access to information.
- Facilitates the availability of information in a form and manner that facilitates its use in analysis, investigations and operations.
- Builds upon existing systems capabilities currently in use across the government.
- Employs an information access management approach that controls access to data rather than just systems and networks, without sacrificing security.
- Facilitates the sharing of information at and across all levels of security.
- Provides directory services, or the functional equivalent, for locating people and information.
- Incorporates protections for individuals' privacy and civil liberties.
- Incorporates strong mechanisms to enhance accountability and facilitate oversight, including audits, authentication, and access controls.

Many of the systems developed to date have achieved their intended goals, and the following discussions provide an abbreviated overview of several systems that are routinely referenced in the open source. Their selection is simply to provide the reader with a high-level introduction to the concepts and scope of some of these systems. It would be impossible to detail and cover each system in this book—and even a list of systems would be out-of-date before the book went to print.

This section is by no means complete and is not intended to deliver a detailed or in-depth overview about the pros/cons, successes/failures, or capabilities offered by such systems. Nor is it an endorsement of any individual system. Rather, it was included to provide the reader with a high-level overview (e.g., a sampling) of representative information sharing systems and programs that have been pursued within the U.S. law enforcement community. These write-ups are merely an introduction to several of these systems or programs and more detail can be found in the references provided.

Furthermore, the technology sector is constantly changing and the status of these systems is forever in flux; therefore, these descriptions are summaries based purely on available *open-source* documents at the time of this writing and the material may no longer reflect the current status of any of these systems. Any inaccurate, erroneous, or incorrect descriptions or misinterpretations of these systems are unintentional and are more reflective of the variance of materials found and the degree of detail openly documented for any system. The reader is strongly encouraged to perform additional research to learn more about these systems if so inclined.

Automated Regional Justice Information System (ARJIS)

The Automated Regional Justice Information System (ARJIS) is a program that operates in Southern California in the two counties, San Diego and Imperial, that border Mexico. With an initial sponsorship[9] from the National Institutes of Justice (NIJ) in the late 1990s, ARJIS became a means for local jurisdictions to share their criminal data. The system has since grown into a larger network (ARJISNet) encompassing 71 local, state, and federal agencies[10] and over 11,500 law enforcement users including police and court and corrections officials, generating 161,000 transactions per month[11] (e.g., system queries, field report submissions, etc.) and is even accessible through secure wireless devices.

The system contains data on crime cases, arrests, citations, warrants, field interviews, traffic accidents, pawn shop slips, fraudulent documents, photographs, gang information, gun data, computer-aided dispatch calls, and stolen property.[12] At the end of 2007,[13] ARJIS contained over 4.5 million names and 2.5 million incidents (suspicious reports, citations, crime cases, arrests, traffic accidents), and delivered more than 38,000 officer notifications.

ARJIS is structured as a "hybrid" system that consists of centralized, distributed, and federated components. There exists a mainframe system to house the data contributed by the participating agencies, as well as access to federated sources, such as the California Law Enforcement Telecommunications System (CLETS), county databases, the Department of Motor Vehicles (with over 32 million photos), the Cal-Photo system (used to access more than 5 million photos[14]), and sex offender registries. The system also supports access to the National Crime Information Center (NCIC) to show wanted persons, violent felons, missing persons, gang members, and terrorists.

ARJIS is constantly improving[15] and has recently been upgraded with additional information sharing enhancements, including access to

---

9 Pamela Scanlon and Rachel Campbell, "A Successful Partnership: When Police and the Feds Team for Technology," *Technology Talk, Police Chief,* October 2000, http://www.iacptechnology.org/Library/TechTalk/TechTalk1100.htm.

10 http://www.arjis.org/ARJISAgencies/tabid/55/Default.aspx?PageContentID=2.

11 http://sandiego.fbi.gov/pressrel/2008/sd012408.htm.

12 Trudy Walsh, "Agencies Put Criminal Justice Data Online for Sharing," *Government Computing News* 7, no. 7 (July 2001), http://www.gcn.com/state/vol7_no7/news/1093-1.html.

13 Pam Scanlon, *Information Sharing in San Diego & Imperial Counties,* 9th Annual Technologies for Critical Incident Preparedness Conference, November 2007.

14 System Documentation for the Automated Regional Justice Information System (ARJIS), Comprehensive Regional Information Sharing Project (CRISP), Mitretek Systems, Supported under Cooperative Agreement 2001-LT-BX-K002, Office of Science and Technology, National Institute of Justice, Office of Justice Programs, U.S. Department of Justice, December 2006.

15 *PSC Dispatch,* Fall 2007, http://www.arjis.org/Portals/0/PSCnewsComp9-11.pdf.

the State Regional & Federal Enterprise Retrieval System (SRFERS) to share booking photos and license plate reader information for Mexico and Canadian borders; the Domestic Violence Communication System (DVCS) for information on the effectiveness of county-funded domestic violence programs; BorderSafe for access to data using wireless personal digital assistants (PDAs) and laptops (currently several hundred units are able to access ARJIS), which also provides for situational team awareness and reporting; and R-DEx, the DOJ's system to share data among federal and state/local law enforcement.

ARJIS is governed by the San Diego Association of Governments (SANDAG) Public Safety Committee (PSC), composed of both elected officials and public safety representatives. ARJIS is funded by membership fees based on a sliding scale for the population area of a participating agency (federal agencies pay a surcharge for their involvement). Overall, the budget of the ARJIS program is approximately $4 million annually, collected mostly from membership fees, some grant funding, and other donations. Important to note, the ARJIS system is not built entirely for use by government officials because it also supports a public area,[16] which provides information to the general public in the form of crime statistics, most-wanted lists, crime maps, online warrants, and inmate logs.

Citizen and Law Enforcement Analysis and Reporting (CLEAR)

Citizen and Law Enforcement Analysis and Reporting (CLEAR) is a system currently in use by the Chicago Police Department (CPD) for collecting, sharing, analyzing, and reporting on crime-related information. It was originally conceived in 2001 as an extension of an existing Criminal History Records Inventory System (CHRIS) built in the mid-1990s and was created in partnership with a commercial vendor. When the system went operational in 2003, it represented a framework of a number of different modules that were created to support an enterprise information system to address three primary areas: police management, criminal justice integration, and community/business partnerships.[17] The system is based on a centralized data warehouse and all access is through browser interfaces (e.g., no client software is required).

16 The incorporation of a public outreach system is becoming a standard offering for many law enforcement programs.

17 Wesley Skogan, Susan Hartnett, Jill DuBois, and Jason Bennis, *Policing Smarter Through IT: Lessons in Enterprise Implementation* (Evanston, IL: The Institute for Policy Research, Northwestern University, 2004), 13.

Overall, the system supports a number of subapplications, including a Crime Mapping tool, a Gang Arrest application, a Juvenile Arrest system, an Automated Rap Sheet system, and several others.[18] The system contains data from automated dispatch systems, fingerprints, arrest databases, investigation reports, traffic violation convictions, criminal warrants, stolen property, gang data, investigative alerts, and contact cards, and has access to a database of more than 6 million mug shots. CLEAR also encompasses a wide range of equipment including cameras, license plate readers, and microphones to triangulate gunshots. The users interact with the system using workstations, portable data terminals (in patrol cars), PDAs, phones, and other wireless devices, which allow patrol officers to quickly query the details or history of a suspect, check photos, compare fingerprints, and even complete their case reports.[19]

The CPD also extended CLEAR to include an outreach to the residents of the city of Chicago with a mapping capability (CLEARmap) to better understand the crime problem and allow citizens[20] to assist in "problem solving and combating crime and disorder in their neighborhoods." CLEARmap provides the ability to search on reported crimes and produce maps, charts, tables, and graphs with the results. There are several other community outreach components[21] and the entire suite of applications and Web sites is referred to as CLEARpath and covers the following:

- Alerts Archive—a collection of past alerts issued by the CPD.
- Cold Cases—details of unsolved homicides in the City of Chicago that allow for citizen input.
- Crime Stopper—a gallery of wanted posters plus the ability for citizens to subscribe to the service to wanted posters via e-mail.
- Crime Watch—a video news magazine covering topics of interest to the public.
- Most Wanted—gallery of most-wanted fugitives w/ photos and physical descriptions.
- Checkerboard Chat—the official blog site of the CPD.
- Prostitution Patron Arrests—the posting of pictures, names, and identities of people that were arrested for soliciting prostitutes.
- Sex Offender Search—a searchable database of registered sex offenders residing in the City of Chicago (defined by patrol beat).

[18] Jessica Ashley, "CLEAR Offers Enhanced Police Efficiencies, Increased Accountability," Illinois Criminal Justice Information Authority, Program Evaluation Summary (Grant #03-DB-BX-0037), May 2006.

[19] Jonathan Walters, "CLEAR Connection: A High-Tech Partnership Is Driving Down Crime in Chicago," *Governing.com,* August 1, 2007, http://www.governing.com/manage/pm/perf0807.htm.

[20] CLEARmap can be found at: http://gis.chicagopolice.org/.

[21] http://www.chicagopolice.org/.

- Tow/Steal Search—a site to help locate towed, impounded, or stolen vehicles where citizens can run the license plate or VIN of a vehicle.
- Wanted—pictures of unidentified people that are wanted for investigation.

CLEAR has grown[22] since its inception and is now in us by more than 400 local, state, and federal law enforcement agencies including those from Illinois, Indiana, Wisconsin, Minnesota, and Washington, D.C. As a testament to its success, officially there are currently more non-CPD users (over 17,000) than actual CPD users (13,800) of the CLEAR system. There is no cost for other agencies to use CLEAR because the CPD covers the expenses for managing and controlling the systems (about 85 percent of the funding for developing CLEAR was from federal and state grants[23]). Furthermore, the CLEAR concept was expanded to create I-CLEAR (Illinois Citizen and Law Enforcement Analysis and Reporting), where the CPD and the Illinois State Police (ISP) created a platform from which to share their data in a common integrated system to serve all 102 counties in Illinois.[24] There is also I-CASE used for uniform incident/case reporting. However, the future status of these systems as an integrated offering throughout the state[25] is unclear.

Comprehensive Regional Information Management Exchange System (CRIMES)

The Comprehensive Regional Information Management Exchange System (CRIMES) was based in the Hampton Roads area of Virginia, one of the world's largest natural harbors. It is home to 2 million residents including the cities of Virginia Beach, Norfolk, and Newport News. The area is heavily influenced by the military, especially the U.S. Navy. The Atlantic Fleet maintains this area as their base port. Not surprisingly, the USS *Cole* (DDG 67), which was attacked by terrorists in Yemen, is based out of Norfolk.

---

[22] Linda Spagnoli, "A New Era in POLICING: Grant Funding Gives Law Enforcement the Opportunity to Cash in on Groundbreaking Technologies," *Officer.com,* October 2007.

[23] System Documentation for the Citizen and Law Enforcement Analysis and Reporting (CLEAR) System, Comprehensive Regional Information Sharing Project (CRISP), Mitretek Systems, Supported under Cooperative Agreement 2001-LT-BX-K002, Office of Science and Technology, National Institute of Justice, Office of Justice Programs, U.S. Department of Justice, December 2006.

[24] I-CLEAR, Illinois Citizen and Law Enforcement Analysis and Reporting, IIJIS Summit, June 25, 2007.

[25] Jill DuBois, Wesley Skogan, Susan Hartnett, Natalie Bump, and Danielle Morris, "CLEAR and I-CLEAR: A Report on New Information Technology in Chicago and Illinois," prepared for the Illinois Criminal Justice Information Authority, August 2007.

Originally conceived in the late 1980s, CRIMES went operational in the early 1990s and initially contained the data from the seven largest jurisdictions in Hampton Roads. CRIMES was built on a grassroots approach and evolved through monthly meetings from the regional police chief association (Hampton Roads Police Chief's Association). Most of the agencies in the region had computerized databases and were capturing incident and arrest data electronically. It was apparent that there was a need to share information given the contiguous nature of the jurisdictional lines (35 municipalities). Ultimately, it was decided that this region would be best served by exploiting the existing technology base and created a sharing protocol to interchange data. Funding for the initial project came from a congressional earmark. As the system expanded to additional municipalities, grant funding and a proportional formula were used to "grow the project." The system eventually grew to include 12 agencies.

A governance structure and operational procedures were formalized where each locality was represented by the law enforcement agency head on the board of directors (who became the policy makers for this system). They adopted the position that *any agency that had data must share that data if they were to participate*. It was also recognized that there were some agencies who, because of hierarchical policy, could not share. Additionally, there were a few agencies who did not have an efficient means to electronically capture their own incident data that would require access to the system. They were evaluated on a case-by-case basis by the board and many received a nonvoting "associate" status with "read-only" capabilities. They included the Federal Bureau of Investigation (FBI), the Virginia State Police, and the Transportation Security Agency (TSA).

CRIMES contained more than 11 million state and local records, including arrests, bookings, incident reports, investigative reports, field interviews, citations, warrants, juvenile data, pawn data, and mug shots. There was no federal data contained in the CRIMES system because federal agencies, due to their rules, could not participate in the network and were therefore not involved with sharing data. Most of the funding for CRIMES came from grant money, some requiring the participating jurisdictions to provide a match of 25 percent. The proportional formula was utilized on a sliding-scale fee based on the number of sworn officers in their organization.[26] Over its life span, less than $2 million was spent on developing and maintaining CRIMES.

[26] System Documentation for the Comprehensive Regional Information Management Exchange System (CRIMES), Comprehensive Regional Information Sharing Project (CRISP), Noblis, Supported under Cooperative Agreement 2001-LT-BX-K002, Office of Science and Technology, National Institute of Justice, Office of Justice Programs, U.S. Department of Justice, January 2006.

The underlying architecture of CRIMES was based on a distributed system where each agency maintained a database server to process the queries it received, allowing them to stay in control of their data, manage access, and monitor system usage. A query would be generated by a user (using fields only from structured data) then sent to the central CRIMES server, which farmed out the request to all other networked servers; each server would then respond with any results; all data sent back to the central server would be consolidated, deconflicted, and ranked before presented to the user.

CRIMES was a successful program and clearly proved its importance. Ultimately, it was decided that LInX (described later) would replace the CRIMES system in the Hampton Roads area, thereby providing a more comprehensive and better-funded program from which to share regional information. It also introduced the concept of incorporating federal data into the mix of state and local records.

Factual Analysis Criminal Threat Solution (FACTS) System

The Factual Analysis Criminal Threat Solution (FACTS) system, based in Tallahassee, Florida, was originally designed in 2001 as a centralized system operated by the Florida Department of Law Enforcement (FDLE), where all data was maintained at a single location. FACTS was designed to combine state and local data into a common repository that also housed public record information. Initially, it was physically located at the facilities of a commercial, for-profit vendor that was responsible for the overall operations of the system, although FDLE always maintained oversight and control on the system.

FACTS ultimately evolved to reflect a distributed architecture that could search a variety of sources including sex offenders, motor vehicles, driver's licenses, criminal histories, and department of corrections, as well as public records,[27] which included data such as pilot licenses issued by the Federal Aviation Agency, aircraft ownership, real-property ownership, U.S. Coast Guard-registered vehicles, corporate filings, Uniform Commercial Code (UCC) filings or business liens, bankruptcy filings, state-issued professional licenses (e.g., real estate, beautician, etc.), Internet domains, hunting and fishing licenses, firearms and explosive permits, DEA-controlled substances licenses, residential and business phone listings, and civil courts records.[28]

---

27 Data provided by Seisent Accurint—since purchased by Lexis/Nexis.

28 System Documentation for the Factual Analysis Criminal Threat Solution System (FACTS), Comprehensive Regional Information Sharing Project (CRISP), Noblis, Supported under Cooperative Agreement 2001-LT-BX-K002, Office of Science and Technology, National Institute of Justice, Office of Justice Programs, U.S. Department of Justice, December 2006.

FACTS was ultimately the core of a program call MATRIX (Multistate Anti-Terrorism Information Exchange), which ceased operation in 2005 due to privacy concerns,[29] data control issues, and even the legality[30] of the program itself. At its peak, it was being considered by 14 states[31] (16 states were invited to participate) and reportedly had access to over 4 billion records[32] representing a combination of state/local and commercial/public records contributed and managed by a private company with law enforcement oversight. After the dissolution of the MATRIX program, the core FACTS system continued operations and is utilized in seven regions throughout the state, each overseen by a special agent in charge (SAC) at FDLE. There were approximately 250 agencies using the FACTS system (circa 2005) throughout Florida with an estimated 1,000 defined end users.

Florida Information Network for Data Exchange and Retrieval (FINDER)

The Florida Information Network for Data Exchange and Retrieval (FINDER) system, based in Orlando, Florida, became operational in 2002 as a means to share pawn data. It was originally conceived as a collaborative effort between law enforcement agencies (e.g., sheriff's departments) and the University of Central Florida, and has since evolved into its own nonprofit entity (The Center for Law Enforcement Technology, Training, and Research [LETTR]). Its initial success allowed the program to expand from a small, regional system with participation from only three counties (Seminole, Hillsborough, and Orange) to a statewide system consisting of more than 140 agencies[33] in early 2008.

FINDER is based purely on existing law enforcement data and is used by police to search for property, motor vehicles, pawn activity, and persons and their known associates[34] through incident reports, accident reports, traffic citations, field interrogations, arrest data, bookings, parking tickets, towed vehicles, contacts/statements, sex offenders, gang reports, computer-aided dispatch (CAD), and other sources. The information is

---

29 MATRIX Report, DHS Privacy Office Report to the Public Concerning the Multistate Anti-Terrorism Information Exchange (MATRIX) Pilot Project. Privacy Office, U.S. Department of Homeland Security, Washington, D.C., December 2006.

30 Attorney General Baker Declares Transfer of Driver Information to MATRIX Database Illegal, Department of Law, State of Georgia, Press Advisory, October 20, 2003.

31 Madeleine Baran, "Fear Real-Life Matrix Will Be Monitoring You," *New York Daily News,* November 23, 2003.

32 Brian Bergstein, "Terrorist Scoring System Sparked Investigations and Arrests," *InformationWeek,* May 20, 2004.

33 http://www.finder.ucf.edu/Home/tabid/36/Default.aspx.

34 http://www.finder.ucf.edu/Default.aspx?tabid=69.

extracted from existing records management systems (RMSs) and converted into a common data format and common code tables.[35]

FINDER is a distributed system operating within a secure network (Florida Criminal Justice Network—CJNet) where each agency maintains control over their own data. Queries are performed through a simple Web interface and are sent to each participating agency using a common software system interface (Data Sharing Server [DSS]). The results are then aggregated back to the requesting entity. Each agency controls the type of data shared and which remote agencies are allowed access based on authorization of the IP address of the participating agency.

Participation in the FINDER program is based on a sliding membership scale, tied to how many sworn officers are affiliated with the department or agency. Several agencies can be associated with one site to offset the costs/fees, albeit very modest.[36] As of 2006 there were over 1.8 million queries processed through the FINDER network of servers. Of course, FINDER is being expanded with new capabilities and features, including compatibility with GJXML. It also supports a hierarchical network routing design that follows national region, state, state region, county, and agency, making it possible to query an entire area or branch within the FINDER network without having to specify all the individual agencies within a region or knowing exactly where they are located.

Ohio Local Law Enforcement Information Sharing Network (OLLEISN)

The Ohio Local Law Enforcement Information Sharing Network (OLLEISN) is a state-level information-sharing system supporting the needs of the majority (almost 90 percent) of local law enforcement agencies in the state of Ohio. The OLLEISN program was started in February of 2004 and went operational less than a year later. It was initially funded with grant money from the Ohio Department of Public Safety, provided by the Department of Homeland Security. OLLEISN is touted as a partnership between public organizations[37] (Ohio Attorney

[35] System Documentation for the Florida Integrated Network for Data Exchange and Retrieval (FINDER) System, Comprehensive Regional Information Sharing Project (CRISP), Noblis, Supported under Cooperative Agreement 2001-LT-BX-K002, Office of Science and Technology, National Institute of Justice, Office of Justice Programs, U.S. Department of Justice, November 2006.

[36] FINDER Information Guide, Law Enforcement Data Sharing Consortium, Florida Integrated Network for Data Exchange and Retrieval, January 15, 2008.

[37] Brett Gerke, "Ohio Local Law Enforcement Information Sharing Network (OLLEISN)," June 2005, http://it.ojp.gov/documents/ucon/ohio.ppt.

General, Ohio Department of Public Safety, Ohio Office of Criminal Justice Services, Buckeye State Sheriff's Association, Ohio State Highway Patrol, and the Ohio Association of Chiefs of Police) and commercial organizations including RMS/CAD vendors, database software companies, hardware companies (e.g., networks, computers), and private consulting firms.

The scope of the system is to focus only on local law enforcement and to have all Ohio agencies participate. OLLEISN is defined as *justice information sharing locally, but on a statewide scale*[38] and has a specific focus on the needs of patrol officers and investigators. Participation in OLLEISN is voluntary; however, in order to use the OLLEISN system, agencies must contribute their own data,[39] also called a "give-to-receive" policy. This ensures that all users have a vested interest in furthering the capabilities and utilization of the system.

The system is able to accept input directly from a number of RMSs and, by design, acts as an RMS for those agencies without the budget or infrastructure required to invest in supporting a full-fledged RMS (approximately 40 percent of local agencies did not have an electronic RMS when OLLEISN was originally implemented). Access to OLLEISN is through an Internet portal available on the Attorney General's Ohio Law Enforcement Gateway (OHLEG),[40] initially launched in 2003. The types of information collected and available within the OLLEISN include wants and warrants, incident data, alerts, field interview notes, suspect/witness/victim information, property types, search warrants, traffic citations, pawn transactions, service calls, registered offenders, concealed carry permits and firearm registrations, evidence, and various biometrics (mug shots, fingerprints, signatures).

The system was designed using national and industry standards,[41] with the ability to scale because it is based on a clustered-server infrastructure that is easily expanded to handle increased demands. The system is operated out of the Attorney General's office and supports over 750 law enforcement agencies[42] submitting more than 25,000 queries daily. A feature of the system requires that all participating agencies update their data submissions at least weekly; for those that don't, a delinquency notice is generated and sent to that agency's point of contact.[43]

---

38 Success Stories in Justice Information Sharing: The Ohio OLLEISN Experience, 2006, http://www.olleisn.org/news/success.pdf.

39 Gary Vest, "Ohio Local Law Enforcement Information Sharing Network: Policy Issues in Data Exchange," *The Police Chief* 72(6): June 2005.

40 http://www.ag.state.oh.us/online_publications/ohleg/05_ohleg_brochure.pdf.

41 OLLEISN JXDM Connection-the-Dots Guide: http://www.olleisn.org/Connect-the-Dots/.

42 Participating OLLEISN agencies: http://www.olleisn.org/about/agencies.php.

43 OLLEISN FAQ: http://www.olleisn.org/faq/.

Law Enforcement Information Exchange (LInX)

The Naval Criminal Investigative Service (NCIS) represents the Navy's law enforcement, counterintelligence, and security division for the U.S. Department of Navy.[44] NCIS is chartered to counteract and investigate a wide range of criminal offenses including, among others, terrorism, espionage, computer intrusion, homicide, rape, child abuse, arson, and procurement fraud. As part of its mission, NCIS works closely with other federal, state, and local law enforcement agencies, providing the foundation for implementing a data-sharing environment. These interactions are crucial and have led NCIS to implement and fund the Law Enforcement Information Exchange (LInX), which is currently deployed regionally throughout the United States with access to over 80 million records nationwide.

LInX is based on creating a centralized data warehouse[45] containing the records for the region it serves, providing new leads to help solve crimes and protect strategic assets. A variety of data, including incident reports, case records, CAD records, citations, mug shots, pawn receipt data, and investigative documents are typically included within a regional warehouse. All of the information is accessed through a "Front Porch" data replication service housed at each participating agency. The data is pushed from these servers into the LInX data warehouse where it is processed (standardized and normalized) as it is loaded, and then made available through Web-based query interfaces with SSL protection for search, analytics, and reporting. LInX uses open standards and relies on existing technology to integrate the different systems together.

The following represent the current and planned LInX deployments:[46]

- Hawaii LInX with eight agencies represented across the state with 250 users.
- Southeast Law Enforcement Alliance Project (SELEAP) spanning Northeast Florida and Southeast Georgia and supporting 39 law enforcement agencies with 3,500 users.
- The Law Enforcement Alliance Project (LEAP) out of South Texas currently supporting 21 agencies with 2,500 users.
- Hampton Roads, Virginia, operating with 45 agencies across Southeastern and Central Virginia[47] with 4,500 users.

---

44 http://www.ncis.navy.mil/about.asp.

45 http://www.ncis.navy.mil/ncis/linx/technical.html.

46 Law Enforcement Information Exchange (LInX) Program Briefing, Naval Criminal Investigative Service, November 2007. http://www.mwcog.org/uploads/committee-documents/uFZWXls20071130151821.ppt.

47 http://www.hrlinx.com/.

- LInX Northwest consisting of more than 168 agencies across Washington State and Northern Oregon with 7,500 users.
- National Capital Region Law Enforcement Information Exchange (NCR-LInX) with 65 local, state, and federal member agencies from Virginia, Maryland, and the District of Columbia with projected users exceeding 5,000.[48]
- New Mexico comprised of 14 agencies, including numerous police departments, sheriff's offices, and the New Mexico Department of Public Safety.
- Southern California (San Diego/Los Angeles) with over 200 agencies.
- New London, Connecticut, North Carolina, and DoD LInX (planned).

OneDOJ, R-DEx, N-DEx

In 2005 the Department of Justice (DOJ) developed the OneDOJ information-sharing policy for electronically exchanging open- and closed-case investigation information with state, local, and other federal law enforcement partners. OneDOJ was uniformly implemented across the Bureau of Alcohol, Tobacco, Firearms, and Explosives (ATF), the Drug Enforcement Administration (DEA), the Federal Bureau of Investigation (FBI), the U.S. Marshals Service (USMS), and the Bureau of Prisons (BOP).[49] During the same time period, the FBI's R-DEx (Regional Data Exchange) program was coming online and was identified as the DOJ's single sharing repository for free-text case information and open interface standards for electronic data sharing.[50] R-DEx was initially targeted for deployment into approximately 15 high-priority metropolitan regions.

As part of the Law Enforcement Information Sharing Plan (LEISP), these two systems are now collectively referenced as OneDOJ where the information from the federal sources is combined with state and local law enforcement data to help facilitate information sharing and improve targeting of criminal activity within a defined region throughout the United States.[51] Overall, the goal is to provide all U.S. law enforcement agencies, from federal agencies down to the local police department, with a means

48 Mary Beth Sheridan, "System Lets Agencies in Area Share Data," *Washington Post*, November 29, 2007.

49 Vance Hitch, "OneDOJ: The Storefront for Federal Law Enforcement Information," *The Police Chief* 74(4): April 2007.

50 Department of Justice E-Government Status Report—FY 2005, http://www.usdoj.gov/jmd/ocio/egovactreport2005.pdf.

51 Vance Hitch, "OneDOJ: The Storefront for Federal Law Enforcement Information," *The Police Chief* 74(4): April 2007.

to access a common system containing case information, suspect profiles and rap sheets, investigative targets, and criminal records. The system was proven successful in 2005 when a system was implemented in Seattle (LInX) and then used in San Diego (ARJIS) and subsequently rolled out to St. Louis, Missouri, and Jacksonville, Florida. A total of 15 sites are targeted for deployment, with about 750 law enforcement agencies gaining access over the next several years.

Important to note, under OneDOJ all data remains under the control and management of the contributing agencies, providing a truly federated search across the data because it allows the agencies to decide what data to share, who to share it with, and under what circumstances it can be shared. At the end of 2006, OneDOJ was reported to have over 1 million case files, and includes investigative reports, criminal histories, offense reports, and the names, addresses, and other pertinent information of criminal suspects or targets.[52] Initial estimates predict the volume to triple within a few years. However, certain types of information will be excluded from the OneDOJ system, including data about public-corruption cases, classified or sensitive topics, confidential informants, administrative cases, and civil rights probes involving allegations of wrongdoing by police.

The National Data Exchange (N-DEx) is a more recent incarnation of a law enforcement sharing system that is designed to collect and correlate incident reports nationally—from federal, state, and local law enforcement agencies—albeit from many of the same sources in use by R-DEx. Instead of being regionally focused, the N-DEx project conceptually will be the national umbrella to tie all of these systems together. Additionally, those agencies who are participating in any regional/state system will be encouraged to participate in N-DEx. The system will contain structured data, plus some basic summary details,[53] and will be made available to law enforcement personnel through Law Enforcement Online (LEO). With over $85 million in funding, it is expected that more than 200,000 users from 15,000 state and local agencies will ultimately have access to N-DEx.[54]

According to the overview published on the FBI's Web site,[55] "N-DEx is a criminal justice information sharing system that will provide nationwide connectivity to disparate local, state, tribal, and federal systems for the exchange of information. N-DEx will provide law enforcement agencies with a powerful new investigative tool to search, link, analyze, and share information (for

---

[52] Dan Eggen, "Justice Dept. Database Stirs Privacy Fears: Size and Scope of the Interagency Investigative Tool Worry Civil Libertarians," *The Washington Post,* December 26, 2006.

[53] Mark Marshall, "Understanding the National Data Exchange (N-DEx) System," *PoliceOne.com,* July 30, 2007.

[54] Robert O'Harrow Jr. and Ellen Nakashima, "National Dragnet Is a Click Away: Authorities to Gain Fast and Expansive Access to Records," *The Washington Post,* March 6, 2008.

[55] http://www.fbi.gov/hq/cjisd/ndex/ndex_home.htm.

example, incident and case reports) on a national basis to a degree never before possible. N-DEx will primarily benefit local law enforcement in their role as the first line of defense against crime and terrorism." It further states that "N-DEx will allow participating agencies to detect relationships between people, places, things, and crime characteristics; to link information across jurisdictions; and to 'connect the dots' between apparently unrelated data without causing information overload. This capability will occur primarily in the realm of structured data, but can also include unstructured data. In addition, N-DEx will provide contact information and collaboration tools for law enforcement agencies that are working on cases of mutual interest."

The overall architecture defined for N-DEx is fairly comprehensive and provides a range of capabilities including data standardization, entity correlation, and entity resolution along with advanced search capabilities, visualizations (e.g., maps, link analysis, charts), alerts and notifications, collaboration, and analytical reporting. Thus, there is significant value added to the data to help organize, manage, and operate large volumes of data.

The N-DEx site goes on to say that "ownership of data shared through N-DEx will remain with the law enforcement agency that provided it. N-DEx will supply controls to allow law enforcement agencies to decide what data to share, who can access it, and under what circumstances. It will allow agencies to participate in accordance with applicable laws and policies governing dissemination and privacy."

Law Enforcement Online (LEO)

Law Enforcement Online (LEO) is an FBI-sanctioned system,[56] originally built in 1995, that is used primarily as an information-sharing and dissemination system for first responders, law enforcement communities, and antiterrorism and intelligence agencies. LEO is primarily a portal environment that supports access to a variety of Sensitive But Unclassified (SBU) data sources, communications, and support tools. According to sources,[57] "LEO members have access to a variety of services via LEO, including LEO Chat (an instant-messaging service), eLearning (for self-paced study), calendar services, e-mail, forums (a bulletin board service), special interest groups, and several crisis-management communication mechanisms." LEO also provides the National Alert Systems, a mechanism that is designed to issue bulk news alerts to pagers, cell phones, and other devices. It provides a virtual command center (VCC), a management tool for tracking, displaying, and disseminating intelligence and tactical

[56] http://www.leo.gov/.
[57] http://www.fbi.gov/hq/cjisd/leo.htm.

information, and acts as a gateway to other networks including RISS, INTELINK[58] (a secure network used by the intelligence community), and the Joint Automated Booking System (JABS).[59]

Joint Regional Information Exchange System (JRIES)

The Joint Regional Information Exchange System (JRIES)[60] was a pilot program, originally created in late 2002, to connect the Department of Defense and state/local law enforcement agencies to improve the sharing of counterterrorism information. Specifically, the Joint Intelligence Task Force for Combating Terrorism (JITF-CT), part of the Defense Intelligence Agency (DIA), reached out to include the California Department of Justice Anti-Terrorism Information Center (CATIC) and the New York Police Department Counterterrorism Bureau (NYPD-CTB).[61] In 2004, the Department of Homeland Security (DHS) set out to connect all U.S. territories, states, and major cities together and adopted the JRIES infrastructure. In 2005, DHS announced the expansion of JRIES as its primary communication, collaboration, situational awareness, and information-sharing system,[62] and renamed the JRIES system to the Homeland Security Information Network (HSIN) in order to reflect the system's broader scope. Its original scope was expanded beyond the law enforcement community and currently provides access to first responders, public safety officials, the National Guard, and private sector communities. Some concern has been raised about the HSIN duplicating efforts of other already established systems such as RISSNET and ATIX.[63]

Joint Terrorism Task Force (JTTF)

The FBI primarily conducts its counterterrorism investigations through its Joint Terrorism Task Force (JTTF) operations, which represent multiple

58 https://www.intelink.gov/.
59 http://www.usdoj.gov/oig/reports/OBD/a0522/exec.htm.
60 U.S. Department of Justice, Office of Justice Programs, The National Criminal Intelligence Sharing Plan, Washington, D.C., October 2003, pp. 45–56, http://it.ojp.gov/documents/National_Criminal_Intelligence_Sharing_Plan.pdf.
61 Harold Relyea and Jeffrey Seifert, "Information Sharing for Homeland Security: A Brief Overview," CRS Report for Congress, January 10, 2005. http://fas.org/sgp/crs/RL32597.pdf.
62 http://en.wikipedia.org/wiki/Joint_Regional_Information_Exchange_System.
63 David Powner, "Information Technology: Homeland Security Information Network Needs to Be Better Coordinated with Key State and Local Initiatives," Testimony before the Subcommittee on Intelligence, Information Sharing and Terrorism Risk Assessment, Committee on Homeland Security, House of Representatives, GAO-07-822T, May 10, 2007, http://www.gao.gov/new.items/d07822t.pdf.

agencies with membership from federal, state, and local groups. JTTFs are designed to act as a frontline defense for terrorist-related events by applying investigative resources to identify targets and suspects, conduct surveillance, monitor, and follow up on terrorist incidents.

The first JTTF was created in New York City in 1980 as a result of the increased terrorist threats and bombings that occurred at banks, missions, and businesses throughout the city by organizations such as FALN, Omega 7, and several others.[64] As of September 2007, there were 101 JTTF locations, including one in each of the FBI's 56 field offices.[65] A JTTF can be comprise of any number of different federal and state/local agencies, including sheriff's departments, city police, county police, state police, university police, and airport police, and some even include beverage control boards and district attorney's offices. For example, the Portland FBI JTTF[66] includes the following representatives:

Portland Police Bureau	Beaverton Police Department
Vancouver Police Department	Oregon State Police
Port of Portland Police	Washington County Sheriff's Office
Bureau of Alcohol, Tobacco and Firearms	Drug Enforcement Administration
Internal Revenue Service	U.S. Department of Agriculture
Defense Criminal Investigative Service	Immigration and Customs Enforcement
U.S. Secret Service	U.S. Coast Guard
Federal Protective Service	Federal Air Marshals Service
Bureau of Land Management	U.S. Attorney's Office

The JTTFs may also participate whenever there are large public activities, such as sporting events including Super Bowls, World Series, and Olympic games; political rallies and demonstrations like the International Monetary Fund-World Bank conferences as well as the Republican and Democratic National Conventions; and other events including New Year's and Fourth of July celebrations, high-profile concerts, or other large-volume gatherings.

Furthermore, the National Joint Terrorism Task Force (NJTTF)[67] was established in 2002, originally located at FBI Headquarters in the

[64] Mary Jo White, "Prosecuting Terrorism in New York," *Middle East Quarterly,* Spring 2001, http://www.meforum.org/article/25.

[65] http://www.fbi.gov/contact/fo/fo.htm.

[66] http://portland.fbi.gov/jttf/jttfqa.htm.

[67] Congressional Testimony for John Pistole, National Commission on Terrorist Attacks upon the United States, April 14, 2004, http://www.fbi.gov/congress/congress04/pistole041404.htm. Also see http://www.proconservative.net/PCVol6Is100PistoleFBITerrorism.shtml.

Strategic Information and Operations Center (SIOC),[68] and is now part of the National Counterterrorism Center (NCTC) in Northern Virginia.[69] The NJTTF was created with the intent to have representation from every federal law enforcement and intelligence agency housed at a single location.[70] The role of the NJTTF[71] is to oversee, liaise, communicate, and coordinate with the local JTTFs to help "fuse" the leads, threats, and information received about ongoing terrorist activities.[72] Currently, there are more than 40 government agencies associated with the NJTTF including those listed in Table 9.1.

Table 9.1 List of NJTTF Associated Agencies

Bureau of Alcohol, Tobacco and Firearms	Bureau of Customs and Border Protection
Immigration and Customs Enforcement	Coast Guard Investigative Service
Defense HUMINT Services	Defense Intelligence Agency
Defense Criminal Investigative Service	Defense Threat Reduction Agency
Department of Energy	Department of Health and Human Services
Department of Homeland Security	Department of Interior
Department of State	Department of Transportation
Drug Enforcement Administration	Environmental Protection Agency
Federal Bureau of Investigation	Federal Bureau of Prisons
Federal Protective Service	Internal Revenue Service
New York Police Department	Naval Criminal Investigative Service
NORAD/NORTHCOM	Nuclear Regulatory Commission
Office of Personnel Management	Railroad Police Department
Transportation Security Administration	Treasury IG for Tax Administration
U.S. Air Force Office of Special Investigations	U.S. Army Criminal Investigative Division
U.S. Army Military Intelligence	U.S. Capitol Police
U.S. Coast Guard	U.S. Department of Agriculture
U.S. Food and Drug Administration	U.S. Marshals Service
U.S. Postal Inspection Service	U.S. Secret Service
U.S. Special Operations Command (SOCOM)	Washington Metropolitan Police Department

68 Strategic Information and Operations Center (SIOC) Fact Sheet: http://www.fbi.gov/hq/siocfs.htm.

69 http://eyeball-series.org/nctc/nctc-birdseye.htm.

70 James Casey, "Managing Joint Terrorism Task Force Resources," Washington, D.C. (November 2004), http://www.fbi.gov/filelink.html?file=/publications/leb/2004/nov04leb.pdf.

71 http://www.fbi.gov/page2/july04/njttf070204.htm.

72 The Department of Justice's Terrorism Task Forces: Evaluation and Inspections Report I-2005-007, Office of the Inspector General, June 2005, http://www.usdoj.gov/oig/reports/plus/e0507/background.htm.

State-Level Fusion Centers

According to the National Information Sharing Environment Implementation Plan,[73] under Action 1.24 DOJ and DHS will work with state governors and other officials (state/local) to "designate a single fusion center to serve as the statewide or regional hub to interface with the federal government and through which to coordinate the gathering, processing, analysis and dissemination of terrorism, law enforcement and homeland security information in an all-crimes approach."

What exactly is a fusion center? According to Office of Justice Programs (OJP),[74] a fusion center is "a collaborative effort of two or more agencies that provide resources, expertise, and information to the center with the goal of maximizing their ability to detect, prevent, investigate, and respond to criminal and terrorist activity." This is a fairly broad statement and is subject to a lot of interpretation. In fact, even though the fusion center guidelines published by OJB define a number of helpful strategies, plans, and procedures for structuring and operating a fusion center, their ultimate implementation is left to the oversight of the individual agencies. Thus, each fusion center is unique and operates according to their specific needs and their scope of operations, which may range from investigating gangs and organized crime to drug trafficking and terrorist events.

The fusion centers run the gamut from basic to elaborate. Some are a bullpen of cubicles, while others support high-tech command centers. Some centers receive only state funds, while others receive federal grants. Some get only minimal funding, whereas others receive millions. Some work alongside federal personnel, while others are entirely staffed by state employees. Some centers focus on counterterrorism, whereas the majority deal with all crimes and all hazards. There is no single blueprint used for establishing a state-level fusion center; they are all tailored to meet the needs of the areas and the requirements of the constituencies they are built to serve.

On September 14, 2006, the DHS reported that 38 state fusion centers were supported by $380 million of initial funding and additional money also provided by sources, such as OJP grants,[75] state budgets,

---

[73] National Information Sharing Environment Implementation Plan, Office of the Director of National Intelligence, Washington D.C. (November 2006), http://www.ise.gov/docs/reports/iseimpplan-200611.pdf.

[74] Fusion Center Guidelines: Developing and Sharing Information and Intelligence in a New Era. Guidelines for Establishing and Operating Fusion Centers at the Local, State, and Federal Levels. Bureau of Justice Assistance (BJA), Office of Justice Programs (OJP), U.S. Department of Justice, August 2006, http://it.ojp.gov/documents/fusion_center_guidelines.pdf.

[75] Fusion Centers: DHS Funded Activities, Fiscal Years 2004–2006. Office of Grants and Training, Preparedness Directorate, U.S. Department of Homeland Security, April 2007, http://www.ojp.usdoj.gov/odp/docs/NPB_Fusion_Centers.pdf.

and other programs. Initial estimates placed the total number of fusion centers expected to be created at 70. In October 2007, GAO delivered a report[76] describing 58 fusion centers and provided an overview of their missions, structures, and staffing. There is even a National Fusion Center Coordination Group (NFCCG), which is designed to provide oversight, resources, and support to the fusion centers to help sustain their infrastructure, and presumably become a means of fusing the fusion centers.

Table 9.2 presents a number of the counterterrorism and fusion centers[77] operating in the United States at the time of this writing. This can only be considered a partial list[78] because the pace of change is rapid and new facilities are being established, new laws are being enacted, and new funding sources are being made available to help promote these centers.

Table 9.2 State-Level Fusion Centers in the United States

Alabama	Alabama Information Fusion Center
	Criminal Information Center (Alabama Bureau of Investigations)
Alaska	Alaska Emergency Coordination Center
Alaska	Statewide Law Enforcement Information Center
Arizona	Arizona Counter Terrorism Information Center (ACTIC)
Arkansas	Arkansas Fusion Center
California	State Terror Threat Assessment Center (STTAC)
	Los Angeles, Joint Regional Intelligence Center (JRIC)
	Sacramento, Regional Terrorist Threat Assessment Center (RTTAC)
	San Diego Regional Terrorism Threat Assessment Center
	San Francisco Regional Terrorism Threat Assessment Center
Colorado	Colorado Information Analysis Center (CIAC)
Connecticut	Connecticut Intelligence Center (CTIC)
Delaware	Delaware Information Analysis Center (DIAC)
District of Columbia	Metropolitan Joint Analytical Center (WAJAC)
	Synchronized Operations Command Complex (SOCC)
	Washington D.C. Metropolitan Fusion Center
Florida	Counter Terrorism Intelligence Center (CTIC)
	Central Florida Intelligence Exchange (CFIX)
	Florida Fusion Center / Florida (FISC)
Georgia	Georgia Information Sharing and Analysis Center (GISAC)
Hawaii	Pacific Regional Information Clearing House (PAC Clear)
Idaho	Use of JTTF and U.S. Attorney's Office (District of Idaho)

(*continued*)

[76] Homeland Security, Federal Efforts Are Helping to Alleviate Some Challenges Encountered by State and Local Information Fusion Centers, October 2007, GAO-08-35, http://www.gao.gov/new.items/d0835.pdf.

[77] http://www.fas.org/irp/agency/ise/state.pdf.

[78] http://www.gao.gov/new.items/d0835.pdf (Appendix II: Operational Fusion Centers).

Table 9.2 *(continued)*

Illinois	Statewide Terrorism & Intelligence Center (STIC)
	Chicago – Crime Prevention and Information Center (CPIC)
Indiana	Indiana Intelligence Fusion Center (IIFC)
Iowa	Iowa Fusion Center
Kansas	Kansas Threat Integration Center (KSTIC)
Kentucky	Kentucky Intelligence Fusion Center (KIFC)
Louisiana	Louisiana State Analysis and Fusion Exchange (La-SAFE)
Maine	Maine Intelligence and Analysis Center (MIAC)
Maryland	Maryland Coordination and Analysis Center (MCAC)
Massachusetts	Massachusetts Commonwealth Fusion Center (CFC)
	Boston Regional Intelligence Center
Michigan	Michigan Intelligence and Operations Center (MIOC)
	Detroit and Southeastern Michigan Information and Intelligence Center (DSEMIIC)
Minnesota	Minnesota Joint Analytical Center (MN-JAC)
Mississippi	Mississippi Analysis & Information Center (MSAIC)
Missouri	Missouri Information Analysis Center (MIAC)
	Kansas City Terrorism Early Warning (TEW)
	St. Louis Terrorism Early Warning Group (TEWG)
Montana	Montana All-Threat Intelligence Center (MATIC)
Nebraska	Nebraska Fusion Center
Nevada	Nevada Analytical Information Center
	Southern Nevada Counter Terrorism Center (LV)
New Hampshire	New Hampshire Intelligence Fusion Center
New Jersey	Regional Operations Intelligence Center (ROIC)
New Mexico	New Mexico All Source Intelligence Center (NMASIC)
New York	Upstate New York Regional Intelligence Center (UNYRIC)
	New York State Intelligence Center (NYSIC)
	New York Police Department (NYPD) Intelligence Division
	Real Time Crime Center (RTCC)
	New York State Intelligence Center (NYSIC)
	New York City UASI Fusion Center
	Rockland County Intelligence Center(RCIC)
	Suffolk County Intelligence Center
	Westchester County Crime Analysis Unit
North Carolina	North Carolina Information Sharing and Analysis Center (ISAAC)
	Charlotte Regional Information Analysis Center
North Dakota	North Dakota Fusion Center
Ohio	Strategic Analysis and Information Center (SAIC)
	Northeast Ohio Terrorism Early Warning Group

Table 9.2 (*continued*)

	Central Oho Terrorism Early Warning Group
	Cincinnati/Hamilton County Regional Terrorism Early Warning Grp
Oklahoma	Oklahoma Information Fusion Center
Oregon	Terrorism Intelligence and Threat Assessment Network (TITAN)
Pennsylvania	Pennsylvania Criminal Intelligence Center (PaCIC)
	Pittsburgh Terrorism Early Warning Group
Rhode Island	Rhode Island Fusion Center
South Carolina	South Carolina Information Exchange (SCIEx)
South Dakota	South Dakota Fusion Center
Tennessee	Tennessee Regional Information Center (TRIC)
Texas	Texas Department of Public Safety – Intelligence Center
	North Texas Fusion Center (NTFC)
	El Paso Intelligence Center (EPIC)
	Houston Regional Intelligence Service Fusion Center (HRISC)
Utah	Utah Criminal Intelligence Center
Vermont	Vermont Fusion Center
Virginia	Virginia Fusion Center
Washington	Washington Joint Analytical Center (WAJAC)
West Virginia	West Virginia Joint Intelligence Fusion Center
Wisconsin	Southeastern Wisconsin Terrorism Alert Center (STAC)
	Wisconsin Statewide Intelligence Center (WSIC)
Wyoming	Use of JTTF and partnership with Colorado's CIAC

Other programs, fusion centers, and systems include the Navy's Multiple Threat Alert Center (MTAC), the Organized Crime Drug Enforcement Task Force (OCDETF) Fusion Center, the National Drug Intelligence Center (NDIC), and the National Gang Intelligence Center. There are a number of others that exist within the industry and government spaces and new ones are constantly forming.

The following discussions provide more detail on a few other programs including the HIDTA, HIFCA, and RISS.

High Intensity Drug Trafficking Area (HIDTA)

The High Intensity Drug Trafficking Area (HIDTA)[79] program was established as part of the Anti-Drug Abuse Act of 1988 and is managed through the Office of National Drug Control Policy (ONDCP). With approximately

[79] http://www.whitehousedrugpolicy.gov/HIDTA.

$220 million of the nearly $13 billion worth of funding[80] allocated in the 2008 federal drug control budget, the HIDTA program is designed to deal with regions and areas that demonstrate serious drug trafficking and drug usage problems that require additional federal resources to help control, reduce, or eliminate the problem. Figure 9.1 shows the current locations of the 32 (28 sites plus 4 on the Southwest Border) HIDTA agencies[81] located throughout the United States followed by the list of the individual agencies (Table 9.3) and their coverage areas.

The areas where HIDTAs operate are set up in response to drug hotspots for the region, and many times do not represent contiguous areas. For example, the two states shown in Figure 9.2 represent Georgia and Louisiana, which correspond to the Atlanta HIDTA and the Gulf Coast HIDTA, respectively. For the Atlanta HIDTA,[82] the coverage area is quite concentrated around a small locale (e.g., the Atlanta metropolitan area), whereas the Gulf Coast HIDTA,[83] which covers a total of three states, shows quite a large diversion of interest across Louisiana where some of its resources are deployed. The dot indicates the location of the HIDTA headquarters.

By design, HIDTAs are independently operated, each has its own budget, and each is governed by an executive board with eight federal members and eight state/local members that regulate how the HIDTA responds to the specific problems encountered in their operating regions. Some HIDTAs are more focused on training, treatment, or prevention programs, while others put more emphasis on enforcement and interdiction activities. However, there is a clear requirement for HIDTAs to promote information sharing as stated in the Office of National Drug Control Policy Reauthorization Act of 2006 (P.L. 109-469), Section 707 [of the Office of National Drug Control Policy Reauthorization Act of 1998 (Public Law 105-277; 21 U.S.C. 1701 et seq.)].[84] Specifically, clause (2) states the following:

> PURPOSE—The purpose of the Program is to reduce drug trafficking and drug production in the United States by (1) facilitating cooperation among Federal, State, local, and tribal law enforcement agencies to share information and implement coordinated enforcement activities; (2) enhancing law enforcement intelligence sharing among Federal, State, local, and tribal law enforcement agencies; (3) providing reliable law enforcement intelligence to law enforcement agencies needed to design effective enforcement strategies and operations; and (4) sup-

[80] http://www.whitehouse.gov/omb/budget/fy2008/.
[81] Image available at http://www.whitehousedrugpolicy.gov/images/hidtamap.gif.
[82] http://www.whitehousedrugpolicy.gov/HIDTA/ga.html.
[83] http://www.whitehousedrugpolicy.gov/HIDTA/la.html.
[84] http://www.whitehousedrugpolicy.gov/HIDTA/statute.html.

porting coordinated law enforcement strategies which maximize use of available resources to reduce the supply of illegal drugs in designated areas and in the United States as a whole.

Additionally, it also states the following under subpart (n):

Coordination of Law Enforcement Intelligence Sharing With Organized Crime Drug Enforcement Task Force Program – The Director, in consultation with the Attorney General, shall ensure that any drug enforcement intelligence obtained by the Intelligence Support Center for each high intensity drug trafficking area is shared, on a timely basis, with the drug intelligence fusion center operated by the Organized Crime Drug Enforcement Task Force of the Department of Justice.

HIDTAs have been a key player in a number of information-sharing initiatives, and because they are focused on local problems and issues they add a considerable amount of value by supporting investigations, providing analytical support, creating regional threat assessments, supporting target deconflictions, and assisting law enforcement through their intelligence systems. HIDTAs also work closely with the DEA, RISS, and a number of other federal and state agencies.

High Intensity Financial Crime Area (HIFCA)

Very similar in concept to the HIDTA program, the HIFCAs are designed to target areas or sectors where there are high risks of money laundering and related financial crimes. Originally created[85] in 1999, by statute of the Money Laundering and Financial Crimes Strategy Act of 1998, HIFCAs were designed to help concentrate law enforcement resources on areas that were "being victimized by, or particularly vulnerable to, money laundering and related financial crime."[86] HIFCAs are composed of all relevant federal, state, and local enforcement authorities; prosecutors; and federal financial supervisory agencies,[87] and they work closely with HIDTAs as well as OCDETF. The current list of seven HIFCAs is shown in Table 9.4.

It should be noted that a HIFCA does not have to be defined solely on geography. There are a number of factors[88] that go into considering the

[85] The Money Laundering and Financial Crimes Strategy Act of 1998, P.L. 105-310 (October 30, 1998) calls for the designation of certain areas as high-risk where money laundering and financial crimes are widespread and present a threat to the stability of financial and economic systems, pursuant to section 5341(b) of the Act. See 31 U.S. Code 5341(b) and 5342(b).

[86] http://www.treas.gov/press/releases/reports/money.pdf.

[87] http://www.irs.gov/compliance/enforcement/article/0,,id=107510,00.html.

[88] http://www.fincen.gov/le_hifcadesign.html.

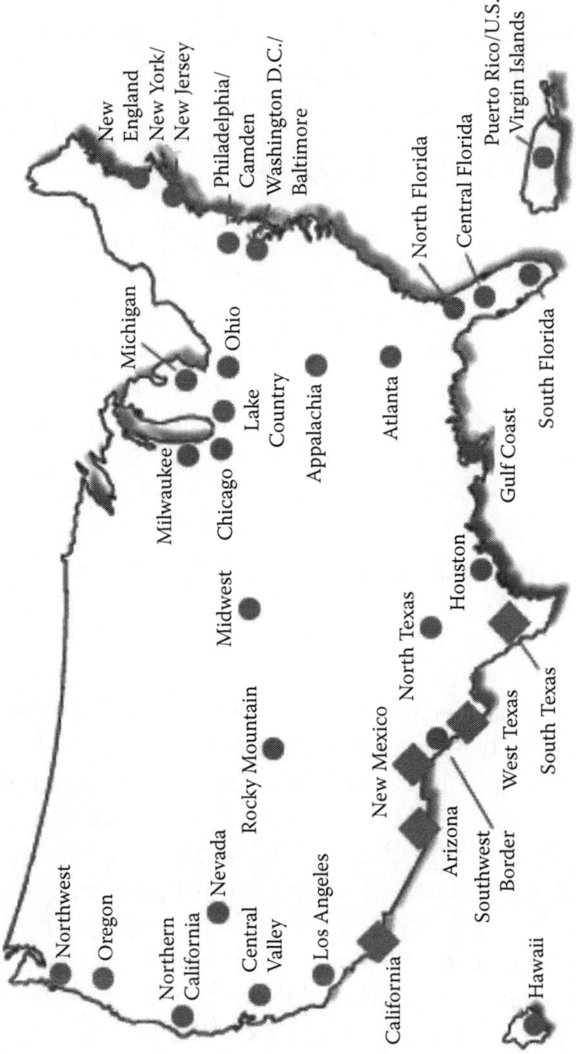

Figure 9.1 HIDTA locations in the United States.

Table 9.3 HIDTA Agencies and Their Designated Coverage Area

HIDTA Agency	*Coverage Area (State/County)*
Appalachia	**Kentucky:** Adair, Bell, Breathitt, Clay, Clinton, Cumberland, Floyd, Harlan, Jackson, Knott, Knox, Laurel, Lee, Leslie, McCreary, Magoffin, Marion, Monroe, Owsley, Perry, Pike, Pulaski, Rockcastle, Taylor, Warren, Wayne, and Whitley counties. **Tennessee:** Bledsoe, Campbell, Claiborne, Clay, Cocke, Cumberland, Fentress, Franklin, Grainger, Greene, Grundy, Hamblen, Hancock, Hawkins, Jackson, Jefferson, Knox, Macon, Marion, Overton, Pickett, Putnam, Rhea, Scott, Sequatchie, Sevier, Unicoi, Van Buren, and White counties. **West Virginia:** Boone, Braxton, Cabell, Gilmer, Kanawha, Lewis, Lincoln, Logan, Mason, McDowell, Mingo, and Wayne counties.
Atlanta	**Georgia:** City of Atlanta, Cobb, Gwinnett, Fulton and DeKalb counties, Atlanta Hartsfield-Jackson International Airport.
Central Florida	**Florida:** Pinellas, Hillsborough, Polk, Osceola, Orange, Seminole, and Volusia counties.
Central Valley	**California:** Fresno, Kern, Kings, Madera, Merced, Sacramento, San Joaquin, Stanislaus, and Tulare counties.
Chicago	**Illinois:** Cook, Grundy, Kendall and Will counties.
Gulf Coast	**Alabama:** Baldwin, Jefferson, Madison, Mobile, Montgomery and Morgan counties. **Louisiana:** Bossier, Caddo, Calcasieu, East Baton Rouge, Jefferson, Lafayette, Orleans and Ouachita Parishes. **Mississippi:** Hancock, Harrison, Hinds, Jackson, Lafayette, Madison and Rankin counties.
Hawaii	**Honolulu,** Maui, Kauai, and Hawaii counties.
Houston	**Texas:** Aransas, Brooks, Fort Bend, Galveston, Hardin, Harris, Jefferson, Jim Wells, Kenedy, Kleberg, Liberty, Nueces, Orange, Refugio, San Patricio and Victoria counties.
Lake County	**Indiana:** Lake County (Northwest Indiana).
Los Angeles	**California:** Los Angeles, Orange, Riverside, and San Bernardino counties.
Michigan	**Michigan:** Wayne, Macomb, Oakland, Washtenaw, Genesee, Kent, Kalamazoo, Allegan and Van Buren counties.
Milwaukee	**Wisconsin:** Milwaukee, Racine, Kenosha, and Waukesha counties.
Nevada	**Nevada:** Clark and Washoe counties.
New England	**Massachusetts:** Suffolk, Essex, Worcester, Plymouth, Hampden, and Middlesex counties. **Connecticut:** Fairfield, Hartford and New Haven counties. **Rhode Island:** Providence County. **Vermont**: Chittenden County. **Maine:** Cumberland County. **New Hampshire:** Hillsborough County.
New York/New Jersey	**New York:** New York City and Albany, Erie, Monroe, Nassau, Onondaga, Suffolk, and Westchester counties. **New Jersey:** Bergen, Essex, Hudson, Passaic, and Union counties.

(continued)

Table 9.3 (*continued*)

HIDTA Agency	*Coverage Area (State/County)*
North Florida	**Florida:** Alachua, Baker, Clay, Columbia, Duval, Flagler, Marion, Nassau, Putnam, and St. Johns counties.
North Texas	**Texas:** Collin, Dallas, Denton, Ellis, Henderson, Hood, Hunt, Johnson, Kaufman, Lubbock, Navarro, Parker, Rockwall, Smith, and Tarrant counties. **Oklahoma**: Cleveland, Comanche, Muskogee, Sequoyah, Oklahoma, and Tulsa counties.
Northern California	**California:** Alameda, Contra Costa, Lake, Marin, Monterey, San Francisco, San Mateo, Santa Clara, Santa Cruz, and Sonoma counties.
Northwest	**Washington:** Benton, Clark, Cowlitz, Franklin, King, Kitsap, Lewis, Pierce, Skagit, Snohomish, Spokane, Thurston, Whatcom, and Yakima counties.
Ohio	**Ohio:** Cuyahoga, Fairfield, Franklin, Greene, Hamilton, Lucas, Mahoning, Montgomery, Stark, Summit, and Warren counties.
Oregon	**Oregon:** Clackamas, Deschutes, Douglas, Jackson, Marion, Multnomah, Umatilla, and Washington counties.
Philadelphia/ Camden	**Pennsylvania:** Philadelphia county. **New Jersey:** City of Camden New Jersey within Camden County.
Puerto Rico/ U.S. Virgin Islands	**Puerto Rico:** the Islands of Puerto Rico, Vieques, and Culebra. **U.S. Virgin Islands:** the Islands of Saint Thomas, Saint Croix, and Saint John.
Rocky Mountain	**Colorado:** Adams, Arapahoe, Boulder, Denver, Douglas, Eagle, El Paso, Garfield, Grand, Jefferson, LaPlata, Larimer, Mesa, Moffatt, Pueblo, Routt, and Weld counties. **Montana:** Cascade, Flathead, Lewis and Clark, Missoula, and Yellowstone counties. **Utah:** Davis, Salt Lake, Summit, Utah, Washington, and Weber counties. **Wyoming:** Albany, Campbell, Laramie, Natrona, Sweetwater, and Uinta counties.
South Florida	**Florida:** Broward, Miami-Dade, Monroe, and Palm Beach counties.
SWB Arizona	**Arizona:** Yuma, Maricopa, Pinal, Pima, Santa Cruz, Cochise, and Mohave counties.
SWB California	**California:** San Diego and Imperial counties.
SWB New Mexico	**New Mexico:** Bernalillo, Hidalgo, Grant, Luna, Dona Ana, Eddy, Lea, Otero, Chaves, Lincoln, San Juan, Rio Arriba, and Santa Fe counties.
SWB South Texas	**Texas:** El Paso, Hudspeth, Culberson, Jeff Davis, Presidio, Brewster, Pecos, Terrell, and Reeves counties.
SWB West Texas	**Texas:** Bexar, Val Verde, Kinney, Maverick, Zavala, Dimmit, La Salle, Webb, Zapata, Jim Hogg, Starr, Hidalgo, Willacy, and Cameron counties and all the municipalities therein.
Washington/ Baltimore	**Maryland:** Baltimore City and Baltimore, Anne Arundel, Howard, Montgomery, Prince George's, and Charles counties. **Washington, D.C. Virginia:** City of Alexandria, Arlington, Chesterfield, Fairfax, Hanover, Henrico, Loudoun, Prince George (Richmond Area), and Prince William counties.

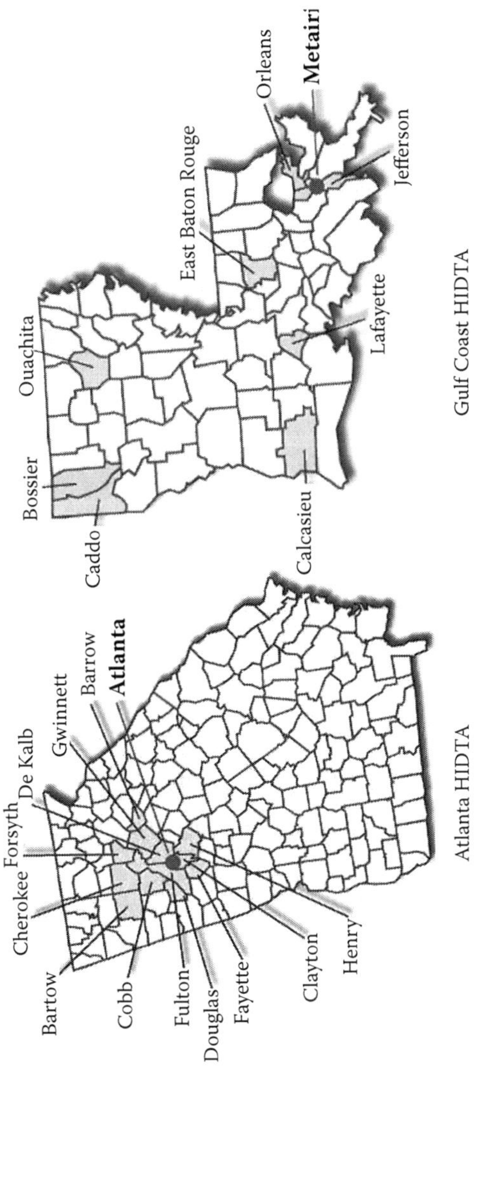

Figure 9.2 Coverage areas for select HIDTAs.

Table 9.4 HIFCA Agencies and Their Designated Coverage

HIFCA	*Coverage Area (State/County)*
California Northern District	Monterey, Humboldt, Mendocino, Lake, Sonoma, Napa, Marin, Contra Costa, San Francisco, San Mateo, Alameda, Santa Cruz, San Benito, Monterey, Del Norte
California Southern District	Los Angeles, Orange, Riverside, San Bernardino, San Luis Obispo, Santa Barbara, Ventura
Southwest Border	**Arizona:** All 15 counties. **Texas:** counties bordering, and adjacent to those bordering, the U.S. and Mexico boundary (30 counties).
Chicago	Cook, McHenry, Dupage, Lake, Will, Kane
New York	**New York** – all 62 counties. **New Jersey** – all 21 counties
Puerto Rico	**Puerto Rico** – all areas. **U.S. Virgin Islands** – all areas
South Florida	Broward, Miami-Dade, Indian River, Martin, Monroe, Okeechobee, Palm Beach, and St. Lucie

designation of a HIFCA and the statutes allow for HIFCAs to be created to address problems related to specific sectors or industries should the need arise based on relevant economic data, patterns of BSA filings, and other descriptive information identifying trends and patterns. For example, a HIFCA could technically be created for investigating cross-border wire transfers, foreign-owned bank accounts, or any class of financial institutions (e.g., Internet banks). Recently, there has also been a lot of consideration given to the Black Market Peso Exchange (BMPE),[89] correspondent accounts, and charitable organizations that are fronting terrorist-financing operations.

One of the more active HIFCAs is based in New York, which is colocated with the HIDTA and is a short distance away from the New York Immigration and Customs Enforcement (ICE) SAC offices. What is unique about this HIFCA is that it represents the intelligence component of the El Dorado Task Force (EDTF), which was established in 1992 as a joint, multiagency (originally 13 agencies) approach to targeting money-laundering operations and financial-crime activities within

[89] Black Market Peso Exchange is heavily used in South America to swap dollars owned in the United States for pesos owned in, say, Colombia. The scheme works purely as an accounting protocol and no money actually leaves the country; only changes in the ledgers are made to credit or debit the accounts based on the needs and purchases in-country.

the New York/New Jersey metropolitan region. The EDTF currently supports over 220 members from more than 40 different law enforcement agencies representing federal, state, and local jurisdictions. Since its inception, it has seized more than $600 million in illegal proceeds and is credited with over 2,200 arrests.

The EDTF helped pioneer some of the initial geographical targeting orders (GTOs) for financial transactions that helped to significantly reduce the flow of drug proceeds using wire-transmitter operations in the New York/New Jersey region. There have been a number of successful operations conducted by the EDTF including the following:

- ***Operation Meltdown***: Task force agents shut down large-scale narcotics and money-laundering operation targeting the New York City jewelry industry in which criminals smuggled gold, disguised as common household goods, to Colombia.
- ***Operation Wire Drill***: This operation required customers wiring money to Colombia to fill out a special remittance form and present identification for any transactions in excess of $750 (identification is mandatory for amounts over $3,000), which virtually blocked the flow of drug money through and forced them to use less established and less secure methods to move their illegal proceeds.[90]
- ***Operation Wirecutter***: This investigation led to the arrest of 42 targets and the seizure of more than $8.2 million. It also led to the first-ever extraditions from Colombia to the United States for money laundering.
- ***Norte Valle Cartel***: El Dorado agents crippled a major New York cocaine supply ring by targeting the money remitters who were sending proceeds of drug sales to Colombia. This investigation led to the indictment and extradition of the hierarchy of the cartel, allegedly responsible for smuggling 1.2 million pounds of cocaine worth over $10 billion into the United States.

The EDTF remains very active, creative, and aggressive in their approach to identifying, detecting, and seizing assets associated with financial crimes and money-laundering operations. One inherent strength of the EDTF is being co-located in one of the world's financial capitals because they are continually working with bank representatives, financial institutions, and other regulators to educate and involve them in the most current issues, approaches, and concerns facing the community.

[90] http://www.ncjrs.gov/ondcppubs/publications/enforce/hidta2001/ny-nj-fs.html.

Regional Information Sharing System (RISS)

The RISS program was established in 1974 to help assist state and local law enforcement agencies address cross-jurisdictional criminal activity and is administered by the Bureau of Justice Assistance (BJA) of the DOJ. The RISS program provides a number of value-added capabilities for the regions they serve, including a wide range of training, technical assistance, analytical support (e.g., telephone toll analysis, computer forensics, financial analysis), information sharing, and the loaning of specialized investigative equipment (e.g., photographic, communications, surveillance).

Typically, RISS centers focus on violent crime, gang activity, and narcotics trafficking, and also help to support terrorist investigations. The RISS program supports over 7,700 law enforcement and criminal justice organizations representing more than 75,000 officers[91] from their six regional centers: MOCIC, MAGLOCLEN, NESPION, ROCIC, RMIN, and WSIN. Each covers specific areas as defined below and in Figure 9.3. Each RISS center is governed by a police board or executive committee made up of members from the region it directly serves.

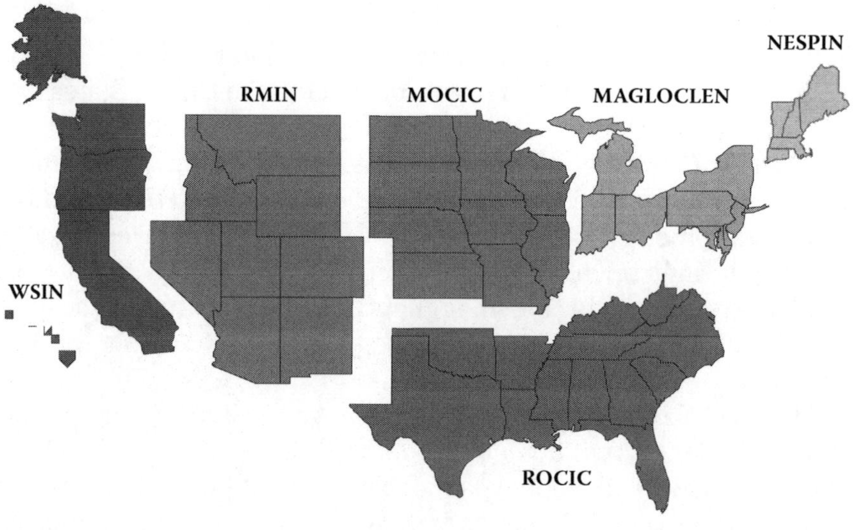

Figure 9.3 RISS centers coverage areas.

[91] Donald Kennedy (NESPIN), Testimony Regarding a Hearing on "Homeland Security Information Network: Moving Past the Missteps Toward Better Information Sharing," Committee on Homeland Security, Subcommittee on Intelligence, "Information Sharing, and Terrorism Risk Assessment," U.S. House of Representatives. May 10, 2007.

1. Mid-States Organized Crime Information Center (MOCIC) supports Illinois, Iowa, Kansas, Minnesota, Missouri, Nebraska, North Dakota, South Dakota, and Wisconsin, plus the bordering Canadian provinces.
2. Middle Atlantic–Great Lakes Organized Crime Law Enforcement Network (MAGLOCLEN) supports Delaware, Indiana, Maryland, Michigan, New Jersey, New York, Ohio, and Pennsylvania, plus the District of Columbia and the bordering Canadian provinces.
3. New England State Police Information Network (NESPIN) supports Connecticut, Maine, Massachusetts, New Hampshire, Rhode Island, and Vermont, plus the bordering Canadian provinces.
4. Regional Organized Crime Information Center (ROCIC) supports Alabama, Arkansas, Florida, Georgia, Kentucky, Louisiana, Mississippi, North Carolina, Oklahoma, South Carolina, Tennessee, Texas, Virginia, and West Virginia, plus Puerto Rico.
5. Rocky Mountain Information Network (RMIN) supports Arizona, Colorado, Idaho, Montana, Nevada, New Mexico, Utah, and Wyoming, plus the bordering Canadian provinces.
6. Western States Information Network (WSIN) supports Alaska, California, Hawaii, Oregon, and Washington, plus Guam and the bordering Canadian provinces.

RISS also supports information sharing through RISSNET, a secure, Web-based, national network, created in 1997 for use by their member organizations. RISSNET provides the communications infrastructure for sharing sensitive and unclassified data and access to a variety of law enforcement data resources. RISSNET is also expanding to become a more mainstream portal for law enforcement to access all resources through a single interface. Additionally, RISS created the Automated Trusted Information Exchange (ATIX)[92] for first responders and public safety personnel (e.g., firefighters, school officials, public utilities, and law enforcement) to share information in a secure, real-time environment.

Conclusion

The systems presented reflect only a small number of the information-sharing capabilities currently in operation around the United States.

[92] Through ATIX, users access the RISS ATIX Web pages and libraries, an ATIX bulletin board, ATIXLive, and secure e-mail.

These discussions did not even overview any foreign systems, protocols, or agencies charted with integrating and sharing data (e.g., SOCA, Europol, SitCen, etc.). Every country has similar issues and concerns and many are working on practical ways to incorporate and share the data they collect.

There has been tremendous progress made over the past several years; however, there is still much room for improvement in terms of standardizations and the quality of the information collected. Imagine being able to access thousands of sources of data in a single query. In an ideal world, the results would provide a complete and accurate accounting for all known details for a target entity. In reality, there is either too much data, due to overgeneralizations for fear of missing a vital piece of data, or too little information due to the inherent inconsistencies, errors, and incompleteness found in most datasets. Ultimately, it comes down to how efficiently and accurately the data can be analyzed to spot patterns, trends, and relationships.

Additionally, as more technologies sectors mature (e.g., text mining, language translation, fuzzy matching, inductive reasoning, etc.), the overall capabilities associated with the intelligence community will vastly improve as will the levels of expectation for delivering better and more accurate analytics. These improvements will be largely based on having a more complete understanding of how to access, interpret, analyze, and report on the data.

A majority of this book was intentionally spent presenting and highlighting different analytical methodologies across a number of domains. It can't be overemphasized how important it is to fully understand the nature of the data, how it was collected, how it is stored, and what can be done with it from an analytical perspective. Having one or a dozen sources of data is inconsequential if the fundamentals of the analysis are flawed. Therefore, more time, effort, and resources need to be invested into creating and supporting better analytical infrastructures. It is a difficult challenge, certainly one of the biggest obstacles that must be addressed, but one that can be overcome with adequate training, updated collection methods, and more consistency in the overall operations of our intelligence and law enforcement agencies.

Analysis is an iterative process that is extremely dependent on data. The higher the quality and consistency of the data, the more likely the analysis will provide tangible results. There are no right answers; there are no wrong answers; only subjective interpretations of the data within a particular context or domain.

Summary

Data mining for intelligence, fraud, and criminal detection requires analysts and investigators to be well versed in a number of technical disciplines (databases, visualizations, etc.) to discover patterns and make effective use of their data. Furthermore, they are dealing with some very complicated and dynamic domains without well-quantified parameters, quantitative examples, or any type of routine or common definitions. Unfortunately, there is no *Easy Button*[1] that automatically discovers patterns of interest. We must continually ask ourselves:

- What does a terrorist look like?
- What does a money launderer look like?
- What does a criminal look like?
- What does a fraudster look like?

Over the past several years, the phrase "connect the dots" has become part of the vernacular within the law enforcement and the intelligence communities. It logically makes sense to find networks of related entities, especially those involved in questionable activities. Keep in mind that seemingly simple networks can often convey very complex meanings. To be effective is to know which dots to connect and how to interpret their results.

Conceptually, there are no real differences in the structure and analysis of data associated with, for example, a border crossing, a financial transaction, a phone call, an insurance claim, or even a terrorist event.

[1] "That was Easy" Staples® (http://www.staples.com).

They all represent transactional (event-based) data and have some type of common element that ties them together (e.g., person, place, or thing). The building blocks are virtually identical. The main difference is in the interpretation, which is based on the context of the analysis being performed.

All organizations have "analytical" data that is used as the foundation for discovering patterns and trends relative to their operations. In addition, there are "referential" data sources that can be integrated and used to help supplement and add value to the analytical data to expose new classes of patterns. The trick is in knowing what sources are available, when to use them, and, ultimately, how to interpret their meaning.

Patterns are actionable, especially in law enforcement, intelligence, and security-related applications. In principle, there only needs to be a single instance of a pattern (e.g., a specific network configuration) to take action (e.g., arrest, seize, etc.). Generally, a pattern can be broken down into discrete parts (e.g., values and relationships) that collectively define the overall pattern. These pieces can be evaluated independently, and entities with larger occurrences of certain configurations (e.g., structures, frequencies, connections) can then be prioritized and reviewed to determine their value or worth to the investigator. Of course, there are always exceptions to the patterns, and many times, exceptions to the exceptions. Therefore, all patterns should be thoroughly reviewed by analysts before any decisions are made.

Some patterns are self-evident; other patterns reveal flaws or errors in the data; sometimes the patterns are not reliable; some patterns are more important (or valuable) than others; yet others simply don't make sense due to illogical data configurations. Understanding the meaning of a network in terms of how the objects are connected, their frequencies, their commonalities, and their structure is vital to identifying and exposing new patterns. Often, networks are created from multiple data sources, so analysts must think multidimensionally because an object can be a composite representation (i.e., instantiation) of dozens of different sources. Each source can help reveal new patterns, enhance existing patterns, or even discredit/invalidate patterns.

There have been literally dozens of systems created over the past decade to share and interchange data. These systems range from local and regional applications to those with statewide or national applications. In general, they have been designed and implemented to address a specific need or purpose. However, to be effective at addressing the information-sharing challenges associated with modern society, systems must standardize on common formats, protocols, and interfaces. This has already proven successful for a few programs. The goal is to obtain further acceptance throughout the analytical community and translate this into operational protocols.

Of course, the integration of different sources is highly dependent on the quality of the data. There are inconsistencies inherent in virtually all data sources due to typos, misspellings, and incomplete values. Data represents the foundation of every analytical system. A strong foundation, in terms of quality, accuracy, and completeness, helps ensure high-quality analytics. A weak foundation makes it difficult to fulfill mission objectives, which realistically costs time, money, and even lives. Organizations need to address the quality of their data and understand how it affects their overall operations. More important, once data quality issues are identified, a plan needs to be defined to mitigate and manage the correction and resolution of the fault. To do anything else will compromise the integrity of the organization.

All of these points are emphasized because, to a certain degree, everything is interrelated. Small adjustments in one area can have profound effects in another; similar to the butterfly effect. A missing period, an abbreviation, an extra letter, a dash or parenthesis, or any other disparity could be the difference between finding a target and dealing with it appropriately, or missing the opportunity with potentially devastating results.

I'll leave you with these final questions to answer on your own:

What is located at the following coordinates?
Latitude = 38.898748
Longitude = –77.037684
Who is associated with this IP address?
198.81.129.100
Where is this ZIP code located?
96616–2876
What are these phone numbers?
(416) 981–0001
(718) 293–4300
(202) 371–0720
What building is at this address?
350 Fifth Avenue, New York, NY 10118
What significant event happened on this date?
March 11, 2004
Who owns this Social Security number?
078–05–1120
Who is this person?
Jorge Alberto Lopez-Orozco

Index

INDEX

D

INDEX

INDEX

I

J

K

L

M

N

INDEX

T

U

X

Z